Migration, Multilingualism and Schooling in Southern Europe

Migration, Multilingualism and Schooling in Southern Europe

Edited by

Sandro Caruana, Liliana Coposescu and Stefania Scaglione

CAMBRIDGE SCHOLARS PUBLISHING

Migration, Multilingualism and Schooling in Southern Europe,
Edited by Sandro Caruana, Liliana Coposescu and Stefania Scaglione

This book first published 2013

Cambridge Scholars Publishing

12 Back Chapman Street, Newcastle upon Tyne, NE6 2XX, UK

British Library Cataloguing in Publication Data
A catalogue record for this book is available from the British Library

ISBN (10): 1-4438-4221-4, ISBN (13): 978-1-4438-4221-1

MERIDIUM
Multilingualism in Europe as a Resource for Immigration
Dialogue Initiative among the Universities of the Mediterranean

Education and Culture DG
Lifelong Learning Programme

This project has been funded with support from the European Commission. This publication (communication) reflects the views only of the author, and the Commission cannot be held responsible for any use which may be made of the information contained therein.

To Margherita and Tudor,
newborn citizens of Europe

TABLE OF CONTENTS

ACKNOWLEDGEMENTS

This volume was published following the International Conference "Multilingualism and migration in Mediterranean Europe", held at the University for Foreigners of Perugia (23-25th November 2011) in conclusion of the MERIDIUM European Project (*Multilingualism in Europe as a Resource for Immigration—Dialogue Initiative among the Universities of the Mediterranean*)[1].

We wish to thank the European Commission, the Directorate General for Education and Culture (DG EAC) and the Education, Audiovisual and Culture Executive Agency (EACEA) who, through their operational and financial support, made possible the implementation of the MERIDIUM Project and the publication of this volume.

We also wish to sincerely thank the members of the Quality Control Board of the MERIDIUM Project, Ingrid Gogolin, Andrei Avram, Louis-Jean Calvet, who gave a fundamental contribution to the Project by following its workings during various stages and through active participation and collaboration.

Finally, we would like to express our appreciation and gratitude to Valentina Seri, MERIDIUM project manager, for her extraordinary work in the administrative coordination of the project and her generous and tireless collaboration to the realization of the Conference and of this volume.

[1] LifeLong Learning Program (LLLP), key-action 2 (Languages), project number 143513-LLP-1-2008-1-IT-KA2-KA2NW.

LIST OF FIGURES

LIST OF TABLES

INTRODUCTION

MIGRATION-INDUCED LINGUISTIC DIVERSITY IN SOUTHERN EUROPEAN COUNTRIES

SANDRO CARUANA, LILIANA COPOSESCU AND STEFANIA SCAGLIONE

0. In this introduction the themes and the reasons for having undertaken the research on which this volume is based shall be presented. After a summary of the conditions which, for several years, have contributed to the implementation of language policies in Europe, and an analysis of the important role such policies have had in various contexts (§ 1.), in § 2 consideration is given to the lines of action promoted by the major continental institutions—and by the European Commission in particular—regarding the themes of support for plurilingualism and the legitimisation of both "endogenous" and "exogenous" linguistic diversity. Some of the critical aspects of the lines of action adopted by the European Commission, including difficulties which have still not been overcome (§3.), are discussed with specific reference to the regional sub-system of Southern Europe, characterized by a comparatively very recent tradition of immigration compared to other European countries (§ 4.). The specificity of this area and the most appropriate strategies in order to promote linguistic diversity effectively within it are the subjects of interest in the MERIDIUM project (§ 5.), from which this book originates. In the last section of this introductory chapter (§ 6.), the structure of the volume is briefly outlined.

1. For at least the last twenty years, the promotion of plurilingualism and the fostering of linguistic diversity have constituted an important priority on the agenda of the European institutions. Against the backdrop of the momentous political and economic processes which developed in

the latter part of the XX century (the break-up of the Soviet Union and the resurgence of nationalisms in regional areas within the European States, the consolidation and enlargement of the European Union, the globalization of markets and of communication circuits, the huge migratory flows towards the Continent)[1], language–understood in its dual function as a communicative resource and an indicator of cultural identity–has acquired an obvious strategic role in mapping out of the European model of citizenship and democratic participation: the solemn proclamation of non-discrimination on a linguistic basis, contained in articles 21,1 and 22 of the *Charter of Fundamental Rights of the European Union* (2000), constitutes, from this point of view, a symbolic goal, with which the member States are called to align their linguistic policies in accordance with shared standards, aiming at promoting intercultural dialogue and eliminating discrimination. The aim, in brief, is to favour the progressive detachment from the *monolingual habitus* (Gogolin, 1994), which relegates plurilingualism to the level of an elitist phenomenon and presents linguistic diversity ("multilingualism") as a real threat to the integrity of State communities.[2]

Overcoming such a concept becomes increasingly necessary in the face of demographic, political, cultural and economic conditions irreversibly marked by internationalization and mobility. The 480 million citizens of the European Union speak 23 different official languages, to which one should add—according to the estimates of the European Commission (2008a: 7)—at least 60 regional or minority languages, utilized by about 50 million speakers (10.6% of the population). This "endogenous" linguistic diversity takes on an unprecedented significance, when one considers the increased internal mobility of European citizens: in 2009, the citizens of the European Union resident in a country different from that of

[1] Cfr. Patten and Kymlicka (2003: 2 ff.).

[2] "Multilingualism", in Council of Europe documentation, is defined as «the presence in a geographical area, large or small, of more than one 'variety of language' i.e. the mode of speaking of a social group whether it is formally recognised as a language or not; in such an area individuals may be monolingual, speaking only their own variety»; on the other hand, "plurilingualism" refers to «the repertoire of varieties of language which many individuals use, and is therefore the opposite of monolingualism; it includes the language variety referred to as 'mother tongue' or 'first language' and any number of other languages or varieties. Thus in some multilingual areas some individuals are monolingual and some are plurilingual» (definitions given in http://www.coe.int/t/dg4/linguistic/Division_EN.asp, accessed September 26, 2012). In the European Commission's documents only "multilingualism" is used, with a broad meaning.

their citizenship constituted 2.4% of the total population (about 12 million people) and 2.8% of the work force.[3] There is also, naturally, the impact of non-EU migration: in the same year, 2009, non-EU citizens resident within the borders of the European Union were almost 20 million (4% of the total population and 4.5% of the work force)[4] and 776,000 individuals, 90% of whom were non-EU citizens, acquired the citizenship of a country of the European Union (Sartori, 2011).

For several years the overall demographic balance of the European Union, as in many of the member States, has benefitted considerably from the input of intra- and extra-European immigration: according to EUROSTAT, in 2009 the migratory balance of the population of the 27-member European Union contributed 1.8% to the overall demographic balance (2.8%), as against a natural balance of 1%. In the long term, the projections of Lanzieri (2011) estimate that in 2061 the percentage of residents with a "foreign"[5] background, in the European Union, will vary between 26.5% and 34.6%, reaching one-third of the population in most of the Countries of Mediterranean and Northern-Central Europe (Lanzieri, 2011: 24). Such a scenario forcefully highlights the outdated nature of the traditional monolingual "territorial" model typical of the nation-State: if, at an individual level, plurilingualism constitutes, more and more, an indispensable exploitable resource for geographical and social mobility, at the level of policies, its real strategic value is represented by the optimization of multilingualism, which can guarantee democratic participation in the life of the State, social cohesion and equal opportunities for all those who–citizens or not–live and work in the European Union.

Such an approach is, after all, in line with the stand taken after the Second World War by the most important international organizations, in supporting respect for individual linguistic identity and safeguarding

---

[3] EUROSTAT data; see:
http://epp.eurostat.ec.europa.eu/portal/page/portal/eurostat/home/,
accessed September 26, 2012

[4] EUROSTAT data.

[5] Following Lanzieri (2011: 6) and «according to international recommendations (UNECE, 2006; §398), persons with a foreign background are '…those persons whose parents were born outside the country. The persons in this group may or may not have directly experienced an international migration.' […] Thus, limiting the analysis to two generations, foreign-born persons whose parents were born abroad (the so-called 'first generation' of migrants), together with native-born persons whose parents were born abroad (the 'second generation'), we can define a group of persons with a foreign background.»

linguistic diversity, within the framework of the principles protecting human rights and conserving humanity's intangible cultural heritage (e.g. United Nations, 1948, 1966, 1992; Council of Europe, 1992, 1995; UNESCO, 2003). Furthermore, international research and reflection have now shown clearly that the phenomena of contact between languages, both in the individual skills of the speakers, and in the widespread communicative practices in the community, constitute the norm, and not the exception, both from a historical perspective and from a synchronic global perspective; the issues related to increasing linguistic diversity in European societies are not therefore due to multilingualism *per se*, but derive, in fact, from «a certain [ideological] context in which this multilingualism is *seen* as a problem, or, rather, creates problems» (Auer and Wei, 2007: 3).

2. In line with this approach, guidance documents such as the *Action Plan 2004-2006 for the promotion of language learning and linguistic diversity* (European Commission, 2003), the *New Framework Strategy for Multilingualism* (European Commission, 2005), the publication *Multilingualism: an asset for Europe and a shared commitment* (European Commission, 2008c) outline a completely "ecological" approach to pluri-multilingualism, in which institutional, economic and social bodies are simultaneously asked to implement structural and cultural conditions which will facilitate and encourage the acquisition, maintenance, use of more than one language on the part of citizens, without prejudice to their status (be they official, regional or minority languages), or their origin ("autochthonous/endogenous" or "allochthonous/exogenous").

The impact of the actions promoted by the European institutions has been remarkable, especially in some sectors. In general terms, the gradual spread of a culture which favours language learning and use among European citizens—especially the youngest and most educated—is borne out by the results of some statistical surveys (EUROBAROMETER 2001, 2006, 2007, 2012), according to which:

- Among European citizens, there is an increase in both the perception of the inherent usefulness of learning foreign languages (in 2001, 80% of the respondents were in favour of this view; in 2005, 83%), and the ability to engage in a conversation in a European language other than their own (47% in 2001; 56% in 2005; 54% in 2012);
- the intention or desire to acquire or improve their proficiency in a foreign language was expressed by 60% of the European citizens interviewed (EUROBAROMETER, 2007: 48).

More specifically, as regards the structural measures adopted by individual national educational systems, with the aim of supporting the plurilingual growth of the young generations, the Eurydice reports (2004; 2009; EACEA-Eurydice, 2008) highlight significant progress:

- the study of a foreign language from primary school level and of at least another foreign language during the period of compulsory education are required in almost all the countries of the European Union; the CLIL (Content and Language Integrated Learning) teaching method has been introduced, at least on an experimental basis, in many countries; and many regional or minority languages are included in the curriculum (EACEA-Eurydice, 2008);
- the vast majority of EU countries have included intercultural dialogue among the general objectives of school curricula and adopt specific measures for the integration of children whose L1 is different from the official language of their country of residence; some countries are also committed to supporting the language and culture of origin of immigrants through organized courses, either at the expense of the host country, or in accordance with bilateral agreements with countries of origin (Eurydice 2004; EACEA-Eurydice, 2009).

In terms of educational policies, the European Union and the European Commission have benefited from the continued collaboration with the Language Policy Division of the Council of Europe, which has produced important operational tools for the development of plurilingual skills among European citizens: the *Common European Framework of Reference for Languages*, the *European Language Portfolio* (2001), reference guides *From Linguistic Diversity to Plurilingual Education. Guide for the Development of Language Education Policies in Europe* (CoE, 2007, I ed. Beacco and Byram, 2003), *Guide for the Development and Implementation of Curricula for Plurilingual and Intercultural Education* (Beacco *et al.*, 2010) and *Language Education Policy Profiles*[6].

3. However, in spite of the considerations presented above, a more analytical consideration of the progress achieved so far is required, in order to understand how the exhortations of the European institutions in favour of pluri- and multilingualism have been implemented, both by the central authorities of individual States and by the citizens themselves. The

---

[6] See http://www.coe.int/t/dg4/linguistic/Profils_en.asp (accessed September 26, 2012).

measures taken towards this goal are mainly grounded on a pragmatic and instrumental vision, which focuses on the formally certified acquisition of foreign languages with economic and professional marketability. From the above-mentioned surveys by the EUROBAROMETER (2006, 2012), for example, it can be seen that, among the languages that respondents believe should be known by young people, English registered an increase from 77% of preferences in 2005 to 79% in 2012, while preferences for the other major European languages decreased (-13% for French, -8% for German, -3% for Spanish). Moreover, minor EU languages, regional or minority languages and non-European languages generally did not improve their position (ranging from 0% to 4%)[7].

Such a "market demand" obviously justifies or supports the choices of education authorities, which, according to the EACEA-Eurydice (2008) report, have greatly favoured English, by making it the most widely taught foreign language, at primary level, in all European countries (except Belgium and Luxembourg). On the other hand, over the years 2001-2006, the European average percentage of pupils studying a foreign language other than English in general secondary education (ISCED 2 and 3) has never exceeded around 24%, compared to an increase from 74% to 86% approximately for English (EACEA-Eurydice, 2008: 74 ff.).

In brief, the paradoxical risk that the emphasis on the economic and employment benefits of plurilingualism will favour only a few supposedly most useful languages is becoming a concrete reality. The deeply-rooted and widespread ideology, that there is a hierarchy of importance among languages could lead to the thwarting of pluralistic principles on which European language policies are based. In fact, giving exclusive prominence to such a market-oriented logic:

- would penalize the dissemination and development of other European languages, limiting their use solely to national contexts and gradually discouraging their utilization in strategic areas for development, such as scientific research and international relations;
- would abate the commitment to the preservation and intergenerational transmission of languages considered "weak" in terms of status, such as regional languages, on the one hand, and non-

[7] The only remarkable exception to this trend is represented by Chinese, which in 2012 obtained 14% of preferences, whereas in 2005 it garnered 2%. Given the current relevance of China in the global economy, such a result seems to demonstrate the substantially instrumental vision underpinning public opinion judgments about language learning.

> autochthonous languages brought in by migration, on the other. This is an indirect, but evident, violation of respect for individual linguistic identity and linguistic diversity.[8]

It is beyond the scope of this research to study in depth the problems regarding EU lesser-used languages as well as those of regional or minority languages.[9] We will focus, instead, on critical issues faced by allochthonous languages, which tend to be greatly amplified both by their complete lack of status within the host society, and by the prejudices related to integration and towards immigration.

In fact, as Extra and Gorter (2007: 23) rightly point out:

> established majority groups often make strong demands on IM [immigrant minority] groups for integration in terms of assimilation and are commonly very reluctant to promote or even accept the notion of cultural diversity as a determining characteristic of an increasingly multicultural environment.

This widespread attitude is matched by a persistent difficulty in recognizing the languages of origin of migrants in terms of public policies of individual countries, with particularly serious effects on education.

According to the EACEA-Eurydice (2009) report, the countries of the European Union still present very varied and, in many cases, objectively difficult conditions as regards the availability of courses to help migrants to maintain/strengthen their skills in their mother tongue. In recent years, the inherent "weakness" of the status of these languages within the host countries has been further aggravated by the limited resources allocated to the school systems: in times of economic hardship, the countries which have not set in motion bilateral agreements with the migrants' countries of origin subordinate the decision on whether or not to start a (migrant) mother tongue course to the demand and availability of human and material resources; also, States that had previously distinguished themselves for their commendable attention to the maintenance of the languages of origin of foreign nationals (e.g. Sweden and the Netherlands) have preferred to use the resources to enhance the teaching of the instructional language as L2, favouring an approach ismuch more based—with regard to immigrant children—on the "deficit theory" (in the instructional language) rather than on the exploitation of the richness of language skills they bring.

---

[8] See, in this regard, the recommendations of the European Parliament (2009).

[9] In the context of the vast bibliography, see, among others, de Swaan (2001), Nic Shuibhne (2002), Hogan-Brun and Wolff (2003), Phillipson (2003).

The educational choices just mentioned contribute to the perpetuation of conditions of disadvantage and exclusion for immigrant minors or children of immigrants, as shown by the data summarized in the recent Green Paper on *Migration and mobility: challenges and opportunities for EU education systems* (European Commission, 2008); moreover, they hinder the growth of a full plurilingual and intercultural awareness in the citizens of the host countries, insofar as they make "invisible" the complexity of the repertoire of a large part of society and of the school population. In its many interventions on these issues, the Council of Europe has never failed to point out that multilingualism brought in by migration can and should contribute to a rethinking of curricula towards a plurilingual and intercultural education for all, which

> realises the universal right to quality education, covering: acquisition of competences, knowledge, dispositions and attitudes, diversity of learning experiences, and construction of individual and collective cultural identities. Its aim is to make teaching more effective, and increase the contribution it makes, both to school success for the most vulnerable learners, and to social cohesion (Beacco *et al.,* 2010: 7)

To this end, an exemplary synthesis of the conceptual key-lines on which the European educational systems should converge is offered by Gogolin (2002: 19 ff.):

1) *Reform of traditional canons of language education* according to the criteria:
   1a. language potential and needs among the given population of a region
   1b. integration of all languages existing on a territory into the canon of officially accepted and taught—i.e. legitimate—school languages;
2) *Language as the medium of instruction*: abandonment of the principle of monolingual organization of school systems;
3) *Education and learning under the conditions of plurilingualism*:
   3a. Recognition and acceptance of the fact that multilingualism is a general condition for all (language) education in European, i.e. linguistically plural, societies;
   3b. Introduction of "heteroglossic literacy" as a general aim of general education.

4. With regard to the above-mentioned issues, the situation of the countries of Southern Europe is particularly interesting, because of the distinctive features of this area of the Continent compared to the rest of the

European Union. In fact, in terms of matters related to the integration of immigrants, Southern Europe is today facing very particular conditions: unlike the States of North-Western Europe, countries in this area have only recently become an immigration destination. On the contrary, until the 1970s, these countries often experienced significant mass migration to other European States or to other continents.

According to estimates by the United Nations Population Division (UNDP), over the last two decades, the percentage of the immigrant population in the Southern European Countries has risen from 2.9% to 9.5%, compared to the current 10.8% in Northern European Countries and the 12.4% of Western European Countries; however, the average growth rate of immigration over the last twenty years has been significantly higher in Southern Europe than in the two European regions mentioned above.

This rapid transition to the condition of immigration-receptor countries has necessitated, with unprecedented urgency, a number of adjustments, particularly in the area of educational policy. In many states in the South of Europe, such policies are often characterized by limitations related, on the one hand, to inadequate teacher training as regards plurilingual and intercultural education and, on the other hand, to the lack of awareness, on the part of school authorities and society as a whole, of the extent and value of immigrant children's language skills in their respective languages of origin. The overall picture is further complicated by the significantly different composition, from country to country, of migration, which may diverge to different degrees in terms of nationality and/or language use. The socio-demographic fabric of the host society, which provides varied conditions for the integration of migrants, may also vary considerably from one area to another.

5. On the basis of the above considerations, seven universities in six countries (Italy, Malta, Portugal, Romania, Slovenia and Spain)[10] have collaborated in the MERIDIUM Project (*Multilingualism in Europe as a Resource for Immigration—Dialogue Initiative Among the Universities of the Mediterranean*), a network project that aims to provide active support for the promotion of the European policy of pluri-/multilingualism in Southern European countries. In this project particular attention has been given to the development of strategies geared to increase awareness of the

[10] The institutions which are participating in this project are the University for Foreigners of Perugia (responsible for coordination), the University of Malta, the Universidade Nova of Lisbon, Transylvania University of Brasov, Babeş-Bolyai University—Cluj-Napoca, the Università del Litorale—Capodistria, the University of Salamanca.

institutions and society towards exogenous linguistic diversity, promote its value and assess the efficacy of measures being taken.

The participation of two Romanian universities is a key aspect of the MERIDIUM network: in fact, it permits, within the network, a direct exchange of information and experience between a country which in recent years has experienced a period of high emigration (IOM, 2008) and countries—above all, Italy and Spain—to which migration flows are directed and from which, in many cases, immigrants are returning home after a longer or shorter stay. The partnership between these universities constitutes an extremely significant instance of the usefulness of creating opportunities for collaboration which can support the maintenance of L1 in the migration setting, while, at the same time, favouring the preservation and the further acquisition of skills in L2 after the return to the country of origin.

In its first three years of activity (2009-2011), the project has had two fundamental aims:

- to analyze, through research in the field, the sociolinguistic contexts and the school culture in areas, in the partner countries, with a high level of migration (inbound and outbound);
- to plan initiatives to promote the dissemination of a plurilingual and intercultural awareness among the institutional parties and the larger society, starting from the specific context of primary education (pupils, teachers, school authorities, families).

6. This book provides a synthesis of the scientific results obtained from the MERIDIUM project, not only through the research and the activities conducted by groups of the network, but also thanks to the reflections arising from the MERIDIUM International Conference "Multilingualism and Migration Flows in Mediterranean Europe" (University for Foreigners of Perugia, 23-25 November 2011).

The first part of the book contains the contributions of European scholars who, while not directly participating in the MERIDIUM Project, provided accounts of important scientific and institutional experiences during the MERIDIUM International Conference. These interventions deal mainly with the problematic implications and the opportunities related to linguistic diversity in the current European context.

In the opening chapter, the contribution of Cornelia Ilie tackles the controversial issue of freedom of expression in a multilingual and multicultural society. It deals specifically with the limits and principles of responsibility that must be identified, so that one can freely express opinions, also and especially when these are in conflict with the views of others. If freedom of speech, like respect for diversity, is an essential value of European democracy, reflecting on the ways in which to combine these two poles in public discourse emerges with particular urgency in a European scenario increasingly exposed to the risk that there will be distinct public spheres separating migrants and citizens.

The role of dominant languages in present-day multilingual societies is discussed by Román Álvarez Rodríguez, who highlights the origins and prospects of the complex interplay between language, identity and power. The existence of a dialectical relationship not only between dominant languages and those which have become minority languages, but also between dominant languages with different status (e. g. English and Spanish) is an inescapable aspect of global communication. This, rather than creating a conflict, could represent an opportunity for cultural progress and openness to others.

In addressing the specific issue of plurilingualism resulting from immigration, the contribution of Joana Duarte draws attention to the need for deeper reflection on the systemic features of the school contexts in which immigrant pupils are placed: in the face of the extensive scientific evidence attesting the difficulties encountered by these students in achieving educational goals, there have been few studies aiming at establishing how much the observed educational disparities are affected by the organizational and aptitude characteristics of the host schools, where, to a great extent, there is still the widespread monolingual habitus which tends to fuel, with regard to immigrant pupils, the "deficit theory".

The other three contributions in the first part of the book are concerned with national contexts directly involved in the MERIDIUM Project.

Within a legal framework such as the Slovenian one, that legitimizes and protects national minorities (Italian and Hungarian) and scattered minorities (Roma), Ana Kralj discusses the foreclosures against new minorities, often from other States of the former Yugoslavia. The author highlights the rifts in the social fabric which originate from this situation and which have repercussions on both the macro-level of the relationships between ethno-linguistic groups, and the micro-level of daily individual interactions.

The contribution of Marina Chini raises, with regard to the Italian context, several issues related to the study of linguistic diversity induced, in recent decades, by migration flows entering the Peninsula: to date, research on linguistic repertoires, customs and linguistic attitudes of immigrants in Italy are still at an early stage and there are few systematic surveys able to provide information comparable with the data already acquired in other European and non-European contexts. Chini addresses the need to plan targeted interventions in order to promote both a better language integration of immigrants, and real possibilities for them to maintain their languages of origin.

Concrete examples of educational activities for the promotion of positive attitudes towards plurilingualism and the development of intercultural skills are discussed by Antoinette Camilleri Grima with regard to the Maltese context: even though bilingualism is present, education in Maltese schools could be further enhanced through the adoption of diversified methodologies, directed at increasing Maltese pupils' motivation to study languages, but, above all, to ensure the integration of students whose L1 is different from the instructional language, through increased attention to the affective and cognitive dimensions in relationship with linguistic diversity.

The second part of the book focuses entirely on presentations resulting from the MERIDIUM Project and on illustrating some of the most significant results obtained from the research carried out in each one of the countries of the network.

Chapters 7 and 8 illustrate the stages of the project and the methodology used for the identification and analysis of case studies; a brief comparative outline of the samples of informants involved in the research in the respective countries being studied is also included.

The final six chapters of this volume, written by the different units of the network, deal with issues of particular significance in the respective national contexts. In fact, as has already been noted, even though all the countries in the network are linked by recent migration dynamics, each has distinctive characteristics, both as regards the organization of the educational systems, and in terms of the patterns of the migratory flows. While bearing in mind the importance of tracing a basic comparative framework, it is only through a context-specific analysis that it will be possible to discuss, in detail, what could be the most suitable instruments and methods of intervention within each individual context.

References

Auer P., and L. Wei. 2007. Introduction: Multilingualism as a problem? Monolingualism as a problem? In *Handbook of Multilingualism and Multilingual Communication,* eds. P. Auer and L. Wei, 1-12. Berlin/New York: Mouton de Gruyter.

Beacco J.-C., and M. Byram. 2003. *Guide for the development of language education policies in Europe. From linguistic diversity to plurilingual education.* Strasbourg: Language Policy Division, Council of Europe (available at www.coe.int/lang, accessed September 26, 2012).

Beacco J.-C., *et al.* 2010. *Guide for the development and implementation of curricula for plurilingual and intercultural Education.* Strasbourg: Language Policy Division, Council of Europe (available at www.coe.int/lang, accessed September 26, 2012).

CoE. 2007. *From Linguistic Diversity to Plurilingual Education: Guide for the Development of Language Education Policies in Europe.* Strasbourg: Language Policy Division, Council of Europe (available at www.coe.int/lang, accessed September 26, 2012).

de Swaan A. 2001. *Words of the World.* Cambridge (U.K.): Polity Press.

EACEA-Eurydice. 2008. *Key Data on Teaching Languages at School in Europe.* Bruxelles: EACEA (available at: http://eacea.ec.europa.eu/education/eurydice/key_data_en.php, accessed September 26, 2012).

—. 2009. *Integrating Immigrant Children into Schools in Europe.* Bruxelles: EACEA (available at: http://eacea.ec.europa.eu/education/eurydice/thematic_studies_en.php, accessed September 26, 2012).

EUROBAROMETER. 2001. *Europeans and Languages*, Special Eurobarometer 147, wave 54.1b. Directorate General for Education and Culture, European Commission (available at: http://ec.europa.eu/public_opinion/index_en.htm, accessed September 26, 2012).

—. 2006. *Europeans and their Languages*, Special Eurobarometer 243, wave 64.3. Directorate General for Education and Culture, European Commission (available at: http://ec.europa.eu/public_opinion/index_en.htm, accessed September 26, 2012).

—. 2007. *European Cultural Values*, Special Eurobarometer 278, wave 67.1. Directorate General for Education and Culture, European Commission (available at: http://ec.europa.eu/public_opinion/index_en.htm, accessed September 26, 2012).

—. 2012. *Europeans and their Languages*, Special Eurobarometer 386, wave 77.1. European Commission (available at: http://ec.europa.eu/public_opinion/index_en.htm, accessed September 26, 2012).

Eurydice. 2004. *Integrating Immigrant Children into Schools in Europe.* Bruxelles: Eurydice (available at:

http://eacea.ec.europa.eu/education/eurydice/thematic_studies_archives_en.php, accessed September 26, 2012).

Extra, G., and D. Gorter. 2007. Regional and immigrant minority languages in Europe. In *Handbook of Language and Communication: Diversity and Change*, eds. M. Hellinger and A. Pauwels, 15-52. Berlin/New York: Mouton de Gruyter.

Gogolin, I. 1994. *Der monolinguale Habitus der multilingualen Schule*. Münster: Waxmann.

—. 2002. *Linguistic diversity and new minorities in Europe*, reference study. Strasbourg: Language Policy Division, Council of Europe (available at: http://www.coe.int/t/dg4/linguistic/Source/GogolinEN.pdf, accessed September 26, 2012).

Hogan-Brun, G., and S. Wolff, eds. 2003. *Minority languages in Europe: Frameworks, status, prospects.* New York: Palgrave Macmillan.

IOM. 2008. *Migration in Romania: A Country Profile 2008.* Geneva: International Organization for Migration (available at: http://publications.iom.int/bookstore/index.php?main_page=product_info&products_id=495, accessed September 26, 2012).

Lanzieri, G. 2011. *Fewer, older and multicultural? Projections of the EU populations by foreign/national background.* Luxembourg: Publications Office of the European Union (available at: http://epp.eurostat.ec.europa.eu/cache/ITY_OFFPUB/KS-RA-11-019/EN/KS-RA-11-019-EN.PDF, accessed September 26, 2012).

Nic Shuibhne, N. 2002. *EC Law and Minority Language Policy. Culture, Citizenship and Fundamental Rights*. The Hague, London, New York: Kluwer Law International.

Patten, A., and W. Kymlicka. 2003. Introduction. Language rights and political theory: context, issues, and approaches. In *Language rights and political theory*, eds. W. Kymlicka and A. Patten, 1-51. Oxford: Oxford University Press.

Phillipson, R. 2003. *English-Only Europe? Challenging Language Policy.* London/New York: Routledge.

Sartori, F. 2011. Acquisitions of citizenship on the rise in 2009. *EUROSTAT. Statistics in Focus*, 24/2011 (available at: http://epp.eurostat.ec.europa.eu/portal/page/portal/product_details/publication?p_product_code=KS-SF-11-024, accessed September 26, 2012).

UNECE. 2006. *Conference of European Statisticians Recommendations for the 2010 Censuses of Population and Housing.* New York/Geneva: United Nations (available at:

http://www.unece.org/fileadmin/DAM/stats/publications/CES_2010_Census_Recommendations_English.pdf, accessed September 26, 2012).

Policy documents

European Commission. 2003. *Action Plan 2004-2006: "Promoting language learning and linguistic diversity".* Communication from the Commission to the European Parliament, the Council, the European Economic and Social Committee and the Committee of Regions, COM(2003) 449 final, 24/7/2003.

—. 2005. *A New Framework Strategy for Multilingualism.* Communication from the Commission to the European Parliament, the Council, the European Economic and Social Committee and the Committee of Regions, COM(2005) 596 final, 22/11/2005.

—. 2008a. *Speaking for Europe. Languages in the European Union.* Luxembourg: Office for Official Publications of the European Communities (available at: http://ec.europa.eu/publications/booklets/move/74/index_en.htm, accessed September 26, 2012)

—. 2008b. *Migration & mobility: challenges and opportunities for EU education systems.* Green paper presented by the Commission, COM (2008) 243 final, 3/7/2008.

—. 2008c. *Multilingualism: an asset for Europe and a shared commitment.* Communication from the Commission to the European Parliament, the Council, the European Economic and Social Committee and the Committee of Regions, COM(2008) 566 final, 18/9/2008.

European Parliament 2009. *Multilingualism: an asset for Europe and a shared commitment.* European Parliament resolution, P6_TA(2009)0162, 24/3/2009.

International Conventions and Declarations

Council of Europe 1992. *European Charter for Regional or Minority Languages,* opened for signature on 5/11/1992, CETS n. 148.

—. 1995. *Framework Convention for the Protection of National Minorities,* opened for signature on 1/2/1995, CETS n. 157.

United Nations 1948. *Universal Declaration of Human Rights*, adopted and proclaimed by General Assembly resolution 217 A (III) of 10 December 1948.

—. 1966. *International Covenant on Civil and Political Rights*, adopted and opened for signature, ratification and accession by General Assembly resolution 2200A (XXI) of 16 December 1966.

—. 1992. *Declaration on the Rights of Persons Belonging to National or Ethnic, Religious or Linguistic Minorities*, Adopted by General Assembly resolution 47/135 of 18 December 1992.

UNESCO 2003. *Convention for the Safeguarding of Intangible Cultural Heritage*, adopted by the General Conference of the United Nations Educational, Scientific and Cultural Organization, 17 October 2003.

PART I

LINGUISTIC DIVERSITY IN THE AGE OF GLOBALIZATION AND CONTEXT-RELATED ISSUES IN SOUTHERN EUROPEAN COUNTRIES

CHAPTER ONE

WHICH FREEDOM? THE CHALLENGES OF KEY WORD CONCEPTUALISATIONS IN A CROSS-LINGUISTIC PERSPECTIVE

CORNELIA ILIE

If liberty means anything, it means the right to tell people what they don't want to hear.
(George Orwell)

To lose freedom is awful; to lose the idea of freedom is even worse.
(George Lakoff)

1.0. Introduction

Historically, freedom and diversity in Europe have been mutually reinforcing, since people whose ideas were not tolerated in one state were able to move to another. Since 1945, freedom has been enshrined as a "European" value—not only in the European Union but also in the Council of Europe, whose 47 members have endorsed the European Convention on Human Rights, thereby accepting the stipulations of the European Court of Human Rights. Over time the notion of freedom has repeatedly been proclaimed as a virtue at the core of European democracy.

Yet nowadays we are witnessing a growing inconsistency between the lofty ideals of freedom-loving nations and the freedom-restricting practices reinforced in several countries due to the fear shared by many Europeans who feel threatened by the large migrations of recent decades. How can freedom be reconciled with diversity in Europe?

Following the recent influx of migrants and refugees from all over the world, Europe has become increasingly multilingual and multicultural. While multilingualism has always been a distinguishing feature of

European societies, many people in Europe have traditionally had less direct contact with individuals from different cultural backgrounds and who speak other languages than their own. Nowadays, however, we are actually witnessing a new reality in which we encounter and interact with individuals belonging to a new category of Europeans, the so-called "hyphenated Europeans" (e.g. Turkish-Germans, North African-French women or Asian Brits). They contribute to the growing number of sub-cultures and languages underpinning modern European nation-states.

When we interact in cross-cultural contexts, we are co-constructing and challenging culture-related meanings in ways which can lead to understanding, but sometimes to misunderstanding, both within and across national borders. In institutions and the media, cultural and linguistic differences are often manipulated for ideological and political purposes by means of stereotypical formulas, false dichotomies or rhetorical dissociation. For a long time the notions of migration and migrants' rights have been associated with the concept of freedom—economic, political, cultural, religious, personal freedom. But how are these rights ensured and reinforced in various European societies? By stipulating coercive legislation or by encouraging and facilitating an open and constructive dialogue between individuals and civil society groups?

1.1. Language, Cognition and Key Words

It is through language that we are able to convey, challenge and negotiate meanings, as well as form concepts, in order to make sense of and structure the world around us. Words that are central to a culture represent the key to understanding how a society takes on new meanings and how these changes reflect values of society. Worth noting in this respect, is Raymond Williams's (1976) pioneering contribution with regard to the interpretation of cultural structures that provide meanings for members of a society by weaving together various aspects of life experience. He examined the historical changes in the meaning of 109 key words, in order to bring out the significance of the facts of these changes. He defined keywords in two ways: as significant, binding words in certain activities, and as significant, indicative words in certain forms of thought. Evans-Pritchard (1982), an anthropologist who focused on the interpretation of history and cultural meaning, is considered the father of symbolic and interpretive anthropology. He considered that the best approach to investigating social structure was to frame it as a series of flexible, logical, cognitive "maps" giving form and meaning to social behaviour. In linguistics, a cross-cultural analysis of the meanings and connotations of related key words, i.e. the British notion of *consensus* and the Swedish *samförstånd* (= *konsensus*) in parliamentary debates (Ilie, 2007), reveals both institutionally based similarities and differences rooted in particular cultural traditions and historically shaped political conventions.

1.1.1. How Can Freedom be Defined?

Many studies of the concept of "freedom" have been carried out by philosophers and anthropologists, and recently by linguists representing different schools of thought. Most of them would agree about the shared generic sense of concepts known as "freedom" and "liberty" in English, "liberté" in French, and "Freiheit" in German, for example. What is lacking in philosophical literature, however, is the cross-linguistic perspective and the contextualised analysis of the actual usages of these concepts.

As was pointed out by etymologists, the Latin concept of "libertas" denotes primarily the status of a "liber", i.e. a person who is not a slave, and it involves the negation of the limitations imposed by slavery. In other words, *libertas* was a privilege and not a right. In ancient Greek and Roman societies some people were granted many liberties, others had very few, and many had none at all. The Roman republic was one in which only a handful of people (senators, magistrates) had the full privileges of free speech, a minority (citizens) had the right to vote on what their superiors had decided, and many people (slaves) had no say at all. The idea reflected in the Latin concept of *libertas* appears to be close to what Isaiah Berlin (1969) calls the notion of "positive freedom", i.e. the wish of the individual to be his/her own master, and what Taylor (1982) refers to as exercising control over one's life.

The words *freedom* and *liberty* are often used interchangeably although they do not necessarily mean the same thing. *Freedom* is generally defined in philosophical literature as the quality or state of being free, or the absence of necessity, coercion, or constraint in making a choice or executing an action. The term may also refer to the state of liberation from slavery or the power of another person or organisation or entity. Freedom is also defined as the state of being outspoken or speaking one's mind. As for *liberty*, the most common definition is that it is a state of being free to do as one pleases. A more basic definition of *liberty* regards that state of being able to make a choice, which presupposes being unrestricted, physically or mentally. A definition mostly used in the context of social, political, or economic situations would encompass being free from arbitrary or tyrannical control. This meaning is derived from the emergence in the 18th century of the English notion of *liberty* or the French notion of *liberté* as the opposite of slavery and oppression, and the rise of democracy. If the word *freedom* focused, primarily, on the rights of an individual to be "left alone" by other people, the word *liberty* became gradually specialised in "public rights", that is, in the rights of social groups, guaranteed by suitable political structures. A significant distinction is made by Wierzbicka (1997) between two expressions: *freedom of speech* and *liberty of the tongue*. The former is assumed to refer to the fact that other people cannot stop us from saying what we want to say. By contrast, the latter is assumed to refer to the fact that one says what one wants to say without taking other people's reactions into account. The current use of the word *liberty* has to do with everybody's inalienable right to do what they think is right and good. The underlying premise is that we are all granted free will by nature, and that no one can take that away from anyone else. However, the basic philosophical, as well as socio-political, issue arises about how we define and identify the "right" and the "good" (Ross 1930).

A major difference between the concept of *freedom* and *libertas* relates to a rather negative orientation of freedom, which can be interpreted in two ways: first, it points to NOT TO DO things that one does not want to do; second, to being able TO DO things that one wants to do WITHOUT INTERFERENCE from other people. This negative view, framed as freedom FROM, has been attributed to classical English philosophers, such as Locke, Adam Smith and John Stuart Mill. The formulation "freedom FROM X" is felicitous if X refers to situations when other people do something to us, thus preventing us from doing what we want to do, e.g. freedom from harassment, from oppression, from tyranny, from coercion, from persecution. The semantics of *freedom* corresponds to the ideal of "non-imposition", or Berlin's notion of "non-interference", which is one of the major cultural themes in the Anglo-Saxon world. According to this ideal, freedom and being free are a matter of what we can do, of what it is open to us to do, whether or not we do anything to exercise these options. In other words, freedom consists in our being able to act, or not to act, depending on what we choose to do.

The concept of freedom of expression displays a dynamic complexity which can be instantiated in two main ways:

(i) **Freedom from X** (e.g. from being offended, insulted, slandered, attacked)
(ii) **Freedom to X** (e.g. to challenge, criticise, accuse, blame, slander)

In both cases, freedom needs to be exercised with:

- **responsibility** (assuming responsibility for what one says)
  and
- **accountability** (being held accountable for what one says)

We often tend to assume that we all know what the word "freedom" or "liberty" means and we take it for granted that the meaning is the same in all languages. However, as Wierzbicka (1997) has convincingly shown, "freedom" is a concept which has different meanings in different languages according to specific cognitive patterns and socio-cultural values. By means of semantic primitives, she has devised a particular metalanguage that is used to define and distinguish various shades of meaning connected with the concept:

[freedom] – English key word
(a) someone X can think something like this:
(b) if I want to do something I can do it
(c) no one else can say to me: "you can't do it because I don't want this"
(d) if I don't want to do something I don't have to do it
(e) no one else can say to me: "you have to do it because I want this"
(f) this is good for X
(g) it is bad if someone cannot think this
(Wierzbicka, 1997: 130)

Components (b) and (c) refer to the range of options which are open to us, whereas components (d) and (e) focus on the benefits of non-interference from other people. According to Wierzbicka, freedom from X can be rhetorically invoked in situations when some condition prevents us from doing what we want to do and what we have the right to do, as in the case of freedom from hunger or freedom from poverty, as well as freedom from persecution, harassment, oppression, coercion or external control.

Expressions of this kind are used to make strong political statements, e.g. "Everyone has the right to do what they want to do and not be prevented from it by X", where X refers to situations when other people prevent us from doing what we think we are entitled to do. This is why "freedom from illness" is not semantically felicitous because it would imply that illness, too, is a social evil, imposed on some people by other people's actions or neglect. Through recurrent use, the modern concept of freedom has developed in opposition to the notions of "interference" and "imposition".

While the word *freedom* tends to focus, above all, on the right of the individual to be "left alone" by other people, the word *liberty* has gradually become associated with civil and political rights that protect individuals from institutional infringement and guarantee respect for personal privacy and integrity. This particular meaning, which applies collectively to all individuals, is represented by Wierzbicka as follows:

[liberty] – English key word
(a) everyone can think something like this
(b) if I want to do something because I think it is good I can do it
(c) no one can say: "this person can't do it because I don't want this"
(d) everyone thinks: this is good
(Wierzbicka, 1997: 134)

Components (b) and (c) refer to control which is actually exercised by someone who is, roughly speaking, his/her own master, and not a person under someone else's control. Component (d) is supposed to account for the positive connotations of the word, which are assumed to apply to "everyone". Whereas most of the distinctions made by Wierzbicka between the semantic denotations and connotations of the two concepts – *freedom* and *liberty* – are supported by actual context-specific usage, her schematic representations do raise important questions. The most problematic is the fact that the meaning of each of the two concepts is envisaged exclusively from the perspective of the individual whose (freedom or liberty) rights are being reinforced, but without being related to the perspective of the interacting agents who participate or are involved in the interaction (interlocutors, audience, and so on). The interpersonal dynamics of the social dialogue, through which freedom- and liberty rights are exerted, has been neglected. This failure results in unidimensional, rather than multidimensional, considerations and conclusions regarding the scope and focus of actual usages of the two concepts. Freedom, like liberty, can only be understood, defined and analysed in relation to the perceptions and interpretations of the agents directly or indirectly involved in contextually situated actions and transactions. Where do we draw the line between freedom of expression, on the one hand, and acknowledgement of other viewpoints, on the other? It is important to realize that freedom is not without limits and that liberty carries with it duties and responsibilities (see 1.2.3, 1.2.4 and 1.2.5 below).

In terms of cross-cultural analysis, Wierzbicka's analytical framework points to idiosyncratic definitions of these words that do not have exact equivalents in other languages. In spite of a core meaning of freedom which is shared by its counterparts in other languages (*libertas* in Latin, *svoboda* and *volja* in Russian, *wolnosc* in Polish), there are a number of context-sensitive semantic differences and culture-specific usages. She also points out that the Russian concept of "svoboda" may apparently correspond exactly to the English concept of freedom since it can sometimes take the negative complement corresponding, roughly, to the English *from*-phrase. However, *svoboda* embodies a different perspective on human and cultural conceptualisation. A central semantic aspect of *svoboda* refers to "ease" or "relaxation", which is said to fit well with the image of a child unwrapped from its swaddling clothes and experiencing the pleasure of being able to move its limbs without any restrictions. According to Wierzbicka (1997: 141), *svoboda*, unlike *libertas* or *freedom*, suggests a feeling of well-being, caused by the perceived absence of external pressure or constraints. The Latin concept focuses on not having a master (not being a slave), whereas the Russian one focuses on not sensing any external constraints. The corresponding English concept focuses on options, and on the absence of interference from other people. It is linked with individual rights, with private space, with being "left alone", with "privacy" and personal independence.

1.2. Freedom of Expression

I may disapprove of what you say but I will fight to death for your right to say it. (Voltaire)

Voltaire believed strongly in freedom of expression and defended the right to engage in debate and controversy over opposite standpoints. His philosophical views on the individual's right to freedom of expression were enshrined in the French Constitution after his death. The right to freedom of expression emerged from the struggle against religious sensitivity, intolerance and tyranny of religion in Medieval Europe. In other words, the emphasis on the right of the individual was historically and politically motivated.

Formal censorship used to be common practice in most states. Autocrats frequently imprisoned critics, shut down the presses, forced authors into exile, or censored written and artistic works. The struggle against licensing requirements in Great Britain in the 17th century, the American Bill of Rights, and the French Declaration of the Rights of Man proclaimed standards of freedom in a way that inspired new realms of independent expression and thought, especially in Europe in the 19th and early 20th centuries, but also in other parts of the world.

The full importance of freedom of expression could perhaps be appreciated only with the rise of totalitarian regimes, such as Adolf Hitler's Germany and Joseph Stalin's Soviet Union, among others. In such regimes, the state not only exerted full control over expression, it also used the media to direct citizens' thoughts and opinions through propaganda, indoctrination, denunciation, and social conformity. After the defeat of Nazi Germany, freedom of expression joined the realm of core freedoms that are now protected as universal standards (Article 19 of the Universal Declaration of Human Rights).

Franklin D. Roosevelt is one of the statesmen who insisted that it is not enough to speak of freedom unless one explains what one wishes to be free from or free for. In 1941 he proclaimed four freedoms as the goals of Allied policy in the Second World War: freedom of speech, freedom of worship, freedom from want and freedom from fear.

Freedom of expression is usually regarded as one of the most fundamental of all freedoms in that it is a basic foundation of democracy. It encompasses not only freedom of speech and media, but also freedom of thought, culture, and intellectual inquiry. Freedom of expression guarantees everyone's right to speak and write openly without state interference, including the right to criticise injustices, illegal activities, and incompetencies. It guarantees the right to inform the public and to offer opinions of any kind, to advocate change, to give the minority the opportunity to be heard, and to challenge the rise of state tyranny by the force of words.

But is complete, unlimited, unconditional, freedom possible? Is it desirable? Is there such a thing as complete freedom to say anything about anything to anybody? Freedom is normally related to constraint, which applies to both the freedom to do things and the freedom to say things. When doing or saying things, we normally engage in an implicit or explicit dialogue with our fellow human beings. Consequently, our freedom emerges through actual interaction with the other(s), who certainly will be affected in various ways by our actions and our words. In the process of exercising our freedom of expression we necessarily get engaged in a relationship with the other(s).

1.2.1. The Challenges of the Danish Cartoons

One of the most recent challenges to freedom of expression was the worldwide reaction to the initial September 2006 publication of a cartoon that mocked the Prophet Muhammad in the Danish daily newspaper *Jyllands-Posten*. The cartoons depicted the Prophet Muhammad as a terrorist with a bomb. As a result, violent demonstrations erupted across the Middle East. Public anger was aimed at Danish embassies, and Muslim leaders demanded that the prime minister of Denmark apologise for the publication of the cartoons and shut down the newspaper. Throughout the world, free speech organisations and some governments defended the right to free expression, although a number of Western leaders criticised the Danish newspaper and called for an apology, persuaded that freedom of expression is a principle to be defended except when violent demonstrations are organised against it. In the end, the Danish paper issued an apology to defuse the international controversy, after an international boycott by Arab countries cost the Danish economy several billion dollars. The Danish Prime Minister decided not to take action against the newspaper, explaining that in free societies, free speech is too important to be interfered with by the state.

Several newspapers in the Netherlands re-published the cartoons in a sign of solidarity for free expression. Most of them received threats of violence as a result. Dutch Prime Minister Jan-Peter Balkenende stated his position, while showing he understood that some images might be provocative, “I regret the threats from the Muslim world. In our world, when someone crosses a line, we take the matter to court. There is no place here for threats and own direction. (I am) Glad there is freedom of speech here. At the same time we have to realize that our images and ideas can be provocative to others” (The Wikipedia Muhammad Cartoons Debate, 15 February, 2006).

France Soir, Germany’s *Die Welt*, *La Stampa* in Italy and *El Periodico* in Spain all carried some of the drawings.

In Italy, Reforms Minister Roberto Calderoli, a leading figure of the anti-immigrant Lega Nord (Northern League) party, said he would wear the T-shirt on which he had imprinted controversial Danish cartoons depicting Prophet Mohammad wearing a bomb-like turban, despite being asked not to do so by Italy’s then Prime Minister Silvio Berlusconi.

The Italian magazine *Studi Cattolici,* close to the influential Catholic conservative Opus Dei group, published a cartoon showing the Prophet Mohammed in hell, sparking outrage among Muslim associations in Italy. According to the Italian news agency Ansa, the cartoon shows the Italian poets Dante Alighieri and Virgil on the edge of a circle of flames looking down on Mohammed, whose body is cut in half. “Isn’t that Mohammed?” Virgil is shown asking Dante. “Yes, and he’s cut in two because he has brought division to society,” replies Dante.

1.2.2. The Reactions to the Swedish Cartoons

In Sweden a controversy started with a series of drawings by Swedish artist Lars Vilks that depicted the Islamic prophet Muhammad as a roundabout dog (it showed the head of Muhammad on the body of a dog). According to Vilks, the art and culture communities in Sweden repeatedly criticise the United States and Israel, whereas Muslim values are rarely even questioned. Several art galleries in Sweden declined to show the drawings, citing security concerns and fear of violence. The controversy gained international attention after the Örebro-based regional newspaper *Nerikes Allehanda* published one of the drawings to illustrate an editorial on self-censorship and freedom of religion. The editorial defended "Muslims' right to freedom of religion" but also said it must be permitted to "ridicule Islam's most foremost symbols —just like all other religions' symbols."

International protests started immediately afterwards. In a statement, the Ministry of Foreign Affairs in Islamabad said Pakistan condemned the publication in very strong terms: "Regrettably, the tendency among some Europeans to mix the freedom of expression with an outright and deliberate insult to 1.3 billion Muslims in the world is on the rise." The Swedish Foreign Ministry spokeswoman Anna Björkander declared that the Swedish Chargé d'Affaires said he was sorry if the publication had hurt Muslim feelings. She also told the Pakistani official that freedom of the press is strongly protected in the Swedish constitution.

The editor-in-chief of *Nerikes Allehanda*, Ulf Johansson, declared that it would be "strange" if the Swedish Chargé d'Affaires had apologised over the cartoon, and would contradict the Swedish government's previous line of not interfering with freedom of the press.

Swedish Prime Minister Fredrik Reinfeldt met with ambassadors from 22 Muslim countries to discuss the issue. Reinfeldt said that he had "explained how Swedish society works and that we don't have elected representatives making editorial decisions", adding that "this is an open country, a tolerant country".

One Muslim woman in western Sweden was arrested on charges of issuing a death threat against Vilks in an e-mail. The woman confirmed during police interrogation that she had written the e-mail and said that she did not have any regrets about it. On the 6th of September, one actual roundabout dog created by Vilks and local children was set alight as an apparent threat.

It was reported that the group Islamic State of Iraq had placed a bounty of at least $100,000 on the head of Lars Vilks and 50,000 dollars on Ulf Johansson, editor-in-chief of *Nerikes Allehanda*. This reward would be raised to $150,000 if he was slaughtered like a lamb, the statement said. The statement also threatened attacks on Swedish companies unless unspecified "crusaders" issued an apology.

The European Council for Fatwa and Research (ECFR) and the Federation of Islamic Organizations in Europe (FIOE) both condemned the death threats against Vilks and Johansson. ECFR also said it planned to issue a "counter fatwa" against the threats.

The World Association of Newspapers (WAN), which represents over 18,000 newspapers around the world, issued a statement where it condemned the death threats and expressed support for *Nerikes Allehanda*'s right to publish the drawing.

1.2.3. The EU Policy in the Cartoon Controversy

In the wake of the affair known as the "Mohammed cartoons" affair, the countries of the Organization of the Islamic Conference (OIC) presented a resolution entitled "Combating defamation of religions."

The European Union is opposed to it: its members do not see the concept of defamation of religions as a valid one in an arena committed to the protection and promotion of human rights and consider that we need to protect the rights of individuals in the exercise of their freedom of religion or belief, rather than the religions as such. By focusing on the obligation to protect a religion, the notion of "defamation of religions" can be used to justify arbitrary limitations imposed on certain human rights or prohibiting the exercise of these rights, in particular the freedom of expression.

In France there is a belief that, since human rights are correlated and indivisible, the freedom of expression and the freedom of religion and belief complement each other. It is assumed that the notion of "defamation of religions" is not compatible with international human rights law, which aims to protect individuals, not doctrines of thought.

With this in mind, it is vital to distinguish between the criticism of religions and beliefs, on the one hand, and the incitement to religious hatred, on the other. Only the latter must be opposed to the extent that it constitutes incitement to discrimination in accordance with articles 19 and 20 of the *International Covenant on Civil and Political Rights*.

That is why France, together with its European partners, has adopted a firm political position which is systematically defended in the international arenas in order to oppose the relativist concept of defamation of religions.

This position was formalised by the adoption of the conclusions of the EU Council on the freedom of religion and belief of the 16th November 2009: this text reflects the values of *laïcité* (secularism). It affirms, in particular, the need to provide adequate and effective guarantees of the freedom of thought, conscience and religion and underlines that the freedom of expression is intrinsically linked to it, citing in particular the right to criticise religion. It also reaffirms that the freedom of religion and belief includes the right to adopt or to abandon a religion, as well as the right not to profess a religion.

The November 2nd 2011 issue of the French satirical weekly *Charlie Hebdo* is entitled “Charia Hebdo” (a play on the French word for sharia), and is apparently “edited” by Muhammad, who is shown to “threaten” the readers with “100 lashes if you don’t die of laughter!” in a front-page cartoon. Inside are dozens of satirical stories and cartoons depicting Muhammad, as well as cartoons featuring women wearing the burqa, the face-covering veil. The idea was to mockingly ‘celebrate’ the victory of Islamists at Tunisia’s recent election, and the introduction of the sharia law in Libya. The following day the publication’s offices in the 20th arrondissement of Paris were firebombed.

Many Muslims did indeed find the cartoons offensive, not least because they breach a convention in Islam that the Prophet should not be depicted. However, Nicolas Sarkozy, former French president who was then interior minister, expressed his view on the 2006 controversy in the following way: he preferred, he said, “an excess of caricature to an excess of censorship”.

1.2.4. How Controversial is Freedom of Expression?

Within democracies, freedom of expression remains controversial: Should there be restrictions on hate speech, on obscenities, or on publishing sensitive national security information? Examining freedom of expression in light of the history of authoritarianism and totalitarianism, past and present, helps place many of these debates in greater perspective and provides deeper understanding of the significance and scope of freedom of expression.

The formal laws constituting freedom of expression in democratic societies are only the tip of the iceberg of unwritten agreements among citizens about what they can express publicly in particular situations and contexts. These agreements differ from society to society: in the case of Denmark, the agreement to allow the publication of the Mohammed cartoons in the Danish newspaper *Jyllands-Posten* has reinforced the proliferation of anti-Muslim prejudice and has served to produce conflict instead of dealing with it. The reactions to the Danish cartoon controversy reveal strong divergences about what the right to free speech is supposed to entail.

If the Danish newspaper *Jyllands-Posten* had instead published anti-Semitic cartoons, very few would have accepted the argument that the newspaper only wanted to manifest its freedom of expression. Nor would the prime minister of Denmark have failed to distance himself from such a manifestation. Most people would have understood that not everything that is theoretically legal to say must also be said, and that freedom of expression has its limits.

As language users, we soon realise that, in order to avoid misunderstanding and conflict, we cannot always say in public what we say in private. The risk of what we say in public being misunderstood is often greater. Moreover, what we say publicly may inadvertently hurt some people or groups of people. When we say something in public, we must also have some notion about how it will be perceived and understood, especially if what we actually say is intended to hurt or wound, which in our tradition of freedom of expression has become a rightful intent in certain public spheres. Someone who has no such notion, and therefore who does not care whether s/he is understood or not, has at best misunderstood the premises of the freedom of expression. Therefore, when a major Danish daily in a country notorious for its fierce anti-Muslim public rhetoric decides to publish cartoons of the prophet Mohammed, with the stated purpose to demonstrate the Danish freedom of expression, it must either not have understood that the purpose would be perceived quite differently by Denmark's already battered Muslims – or it must have had a different purpose. To many it demonstrated not the strength of Danish freedom of expression, but rather its weakness.

1.2.5. Dimensions of the Freedom of Expression

Concrete manifestations of the freedom of expression can take different forms in terms of:

- the sphere of the interaction: Public vs. Private (we cannot always say in public what we say in private)
- the target of the interaction: Individual vs. Collective (the emphasis may be on an individual's personal characteristics or on group/ethnic stereotypes)
- the nature of the potential offence: Intentional vs. Non-intentional (the targeted person/s is/are expected or not expected to feel insulted, get hurt, etc.)

In connection with freedom of expression the following questions arise: What may a tabloid print on its posters? What may a daily newspaper write about particular religious groups, such as Muslims, and about religions, such as Islam? The answers to such questions will depend on different shared understandings and agreements retrievable in different public arenas. In the Danish public sphere, it has long been possible to say things about Muslims and Islam that are not always possible to say in the Swedish public arena, for example. This does not necessarily mean that Denmark has more freedom of expression than Sweden, but only that public Denmark has stretched the limit for tolerating the expression of challenging opinions in the public sphere. In Denmark this may have been done at the cost of excluding its Muslim population from the process of tuning and adjusting the pragmatic rules of public discourse.

France, unlike Denmark and Sweden, has very explicit laws delimiting the freedom of expression. According to article R 625-4 of the French Penal Code, individuals who are perceived to insult others based on their race or origin are subject to fines and trial in French court. This also applies to the propagation of hatred.

Two public arenas that are kept apart in Scandinavian and other European countries are politics and the media. In Denmark freedom of expression is not submitted to state control. It is up to the free media to take the responsibility. Though frowning on those who reproduced images first circulated in Denmark's *Jyllands-Posten*, several politicians insisted that editors were within their legal rights to do so. Governments refrained from apologising to the Islamic community because they consider publication to be a matter for editors, not politicians. In countries like France, however, there is a separation between the state and the church, which is known as *la laïcité*. Hence the emphasis is placed on the neutrality of the state and the public sphere.

When citizens are unable to talk to and with each other, or see no need to do so, they will increasingly talk past and against each other, and thereby will increasingly misunderstand and mistrust each other. A major challenge to the freedom of expression is the lack of informal controls and agreements, a result of the rapid division of our societies into separate public spheres that no longer communicate with each other.

1.3. Final Remarks

As has been argued throughout this chapter, the notions of *freedom* and *liberty* are historically, socially and culturally determined, but they are increasingly used with reference to situations and events that acquire cross-cultural scope and significance. Thus moral values, norms and expectations reflected in the pragma-semantic meanings of these concepts are being submitted to scrutiny and debate across cultural and political borders.

The essence of freedom of expression is not the right to express offensive views about the beliefs of others, but rather the freedom to report or convey facts, opinions, philosophies, and worldviews with the support of valid arguments. Freedom of expression is supposed to empower citizens through knowledge, opinion, and the possibility to use their own voice. Within democracies, free expression allows citizens to challenge political leaders, journalists to uncover information for the public, and the public to require the accountability of their government. A set of basic stipulations with regard to freedom of expression have been put forward in the *White Paper on Intercultural Dialogue* launched in 2008 by the Council of Europe:

> The exercise of this freedom [of speech], which comes with duties and responsibilities, may be limited in certain specific conditions defined in Article 10 paragraph 2 of the European Convention on Human Rights. "Hate speech" has been an increasing concern of the European Convention on Human Rights in recent years, and in its jurisprudence the Court has drawn the boundary, case by case, beyond which the right to freedom of expression is forfeited.
>
> Some expressions are so gratuitously offensive, defamatory or insulting as to threaten a culture of tolerance itself – indeed that may inflict not only unconscionable indignity on members of minority communities but also expose them to intimidation and threats. Inciting hatred based on intolerance is not compatible with respect for fundamental rights and freedoms guaranteed by the Convention and the Court's jurisprudence.
>
> The European Convention on Human Rights has however set a high bar against restrictions on free expression, indicating that even expressions that "offend, shock and disturb" should be protected. This means, for example, a certain licence to criticise another's religion (as a system of ideas which they can choose to embrace). The Court takes into account the impact and context of the expressions made, in particular when they contribute to a pluralistic public debate on matters of general interest.
>
> As for the media, the basic principle is the defence of freedom of expression even if there is however a recognition of the special duties and responsibilities of journalists who must be free to express their opinions – including value judgements – on matters of public concern, but who are also responsible for the collection and dissemination of objective information.

Freedom of expression is essential in enabling citizens to participate in democratic debates and decision-making processes. In order to ensure the respect for and exercise of our rights and freedoms, we need to have free access to information and ideas, and to be able to express our views freely. We are sometimes faced with some extreme forms of expression which incite intolerance or hatred between groups, and which need to be curtailed for the protection of other human rights. Restricting the freedom of expression in such situations is always a fine balancing act. This is why we should continuously scrutinise, expose and discuss the concrete implications of instances of restriction or violation of freedom of expression.

References

Berlin, I. 1969. *Four essays on liberty*. Oxford: Clarendon Press.

Evans-Pritchard, E. 1981. *A history of anthropological thought*, ed. André Singer. New York: Basic Books.

Ilie, C. 2007. British 'consensus' versus Swedish 'samförstånd' in parliamentary debates. In *The use of English in institutional and business settings: An intercultural perspective*, eds. G. Garzone & C. Ilie, 101-125. Bern: Peter Lang.

Lakoff, G. 2006. *Whose freedom? The battle over America's most important idea*. New York: Farrar, Straus and Giroux.

Roosevelt, F. D. 1941. Address to Congress on January 6, 1941. In *Congressional Record,* 1941, Vol. 87, Pt. I. (available at: http://www.wwnorton.com/college/history/ralph/workbook/ralprs36b.htm, accessed September 26, 2012)

Ross, W. D, 1930. *The Right and the Good*. Oxford: Oxford University Press,

Taylor, Ch. 1982. *Philosophical papers, Vol. 2: Philosophy and the human sciences*. Cambridge: Cambridge University Press.

Wierzbicka, A. 1997. *Understanding cultures through their key words: English, Russian, Polish, German and Japanese*. Oxford: Oxford University Press.

Williams, R. 1976. *Keywords: A vocabulary of culture and society*. London: Flamingo, Fontana.

CHAPTER TWO

DOMINANT LANGUAGES IN A MULTILINGUAL SOCIETY[1]

ROMÁN ÁLVAREZ RODRÍGUEZ

2.1. European Cultural Identity

In the 21st century, we find ourselves in a world in which the homogenizing humanist ideology that has been prevalent since the Age of Enlightenment has given way to a new space in which intellectuals are more prone to posing questions than to offering answers, where there is a more heterogeneous and open way to see and analyze things, where differing opinions would seem to be accepted more easily. If we consider Europe as a common homeland, we must assume that both World Wars were European Civil Wars, wars that took place as a consequence of different views of the world. If, with the passing of time, we now defend a common identity, it would seem logical to assume that a post-nationalist phase will open before us. However, this does not seem to be the case, but quite the opposite. Let us observe the splitting process and the political quasi-dismemberment affecting some countries, as well as the stubborn pro-independence attempts of other regions that, of course, clearly state their respective adherence and attachment to different European identities. This may lead us to wonder whether Europe continues to be a focal point that hopes to maintain a sense of universality. In this regard, the identity of the "Self"—i.e. Europe—would be defined by its opposition to the "Other", to the others that have been historically subject to what some authors have called "metaphysical cannibalism". However, if we choose a European post-nationalist re-definition, then we will be erasing the binary classification of the "Self" versus the "Other", or "Us" versus "Them". We

[1]This paper forms part of research Project GR277, titled "Immigration and Translation Policies: New Cultural Mediation Challenges in the 21st Century", which is funded by the Spanish Regional Government of Castile and Leon.

would be assuming the legitimate European membership of the "immigrant subject", of the "hybrid" citizens we are turning into full members. We would be bringing into question the old and unclear concept of "Europeanness"—if it ever existed at all—, "unity in diversity", or Europe as a cultural term. We would, in short, be redefining a new political concept, once the old equation stating that one nation equals one language and one culture becomes outdated. The "pure" identity would then give way to a hybridization within the framework of a new European multiculturality in which there is room for new subjects, a multilingual Europe whose organizations and institutions work in 22 languages (Romance, Germanic and Slavic languages, as well as two non-Indo-European languages) and three alphabets (Latin, Greek and Cyrillic), with a total of 462 possible language combinations for translation and interpreting. Some of the languages are within states, but others cross borders. And there are other languages as well, such as Turkish, knocking at the Union's door.

Borders have always been changeable, mutable and unpredictable entities that have created countless conflicts throughout History. On a linguistic level, this has significant implications, which are sometimes the origin of debates that cannot be resolved, such as the French and Flemish border in Belgium, for example, which, from a political point of view, goes far beyond the simple use of one language over another by the speakers. Let me just refer to the latest election results and their potential consequences and imbalances in the political panorama of a highly fragmented country that has managed to survive for a year and a half without a government. In some cases, borders are given to us by the evolution of History: great empires and their subsequent dismantling, which have reached high levels of fragmentation (the Roman Empire, the Ottoman Empire, the Austro-Hungarian Empire, etc.), accounts for many of the current political and linguistic boundaries. In other cases, such as Africa, frontiers have been traced over maps; they are artificial borders that were once established according to certain criteria that did not take into account cultural and linguistic affinities, ethnic or identity groups. These are borders created by politicians and administrators with drawing pens, rulers and set squares, the final result of violent colonizations, rushed decolonizations or illegitimate economic interests. There are also other borders that separate speakers of the same language, borders that set apart people who shared the same culture for centuries, and that divided members of the same family for political reasons. A close example would be the Iron Curtain in Eastern Europe, with Berlin as the epitome of this situation. There are borders with a similar origin, that were drawn as the consequence of fratricidal wars, and that are still in force in the world today: at one end of Asia, for instance, both Koreas are separated by an impassable wall of concrete, steel and minefields that represent a completely unbreakable barrier, although inhabitants from both sides speak the same language.

At the beginning of the 20th century, the European powers controlled a high percentage of the surface of the earth. And, although in the second half of that same century there were different—and more or less traumatic—decolonization processes (which could be euphemistically called "power transfers") that altered maps and borders, the mark of dominant languages remained, especially in those places in which the language imposed by the colonizers was used for communication after the structures of power were altered. Thus, we have built a world in which dominant languages coexist with minoritized languages, a world in which, from different languages and different cultures, we regard those who do not share those same codes as us with suspicion, and we forget that, since the Enlightenment, plurality has been regarded as an asset instead of a burden. However, it is also true—and even paradoxical—that the age of Enlightenment was the origin of the great colonizing empires that subjugated thousands of peoples and took advantage of their economies and resources.

After World War II there were some forced displacements of entire populations: Poles, Ukrainians, Germans, Czechoslovaks, Serbs, Bosnians, etc. Some of those migrations are the root of subsequent ethnic conflicts that are still alive today. The stereotypical images finally put the Other back into fashion, they turned it into a commodity, they turned multiculturalism into a banality, they propagated simplistic ideas of exoticism, of "strangeness", but, ultimately, what they did was maintain a political, social, military and economic control over minoritized cultures. After decolonization, crowds of immigrants from decolonized countries went to the old metropolis, in the belief that they had some hypothetical rights as previous subjects. However, they found that colonial humiliation was now paired with a new kind of humiliation: the land that, much to its regret, received them was far from being the Promised Land.

The term "repatriated person" was coined in order to allude specifically to the selection that was carried out in order to accept expatriates: some of them showed a higher degree of "belonging" to the land that was receiving them than others, depending on how fast they could integrate into it. Basically, it was a matter of ethnic and cultural differences, rather than linguistic differences. Years later, a similar situation took place when the subjects of old colonies came back to their respective metropolis, as a consequence of decolonization processes. In the Netherlands, for example, white citizens received a different treatment to other citizens when they came back from Surinam (former Dutch Guiana). To be perfectly honest, we must point out that there were no legal differences at the beginning. However, wide sectors of society soon voiced their reluctance. On the other hand, this problem had not been detected when, in 1949, after the independence of Indonesia, many citizens came back to the land of their ancestors, especially if they were white and had not mixed with native ethnic groups. In the United Kingdom, the double process of admission to the heart of British citizenship was determined by membership of either the old or the new Commonwealth. Therefore, the old—and white—Commonwealth included countries such as Australia, New Zealand and Canada, whereas the new one—non-white—included countries from Africa and Asia. The reception of this last group in the colonial country was much more problematic and, in some cases, simply impossible. Only some years ago, and on our doorstep, the war of the old Yugoslavia triggered a diaspora of five million refugees (data provided by the UN), which represents the biggest population movement since the end of World War II in Europe. The consequences can still be felt today.

Religious differences, on the other hand, lie beneath some of the conflicts that threaten world peace nowadays, in a world in which radical ideologies arouse a great deal of interest and in which difference and diversity represent a significant part of it. It would be absurd to deny that these and other differences have determined the historical existence of all peoples. Collective differences are likewise changeable, as well as identities and even the sense of belonging. A global culture unifies, standardizes and controls potential dissidents. Everything tends to be homogeneous, standard and repetitive as a result of the loss of originality. However, there are many other deficiencies, such as the lack of social sensitivity that does not affect our consciences—or even our appetites—when, at dinner time, the television screen shows scenes of famine in the Horn of Africa or the crowds that flee from Libya and are crammed in Lampedusa, in the hope that they can reach the European continent. What we see is misery and injustice amidst western superabundance. Even misery itself can become a commodity and a frequent topic for conversation with which, supposedly, we silence the voice of our consciences. Values become mixed up and disrupted in an endless dance. Advanced societies in the so-called First World are threatened by dangers that were not even detected before. For this reason, dominant powers are confused in view of the risks represented by the progressive and unstoppable incorporation of the Other crossing our borders or reaching our shores aboard fragile rafts or crammed open boats. It is no wonder that alarms are raised and xenophobic feelings come to the surface when certain leaders of Islamist movements talk about the future *Reconquista* of Al-Andalus, all the way up to Poitiers, or when they state that, halfway through the 21st century, the conquest of the Netherlands will be concluded by the demographic growth of Muslims within the borders of the country itself.

2.2. Language and the Consolidation of Power

How is an identity built? In *La peur des barbares* (2008), Tzvetan Todorov states that the concept of a collective identity has become a suspicious one, because it seems to infringe individual liberties. In a plurality of cultures we must distinguish between cultural belonging and civic identity. Cultural belonging is something we feel from childhood when we internalize certain habits, codes and lifestyles. This does not mean that we have a single cultural identity, but several different ones that overlap or intertwine through life, because, all in all, every culture is changeable, agglutinative, hybrid, crossbred or half-breed, because it is the result of previous cultures and is subject to a perpetual transformation, although some of the so called "traditional" cultures have changed at a slower pace than "modern" ones. However, no identity is immutable. Culture is the image that society has of itself, according to Todorov. Nevertheless, from the point of view of our individual identity, changes that directly involve the culture we live in are received with suspicion, or even with open hostility. This is the case when, in the cultural environment in which we usually live, we suddenly perceive the continuous arrival of new neighbors, speakers of a different language that is incomprehensible to us, who probably profess a different religion, who are slowly settling in the area. The defining features of their identity—language and religion—may not be identifying features of the culture they are entering, which may generate hostile reactions by both parties and trigger an action-reaction effect, which gives way to interethnic discordance, to resentment and conflicts that are not easily resolved. Edward Said, among many others, speaks about the lack of understanding, banishment and exile, and the identity complexity. In sum, what he suffered himself as an engaged intellectual, and what he reflects in the memories that have the significant title *Out of Place*. For his part, in *La défaite de la pensée* (1987), Finkielkraut states that we cannot deny that the presence in Europe of a growing number of immigrants from the Third World poses unprecedented problems, and that people who are expelled from their homes by misery and who are traumatized by colonial humiliation cannot harbour feelings of gratitude towards the country that takes them in, contrary to what happened with the refugees from Eastern Europe. Building an identity is not easy, least of all in this new century in which identity is far from homogeneous, but emerges from the dialogue—sometimes a bitter and forced one—between collective experiences that are very different.

How do we build an identity with language? Human beings are characterized by their ability to use language. The plurality of voices implies that there are some differences, but not superiority of one of them—the norm—over that of the Other. Reductionist and simplistic views, far from recognizing the plurality of cultures and identity, promote the clash between the Self and the Other. These reductionisms can be seen in the policies that oppose the declaration of equal rights and duties, those that bring into question the plurality of voices and cultural identities and that deny the most privileged manifestation of those languages which is literature. K. A. Appiah reminds us that the fact that a territory may be populated by twenty or thirty languages is neither good nor bad. The fact that one of them may disappear because the people who use it are being abused is the true tragedy. This reasoning can also be applied to the loss represented by the disappearance of certain species from the Earth. George Steiner, for his part, fears that we may reach a situation of monolingualism—which many have yearned for—, which would represent an extremely serious danger for liberties because, in fact, it would mean falling into the clutches of Anglo-American economic dominance, which can be seen as the Esperanto of commerce. The West wants to homogenize other identities, to fix some cultural parameters and guarantee a unitary space against fragmentation.

Language is an essential instrument in the consolidation of those power structures. For this reason, cultural or political subordination continued to place certain nations or social groups in a position of dependence on the hegemonic culture, even when this culture had officially left the field clear for the autonomous development of those nations and groups. For this reason, many cultures that were dominated by colonizing powers look for their own ways of self-representation and identity through the promotion of national languages, although they do not neglect the colonizing language—mainly due to practical reasons. However, we cannot deny that power and dominance relationships have always been present between languages, and that the use of one language over another is a reflection of the asymmetries at work in the political arena. And, of course, if we talk about the political arena we might as well talk about the economic one, because both powers usually go hand in hand. Dominant languages adhere to certain continuous, constant and homogeneous norms and standards that strengthen that feeling of superiority they feed on.

Many authors who live in a context of cultural crossbreeding rebel against language as an instrument of power. Therefore, we can see Indians who write in English, Maghrebis who write in French, Turks who write in German, Iranians who write in Dutch, Africans who write in Spanish… They all inhabit ambiguous territories and they suffer certain tensions when they write in "strong", dominant languages. They find a potential escape route from these tensions when they try to create a language in which there can be no doubt that there is an underlying asymmetry, in which there can be no doubt that, although they may yield to a language, they do so by peppering it with "rebelliousness", with quirks that are exclusively found in the culture of the writer. The writer, then, tries to reassert his or her personality through certain hybrid or local nuances that emphasize the element of otherness, the interferences, the mixture of acceptance and rejection of the colonizer's language, which is the language of success on the social scale.

Language is not innocent. It crystallizes in the form of metaphors, and these metaphors carry connotative elements that are a reflection of many other things. In today's world, the balancing elements between different languages have changed. Nowadays, many people feel, so to speak, like nomads in their own languages. Minoritized languages and dominant languages come into conflict, because they represent a reality that goes far beyond some specific linguistic uses: they represent relations of power in the broadest sense, they bring the Self face to face with the Other, and they demand a change in these relations. Let us consider an example: in the United States, where the "English only" doctrine prevailed for decades, Arabic is a minoritized language, even if there are more than 200 million Arabic speakers in the world (in 25 countries). Less than 1% of all students of foreign languages choose Arabic in the United States. However, after September 11, Americans realized that national security was being threatened, and that there were security breaches because dangers were not being detected in time due to a lack of translators and interpreters of Arabic.

With regard to languages, European citizens—if they really consider themselves European—should learn one of the majority languages and also at least one of the languages used in the smaller countries. This would counteract the lack of willingness to try to understand the Other, starting with the language. There is nothing worse than a "mute" world faced with the voices of the minorities or those that come from the periphery.

Something similar could be said of the study of those literatures that contributed to the creation of a European identity, not only the great canonical literatures of dominant languages, but also those literatures written in the minoritized languages I have just referred to. All of them—the big ones and the small ones—have contributed to the establishment of a European spirituality, and they contribute to the understanding of the Other. They let us listen to the Other, respect him and integrate everything that is located in the margins, far away from the centers of power. These literatures help us destroy, in sum, that monolithic image of the Other that we have built from stereotyped and decadent binary assumptions: good versus evil; civilized versus primitive; western white versus savage black, etc. Minoritized cultures claim their own spaces, but not only those commercial spaces that may arise because the minoritized reality has come into fashion. Cultural differences also become diluted when a common language is shared in the post-colonial world.

2.3. Spanish Versus English?

Can we defend today the principle that states that a language is important whenever the nation that speaks it is also important in the international arena? If we assume this point of view, there is no doubt that Spanish is the main vertebrating instrument of a linguistic community which has over four hundred million speakers, many of whom defend their own identity precisely through the use of a common language. Languages do not only communicate, they also contribute to the placement of countries where they belong in the global panorama. In this regard, we can rightly declare that "language is money". Empires, conquests and their respective colonization processes, political and economic power, in sum, consolidate the preeminence of languages and they guarantee their survival. The Spanish scholar Antonio de Nebrija was perfectly aware of this reality when he defined language as the partner of Empires. The two great powers that held political control for centuries in large areas of the planet—Spain and Great Britain—defined both an economic and linguistic hegemony with their presence.

The Spanish language was considered in Spain to be so strong in the mid-20th century that the so-called "State exams" that enable students to access university education did not even include a test for other modern languages. Even during the two last years of secondary education, teachers of classical languages earned more than those who were in charge of modern languages. English, on the other hand, was at that time present in all teaching levels in the curriculums of most of the Western world. In the last decade of that century, British leaders led an effort to position themselves in what they called "Eastern Europe emerging democracies" after the collapse of the Soviet Union. In virtually no time, prestigious institutions for linguistic and cultural diffusion, such as the British Council, dismantled or cut down many of their facilities in countries where their presence was firmly rooted and quickly moved to Eastern Europe in order to occupy the space left by the Russian influence that had been imposed on them through military force. The so-called "Euro-English" continued then its unstoppable pace through the European continent.

When assessing the relevance of a language, the following parameters can be taken into account: number of native speakers; number of countries in which the language is spoken and number of inhabitants of those countries; number of "secondary" speakers (i.e. foreign students, immigrants, etc.); economic power of the countries in which the language is used; number of areas of human activity in which the language is important; and prestige of the language in fields such as literature, social sciences and other areas of culture.

An empirical proof of the importance of a language is the number of translations made from it towards other languages. The authority, prestige and status of a dominant language materialize in the amount and variety of texts that are transferred to other languages. There are some data that are self-explanatory. Approximately one quarter of all books published in Spanish are translations, and from these translations, approximately one half come from English. This includes children's and young adult literature, conventional literary creation, social science texts, technical and scientific texts, etc., and these numbers from Spain are similar to those of Italy, for example. On the other hand, translations into English represent one tenth of the volume of texts translated from English into Spanish.

The European Union's policy tries to reflect Europe's diversity, with its multiple languages, through a democratic multilingualism, because it considers that the existence of a dominating language imposed from outside would remind us of the forced adoptions carried out by subjugated populations in the old colonizing powers. However, we cannot forget that any *lingua franca* is a freely accepted communication system. The diffusion of new knowledge, both in the field of science and technology must take place, not only in our linguistic and cultural environment, but also within the global scientific community. However, the instrument of communication and diffusion that has been universally accepted was—and is—the English language.

The English language underwent a great advance when it was decreed that it could be used in the field of science and for the transmission of all kinds of knowledge by the Royal Society (1662), as well as with the introduction of new vocabulary for the new ideas and concepts that appeared in the scientific and technical areas. In this context, the "Plain English Movement" was also important because of the influence it exerted on the journals and novels of the 18th century. Let us remember, however, that, in the first third of the 17th century, the philosopher Francis Bacon wrote his philosophical work, *Novum Organum* in Latin, and that at the end of that same century, Isaac Newton also used Latin for the presentation of his findings in the field of calculus and mechanics, under the title *Philosophiae Naturalis Principia Mathematica* (1687). Even then, those in favour of the English language were opposed to the old idea that some disciplines, such as Philosophy or scientific advances should be expressed in Latin because English was not an adequate or accurate language. It was in the Age of Enlightenment that they championed the triumph of English, and were convinced that this language was perfectly valid for the expression of any concept or thought, regardless of how abstract, deep or complex it was.

Nowadays we talk about "World English", "Global English" and "International English". I believe that it is worth paying close attention to a language that might serve as an example because it set a precedent of what seems to be an unstoppable and undeniable international expansion. English, as Steiner points out, is the language that a South Korean pilot uses to speak with the control tower of a Greek airport. However, it is also a language of business, and the language that many European universities consider as the most adequate for the transmission of knowledge and the recruitment of international students.

The universities themselves, as we know, promote teaching in English under the pretext of the European Convergence and its hypothetical requirements. Some Spanish universities are proud to include English in part or all of their studies. The University of Salamanca urges those responsible for the studies to do their part, and in the near future we can foresee a sufficiently representative presence of English as a vehicular language in many subjects, which will undoubtedly require adequate motivation and counseling for the teaching staff.

However, we must not forget that Spanish is the language of a large international community of more than four hundred million speakers and that it can structure the diffusion of scientific and technological knowledge with the aid and the support of the authorities who, paradoxically, seem to be the first to mistrust that ability of the Spanish language to compete with

English. According to Spain's Interministry Commission for Science and Technology (2007), "Scientific and technical knowledge, as well as their application to all the fields of life in our societies are one of the driving forces of the processes of economic growth and improvement of social welfare". So far, so good, but the treatment received by the Spanish language within the country, in the communities with a different official language may lead us to think that Spanish is an "enemy language". The Spanish Ministry of Science and Innovation, in its *Guidelines for R&D&I Projects 2009*, which can be accessed through their webpage, states the following in the 2nd point of its 2nd section, which refers to the presentation of applications: "Also, if the budget exceeds the sum of € 150,000, applicants must include the scientific and technical report in English". We can interpret, therefore, that all "scientific and technical" knowledge must be reported in English, because in this case, unlike in the projects with smaller budgets in which an abstract of the proposal must be included *also* in English, the applicants must write the report in English alone.

If we start from these premises, what can we expect from the promotion of Spanish as a capable and adequate language for the international scientific community? And what about the promotion and presence of the other European languages? European languages can contribute to the diffusion of new knowledge, but they must prove that they can act as instruments in order to put their respective countries in the vanguard of knowledge and international competitiveness. The authorities must implement all necessary mechanisms and infrastructures for this purpose, and while improving the funding of research programs, they will have to support all scientific organizations that promote excellence in research, or increase the relations between the university and the productive sector, for example. The problem lies in the fact that international networks of research projects operate in English, and for this reason the participation and inclusion of groups or individuals who speak other languages presupposes the acceptance of English as a natural vehicle for science and technology. On the other hand, statistics show that the entire corpus of publications in Romance languages (used by more than one billion speakers) represents one tenth of the number of works published in English.

Therefore, there is a clear predominance of English in scientific databases, in scientific and technological discussion forums, in computer jargon, etc. In all those fields we have yielded with almost no resistance to the entry of words, expressions and acronyms that came from the English language, and we have not tried—or we have tried too feebly—to impose our linguistic equivalents, which were perfectly adequate. My view, in this sense, is that our brothers from Latin America have been more alert and have remained stronger defenders of the language than the Spaniards themselves. On the other hand, entries in a tool as popular as *Wikipedia* are much more common, not only in English (in which the number of articles is around ten times higher), but also in languages such as German, French, Japanese, Italian or even Polish and Portuguese.

But there is no doubt that English itself has been subjected to a hybridization process that can be seen in the literature corpus of the Commonwealth. Something similar could be said about the Spanish language with regard to the entire Spanish-speaking community. And regarding the recent diffusion of the language, let us remember that, in a matter of a few years, the number of Spanish language students in Brazil has increased at least fivefold, and that these numbers have also grown considerably in many other countries, as shown by statistics and the increasing demand that is barely met by the Institutos Cervantes all over the world.

The Spanish language, through its different geographical varieties, seems to be becoming more and more international. We can, therefore, refer to a "global Spanish" which is, to some extent, an "eccentric" or multicentric variety, a kind of International Spanish in which the Pan-Hispanic linguistic standard has been promoted. This is a variety that recognizes the blunt reality that states that variation does not endanger the standard language. I believe that, in this process of internationalization, many advances are due to the efforts of the Instituto Cervantes, as well as those of the five World Conferences of the Spanish Language that have been organized so far in Zacatecas, Valladolid, Rosario, Cartagena de Indias and Valparaiso.

The projection of Spanish in the English-speaking world is clear in several cases. Let us consider two significant examples: we can assert that the introduction of Spanish in the United States is unstoppable in quantitative terms. Back in 1978, *Time* published a report on this subject, and it stated that in some counties of Miami (such as Dade, for example), Spanish threatened to replace English completely[2]. In this country, the students of Spanish outnumber all other students of foreign languages (French, German, Italian, Portuguese, Russian, Japanese, Chinese, etc.) as a whole. However, in my opinion, too much emphasis is placed on merely quantitative factors, because the important fact is whether those millions of Spanish-speaking people in the United States will act as bilingual individuals in the future or will abandon their mother tongue. Another

---

[2] See Lorenzo (1980: 151).

interesting case is that of New Zealand where, according to official data from the year 2009, Spanish is already the second most taught foreign language in primary and secondary schools, only surpassed by French. Japanese, which had traditionally been in the second place as a foreign language, has now been pushed out. Data from the year 2009 show that there are 25,979 French students, 23,778 Spanish students and 17,647 Japanese students as well as 8,830 German students and 4,838 students of other languages. True, there are still many more centers that teach French (252) than Spanish (161), but the number of people interested in Spanish is clearly growing on a daily basis. The recent inauguration of a Center of the University of Salamanca in Auckland will mean a new boost for the promotion of Spanish in the Oceanic country, because the University of Salamanca is rightly known as "the University of Spanish".

The Spanish language, in its struggle with English, needs the support of institutions with which it can reach larger areas of influence in the globalized world. A stronger promotion of Spanish in the networks of the society of information and knowledge, for example, would be advisable, thus creating new alternatives in cyberspace, the world of e-business, telemedicine, telework, mobile devices and electronic support (PDAs, iPhones, etc.). Also, another useful initiative would be the coordination of efforts and synergies with other countries of our same linguistic environment (Argentina, Mexico, Colombia and Chile, mainly), which are strongly committed to the development of Spanish as a foreign language, and have recently been opening up a very considerable market in this area. Similarly, it would be a good idea to promote the Spanish language in African countries, where its presence is barely noticeable, except for Equatorial Guinea, although this country is veering towards French under the apparent indifference of the Spanish authorities. There are some countries, such as Cameroon, for example, where there is a considerable demand for Spanish language. The creation of university chairs for African Studies might act as a stimulus for linguistic contacts, and it would also bring those countries closer and gain new markets for our language. Another aspect that should be taken into account is the establishment of agreements between institutions or public services and Spanish business with branches in countries that might be interested in our offer of Spanish. The business world would be the first to benefit from this, because companies would have Spanish-speaking workers in their environment, not to mention the potential fiscal benefits that might derive from it. The collaboration of diplomatic representations in these countries is essential in the early stages of these relations. In view of the facts that we have mentioned before, there should be a promotion of the translation of Spanish books to other languages, either by means of incentives for publishing houses or other means of support, such as financial aid for conferences like "*El español, lengua de traducción*", that takes place every two years, or for projects, such as TERMINESP, backed by the Spanish Association of Terminology, which aims to spread the scientific and technical terminology of the Spanish language. Along this same line, some events should be institutionalized, like "*2010 Año Internacional del Español*". This would represent a great support for the Spanish language as well as for its international projection. Also, these projects could receive European funding and count on the support of Latin American governments. It is a satisfaction to see that, in the Department of Public Information of the United Nations headquarters in New York, Spanish is the second language with the highest number of requests, immediately after English.

We must admit that counteracting the influence of the English language as a centralizing force in an international reality, with the current state of communications, Internet, etc. is a very difficult task, at least in certain areas. However, History has shown that there is nothing completely foreseeable in the diachronic evolution of languages. David Crystal already reminded us, in a conference back in the year 2000, that no one would have thought, one millennium ago, that there would be almost no people who understood Latin one thousand years later.

References

Alvarez Rodríguez, R., and M. C. Á. Vidal Claramonte, eds. 1996. *Translation, Power, Subversion*. Clevedon: Multilingual Matters.

Appiah, K. A. 2008. *Mi cosmopolitismo*. Buenos Aires: Katz Editores. Trad. Lilia Mosconi.

Bhabha, H. 1994. *The Location of Culture*. London and New York: Routledge.

Beck, U. 2007. *Pour un Empire européen*. Paris: Flammarion.

Carbonell, O. 1997. *Traducir al Otro. Traducción, exotismo, poscolonialismo*. Cuenca: Ediciones Universidad de Castilla-La Mancha.

Crystal, D. 1997. *English as a Global Language*. Cambridge: Cambridge University Press.

Finkielkraut, A. 1987. *La derrota del pensamiento*. Barcelona: Anagrama. Trad. Joaquín Jordá.

Lorenzo, E. 1980. *El español y otras lenguas*. Madrid: Sociedad General Española de Librería.

Said, E. 1999. *Out of Place*. London: Granta Publications.
Steiner, G. 2002. Errante entre lenguas. Una entrevista de Ramón Jahanbegloo a George Steiner. *Debats* 75. 60-66.
Todorov, T. 2008. *El miedo a los bárbaros*. Madrid: Galaxia Gutenberg. Trad. Noemí Sobregués.
Torres Robles, A., ed. 2006. *I Acta Internacional de la Lengua Española. El español: activo cultural y valor económico creciente*. San Millán de la Cogolla.
Vidal Claramonte, M. C. Á. 2007. *Traducir entre culturas. Diferencias, poderes, identidades*. Frankfurt: Peter Lang.

CHAPTER THREE

MIGRATION AND EDUCATIONAL SUCCESS THE CHALLENGE OF LANGUAGE DIVERSITY FOR EUROPEAN EDUCATION SYSTEMS

JOANA DUARTE

3.1. Introduction

Recent migration phenomena, which have taken place since the end of the Cold War, are a consequence of increasing globalisation movements and are characterised by an intensification of migration typologies (in terms of countries of origin, language, ethnicity and religion, as well as of motives, patterns and itineraries of migration, processes of integration into host communities, etc. (Vertovec, 2007). This shift in migration types launched a discussion on the adequateness of the multiculturalism paradigm, widely used in order to describe migration-induced phenomena and very much focused on the study of so-called ethnic minorities in precarious social conditions (Vertovec, 2010). According to Vertovec, new phenomena require a new paradigm—one which is more appropriate to encompass the complexity of recent migration trends. In this post-multicultural globalised era, the term super-diversity offers a strong alternative to the multiculturalism paradigm in its attempt to describe and capture the migration-induced phenomena of the last two decades (Vertovec, 2006).

The investigation of the complex phenomena of super-diversity was mostly carried out from a sociological (or sociolinguistic) and anthropological perspective (see Blommaert and Rampton, 2011 for an overview). However, less attention has been given to the repercussions of super-diversity, particularly concerning language use, on educational institutions and systems. Against this backdrop, this paper tackles recent migration trends and its consequences for educational settings across Europe. The first section provides an overview on migration trends in Europe and their consequences for language diversity, followed by some results on migration and school outcomes. Furthermore, it focuses on explanations for certain educational gaps that particularly affect pupils with a migration background. The conclusions will sum up the main issues raised, linking them up to the European Union discourse on language diversity.

3.2. Recent Trends in European Migration

One of the most relevant traits of migration in and towards Europe, particularly when considering the age structure of the population of most countries with migratory influx, is the fact that migrants represent a relatively young population group[1]. The age pyramids of the EUROSTAT data portrayed in Fig. 3-1 (next page), although not really considering the full complexity of migratory phenomena as described by Vertovec (2007)[2], clearly show that most foreign citizens are between 20 and 40 years old, which, on the one side, very much contrasts with the aging tendency of resident population and, on the other, counterweights the low birth rates of autochthonous citizens. Furthermore, this tendency can mostly be observed in large urban areas, where the amount of young migrants can reach 60% (Bildungsberichterstattung, 2010).

When taking into account migration background rather than only nationality data, about one-third of the European population under the age of 35 belongs to an immigrant minority group (Gogolin, 2002). In addition, if one considers the group of the first-graders in large urban areas, about every second child has a migration background (see for example the Hamburger Schulstatistiken 2011[3] for the case of Hamburg).

Due to fact that most migrants are relatively young, Europe needs migration. According to the Third Demography Report of the European Commission (Messer *et al.*, 2011), not only is Europe's population growing older, but in addition life expectancy is increasing at as much as three months per year. Both of these phenomena produce shrinkage in the workforce. The report also confirmed trends about fertility, life expectancy, and migration. Fertility rates are low in Europe, contributing

---

[1] This fact has been confirmed by the MERIDIUM results.

[2] Data collected referred to population stocks of national and foreign (non-national) citizens, and to the acquisition of citizenship. They do not include migration background based on language use or place of birth of parents. See Kemper (2010) for an overview of the most common variables used to define migration background.

[3] Available at:
http://www.hamburg.de/contentblob/2976252/data/pdf-gesamtinfo-ueberblick-2010-11.pdf (accessed September 26,2012)

to a higher average age in the population. It is predicted that the population will begin to decline by 2030, when roughly two active people (15-65) will have to take care of one inactive person (65+). Europe will have 18 million children and adolescents less than today. As a consequence, migration and especially young migration counteracts the aging population, as European policies to increase birth rates have failed so far.

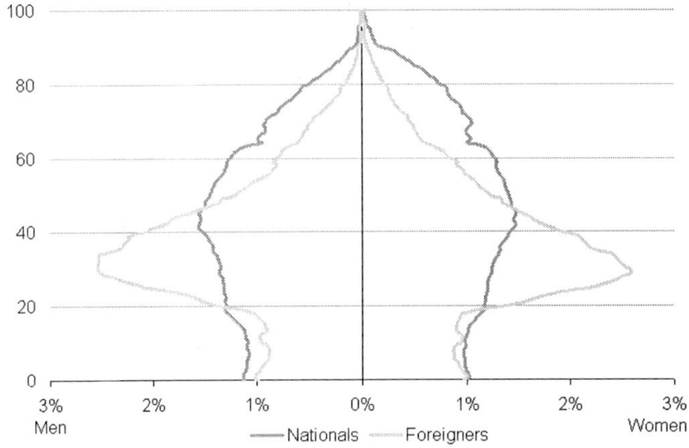

Fig. 3-1: Age structure of the national and non-national populations in the EU (Messer, Leseman, Boom, & Mayo, 2011)

Additionally, migration is becoming an increasingly complex modern phenomenon. In the 1960s migrants moved in search of work and either returned to their countries after a few years or settled permanently in the host country. These migrants came with work contracts and were recruited from a few countries. Nowadays migration channels are becoming more and more diversified and new phenomena are arising. In this respect, Martiniello speaks of the diversification of diversity (Martiniello, 2004). As a consequence, there is also a growing proliferation of legal statuses for migrants with differing consequences for their possibilities to work in the host country (see, for example, Vertovec, 2007). Within his framework of super-diversity mentioned above, he analysed diachronically migration movements towards Germany and looked closely at the changes in the top 50 nations of origin of migrants from 1960 to 2006. While in 1960 there were large recognisable groups of migrants coming from a relatively small number of different countries (Poland or Turkey, for example), in 2006 the amount of groups with an identifiable country of origin has reduced considerably. As a consequence, in super-diverse societies, there are currently more migrants coming from a growing number of countries of origin, through an increasing number of migration channels and with very many legal statuses. Furthermore, there is a growing number of so-called transmigrants, who have either been in some other country or intend to migrate further and who organise their lives plurilocally (Fürstenau, 2004).

The most quoted example for super-diversity is the city of London, where people from more than 300 nations live together in a densely populated space. The metaphor "the world in one city" has been often used to describe this city.

3.3. Migration and Language Diversity

The use of the nationality variable to collect data on migration brings about two major obstacles for research, especially in the field of language diversity. On the one hand, data on nationality are increasingly becoming an obsolete tool to capture social heterogeneity, particularly when addressing younger children, as most European countries have either recently altered naturalization laws[4] or have made adjustments regarding the status of citizens of the ex-colonies. On the other hand, nations are not equivalent to languages, since national territories may contain different groups speaking different languages or even dialects. Ethnologue's (Ortega and Iberri-Shea, 2005, or the interactive web version[5]) categorisation of world languages, shows that in Turkey, for example, 34 different languages are spoken, in India 438 and in Papua New Guinea even 830. Thus, neither nationality nor migration background data offer reliable information on language diversity, and this emerges only if data on language use are collected (Gogolin, 2010). Consequently, it can happen that a Turkish migrant in Germany (a) does not have the Turkish but rather the German nationality; (b) speaks Turkish and another language spoken in Turkey, for example Kurdish; or (c) speaks one, two or more languages spoken in Turkey but not necessarily Turkish.

In short, much is known on nationality-driven data but little of it can be used to draw conclusions on migration-induced language diversity. The particular case of large urban areas, where most migrants are concentrated, thus poses a special case of interest for research on language diversity.

---

[4] The observed tendency is towards *jus soli* over *jus sanguinis* in the attribution of citizenship. Furthermore, many migrants are allowed double citizenship, especially within the EU.

[5] Ethnologue (http://www.ethnologue.com) is a website in which information on languages per region can be found.

3.3.1. Language Diversity in Urban Areas

A great deal of research on language diversity has been conducted in regions of the world with either a high concentration of different languages from different language families, as is the case in Papua New Guinea mentioned above, or isolated languages of indigenous people with little contact with the outer world, as is the case of some tribes in the Amazonian region. However, less systematic studies have been held to investigate migration-induced language diversity in densely populated areas. As a result, although complex cultural and linguistic constellations may be housed in one multi-storey building, not much is known about language practices amongst its inhabitants. In order to understand many of the phenomena surrounding language diversity today, it is necessary to look at some historical processes.

Although linguistic and cultural plurality has always been a key feature in European history, as in most other regions of the world (Graf Estes, Evans and Else-Quest, 2007), the processes leading to the formation of European nation-states in the 18th and 19th centuries, brought about a new ideological triad which has since then harshly affected attitudes towards migration-induced language diversity: nations became associated with one national language and one homogeneous people proficient in that language (Gogolin, 2002). Hence, although diversity had always been a trait in Europe, attaining cultural and linguistic homogeneity became the primary objective for most nation-states (Hobsbawm, 1991). As a consequence, national languages acquired the status of privileged languages, whereas other languages, especially minority languages, were seen as devalued languages, which were forced to operate in the periphery of what Bourdieu has termed the linguistic market (Bourdieu, 1992).

Accordingly, nation-state building processes have a large influence on how language diversity is perceived in Europe today. On the one hand, the state is a political and geopolitical entity; on the other, the nation is a cultural and/or ethnic entity. So, the term "nation-state" implies that the two geographically overlap, thus distinguishing the nation-state from the other types of state organisation that historically preceded it. This notion caused a conscious choice of national languages, mostly deriving from the most prestigious dialects at the time, as well as the emergence of privileged languages on the one hand and devalued languages on the other.

Europe's historical burden is, therefore, at the root of what Gogolin (1994) has called the "monolingual Habitus", drawing on Bourdieu's notion of Habitus as a set of socially learnt dispositions, skills and ways of acting that are often taken for granted, and which are acquired through everyday activities and experiences (Bourdieu, 1991). The concept of "monolingual Habitus" describes the fact that the core of the nationalistic self-understanding of the school system of a nation-state leads to the non-recognition and non-promotion of the pupils' multilingualism and cultural plurality, as in the case, for example, of family socialisation. Multilingualism is thus perceived as a threat to the "imagined" unity of a nation and the co-existence of many languages as a risk factor for the maintenance of this fictive homogeneity.

To sum up, if one is to imagine a hierarchical ladder of Europe‘s languages, one would have the national languages occupying the highest position, then foreign languages taught at school, followed by autochthonous minority languages (some of which may have a long tradition in some of the countries, as is the case of Danish in the border regions of northern Germany) and, at the lowest position, immigrant or minority languages. Furthermore, and although multilingualism is officially accepted and celebrated at a European level, what actually is celebrated are the languages of European nations, not the languages of non-European peoples living in Europe.

3.4. Migration and School Outcomes—An Overview

In international large scale school performance studies, such as PISA (Programme for International Student Assessment) for the 15-year-olds or PIRLS (Progress in Reading Literacy Study) for the 10-year-olds, pupils with a migration background achieve systematically lower results in both language and content-matter subjects than their monolingual peers (see Bos *et al.*, 2008; Klieme *et al.*, 2010; Bos *et al.*, 2007). These studies successfully drew public attention to the performance gap between pupils with and without a migration background. In addition, they also showed great variety across countries regarding educational disadvantages of migrant pupils. While in some countries (mostly traditional immigration countries), immigrants outperform, or show a comparative performance to, monolingual pupils, in the majority of European countries they tend to underperform (Schnepf, 2007).

In fact, such data are mostly collected cross-sectionally, but if one attempts to gather diachronic information on the situation of migrant pupils throughout educational systems, additional and cumulative aspects of inequalities become evident. In what follows, a brief overview of these will be provided (see Baumert, Stanat and Watermann, 2006; Diefenbach, 2010 for a complete survey).

During the pre-school system, enrolment of migrant pupils happens, in average, at a later age and at a lower ratio when compared to the situation of their monolingual peers. During primary school, they attain lower results in international monitoring studies, such as PIRLS (Bos *et al.*, 2007), and experience school retention more often (Auernheimer, 2006). During secondary school, migrant pupils are often found in school forms/classes which are academically less demanding and of shorter duration. Furthermore, they stay at school on average for a shorter period of time. In addition, they are over-represented in schools for special education and under-represented in school forms/classes leading to higher academic degrees. They are also often placed in lower grades than age-appropriate.

When considering the end of compulsory education and the transfer of these migrants to the labour market or to further studies, one can see that around 20% drop out of school without having attained any certificate, although this varies strongly throughout Europe and also within the different groups (OECD, 2010b). Once having successfully entered the labour market, migrants have reduced chances of access to and completion of technical education.

Generally speaking, it is a fact that, in most systems, migrant pupils suffer from educational inequality. At a societal level, these educational disparities lead to processes of social exclusion, which are a sign of inappropriate use of existing resources, therefore leading in the long term to economic losses. For example the EU commissioned study ELAN (Effects on the European Economy of Shortages of Foreign Language Skills in Enterprise) has proved that small and medium-sized companies in the European Union lose contracts worth several millions each year due to language and culture barriers. The study clearly shows that investment in foreign language skills has a significant positive impact on the competitiveness and commercial success of a company (Pickering, 2006). Other studies provide evidence that enriched human capital has the potential to improve substantially the long-run economic well-being of the OECD (Organisation for Economic Co-operation and Development) countries (OECD, 2010a).

3.4.1. Explanations for Educational Disadvantages

Research has identified several factors contributing to the low school performance of migrant pupils in European countries, as opposed to their performance for example in Australia or Canada, as demonstrated in the PISA data. In the early research on intercultural education, contextual factors stemming from the social or cultural background of the migrants themselves were held responsible for the educational failure of their children. Examples of these are studies on linguistic and religious differences or on aspiration and motivation and school performance.

However, no empirical evidence has been found to support the hypothesis that migrants' own characteristics and dispositions are to blame for their own failure or success. So, as Diefenbach puts it:

> It has not been empirically verified that the disadvantages of children and youth from migrant families can be satisfactory explained by the assumption that their cultural or religious predispositions do not match the expectations of the schools or by the comparatively poor socio-economic situation of their families (Diefenbach, 2007: 153)

In fact, as far as aspirations and motivation are concerned, research has proved that migrant families in fact have high aspirations and are highly motivated to invest in the educational career of their children. Furthermore, and when taking studies on educational aspirations and motivation into account, both migrant families and pupils have been found to be highly motivated in attaining school success and in investing in educational careers (Stanat, 2003).

Other studies have tried to describe legal and political measures leading to better or worse school results. For example, Canada is a multilingual nation by definition and has other immigration laws and acculturation strategies, therefore results are different from those in typical monolingual countries (OECD, 2003).

Studies based on Bourdieu's theory of class distinction have attempted to explain the reproduction of educational disadvantages at a sociological level. Bourdieu theorises that class divisions are set by a combination of varying degrees of social, economic, and cultural capital. Society assigns symbolic goods – especially those considered as the attributes of excellence – a major role in the process of class distinction. Attributes associated with excellence are thus moulded by the interests of the dominating class (Bourdieu, 1991). Bourdieu emphasizes the dominance of cultural capital early on by assuming that differences in cultural capital are also at the borders of class stratification. This would accordingly mean that across time societies reproduce inequalities and those occupying lower positions within a society will pass on their position to their children.

Another set of factors identified as a possible cause for educational inequalities is related to several systemic aspects of teaching and learning. The fact that an educational system has a monolingual self-understanding, although its population is largely multilingual, acts as one of the subtle mechanisms leading to educational failure (Gogolin, 1994). Migrant languages are thus often seen as an impediment to the learning of the language of the host society and not as valuable instruments in the acquisition of all other languages. It has also been suggested that institutional discrimination mechanisms within educational systems, as, for example, early tracking of pupils, affect migrants more often than their monolingual peers (Gomolla and Radtke, 2002). Furthermore, research has shown that the linguistic register used at and required in school is often inaccessible for second language learners and is not explicitly taught, leading to educational disparities (Gogolin and Lange, 2010). This aspect will be further explored in the following section.

3.4.1.1. The Issue of Language and School Success in Multilingual Contexts

The concept of academic language intends to describe the register used in formal communicative settings in educational contexts or in comparable situations in public communication, both in oral and written forms (Gogolin and Lange, 2010). In educational settings it takes up a rather central role, as it is used in learning tasks, textbooks and other teaching materials, as well as in assessments and exams. So, this register has a double function within educational institutions: on the one side, it is the object of learning and, on the other, the medium for learning.

School academic language can be defined according to Halliday's depiction of written language (Halliday, 1989): it is characterized by a high lexical density; it is not situation- or context-specific and functions strongly with symbolic, generalizing and abstract linguistic expressions. Unlike academic language, everyday communication is dominated by associative, concrete and illustrative elements, which are highly context-embedded. Using Halliday's systemic functional theory of language (Halliday, 1994) Schleppegrell (2004) addressed the concrete use of academic language in educational contexts, such as different exercises, text books and essays both from primary and secondary school, while contrasting it to language features used in everyday interpersonal communication. He then characterised the academic language used in schools at a lexical, morpho-syntactic and textual level. At the lexical level, common academic language features are the use of precise, technical words which might be discipline-related, of lexical and grammatical approaches to condense information, as well as the use of explicit and specific references to time and space which serve to establish a frame of reference shared by the speaker and the audience. As a consequence, academic language utterances contain more content words than everyday interactive discourse and are thus formed by information-dense sentences. At the morpho-syntactic level, academic language makes use of elaborate forms of tense and aspect to intensify the frame of reference, as well as of persuasive, declarative or argumentative mood of the verb predicate, and the use of adverbs and auxiliaries to represent the speaker's attitude. Furthermore, academic language is marked by a more repeated use of coordinate, relative and subordinate clauses, mostly combined to express complex meanings in a relatively condensed manner. As a result, sentence connectors are often applied to articulate logical relations, such as temporal and logical conditionality, causality, contrast, or comparison. Lastly, at the textual level, academic language was found to be more monological than dialogical in nature, thus obliging the interlocutors to construct long pieces of discourse.

Leseman *et al.* (Leseman, 2007) based their considerations on the same theoretical construction and relied on Schleppegrell's results to investigate the influence of home literacy practices for the emergence and development of academic language in early childhood of Dutch-speaking children. Their study confirmed the importance of home literacy practices with young children for the development of academic language and, consequently, for school success. The effects of such practices were found to be stronger than the socioeconomic status of the families and to compensate for low working memory capacity. Furthermore, their construct of academic language appeared to be rather homogenous, "with all different aspects being moderately to strongly intercorrelated" (Leseman, 2007: 351).

The Council of Europe has recently suggested the term "language of schooling", with the overall aim of promoting "effective skills in the language(s) of instruction which are essential for successful learning across the whole curriculum"[6]. The term was first used to describe the subject-specific technical language which may cause problems to second language learners and has recently acquired a similar meaning to the term "academic language" as used by Schleppegrell (2004) and Leseman (2007), as well as "Bildungssprache" as defined by Gogolin (Gogolin, 2009; see also Gogolin and Lange, 2010). In the policy paper of the Strasbourg language policy division (Thürmann, Vollmer and Pieper, 2010), the term "language of schooling" is described as the "varieties of academic language that constitute the fabric of the different curriculum subjects" (2010: 30). The rationale behind the creation of the concept is that "all teachers must be language teachers in the sense that they are sensitive to the language of their subject(s) and help their learners to master it" (*ibidem*). Thus, the concept of academic language from a school perspective seems to be gaining more and more visibility also in the discourse at a European level.

---

[6] For more information, see http://www.coe.int/t/dg4/linguistic/Schoollang_en.asp (accessed September 26, 2012).

The notion that academic language and school achievement are related is well accepted in the English-speaking research community (Cummins, 2000; Gibbons, 2006; Thomas and Collier, 1997) and is increasingly becoming the centre of attention in the German speaking context (Dehn, 2011; Duarte, 2011; Gantefort and Roth, 2010; Gogolin and Lange, 2010). An adequate access to this register is thus a contribution to educational equality and social cohesion at large. In Bourdieu's sense (1991), it would contribute to reduce the mechanisms of reproduction of inequality.

3.5. Conclusions

Due to historical reasons, monolingualism is still considered the normal case in most European countries (Gogolin, 1994). Migration-induced multilingualism is thus perceived as a threat to the unity of many European nations. Migration movements have changed radically over the past 50 years. In fact, as mentioned above, the recent forms of migration have even been defined by using the term "super-diversity" (Vertovec, 2006). Within this framework, the additional languages of migrants are mostly devalued and seen as an obstacle to learning the host community's language, which in turn leads to educational and professional disadvantages for migrant pupils.

In the so-called Lisbon strategy, involving an action and development plan for the economy of the EU between 2000 and 2010, representatives of the Member States proposed to turn Europe into the most competitive economy in the world, with more and better jobs as well as greater social cohesion. They have clearly failed!

Furthermore, research found a positive correlation between educational attainment and economic growth. Thus, educational inequalities and failures cause long-term financial costs of incalculable value. Educational institutions are the only societal instances, which can compensate for existing discrepancies in a growingly heterogeneous population, as they attribute cultural capital (Bourdieu, 1991) in the form of certificates. Thus, an educational policy focused on the support of academic language proficiency should be considered to be a contribution towards equality.

References

Auernheimer, G., ed. 2006. *Schieflagen im Bildungssystem. Die Benachteiligung der Migrantenkinder*. Wiesbaden: VS Verlag.

Baumert, J., P. Stanat and R. Watermann. 2006. *Herkunftsbedingte Disparitäten im Bildungswesen: Differenzielle Bildungsprozesse und Probleme der Verteilungsgerechtigkeit*. Wiesbaden: VS Verlag.

Bildungsberichterstattung, A. 2010. *Bildung in Deutschland 2010. Ein Indikatorengestützter Bericht mit einer Analyse zu Perspektiven des Bildungswesens im demografischen Wandel*. Bielefeld: W. Bertelsmann Verlag.

Blommaert, J., and B. Rampton. 2011. Language and superdiversity: A position paper. *Working Papers in Urban Language & Literacies*, Paper 70.

Bos, W., S. Hornberg, K. Arnold, G. Faust, L. Fried, E.-M. Lankes, eds. 2007. *IGLU 2006. Lesekompetenzen von Grundschulkindern im internationalen Vergleich*. Münster: Waxmann.

Bos, W. *et al.* 2008. TIMSS 2007. *Mathematische und naturwissenschaftliche Kompetenzen von Grundschulkindern in Deutschland im internationalen Vergleich*. Münster: Waxmann.

Bourdieu, P. 1991. *Language and Symbolic Power*. Cambridge: Polity Press.

CILT. 2006. ELAN: *Auswirkungen mangelnder Fremdsprachenkenntnisse in den Unternehmen auf die europäische Wirtschaft*. Bristol: National Centre for Languages.

Cummins, J. 2000. *Language, Power and Pedagogy. Bilingual Children in the Crossfire*. Clevedon: Multilingual Matters.

Dehn, M. 2011. Elementare Schriftkultur und Bildungssprache In *Migration und schulischer Wandel: Mehrsprachigkeit,* eds. S. Fürstenau and M. Gomolla, 129-151. Wiesbaden: VS Verlag.

Diefenbach, H. 2007. *Kinder und Jugendliche aus Migrantenfamilien im deutschen Bildungssystem - Erklärungen und empirische Befunde*. Wiesbaden: VS Verlag für Sozialwissenschaften.

—. 2010. *Kinder und Jugendliche aus Migrantenfamilien im deutschen Bildungssystem: Erklärungen und empirische Befunde*. Münster: Waxmann.

Duarte, J. 2011. *Bilingual language proficiency. A comparative study*. Münster: Waxmann.

EUROSTAT. 2010. *Demography report 2010. Older, more numerous and diverse Europeans*. Luxemburg: Publications Office of the European Union (available at: http://ec.europa.eu/social/BlobServlet?docId=6824&langId=en, accessed September 26, 2012).

Fürstenau, S. 2004. *Mehrsprachigkeit als Kapital im transnationalen Raum. Perspektiven portugiesischsprachiger Jugendlicher beim Übergang von der Schule in die Arbeitswelt*. Münster: Waxmann.

Gantefort, C., and H. J. Roth. 2010. Sprachdiagnostische Grundlagen für die Förderung bildungssprachlicher Fähigkeiten. *Zeitschrift für Erziehungswissenschaft* 13. 573–591.

Gibbons, P. 2006. Unterrichtsgespräche und das Erlernen neuer Register in der Zweitsprache. In *Die Macht der Sprachen. Englische Perspektiven auf die mehrsprachige Schule,* eds. P. Mecheril and T. Quehl, 269-290. Münster: Waxmann.

Gogolin, I. 1994. *Der monolinguale Habitus der multilingualen Schule.* Münster: Waxmann.

—. 2002. Linguistic and cultural diversity in Europe: a challenge for educational research and practice. *European Educational Research Journal* 1/1. 123-138.

—. 2009. "Bildungssprache" - The Importance of Teaching Language in Every School Subjekt. In *Science Education Unlimited. Approaches to Equal Opportunities in Learning Science,* eds. T. Tajmel and K. Starl, 91-102. Münster: Waxmann.

—. 2010. Stichwort: Mehrsprachigkeit. In *Zeitschrift für Erziehungswissenschaft* 13/4. 529 – 547.

Gogolin, I., and M. Krüger-Potratz. 2010. *Einführung in die Interkulturelle Pädagogik.* Opladen: Barbara Budrich/UTB.

Gogolin, I., and I. Lange. 2010. Bildungssprache und Durchgängige Sprachbildung. In *Migration und schulischer Wandel: Mehrsprachigkeit,* eds. S. Fürstenau and M. Gomolla, 107-128. Wiesbaden: VS Verlag.

Gogolin, I., I. Dirim, T. Klinger, I. Lange, D. Lengyel, U. Michel, *et al.* 2011. *Förderung von Kindern und Jugendlichen mit Migrationshintergrund FörMig. Bilanz und Perspektiven eines Modellprogramms.* Münster: Waxmann.

Gomolla, M. and F. O. Radtke. 2002. *Diskriminierung. Die Herstellung ethnischer Differenz in der Schule.* Opladen: Leske+Budrich.

Halliday, M. A. K. 1989. *Spoken and Written Language.* Oxford: Oxford University Press.

—. 1994. *An introduction to Functional Grammar.* London: Edward Arnold.

Hobsbawm, E. J. 1991. *Nationen und Nationalismus. Mythos und Realität seit 1780.* Frankfurt/ M.: Campus.

Kemper, T. 2010. Migrationshintergrund—eine Frage der Definition. *Die Deutsche Schule. Zeitschrift für Erziehungswissenschaft Bildungspolitik und pädagogische Praxis* 102/4. 315-326.

Klieme, E. *et al.,* eds.. 2010. *PISA 2009: Bilanz nach einem Jahrzehnt.* Münster: Waxmann.

Leseman, P. P. M. *et al.* 2007. Home literacy as a special language environment to prepare children for school. *Zeitschrift für Erziehungswissenschaft,* 10/3. 334-355.

Lewis, M. P. 2009. *Ethnologue: Languages of the world*, 16th edition. (available at: www.ethnologue.com, accessed September 26, 2012).
Martiniello, M. 2004. The many dimensions of Belgian diversity. *Canadian Diversity/Diversité Canadienne* 3/2. 43-46.
OECD. 2003. *Education at a Glance. OECD Indicators*. Paris: OECD Publishing.
—. 2010a. *The High Cost of Low Educational Performance. The long-run economic impact of improving PISA outcomes*. Paris: OECD Publishing.
—. 2010b. *OECD Reviews of Migrant Education - Closing the Gap for Immigrant Students: Policies, Practice and Performance*. Paris: OECD Publishing.
Schleppegrell, M. J. 2004. *The language of schooling: a functional linguistics perspective*. Mahwah, NJ: Erlbaum.
Schnepf, S. 2007. Immigrants' educational disadvantage: an examination across ten countries and three surveys. *Journal of Population Economics* 20/3. 527-545.
Stanat, P. 2003. Schulleistungen von Jugendlichen mit Migrationshintergrund. Differenzierung deskriptiver Befunde aus PISA und PISA-E. In *PISA 2000. Ein differenzierter Blick auf die Länder der Bundesrepublik Deutschland,* ed. Deutsches PISA-Konsortium, 243-260. Opladen: Leske+Budrich.
Thomas, W. P., and V. Collier. 1997. *School effectiveness for language minority students*. Washington D. C.: National Clearing House for Bilingual Education.
Thürmann, E., H. Vollmer and I. Pieper. 2010. *Language(s) of Schooling: Focusing on vulnerable learners*. Strasbourg: Language Policy Division.
Vertovec, S. 2006. *The Emergence of Super-Diversity in Britain*. ESRC Centre on Migration, Policy and Society Working Papers, 25. Oxford: University of Oxford (available at: http://www.compas.ox.ac.uk/fileadmin/files/Publications/working_papers/WP_2006/WP0625_Vertovec.pdf, accessed September 26, 2012)
—. 2007. Super-diversity and its implications. *Ethnic and Racial Studies* 30/6. 1024-1054.
—. 2010. Towards post-multiculturalism? Changing communities, conditions and contexts of diversity. *International Social Science Journal* 199. 83-95.

CHAPTER FOUR

"TO BE ACCEPTED FOR WHO WE ARE": THE SITUATION OF UNRECOGNIZED NATIONAL MINORITIES IN SLOVENIA

ANA KRALJ

4.1 Introduction

> I have always had a problem with this differentiation between Slovenians and Non-Slovenians. Non-Slovenians are not Englishmen or Hungarians; they are always 'the ones from the South'.
> (Montenegrin representative)

The Republic of Slovenia is a multiethnic community that was never ethnically and culturally homogenous. The number of ethnic minorities, their extent and real economical and political power varied through different historical periods with respect to changes of state borders and the sovereignty over this area (Komac, 2005). After Slovenia's independence there are members of several non-Slovenian ethnic communities living within the boundaries of the state. These communities can roughly be divided into two groups:

- historical or territorial national minorities (or the autochthonous[1] national communities as defined by the Constitution) including the Italian, the Hungarian and the Roma community;

---

[1] The Slovenian Constitution does not specifically define the term "autochthonous"; in the context of ethnic minorities the term is used when referring to an ethnic community, which has occupied a certain geographical area "from old". However, due to numerous difficulties and dubious explanations (the definition of "autochthonous", for instance, is largely arbitrary) the term is criticized by several authors. For further explanation see Klinar (1986), Kržišnik-Bukić (2003), Komac (2005). Due to its arbitrary and manipulative nature the term "autochthonous" is no

- the so-called "new" national communities, members of which belong to the nations and nationalities of the former common state of Yugoslavia. Most of them immigrated to Slovenia during the 1960s and the 1970s as economic migrants[2].

The assurance and protection of rights of (national and ethnic) minorities in Slovenia can be categorized into three spheres:

1. the relatively integral legislative protection of historical or autochthonous minorities (Italian and Hungarian), including constitutional provisions and about 80 laws and regulations, concerning various aspects of everyday life of minorities. Special rights are of dual nature, being collective and individual rights simultaneously. The recognition of the dual nature of minority rights and the implementation of the "positive concept of protection of minorities" is defined in the article 64 of the Constitution of Republic of Slovenia which establishes also an obligation on the state to ensure the realization of these special rights, morally and materially.
2. the article 65 of the Constitution, which establishes that the special rights of the Roma community in Slovenia are regulated by a special law[3];
3. members of national communities from the former common state of Yugoslavia do not possess a collective social status in Slovenia. The Slovenian Constitution does not include particular regulations regarding the protection of their (collective) rights and their minority communities. When preserving their national identity, the "new" national communities are only supported by the articles 61 and 62 of the constitution determining the right to express their

---

longer used in EU's documents in regard to national and ethnic minorities. In this sense, Slovenia is a discernible exception.

2 When using the term "new" national communities we are referring to the definition of Miran Komac (2003, 2007), though it has to be noted that this terminology too is perhaps a relic of the past rather than an adequate expression of the present times. The members of nations and nationalities of the former Yugoslavia have lived in Slovenia for several generations, so the use of the term "new" national communities is disputable. As noted by Medica (2004: 98): «the current terminology is diverse, inaccurate and often degrading in everyday life ... and thus—by all means and among other things—rather manipulative because of its poor determination».

3 The law regulating the rights of the Roma community was passed through parliament as late as 2007 and only after a long-lasting and heated debate.

national appurtenance and the right to use their language and writing.

From a historical point of view the present legal and formal situation of members of other nations and nationalities of former Yugoslavia represents a clear deterioration of the possibilities of exercising their cultural and linguistic identities. Namely, the Constitution of the Socialist republic of Slovenia from 1974 provided that citizens of other republics of Yugoslavia had the same rights and obligations in Slovenia as the citizens of Slovenia, including the right to cultivate and express their culture and use their language and script. Furthermore, members of other Yugoslav nations and nationalities had the right to education and schooling in their own language.[4] In December 1990, before the referendum on Slovenia's independence, the Assembly of the Socialist Republic of Slovenia invited all citizens and voters in the republic of Slovenia to take an active part in the forthcoming referendum. At the same time, the Assembly issued the Statement of Good Intents in which it declared that the Slovenian state would ensure "to all members of other nations the right to multifarious cultural and linguistic development"[5].

After Slovenia's independence in 1991 and after the adoption of the new Constitution, all provisions that pertained to other nations and nationalities of the former Yugoslavia were omitted from the new legal and formal framework. Since independence and up to the present this population has been labelled in a number of different categories, all of which indicate some sort of temporality and instability of their stay in Slovenia: immigrants from the other republics of Yugoslavia, migrant workers, first/second/third generation immigrants, third country nationals etc. (Petković, 2011: 76). This development indicates that the status of this population changed from one that guaranteed relatively adequate protection of their cultural and linguistic rights to the present status where the Constitution no longer mentions members of other nations and nationalities of former Yugoslavia.

This paper discusses the situation of members of "new" national communities in Slovenia, focusing particularly on their experience regarding discrimination in the spheres of everyday life. We are arguing

---

[4] Articles 6, 212 and 213 of the Constitution of the Socialist Republic of Slovenia. Source:
http://sl.wikisource.org/wiki/Ustava_Socialisti%C4%8Dne_republike_Slovenije_(1974) (accessed September 26, 2012).

[5] The Statement of Good Intents, paragraph 2. Source: http://www.bivsi-predsednik.si/1992-2002/izjava_o_dobrih.htm (accessed September 26, 2012).

that discrimination, encountered by members of the "new" national communities in Slovenia is often rooted in the lack of systemic regulation of their status as a minority. To gain maximum insight into the sort, the extent, the circumstances and the consequences of the social, civil and political discrimination based on national or ethnic appurtenance we have decided to perform semi-structured interviews with members of minority associations, who are more active in representing the interests of minority communities and appear in the media.

4.2 Discrimination in Everyday Life

When speaking about discrimination or unequal treatment, which occurs to members of national/ethnic communities in everyday life, our informants emphasized the distinction between the overt and covert discrimination. The discrimination they are facing with in everyday life is often rooted deep within the institutional level.

> They say that there are two sorts of discrimination, hard and soft discrimination. Hard discrimination is present in legislation, in laws and other legal regulations, while soft discrimination is something we meet in everyday life. The literature says, and I would agree, that soft discrimination is more common than hard discrimination … which is, nevertheless, present as well. Hard discrimination is present in a sense that our national communities are not acknowledged as national minorities in the Slovenian Constitution. This is the first level of discrimination we are facing. We are not present in the Constitution, though, in a way, we should be, as we were among the constitutive nations of the former Yugoslavia and the present-day Slovenia. In the first place the absence from the Constitution. Then this continues in legislation.
> (Serbian representative)

Another problem that comes to the fore is the use of mother tongue in public, which is often the reason why members of ethnic/national communities are regarded with disapproval, contempt or subjected to outright rejection. This happens despite the fact that the Article 61 of the Constitution of the Republic of Slovenia states that «Everyone has the right to freely express affiliation with his nation or national community, to foster and give expression to his culture and to use his language and script»[6].

---

[6] Source: Official Gazzete of the Republic of Slovenia, no. 33/1991, http://www.uradni-list.si/1/objava.jsp?urlid=199133&stevilka=1409 (accessed September 26, 2012).

> There are remarks in the sense 'How dare you [speak in your mother tongue; author's note], this is Slovenia!' Most of us use our mother tongue when we speak on the telephone. … But a certain discomfort is always present. If you speak in English, then everything is fine. This is the problem of small nations, which are very homogenous.
> (Bosnian representative)

People we interviewed drew our attention to the indirect or direct pressures exerted upon the members of national/ethnic communities because of the use of their mother tongue on their work post, which can lead to different forms of self-censorship:

> As far as public use of our mother tongue is concerned, of course, it can represent a problem. For instance, when I am at work and my phone rings and I know that a Serb is calling me, I will always carefully observe who is around to hear me speak. There is nothing spontaneous about answering the call. On one occasion it happened that I left the office and spoke on the phone in Serbian in the corridor, when a co-worker approached me and told me to be careful, when I speak, as someone could hear me.
> (Serbian representative)

> When we call someone on the telephone, the first thing we ask, is 'Možeš da pričaš?', 'Can you speak?' and this does not mean 'Do you have time to talk?', but 'Can you speak in Serbian?'
> (Serbian representative)

According to our informants, experiences with different sorts of discrimination in everyday life vary among different generations of members of ethnic/national communities, living in Slovenia. The perception of discriminatory practices varies between the members of the first, second and third generation. The first generation has faced specific problems, mostly deficient knowledge of Slovenian language. As Petković (2011: 75) explains:

> This phenomenon is quite understandable, given that these people came to Slovenia as workers during the socialist era when Slovenia was still part of Yugoslavia. Their labour was included in Slovenian industry, but the system did not provide mechanisms for their complete inclusion in Slovenian society.

The next generations of young people, born and educated in Slovenia, usually do not have this problem; however, they are facing other difficulties. All the people we spoke to point out that the second and the third generation are in a very stressful situation of the identity crisis, which is best described with a question «Who am I?».

> Then we have the second generation, which is hurt, which does not receive enough of our attention and is torn apart between different worlds, without the possibility to draw knowledge and strength from the cultural identity of their ancestors. On the other hand they are stigmatized and cannot fit inside the wider younger generation. The young have to struggle to be accepted for who they are but without any scorn.
> (Serbian representative)

> The younger generation is in some severe distress. They live in this conflict. Let us say that they speak Slovenian at home and then a question arises 'Who am I?' and it is easiest just to say 'I guess I am Slovenian.' On the other hand the environment does not perceive these kids as Slovenians, but rather as a sort of a foreign body in the national corpus. They will always remain immigrants. Sadly, it is the surname that defines the attitude of the environment towards an individual.
> (Macedonian representative)

To gain further insight into the blurred boundaries of ethnic identities we created a focus group with seven youngsters, whose parents immigrated to Slovenia in search for work in the late 1970s and 1980s.

> I proudly declare myself Albanian! People tell me I was born and educated here in Slovenia, but no! No way, I am Albanian and proud to be one! I am living here, I know one additional culture, I speak one additional language, but I could never declare myself Slovenian. ... but I would never want to live in Kosovo, either. Recently, I was there for two weeks and I started to miss Slovenia, I started to miss my way of life. Maybe I am partly Slovenian, after all. I am Albanian but part of me is Slovenian, too. Maybe not just a small part. You see, only now that we are talking about this, I am starting to realise I am partly Slovenian, too.
> (Albanian youngster)

> It's difficult to decide... What does it mean to be Slovenian – culture, traditions, language, religion? I like Bosnian culture; it feels so close to me, we even have a prayer rug at home. I would say I am somewhere in between. I am not a real Slovenian, but I am not a real Bosniac, either. In a way, I am Slovenian, I have Slovenian citizenship, I like Slovenia... But to declare myself Slovenian, this is a tough one! You simply cannot – the culture is different.
> (Bosnian youngster)

> Hmm, this is a difficult question. I would put it this way: 'Macedonia is my mother, Slovenia is my step mother. Macedonia could not provide me for a living, Slovenia can. Otherwise, I feel Macedonian, living in Slovenia. But I could never go back, living in Macedonia. Only for a vacation, but living there, no, no way. (Macedonian youngster)

The emotional distress of the second and the third generation, trying to be recognized as equal in the wider society, is also apparent in the process of quiet assimilation or self-assimilation, which is well illustrated by the alteration of personal first names and/or surnames[7].

> In my experience, the alteration of surnames, I think, is rather common in the second or the third generation. Then this voluntary assimilation takes place, when a person wants to have an easier life and says to oneself: 'Why did my parents give me this first name or this surname?' And of course if there is an opportunity, these kids write č instead of ć and thereby participate in a sort of soft assimilation. The second and the third generation can have this aversion towards the members of the nations they originate from. … I think this is a consequence of this soft assimilation, of the desire to be closer to the majority population and then this represents a burden. A child with such a surname gets a feeling of inferiority, is labelled for life with this mark. In the first generation we are aware of this from the first moment - we know, where we came from, but the third generation… they are in a very difficult situation, it is hard for them to identify themselves as they have lived here since they were born. They could be Slovenian, but are not and so they ask themselves: 'Why am I not Slovenian?' This represents an enormous emotional pressure for young generations.
> (Serbian representative)

> Sometimes I felt like... in the primary school, even though half of my schoolmates came from the other republics of Yugoslavia, I had a feeling that I am surrounded by Slovenians, that I am the only Bosnian child. I was ashamed; I didn't want to say my mother's name, because it sounded so different. I had a feeling of inferiority.
> (Bosnian youngster)

> This pressure is huge. The son of my friend is 25 and could not get a job anywhere. So he gave up his father's surname and took the one from his mother. There are some examples … for instance, Rasim becomes Rastko.
> (Bosnian representative)

---

[7] The results of the research project Perceptions of Slovenian Integration Policies (PSIP, 2003) indicate that more than a third of the sample population has found themselves in a situation, where they considered it best not to reveal their ethnicity. At the same time, over 5% of the sample population answered that they had changed their name and/or surname to a more Slovenian sounding form to avoid discrimination of the majority population; and over 15% of the population answered that they occasionally think about doing so. They usually mentioned one of the following three reasons: marriage, adaptation to life in Slovenian society and providing a better perspective to their children (Medvešek and Komac, 2005: 203).

> I know some people that changed their surnames in order to have better possibilities, to achieve more in society. Many people told me to at least change my surname, to change the 'ć' into 'č' but I don't want to. I am who I am, I want to show other people that my surname is not important. I am not inferior because my surname ends with 'ć'.
> (Croatian youngster)

> In the absence of minority status and efforts towards achieving an integral model of minority protection for the communities of the peoples of the former Yugoslavia, Slovenia implements partial measures in the field of cultural and education policies that could be considered to be a contribution to the preservation of culture and language among these communities (Petković, 2001: 79-80).

In the sphere of education, the question of (additional) classes of mother tongue and culture is of particular interest. The right to use their own language in upbringing and education is assured exclusively for members of the Italian and the Hungarian national minority, while members of other ethnic communities can only rely on eventual bilateral agreements and international conventions[8] and above all, on the self-organization and self-funding of such additional classes. The representative of the Albanian national community emphasised the following problems:

> Additional classes of Albanian language for instance. The government approves, of course, providing that the assembled group of children is large enough… But we cannot pay the teacher! We do have a teacher, but look, she also has a family to support. The Ministry of Education, they paid 150 Euros to our teacher … That does not even cover travelling expenses. So teachers feel uninspired, they are not motivated and find no satisfaction in teaching.
> (Albanian representative)

Similar problems were pointed out by the representative of the Croatian community:

> The Slovenian authorities considered our suggestion and sent a list of particular schools to the Ministry of Education, which were instructed to host our teachers on a certain day of the week. The Slovenian state only

---

[8] According to the 8th article of the Elementary School Act (Official Gazette, no. 12/96, 33/97 in 59/01) and on the basis of international treaties and bilateral agreements, children, belonging to the Albanian, Croatian or Macedonian community, who are included in the Slovene elementary school programmes, have the opportunity to follow additional lessons of their mother tongue and culture organized for them.

> provides the place in some primary schools… and our teacher travels from Maribor through Ljubljana to Piran. The teacher's salary, books, teaching materials and travel expenses are financed by the Republic of Croatia. …We say: adopt some new laws and include the Croatian language among other optional subjects in schools … and we will see to it, that Croatian children will register for them, but Slovenian children will also be able to register and this is something completely different.
> (Croatian representative).

However, even within the Croatian community, there are certain reservations regarding the organization of an additional subject in selected schools.

> Some schools have been instructed to offer us room for the organization of classes. … in a way, to us, this resembles ghettoization. If you appoint the school and then let us, the national community, organize additional classes, then only our children will come. We would like to have Slovenian children or anyone else who would like to, would be able to join too. And then what happens—parents are afraid that their children will be labelled, marked, and that is why instead of one hundred, twenty kids turn up and results are modest.
> (Croatian representative)

Other national communities, whose countries have no bilateral agreements with Slovenia, usually find themselves being dismissed as there is no legal basis to support the organization of additional classes in their language.

> Five or six years ago we demanded the organization of additional classes of our mother tongue in primary schools and when we visited the Basic Education Directorate … well, there the conversation ran on and on and this was the result: there is no legal basis… We would agree, for instance, to a Serbian or a Croatian teacher being appointed in Koper or in Jesenice. And lessons should be open to all, ultimately, why shouldn't other children join the classes if they want to?
> (Bosnian representative)

4.3 Conclusion

The basic problem of the members of the nations and nationalities of the former Yugoslavia living in Slovenia is – as previously mentioned – that they are not acknowledged by the Slovenian Constitution as a legal group entity, as a minority, so they have no legal background to support the cultural and lingual expression of their national particularities. That is why in 2003 at the Round Table of the European Commission against

Racism and Intolerance (ECRI) the representatives of Albanians, Bosniacs, Montenegrins, Croats, Macedonians and Serbs in Slovenia, organized within The Association of Unions of Cultural Societies of the Constitutive Nations and Nationalities of the Former Yugoslavia in Slovenia, have presented a public appeal to the National Assembly of the Republic of Slovenia to "initiate and perform the procedure and change the Constitution of Slovenia so as to include us, the Albanians, Bosniacs, Montenegrins and Serbs living in Slovenia and to declare our status as national communities/national minorities living in the Republic of Slovenia".[9]

During the continuation of the public appeal it was pointed out that members of nations from the former Yugoslavia represent a considerable proportion of the inhabitants of Slovenia, that they have lived in Slovenia for a long time, that they are concentrated in larger cities, industrial and mining centres, that they are loyal citizens, that they want to preserve their national identity and that they do not want to be assimilated.[10] The public appeal did not receive any response in the National Assembly; none of its suggestions were implemented or even taken into consideration.

Though it seems that the establishment of integrated model of minority protection for these populations is a challenge too great for any government of Slovenia so far to tackle, some steps forward were being made in the beginning of 2011, when the National Assembly adopted the "Declaration of the Republic of Slovenia on the policies toward new national communities".[11] Even though the Declaration can be seen as a very abstract legal document with little specific provisions or practical value it still represents a formal framework for negotiations, as it calls upon the government to establish a special advisory body that would serve as a platform for dialogue between representatives of new national communities and the government. Last but not least, further efforts should be made in changing the stereotypically negative attitude of a part of the majority society towards these communities by emphasizing the significance of transculturalism and multilingualism in order to develop an open, pluralistic society and social solidarity.

---

[9] The public appeal was presented at the round table organised by Council of Europe - European Commission against Racism and Intolerance. Ljubljana, October 14th, 2003, page 1.

[10] Public appeal of Albanians, Bosniacs, Montenegrins, Croats, Macedonians and Serbs, living in Slovenia, page 2, points 4 - 8.

[11] Official Gazzette, no. 7/2011:
http://www.uradni-list.si/1/objava.jsp?stevilka=210&urlid=20117
(accessed September 26, 2012).

References

Bešter, R. 2007. Socialnoekonomska integracija priseljencev iz prostora nekdanje Jugoslavije in njihovih potomcev v Sloveniji. In *Priseljenci*, ed. M. Komac, 219-255. Ljubljana: Inštitut za narodnostna vprašanja.

Eriksen, T. H. 1993. *Ethnicity and Nationalism. Anthropological Perspectives*. London: Pluto Press.

Klinar, P. 1986. Sociologi o migracijah. *Teorija in praksa* 23/12. 1566-1568.

Komac, M. 2003. Varstvo »novih« narodnih skupnosti v Sloveniji. *Razprave in gradivo* 43. 6–33.

Komac, M. ed. 2007. *Priseljenci*. Ljubljana: Inštitut za narodnostna vprašanja.

Komac, M., and M. Medvešek, eds. 2005. *Percepcije slovenske integracijske politike*. Ljubljana: Inštitut za narodnostna vprašanja.

Kržišnik-Bukić, V., ed. 2003. *Albanci, Bošnjaki, Črnogorci, Hrvati, Makedonci in Srbi v Republiki Sloveniji. Položaj in status pripadnikov narodov nekdanje Jugoslavije v Republiki Sloveniji*. Ljubljana: Inštitut za narodnostna vprašanja.

Medica, K. 2004. Perspektive medijev etničnih skupin/manjšin z območja bivše Jugoslavije v Sloveniji. *Monitor ISH* VI/1. 93-122.

Petković, B. 2011. Erased languages, aroused alliances – language policy and post-Yugoslav political and cultural configurations in Slovenia. In *Cultural Identity Politics in the (Post-) Transitional Societies*, eds. A. Milohnić and N. Švob-Đokić, 71-84. Zagreb: Institute for International Relations & Peace Institute.

Švab, A. *et al.* 2008. *Posledice diskriminacije na družbeno, politično in socialno vključenost mladih v Sloveniji: analiza glede na spol, spolno usmerjenost in etnično pripadnost. Zaključno poročilo ciljno-raziskovalnega projekta v okviru programa Konkurenčnost Slovenije 2006-2013*. Ljubljana: Fakulteta za družbene vede, Center za socialno psihologijo.

Toš, N. *et al.* 2002. *Slovensko javno mnenje. Sumarnik raziskav*. Ljubljana: Univerza v Ljubljani, Fakulteta za družbene vede. Arhiv družboslovnih podatkov.

Zavratnik, S., and A. Kralj. 2008. *Integracijske politike – vzpostavitev evalvacijskega modela in instrumentov longitudinalnega monitoringa. Sumarnik javnomnenjske raziskave – ankete in interpretacija rezultatov*. Koper: Univerza na Primorskem, Znanstveno-raziskovalno središče Koper

CHAPTER FIVE

FOSTERING PLURILINGUALISM AND INTERCULTURAL COMPETENCE: AFFECTIVE AND COGNITIVE DIMENSIONS

ANTOINETTE CAMILLERI GRIMA

5.1. Introduction

The benefits of linguistic and cultural diversity are multiple and multi-faceted (Skutnabb-Kangas, 2002; Starkey, 2002; Gogolin, 2002; Pavlenko, 2005; Edwards, 2010). In almost every recent book that deals with multilingualism and cultural diversity lies an emphasis on the extent of cultural diversity in many regions around the world, and the need to tackle this issue with urgency and with a positive outlook (Pattanayak, 2003; Ouane, 2003; Miller *et al.*, 2009; Hélot and Ó Laoire, 2011). Indeed, important international organisations such as UNESCO (e.g. Ouane, 2003), the Council of Europe (e.g. Raasch, 2002; Ó Riagáin, 2002), the European Centre for Modern Languages (e.g. McPake and Tinsley, 2007), as well as the European Union (e.g. Europublic, 2009) have delegated experts to produce studies, and thereafter made recommendations for the implementation of a variety of policies, projects and actions aimed at fostering plurilingualism and intercultural competence (e.g. Beacco and Byram, 2003; Camilleri Grima, 2007; Newby, 2007).

Among the advantages commonly publicised in recent years to encourage the learning of additional languages, and the maintenance and revitalisation of languages spoken by minority communities, are: economic incentives (Grin, 2002), cognitive benefits (Europublic, 2009; Clyne, 2011), better social prospects and enhanced communication (Raasch, 2002), and also a delay in the slow-down of mental functioning (Bialystok, 2010). Individuals are thus encouraged to sustain and enhance their plurilingualism, and societies are stimulated to support language and cultural diversity.

This paper is anchored in an educational milieu, and aims to contribute to the endeavour of supporting and promoting diversity through pedagogical activities. It will describe three projects: (i) one conducted with primary school children (story sacks); (ii) another one that took place in a secondary school for boys (storyline); (iii) and finally a project which was part of teacher education (image theatre). I participated in all three projects: I was a parent of two children in the primary school at the time of the project; I was a course supervisor of the newly qualified teacher who embarked on the storyline project at secondary level; and I co-organised the in-service teacher training course. In what follows, I will describe the context and the general aims of the three projects. Following that, while focusing on the activities themselves, I will draw on the theoretical underpinning in order to illustrate that there are both cognitive and affective dimensions involved, and that it is efficacious for pedagogists to keep both aspects in focus.

5.2. The Context of the Projects

All three projects described in this paper took place in Malta where the context is one of nation-wide bilingualism, involving Maltese and English, and where the community is, by and large, mono-ethnically Maltese, with less than 3% of the population being non-Maltese (National Statistics Office, 2005). As a result, the awareness of linguistic and cultural differences is limited mainly to a view of otherness experienced locally thanks to a flourishing tourist industry, and by virtue of travel abroad. Although the phenomenon of illegal immigration has been hotly debated in recent years, there has been limited contact, and even more limiting approaches and perceptions, between the (unwelcome) foreigners and the local population. Overall, one cannot say that children from different cultural backgrounds are particularly visible in schools, although there seems to be increasing diversity in a small number of schools, depending on the location of the school. I will now describe the context within which each project took place.

The primary school where the "story sack project" took place is a village school in a rural area. It caters for about three-hundred pupils aged three to eleven, and according to the Head of School, at the time of the project, there was only one foreign pupil in the school whose parents came from Lithuania. The rest of the pupils were all Maltese and the parents of the majority of them had also grown up in the same village. The objectives of the story sacks in primary school were elementary, in the sense that the children were introduced to language diversity through books and films and not through direct, first-hand contact with diversity. In fact, this 'mono' reality was the main issue that we wanted to tackle: we felt it was becoming urgent to expose the village children to linguistic and cultural diversity in a positive and encouraging way before they became hostages to prejudices about foreigness, an approach that was not totally unknown in the environment and on the media. Furthermore, an added value of this project was the involvement of parents such that awareness was raised among a wider audience including teachers and parents.

In the secondary school for boys there was a different reality[1]. The "storyline project" was conducted during October 2011 with Form 2 and Form 3 students, aged 12 to 14. Among the fifty or so students that took part, one-third originated from other countries: Bulgaria, Italy, France, Germany, Spain, the UK, Ukraine, Tunisia, the USA, Australia and China. This particular school is located in the harbour area and hosts lower academic ability students, namely those who failed the entrance examination to the higher ability lyceums at age 11[2]. One newly qualified teacher who was working in this school, and whom I had tutored during the previous year, approached me because she was worried about the kind of relationship that was developing between the Maltese boys on one hand, and the foreign boys on the other. She had witnessed one critical incident and was willing to do something about it. During break time the boys normally play football. The Maltese boys are rather rough and for them it is common practice to push and pull each other, and they even tear each others' clothes, without worrying about it. However, when they pushed one of the foreign boys, and roughly pulled his clothes, he was gravely offended. It became clear that cultural differences were at play, and that no one had been, up to that point, aware of the dangers of a lack of intercultural competence among the boys. The project reported here was a first step in an attempt to consciously deal with plurality within the school. An added value was that while the Maltese and foreign boys were normally separated for the Maltese lesson, during this project they worked together in a collaborative manner during the time allotted for Maltese, and worked with the teacher of Maltese.

The "teacher education project" was based on the belief that in order for teachers to be able to act as effective educators of diversity in school they needed to have an educational experience themselves. Normally, intercultural competence is included as part of foreign language learning

---

[1] State seconday schools in Malta are not co-educational, i.e. they cater for boys and girls separately.

[2] As from 2011 this selective system has been abolished for students entering secondary school for the first time.

with a view to being able to travel for work or for pleasure, and to understand and integrate in the target culture (Council of Europe, 2001). The perspective we took in the project described here was broader. First of all, intercultural competence is considered here to be an essential element of mother-tongue education and not simply as part of the content knowledge of foreign languages[3]. Secondly, everyone needs to be well-prepared in advance for the occasion of facing otherness, irrespective of whether they will travel or migrate or continue inhabiting their own corner of the world.

Languages and cultures encompass both cognitive aspects as well as affective dimensions. Traditionally, apart from language learning, intercultural competence tackles three domains of knowledge, skills and attitudes: 'savoir', 'savoire-faire' and 'savoir-être' (Council of Europe, 2001; Sercu, 2002). The range of 'savoirs' can be further expanded to include learning how to learn or 'savoir-apprendre' (Zarate, 2003), skilfully amplified and illustrated in Candelier (2011). Neuner (2003) describes the paradigm shift in language teaching methodology over the past decades, and the functions and outcomes of the various methodologies. With regard to intercultural competence he focuses in some depth on the interdependence between the cognitive (e.g. selection of information, analysis of structures of a socio-cultural phenomenon), and the affective (e.g. empathy, role distance, tolerance of ambiguity) aspects. Similarly, in Camilleri Grima (2002) I specify that as a means of fostering intercultural competence there is a need for:

a) Developing cognitive complexity in responding to new environments
b) Motivating affective co-orientation towards fresh encounters
c) Directing behaviour to perform various interactions with additional social groups

Each of the projects described below highlights a selection of cognitive and affective objectives, that are age-appropriate, and that are best fitted to the activity concerned. Furthermore, each project was designed with a consideration of the sociolinguistic context for which it was intended. Each project was planned for the classroom as a safe laboratory, a place to explore and dissect differences in an appropriate way, avoiding negative judgement and the related consequences. More than that, it allows plenty of opportunity for personal enrichment in terms of knowledge, and for a growing maturity as social beings.

[3] For several years I have been coverng a component of intercultural competence within the L1 programme in pre-service education.

5.3. Cognitive Processes

One of the fundamental principles taken into consideration in these projects is that in order to foster plurilingualism and intercultural competence, we need to give attention to the way the human mind works. The inputting of data into the mind must be carried out efficiently because this operation establishes a platform for the mind's further processing of the information, and for producing reactions later on. In fact, Abkulut (2007) emphasises that language and cognition are interdependent. Willingham (2007) explains that the human mind works like a computer: it takes in information, manipulates it, and then produces responses. The cognitive processes that are of interest to us here relate to ways in which the human mind gains access to knowledge about the world, how it processes it for instance by using attention, memory and association, and then acts on the basis of the responses created in the mind. Indeed, the *Common European Framework of Reference for Languages: Learning, teaching, assessment* (Council of Europe, 2001:104) proposes that users of the Framework consider and state:

- What prior sociolcultural experience and knowledge the learner is assumed/required to have;
- What new experience and knowledge of social life in his/her community as well as in the target community the learner will need to acquire in order to meet the requirements of L2 communication;
- What awareness of the relation between home and target cultures the learner will need, so as to develop an appropriate intercultural competence.

Prior knowledge makes things easier to remember, and also guides what details the mind is likely to pick out in a complex situation (Willingham, 2007). In relation to this, the storyline project and the teacher education project start off by foregrounding the prior knowledge of the learners. The relation between familiar and new knowledge can be described as anchoring (Augoustinos *et al.*, 2006), that is, the classification and naming of new and unfamiliar objects or social stimuli by comparing them with existing stock of familiar and culturally accessible categories.

For these reasons, cognitive processes like identifying, comparing, explaining and so on, have been purposefully built into each of the pedagogical activities, with a view to training the mind toward effective anchoring of cultural and linguistic information. In Camilleri (2000) I present a list of cognitive processes, such as discovering, completing, accepting, being creative and solving problems, as examples of the kind of mental activity that takes place during pedagogical activities that form part of language learning and culture-related exercises. Similarly, the publication by Europublic (2009) highlights cognitive functions such as divergent and convergent thinking, conceptual expansion, creativity and innovation as typical of a plurilingual mind. These are cognitive assets very much desirable in a context of cultural diversity.

The reactions of participants, which are in part dependent on the cognitive processes used for the inputting and manipulation of information, were also guided with care throughout the projects because the outcomes of the activities had been planned with specific targets in mind.

5.4. Affective Dimensions

The affective dimension in intercultural competence refers to the emotional side of the experience and the motivational readiness of the participants in an interaction. It is closely related to values, attitudes, and feelings embedded in messages of a verbal and non-verbal nature. In agreement with Neuner (2003:35) we believe that

> the emotional-affective dimension with its emphasis on the development of attitudes toward the target language and socio-culture, is especially closely tied in with the all-encompassing socio-political and educational objectives

Furthermore, a lot of care was taken throughout the projects for the "emotional-affective dimension" which "...relates to... the imaginary participation in exciting events and the appeal to feelings, to soul and heart" (Neuner, 2003:35). For this reason, the motivational aspect of the projects involving the emotional-affective dimension was particularly catered for, and both the secondary school project and the teacher education project also included the imaginary participation in exciting events as part and parcel of the activity.

Indeed, this pedagogical claim has been substantiated by research in psychology. There is a positive correlation between how vivid a memory seems, and how emotional it is (Willingham, 2007), and thus emotion clearly makes things more memorable. In each of the projects the emotions are guarded: we wanted them to be there because this promotes learning, and we wanted them to be positive, because this will colour future reactions to difference. The theory of social representations (e.g. Augoustinos *et al.*, 2006) departs from the belief that the individual cannot be properly and fully understood in abstract isolation from the social, and that this internalized social knowledge in turn guides and facilitates the processing of social information. Furthermore, representations are conceptualized as affective structures with inherent normative and evaluative dimensions. Attitudes are first and foremost evaluations, which we commonly refer to as stereotypes and prejudices. Of fundamental concern to us is that such attitudes will result in behaviour, which might not always be laudable in a multilingual and multicultural environment. The kind of activities described here, are therefore, a means for instilling a propensity in participants to avoid hasty judgements on encountering diversity.

Similary, while departing from a more linguistic point of view, Pavlenko (2005) illustrates very vividly how emotions, languages and cultures, are intertwined. While she convinces us that an education in multilingualism and diversity is a lifelong endeavour, she also gives plenty of examples to show how the effects of both the cognitive processes and the affective aspects present when learning a language, or when dealing with a new culture at some point in someone's life, continue to be felt throughout one's life. Of particular relevance to us is her discussion of foreign language learning and anxiety, apathy and emotional vulnerability, which she illustrates and explains through examples of individuals who learned German during the Nazi era. Such emotions like anxiety are what we are trying to avoid in the future lives of our learners upon encountering diversity. Furthermore, we are concerned with developing pedagogical contexts that positively shape learners' emotional evaluations and subsequent actions.

One approach to prepare a learner for affective co-orientation is explained by Gaston (1992) as a four stage procedure that allows the teacher and the learners to methodically attain specific skills and attitudes. The four stages that lead to intercultural competence are: Recognition, Reaction, Empathy, Respect. This four-step approach is particularly evident in the secondary school project and in image theatre for teacher education. Furthermore, all the cognitive and affective objectives identified for each project are taken from the *Framework of reference for pluralistic approaches to languages and cultures*, known as the CARAP (Candelier, 2007/2011), henceforth referred to as the CARAP. Each learning objective or descriptor (as they are known in the CARAP) is preceded by the same number used in the CARAP.

5.5. Story Sacks in Early Childhood and Primary Education

The story sack project was an initiative taken by a group of parents who felt the necessity to introduce an innovative and motivational aspect into the life of the child at school; to include a window opening onto the world. The general aim of the project was to create story sacks as a means of stimulating curiosity about other languages while inculcating a sense of pleasure in intercultural competence and language learning. The objectives of the story sacks were multiple, especially as parent education was brought into the equation. However, for the purposes of this paper we will narrow down our focus to the cognitive and affective aspects specifically chosen from the CARAP (2007) for the linguistic and cultural content of the sacks. The cognitive aims were that the child would come to know:

5.1	that there are many different languages in the world
5.3	that there are different kinds of script
11.1	that cultural differences exist

The affective dimension was also considered to be very important. Following Pavlenko (2005:198) the parents believed that "language-related emotions are likely to influence individual decisions and choices in situations like ethnic conflict or immigration...". Whether positive or negative, sensations and feelings that are aroused by languages and cultures predispose an individual to particular behaviour, and continue to dominate one all through one's life. The project intended to catch these children early enough in order to gently prod them forward in a very positive and profitable way into the world of otherness. The specific affective aims concerned:

1.1	Attention to language and manifestations of culture
3.2.1	Curiosity about the similarities and differences between one's own language/culture and the target language/culture
9.5	Desire to find out about other languages/cultures

The cognitive and emotional development of the child was catered for by the various elements involved in the story sack project. Katz and Chard (2000:6) explain that an appropriate education for young children should address the full scope of their growing minds as they strive to make better and fuller sense of their experiences. It encourages them to pose questions, pursue and solve puzzles, and increase their awareness of significant phenomena around them". The story sacks tried to capture the four essential categories of learning goals as defined by Katz and Chard (2000), that is (a) Knowledge, by including an information card on the topic for each sack; (b) Skills, appropriate to the age group, mainly activated through the games, puzzles or other activities inserted in each sack; (c) Dispositions relevant to social competence, such as inquisitiveness, which was in-built in the fact that the objects came out of the sack with a great deal of expectation and surprise, and the books and other objects that lead the children to ask questions; and finally (d) Feelings, i.e. the affective states such as feeling confident and important, like the children felt when coming out of school every Tuesday with a story sack on their back.

The procedure to produce the story sacks was rather lengthy, and the whole project took a year from beginning to end. As a start, the parents asked the national education authority for assistance who, in fact, recommended a presentation by another parent from another school who had been involved in a literacy project for children. Following her presentation it was decided to create story sacks for children aged 7, such that each child of that age in the school would take a story sack home every week. A series of workshops for the parents of the 7 year old children was organised, initially to explain the project, and eventually to get everyone involved. For example, some parents helped by sewing the sacks, or by collecting games, preparing the instructions for each sack, puppets etc. Each sack was given a number and assigned a topic, and in each sack as a minimum there were: a big book; commercially available books in different languages, always including Maltese, English and another language; a game; an instruction card; a toy and/or a soft-toy; a puppet; and a DVD. A total of thirty-five sacks were prepared. The big books, which were made by the parents together with the children during some of the evenings spent in school, were either in Maltese or in English, and the stories they invented narrated some cultural behaviour or event, often described from the point of view of animals or objects. The story sacks were useful because in that way more cultural content could be covered, and children could be gently introduced to a diversity of languages and scripts.

The following diagram (Fig. 5-1) illustrates the procedure, which was kicked off with one parent from another school sharing her experiences, and continued in a cyclical fashion when two of the parents involved in the story sack project were, in turn, invited to make a presentation about it at a private school.

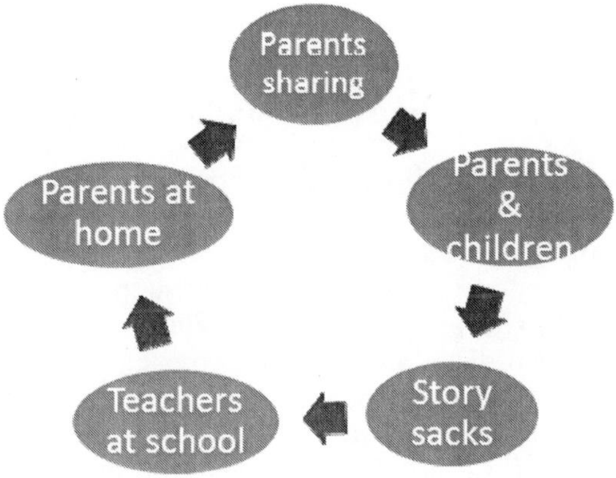

Fig. 5-1: The story sacks project

Once the sacks were ready, a couple of parents tried out the sacks with a group of pupils at the school, showing other parents how the surprise element and the contents could be dealt with by the parents and the child at home. Every week the parents took it in turns to collect, check, clean and re-distribute the sacks to the children. The teachers also got involved and used the sacks with the other classes whose parents were not involved in the project.

The reactions of some of the children who took part in the project and that were reported to us are well worth mentioning. For instance, a common question was: "What is this language?", or trying to guess, "Is this German?". Some children asked about learning foreign languages: "When can I start learning French?" or "Isn't it too long to wait until I'm 10 to start learning French?!". One of the books in the story sacks was called Hilarious Estonia. It is a publication of the Estonian Institute (Debelakk, 2001), and it's a very colourful and funny representation of modern life in Estonia, narrated visually in comic-style drawings with comments in English. We could observe the children's reactions to manifestations of culture in this book, and one of the boys couldn't contain himself with surprise: "What? They make fun of themselves? No, I wouldn't want Malta to be laughed at!". Indeed, we realised that as a nation the Maltese do not normally enjoy self-derision. The different approaches taken by the different languages and literacy cultures in children's books was fascinating in itself. The adults that were involved in the project also found themselves embarking on a journey of discovery and self-discovery, just like the children!

5.6. Storyline at Secondary Level

As explained in sections 2 and 3 above, personal involvement through recall of past experiences and knowledge has an important role to play in intercultural competence and foreign language learning. The secondary school project intended to involve the learners personally, through a sharing of intercultural experiences, and by giving them an opportunity for creative output. One of the global cognitive competences described in the CARAP (2007:35) is the "competence in profiting from one's own intercultural and inter-language experiences". Therefore, this project took the view that the experience of the learners is a resource, and that the school needs to utilise this human resource with profit.

As mentioned above, there was an increasing number of non-Maltese boys attending this school. For this reason, the targets of the storyline project were more closely related to the context in which the project was taking place. For instance, it was relevant to mention the diversity of languages and cultures in one's own environment given the range of countries of origin of the learners taking part. Besides, considering that some children came from European countries and from the Mediterranean region, while others came from as far as the USA, Australia and China, it was important to make explicit reference to lands near and far. Indeed, the CARAP specifies descriptors for these aspects. Thus, the cognitive aims of the storyline project were that the learner:

5.7	Knows that there are multilingual, plurilingual situations in one's own environment and in other places near or far
10	Has knowledge concerning different cultures
11.4.2	Becomes familiar with the historical and geographical factors which determine aspects of different cultures

The affective objectives were also directly related to what the school wanted to achieve given the increasing diversity of languages and cultures among the students:

5.2	Receptiveness towards people with other languages
4.2.1	Acceptance of the value of all languages/cultures in the school
7.3.1	Growing confidence to 'go to meet' what is new and strange in language behaviour and cultural values of others

The project was elaborated in three phases as shown in Fig. 5-2. First of all it focussed on the personal experiences of the students. The activity was introduced through a brainstorming session about what they had considered to be strange while visiting other countries, and then slowly developed into a methodology that encompassed cognitive processes like remembering what had happened, describing the event, sharing how they felt, and explaining the reasons why they thought it was strange. The students were guided in their activities in order to help them identify possible geographical, historical, political or other factors that play a role in the way of life of a cultural group.

In the second phase they worked in national groups in order to collate a choice of cultural information in such a way that they could present it visually to their peers. All the boys took particular interest in this activity and talked with pride about their country of origin. Each presentation almost developed into an advertisement! The material took the form of charts which they later used in a class discussion in order to identify and compare how geographical and other factors impact on culture. The linguistic element was brought into the activity when the boys decided that each group should translate a list of words they had chosen into the various languages. In the third phase they worked in mixed groups and their task was to invent a story where everything had to be fictional: the place, the characters and the plot. The idea was to foster further cognitive flexibility through an imaginative scenario, and thus foster their readiness to engage with things that are new and strange.

1. PERSONAL EXPERIENCE	remembering identifying describing sharing

⇩

2. COLLABORATIVE PRODUCTION	collating information presenting comparing

⇩

3. CREATIVE WRITING	imagining creating

Fig. 5-2: The storyline project

During the second phase, the students of a non-Maltese cultural background were particularly keen to learn more about the local culture. Interestingly, they emphasized the fact that given the bilingual situation in Malta they found it easier to integrate with the local population. In fact, most of them expressed themselves in English throughout the activity. The cultural factor that interested the boys most was geographical distance, how it varied greatly from one country to another, and how it had an impact on private and public transport. The Maltese boys were paticularly impressed by the fact that some countries are so huge that one needs to travel by air to get from one place to another, and that it can take up to seven hours to get to the beach. Some of the comments made by the Maltese boys were: "I really didn't know that!" and "How lucky we are that we can get to the beach in minutes". The Maltese boys expressed their satisfaction with regard to the short distances in Malta and the pleasant climate, but on the other hand, some of them said they wished there were trains and other means of transport that were lacking in Malta. From a linguistic point of view, the boys took particular interest in Bulgarian and Ukrainian, and found the Chinese language most fascinating and wanted to hear more Chinese spoken by their peers. They wanted to know more about naming practices and each national group was asked to give a list of typical boys' names in their culture. Some discussion centred around the Arabic alphabet and the fact that in Arabic writing takes place from right to left.

In the final phase of the project the boys worked very well together in mixed national groups. Each group wrote about an imaginary country, gave it a name, fantasised about what it was like to live there, and described items like food, sport, work and pleasure activities. Above all, it was worth observing how they made an effort to describe the physical geography of the land, to include rivers, mountains, forests and sandy beaches, as well as plenty of different means of transport. They also focussed on how history and national memories, for instance, are of daily relevance because in every country there are major squares and streets named after historical events and personalities. In their creative writing, for example, one country was called "Chukvers", its language was called "Chukvernish", the favourite food was a "chukvers pizza with sauce, sausages, mushrooms and, of course, chukvers", and the typical drinks were "chukspresso" and "chukshot"!

In the end, a major outcome of the storyline project was a surprise. The school decided to organise a Culture Week so that diversity could be given more space, plenty of visibility, and more importantly, in order to continue inculcating and fostering the affective dimensions that this project had set going.

5.7. Image Theatre in Teacher Education

The education of teachers with a view to diversity cannot be underestimated. As teacher educators we were aware that up to that point our teachers had had very little formal training in intercultural competence. Therefore, we felt that before we could ask them to put theory into practice we needed to bring them together in order to act and reflect on the basis of first-hand experiences. One of the competences mentioned in the CARAP (2007: 37) refers to the "competence in applying systematic and controlled learning approaches in a context of otherness". Without a doubt, the application of theory to practice with regard to intercultural competence and language diversity needs to be part and parcel of teacher education. In fact, Siegel (2005) reports that educating teachers about language diversity and issues of language and power was the first step in most of the successful programmes he describes, all of which were directed toward the promotion of language diversity in the classroom. Teachers are normal social actors who have accumulated a lot of cultural and linguistic knowledge over the years, but who also entertain their own prejudices and limiting perceptions. This needs to be tackled during their training, or as part of an in-service offer.

The aim of image theatre[4], in this case, was to develop mental flexibility in dealing with ambiguity and bizarre situations. An individual's cognitive fexibility is dependent on their ability to make sense of, and to integrate new information, into a pre-existing cognitive structure, that is, their ability to bend their way of thinking and to be receptive to new cultural patterns. This fexibility in perception and thought patterns is a key to openness and acceptance of another culture, and thus to successful cross-cultural adaptation (Camilleri Grima, 2002).

The inclusion of creativity as a cognitive objective is fundamental. Creativity is defined by the Europublic study (2009) as the ability of think of something new by conceptual expansion. This study (ibid.) also explains that creativity generally precedes innovation, and in the Europe of the future as envisaged by the European Commission, innovation will be one of the cornerstones of European success. Furthermore, from a language learning point of view, the existence of more than one language in the brain suggests that bilinguals are able to see the world through

[4] Image theatre is the brainchild of Augusto Boal (1992).

different lenses, they have enhanced cognitive control, they are better at multitasking and focusing, and plurilingualism helps in nurturing interpersonal communication, awareness and skills. Cognitive differences in bilingual speakers when compared to monolinguals seem to be linked to differences in their brain's physical make-up (presumably resulting from the number of languages they are fluent in), as has been shown by Mohades *et al.* (2012).

The cognitive objectives of the teacher education project were that, as a result of this experience, the learner comes to:

10.1	Possess cultural references enabling one to structure the implicit and explicit knowledge about the world
13.2.1	"Decentre" oneself in relation to one's own language/culture and to put oneself in another person's place

The affective dimensions involved:

6.10	Becoming familiar with one's own reactions towards linguistic/cultural differences
8	Motivation to observe, study, analyse features of linguistic/cultural diversity

Even in teacher education, not only is prior knowledge put at the forefront because "it is crucial to how you process new experences" (Willingham, 2007), but the innovative slant in methodology ascertains that the emotions are at high alert, because "emotion does make things more memorable...emotion provides a memory boost" (Willingham, 2007: 179). Indeed, the teachers participated with a lot of enthusiasm, and they commented that the training workshops were fun. Having enjoyed the learning process, they are tuned in to more pleasurable encounters with diversity in future.

This project comprises a number of steps:

(i) In small groups each participant is invited to narrate a personal experience that occurred in a context of otherness, and that resulted in a reaction of surprise and a feeling that something bizarre was happening. These personal anecdotes are used as a springboard for the participants to probe further into foreign languages and cultures in a way that interests them, because it has already touched them personally.

(ii) They then compare and contrast languages and cultures. What is strikingly different inherently brings to the surface the shape of one's own language and culture. The anecdotes are used not only to describe the foreign features and the emotions they caused, but for the participants to delve deeper into the causes for such emotions, namely by trying to answer the question: Why is that event, behaviour, occurrence, tradition etc. strange? What does it help me realise about my own language/culture? How do others see me, my culture, my language, my behaviour, etc.?
(iii) Accepting that people's reactions, one's own and those of others, are shaped by the culture they operate in.
(iv) Decentring and being creative. In groups of 5-7 the participants choose one critical incident from those narrated by their colleagues. They prepare a sequence of five still pictures that they have to act out, as a way of reciting the anecdote. The performance is carried out in silence. At this stage the participants are expected to decentre in the sense that they take on the persona of someone else, in an unknown culture, and behave in a non-customary fashion.
(v) Each group presents their narrative, and the class has to interpret the cultural event. A discussion then ensues about the key features of cultural (mis)understanding.

Sometimes, the enactment involves language issues, such as the different meaning of homonyms or cognates. For instance, one anecdote centred around the different meaning and use of 'mela' in Maltese and Italian. An Italian family were placing an order in a Maltese restaurant, but they were rather surprised that the waitress said she was going to offer them an apple ("mela"). In fact, when the waitress said "mela" she was simply uttering a Maltese discourse marker of no consequence, equivalent to "so" or "therefore" in English! Similarly, when a Maltese student with some knowledge of Italian was visiting Spain and wanted some butter he asked for "burro", but was met with utter bewilderment because, apparently, in Spanish he was asking for a donkey!

This project took about thirty hours and was conducted in evening sessions[5]. All the gatherings were enjoyable and increased the participants' motivation toward issues of diversity (Camilleri Grima *et al.*, 2006). Course participants appreciated the novel approach to learning which was based on active participation and involved physical activity; the respect

---

[5] This project was partly financed by the European Union, and was an element of the COALA project: "Communication and language promotion in training pre-school teachers" (Comenius 2.1 Action, Training of Education School Staff).

shown to their experience and the way it was brought into the teaching-learning process; and the relevance of the content and of the methodology to classroom practice.

5.8. Conclusion

In conclusion, I would like to point out four junctures that transpire from these three projects: venturing toward a wholistic approach to school development; intercultural education as part of first language instruction; educating for diversity in one's own region; and the importance of both the cognitive and affective dimensions in learning.

Whole-school development (Camilleri Grima, 2007) is an important element in innovation, for instance, when trying to introduce a specific form of continuity between home and school. The story sacks project found a place in this primary school's School Development Plan, and was accompanied by the upgrading of the school's reading room in such a way that the teachers could also contribute to the efforts of the parents. A whole-school approach seeks to accomplish the goals by involving all stakeholders through community building and by sharing responsibility. This means that school administrators, teachers, learners, parents, researchers, and experts all have a part to play. As detailed by Fleishmann (2007), the Head of School can be the main instigator of change. On the other hand, parents and grandparents can have a crucial role, as in the examples described by Young and Hélot (2007) where parents came into the school to show and tell about their different cultures, and by Huss (2007), who reports an interesting case where the grandparents were indispensable for language revitalisation at kindergarten level. Even researchers and experts can give a hand, as illustrated by Norberg (2007) who explains how applied linguists contributed to the success of bilingual education through German and Sorbian in Sorbian speaking areas in Germany. As Edwards (2010: 288) concludes, "It is impossible to understand the school by remaining within its gates". Moreover, children cannot understand diversity and interact with otherness unless the school gates open up their world to what lies outside.

As many scholars point out, intercultural competence and plurilingualism are lifelong endeavours, which means that one must start early and then needs to continue sharpening one's skills, and enhancing competences, even after leaving school. We also believe that this is so important to the extent that we wish it would become part of first language instruction. One has to be prepared, albeit, as prepared as possible, not with the actual details about the language structures and the cultural cues of other languages than one's own, but indeed, with the mental flexibility and the affective readiness to face differences and avoid social failures. If anything, it is impossible to obtain all the information and knowledge required for cross-cultural and cross-linguistic encounters. Therefore, it is mental flexibility and emotional readiness that we must aim for. Besides, we have also noted how becoming receptive to otherness includes a deeper reflection about one's own language and culture.

We have also mentioned that an education in favour of intercultural competence and language diversity must take into account one's own environment. We have to move away from the idea that learners need to learn about cultures and other languages because they will need them in their future, for work and travel. An education that backs diversity needs to start and to continue in one's own milieu, and to cater for the related skills needed within one's own environment.

Finally, given the interdependence of the affective and cognitive dimensions it is worthwhile bringing both of them to the fore in pedagogical activities. They cannot be separated, and they are both fundamental in the development of intercultural competence and plurilingualism. Intercultural competence can be inculcated whatever the age of the participants. To enhance this there is a wide variety of methodologies that can be applied, adapted, expanded and created such that every learning event is calibrated to the needs of the learners, at the right level of development, and with the most appropriate cognitive and affective objectives in mind.

References

Abkulut, Y. 2007. Bilingual acquisition and cognitive development in early childhood: challenges to the research paradigm. *Elementary Education Online* 6/3. 422-429.

Augoustinos, M., Walker, I., and N. Donaghue 2006. *Social Cognition. An Integrated Introduction*. London: Sage Publications.

Beacco J.-C., and M. Byram. 2003. *Guide for the development of language education policies in Europe. From linguistic diversity to plurilingual education.* Strasbourg: Language Policy Division, Council of Europe (available at www.coe.int/lang, accessed September 26, 2012).

Bialystok, E. 2010. Delaying the onset of Alzheimer disease: Bilingualism as a form of cognitive reserve. *Neurology* 75. 1726-1729.

Boal, A. 1992. *Games for actors and non-actors*. London: Routledge.

Camilleri, A. 2000. The development of cognitive processes. In *Approaches to Materials Design in European Textbooks: Implementing*

Principles of Authenticity, Learner Autonomy, Cultural awareness, eds. A.-B. Fenner and D. Newby, 13-14. Strasbourg: European Centre for Modern Languages/Council of Europe.

Camilleri Grima, A. 2002. *How Strange! The use of anecdotes in the development of intercultural competence.* Strasbourg: European Centre for Modern Languages/Council of Europe.

—, ed. 2007. *Promoting Linguistic Diversity and Whole-School Development.* Strasbourg: European Centre for Modern Languages/ Council of Europe.

Camilleri Grima, A., V. Sollars, and A. Mallia. 2006. Storyline through Image Theatre: A Maltese case-study. In *Intercultural competence & Communication in teacher training for early childhood educaion. Theory and Practice,* 50-54. Malta: Faculty of Education, University of Malta.

Candelier, M., ed. 2007. *Across Languages and Cultures. CARAP. Framework of reference for pluralistic approaches to languages and cultures.* Strasbourg: European Centre for Modern Languages/Council of Europe.

—, ed. 2011. *CARAP Cadre de Référence pour les Approches Plurielles des Langues et des Cultures Compétences et ressources.* Strasbourg: European Centre for Modern Languages/Council of Europe.

Clyne, M. 2011. Three is Too Many in Australia. In *Language Policy for the Multilingual Classroom. Pedagogy of the Possible,* eds. C. Hélot and M. Ó Laoire, 174-187. Bristol: Multilingual Matters.

Council of Europe. 2001. *Common European Framework of Reference for Languages: Learning, teaching, assessment.* Cambridge: Cambridge University Press & Modern Languages Division, Strasbourg.

Debelakk, R. 2001. *Hilarious Estonia*. Estonia: Estonian Institute.

Edwards, J. 2010. *Language Diversity in the Classroom.* Bristol: Multilingual Matters.

Europublic. 2009. *Study on the Contribution of Multilingualism to Creativity.* Brussels: European Commission (available at: http://eacea.ec.europa.eu/llp/studies/study_on_the_contribution_of_multilingualism_to_creativity_en.php, accessed September 26, 2012).

Fleischmann, E. 2007. The growth of a bilingual school: a principal's perspective. In *Promoting linguistic diversity and whole-school development*, ed. A. Camilleri Grima, 45-56. Strasbourg: Council of Europe.

Gaston, J. 1992. *Cultural Awareness Teaching Techniques.* Vermont: Pro Lingua Associates.

Gogolin, I. 2002. *Linguistic diversity and new minorities in Europe*, reference study. Strasbourg: Language Policy Division – DGIV, Council of Europe (available at: http://www.coe.int/t/dg4/linguistic/Source/GogolinEN.pdf, accessed September 26, 2012).

Grin, F. 2002. *Using language economics and education economics in language education policy*. Strasbourg: Council of Europe (available at http://www.coe.int/t/dg4/linguistic/Source/GrinEN.pdf, accessed September 26, 2012).

Hélot, C., and M. Ó Laoire, eds. 2011. *Language Policy for the Multilingual Classroom. Pedagogy of the Possible.* Bristol: Multilingual Matters.

Huss, L. 2007. "Let's Begin with the Youngest!" Minority language revitalisation through preschool. In *Promoting linguistic diversity and whole-school development* (CD-Rom), ed. A. Camilleri Grima, Strasbourg: Council of Europe.

Katz, L., and S. Chard. 2000. *Engaging Children's Minds: The Project Approach*. Stamford, Connecticut: Ablex Publishing Corporation.

McPake, J., and T. Tinsley, eds. 2007. *Valuing All Languages in Europe.* Graz: European Centre for Modern Languages of the Council of Europe (available at: http://archive.ecml.at/mtp2/publications/Valeur-report-E.pdf, accessed September 26, 2012).

Miller, J., A. Kostogriz, and M. Gearon, eds. 2009. *Culturally and Linguistically Diverse Classrooms. New Dilemmas for Teachers.* Bristol: Multilingual Matters.

Mohades, S.G., Struys E., Van Schuerbeck, P., Mondt, K., Van de Craen, P. And R. Luypaert. 2012. DTI reveals structural differences in white matter tracts between bilingual and monolingual children. In *Brain Research* 1435. 72-80.

National Statistics Office. 2005. *Census of Population and Housing, Vol. 1*. Malta: NSO.

Neuner, G. 2003. Socio-cultural interim worlds in foreign language teaching and learning. In *Intercultural competence*, ed. M. Byram, 15-62. Strasbourg: Council of Europe.

Newby, D. 2007. *European Portfolio for Student Teachers of Languages.* Strasbourg: European Centre for Modern Languages/Council of Europe.

Norberg, M. 2007. The Sorbian WITAJ project and the role of applied linguistics in the development of materials. In *Promoting linguistic diversity and whole-school development,* ed. A. Camilleri Grima, 33-44. Strasbourg: Council of Europe.

Ouane, A. 2003. By way of conclusion: the normality of multilingualism and its political ad educational implications. In *Towards a Multilingual Culture of Education,* ed. A. Ouane, 451-469. Hamburg, Germany: UNESCO Institute for Education.

—. ed. 2003 *Towards a Multilingual Culture of Education*. Hamburg, Germany: UNESCO Institute for Education.

Ó Riagáin, P. 2002. *The consequences of demographic trends for language learning and diversity*. Strasbourg: Council of Europe.

Pattanayak, D. P. 2003. Multilingual contexts and their ethos. In *Towards a Multilingual Culture of Education,* ed. A. Ouane, 49-58. Hamburg, Germany: UNESCO Institute for Education.

Pavlenko, A. 2005. *Emotions and Multilingualism*. Cambridge: Cambridge University Press.

Raasch, A. 2002. *Europe, Frontiers and Languages*. Strasbourg: Council of Europe (available at: http://www.coe.int/t/dg4/linguistic/Source/RaaschEN.pdf, accessed September 26, 2012).

Sercu, L. 2002. Autonomous learning and the acquisition of intercultural communicative competence: some implications for course development. *Language, Culture and Curriculum* 15/1. 61-74.

Siegel, J. 2005. Keeping Creoles and Dialects Out of the Classroom: Is It Justified?. In *Dialects, Englishes, Creoles, and Education*, ed. S. J. Nero, 39-70. New Jersey: LEA.

Skutnabb-Kangas, T. 2002. *Why should linguistic diversity be maintained and supported in Europe?*. Strasbourg: Council of Europe (available at http://www.coe.int/t/dg4/linguistic/Source/Skutnabb-KangasEN.pdf, accessed September 26, 2012).

Starkey, H. 2002. *Democratic citizenship, languages, diversity and human rights*. Strasbourg: Council of Europe (available at: http://www.coe.int/t/dg4/linguistic/Source/StarkeyEN.pdf, accessed September 26, 2012).

Willingham, D. 2007. *Cognition. The Thinking Animal*. New Jersey: Pearson.

Young, A., and C. Hélot. 2007. Parent power: parents as a linguistic and cultural resource at school. In *Promoting linguistic diversity and whole-school development,* ed. A. Camilleri Grima, 17-32. Strasbourg: Council of Europe.

Zarate, G. 2003. Identities and plurilingualism: preconditions for the recognition of intercultural competences. In *Intercultural competence*, ed. M. Byram, 85-118. Strasbourg: Council of Europe.

CHAPTER SIX

SOME REMARKS ON IMMIGRATION, IMMIGRANTS' LANGUAGES AND REPERTOIRES IN ITALY, AT THE BEGINNING OF THE XXI CENTURY

MARINA CHINI

6.1. The Context of Immigration in Contemporary Italy

Like many other EU countries, in the last twenty years, Italy has received a growing number of immigrants mainly from the Mediterranean area and from Eastern Europe (Romania, Albania, Morocco, Ukraine), but also from more distant regions of Africa, Asia and Latin America. According to the last official ISTAT[1] data (January 2011) 4,570,317 immigrants live in Italy, over a population of 60 million people (7.5% of the entire population). The Caritas/Migrantes Dossier on 2011 estimates that there were about 5 million immigrants in Italy in 2010, among which 3 million came to Italy in the last 10 years. 150 years ago, when Italy was unified (1861), its population included only 88,639 immigrants (0.4% of the population). The quantitative evolution of this section of population and its origin are presented in Tab. 6-1 (next page).

The developments outlined in the table are in line with the international scenario: in the last 10 years the immigrant population in the entire world has grown conspicuously (+ 64 million immigrants), so that now there are 214 million immigrants in the world and more than 15 million refugees. In the EU, almost one inhabitant out of ten was born in a country different from the country he/she is living in now: in 2009, 32.5 million people in the EU had a foreign citizenship (6.5%) and almost 15 million were naturalized.

---

[1] ISTAT, the National Institute for Statistics, is the official agency that collects data for statistical analyses in Italy.

YEAR	ORIGIN (%)						TOTAL N
	Europe	Africa	Asia	America	Oceania	others	
1980	*53.2*	*10.0*	*14.0*	*21.0*	*1.4*	*0.4*	298,749
1990	*33.5*	*30.5*	*18.7*	*16.4*	*0.8*	*0.1*	781,138
2000	*40.7*	*28.0*	*19.2*	*11.8*	*0.2*	*0.0*	1,388,153
2003	*47.9*	*23.5*	*16.8*	*11.5*	*0.1*	*0.1*	2,193,999
2008	*53.6*	*22.4*	*15.8*	*8.1*	*0.1*	*0.1*	3,891,295
2011	*53.4*	*21.6*	*16.8*	*8.1*	*0.1*	*0*	4,570,317

Tab. 6-1: Immigrants with residence permit living in Italy (1980-2011) (Source: Caritas/Migrantes based on ISTAT)

The distribution of immigrants on the national territory in Italy is unequal (see Tab. 6-2): 35% of them live in the North West, 26.3% in the North East, 25.2% in the Centre and 13.5% in the South and on the Islands. The regions in which the highest presence is registered are Lombardy (23% of the whole immigrant population in 2010), followed by Lazio, Veneto and Emilia Romagna, as shown in Tab. 6-2.

REGION	MIGRANTS WITH RESIDENCE PERMIT - BEGINNING 2010
Piedmont	377,241
Lombardy	982,225
Veneto	480,616
Friuli-Venezia Giulia	100,850
Emilia Romagna	461,321
Tuscany	338,746
Lazio	497,940
Campania	147,057
Abruzzo	75,708
Apulia	84,320
Sicily	127,310
Sardinia	33,301
ITALY	4,235,059 22% minors

Tab. 6-2: Migrants with residence permit in some Italian regions (Source: Dossier Caritas/Migrantes, 2010)

In some regions and towns the concentration of immigrants is quite high: migrants represent about 10-12% of the whole population in regions such as Emilia Romagna, Lombardy and Umbria, and in towns such as Brescia, Mantova, Piacenza, Reggio Emilia, Prato, which are all in the North or in the Centre of the country. In the South of Italy the concentration of immigrants, on the contrary, is very low, as it amounts to about 3%. The areas with the higher migrant concentration are potentially the most suitable for the development of linguistic communities of immigrants (see discussion in Chini, 2009a and Chini, 2011).

Other relevant socio-demographic variables have also to be considered, in a sociolinguistic perspective, in particular the young age of this population and the growing stability of the phenomenon. We can describe this in short with some figures:

- the age of more than one fifth of immigrants is less than 18 years old;
- the average age of migrants is low: 32 years (vs. 44 years of Italians);
- only 2% of immigrants are older than 65 (vs. 20% of the Italian population);
- 78.8% of them are of working age;
- almost 1 out of 10 of the whole working population of Italy is immigrant;
- there are frequent mixed marriages in Italy (in 2009, 1 out of 10);
- the number of those who are less than 18 years old is growing: almost 1 million;
- the number of second generation people is also increasing: almost 650,000;
- according to ISTAT, 600,000 immigrants have been granted Italian citizenship (66,000 in 2010).

Italian schools have a very important role in integrating the young immigrant population in Italy and in its culture. They are also crucial in developing these immigrants' competence in Italian. The amount of foreign pupils in schools in 2010-11 is as follows: 711,046 pupils with non-Italian citizenship, that is almost 8% (7.9%), which is not far from the percentage in other large European countries which are traditional destinations for migrants (for instance, Germany 8.6%). The distribution of immigrant pupils is different according to their level of schooling: 35.8% of the total number of foreign pupils attend primary schools (5/6-10 years old); 20.3% attend preschools (2/3-5 years old), 22.3% junior high schools (11-14 years old), 21.6% senior high schools (14-19 years old), where there has been a consistent increase in the last years (14% in 2001-02, 21.6% in 2010-2011). There are a large number of nationalities which are represented in Italian schools. The native countries with the highest number of students are listed in Tab. 6-3:

NATIVE COUNTRY	N OF PUPILS (2010-2011)	TOTAL N OF IMMIGRANTS COMING FROM THESE COUNTRIES	
		I.1.2010	2011
Romania	126,452	887,763	968,576
Albania	99,205	466,684	482,627
Morocco	92,542	431,529	452,424
China	32,691	188,352	209,934
Moldova	20,580	105,600	130,948
India	20,536	105,863	121,036
Philippines	19,766	123,584	134,154
Ecuador	19,537	85,940	91,625
Tunisia	18,333	103,678	106,291
Ukraine	17,408	174,129	200,730

Tab. 6-3: First native countries of pupils with non-Italian citizenship, 2010-2011.
Total number of immigrants from the same countries (I.1.2010, 2011) (Source: MIUR; Caritas/Migrantes, 2010)

Second generation pupils are increasing in number: they represented 42% of the foreign pupils in 2010-11, with a much higher percentage among kindergarten pupils (78.3%). Immigrant pupils are concentrated in large numbers in the same regions and towns mentioned before, especially in Milan, Rome, Turin, Brescia, Bergamo, and in the regions of Lombardy (173,051, almost one foreign pupil out of four attends a school in Lombardy = 24%), Veneto (almost 85,000 pupils), Emilia Romagna (almost 83,000), and Piedmont and Lazio (with 67-68,000 foreign pupils each). As for their origin (see Tab. 6-3), the main home countries are Romania, Albania and Morocco: 40% of the total number of foreign pupils come from these three countries. Recently, there has been a significant increase in pupils coming from Romania, Moldova and India, while pupils of whom both parents come from Morocco, Albania or Philippines, are often born in Italy or came here several years ago. On the contrary, countries of recent migration such as Ukraine are underrepresented in schools.

In this context Italian educational policy has focussed more on teaching Italian L2 and on intercultural education and dialogue, than on L1 maintenance (although some pertinent indications are provided in several laws[2]). In January 2010, the Italian Ministry of Education, University and Research (MIUR) established that 30% is the maximum percentage of foreign pupils in a class, in order to avoid ghettoisation, and so that schools "can organize a first phase of language learning for foreign pupils [newly arrived in Italy], before they enter the class or in parallel to their settling-in phase, in order to facilitate their integration"; furthermore schools "can organize enhancement courses where it is possible, resorting to teachers from the same school. Therefore it is convenient, in teacher training, to give special attention to methodologies and teaching measures suitable for promoting integration"[3]. The main principles inspiring the MIUR official policy are the following[4]:

- inclusive policy;
- promotion of the acquisition of Italian L2 and of intercultural dialogue;
- care to the uniqueness and relational character of every pupil;
- the development of multilingualism;
- parental involvement.

Some innovative national projects on Italian L2 teaching have been pursued in the Nineties (for instance the MILIA Project) and at the beginning of the new century, namely the integrated e-learning teacher training project *Italiano L2: lingua di contatto, lingua di culture* 'L2 Italian: language of contact, language of cultures', 2003-2006[5]. Together with other local refresher courses, these projects have contributed to

[2] The following are some Italian laws and regulations which deal with the issue: CM 301, 8.9.1989; law 40/1998; Regulations DPR 394/1999; CM 24 of the Italian Ministry of Education, University and Research MIUR, I.3. 2006, *Linee guida per l'accoglienza e l'integrazione degli alunni stranieri* ['Guidelines for welcoming and integrating foreign pupils']; the 2007 document of the Italian Ministry of Education MPI, *La via italiana per la scuola interculturale e l'integrazione degli alunni stranieri* ['The Italian way to intercultural schooling and integration of foreign pupils'].

[3] See http://www.istruzione.it/web/ministero/cs080110, accessed September 26, 2012.

[4] See MPI document, *La via italiana per la scuola interculturale e l'integrazione degli alunni stranieri*, October 2007.

[5] See:
http://venus.unive.it/italdue/index.php?name=EZCMS&page_id=326&menu=100, accessed September 26, 2012.

promote greater intercultural awareness among Italian teachers. However, some extant problems have to be mentioned, among which:

- there are still few resources at financial and organizational level in order to promote multilingualism and intercultural dialogue;
- often teachers do not have enough competence at a pedagogical and linguistic level in order to deal appropriately with pupils in multicultural and multilingual classes;
- the intervention in this field is often non-systematic;
- teachers are often not qualified specifically to teach Italian L2;
- a certain underestimation of the importance of having teachers trained in Italian L2 and in intercultural and multilingual education is attested in a recent Ministerial decree (DM 249/2010) on teacher training.

Nevertheless, there are also some positive aspects which deserve mention:

- there is growing expertise and awareness among teachers;
- there is a significant involvement of the civil society and of volunteers;
- some free of charge public courses for immigrant adults have been organized, aimed at obtaining certification (for instance in Lombardy; cf. www.certificailtuoitaliano.it)[6].

Having described the overall socio-demographic and institutional representation of immigration in Italy, attention will now shift to sociolinguistic contributions to this field of enquiry.

6.2. Immigration and Multilingualism in Italy: Some Research Trends

During the Eighties and the Nineties, linguistic studies on migration to Italy focussed essentially on immigrants' acquisition of Italian as a second language (Banfi, 1993, Giacalone Ramat, 2003), sometimes also with a

---

[6] In recent years regions such as Lombardy have organised such courses for levels A1, A2, B1 and also B2 of the Common European Framework. Unfortunately these courses are quite short, as they range from a minimun of 20 hours to a maximum of 40. These courses aim to help immigrants to sit for the A2 level test in Italian, which, according to a recent law (art. 22 bis of the law n. 94, 15/7/2009), is necessary for them in order to obtain a long-term residence permit.

sociolinguistic perspective on pidginized learner varieties (Orletti, 1988); later studies were carried out on the possible development of Italian ethnolects in some specific communities (Vietti, 2005). Especially since the Nineties, researchers of the so-called 'Pavia Project' documented developmental regularities at morphological and syntactic level, then also at lexical and discourse level, in Italian L2 (see Giacalone Ramat, 2003, Bernini *et al.*, 2008). A close interaction with European networks on second language acquisition began and studies on Italian L2 were carried out also in a comparative perspective. Among these there are both the Vigoni-Project on the acquisition of Italian L2 by German learners and of German L2 by Italian learners, a project coordinated by Norbert Dittmar and Anna Giacalone Ramat (Dittmar and Giacalone Ramat, 1999), and the so-called *Learner varieties project*, coordinated at the Max-Planck Institute for Psycholinguistics of Nijmegen (NL), by Wolfgang Klein, Clive Perdue, and subsequently by Henriëtte Hendriks and Christine Dimroth (cf. http://www.learner-varieties.eu/). This project included various phases: "The structure of learner varieties" (1994-1999), "The dynamics of learner varieties" (1999-2004), and "The comparative approach to L2 acquisition" (2004-2009). It involved about 40 researchers from different European countries, working on different L2s (mainly English, German, French, Dutch, Italian) from a cognitive-functional approach. Several interesting common principles and phases (in particular the well-known *Basic Variety*, Klein and Perdue 1997) were identified for the whole range of the L2s studied[7].

It was only during the last decade that an interest towards the entire immigrants' linguistic repertoire developed in Italy. After a seminal sociolinguistic outline of the linguistic situation of migrants in Italy (Mioni, 1998) and after the first presumptive list of migrants' native languages (Vedovelli and Villarini, 2001), a national project funded by the Italian National Research Council (CNR-Agenzia 2000 Project "Le lingue straniere immigrate in Italia" [lit. 'Foreign languages that immigrated to Italy']) was coordinated by Massimo Vedovelli (University for Foreigners of Siena) and involved six Italian Universities (Bergamo, Cagliari, Milano Bicocca, Pavia, Siena, Verona). It analysed the migrants' linguistic repertoires (Chini, 2004, 2009a; Guerini, 2006; Berruto, 2009) and some dynamics of language maintenance and language shift in Northern Italy contexts such as Turin, Pavia, Bergamo, Verona (Chini, 2003, 2004, 2009b, 2009c, 2011; Massariello Merzagora, 2004; Valentini, 2005,

[7] The main results of the research are gathered in some (joint) publications, among which, Giacalone Ramat and Crocco Galèas (1995), Dimroth and Starren (2003), Hendriks (2005) and Dimroth and Lambert (2008).

2009), as well as the presence of immigrant languages in the linguistic landscape of Central Italy (Bagna *et al.*, 2004) and the possible rise of ethnolects and their internal variation in Northern Italy (Vietti, 2005, 2009; see also Chini, 2011 for a synthetic review of research done). The Pavia research Unit (coordinated by the author) investigated some sociolinguistic aspects of migration in the Province of Pavia (Lombardy) and in Turin (Piedmont). After some qualitative investigations (e.g. Chini, 2003), a quantitative research based on a questionnaire studied the linguistic repertoire, the (self-assessed) linguistic competence and language uses of 414 immigrant pupils of public schools (9-20 years) and of 171 adults in the same areas, Pavia and its province, and Turin (Chini, 2004). In this context, given MERIDIUM's focus on immigrants' repertoires and multilingualism, the results of this last research trend will provide the main focus of further reflection.

6.3. The Native Languages of Immigrants and the Main Immigrant Linguistic Communities

If we consider the immigrants' countries of origin according to the latest census data, a first presumptive list of their main native languages can be proposed:

(1)
1) Romanian (21%);
2) Albanian (11%);
3) Moroccan and Tunisian Arabic, various Arabic dialects (13%);
4) Chinese, different Chinese varieties and dialects (5%);
5) Ukrainian (and Russian) (4-5%),
6) Tagalog/English (3%),
7) several varieties of Spanish (ca. 6%).

Given that the countries of origin are almost 200 and given their often multilingual repertoire, the global number of languages is much higher (even more so, if we consider also dialects and regional varieties). On the whole 120 to 140 languages could be attested on the Italian territory (see Vedovelli and Villarini, 2001: 228-229), but no official data on the immigrants' languages have been collected to date, not even during the last official census (October 2011).

The immigrants' languages are differently rooted in Italy: some of them have arrived only recently, such as Ukrainian. Others, such as Moroccan and Tunisian Arabic, have been attested in Italy for decades. For some of them we can clearly apply Vedovelli's and colleagues' label "lingue immigrate" [lit. 'immigrated languages'], i.e. languages socially rooted and potentially able to influence the local linguistic setting (lit. *lingue "di sicuro radicamento sociale" in grado "di condizionare l'assetto idiomatico locale"*; Bagna *et al.*, 2003: 203).

We can suppose that proper linguistic communities exist in Italy (or are about to settle) for at least some of these languages, for instance in contexts where there are a certain amount of immigrants of the same origin and L1. Some criteria for identifying proper immigrant minorities have been proposed and could be applied also in this case (cf. Lüdi, 1990; Chini, 2004: 23; Chini, 2009a: 295):

1) a sufficiently high number of immigrants (which has to be established);
2) existence of a migrant community sharing the same culture and language;
3) quite regular and frequent interactions also in the L1 within the immigrants' community;
4) the migratory project should be definitive (this means, in particular: long duration of stay; high number of young immigrants attending schools; important number of naturalizations);
5) creation of (cultural, religious, sport, recreational, union, media) institutions specifically pertaining to the immigrant community;
6) clear intention to maintain the L1.

If we consider as possible locations for immigrants' minorities towns with at least, for instance, 5,000 immigrants coming from the same country, we would obtain the presumptive list of immigrants' minority communities in Italy displayed in Tab. 6-4 (next page).

Therefore there are large communities of Romanians in Rome, Turin and Milan, of Chinese in Milan, Rome and Prato, of Philippines in Milan and Rome, and so on. Almost in all Italian regions the first three groups of immigrants (by size of the community) are Romanian, Albanian and Moroccan, potentially forming also linguistic communities. For some nationalities we find high concentrations of immigrants (often working in families) in a few towns, mainly in regional capitals (e.g. migrants from the Philippines, Ecuador, Peru living in Milan and Rome), where the rise of language minority communities is probable. For others there is sometimes a more dispersed presence on the territory (e.g. people from India, Morocco, Albania, Tunisia), which could discourage the birth of language communities linked to the native language. Field research, also through ethnographic means, on single immigrants' groups in various Italian contexts is necessary in order to obtain a realistic representation of these presumptive communities.

COUNTRY	% LIVING IN THE PROVINCIAL OR REGIONAL CAPITALS	FIVE FIRST TOWNS WITH AT LEAST 5,000 IMMIGRANTS IN 2011
Romania	*30.6*	Rome, Turin, Milan, Padua, Verona
Albania	*27.1*	Rome, Turino, Genoa, Milan, Florence
Morocco	*22.2*	Turin, Milan
China	*46.8*	Milan, Rome, Prato, Turin
Ukraine	*38.6*	Rome, Naples, Milan
Philippines	*80.1*	Milan, Rome
Moldova	*45.2*	Rome
Poland	*35.1*	Rome
Peru	*62.3*	Milan, Rome, Turin, Florence
Ecuador	*56.9*	Genoa, Milan, Rome

Tab. 6-4: Main native countries of immigrants, their concentration in the regional and provincial capitals; towns with at least 5,000 immigrants coming from the same country (source: ISTAT, 2011) [8]

A look at immigrants' media in Italy can also be revealing. Immigrants' media in Italy according to Fiorentini (2005) include about 50 newspapers and magazines, printed (with a circulation of 3,000-20,000 copies each) or on the internet, on the whole resulting in a total circulation of 350,000 copies in the country; 70% of them are distributed free of charge and are thus very easily accessible to immigrants. The main languages used in these publications are the following:

- English and French in the media for Africans;
- Albanian for Albanians;
- Romanian and Italian for Romanians;
- Spanish for Latin-American immigrants;
- Portuguese for immigrants from Brazil and Portuguese-speaking African countries;
- Chinese and sometimes Italian in the media for Chinese people;
- Arabic, French, Italian for people from Arabic speaking countries;
- English and Tagalog for immigrants from the Philippines;
- Polish for Polish immigrants;

[8] See http://demo.istat.it/, sub *Cittadini stranieri – Bilancio demografico.*

- Urdu, Bengali, English, Punjabi, Sinhalese for immigrants from the Indian Region;
- Russian, Ukrainian and Italian for Ukrainians [and Russians] in Italy.

A further survey carried out after the one referred to above, the 2007 survey of the Cospe organization (*Cooperazione per lo Sviluppo dei Paesi Emergenti*; see Caritas/Migrantes, 2008), reveals that there are about 150 newspapers and magazines in immigrants' languages. Two thirds of them started being published in the last 5 years: 63 magazines, 59 radio broadcasts, 24 TV programmes. All this testifies the vitality of the immigrants' communities and of their languages in Italy.

If, on the whole, the most represented immigrants' languages are those listed in (1), with differing percentages, in particular regions some peculiarities are attested. For instance in Friuli, in the North East, besides Albanian, South Slavic languages such as Serbian and Croatian are also heavily represented.

In several Italian contexts, besides the most represented immigrant languages listed earlier, there is a clear dispersion among a high number of lesser represented languages. In order to provide an approximate indication of the phenomenon, Tab. 6-5 includes a list of the most representative immigrant language communities in Italy (at the national level and in some contexts in the North and the Centre), according to some recent investigations.

RANK	ITALY (2008)	VERONA[9] (2000/01)	PROVINCE OF SIENA[10] (2002)	PAVIA-TURIN[11] (2002)	BERGAMO[12] (2003)
1.	Romanian	Moroccan Arabic	Albanian	Albanian	(Latin American) Spanish
2.	Albanian	Spanish	Serbian	(Latin American) Spanish	Moroccan Arabic

Tab. 6-5: The most representative immigrant language communities in Italy (national and local level) according to some recent investigations (over 3% of immigrants)

[9] Source: Massariello (2004).
[10] Source: Bagna *et al.* (2004)
[11] Source: Chini (2004). Data concerning minors.
[12] Source: Valentini (2009)

RANK	ITALY (2008)	VERONA (2000/01)	PROVINCE OF SIENA (2002)	PAVIA-TURIN (2002)	BERGAMO (2003)
3.	Moroccan Arabic	Albanian	Romanian	Moroccan Arabic	Albanian
4.	Chinese varieties	English	German	Romanian	Serbian
5.	Ukrainian	Serbian	English	Chinese varieties	Chinese varieties
6.	(Latin American) Spanish	Romanian	Tunisian Arabic		Romanian
7.	Tagalog-English	Sinhala	French		Tunisian Arabic
8.	Tunisian Arabic	Portuguese	Tagalog-English		French
9.	Polish	Kosovian [Albanian]	Macedonian		
10.	Macedonian	Ashanti	Polish		
11.	Egyptian Arabic	Bosnian			
12.	French	Croatian			
13.	Sinhala	Chinese (Zhejiang dialect)			
14.	Bengali	Fant			
15.	Serbian	Berber			

Tab. 6-5 (cont.): The most representative immigrant language communities in Italy (national and local level) according to some recent investigations (over 3% of immigrants)

In a 2002 research on immigrants' languages and repertoires in the Province of Pavia and in Turin (North West Italy; Chini, 2004) approximately 40 languages (Tab. 6-6 below) were attested, not to mention the local varieties and dialects spoken by 414 young immigrants both before they migrated and also once they settled in Italy. The languages listed in the following table (see Chini, 2004: 119-120) belong to several language families and groups:

LANGUAGE FAMILY	LANGUAGES	GROUP
Indoeuropean	Spanish and its varieties	Romance
	French	Romance
	Haitik	French based creole
	Romanian and its dialects	Romance
	Moldavian	Romance
	Italian	Romance
	Portuguese	Romance
	Albanian (its varieties)	Albanese
	English and its varieties	Germanic
	Pidgin English	English based creole
	German	Germanic
	Kurdish	Indoiranian/iranian
	Sinhalese or Sinhala	Indoiranian/iranian
	Urdu	Indoiranian/iranian
	Panjabi	Indoiranian/iranian
	Zagon (rom)	Indoiranian/iranian
	Russian	Slavic
	Serbian	Slavic
	Bosnian	Slavic
	Croatian	Slavic
	Macedonian	Slavic
	Bulgarian	Slavic
	Polish	Slavic
	Ukrainian	Slavic
	Greek	Greek
Afroasiatic	Arabic (varieties and dialects)	Semitic
	Amharic	Semitic
	Tigrinya	Semitic
	Berber	Berber
Sino-tibetan	Mandarin Chinese	Chinese
	Chinese wú	Chinese
	Chinese dialects	Chinese

Tab. 6-6: Source languages of young immigrants in the Province of Pavia and in Turin
(Chini, 2004: 119-120)

LANGUAGE FAMILY	LANGUAGES	GROUP
Niger-Congo	Diula/Dioula/Jula	Mande
	Lingala	Atlantic-congo
	Twi (Akan)	Kwa
	Yoruba	Atlantic-congo
	Edo or Bini	Atlantic-congo
Austronesian	Pilipino or Tagalog	Polinesian Malese
Altaic	Turkish	Turkish
Quechuan	Quechua	Quechuan II
Uralic	Hungarian (and Hung. dialect)	Ugrofinnish

Tab. 6-6 (cont.): Source languages of young immigrants in the Province of Pavia and in Turin (Chini, 2004: 119-120)

Approximately the same languages have been found in a group of 171 adults' in the Province of Pavia and in Turin (Andorno, 2004: 241). They are mainly Indo-European and Afro-Asiatic languages, but some Niger-Congo and Sino-tibetan languages of different groups were also attested. Besides (more or less) standard languages, our subjects sometimes mention regional or sovra-regional varieties of Arabic, Chinese, Portuguese, Spanish, along with several dialects (of Albanian, Chinese, Romanian, Spanish). One out of 6 subjects (16%) was already plurilingual when he/she arrived in Italy, speaking, for instance, a certain language (such as Kurdish, Moldavian, Tigrinya, Berber, Yoruba) in the family, or only with the parents and the grand-parents, and another one outside the family (such as Arabic, Ukrainian, Amharic, English). Mixed language choices have also been attested, mainly with parents and siblings (see Tab. 6-7).

COUNTRY	WITH PARENTS	WITH SIBLINGS	WITH GRAND-PARENTS	WITH FRIENDS
Syria	Kurdish/ Syrian Arabic	Kurdish/ Syrian Arabic	Kurdish/ Syrian Arabic	(Syrian) Arabic
Romania	Zagon	Zagon	Zagon	Romanian
Ukraine	Moldavian F/ Moldavian + Russian M	-	Moldavian/ Russian	Ukrainian
Ethiopia	Amharic/ Tigrinya	Amharic/ Tigrinya	Amharic/ Tigrinya	Amharic
Nigeria 1	Bini F/Edo M	-	Edo	English/ pidgin
Ukraine	Moldavian F/ Moldavian + Russian M	-	Moldavian / Russian	Ukrainian
Nigeria 2	English	Yoruba/ English	Yoruba	English
Ghana	English /Twi	English /Twi	Twi	English /Twi
Angola	Portoguese	Portoguese	Lingala	Portoguese
Congo 1	French	-	Lingala	French
Congo 2	French /Lingala	Lingala	Lingala/ French	French/ Lingala
Pakistan	Urdu/Panjabi	Urdu/Panjabi	Panjabi	Urdu
Morocco 1	Tunisian Arabic F/ Moroccan Arabic M	Moroccan Arabic.	Tunisian Arabic/ Moroccan Arabic	Moroccan Arabic
Morocco 2	Moroccan Arabic + Berber	Moroccan Arabic	Moroccan Arabic + Berber	Moroccan Arabic

Tab. 6-7: Language choices (before migration) in young immigrants with bilingual background (Chini, 2004)

For many immigrant pupils, TV and school have also been an important source for other linguistic experiences and for multilingualism, also before migration: 34% of them have had their first contact with English and 18% with French in this way. About one out of ten (11%) says that his/her contact to Italian began already in the home country, often through TV or school (this is true mainly for Albanian and Romanian pupils). It is highly probable that today pre-migration contact with the L2 and also with international languages is more plausible, as this contact is far more accessible than it was 10 years ago, especially through the internet. In order to provide an indication of the linguistic choices of young immigrants in the migration context, in Tab. 6-8 data pertaining to a group of immigrant pupils (in the Province of Pavia and in Turin; Chini, 2004) and to a similar group in Verona (cf. Massariello Merzagora 2004; IT = Italian; L1 = first language, language of origin) are provided.

Interlocutor	**Languages used by immigrant children (%) in Verona (N 267), Pavia (N 309), Turin (N 105)**								
	L1			**IT**			**L1+IT**		
	VR	**PV**	**TO**	**VR**	**PV**	**TO**	**VR**	**PV**	**TO**
father	*59.6*	*48.5*	*53.3*	*10.9*	*14.6*	*12.4*	*14.2*	*26.2*	*27.6*
mother	*58.4*	*47.9*	*46.7*	*9.4*	*10.4*	*19.0*	*20.2*	*35.6*	*27.6*
siblings	*25.5*	*28.2*	*31.4*	*28.1*	*19.7*	*24.8*	*18.4*	*35.0*	*22.9*
grand-parents	*79.4*	*80.9*	*80.9*	*2.2*	*2.2*	*2.2*	*1.1*	*8.5*	*8.5*
friends	*4.1*	-	-	*62.6*	-	-	*24.7*	-	
(non-It friends)	-	*33.7*	*39.0*	-	*29.1*	*25.7*	-	*24.6*	*27.6*
(It. friends)	-	*1.0*	-	-	*91.9*	*97.1*	-	*1.9*	-
neighbours	*6.0*	-	-	*79.8*	-	-	*4.5*	-	-

Tab. 6-8: Languages used by immigrant children with different interlocutors in Verona, in the Province of Pavia and in Turin: main possibilities (Massariello Merzagora, 2004 for Verona; Chini, 2004: 157, 184-185 for the Province of Pavia and Turin)

The language choices differ according to the interlocutor in all the three contexts, with an important L1 maintenance when speaking to parents (50-60%) and to grand-parents (about 80%). In Pavia and Turin the scale of L1 maintenance is the following (Chini, 2004: 307; Chini, 2011: 61):

(2) grand-parents> father/mother > non Italian friends > brothers/sisters > school, Italian friends, transactions

According to our investigation, language choices vary also in relation to the country of origin and to other factors, such as sex (mother and daughters are more prone to use both L1 and L2 in the family than fathers and sons; see Chini, 2006, 2009b), generation (parents are more conservative), length of stay in Italy, endogamy, parents' occupation, school attendance in the native country, social context of life, etc. (Chini, 2004: 317-331). Looking now at the language shift towards Italian, a complementary scale could be identified among immigrant children in the Province of Pavia and in Turin:

(3) school, Italian friends > transactions > non Italian friends > family (brothers/sisters > father > mother > grand-parents)

In the following section the configuration of the linguistic repertoires of immigrants in Italy will be presented.

6.4. The Linguistic Repertoire of Some Immigrant Groups

As already said, in frequent cases the linguistic repertoires of immigrants in Italy often include different languages: not only their native language and Italian, but also other languages (exolanguages, pidginized varieties of those, minority languages, etc.). Their linguistic repertoires before migration typically include (Chini, 2004, ch. 4; Chini, 2011: 55-56; D'Agostino, 2005: 78-87):

1) a *national language* and *local related varieties and dialects*, sometimes in a diglossic relationship;
2) a *national language*, (local related varieties) and a *minority language*;
3) an (international) *exolanguage* (also in pidginized varieties), sometimes one or more vehicular languages or lingua franca (ex. Wolof in Senegal), *national languages*, and *local varieties and dialects*;
4) *two widely spread languages*, and sometimes more local varieties (i.e. Standard Arabic together with French, besides regional varieties of Arabic, among educated people from Morocco and Tunisia).

Following Berruto (2009), one may distinguish the repertoire of languages used for intra-group communication (*repertorio endocomunitario*), in which the L1 still has an important role and Italian has a growing importance, and the repertoire for inter-group communication (*repertorio esocomunitario*). The latter often includes Italian and sometimes international languages such as English, French or Spanish, occasionally used as bridging languages. Given this situation, the everyday discourse of immigrants can show various phenomena of language contact, such as code alternation, code switching and code mixing, the latter being sometimes due mainly to lack of competence (as in the case (4)) and sometimes to a creative indexation of a new mixed identity. The following example is reported from a Pakistani immigrant living in South Tyrol/Alto Adige, an Italian trilingual region with a German speaking majority (insertions in italics are in English, those in bold are in German):

(4) mio fratello eh *before* **arbeit** lavora Pakistan + tre/äh du/+ anno + Germania ++
'my brother eh before work Pakistan + three/ äh two/+ year(s) + Germany'

++*and then go/and then* **gehen** Pakistan *and* eh + una fabbrica + fabrica
'and then go/and then go Pakistan and eh + a factory + factory'

and then **arbeit ålf [elf] person**
'and then work eleven eleven persons'
(Banfi, 1995: 146-147)

Language repertoires and language choices differ substantially among different immigrants' groups, especially according to their native country. For instance, among minors, but often also among adult immigrants, from Romania and Albania, language shift to Italian within the family is more frequent than among minors and adults from Morocco (i.e in Turin and Pavia, Chini, 2004: 319-322). In these cases the space for Italian even in the intra-group repertoire can be quite relevant.

In a recent work, Berruto (2009) proposed some models of language repertoire for immigrant communities living in Northern Italy (mainly for first generation migrants); these often include two or three levels (high H, middle M, low L). The following two examples, one for the Ghanaian community in Bergamo (see also Guerini, 2006) and one for Nigerian immigrants in Turin, illustrate this point:

(5) Language repertoire of the Ghanaian community in Bergamo and its province (Guerini, 2006: 65)

H	*GHANAIAN ENGLISH* | ITALIAN
M	AKAN/TWI |*Student Pidgin (?)* | (*Bergamasco* dialect?)
L	GHANAIAN LANGUAGES AND VERNACULARS | *GHANAIAN PIDGIN ENGLISH* | (*Bergamasco* dialect?)

(6a) Language repertoire of the Nigerian community in Turin (Berruto, 2009: 13)

H	NIGERIAN ENGLISH	ITALIAN
M	IGBO	ITALIAN
L	LOCAL VERNACULARS	*NIGERIAN PIDGIN ENGLISH*

In the post-migration repertoire there is a reduction of the number of levels and a downgrading of the languages (from level M to L), as in the case of the Nigerians in Turin. In the migrants' intra-group post-migration repertoire, Italian can be placed at the H level, next to the H language of the original pre-migration repertoire, which is often an exolanguage (English, French), while some M languages (like Igbo for Nigerians) are downgraded to L languages (cf. 6b with 6a):

(6b) Intra-group language reportoire of Nigerian immigrants in Turin (Berruto, 2009: 15)

H	NIGERIAN ENGLISH	Italian	
L	IGBO	*NIGERIAN PIDGIN ENGLISH*	local vernaculars

This kind of dynamics can result in a gradual loss and in a disappearance of languages with low prestige and marginal utility in the Italian context, as in the case of local African vernacular for Ghanaian immigrants (Guerini, 2006: 243-244).

At the lower level of the immigrants' repertoire we can also find Italo-Romance dialects (such as the *Bergamasco* dialect for Ghanaians in Bergamo), but this has to be ascertained from case to case. Their presence in these repertoires depends very much on the vitality of the single dialects in the local native speakers' community and on the migrants' attitudes towards these dialects, which often are not positive, especially in the North West of Italy (Chini, 2009a: 299-301). In other areas (North East, South, little towns) it is highly probable and also (although not systematically) attested that the Italo-Romance dialects enter the migrants' (mainly extra-group) repertoires, acting as a significant means of integration, as documented for instance in Palermo by D'Agostino (2004) and in some villages near Pavia by Chini (2003; see also Chini, 2011: 59-60).

Another aspect still to be verified concerns the position of historical minority languages of Italy in the repertoire of immigrants who live in regions where these languages are normally spoken (for instance German varieties in South Tyrol/Alto Adige, Friulian in Friuli, Sardinian in Sardinia, French and Franco-Provençal in Aosta Valley; see Iannaccaro and Dell'Aquila, 2011 for such minorities).

In general, the structure of immigrants' linguistic repertoires in Italy depends on various factors (Chini, 2009a: 296):

1. number of languages in the pre-migration repertoire and its complexity;
2. status, prestige, function and resistance of the pre-migration codes in the current situation (also in terms of different types of diglossia);
3. presence, functions and penetration of Italian and of Italo-Romance dialects in the migrants' current repertoire;
4. structural distance between the codes of the current repertoire. If it is reduced, language contact phenomena and probably also mixed (ethnic) varieties are very likely to emerge (see Vietti, 2005 and 2009, for the Italian L2 varieties of Peruvian immigrant women living in Turin, possibly the first step towards a Peruvian ethnic variety of Italian).

6.5. Conclusion, with Some Comparative Remarks

The sociolinguistic study of migration in Italy is quite recent and research projects such as MERIDIUM give an important contribution to its progress. To date, we still lack a global representation of the language uses and of the linguistic competence of the various immigrants' groups in Italy and of their plurilingualism. Research has focussed mainly on identifying the principal immigrants' languages and on describing the repertoire of some communities, as well as on some dynamics of language maintenance, shift and use in several domains and in some areas of the country, mainly in the North and in the Centre (see Chini, 2004, 2009a; Massariello Merzagora, 2004; Valentini, 2009). In various immigrant contexts an initial language shift has been attested, mainly in the inter-ethnic domains (transactions, school, work), but also in intra-ethnic domains, especially among immigrants' children or sometimes in the speech between these children and their parents. There are signs that Italian has started to be accepted not only as a *they-code* among immigrants, especially among younger individuals and those living with their family and children in Italy. However, the field still requires extensive study, especially in South and North East Italy, among the first and the second generations of migrants of different origins. More precisely, the aspects to investigate further in the years to come are the following, among others:

- statistical data on native languages and on language use of immigrants in Italy (unfortunately to date these data are not registered by the national population census);
- language attitudes of immigrants (and also of native residents) with regard to the languages of their repertoires, to multilingual practices and multilingualism;
- possible emergence of new linguistic minorities and in depth analysis of their sociolinguistic situation.

Finally, in order to understand better the Italian situation of migrants, a comparison with other parallel cases could also be useful. Seemingly, the migrants' situation in Italy shares some features with other migratory contexts, but it also displays some peculiar characteristics. For instance, we can consider some results of the Nordic project NISU (Boyd and Latomaa, 1999) on immigrants in Scandinavia (people from Turkey, Vietnam, Finland and United States) and of research trends on migration to Australia (Clyne, 2003).

According to the NISU Project (Boyd and Latomaa, 1999), intra-ethnic friendship networks are very conservative in relation to L1 (here called minority language, ML) maintenance in Scandinavia; this turns out to be true also in different Italian contexts, but seemingly to a smaller extent (see Tab. 6-8). Furthermore, the use of the minority language (ML or L1) among partners from the same country seems to be very high (90-100%) in Scandinavia. This is much higher than among migrants in Italy (Pavia and Turin; see Chini, 2004; Andorno, 2004), where parents from the same country often use their L1 only among themselves (sometimes also together with other languages, excluding Italian), but much less often than their counterparts in Scandinavia (in 59-68% of the cases vs. 90-100%); in frequent circumstances immigrant parents use both their L1 and Italian (and in case also other languages) in order to talk to each other (in 23% of the cases), while a complete shift to Italian only is very low (2-4%; see Andorno, 2004: 279, table 7.30). Thus language shift to L2, in this case a secondary shift, turns out to be more frequent in Italy than in Scandinavia. The reasons for this are to be investigated through a rigorous comparison, taking into consideration various contextual, social and cultural data. As for language maintenance in Scandinavia, the NISU project has proposed the following scale of decreasing L1 maintenance:

(7) *Maintenance of minority language among immigrants' children in the Nordic area*:
father or mother of the minority language [ML] > adult of ML > brothers and sisters [younger > older] > father or mother of the majority language (Boyd and Latomaa, 1999: 309-311)

This scale is similar to the scale in (2) for Pavia and Turin, especially as it shows the greater propensity of immigrants' children to maintain the ML (or L1) with their parents than they do with their brothers and sisters (see Chini, 2004: 307; Chini, 2011: 61).

Also in many immigrants' communities in Australia, the L1 is used more often by children in order to talk to their parents (or among parents) than by children when talking to brothers and sisters (Clyne and Kipp, 1999; Clyne, 2003: 42-46). Furthermore, a high L1/ML maintenance index among parents does not necessarily imply a high L1 maintenance among children's generation in Australia; this seems also to be true for Moroccan families in Italy, given that their parents use their L1 very often, also with their children (71-77%; Chini, 2004: 171) and their children use just the L1 also very often with their parents (63% with their fathers, 68% with their mothers), but much less often with their brothers and sisters living in Italy (34%; Chini, 2009b: 119).

The factor "native country" turns out to be very significant in data about (North-West) Italy, as well as in other contexts: Chinese immigrants and often Moroccan Arabic immigrants, for instance, show high L1 maintenance in Italy, as well as in the Netherlands and in Australia (Extra and Verhoeven, 1999: 19; Clyne, 2003: 35). On the contrary, language choices among Spanish speaking immigrants seem to be less coherent in various areas of the world, most likely because of different factors that come into play.

Some explaining factors, which have been mentioned by the literature on migration, are partially confirmed by investigations on some Italian contexts (factors such as endogamy, length of schooling in Italy and in the native country, parents' profession, degree of social integration, sex, generation; see Chini, 2004: ch. 8; Chini, 2009a). Others have still to be better investigated, for instance linguistic and cultural distance, socio-cultural condition, settlement patterns in the new country, migration models and migration phase. More research is therefore necessary, for example to investigate the situation in different regions of the country as well as that within specific migrant communities. Such research would provide a more in-depth understanding of the complex phenomenon of migration in present-day Italy and to foresee possible developments in the future.

References

Ambrosini, M. 2005. *Sociologia delle migrazioni.* Bologna: Il Mulino.

Andorno, C. 2004. I repertori e gli usi linguistici. In *Plurilinguismo e immigrazione in Italia. Un'indagine sociolinguistica a Pavia e Torino*, ed. M. Chini, 239–298. Milano: FrancoAngeli.

Bagna, C., M. Barni and R. Siebetcheu. 2004. *Toscane favelle. Lingue immigrate nella provincia di Siena.* Perugia: Guerra.

Bagna, C., S. Machetti and M. Vedovelli. 2003. Italiano e lingue immigrate: verso un pluriliguismo consapevole o verso varietà di contatto. In *Ecologia linguistica*, eds. A. Valentini, P. Molinelli, P. Cuzzolin and G. Bernini, 201–222. Roma: Bulzoni.

Banfi, E. 1993. Italiano come L2. In *L'altra Europa linguistica. Varietà di apprendimento e interlingue nell'Europa contemporanea*, ed. E. Banfi, 35-102. Firenze: La Nuova Italia.

—. 1995. Alternance des codes chez un sujet Pakistanais apprenant l'italien et l'allemand. *Acquisition et Interaction en Langue Etrangère* 5. 143-162.

Barni, M. In press. Diritti linguistici, diritti di cittadinanza: l'educazione linguistica come strumento contro le barriere linguistiche. In *Linguistica educativa*, ed. S. Ferreri. Roma: Bulzoni.

Bettoni, C., and A. Rubino. 1996. *Emigrazione e comportamento linguistico. Un'indagine sul trilinguismo dei Siciliani e dei Veneti in Australia*. Galatina (LE): Congedo.

Bernini, G., L. Spreafico and A. Valentini, eds. 2008. *Competenze lessicali e discorsive nell'acquisizione di lingue seconde*. Perugia: Guerra.

Berruto, G. 1993. Le varietà del repertorio. In *Introduzione all'italiano contemporaneo. La variazione e gli usi*, ed. A. A. Sobrero, 3-36. Bari: Laterza.

—. 2009. Ristrutturazione dei repertori e 'lingue franche' in situazione immigratoria. Appunti di lavoro. *Studi Italiani di Linguistica Teorica e Applicata* 38/1. 9–28.

Bombi, R., and F. Fusco, eds. 2004. *Città plurilingui. Lingue e culture a confronto in situazioni urbane*, Udine: Forum.

de Bot, K., and W. Fase, eds. 1991. Migrant languages in Western Europe. *International Journal of the Sociology of Language* 90 (Monographic issue).

Boyd, S., and S. Latomaa. 1999. Fishman's diglossia and bilingualism in the light of language maintenance and shift in the Nordic Region. In

Bilingualism and Migration, eds. G. Extra and L. Verhoeven, 303-324. Berlin: Mouton de Gruyter.

Caritas/Migrantes. 2002. *Immigrazione – Dossier Statistico 2002.* Roma: Anterem.

—. 2008. *Immigrazione – Dossier Statistico 2008.* Roma: IDOS.

—. 2010. *Immigrazione – Dossier statistico 2010.* Roma: IDOS.

Chini, M. 2003. Rapporti fra italiano e lingue d'origine nel repertorio di immigrati in area lombarda: un sondaggio qualitativo. In *Ecologia linguistica*, eds. A. Valentini, P. Molinelli, P. Cuzzolin and G. Bernini, 223–246. Roma: Bulzoni.

—. 2006. Genere e comportamento linguistico di immigrati. In *Linguaggio e genere*, eds. S. Luraghi and A. Olita, 186-206. Roma: Carocci.

—. 2009a. L'italiano L2 nel repertorio delle nuove comunità alloglotte: riflessioni su alcune dinamiche in atto. In *Alloglossie e comunità alloglotte nell'Italia contemporanea. Teorie, applicazioni e descrizioni, prospettive*, eds. C. Consani, P. Desideri, F. Guazzelli and C. Perta, 279–315. Roma: Bulzoni.

—. 2009b. Scelte di lingua e atteggiamenti di immigrati a Pavia e Torino: l'incidenza della variabile del genere in famiglie di minori stranieri. *Studi Italiani di Linguistica Teorica e Applicata* 38/1. 107–133.

—. 2011. New linguistic minorities: repertoires, language maintenance and shift. *International Journal of the Sociology of Language* 210. 47-69.

—, ed. 2004. *Plurilinguismo e immigrazione in Italia. Un'indagine sociolinguistica a Pavia e Torino.* Milano: FrancoAngeli.

—, ed. 2009c. Plurilinguismo e immigrazione nella società italiana. *Studi Italiani di Linguistica Teorica e Applicata* 38/1 (Monographic issue).

Clyne, M. 1991. *Community languages: The Australian experience.* Cambridge: Cambridge University Press.

—. 2003. *Dynamics of language contact.* Cambridge: Cambridge University Press.

Clyne, M., and S. Kipp. 1999. *Pluricentric languages in an immigrant context: Spanish, Chinese, Arabic.* Berlin: Mouton de Gruyter.

Cortinovis, E. 2010-2011. *Lingua, etnicità e stile. Usi linguistici di adolescenti albanofoni a Bolzano*. Unpublished PhD thesis, Università di Pavia.

D'Agostino, M. 2004. Immigrati a Palermo. Contatti e/o conflitti linguistici e immagini urbane. In *Città plurilingui. Lingue e culture a confronto in situazioni urbane*, eds. R. Bombi and F. Fusco, 191–211. Udine: Forum.

—. 2005. Nuove condizioni linguistiche. Gli effetti dell'immigrazione. In *Gli italiani e la lingua*, eds. F. Lo Piparo and G. Ruffino, 70-92. Palermo: Sellerio.

Dal Negro, S., and P. Molinelli, eds. 2002. *Comunicare nella torre di Babele. Repertori plurilingui in Italia oggi.* Roma: Carocci.

Dimroth, C., and M. Lambert, eds. 2008. La structure informationnelle chez les apprenants L2. *Acquisition et Interaction en Langue Etrangère* 26 (Monographic issue).

Dimroth, C., and M. Starren, eds. 2003. *Information structure and the dynamics of language acquisition.* Amsterdam: Benjamins.

Dittmar, N., and A. Giacalone Ramat, eds. 1999. *Grammatik und Diskurs/Grammatica e discorso*. Tübingen: Stauffenburg..

Extra, G., and L. Verhoeven, eds. 1999. *Bilingualism and Migration.* Berlin: Mouton de Gruyter.

Fiorentini, B. 2005. I giornali degli stranieri. Alcune indicazioni per le biblioteche multiculturali. *Bibliotime* 8/2 (available at: http://www2.spbo.unibo.it/bibliotime/num-viii-2/fiorenti.htm, accessed September 26, 2012).

Giacalone Ramat, A., ed. 2003. *Verso l'italiano. Percorsi e strategie di acquisizione.* Roma: Carocci.

Giacalone Ramat, A., and G. Crocco Galèas, eds. 1995. *From Pragmatics to Syntax. Modality in Second Language Acquisition*. Tübingen: Narr.

Guerini, F. 2006. *Language alternation strategies in multilingual settings. A case study: Ghanaian immigrants in Northern Italy.* Bern: Lang.

Guerini, F., and S. Dal Negro, eds. 2011. Italian sociolinguistics: twenty years on. *International Journal of the Sociology of Language* 210. Special Issue.

Hendriks, H., ed. 2005. *The structure of Learner Varieties*. Berlin: Mouton de Gruyter.

Iannaccaro, G., and V. Dell'Aquila. 2011. Historical linguistic minorities: suggestions for classification and typology. *International Journal of the Sociology of Language* 210. 29-45.

Klein, W., and C. Perdue. 1997. The basic variety (or: Couldn't natural languages be much simpler?). *Second Language Research* 13. 301-347.

Lüdi, G. 1990. Les migrants comme minorité linguistique en Europe. *Sociolinguistica* 4. 113–135.

Massariello Merzagora, G. 2004. Le "nuove minoranze" a Verona. Un osservatorio sugli studenti immigrati. *Le città plurilingui. Lingue e culture a confronto in situazioni urbane*, eds. R. Bombi and F. Fusco, 353–376. Udine: Forum.

Ministero dell'Istruzione, dell'Università e della Ricerca (MIUR). 2006. *Linee guida per l'accoglienza e l'integrazione degli alunni stranieri.* (available at: http://archivio.pubblica.istruzione.it/normativa/2006/cm24_06.shtml, accessed September 26, 2012)

Ministero della Pubblica Istruzione (MPI). 2007. *La via italiana per l'educazione interculturale e l'integrazione degli alunni stranieri.* (available at: http://archivio.pubblica.istruzione.it/news/2007/allegati/pubblicazione_intercultura.pdf, accessed September 26, 2012).

Mioni, A. M. 1998. Gli immigrati in Italia. Considerazioni linguistiche, sociolinguistiche e culturali. In *Ars linguistica. Studi offerti da colleghi e allievi a Paolo Ramat*, eds. G. Bernini, P. Cuzzolin and P. Molinelli, 377–409. Roma: Bulzoni.

Orletti, F. 1988. L'italiano dei filippini a Roma. In *L'italiano tra le altre lingue: strategie di acquisizione*, ed. A. Giacalone Ramat, 143-159. Bologna: Il Mulino.

Valentini, A. 2005. Lingue e interlingue dell'immigrazione in Italia. *Linguistica e Filologia* 21. 195–208.

—. 2009. La vitalità delle lingue immigrate: un'indagine a campione tra minori stranieri a Bergamo. *Studi Italiani di Linguistica Teorica e Applicata* 38/1. 89–106.

Valentini, A., P. Molinelli, P. Cuzzolin, and G. Bernini, eds. 2003. *Ecologia linguistica.* Roma: Bulzoni.

Vedovelli M., and A. Villarini. 2001. *Le lingue straniere immigrate in Italia.* In *Immigrazione–Dossier statistico 2001*, Caritas/Migrantes, 222–229. Roma: Nuova Anterem.

Vietti, A. 2005. *Come gli immigrati cambiano l'italiano. L'italiano di peruviane come varietà etnica.* Milano: FrancoAngeli.

—. 2009. Contatto e variazione nell'italiano di stranieri: la formazione di una varietà etnica. *Studi Italiani di Linguistica Teorica e Applicata* 38/1. 29-53.

PART II

A RESOURCE-ORIENTED PERSPECTIVE ON LINGUISTIC DIVERSITY: THE MERIDIUM PROJECT

CHAPTER SEVEN

THE MERIDIUM FOCUS ON PRIMARY SCHOOLS: CHILDREN AND FAMILIES CONFRONTED WITH LINGUISTIC DIVERSITY

STEFANIA SCAGLIONE

The second part of the book focuses on the MERIDIUM project, which is introduced in this chapter. After a description of its general premises and aims (§ 7.1), a detailed account of the field research carried out in the countries represented by MERIDIUM universities (Italy, Portugal, Spain, Slovenia, Malta, Romania) is given. The research has been conceived as a "snapshot" of linguistic repertoires and language use, perceptions and attitudes within selected areas in participating countries, in order to gain preliminary indications about the extent to which plurilingualism and linguistic diversity are actually present, perceived and promoted at a local level. To this end, informants have been selected among primary school children and their families.

In §7.2 the methodological background of the research is described; in §7.3 terminological choices and categorization procedures are outlined.

Finally, §7.4 presents a general overview of collected samples (children and parents) and puts forward some preliminary observations in a comparative perspective among national sub-samples.

7.1. The MERIDIUM Project: A General Description

MERIDIUM (*Multilingualism in Europe as a Resource for Immigration —Dialogue Initiative among the Universities of the Mediterranean*) is a three-year project (2009-2011) financed by the European Commission as part of the Life-Long Learning Program (LLLP), key-action 2 (Languages).

The conceptual framework that constitutes the basis of the creation of the project takes into consideration, in its fundamental aspects, the line of intervention promoted by the European Commission and by the European Council on plurilingualism and linguistic diversity during recent years (see the Introduction to the volume). This strategy includes giving value to multi- and plurilingualism as a resource for social cohesion and as a fundamental condition in the formation of a true "European citizenship", that is a common heritage of those who have been living in Europe for generations, as well as of those who migrated to Europe.

Institutional contributions highlight strongly the existence of two distinct yet interacting levels, which ought to be pursued simultaneously:

a. Structural promotion of individual plurilingualism for all, through the implementation of strategies and by employing instruments which concretely facilitate language learning;
b. Cultural promotion to foster multilingualism in societies (linguistic diversity), with specific attention to the "new" non-autochthonous languages, to be implemented through adequate initiatives in order to create awareness among the public.

In recent years, much has been done as far as structural promotion is concerned, especially within individual national educational systems, even in a context which tends, inevitably, to favour a few international European languages. On the other hand, interventions aimed at reaching the second level outlined above have proven less effective, and the situation of countries in the South of Europe is particularly problematic in this respect, as conditions for the linguistic, educational and social integration of migrants still present difficulties and challenges, due to the intensity and recentness of migratory influxes in this area.

In these countries, public discourse on immigration is still largely characterized by alarmist tones that amplify the problems related to immigration, leaving little room for reflection on how integration could be better understood; there is, in public opinion, a resulting climate of mistrust which, in fact, promotes attitudes tending towards assimilation, while diversity is viewed with suspicion.[1] Against such a backcloth, the

[1] For some general considerations about the responsibilities of the public and social players in intercultural relations in Europe, cf. European Commission-EUMC (2006).

Interesting data, updated to 2005, regarding attitudes towards immigrant citizens in the countries of Southern Europe, are available in EUMC (2005). In particular, it is noted that «resistance to immigrants and asylum seekers was widely

linguistic and cultural background of migrants receives scant attention; it is therefore very difficult for educational authorities to promote, in the school systems, innovations directed at plurilingual education and the preservation of the immigrant pupils' original languages. Also because of the recent crisis in public funding, among other reasons, schools give priority to investments in teaching foreign-born pupils the language of instruction, rather than focusing on creating the necessary environment in order to help these students maintain their language/s of origin; the lack of a "systemic" balance between the need to learn the majority language and creating possibilities and conditions for these students to enhance and maintain their L1, however, makes integration particularly difficult for pupils with foreign background, possibly leading to "inadequate" academic performance and contributing, in the long term, to their educational failure (see Duarte, Ch. 3, in this volume; Queirolo Palmas and Chaloff, 2006). At the same time, "autochthonous" students, who also experience daily opportunities for contact with linguistic diversity, are not helped to acquire the cognitive and cultural tools necessary to deal with such diversity constructively, ending up perceiving it as a social obstacle and a disadvantage.

In the end, a vicious cycle emerges, whereby the *monolingual habitus* (Gogolin, 1994) is perpetuated to the detriment of the development and cohesion of the societies that nurture it.

The objective of contributing to the creation of a climate conducive to linguistic diversity among the subjects directly involved in the management and use of educational systems (school authorities, teachers, pupils, families) within the countries of Southern Europe is at the heart of the MERIDIUM experience, involving seven universities in six States:

- Università per Stranieri di Perugia, Italy (coordinator)

---

shared by respondents from Mediterranean countries – in particular Greece showed marked resistance to immigrants. These stances were also strongly supported by people living in east European countries. In comparison, people from Nordic countries tended to dissociate themselves from these stances.» (EUMC, 2005: 14); it is also pointed out that «In western and eastern European societies, a minority of one in five respondents avoid social interaction with migrants and minorities – ethnic distance. Support for ethnic distance was particularly strong in some Mediterranean countries and some east European countries» (EUMC, 2005: 15). The Mediterranean countries included in this study were Portugal, Spain, Italy, Greece; the countries of Eastern Europe were represented by Slovenia. It is interesting to note that these countries, without exception, also occupied the top positions in relation to "resistance to diversity" (EUMC, 2005: 35).

- Università ta' Malta, Malta
- Universidade Nova de Lisboa, Portugal
- Universitatea Transilvania din Brasov, Romania
- Universitatea Babes-Bolyai, Cluj-Napoca, Romania
- Univerza na Primorskem, Slovenia
- Universidad de Salamanca, Spain

For the purposes of the Project, the participation of two universities located in Romania is particularly important, as, in recent years, this country has gone through a period of intense emigration (IOM, 2008), much of which is directed to States in Southern Europe (Italy and Spain). Not only do children of Romanian origin constitute one of the most numerous foreign groups in Italian and Spanish schools, but many of them have returned or are returning to their country of origin with their families, because of the global financial crisis which, since 2009, has progressively reduced employment opportunities in countries towards which they had migrated: this situation constitutes an extremely significant scenario as regards the need to build collaborative networks which will support the maintenance of the L1 of foreign-born nationals in the countries to which they have migrated, favouring, at the same time, the retention and further acquisition of skills in one L2 or more after they return home.

In its specific objectives, the project draws inspiration from the indications of Gogolin (2002: 19 f.) referred to in the Introduction, § 3:

1. Helping to promote, in schools, a new model of language education, aimed at optimizing the linguistic potential of the reference population, through the legitimization of all the languages in the territory in the role of “school languages”, if not real "languages of schooling";
2. Fostering the idea that education and learning develop within the framework of widespread multilingualism, which has become a structural feature of all European societies. Promoting, therefore, the inclusion of activities in school curricula which aim at the development of metalinguistic skills and at improving the ability to interact in multilingual contexts, even with a poor command of the language of interaction.

The implementation of these objectives required the integration of two distinct levels of action:

1. Documentation and research, in relation to each of the contexts of national interest, with respect to:

   a. Background elements: the features and integration conditions of migrants; the language policies being devised and being implemented; the organization of educational systems and language courses; demographic and socio-linguistic features of the national population;
   b. The reference population's language repertoire and use, experiences, attitudes and perceptions regarding plurilingualism and linguistic diversity.

2. Dissemination and discussion of the information which emerged within each national context with school authorities, teachers, other institutional leaders and representatives of immigrant associations, in order to plan targeted educational campaigns.
   For this purpose, two initiatives were undertaken:
   a. setting up a permanent Documentation and Research Centre on Multilingualism in Mediterranean Europe at the University for Foreigners of Perugia. The Centre aims to conduct activities and offer consultation on multilingualism and linguistic diversity to institutions and private enterprises in the partner countries. Currently the main activities of the Centre consist in the collection and publication of information and of examples of good practice through a bi-monthly newsletter.
   b. designing:
      - informative materials on the results of the data collected and analysed, targeting principally national and local institutions;
      - teaching tools aimed at helping students to reflect on linguistic diversity and to develop positive attitudes towards multilingualism, languages and language acquisition.

Materials referred to in 2b. were disseminated in the partner countries of the MERIDIUM network during national seminars which were addressed to representatives from educational institutions, from local associations, from the tertiary sector, from industry and from migrant associations. Due to the interest shown especially by those involved in the educational sphere, additional activities have been carried out in some countries of the network, including the organization of in-service courses for school personnel.

In this second part of the book, starting from the present contribution, particular attention is paid to the research efforts undertaken within MERIDIUM. The primary aim of this is to make available to the scientific community some descriptions and analysis of language repertoire, use, perceptions and attitudes from the countries participating in the Project. It should be noted, in fact, that studies in the field of the sociolinguistics of migration are still at an early stage as regards the countries of Southern Europe, and lack, to date, systematic research comparable to that conducted in North-Western European countries, not to mention contributions from the U.S. and Australia.[2]

7.2. MERIDIUM Sociolinguistic Research

The first phase of the MERIDIUM research involved obtaining information about the aspects that in 1a. above have been defined as "background elements", pertaining to each country's migrant population, national and regional legislation regarding migration, linguistic and educational policies, demo-linguistic information etc. A country report was compiled by each partner on the basis of this information[3].

Through this report, areas showing a relatively high immigration rate were identified; in the case of Romania, areas with a relatively high rate of emigration/remigration were selected. Each area was further investigated for an in-depth context analysis, through which the extent of the implementation of national, regional or local linguistic and educational policies was investigated.

The second phase of the research consisted in collecting field data, aimed at describing language repertoire and use, experiences, perceptions and attitudes concerning plurilingualism and linguistic diversity of people living in localities in selected areas.

Given the aims of the project, these data were collected from pupils attending either the penultimate or the final year of primary schooling (10-11 year-old) and their families. In fact, primary school is—for all the countries of the network—the first cycle of compulsory schooling and, therefore, the first opportunity, for children and their families, to come face to face with the linguistic and educational culture of the schools, as well as their evaluation system: in this phase, to a great extent, the cognitive, aptitude and emotional preconditions of children are established. The beginning of the path of literacy also prepares the child to internalize language ideologies which permeate the community and give different degrees of legitimacy to the varieties and languages present in it:

---

[2] Among the many possible works which could be consulted, see Clyne (1991, 2003), Extra and Verhoeven (1993), García and Fishman (1997), Baker and Eversley (2000), Extra and Yağmur (2004).

[3] In this regard, refer to the *Country Reports* published on the official site of the Project: http://meridium.unistrapg.it/.

it is therefore an extremely delicate phase, in which it is necessary to promote an approach to language education which will be, as far as possible, plural and inclusive. Moreover, it must be taken into account that, according to available official data pertaining to the school year 2009-2010 (the year in which the data collection was carried out), in many countries of the MERIDIUM network the highest rate of students of different nationalities were concentrated in primary schools (see, for example, MIUR-ISMU, 2011; IFIIE, 2011), which, therefore, emerge as ideal settings where to grasp dynamics of contact and exchange between different linguistic identities.

In this perspective, the survey sought to gather evidence to build a picture of the circuit of the relationships that contribute to shape children's linguistic repertoires, perceptions, attitudes; for this reason, in addition to handing out questionnaires to all the pupils of each class (Questionnaire A), specific questionnaires were also designed for the children's parents to fill in (Questionnaire B); there were also preliminary interviews, with school administrators and teachers responsible for the classes involved, which were followed by further meetings to discuss the results of the survey.

The sampling criteria and the data collection instruments used for field research are described in detail in Ch. 8.

7.3. Terminology

Before presenting some results from the data analysis, it is necessary to make some preliminary remarks regarding the choice of terminology adopted in categorizing our informants, mainly those who, until now, we have informally defined as "(im)migrants," people of "non-autochthonous" origin or with "foreign/ non-native backgrounds".

As Extra and Gorter (2007: 21 f.) have rightly pointed out, the nomenclature in this field, both in the scientific literature, and in institutional parlance, is still far from being homogeneous. In part, this is due to the objective need to highlight different perspectives in dealing with the same objects of discourse: the term "non-national residents" is useful to emphasize the (non-)correspondence between nationality and country of residence when discussing legal-administrative issues; on the other hand, the term "(economic) immigrants", which highlights the experience of leaving the country of origin under the pressure of economic needs, can be functional in a sociological discourse that focuses on the reasons why people choose to live outside their country of birth, making a distinction between this category of foreign nationals, and—for example—

"international students" or "asylum-seekers". The multiplicity of the possible choices of terminology is, in fact, intrinsically linked to the situation of "super-diversity" (Vertovec, 2007) that characterizes contemporary societies, in which the sharp increase of international mobility has led to

> a multiplication of significant variables that affect where, how and with whom people live. [...] Such additional variables include differential immigration statuses and their concomitant entitlements and restrictions of rights, divergent labour markets experiences, discrete gender and age profiles, patterns of spatial distribution, and mixed local area responses by service providers and residents (Vertovec, 2007: 1025).

What variables, therefore, are relevant for defining the subjects surveyed in the MERIDIUM Project? If the objective is to describe repertoires and linguistic habits, experiences, attitudes and perceptions related to plurilingualism and linguistic diversity, it is clear that adopting analytical and definitional criteria based on nationality/citizenship is useless: in fact, these instances of legal status are not necessarily indicative of an individual's linguistic identity. On the contrary, the places and environments of the subjects' life are significant: being born in a given country raises important preconditions for the development of language skills; living in a household whose members are or are not from the same country is similarly significant. The cases of foreign-born children who reach a given country at a (pre-)school age, as a result of international adoption, or who return to their parents' homeland after a period of emigration, effectively demonstrate the diverse importance of the two criteria, namely citizenship *vs.* place of birth of the subject and of his/her parents: in such cases, the criterion of citizenship makes both the former and the latter group of children "invisible", since, in the countries of the MERIDIUM network and in many others, parents' citizenship is transmitted to children, whether adopted or natural; on the contrary, place of birth could be an indication of potentially complex linguistic experiences that characterize children from the very day when they are born.

Therefore, in categorizing our main sample of informants, constituted by children attending the penultimate or last grade of primary school, we will adopt a criterion based on the country of birth of the subject (BC), of his/her mother and of his/her father, as shown in Tab. 7-1 (see p. 131). This criterion will be applied following some of the methodological and terminological choices adopted in EUROSTAT (2011).

A first categorization put forward in EUROSTAT (2011) and concerning exclusively the BC of the person distinguishes between "foreign-born persons" and "native-born persons":

> [Foreign-born persons] This is the population most commonly described as migrants, as these persons have migrated to their current country of residence at some stage during their lives. The foreign-born population includes both persons with foreign citizenship and persons with the citizenship of their country of residence, either from birth or acquired later in life. […]» (EUROSTAT, 2011: 6)

A second categorization takes into account also the BC of a person's parents ("background" in EUROSTAT terminology), defining "second generation immigrants" as

> the descendants of foreign-born parents, who are themselves born in their country of residence. Some of them have foreign citizenship, whereas others have the citizenship of the country of residence." (EUROSTAT, 2011: 6)

By contrast, persons born in the country of residence from native-born parents are "persons with native background" (2011: 122). EUROSTAT (2011) also proposes a sub-categorization among these subjects, distinguishing between "persons with mixed background" and "persons with foreign background":

> The first group, with a mixed background, is defined as persons who are native born and who have one foreign-born parent and one native-born parent. The second group, with a foreign background, is defined as persons who are native born with both parents being foreign-born.» (EUROSTAT, 2011: 121)

This distinction may also prove useful in a sociolinguistic research, assuming that having both parents, or just one of them, who speak a language which is different from the official language of the country of residence can lead to quite different results in terms of the maintenance of this language by children.

		PUPIL	
		BC = RESIDENCE COUNTRY	**BC ≠ RESIDENCE COUNTRY**
PARENTS	**BC = RESIDENCE COUNTRY IN BOTH CASES**	Native-born children with native background (NNb)	Foreign-born children with native background (FNb)
	BC = RESIDENCE COUNTRY IN ONE CASE; BC ≠ RESIDENCE COUNTRY IN THE OTHER	Native-born children with mixed background (NMb)	Foreign-born children with mixed background (FMb)
	BC ≠ RESIDENCE COUNTRY IN BOTH CASES	Native-born children with foreign background (NFb)	Foreign-born children with foreign background (FFb)

Tab. 7-1: Categorization of MERIDIUM sample A subjects (pupils) by birth country (BC) of theirs and of their parents ("background")

When referring to languages spoken by foreign-born informants, the term "(im)migrant (minority) languages" (Extra and Gorter, 2007; Barni and Extra, 2008) will not be used; in this respect, we totally agree with considerations expressed by the authors of the VALEUR Project report *Valuing all languages in Europe* (McPake and Tinsley, 2007: 20):

> the term 'migrant' or 'immigrant' language is frequently generalised to include other circumstances too, and perhaps used as a means of eschewing responsibility for developing children's plurilingual abilities. The word 'migrant' carries with it the sense that people will return to their country of origin, or move on somewhere else, and that therefore the host country bears no responsibility for ensuring children can maintain their languages. (In fact, in a situation in which children's parents are genuinely migrants, the need for them to maintain their language of origin will be of crucial importance to them, alongside acquiring the language of the host country.) But in many cases so-called 'migrant' languages are the languages of settled communities, with second and third generation citizens using them for different purposes in their daily lives. For such people, the term 'migrant' or 'immigrant' is insulting and appears to question their rights as citizens. Similarly, it casts the language in a role linked only to immigrant communities, rather than including a sense of its wider usefulness and value.

Members of VALEUR project use the hypernym "additional languages" to term these languages, as well as other non-dominant languages in a given country (regional or minority languages, non-territorial languages, sign languages): although we deem this choice opportune and applicable to our study, when a more specific term is needed for analytical purposes, we will also adopt other terms, mainly focusing on geographical distribution and socio-political status of languages:

- autochtonous languages (to be eventually differentiated into official l., national l., regional l., minority l., non-territorial l., national sign l., local dialects);
- non-autochtonous languages (to be eventually differentiated into non-national varieties of the State-official language/s, EU official l., non-EU European l., extra-European l. and their varieties and so forth)

On the one hand, such a categorization allows us to underline, in the first place, the (increasing) share of linguistic diversity due to transnational mobility, without implying value judgments on single languages. On the other hand, it gives due attention to the historical rootedness of each language and its institutional status both at a national and international level, these being important elements affecting (de)legitimizing linguistic ideologies and ethnolinguistic vitality (Giles, Bourhis, Taylor, 1977).

As to references to single languages, we have chosen to report them as originally formulated by informants in open questions asking "Which language/s ….?". Since this research is aimed at obtaining self-reported data of language use as well as information regarding experiences, perceptions, attitudes about linguistic diversity (also in order to raise awareness towards it), we have deemed relevant to provide a picture of all the linguistic forms perceived by children and adults as "languages". These include dialects and different non-national varieties of the same language, as well as "non-existent" languages, which are named by derivation from the name of the State or continent where they are supposedly spoken (e.g. "African"). When these "pseudo-glottonyms" (always cited in quotes) are included in responses to a questionnaire, it may be problematic to enumerate precisely the languages which are being referred to by informants; they give, nonetheless, significant indications about "linguistic imagination" and attitudes of informants themselves.

A second and a third type of denominations are, respectively, "proxi" items (extemporaneous derivations such as "Bangladeshan", which reveal informants' unfamiliarity with the correct glottonym, but also their clear perception of a relationship "State-language"), and "other" items, mainly represented by religion's names (e.g. "Muslim") intended to designate the supposedly corresponding language, or invented glottonyms ("extraterrestrian")[4]. These two types have been classified in separate categories, which show a highly variable distribution depending on the nature of related questions.

7.4. Profile of the Samples and Comparative Analyses

The overall outcome of the fieldwork phase is presented in Tab. 7-2:

SURVEY COUNTRY	N OF MUNICIPALITIES	N OF SCHOOLS	N OF COLLECTED A QUESTIONNAIRES	N OF COLLECTED B QUESTIONNAIRES
Italy	14	17	697	613
Spain	11	12	429	284
Portugal	5	6	316	316
Romania	11	15	305	292
Malta	3	3	164	164
Slovenia	2	4	156	137
TOTAL	**46**	**57**	**2067**	**1806**

Tab. 7–2: Quantitative overview of the MERIDIUM survey

The questionnaires of each type were inserted into the respective matrix (database A and database B), together with codes enabling one to trace the area/location of data collection (country, region, district, city, school, class).

7.4.1. Sample A (pupils)

The composition of the sample of children by country of birth of the informant and of his/her parents is shown in Tab. 7-3:

[4] Some children did actually use invented glottonyms of this kind, being probably influenced by Babel, our alien comic-strip character.

Survey country		Native-born informants			Foreign-born informants			Tot.	Missing data	Grand total
		NNb	NMb	NFb	FNb	FMb	FFb			
IT	N	450	31	92	4	3	116	696	1	697
	%	*64.7*	*4.5*	*13.2*	*.6*	*.4*	*16.7*	*100.0*	-	
ES	N	293	36	8	2	6	72	417	12	429
	%	*70.3*	*8.6*	*1.9*	*.5*	*1.4*	*17.3*	*100.0*	-	
PT	N	194	58	14	1	2	41	310	6	316
	%	*62.6*	*18.7*	*4.5*	*.3*	*.6*	*13.2*	*100.0*	-	
RO	N	276	8	0	8	3	0	295	10	305
	%	*90.5*	*2.7*	-	*2.7*	*1.0*	-	*100.0*	-	
MT	N	104	22	8	0	6	7	147	17	164
	%	*70.7*	*15.0*	*5.4*	-	*3.7*	*4.3*	*100.0*	-	
SI	N	98	28	14	1	3	7	151	5	156
	%	*64.9*	*18.5*	*9.3*	*.7*	*2.0*	*4.6*	*100.0*	-	
Tot	**N**	**1415**	**183**	**136**	**16**	**23**	**243**	**2016**	**51**	**2067**
	%	***70.2***	***9.1***	***6.7***	***.8***	***1.1***	***12.1***	***100.0***	-	

Key: NNb = native-born with native background; NMb = native-born with mixed background, NFb = native-born with foreign background; FNb = foreign-born with native background; FMb = foreign-born with mixed background, FFb = foreign-born with foreign background.

Tab. 7–3: MERIDIUM sample A (pupils) stratified by survey country, birth country of informants and of their parents ("background")

As one may observe, all national sub-samples, except the Romanian one, include at least 30% of subjects whose birth country is not the one in which they live, or whose background is not entirely native, or not native at all. Moreover, all possible combinations between informant's BC and the BCs of her/his parents are represented: there are practically no empty cells, with the exception of the Romanian sub-sample, where we find no pupils with foreign background (whether native-born, or foreign-born), and in the case of Malta, where we find no subjects born abroad of Maltese parents. However, in the Romanian sub-sample, we find a percentage of foreign-born children with native-background (2.7%) which is considerably higher than that registered in other sub-samples.

Sub-samples collected in the so-called "countries of immigration" represent an example of how international mobility has led to the erosion of the imaginary boundary between "natives" and "foreigners", even in non-metropolitan contexts, such as those in which data were collected, mainly including small and medium-size localities.

The linguistic aspect of this process of erosion is evident when one compares the languages that native-born and foreign-born children use at home with their parents (Tabs. 7-4a-f, p. 136 ff.)

The notable differences in background detected among native-born children in Tab. 7-3 correspond, in all the national sub-samples, to an equally noteworthy linguistic diversity in Tabs. 7-4a-f, where the home-languages of native-born children are, in many cases, just as numerous and diverse as those of foreign-born children. These data effectively suggest the great variety of cultural and linguistic backgrounds which already characterizes native-born schoolchildren, besides that which derives through the presence of foreign-born "newcomers".

The phenomenon of diversification of languages used by native children in the family environment is also to be found in the Romanian sub-sample, where, moreover, there are no informants with foreign background (see Tab. 7-3). In this case, the recorded linguistic diversity is partly due to the presence of national linguistic minorities (German, Hungarian) or non-territorial minorities (Rroma), but it also demonstrates, in a number of cases, the maintenance of languages acquired by children or by their parents during migration experiences (Italian and Spanish).

ITALY HOME-LANGUAGES OF NATIVE-BORN PUPILS		CATEGORY	ITALY HOME-LANGUAGES OF FOREIGN-BORN PUPILS	
LANGUAGE	N		LANGUAGE	N
Italian	452	AUTOCHT.	Italian	46
local It. dialect	107	LGS.	other It.dialect	2
other It. dialect	51		local It. dialect	1
Sardinian	2			
English	27	EU LGS.	Romanian	18
German	6		English	4
Spanish	6		French	3
French	4		Spanish	3
Romanian	2		Bulgarian	1
Bulgarian	1		German	1
Portuguese	1			
Danish	1			
Greek	1			
Polish	1			
Albanian	16	NON-EU	Albanian	17
Serbian	9	EUROPEAN	Macedonian	9
'Kosovan'	3	LGS.	Serbian	6
Macedonian	1		'Kosovan'	4
			Moldavian	3
			Croatian	1
			Russian	1
Arabic	13	EXTRA-	'Indian'	10
'Moroccan'	8	EUROPEAN	'Bangladese'	4
'Ghanaian'	7	LGS.	Arabic	5
'Indian'	7		'Pakistani'	3
'Pakistani'	2		Bengali	3
'Tunisian'	2		Chinese	3
Chinese	2		'African'	2
'Bangladese'	1		'Ghanaian'	2
Bengali	1		Panjabi	2
Turkish	1		Urdu	2
Urdu	1		'Guinean'	1
Yoruba	1		'Moroccan'	1
'Togolese'	1		'Senegalese'	1
Pilipino	1		'Tunisian'	1
Ukrainian	1		Bissa	1
			Hindi	1
TOTAL RESPONDENTS	**563**		**TOTAL RESPONDENTS**	**121**

Tab. 7-4a: Self-reported languages used by pupils with mother and/or with father (home-languages) in Italy

SPAIN HOME-LANGUAGES OF NATIVE-BORN PUPILS		CATEGORY	SPAIN HOME-LANGUAGES OF FOREIGN-BORN PUPILS	
LANGUAGE	N		LANGUAGE	N
Spanish	280	AUTOCHT. LGS.	Spanish	41
Galego	6		Catalan	1
Canario	2			
Bable	1			
Valencian	1			
'Argentinian'	2	VARIETIES OF THE OFFICIAL LG.	'Argentinian'	1
'Mexican'	1		'Chilean'	1
			'Columbian'	1
			'Ecuadorian'	1
			'Peruvian'	1
English	20	EU LGS.	Portuguese	9
French	10		Romanian	6
German	2		Polish	3
'Hollander'	1		English	2
Luxembourgish	1		Italian	1
			Lithuanian	1
			French	1
Arabic	2	EXTRA-EUROPEAN LGS.	Chinese	3
Korean	2		Arabic	2
Pilipino	1		Georgian	1
			Guaraní	1
			Manjaku	1
			Quechua	1
TOTAL RESPONDENTS	**292**		**TOTAL RESPONDENTS**	**69**

Tab. 7-4b: Self-reported languages used by pupils with mother and/or with father (home-languages) in Spain

PORTUGAL HOME-LANGUAGES OF NATIVE-BORN PUPILS		CATEGORY	PORTUGAL HOME-LANGUAGES OF FOREIGN-BORN PUPILS	
LANGUAGE	N		LANGUAGE	N
Portuguese	259	AUTOCHT. LGS.	Portuguese	20
'Brazilian'	1	VARIETIES OF THE OFFICIAL LG.	'Brazilian' Brazilian Portuguese	8 1
English French German Spanish Dutch	18 8 3 2 1	EU LGS.	English Romanian Bulgarian French	2 1 1 1
-	-	NON-EU EUROPEAN LGS.	Russian Ukrainian Moldavian	4 4 2
Chinese 'Angolan' Cape Verde Creole	1 1 1	EXTRA-EUROPEAN LGS.	Cape Verde Creole Guinea Bissau Creole S. Tomé e Principe Creole	10 1 1
TOTAL RESPONDENTS	**263**		**TOTAL RESPONDENTS**	**43**

Tab. 7-4c: Self-reported languages used by pupils with mother and/or with father (home-languages) in Portugal

ROMANIA HOME-LANGUAGES OF NATIVE-BORN PUPILS		CATEGORY	ROMANIA HOME-LANGUAGES OF FOREIGN-BORN PUPILS	
LANGUAGE	N		LANGUAGE	N
Romanian	273	AUTOCHT. LGS.	Romanian	8
Hungarian	7		Romani	1
German	3			
Romani	1			
Italian	19	EU LGS.	Italian	4
English	13		Spanish	1
Spanish	5			
French	4			
Greek	1			
Russian	1	NON-EU EUROPEAN LGS.	-	-
-	-	EXTRA-EUROPEAN LGS.	Turkish	2
TOTAL RESPONDENTS	**284**		**TOTAL RESPONDENTS**	**9**

Tab. 7-4d: Self-reported languages used by pupils with mother and/or with father (home-languages) in Romania

Malta Home-languages of native-born pupils		Category	Malta Home-languages of foreign-born pupils	
Language	N		Language	N
Maltese	137	autocht. lgs.	English	6
English	53		Maltese	3
other Mt. dialect	1			
'American'	1	varieties of the official lg.	-	-
Italian	11	EU lgs.	Bulgarian	1
Dutch	1		Italian	1
German	1			
-	-	non-EU European lgs.	Serbian	1
			Russian	1
'Moroccan'	2	Extra-European lgs.	'Egyptian'	1
			'Iranian'	1
			Thai	1
Total respondents	**145**		**Total respondents**	**12**

Tab. 7-4e: Self-reported languages used by pupils with mother and/or with father (home-languages) in Malta

Slovenia Home-languages of native-born pupils		Category	Slovenia Home-languages of foreign-born pupils	
Language	N		Language	N
Slovene	139	autocht. lgs.	Slovene	8
Italian	4		Italian	2
English	1	EU lgs.	-	-
German	1			
Bosnian	6	non-EU European lgs.	Bosnian	3
Croatian	2		Serbian	2
Serbian	2		Croatian	1
Albanian	1			
Russian	1			
Total respondents	**141**		**Total respondents**	**11**

Tab. 7-4f: Self-reported languages used by pupils with mother and/or with father (home-languages) in Slovenia

The multilingualism which characterizes the language use of pupils within the family domain is greatly reduced in the school environment. The languages that children said they use with their classmates are summarized in Tabs. 7-5a-f, those used with teachers, in Tabs. 7-6a-f.

ITALY LANGUAGES USED WITH CLASSMATES BY NATIVE-BORN PUPILS		CATEGORY	ITALY LANGUAGES USED WITH CLASSMATES BY FOREIGN-BORN PUPILS	
LANGUAGE	N		LANGUAGE	N
Italian	519	AUTOCHT. LGS.	Italian	116
local It. dialect	51		other It. dialect	1
other It. dialect	9			
English	7	EU LGS.	Bulgarian	1
Spanish	3			
French	1			
Romanian	1			
Albanian	3	NON-EU EUROPEAN LGS.	Albanian	1
Macedonian	1			
Serbian	1			
'Ghanaian'	2	EXTRA-EUROPEAN LGS.	Arabic	1
'Moroccan'	2		Chinese	1
			'Indian'	1
			'Pakistani'	1
TOTAL RESPONDENTS	**556**		**TOTAL RESPONDENTS**	**117**

Tab. 7-5a: Self-reported languages used by pupils with classmates in Italy

SPAIN LANGUAGES USED WITH CLASSMATES BY NATIVE-BORN PUPILS		CATEGORY	SPAIN LANGUAGES USED WITH CLASSMATES BY FOREIGN-BORN PUPILS	
LANGUAGE	N		LANGUAGE	N
Spanish Galego Andaluz Bable Canario Murcian	238 3 1 1 1 1	AUTOCHT. LGS.	Spanish	65
English French Polish	24 3 1	EU LGS.	English Portuguese	1 1
Ukrainian	1	NON-EU EUROP. LGS.	-	-
Arabic Chinese	1 1	EXTRA-EUROP. LGS.	-	-
TOTAL RESPONDENTS	**253**		**TOTAL RESPONDENTS**	***65***

Tab. 7-5b: Self-reported languages used by pupils with classmates in Spain

PORTUGAL LANGUAGES USED WITH CLASSMATES BY NATIVE-BORN PUPILS		CATEGORY	PORTUGAL LANGUAGES USED WITH CLASSMATES BY FOREIGN-BORN PUPILS	
LANGUAGE	N		LANGUAGE	N
Portuguese	264	AUTOCHT. LGS.	Portuguese	39
'Brazilian'	3	VARIETIES OF THE OFF. LG.	'Brazilian'	2
English Romanian Spanish	3 1 1	EU LGS.	English	1
-	-	NON-EU EUROP. LGS.	Moldavian Ukrainian	1 1
Cape Verde Creole	2	EXTRA-EUROP. LGS.	Cape Verde Creole	7
TOTAL RESPONDENTS	**267**		**TOTAL RESPONDENTS**	**42**

Tab. 7-5c: Self-reported languages used by pupils with classmates in Portugal

Romania languages used with classmates by native-born pupils		Category	Romania languages used with classmates by foreign-born pupils	
Language	N		Language	N
Romanian	277	autocht. lgs.	Romanian	10
Romani	1			
English	11	EU lgs.	-	-
Total respondents	**283**		**Total respondents**	**10**

Tab. 7-5d: Self-reported languages used by pupils with classmates in Romania

Malta languages used with classmates by native-born pupils		Category	Malta languages used with classmates by foreign-born pupils	
Language	N		Language	N
Maltese	121	autocht. lgs.	Maltese	5
English	39		English	3
Russian	1	non-EU Europ. lgs.	-	-
Total respondents	**129**		**Total respondents**	**9**

Tab. 7-5e: Self-reported languages used by pupils with classmates in Malta

Slovenia languages used with classmates by native-born pupils		Category	Slovenia languages used with classmates by foreign-born pupils	
Language	N		Language	N
Slovene	136	autocht. lgs.	Slovene	9
English	1	EU lgs.	-	-
Bosnian	1	non-EU Europ. lgs.	-	-
Total respondents	**136**		**Total respondents**	**9**

Tab. 7-5f: Self-reported languages used by pupils with classmates in Slovenia

As can be seen by comparing Tabs. 7-5a-f to Tabs. 7-4a-f, many of the languages that the informants claim to use with their parents are not used in the interaction with their classmates. The fact that children often use a more limited number of languages at school is certainly due to the fact that they interact with peers with diversified linguistic backgrounds and that at school the instruction language/s act/s as a sort of "lingua franca". Nevertheless, it is equally clear that, in such a situation, many of the children's native languages tend to disappear totally within schools and classes.

In fact, it should be noted that, despite the recommendations of the national educational authorities to support native tongues of pupils with foreign background, language courses other than those envisaged by the curricula established at a central or regional level are present in very few schools included in the MERIDIUM Project.[5] Interaction with teachers is not conductive to exploit children's linguistic resources: the data in Tabs. 7-6a-f show that the languages used by informants with teachers are solely, or mainly, those included as subjects to be studied in the schools' curricula (these languages are italicized in the following tables).

ITALY LANGUAGES USED WITH TEACHERS BY NATIVE-BORN PUPILS		CATEGORY	ITALY LANGUAGES USED WITH TEACHERS BY FOREIGN-BORN PUPILS	
LANGUAGE	N		LANGUAGE	N
Italian	539	AUTOCHT. LGS.	*Italian*	103
local It. dialect	11		local It. dialect	1
other It. dialect	3			
English	86	EU LGS.	*English*	14
French	1		French	1
			Romanian	1
-	-	NON-EU EUROP. LGS.	Albanian	1
'Ghanaian'	3	EXTRA-EUROPEAN LGS.	'Guinean'	1
Arabic	1		'Indian'	1
Bengali	1		'Pakistani'	1
TOTAL RESPONDENTS	**550**		**TOTAL RESPONDENTS**	**110**

Tab. 7-6a: Self-reported languages used by pupils with teachers in Italy

[5] See Ch. 9-14 for details.

SPAIN LANGUAGES USED WITH TEACHERS BY NATIVE-BORN PUPILS		CATEGORY	SPAIN LANGUAGES USED WITH TEACHERS BY FOREIGN-BORN PUPILS	
LANGUAGE	N		LANGUAGE	N
Spanish	225	AUTOCHT. LGS.	*Spanish*	53
Galego	8			
Andaluz	1			
Canario	1			
English	59	EU LGS.	*English*	4
French	18		*French*	3
Arabic	1	EXTRA-EUROP. LGS.	-	
Punjabi	1			
TOTAL RESPONDENTS	**254**		**TOTAL RESPONDENTS**	**57**

Tab. 7-6b: Self-reported languages used by pupils with teachers in Spain

PORTUGAL LANGUAGES USED WITH TEACHERS BY NATIVE-BORN PUPILS		CATEGORY	PORTUGAL LANGUAGES USED WITH TEACHERS BY FOREIGN-BORN PUPILS	
LANGUAGE	N		LANGUAGE	N
Portuguese	266	AUTOCHT. LGS.	*Portuguese*	39
-	-	VARIETIES OF THE OFF. LG.	'Brazilian'	2
English	7	EU LGS.	*English*	1
-	-	EXTRA-EUROP. LGS.	Cape Verde Creole	1
TOTAL RESPONDENTS	**267**		**TOTAL RESPONDENTS**	**42**

Tab. 7-6c: Self-reported languages used by pupils with teachers in Portugal

ROMANIA LANGUAGES USED WITH TEACHERS BY NATIVE-BORN PUPILS		CATEGORY	ROMANIA LANGUAGES USED WITH TEACHERS BY FOREIGN-BORN PUPILS	
LANGUAGE	N		LANGUAGE	N
Romanian	263	AUTOCHT. LGS.	*Romanian*	10
English	107	EU LGS.	*English*	4
French	37			
German	13			
Italian	1			
Spanish	1			
TOTAL RESPONDENTS	**281**		TOTAL RESPONDENTS	**11**

Tab. 7-6d: Self-reported languages used by pupils with teachers in Romania

MALTA LANGUAGES USED WITH TEACHERS BY NATIVE-BORN PUPILS		CATEGORY	MALTA LANGUAGES USED WITH TEACHERS BY FOREIGN-BORN PUPILS	
LANGUAGE	N		LANGUAGE	N
Maltese	116	AUTOCHT. LGS.	*English*	8
English	39		*Maltese*	5
Italian	1	EU LGS.	-	
TOTAL RESPONDENTS	**124**		TOTAL RESPONDENTS	**10**

Tab. 7-6e: Self-reported languages used by pupils with teachers in Malta

SLOVENIA LANGUAGES USED WITH TEACHERS BY NATIVE-BORN PUPILS		CATEGORY	SLOVENIA LANGUAGES USED WITH TEACHERS BY FOREIGN-BORN PUPILS	
LANGUAGE	N		LANGUAGE	N
Slovene	135	AUTOCHT. LGS.	*Slovene*	8
Italian	10			
English	10	EU LGS.	-	
German	1			
TOTAL RESPONDENTS	**136**		TOTAL RESPONDENTS	**8**

Tab. 7-6f: Self-reported languages used by pupils with teachers in Slovenia

On the whole, the data reported in this section show some interesting tendencies, which merit further analyses in the light of the educational situation characterizing each country involved in the survey. These include:

- the complexity of the linguistic and cultural background of the student population;
- noteworthy changes in language choice and use according to the domain of interaction (family *vs*. school);
- scant recognition and optimization of children's home-languages at school.

A brief analysis of sample B (parents) provides further insight into the context in which the research took place and into the children's family background.

7.4.2. Sample B (parents)

The composition of the sample of adults, by country of birth of the informant, is shown in Tab. 7-7:

SURVEY COUNTRY		NATIVE-BORN INFORMANTS	FOREIGN-BORN INFORMANTS	TOT.	MISSING VALUES	GRAND TOTAL
IT	N	423	186	609	4	613
	%	*69.5*	*30.5*	*100.0*		
ES	N	212	70	282	2	284
	%	*75.2*	*24.8*	*100.0*		
PT	N	228	88	316	0	316
	%	*72.2*	*27.8*	*100.0*		
RO	N	285	5	290	2	292
	%	*98.3*	*1.7*	*100.0*		
MT	N	131	33	164	0	164
	%	*79.9*	*20.1*	*100.0*		
SI	N	111	25	136	1	137
	%	*81.6*	*18.4*	*100.0*		
TOT	**N**	**1390**	**407**	**1797**	**9**	**1806**
	%	*77.4*	***22.6***	***100.0***		

Tab. 7–7: MERIDIUM sample B (parents) stratified by survey country and birth country of informants

All the national sub-samples include informants born outside of the country being investigated, ranging from 18.4% of the Slovenian sub-sample to 30.5% of the Italian sub-sample; the exception, easily foreseeable on the basis of the data previously discussed, is the Romanian sub-sample, which has a negligible non-native percentage (1.4%)[6].

The distribution of adult informants by gender shows a prevalence of female subjects in all the national sub-samples, amounting to 74.8% of the total sample. It should be noted, however, that there are more foreign-born fathers represented in the sample, than native-born fathers (34.2% *vs.* 21.8% in the total sample), possibly because of their enhanced knowledge of the language of the country of residence compared to their spouses, some of whom might have joined them at a later date, thereby reuniting the family.

The responses of the adult informants to the question "What is your native language?" (see Tabs. 7-8a-f, p. 149 ff.) provide information which leads to a meaningful comparison with the home-languages declared by the children (Tabs. 7-4a-f).

[6] However, within the Romanian sub-sample, the percentage of native people who have lived/worked abroad for a year or more (16.3%) is considerable.

ITALY NATIVE LANGUAGES OF NATIVE-BORN PARENTS		CATEGORY	ITALY NATIVE LANGUAGES OF FOREIGN-BORN PARENTS	
LANGUAGE	N		LANGUAGE	N
Italian	396	AUTOCHT. LGS.	Italian	5
other It. dialect	11			
local It. dialect	1			
German	1	EU LGS.	Romanian	22
			French	6
			Spanish	6
			English	5
			Bulgarian	2
			German	2
			Polish	2
			Portuguese	1
-	-	NON-EU EUROPEAN LGS.	Albanian	31
			Serbian	12
			Macedonian	9
			'Kosovan'	4
			Moldavian	3
			Croatian	1
-	-	EXTRA-EUROPEAN LGS.	Arabic	22
			Punjabi	7
			'Indian'	6
			Urdu	5
			Bengali	4
			'Pakistani'	3
			'Bangladese'	2
			'Senegalese'	2
			Chinese	2
			'African'	1
			'Ghanaian'	1
			'Moroccan'	1
			'Tunisian'	1
			Edo	1
			Éwé	1
			Turkish	1
			Yoruba	1
TOTAL RESPONDENTS	**409**		**TOTAL RESPONDENTS**	**172**

Tab. 7–8a: Self-reported native languages of parents in Italy

SPAIN NATIVE LANGUAGES OF NATIVE-BORN PARENTS		CATEGORY	SPAIN NATIVE LANGUAGES OF FOREIGN-BORN PARENTS	
LANGUAGE	N		LANGUAGE	N
Spanish	198	AUTOCHT. LGS.	Spanish	39
Galego	5			
Andaluz	1			
-	-	VARIETIES OF THE OFF. LG.	'Columbian'	1
			'Ecuadorian'	1
-	-	EU LGS.	Portuguese	7
			Romanian	4
			French	1
			Italian	1
			Polish	1
-	-	EXTRA-EUROPEAN LGS.	Arabic	6
			Chinese	3
			Guaranì	1
			Manjaku	1
			Pilipino	1
TOTAL RESPONDENTS	**204**		**TOTAL RESPONDENTS**	**67**

Tab. 7–8b: Self-reported native languages of parents in Spain

Portugal Native languages of native-born parents		Category	Portugal Native languages of foreign-born parents	
Language	N		Language	N
Portuguese	217	Autocht. lgs.	Portuguese	33
-	-	varieties of the off. lg.	Brazilian Portuguese	12
English	3	EU lgs.	French	6
			Romanian	3
			English	3
			German	2
			Bulgarian	1
-	-	Non-EU European lgs.	Ukrainian	4
			Russian	2
			Moldavian	1
-	-	Extra-European lgs.	Cape Verde Creole	13
			Guinea Bissau Creole	2
			'Capeverdean'	1
			'Guinean'	1
			Chinese	1
Total respondents	**220**		**Total respondents**	**85**

Tab. 7–8c: Self-reported native languages of parents in Portugal

Romania Native languages of native born parents		Category	Romania Native languages of foreign born parents	
Language	N		Language	N
Romanian	264	Autocht. lgs.	Hungarian	1
Hungarian	8		Romanian	1
Romani	2		Romani	1
English	1	EU lgs.	-	-
Total respondents	**275**		**Total respondents**	**3**

Tab. 7–8d: Self-reported native languages of parents in Romania

MALTA NATIVE LANGUAGES OF NATIVE BORN PARENTS		CATEGORY	MALTA NATIVE LANGUAGES OF FOREIGN BORN PARENTS	
LANGUAGE	N		LANGUAGE	N
Maltese	108	AUTOCHT. LGS.	English	10
English	5		Maltese	9
Italian	3	EU LGS.	Bulgarian	1
French	1		Dutch	1
			Flemish	1
-	-	NON-EU EUROP. LGS.	Russian	2
			Serbian	2
-	-	EXTRA-EUROPEAN LGS.	Arabic	3
			'Moroccan'	1
			Thai	1
TOTAL RESPONDENTS	117		TOTAL RESPONDENTS	31

Tab. 7–8e: Self-reported native languages of parents in Malta

SLOVENIA NATIVE LANGUAGES OF NATIVE BORN PARENTS		CATEGORY	SLOVENIA NATIVE LANGUAGES OF FOREIGN BORN PARENTS	
LANGUAGE	N		LANGUAGE	N
Slovene	107	AUTOCHT. LGS.	Slovene	5
Italian	1		Italian	1
Bosnian	1	NON-EU EUROPEAN LGS.	Croatian	8
Croatian	1		Bosnian	4
			Serbian	2
			Albanian	1
			Macedonian	1
TOTAL RESPONDENTS	110		TOTAL RESPONDENTS	22

Tab. 7–8f: Self-reported native languages of parents in Slovenia

In all the sub-samples—except for the Romanian one—the variety of languages that are found among native-born parents is much lower than the one reported by native-born children: over approximately a thirty-year period, therefore, population shifts due to immigration has resulted, in the zones being investigated, in increasing cultural and linguistic diversity. This is highly remarkable in some cases, especially as far as the Italian, Spanish and Portuguese sub-samples are concerned.

The parents involved in the survey are generally highly aware of the importance of acquiring "additional languages" to improve their prospects, particularly in the Maltese and Slovenian sub-samples (see Fig.7-1). In the latter, moreover, the percentage of employed informants who report having used, in the week preceding the survey, a language different from the official language of the country of residence in order to work reaches 66.4%[7], while in the other sub-samples lower percentages are found, ranging from 7.9%, in Italy, to 25.9% in Portugal.

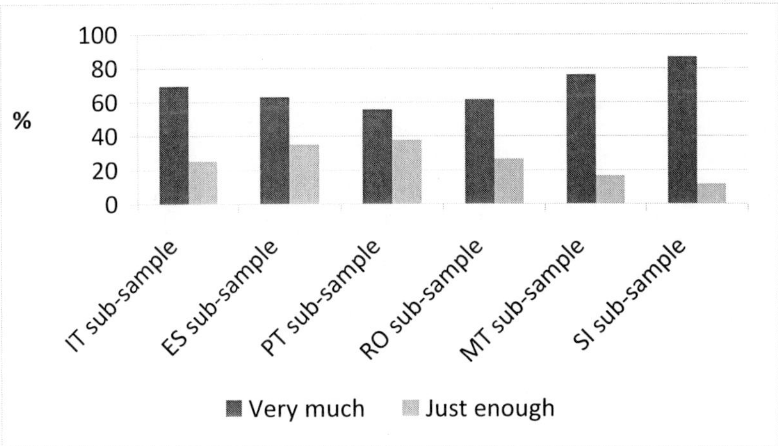

Fig. 7-1: Percentages of positive answers provided by parents to question BQ39 "According to you, how important is it to speak well at least one language, besides your native language/s?"

The adult informants were also asked which language(s) they consider most useful to get a good job and a higher income: in all the sub-samples, both among native-born and foreign-born informants, English is the language deemed to be the most suitable for these purposes, followed, at a considerable distance, by the official languages of the respective countries of residence and, in the lowest positions, in varying order, by languages of the European Union that enjoy an established prestige and widespread international diffusion (French, German, Spanish).

Other non-autochthonous languages are mentioned by a negligible number of informants in all the sub-samples. In this regard it should be noted, however, that there is an interesting difference between the responses to questions about work and the answers to the questions on income. In the former case (languages for work), the languages mentioned

[7] As will be explained further in Ch. 14, it should be borne in mind, in this regard, that the area being surveyed is Istria, near the Italian border.

by more than one informant are only Russian (4 instances in the entire sample) and Chinese (16 occurrences in the entire sample, including 10 just in the Italian sub-sample); in the latter case (the languages to earn a higher income), Russian is indicated by 11 informants and Chinese by 42 (31 of whom are in the Italian sub-sample); the list also includes Arabic and Japanese (each referred to 5 times). For a small group of subjects, therefore, these languages are of little value for finding satisfactory employment, but seem to be associated with highly qualified and profitable activities. Obviously, the totally marginal position of Arabic in contexts such as those of Italy, Spain and Malta is worth noting.

The albeit cursory general evaluation of the data presented in this section leads to the conclusion—apart from indispensable clarifications in Ch. 9-14—that the attitude of adults involved in the MERIDIUM investigation, though generally favourable to language learning, appears influenced by a markedly hierarchical view of the value of languages, in which English has an absolute primacy, while the non-hegemonic EU languages, the non-EU European languages and the extra-European languages are virtually excluded. The datum, which fits perfectly with what emerged in the EUROBAROMETER surveys (2006, 2012), is particularly critical and deserving of in-depth study, because it was collected:

- in areas with high levels of immigration, where the services sector, but even more so many productive and commercial sectors, increasingly need staff with "additional" linguistic skills apart from the knowledge of English;
- in a country, such as Romania, where the outgoing migratory flows are directed largely to non-Anglophone States, which are relatively close geographically and, at least in the case of Italy, for some time oriented towards a policy of relocating production activities precisely in Romania.

In the chapters that follow, each MERIDIUM research unit will present a detailed analysis of the respective sub-samples, contextualizing, by providing the background of the relevant national and local contexts, the interpretation of the data discussed. In fact, as has already partly emerged from the comparative profiles, all the countries in the network have experienced recent migratory flows, but each displays distinctive characteristics, both as regards the organization of educational systems, and also in terms of migratory patterns. The basic comparative outline provided in this chapter is therefore accompanied by these context-specific analyses, in which the most relevant findings are discussed in detail.

Furthermore, the most appropriate tools and intervention methods to heighten awareness of the value of linguistic diversity in school communities and families are also discussed in some chapters.

References

Baker P., and J. Eversley. 2000. *Multilingual capital. The languages of London's school children and their relevance to economic, social and educational policies.* London: Battlebridge Publ.

Barni M., and G. Extra, eds. 2008. *Mapping linguistic diversity in multicultural contexts.* Berlin/New York: Mouton de Gruyter.

Chaloff J., and L. Queirolo Palmas, eds. 2006. *Scuole e migrazioni in Europa*. Roma: Carocci.

Clyne M. 1991. *Community languages: The Australian experience.* Cambridge: CUP.

—. 2003. *Dynamics of language contact.* Cambridge: CUP.

EUMC. 2005. *Majority populations' attitudes towards migrants and minorities*. Wien: European Monitoring Centre on Racism and Xenophobia.

EUROBAROMETER. 2006. *Europeans and their Languages*, Special Eurobarometer 243, wave 64.3. Directorate General for Education and Culture, European Commission (available at: http://ec.europa.eu/public_opinion/index_en.htm, accessed September 26, 2012).

—. 2012. *Europeans and their Languages*, Special Eurobarometer 386, wave 77.1. European Commission (available at: http://ec.europa.eu/public_opinion/index_en.htm, accessed September 26, 2012).

EUROSTAT. 2011. *Migrants in Europe. A Statistical Portrait of the first and second generation.* Luxembourg: Publications Office of the European Union (available at: http://epp.eurostat.ec.europa.eu/cache/ITY_OFFPUB/KS-31-10-539/EN/KS-31-10-539-EN.PDF, accessed September 26, 2012).

Extra G., and D. Gorter 2007. Regional and immigrant minority languages in Europe. In *Handbook of Language and Communication: Diversity and Change*, eds. M. Hellinger and A. Pauwels, 15-52. Berlin/New York: Mouton de Gruyter.

Extra G., and L. Veroheven, eds. 1993. *Immigrant Languages in Europe.* Clevedon: Multilingual Matters.

Extra G., and K. Yağmur, eds. 2004. *Urban Multilingualism in Europe. Immigrant Minority Languages at Home and School*. Clevedon: Multilingual Matters.

García, O., and J. A. Fishman, eds. 1997. *The Multilingual Apple: Languages in New York City*. Berlin and New York: Mouton.

Giles, H., R.Y. Bourhis, D. M. Taylor 1997. Towards a Theory of Language in Ethnic Group Relations. In *Language, Ethnicity and Intergroup Relations,* ed. H. Giles, 307-348. London: Academic Press..

Gogolin, I. 1994. *Der monolinguale Habitus der multilingualen Schule*. Münster: Waxmann.

—. 2002. *Linguistic diversity and new minorities in Europe*, reference study. Strasbourg: Language Policy Division – DGIV, Council of Europe (available at: http://www.coe.int/t/dg4/linguistic/Source/GogolinEN.pdf, accessed September 26, 2012).

IFIIE. 2011. *Evolución y situación actual de la presencia del alumnado extranjero en el sistema educativo español (2000-2011)*. Madrid: Instituto de Formación del Profesorado, Investigación e Innovación Educativa (available at: http://www.educacion.gob.es/educacion/sistema-educativo/educacion-inclusiva/educacion-intercultural/informes.html, accessed September 26, 2012)

IOM. (2008). *Migration in Romania: a country profile 2008*. Geneva: International Organization for Migration (available at: http://publications.iom.int/bookstore/index.php?main_page=product_info&products_id=495, accessed September 26, 2012).

McPake, J., and T. Tinsley, eds. 2007. *Valuing All Languages in Europe*. Graz: European Centre for Modern Languages of the Council of Europe (available at: http://archive.ecml.at/mtp2/publications/Valeur-report-E.pdf, accessed September 26, 2012).

MIUR-ISMU. 2011. *Alunni con cittadinanza non italiana. Verso l'adolescenza. Rapporto nazionale a.s. 2010/2011*. Milano: Fondazione ISMU (available at: http://www.ismu.org/file-download.php?id=5537, accessed September 26, 2012).

Vertovec, S. 2007. Super-diversity and its Implications. *Ethnic and Racial Studies* 30/6. 1024-1054.

CHAPTER EIGHT

THE MERIDIUM PROJECT: RESEARCH PLAN AND METHODOLOGICAL CONSIDERATIONS

STEFANIA TUSINI

8.1. Sampling Criteria

It is not always necessary to select a sample to carry out research. In cases of small population or in the presence of considerable resources, the investigation can also be done with complete enumeration, i.e. involving all the cases. When the population size exceeds the possibilities of direct contact or resources are limited, it is necessary to sample, i.e. to extract a small number of cases (sample) from a larger set (population) on the basis of a set of criteria.

Before illustrating how the MERIDIUM research team has selected its sample, it is useful to call to mind some remarks about sampling.

Samples are generally distinguished between probabilistic and not probabilistic. In the first case, each member of the population has a known and non-zero probability of being chosen to be part of the sample. The non-probability sampling, on the contrary, does not provide all members of the population an equal chance of being chosen and, in fact, some groups or individuals are more likely to be selected than others.

Among probability samples, representative sampling is often identified as the most appropriate procedure to scientific practice because it is generally believed that the results obtained by the sample can be simply extended to the whole population. However, representativeness has some features and some limitations that are often not mentioned in spite of their relevance in order to put this concept in its right perspective. In fact, this term is loaded with extra-statistical meanings and values, that give it an importance that goes beyond mere technical issues: above all, the conviction that, without representativeness, one cannot reasonably be in presence of scientific activity. This belief, also widespread within the humanities, is based on a "category mistake" (Ryle, 1938) which assigns inappropriate features to the representative sample.

A sample is considered representative if it reproduces some characteristics of the general population on a smaller scale. This means that, for instance, if the population is 60% females and 40% males, even the sample must have (more or less) this proportion. Normally, however, representative samples are stratified, i.e. built taking into account a set of variables, not just one. Therefore, in addition to gender, one may consider the distribution of other variables (such as age, educational level, marital status, and so on) and place them in the sample proportionally.

Once the frequency of selected variables is determined, and each variable has been reproduced in the sample proportionally, is it possible to claim that the sample so built is representative also of all other variables (endless minus ones considered) in the general population? Of course this is not the case.

The point is that this type of sample can reproduce some variables whose statistical distribution in the population is already known (and cannot be otherwise). For instance, one may use gender and marital status to stratify the sample only if one knows how many men and women make up the population, and how many individuals are single, widowed, married or divorced.

Unfortunately, the crucial variables for research (for MERIDIUM, for instance, attitudes towards multilingualism or towards otherness) whose statistical distribution in the population is unknown—and it can only be so, given that each survey is carried out in order to produce knowledge on a topic which is still unknown (or partially so)—cannot be used for the sample building.

The most direct consequence is that a sample so selected is not representative of the most meaningful variables for research, but of others (gender, age, marital status, and so on). However, at the end of the survey, the findings concerning attitudes towards multilingualism or toward otherness will be inferentially attributed to the population as a whole (from which the sample was extracted).

Building a representative sample, in the absence of other criteria, helps to maintain a balance in the selection of cases (based on variables with known distribution), but unfortunately it does not mean that one can establish inferences from the sample to the whole population, because representativeness is not transmitted from one variable to another (Marradi, 1989: 60; 2007: ch. 5).

Therefore it is necessary to be aware that a perfectly representative sample of variables with known distribution (such as gender, age, marital status) is not sufficient to guarantee representative results for the variables under investigation[1]. This is because—to reinforce the concept with an example—two individuals may be perfectly equivalent from a statistical point of view (both male, both 40-year old, both single, and so on), but they may have opposite opinions on foreign immigration. From a statistical point of view they are substitutes: it makes no difference to put one or the other in the sample; on the contrary, from a substantive point of view the difference is much greater: interviewing one or the other shifts remarkably the outcome of the investigation.

In some studies, such as MERIDIUM, it seems much more useful to think in terms of prototypicality. This concept, coined by anthropologist Eleanor Rosch (1973, 1977, 1978), proposes an alternative perspective in order to consider individuals' categorization procedures for sampling. It subverts the idea that each member of a class has a representativeness capacity which is equal to all others (Tusini, 2006).

Following classical theory in the field, all members of a category are considered to be logically equivalent; they have the same degree of categorical membership by definition. In the Rosch proposal, by contrast, the categories are designed as continua on which prototypes are placed—i.e. exemplary members of the class—and also other individuals which deviate from that exemplarity.

To give an example, if it comes to birds, it is patent that a finch is more "bird" (it is more prototypical) than a penguin, although the latter has all the requirements to fit into the birds' category. Prototypes merely are subjects which represent better their own category than others—because they possess most of the essential characteristics, or most of the characteristics, possessed by the largest number of the members of the class—but not entirely fill it.

So, following the Rosch proposal, boundaries of the conceptual categories seem much more vague and blurred: Wittgenstein talked about "family affinity" (1953) and Waismann about "family of concepts" (1936). On the contrary, the idea behind inferential logic (which supports the representative sampling procedures) simplifies the complexity and highlights the vagueness of certain concepts: it therefore deserves to be

[1] In addition to this, the sampling plan seldom, if ever, matches exactly the empirical cases actually involved in the investigation. This is fundamentally because, not all individuals who one would like to include in the sample are willing to participate.

debated as it can be deemed to be inappropriate in some contexts of investigation.

It should therefore be clear that a representative sample cannot guarantee *per se* the "scientific" (whatever this may mean and imply) nature of research and the transferability of the findings from the sample to the entire population.

This was a necessary theoretical introduction before illustrating how the MERIDIUM research team has selected its sample.

The reference population for each MERIDIUM research team is theoretically represented by all the children attending the final year of primary school, throughout the countries involved in the project, and their parents/guardians. These are two separate populations (despite the fact that one is related to another) requiring different selection criteria.

To this aim, it is useful to employ the concepts of "social world" and "situational category" proposed by Bertaux (1998). A social world is a group built around a specific kind of activity (professional, cultural, sports, club membership, political, and so on)[2]. Each social world is characterized by its own logic of action, relationship, change, that makes it a sociologically recognizable object.

Instead, the concept of "situational category" which identifies people who share life experiences under specific conditions, such as the chronically ill , families with adopted children, young people seeking their first job, illegal immigrants, teenage mothers, elderly people, and so on. In this case people do not carry out shared activities; they just live the same social situation that generates constraints and logic of action that become elements common to all the members.

The MERIDIUM project surveyed members of social worlds (the children attending the school) and, also, members of situational categories (the parents of the children attending the school).

While the individuals belonging to social worlds are potentially easy to find, because in many cases there are places where they assemble (in our case, the classroom), this is not the case for members of situational categories, because they are scattered throughout the population, they do not have common meeting places and therefore it is necessary to determine appropriate criteria for their recruitment. In our case, the most effective way of reaching the adult population was through their children, who were instructed to give their parents/guardians the questionnaire to be filled in.

---

[2] It is obvious that each individual can simultaneously belong to various social worlds.

Given the size of the reference population (for some partners it was very large)—all the children attending the last or penultimate class of primary schooling—and its territorial dispersion, setting oneself the objective of structuring the sample taking into account a criterion of representativeness would have involved a number of cases which would have been far too high for the resources available.

Moreover, and more importantly, we wondered whether—in the context of a sociolinguistic investigation such as MERIDIUM, in which one of the main criteria is the respondents' origin and, in particular, the languages they speak—it made sense to develop a sample based on statistically known but not necessarily meaningful variables. Consequently, it was necessary to focus on the choice of sampling points that would have particularly suitable characteristics for the research aims.

In other words: the idea of putting questions to those who—because of some of their characteristics—would be potentially able to provide answers (and not, indiscriminately, to subjects selected on a purely statistical basis), is the guiding criterion of the sampling approach used in the MERIDIUM survey, and this criterion could not fail to consider the presence of migrant subjects within these samples.

This presence has therefore been conceptualized as "migration density" and evaluated according to the number of students with non-autochthonous origins in the classroom. This concept has been applied differently by the individual research teams according to the situation present in their context and to the procedures used for collecting data by their respective national statistical offices[3]. This will be dealt with in greater detail later. In the meantime it seems important to emphasize that the sampling procedure adopted is loosely based on theoretical sampling proposed by Glaser and Strauss (1967), whereby the subjects to be included in the survey are selected according to certain characteristics assessed as important from a theoretical point of view, with particular regard to the cognitive question(s) posed by the research. This is therefore a selection that is not at all concerned with statistical representativeness, but is rather guided by the theoretical relevance of the cases in relation to the aims of the investigation. In other words, the cases are selected on the basis of their problematic-categorial centrality, for which the criteria

[3] For example, according to the Italian Ministry of Education, foreign pupils (or, more recently, pupils "having non-Italian citizenship"), are those whose parents are not Italian nationals, even if born in Italy. Students with dual citizenship (one of which is Italian), stateless persons and nomads with Italian nationality are not defined as foreigners.

dictated by the theory of probability are not important, whereas those viewed from the perspective of sociological theory are.

The sample built for the MERIDIUM project does not therefore intend to generalize its results statistically to the population, but to reconstruct paths, meaning, value-positions, concepts, with the reasonable hope that the conclusions which can be drawn will also apply to other "landscapes" with similar characteristics. This exempts one from seeking a statistical projection and urges the adoption of the awareness that, in some cases, the transferability of the results of a study relates to the possibility of identifying a set of statements—which are usually very general—that, *mutatis mutandis*, can shed light on the behaviour, values, beliefs, of similar cultures and forms of life.

Any empirical research aims to make generalizations that tend to release the knowledge produced in a concrete frame of reference and make it applicable to wider areas. This aim can be pursued in various ways, including the statistical approach which is probably the least relevant for the social sciences. Morris Rosenberg (1968), in dealing with the relationship between theory and empirical basis, believes we can speak of two types of generalization (descriptive/statistical, and theoretical), to which we can add a third.

In the first case (the simplest form), we generalize an observation based on a reduced number of cases drawn from a wider population. In other words, "a descriptive generalization refers to the relationship between specific categories under consideration, generalized to the population on which the sample is based" (Rosenberg, 1968). This is the meaning prevalent among statisticians.

Another type of generalization (which we could call "ecological") is related to the fact that the researcher can achieve similar results by checking similar hypotheses in different spatio-temporal contexts and then expanding the empirical foundation on which the same generalization is based, that is, providing a growing corroboration of the findings.

Last but not least, we can talk about a theoretical or conceptual generalization when more specific concepts are replaced with more general ones that allow one to "expand" the boundaries of the theory.

> Often [in fact] our interest in generalizing is not simply to draw conclusions about the broader population ... [based on] a small number of cases, but rather to draw conclusions about the relationship between variables that are conceptually, rather than phenomenologically, defined (Jahoda, Deutsch, Cook, 1951: 87).

To develop a concept (or, rather, a constellation of concepts) encompassing a variety of situations means operating a theoretical generalization based on the data; in this case, in fact, the concrete variables are seen as mere indicators of broader concepts, which nevertheless take shape thanks to the empirical findings of the survey.

The last two types of generalization (ecological and theoretical) are those most intimately involved with the social sciences and go hand in hand: progressively more generalized concepts will prove to be applicable to ever more vast spatio-temporal areas. Even Robert K. Merton (1949), in dealing with the theme of the relationship between empirical research and generalization procedures, has highlighted their circularity and cross-fertilization.

Following this theoretical line, the sample used for the MERIDIUM survey is based on theoretical sampling; in particular, it is a purposive sampling (or based on dimensions; Silverman 2000) built by electing one or more variables as discriminating and selecting subjects that have that same characteristics. Among so selected subjects it is possible to choose cases with extreme states, or individuals who have maximally homogeneous profiles compared to the baseline, or maximally heterogeneous ones; or even select cases that cover the entire range of states.

As mentioned before, the criterion used to build the MERIDIUM sample is migration density, a concept that has led to a funnel procedure with the aim of selecting a certain number of children aged 10-11 years and their parents, and selecting them—a nullifying point—so as to ensure a fair presence of immigrant children, or children with a "foreign background"[4].

As already stated, the starting point of the selection process involved an examination of the areas to be included in the survey: the choice was made focusing on those in which, according to official statistical sources, there were relatively high concentrations of foreign immigration (or emigration, in the case of Romania). Within these zones, the areas of data collection were defined by excluding those with settlements of predominantly mono-ethnic migrants and, where possible, avoiding big cities.

There were two reasons for this latter choice. Firstly, given the strong power of attraction of the great urban centres, in relation to immigration, they tend to be privileged objects of research on multilingualism, while cities, towns and villages of small-medium size are largely unexplored. On the other hand, large urban centres have a complex relational and spatial

[4] Regarding this choice of terminology, see Ch. 7, §7.3.

heterogeneity (e. g. strongly ethnic neighbourhoods) such as to be identified as a separate case, with respect to contexts of more limited proportions, in which the contact with groups of the allochthonous population is generally very recent. Furthermore, we also considered that migrant settlements tend to be more widespread in urban settings than in rural ones.

Secondly, and in line with the above, the socio-cultural centrality of big cities allows educational staff and citizens to have relatively immediate access to structural and cognitive resources appropriate to increase their intercultural awareness; in the same way, immigrant residents are favoured by their own concentration in organizing cultural and linguistic support networks or associations able to interact in a systematic and consistent way with local institutions. On the contrary, in the small-medium size centres, opportunities of this type are very limited. This aspect is particularly important for the project, inasmuch as MERIDIUM aims precisely at spreading a plurilingual and intercultural awareness also through the involvement of schools and families in the research.

Naturally, given the diversity that characterizes each of the countries of the network, while maintaining the basis of these general criteria, each unit could make autonomous choices, dictated by special considerations or interests, which each group will explain in its own respective contribution (Ch. 9-14, this volume).

After a first territorial screening, it was necessary to establish an adequate concept for selecting the sampling sites, namely schools. The criterion of migration density in schools as a guiding criterion for sampling procedures was discussed among the partners during the first meeting of the MERIDIUM project and it was considered appropriate for the aims of the investigation. Apart from being suitable for identifying the individuals to be involved in the survey, this selection criterion permits (in some countries) the inclusion of irregular migrant families, thanks to the fact that, despite their legal status, children are still guaranteed school attendance. Otherwise, a discrimination which is meaningless from a scientific and ethical point of view, would have been introduced.

The decision to select "children" as the first empirical level has proved to be extremely effective, because their mediation has made it possible to reach, in a relatively easily manner, their parents/guardians (whether immigrants or not), who represent an additional target in the data collection and will be dealt with shortly.

The schools within which the survey could be conducted were identified primarily on the basis of data provided by local education authorities regarding the composition of the student population by citizenship, being careful to select institutions for which the percentage of non-autochthonous children, however high, was not predominant.

A further step regarding the sampling stage concerned the involvement of adult informants, the parents/guardians of the children actually interviewed. Even in this case purposive sampling, which only included the parents/guardians of the children involved in the investigation, was used. In particular, the empirical sample turned out to be self-selected, since the MERIDIUM research group chose not to give guidance as to which of the two parents/guardians should fill in the questionnaire.

This choice was dictated by the following reasons:

a. avoiding creating difficulties for the children if the parent/guardian chosen *a priori* to fill in the questionnaire was not present;
b. allowing families with non-autochthonous origins to decide freely who would fill in the questionnaire, on the basis of linguistic skills and cultural prerogatives;
c. avoiding turning into a constant a characteristic (the gender of the adult informant) of which, instead, it was interesting to evaluate the variability[5].

The quantitative limitations on the number of areas and centres in which to select the schools inevitably had to take into account the financial and human resources available to each research unit for the field survey; moreover, a criterion of proportionality with respect to the size and administrative organization of each country has been adopted. A distinction was therefore made among:

1. large countries, with a primarily regionally based administrative organization, i. e. territorial units corresponding to NUTS level 2 (EUROSTAT, 2011): Italy, Spain;
2. large/medium sized countries, with a district administrative organization, that is divided on territorial units corresponding to NUTS level 3 or LAU level 1: Romania and Portugal;

[5] In this sense, the empirical findings are encouraging: in all the countries, the questionnaires were filled in more by female respondents (mostly mothers) than by male respondents, but among those who filled in questionnaires, the native female respondents are systematically more numerous than the female respondents of non-autochthonous origin. This raises interesting questions of a sociological and socio-linguistic nature.

3. small countries, with a mainly municipally based administrative organization, i. e. divided on territorial units corresponding to the LAU level 2: Slovenia and Malta.

For each category, minimum quantitative limits, regarding the typology of the data-collection points and the number of questionnaires to be collected from the children (questionnaire A, see Tab. 8-1) were established.

SURVEY COUNTRIES (BY CATEGORY)	NUMBER OF ADMINISTRATIVE UNITS TO BE SELECTED FOR THE SURVEY			QUESTIONNAIRES 'A' TO BE COLLECTED	
	Regions (NUTS 2)	**Districts** (NUTS3/ LAU1)	**Municipalities** (LAU2) **per territorial unit**	**N per region or district**	**Total N per country**
A. Italy, Spain	3	N. d.			450
B. Portugal, Romania	-	2	2	150	300
C. Malta, Slovenia	-	-			150

Tab. 8-1: Minimum quantitative limits established for the MERIDIUM survey

Tabs. 8-2a-f (presented in the following pages) show the locations in which data were collected, the number of schools visited and the number of questionnaires collected for each country of the network. The minimum quantitative criteria initially established (see Tab. 8-1) were generally respected, and the number of "A questionnaires" collected is well above the minimum required. The fact that the "B questionnaires" (filled in by the parents) were less numerous depends upon the different criteria of distributing the questionnaires (see *infra*, §8.2): the independent filling in of these questionnaires obviously led to a loss, which in some cases was significant (e. g. Spain).

In the comparative analyses which will be carried out, the individual national sub-samples will always be presented in decreasing order of size (IT, ES, PT, RO, MT, SLO), so as to facilitate a direct visual comparison between comparable sets.

REGIONS (NUTS 2)	MUNICIPALITIES (LAU 2)		N OF SCHOOLS	N OF COLLECTED QUESTIONNAIRES	
	NAME	N		A	B
Lombardy	- Bagnolo Mella - Montichiari - Asola - Suzzara	4	4	241	210
Veneto	- Arzignano - Lonigo - S. Biagio Callalta - Susegana	4	5	211	195
Umbria	- Castiglione del Lago - Marsciano - Umbertide	3	5	141	117
Marche	- Corridonia - Matelica - Urbania	3	3	104	91
	TOTAL	**14**	**17**	**697**	**613**

Tab. 8-2a: Italy: MERIDIUM survey profile

REGIONS (NUTS 2)	MUNICIPALITIES (LAU 2)		N OF SCHOOLS	N OF COLLECTED QUESTIONNAIRES	
	NAME	N		A	B
Andalucía	- Vera - Lepe	2	2	118	76
Asturias	- Gijón - Oviedo	2	2	48	34
Castilla-León	- Miranda de Ebro - Salamanca - Segovia	3	3	70	49
Galicia	- Cangas do Morrazo	1	1	25	15
Islas Canarias	- Las Palmas de Gran Canaria - Vecindario	2	2	60	44
Murcia	- Murcia	1	2	108	66
	TOTAL	**11**	**12**	**429**	**284**

Tab. 8-2b: Spain: MERIDIUM survey profile

Districts (NUTS3/ LAU 1)	Municipalities (LAU 2)		N of schools	N of collected questionnaires	
	Name	N		A	B
Grande Lisboa	- Amadora - Mafra - Sintra	3	3	119	119
Península de Setúbal	- Setúbal	1	1	80	80
Algarve	- Faro	1	2	117	117
	Total	**5**	**6**	**316**	**316**

Tab. 8-2c: Portugal: MERIDIUM survey profile

Districts (NUTS3/ LAU 1)	Municipalities (LAU 2)		N of schools	N of collected questionnaires	
	Name	N		A	B
Braşov	- Făgăraş - Buneşti - Cuciulata - Dacia - Feldioara - Hoghiz - Jibert	7	11	156	154
Bacău	- Oneşti - Lupeşti -Mănăstirea Caşin - Stefan cel Mare	4	4	149	138
	Total	**11**	**15**	**305**	**292**

Tab. 8-2d: Romania: MERIDIUM survey profile

MUNICIPALITIES (LAU 2)		N OF SCHOOLS	N OF COLLECTED QUESTIONNAIRES[6]	
NAME	N		A	B
- Birżebbuġa - San Pawl il-Baħar - Sta. Venera	3	3	194	168
TOTAL	**3**	**3**	**194**	**168**

Tab. 8-2e: Malta: MERIDIUM survey profile

MUNICIPALITIES (LAU 2)		N OF SCHOOLS	N OF COLLECTED QUESTIONNAIRES	
NAME	N		A	B
- Koper - Piran	2	4	156	137
TOTAL	**2**	**4**	**156**	**137**

Tab. 8-2f: Slovenia: MERIDIUM survey profile

8.2. Tools and Method of Data Collection

For the data collection, we mainly used questionnaires because the research sought to bring out, in the first instance, quantitative elements in order to evaluate the features of interest in the populations under consideration. The data collected would enable us to present, so to speak, a "snapshot" of the current situation in the various countries.

Some may be surprised that we opted for the questionnaire as a survey tool, having adopted a sampling procedure based on a reasoned choice. However, it is not correct to assume that the sampling system imposes the use of a particular survey tool. Starting from a representative sample, one can proceed with data collection through in-depth interviews, as well as with questionnaires (self-administered, face-to-face, by telephone), both approaches being scientifically correct.

It is understandable that the practice of usually having a representative sample paired with a questionnaire survey engenders the idea that they are scientifically inseparable options, but this is not the case. It is instead a question of two terms that come to be matched with a very stringent field

[6] The questionnaires that were considered valid for analysis by the Maltese unit, as explained in Ch. 13, are those which were filled in by both children and their parents/guardians (164 for each category).

logic, which is obviously based on many good reasons; but there is no reason why "the cards should not be shuffled", especially if data collection by questionnaires is supported by a sample designed to select informants with characteristics appropriate to the investigation, as for the MERIDIUM project.

Furthermore, just as the type of sample chosen is not automatically linked to the type of instrument used for data collection, it also does not imply that one has to use a specific technique of data analysis. These research issues, found in every investigation, are each related to a specific query:

a) How does one select the cases to be investigated?
b) With which tool should the data be collected?
c) Through which technique should these data be analyzed?

Answers to question (a) are obviously related to those to (b) and (c), but it does not imply that (b) and (c) are inexorably bound by (a). However, choosing a particular data-collection tool over another unavoidably affects the choice of the analysis technique. In other words, the fact of having adopted a sample based on a reasoned choice in the MERIDIUM project does not dictate the rules of the data analysis. It simply places the research on a different track from that of the statistical generalization; this, obviously, as has been said, does not mean putting aside the possibility of considering theoretical generalizations.

However, the use of the questionnaire for the data collection—as is the case for MERIDIUM—strictly obliges one, in the analysis phase, to follow the rules dictated by a matrix: this, besides simplifying matters, inevitably leads to quantitative considerations. Operating in this area (quantitative), the data can be processed as monovariate, bivariate (crossing two variables), or multivariate, building indices both of the summation and typological type, as well as other synthetic configurations. Data so analyzed are suitable, therefore, to be presented by graphs or tables.

Since, as mentioned above, the investigation involved two different samples of subjects (children and adults), two distinct questionnaires were prepared, each for a different sample.

From the point of view of the questions that the informants were required to answer, there is only a partial overlap between two questionnaires although they are very similar if one analyzes the conceptual dimensions, which are the object of the data collection. In other words, the cognitive objectives pursued by both questionnaires are essentially homogeneous, but their operational definitions take into account the specific characteristics of the two populations being investigated.

The two questionnaires, both composed of closed and open-questions, were designed to collect:

- sociolinguistic data: repertoire and language use;
- identity data: self-definition, identification centres (family/local/ global);
- experiences of contact with linguistic diversity: friends and/or proximity to speakers of different languages, linguistic connotation of their own world;
- perceptions of linguistic diversity in the local and global context: the quantitative and qualitative perception of diversity;
- opinions and attitudes towards linguistic diversity in an everyday-life context: the hierarchy and reputation of languages, language learning motivation;
- socio-demographic data: country of birth, age, gender, family composition, length of stay in the country; (for adults) educational level, employment status.

The children's questionnaire (Questionnaire A) consists of 48 items; the one for adults (Questionnaire B) is composed of 53 items. The questionnaires used in Romania contain additional questions, designed to collect information on the repertoires, the habits and attitudes of migrants who have returned to their country of origin[7].

The preparation of the questionnaires resulted in structural, conceptual and linguistic problems.

In the first place, it was necessary to build data-collection tools adapted to the reference targets. For the children's questionnaire, we tried to make the formulation and structure of the questions as simple as possible; in order to make the tool more attractive, a cartoon character, Babel, was created, which featured in the questionnaire. Operational definitions, that would make the questions easy to understand, were also necessary for adults, as the questionnaires were only translated into the official languages of the countries of the data collection, of which some migrants might only have had a limited knowledge.

The decision to use questionnaires formulated only in the educational and official language(s) of the country being surveyed is obviously a critical element that can be justified only by invoking the limits imposed by the available time and financial resources. On the other hand, despite

[7] See Appendices A and B, this volume.

the variety of non-autochthonous languages used as L1 by pupils and/or their families, none of the schools involved were able to provide competent personnel with whom to work to prepare translations. An attempt was made to overcome this drawback by adopting suitable measures in administering the questionnaire.

To ensure semantic consistency of the questionnaires, despite the linguistic diversity, researchers discussed and agreed upon basic semantic concepts involved in each question. To this end, conceptual dimensions, sets of indicators aimed at detecting dimensions, and a description of the goals to be pursued were developed. Finally, operational definitions were proposed, in order to have common indications in order to word the questions. Thanks to the procedure adopted, it can be reasonably affirmed that research teams have conducted the survey with semantically consistent questionnaires.

The draft questionnaires were submitted to a pre-test, by being given to at least 40-50 subjects per sample in each country. The analysis of the results brought to light some problems, mainly related to the formulation of the questions, which in some cases were too generic for the children's level of understanding. The final versions of both questionnaires were then corrected and approved, and are reproduced in the Appendix of this book, in an English version with the complete set of additional questions set in Romania.

The defined operational phases of the data collection, carried out in spring 2010, may be summarized as follows.

Before the questionnaires were handed out in class, in each school a preliminary meeting was held between a MERIDIUM researcher, the head teacher and the teachers of the classes involved, which aimed at: describing in detail the aims of the project, collecting information on school policies (criteria for the composition of classes, availability of courses in/of languages other than the official language, specific measures for the integration of children with a different L1 and their families, measures to promote plurilingual and intercultural education, teacher training, school-community relationships); formally acquiring the necessary permits to conduct the investigation; instructing the teachers directly involved in the process of handing out the questionnaires, agreeing upon the timing and mode of presentation of the project to the classes.

The handing out and filling in of questionnaire A took place under the guidance of a MERIDIUM researcher: each child was given a numbered questionnaire and the pupils filled in the questionnaires in class, in the presence of a teacher and, when necessary and available, of a language mediator to assist newly-arrived pupils with limited skills in the official language. This methodological approach was necessary to ensure good data quality, bearing in mind the complexity of the issues addressed in the questionnaire and the young age of the informants. The protocol of data collection meant that some of the rules regarding the filling in of the questionnaires were respected, where the children could easily have ignored them (for example, in the questions where a single answer had to be selected) and prevented the children from consulting each other before selecting the answers. Moreover, in an even more delicate task, the researchers who oversaw the survey provided the children with semantic explanations, specifying the meaning of certain terms and clarifying the meaning of certain questions. This favoured the uniformity of the data-collection conditions in schools and between countries.

After questionnaire A had been completed, each child was also given a questionnaire B, with the same number which had been assigned to the questionnaire A which he/she had just filled in. The children were asked to deliver the questionnaire B to one parent/guardian, for self-completion, and return it to the teacher, who then arranged for the questionnaires to be sent to the university responsible for the data collection in the country.

The information in both questionnaires was collected fully respecting the anonymity and privacy of the respondents.

8.3. Data Processing

Generally, a high percentage of A and B questionnaires were completed. During the initial screening, prior to the entering of the data, some B questionnaires were excluded from the survey because, although they had been returned to the school, they had not been completed, or because they had been filled in by someone clearly different from the one indicated (for example, an elder sister rather than a parent).

With regard to consistency checks, it was decided not to make any corrections, apart from mere clerical errors. There are many reasons for this. One is the concept of consistency which, in its original meaning, refers to the idea of a relationship of equivalence between objects (numbers or geometric figures); its application in the sociological field, in particular in estimating the effectiveness of the questions in a questionnaire, should help to determine whether the respondent has provided more or less consistent answers. This possibility seems to presuppose the existence of shared (universal?) models of reasoning, on the basis of which one could identify any deviations; an intellectually daring operation, since admitting the existence of such models would mean wiping out, with a single blow, all the concepts related to the cultural nature of human beings.

At a less general level, and more intimately concerned with the MERIDIUM research, it was felt that a pattern of responses, judged to be inconsistent by others, could be devoid of contradictions for the person who gave those answers. In other words, we consider that the respondents, given their experiences, their resources and environment, have "good reasons" (Boudon, 1995, 2003) to express certain opinions or attitudes.

After all, the objects of study of the life sciences are sentient beings, capable of choosing and simultaneously undergoing conditioning in non-controllable ways; consequently, the context in which social research takes place does not possess the characteristics of an experimental situation. In the literature, there are very numerous, well-documented instances of "distortions" which, caused by one (or more) of the field elements (interviewer, interviewee, data-collection tool and context), can lead to inaccuracies in the data (Fideli and Tusini, 1997; Tusini, 2002, 2004). Some of these are predictable, others much less so. Their manifestation does not, however, involve a judgment of inadequacy of all the empirical material, since, as is obvious, this takes into consideration each and every question.

The significance of the topic would deserve much more in-depth discussion; in any case one can reflect on the fact that the MERIDIUM questionnaires have been prepared to detect opinions and attitudes on multilingualism, rather than a mere list of language repertoires or baseline characteristics. Through this aim individual respondents (children and adults) provided not only facts (about which distortions can still occur), but assessments, self-assessments, evaluations, opinions, which, as such, have an undeniable weight of subjectivity. However, this subjectivity is precisely what we are interested in detecting: research, in fact, usually does not deal with constants but with variables.

Matrices for data entry were constructed on the basis of the two questionnaires:

- database A (pupils);
- database B (parents/guardians);
- database AB, in which the questionnaires A and B, marked with the same number, have been combined.

Each database is shared by all the partners and includes a Drupal module that allows the data to be entered in a hierarchical mode, a control panel for data export and the possibility to manage permissions.

Databases were pre-tested by all the research teams and after this phase, the data collected in each country were included in the matrices by the corresponding research unit.

The SPSS (Statistical Package for Social Science) or Excel was used for data extraction. Data analysis was performed by SPSS.

References

Bertaux, D. 1998. *Les Récits de vie.* Paris: Editions Nathan.

Boudon, R. 1995. *Le juste e le vrai*. Paris: Fayard.

—. 2003. *Raison. Bonnes raisons*. Paris: PUF.

EUROSTAT. 2011. *Regions in the European Union.* Luxembourg: Publications Office of the European Union (available at: http://epp.eurostat.ec.europa.eu/cache/ITY_OFFPUB/KS-RA-11-011/EN/KS-RA-11-011-EN.PDF, accessed September 26, 2012)

Fideli, R. and S. Tusini 1997. L'infedeltà delle risposte: cause e possibili rimedi. *Sociologia* 31/3. 69-101.

Glaser, B.G. and A. L. Strauss 1967. *The Discovery of Grounded Theory: Strategies for Qualitative Research*. Chicago: Aldine.

Jahoda, M., M. Deutsch and S. W. Cook 1951. *Research Methods in Social Relations*. New York: Dryden Press.

Marradi, A. 1989. Casualità e rappresentatività di un campione: contributo a una sociologia del linguaggio scientifico. In *I sondaggi elettorali e le scienze politiche. Problemi metodologici*, ed. R. Mannheimer, 51-134. Milano: Franco Angeli.

—. 2007. *Metodologia delle scienze sociali*. Bologna: il Mulino.

Merton, R. K. 1949. *Social Theory and Social Structure.* Glencoe: The Free Press.

Ryle, G. 1938. Categories. In *Proceedings of the Aristotelian Society*, 189-206.

Rosch, E. 1973. *On the Internal Structure of Perceptual and Semantic Categories*. In *Cognitive Development and the Acquisition of Language*, ed. T. E. Moore, 111-144. New York: Academic Press.

—. 1977. Human Categorization. In *Advances in Cross-Cultural Psychology*, ed. N. Warren, I, 1-49. London: Academic Press.

—. 1978. Principles of Categorization. In *Cognition and Categorization*, eds. E. Rosch and B. B. Lloyd, 27-48. Hillsdale: Erlbaum.

Rosenberg, M. 1968. *The Logic of Survey Analysis*. New York: Basic Books.

Silverman, D. 2000. *Doing Qualitative Research. A Practical Guide*. London: Sage.

Tusini, S. 2002. Sorprese semantiche: gli intervistati e le domande. *Sociologia e ricerca sociale* 23/67. 141-67.

—. 2004. Contesti, domande e intervistati. In *Giovani Sociologi 2003*, ed. Associazione Italiana di Sociologia, 185-198. Milano: Franco Angeli.

—. 2006. *La ricerca come relazione. L'intervista nelle scienze sociali.* Milano: Franco Angeli.

Waismann, F. 1936. *Einführung in das mathematische Denken*. Wien: Gerold & Co.

Wittgenstein, L. 1953. *Philosophische Untersuchungen*, eds. E. Anscombe and R. Rhees. Oxford: Blackwell.

CHAPTER NINE

BILINGUAL PUPILS AND PARENTS IN ITALIAN SCHOOLS: AN OPPORTUNITY FOR THE EDUCATIONAL SYSTEM

STEFANIA SCAGLIONE

Much has been debated, in the last twenty years, about an alleged "immigrants' problem" in the Italian school system: media discourse on the so called "invasion" of foreign pupils, the obvious difficulties faced in the early period, the reduction in public schools' funding, all have had an important role in convincing public opinion that pupils and families "with non-Italian citizenship" (following the circumlocution being used by the Italian Ministry of Education) just represent an additional problem for schools, teachers, schoolmates.

Although progress has been made in order to welcome these students in schools and to teach Italian as a second language to allophone pupils, as well as in developing intercultural education, the main problem, today, is represented by the substantial difficulty of the Italian educational system to dismiss the monolingual and homoglottic ideology which permeates management, curricula and attitudes at every school level.

Institutional priorities have not changed, even in the face of a remarkable gap in performance and educational success between "Italian pupils" and pupils with an immigrant background (OECD, 2010: 65 ff.; MIUR-ISMU, 2011: 40 ff.), and notwithstanding the fact that in the last few years the percentage of newly-arrived foreign-born children in the Italian school system has been gradually declining, compared to that of native-born children with foreign background. Any consideration about structural measures aimed at meeting the challenges posed by increasingly multilingual school communities is invariably evaded.

Against the background of a European policy pressing for the adoption of plurilingual education as a resource for children's cognitive development as well as for social cohesion, the methodology and the data of the MERIDIUM sociolinguistic research carried out in 17 Italian primary schools will be presented in order to focus on two fundamental issues:

1) To measure the extent of the multi- and plurilingualism characterizing pupils with foreign background in survey schools and classes;
2) To verify if, for these pupils, plurilingualism represents just an individual and family matter, or if it is also significantly present and experienced regularly within the school community.

In the first section of this paper, some general information is provided about Italian educational policies aimed at creating favorable conditions for the integration of pupils with foreign background (§ 9.1.). After a short presentation of the MERIDIUM research methodology (§9.2.), data are discussed which pertain to the use of "family tradition languages" (FTL) spoken by the informants with foreign background (§9.3.). Furthermore, sections 9.4. and 9.5. provide data concerning, respectively, pupils' proficiency in family tradition languages and ongoing extra-curricular experiences of language learning, be it FTL learning, or learning an additional language (with the exception of Italian).

In §9.6. these data will be discussed in the light of educational practices and attitudes towards linguistic diversity that have been noticed in survey schools.

Finally, in § 9.7., some conclusions will be drawn, in an attempt to provide a critical and constructive interpretation of these results. In this section I will also refer to the outcomes of seminars for in-service primary and lower-secondary school teachers, carried out by the members of the MERIDIUM research unit of the University for Foreigners of Perugia.

9.1. The National Context

According to the data published by the Italian National Statistical Institute (ISTAT), between the end of 2002 and the end of 2010, the non-national resident population in Italy has increased from a little more than one and a half million individuals to almost 4 million and 600 thousand[1];

[1] These figures refer to resident foreign citizens, and do not therefore include refugees and those who entered the country illegally, or those who have a residence in another country.

in eight years, the percentage of non-national residents in the total population grew from 2.7 to 7.5 percent.

The increase in number of non-national citizens in Italy is mainly due to the steadiness of large immigration flows, but also to the fact that in Italy in these years many children were born from foreign parents, and, by law (*ius sanguinis*)[2], they acquired the citizenship of their parents. According to the most recent ISTAT figures, by December 31st 2009, 572,720 (13.5%) of 4,235,059 non-national resident citizens were born in Italy.

As a result of the natural growth of the foreign resident population in Italy and of the new arrivals of foreign-born children who join their parents who would have emigrated previously, in the last years Italian schools have registered a steady growth of the co-called "pupils with non-Italian citizenship": according to the report by MIUR-ISMU (2011: 9 ff.), the percentage of these pupils in Italian schools has grown from 2.7% in the school year 2002/03 to 7.9% in 2010/11, with an increment of 60-70 thousand individuals a year.

General conditions for school enrolment of non-national students are established in accordance with the Presidential Decree n. 394 dated August 31, 1999, art. 45, *Regulation concerning implementation rules of the consolidated act of provisions governing immigration and the condition of non-nationals*[3]. On the basis of these measures, non-national minors living within the national territory:

a. have the right to attend school independently from the regularity of their stay, following modalities and conditions granted for Italian citizens; they are subject to compulsory school attendance;
b. can be enrolled in Italian schools at any period of the school year and must be placed in the year-class corresponding to their age, unless the teaching staff decides to enrol them in a different year-class, having considered school programmes of the country of

---

[2] Law 1992-02-05, n. 91. The same law establishes that a foreign citizen born in Italy and residing uninterruptedly in the country can opt for the Italian citizenship on reaching the age of 18.

[3] The above mentioned "consolidated act" ("testo unico") is the Legislative Decree dated July 25, 1998, n. 286 *Consolidated Act of Provisions concerning immigration and the condition of non-nationals*, that brings together and coordinates various measures currently in force with the immigration law n. 40 dated March 6, 1998. The so-called "Bossi-Fini law", dated July 30, 2002, n. 189, modifies previous regulations concerning immigration and asylum, without changing school registration procedures for foreign pupils, which are still defined by Regulation n. 394 of 1999.

origin of the pupil, his/her educational qualifications, and having assessed the general level of his/her knowledge and abilities;

c. must be assigned to classes taking into account that the number of foreign pupils in the class cannot exceed the number of Italian pupils;

d. can attend specific teaching programmes in order to learn Italian.

Furthermore, the *Regulation* considers the importance of broadening initiatives on the topic of intercultural education, as indicated in paragraph 3, art. 38 of the *Consolidated Act of Provisions concerning immigration and the condition of non-nationals* (1998):

> The school community considers linguistic and cultural differences as fundamental values to build mutual respect, exchanges between cultures and tolerance; for this purpose the school community promotes and helps initiatives aimed to welcome [*scil.*: pupils with non-Italian citizenship], to protect the [their] culture and language of origin and to implement common intercultural activities.

The relevance given to intercultural education features regularly in ministerial guidelines since the beginning of the Nineties[4] and it prompted the Italian school system to adopt initiatives promoting dialogue and interchange between cultures: by means of the administrative autonomy given to educational institutions, most schools engage linguistic and cultural mediators, in order to support the integration of foreign-born pupils and the involvement of their parents in school activities; many schools offer educational projects in their course programme, stimulating children's curiosity and open-mindedness towards different cultures; the production of text books and fiction introducing cultural pluralism and intercultural topics for children and teenagers has significantly increased and many schools set up multicultural bookshelves in their libraries.

It is necessary to clarify that the prospect of carrying out these measures depends largely on the financial means of each school, as well as on the presence of teachers and school directors who are adequately prepared or who are disposed to invest in instruction on the subject of

---

[4] See Ministerial Circular Letter (MCL) of July 22, 1990, n. 205 *Compulsory education and foreign pupils. Intercultural education*; MCL of March 2nd, 1994, propagating the document *The intercultural dialogue and democratic coexistence*; MCL of March 1st, 2006, n. 24, *Guidelines to welcome and integrate foreign pupils*; the Directive *The Italian way for an intercultural school and integration of foreign pupils*, written by the National Observatory for the integration of foreign pupils (October 2007).

intercultural education: although the Ministry of Education took action on these issues over the years[5], to date results are not homogeneous if one examines the situation in different schools in Italy.

On the other hand, there are rather few initiatives concerning the protection of the language of origin of pupils with non-Italian citizenship: while we can say that by now all the schools organize courses of Italian as a second language for allophone pupils, there are very few cases of schools offering, in collaboration with associations present in the territory, or on the basis of bilateral agreements with some countries, lessons of the languages of origin of foreign-born children or of children with foreign background. If any are held, they are mostly extra-curricular classes.

This extensive lack of commitment towards multilingualism as a result of immigration in Italy mirrors the substantial indifference of the Ministry of Education on the issue: even though the circular letters quoted previously mention the necessity to grant adequate recognition of non-Italian pupils' languages of origin, there have not been structural measures directed explicitly toward this goal, by means of in-service teachers' training and appropriate funding.

In the Italian educational system the highest percentage of pupils with non-Italian citizenship is registered in primary schools, where in the school year 2010-2011 they constituted 9% of the total students' population and 35.8% of the population of students with non-Italian citizenship enrolled in the Italian school system (MIUR-ISMU, 2011: 10 ff.).

Plurilingualism and language diversity, therefore, represent an everyday experience for primary school pupils; and it is at school that they should be taught to appreciate the value and potentiality of them. On the contrary, in the absence of adequate educational and teaching programmes, these individual and collective linguistic resources risk to remain largely external to the school community, or to be regarded even as limitations to overcome, within a school system which conserves—not only in the primary education—a traditionally monolingual approach, enhanced merely by teaching one or two European languages of wider communication[6].

---

[5] See Ministerial Circular Letter n. 155/2001, aimed at supporting staff serving in schools experiencing consistent immigration flow; incentives for projects regarding areas at risk, with consistent immigration flows and against marginalisation in schools.

[6] English language is compulsory since the first year of the primary school (ISCED 1), whereas in the lower classes of secondary school (ISCED 2) two European languages are taught (English+French/German/Spanish). In high school (ISCED 3), only one European language is taught, except in the so-called "linguistic high

This situation seems even more incongruous, if one considers that an increasing number of bilingual children joins educational institutions every year: they are children born in Italy from foreign parents, and in the school year 2010-2011 they represented 42.1% of the entire school population of foreign origin (299,565 pupils out of 711,046, +3% compared to the previous year); in the same year, they constituted 78.3% of registered pupils with foreign citizenship in preschool and 52.9% in primary school (MIUR-ISMU, 2011: 11 ff.).

Based on these preliminary considerations, the MERIDIUM research carried out in 17 Italian primary schools by the research unit of the University for Foreigners of Perugia proposed to focus closely on language use, experience and perception, as well as linguistic attitudes of pupils and their parents in schools and social contexts characterized by an increasing linguistic and cultural diversity. This research aims to produce critical reflection which will lead to further awareness regarding plurilingualism and language diversity inside school communities and pupils' families[7].

9.2. Selection Criteria and Profile of the Territorial Units and Schools under Study

9.2.1. Regions, Provinces and Municipalities

Recent migratory flows have not been homogeneous in Italy, as they are concentrated mainly in the North and in the Centre of the country, where socio-economic conditions are comparatively better and work opportunities are more numerous compared to the South and the islands.

For these reasons, the Italian research unit of the MERIDIUM project selected the following regions for the survey: Lombardy and Veneto in the North, Umbria and Marche in the Centre, according to the guidelines described in Ch. 8. In these regions, in the last decade the percentage of

---

schools", where, besides a classical language (Latin), three foreign languages are taught.

[7] Although this paper has been written by the coordinator of the MERIDIUM research unit of the University for Foreigners of Perugia, it must be duly noted that the following researchers have participated as active members of the group in all phases of the project: Stefania Tusini, Alejandro Marcaccio, Borbala Samu, Jessica Cancila. An important contribution was also made by Federica Venier (University of Bergamo) and by Eleonora Lucibello, who participated in the project as consultants.

non-national residents ranks among the highest at a national level (Tab. 9-1).

REGION	YEAR		
	2002	2006	2010
Lombardy	*4.0%*	*7.6%*	*10.7%*
Veneto	*4.0%*	*7.3%*	*10.2%*
Umbria	*3.9%*	*7.3%*	*11.0%*
Marche	*3.7%*	*6.5%*	*9.3%*
ITALY	***2.7%***	***5.0%***	***7.5%***

Tab. 9-1: Percentages of non-national residents on the total population: years 2002–2006–2010 (Source: ISTAT)

According to data from the Ministry of Education, in the school year when data collection has been carried out (2009-2010), children with non-Italian citizenship constituted 8.7% of total pupils enrolled in primary schools: the percentage reached 14.5% in Umbria, 13.5% in Lombardy, 13.3% in Veneto, 12.8% in Marche (MIUR, 2010: 20).

The selection of administrative districts and municipalities in these regions was made in compliance with the latest ministerial data available regarding numbers of non-national pupils in Italian provinces (MIUR, 2009b: 23 ff.) and in municipalities not being provincial capitals[8], but having at least 1,000 pupils enrolled in state schools (MIUR, 2009a: 37 ff.). The outcomes of the selection are shown in Tab. 9-2:

[8] Regional and provincial capitals were excluded on the basis of dimensional hypotheses illustrated in Ch. 8 for survey municipalities. Municipalities under study in Italy have a population between 9,000 and 25,000 inhabitants.

SURVEY REGION	BEST TERRITORIAL UNITS BY % OF PRIMARY-SCHOOL PUPILS WITH FOREIGN CITIZENSHIP			
	ADMINISTRATIVE DISTRICTS	%	MUNICIPALITIES	%
LOMBARDY	Mantova (MN)	*19.4*	Asola Suzzara	*18.7* *17.5*
	Brescia (BS)	*17.0*	Bagnolo Mella Montichiari	*19.0* *17.3*
VENETO	Treviso (TV)	*15.7*	Susegana San Biagio di Callalta	*24.8* *16.7*
	Vicenza (VI)	*14.7*	Arzignano Lonigo	*17.4* *16.7*
UMBRIA	Perugia (PG)	*15.1*	Castiglione del Lago Umbertide Marsciano	*18.3* *18.2* *15.7*
MARCHE	Macerata (MC)	*15.3*	Matelica Corridonia	*16.2* *15.8*
	Pesaro-Urbino (PU)	*11.8*	Urbania	*17.3*

Tab. 9-2: Results of the selection of administrative districts and municipalities in Lombardy, Veneto, Umbria, Marche (sources: MIUR, 2009a; MIUR, 2009b)

In municipalities under study, pupils with foreign background belong to a great number of different nationalities: in Tab. 9-3 (p. 185) one may acknowledge the socio-demographic complexity of these contexts, where many groups of different origin cluster together, following consolidated "chain migrations", often influenced by the needs of the local economy:

MUNICIPALITY	RANKING OF THE FIVE MOST REPRESENTED NATIONALITIES BY % OF RESIDENT CITIZENS ON THE TOTAL OF NON-NATIONAL RESIDENTS									
	1st		2nd		3rd		4th		5th	
Asola (MN)	Albania	*22.4*	Macedonia	*19.6*	Romania	*15.0*	Morocco	*11.6*	India	*6.7*
Suzzara (MN)	India	*37.9*	Bangladesh	*14.9*	Morocco	*11.7*	Pakistan	*7.8*	Albania	*7.8*
Bagnolo Mella (BS)	India	*16.5*	Morocco	*16.0*	Pakistan	*11.5*	Senegal	*8.4*	Albania	*7.8*
Montichiari (BS)	Romania	*22.7*	Albania	*12.8*	Morocco	*11.4*	Macedonia	*8.4*	India	*8.0*
Susegana (TV)	Macedonia	*25.7*	Morocco	*11.2*	China	*9.7*	Serbia	*6.9*	Albania	*6.7*
San Biagio Callalta (TV)	Morocco	*14.4*	Serbia	*12.9*	Romania	*11.0*	Albania	*8.4*	Senegal	*4.7*
Arzignano (VI)	Serbia	*21.2*	Bangladesh	*21.1*	India	*18.8*	Albania	*8.2*	Ghana	*6.9*
Lonigo (VI)	Romania	*20.8*	Bangladesh	*17.2*	Serbia	*16.2*	India	*11.7*	Albania	*9.6*
Castiglione del Lago (PG)	Albania	*31.0*	Romania	*22.6*	Morocco	*14.1*	U.K.	*7.6*	Bulgaria	*2.8*
Umbertide (PG)	Morocco	*25.2*	Albania	*22.4*	Romania	*15.6*	Algeria	*6.6*	U.K.	*4.0*
Marsciano (PG)	Romania	*39.4*	Morocco	*15.0*	Albania	*9.9*	Poland	*5.3*	Ecuador	*3.8*
Matelica (MC)	Albania	*41.9*	Macedonia	*28.1*	Romania	*8.9*	Ukraine	*3.1*	Nigeria	*2.3*
Corridonia (MC)	Pakistan	*32.2*	Macedonia	*16.6*	Romania	*15.1*	China	*11.1*	Morocco	*4.9*
Urbania (PU)	Albania	*31.9*	Morocco	*20.6*	Moldova	*11.1*	Romania	*8.3*	Macedonia	*6.2*

Tab. 9-3: Ranking of the five most represented nationalities by % of resident citizens on the total of non-national residents in survey municipalities at 1st January 2010 (source: ISTAT)

9.2.2. Schools and Classes Involved in the Survey

In each municipality, primary schools were selected on the basis of lists provided by Regional School Offices ("Uffici Scolastici Regionali") and including state schools with the largest number of pupils "with non-Italian citizenship"[9]. In each school which participated in the project (17 institutes), the school director was asked to indicate, in accordance with the teachers, one or more classes of the final year of primary schooling (fifth class in the Italian school system) to be involved in the survey.

At the time of the survey, in each school included in the project pupils with a mother tongue different from Italian were offered classes of Italian L2, generally taking place during the hours of the school timetable; in some cases, assistance of linguistic mediators was also provided for newly arrived children. Moreover, all the schools carried out projects on intercultural education, often involving the families of the pupils. Courses for the maintenance of some of the most widespread languages of origin were only being held in three schools (BS1, VI11, PG3)[10]; however, such initiatives lack continuity, since they are re-scheduled each year according to the financial resources. Besides, they are not held during school hours. In all the survey schools, English language constitutes the only compulsory foreign language included in the curriculum for every pupil (2/3 hours a week).

The placement of non-national pupils in classes is decided in each school taking into account the requirement to avoid an excessive concentration of such pupils in a single class; in particular, the Ministerial Circular Letter (MCL) of January 8, 2010 n. 2 states that—with effect from the school year 2010/11—the percentage of pupils with non-Italian citizenship in each class must not exceed 30%.

---

[9] In Italy there are two parallel educational systems: "state schools" (free of charge) and "private schools" (fee paying). Private schools may be officially recognized by the Ministry of Education if they adopt the same system of organization of state schools; otherwise, they are not recognized and the qualifications they issue have no legal value. According to the Ministry of Education, in the school year 2009/10 only 4.2% of pupils with non-Italian citizenship were enrolled in private schools (MIUR, 2010b: 10).

[10] For the sake of conciseness, a code has been assigned to each survey school, including the abbreviation of the province (e.g. VI = Vicenza) and a number which represents the municipality (e.g. VI-1 = Arzignano; VI-2 = Lonigo). If in a single municipality two different schools have been selected, another number will follow (e.g. VI-1-1 = Arzignano, Primary School "A. Fogazzaro"; VI-1-2 = Arzignano, Primary School "V. da Feltre").

Tab. 9-4a shows the percentages of pupils with non-Italian citizenship registered in the 36 survey classes in the school year 2009/10; if one considers them in the light of the parameters put forward by the MCL 2/2010 and in effect from the following school year, one may observe that 16 classes out of 36 would have been beyond the established limit.

REGION	DISTRICT	SCHOOL CODE	% OF PUPILS WITH NON_ITALIAN CITIZENSHIP PER CLASS				
			A	B	C	D	E
Lombardy	BS	BS1	***33%***	*16%*	-	-	-
		BS2	***40%***	***46%***	***37%***	-	-
	MN	MN1	***41%***	***38%***	-	-	-
		MN2	*24%*	*17%*	*14%*	*22%*	-
Veneto	VI	VI11	***37%***	-	-	-	-
		VI12	*14%*	-	-	-	-
		VI2	***42%***	***37%***	***32%***	*26%*	*30%*
	TV	TV1	*29%*	*22%*	-	-	-
		TV2	***37%***	***32%***	-	-	-
Umbria	PG	PG11	***33%***	-	-	-	-
		PG12	*22%*	*22%*	-	-	-
		PG21	*22%*	-	-	-	-
		PG22	***50%***	-	-	-	-
		PG3	*16%*	*21%*	***35%***	-	-
Marche	MC	MC1	***42%***	-	-	*25%*	-
		MC2	-	-	-	*29%*	-
	PU	PU1	*11%*	*17%*	*29%*	-	-

Tab. 9-4a: Percentages of pupils with non-Italian citizenship enrolled in survey classes (school year 2009/10)

It must be noted, however, that the dichotomy based on citizenship poses too narrow limits to the composition of classes: many of the pupils classified as “foreigners” were in fact born in Italy from foreign-born parents and, although they do not have Italian citizenship, their situation is quite different from the one of foreign-born and newly arrived pupils, who—in most cases—do not speak Italian.

If the percentages presented in Tab. 9-4a were re-calculated omitting the citizenship criterion, and focusing on the ratio between pupils born in Italy and pupils born abroad from foreign-born parents, only 3 of the 36 classes under study would exceed the 30% limit (see Tab. 9-4b).

REGION	DISTRICT	SCHOOL CODE	% OF PUPILS BORN ABROAD FROM FOREIGN PARENTS PER CLASS				
			A	B	C	D	E
Lombardy	BS	BS1	*29%*	*12%*	-	-	-
		BS2	*28%*	*23%*	*26%*	-	-
	MN	MN1	*9%*	*12%*	-	-	-
		MN2	*24%*	*9%*	*9%*	*9%*	-
Veneto	VI	VI11	***32%***	-	-	-	-
		VI12	*5%*	-	-	-	-
		VI2	*17%*	*21%*	*16%*	*13%*	*9%*
	TV	TV1	*14%*	*6%*	-	-	-
		TV2	*16%*	*21%*	-	-	-
Umbria	PG	PG11	*19%*	-	-	-	-
		PG12	*11%*	*11%*	-	-	-
		PG21	*22%*	-	-	-	-
		PG22	***31%***	-	-	-	-
		PG3	*5%*	*10%*	*15%*	-	-
Marche	MC	MC1	***37%***	-	-	*6%*	-
		MC2	-	-	-	*21%*	-
	PU	PU1	*5%*	*11%*	*23%*	-	-

Tab. 9-4b: Percentage of pupils born abroad from foreign-born parents and enrolled in survey classes (school year 2009/10)

As illustrated above in §9.1., native-born pupils with foreign background currently represent the majority of the so-called "foreign pupils" enrolled both in pre-school and in primary school. According to the Ministry of Education, at the time of the survey (school year 2009/10) they represented 48.6% of pupils with non-Italian citizenship in primary schools; in the MERIDIUM sample, they actually represent 44.2% (208 pupils out of 697).

9.3. The Use of "Family Tradition Languages" among Pupils with Foreign Background

As shown in §7.4.1., languages which both native-born and foreign-born pupils declare to use with parents ("home-languages") give rise to a rich multilingual and polydialectal patchwork. On a total of 697 informants, 229 (32.8%) use a language which is different from Italian with their mother and/or their father: among them, there are obviously pupils with a foreign background, but also children of mixed-nationality couples, or children of Italian parents.

In this section, focus will be made specifically on pupils with a foreign background, with the aim to ascertain the extent to which their "family tradition languages" (FTL) are actively used by them, within and outside the family circle.

With the term "family tradition language", I am referring to all the languages different from Italian that children with foreign background may be familiar with because they are normally used by their parents in interacting with each other, with their children, with relatives. These languages may be conceived as the components of the family linguistic repertoire before migration; analyzing the self-reported language use of children against this broader background may therefore help to obtain a clearer picture of their language preferences and choices within the migration context.

For each pupil with foreign background, the respective "family tradition language/s" have been identified by means of two sets of data:

- the answers provided by the pupil, concerning her/his language use with parents, siblings, grandparents and other relatives (questions AQ36 a-d and AQ37a);
- the answers provided by the pupil's parent, concerning her/his own language use with children, partner, parents, siblings and relatives (questions BQ52 a-d and BQ53a).

In the MERIDIUM pupils' sample (A sample) there are 208 pupils with foreign background; their birth-countries, and the birth countries of their parents, are listed in Tab. 9-5 below:

BIRTH-COUNTRY	PUPILS	MOTHERS	FATHERS
Italy	92	-	-
Romania	20	22	21
Albania	13	32	32
Macedonia	13	15	14
India	11	17	18
Bangladesh	8	10	10
Serbia	7	14	12
Morocco	6	26	26
Pakistan	5	8	8
Kosovo	5	7	8
Ghana	3	9	10

Tab. 9-5: Birth-countries of pupils and parents with foreign background

BIRTH-COUNTRY	PUPILS	MOTHERS	FATHERS
Cina	3	5	4
Moldova	3	3	3
Ecuador	3	2	2
Tunisia	2	5	5
United Kingdom	2	3	3
‘Africa’	2	2	2
Greece	2	-	-
Senegal	1	1	2
Cameroon	1	1	1
Côte d’Ivoire	1	1	1
Guinea (Conakry)	1	1	1
Venezuela	1	1	1
Croatia	1	-	1
Burkina Faso	1	-	-
Algeria	-	2	2
Togo	-	2	2
Bulgaria	-	2	1
Germany	-	2	1
Bosnia and Herzegovina	-	1	2
Brazil	-	1	2
Dominican Republic	-	1	1
Nigeria	-	1	1
Syria	-	1	1
Egypt	-	-	1
Poland	-	-	1
Switzerland	-	-	1
Turkey	-	-	1
Guinea-Bissau	-	1	-
Argentina	-	1	-
France	-	1	-
Liberia	-	1	-
Slovenia	-	1	-
not specified	1	5	6
TOTAL	208	208	208

Tab. 9-5 (cont.): Birth-countries of pupils and parents with foreign background

44.2% of the 208 pupils with foreign background were born in Italy, while—among those born abroad—78 (37.5% of the total) come from seven countries (Romania, Albania, Macedonia, India, Bangladesh, Serbia, Morocco), which prevail also among parents (65.4% of mothers and 63.9% of fathers come from these countries). The correspondence between occurrences in mothers’ and fathers’ data shows that in most cases pupils’ parents share the same national origin.

In order to identify as accurately as possible the "family tradition languages" of pupils, language names used by these informants have been compared to those used by parents, as in our database children often make use of "pseudo-glottonyms" derived from the name of the country where the language is spoken. For example, many pupils from India call "Indian" the language that their parents refer to as *Panjabi*; all the pupils from Kosovo call "Kosovan" the language that their parents refer to as *Albanian*[11]. In Tab. 9-6 family tradition languages that it was possible to identify are listed, as well as the "pseudo-glottonyms" (within quote marks), in cases where the language being referred to was not clear:

MAIN FTL	N OF PUPILS	OTHER FTL	N OF PUPILS
Albanian	45	-	
Arabic	32	French	3
Romanian	23	Serbo-Croatian	2
Serbo-Croatian	16	Albanian	1
Hindi	11	-	
Bengali	10	English	1
'Ghanaian'	9	English	4
Panjabi	8	Urdu Hindi English	1 1 1
Macedonian	8	-	
Urdu	8	-	
Spanish	6	-	
Chinese	5	German	1
French	5	Arabic Polish	1 1
English	4	-	
Moldavian	3	-	
Bulgarian	2	-	
'African'	2	-	
'Senegalese'	2	-	

Tab. 9-6: "Family tradition languages" (FTL) of pupils with foreign background

[11] Kosovo was an autonomous province of Serbia and Montenegro, which proclaimed itself an independent State in 2008. Albanians are the largest ethno-linguistic group (85.2% according to Leclerc, 2012), and Albanian is *de facto* the only official language, while being *de jure* co-official with Serbian. It must be noted, however, that the variety of Albanian spoken in Kosovo differs from standard Albanian in that the latter is based on the Tosk variety, while the former is a Gheg dialect (see also Toso, 2006: 49 ff.).

MAIN FTL	N OF PUPILS	OTHER FTL	N OF PUPILS
Bisa	1	French	1
Ewé	1	French	1
German	1	-	
'Guinean'	1	-	
Portuguese	1	-	
'Togolese'	1	French	1
Turkish	1	Albanian	1
Yoruba	1	English	1
[not specified]	1	-	
TOTAL	208	TOTAL	22

Tab. 9-6 (cont.): "Family tradition languages" (FTL) of pupils with foreign background

There are seven cases where pupils never declare to use their FTL, although their parents claim they use it on a regular basis when speaking to their children or to other family members. Interestingly enough, these pupils have intentionally avoided to declare their language use with the different (categories of) family interlocutors (giving no answer at all), or answered only to questions where they could report a monolingual use of Italian (e.g. with siblings). Such a behavior might therefore be implying a situation of conflict with their own "other-than-Italian" identity.

For the most part, however, pupils with foreign background involved in the research seem to actively use at least one family tradition language; actually, 22 of them declare two FTLs, which can be related to the different national origin of their parents (6 cases), or to a family linguistic repertoire including a national or minority language and an official language (normally a former-colonial one), as frequently happens in multilingual countries, as India, Pakistan or African States (16 cases).

9.3.1. The "Family Usage Index" of Family Tradition Languages

A conventional value has been assigned to the language use declared by pupils in the interaction with a single (category of) interlocutor(s) ("usage index", UI). This value has been assigned in order to quantify the use of the family tradition language/s against the use of Italian: when an informant states that s/he uses only his/her FTL(s) when talking to a specific interlocutor, the "usage index" for that FTL(s) is 1; if—on the contrary—the informant uses only Italian, the value of the "usage index" for his/her FTL(s) is 0. When an informant declares an alternate use of his/her FTL(s) and Italian, the "usage index" is 0.5.

Tab. 9-7a below shows the frequencies of the values pertaining to the "FTL family usage index": these values have been obtained as the arithmetic mean of usage indexes assigned to uses declared by pupils in interactions with each (category of) interlocutor(s) within the family (UI mother, UI father, UI siblings, UI grandparents, UI relatives). In order to obtain complete comparability among the informants, only those who have provided valid answers for all the (categories of) interlocutors will be taken into account (162 subjects out of 208).

VALUES OF THE "FTL FAMILY USAGE INDEX"	PUPILS	
	N	%
ZERO (0.0)	1	*0.6*
LOW (0.1-0.3)	6	*3.7*
BALANCED (0.4-0.6)	42	*26.0*
HIGH (0.7-0.9)	78	*48.1*
FULL (1.0)	35	*21.6*
TOTAL	162	*100.0*

Tab. 9-7a: Values of the "family usage index" for the family tradition languages (FTLs) spoken by pupils with foreign background

On the whole, the family usage of the FTLs is good, as 113 informants out of 162 (69.8%) score "high" or "full" values for this index.

The fact that an informant was born in Italy or abroad affects the FTL family usage index value, although not in a dramatic way (see Tab. 9-7b); comparing pupils born abroad to pupils born in Italy, full values halve and middle values almost double.

VALUES OF THE "FTL FAMILY USAGE INDEX"	FOREIGN-BORN PUPILS		PUPILS BORN IN ITALY	
	N	%[12]	N	%
ZERO (0.0)	0	-	1	*(1.3)*
LOW (0.1-0.3)	5	*(5.8)*	1	*(1.3)*
BALANCED (0.4-0.6)	16	*(18.6)*	26	*(34.2)*
HIGH (0.7-0.9)	40	*(46.5)*	38	*(50.0)*
FULL (1.0)	25	*(29.1)*	10	*(13.2)*
TOTAL	86	*(100.0)*	76	*(100.0)*

Tab. 9-7b: Values of the "family usage index" for the family tradition languages (FTLs) spoken by pupils with foreign background: birthplace-disaggregated data

9.3.2. The "Home Usage Index" of the Family Tradition Languages

In parallel with "family usage index"—which takes into account the "conservative influence" exerted on pupils' language use by grandparents and relatives (often still living in the family's country of origin)—the "home usage index" of the family tradition languages was calculated. Values for this index have been obtained as the arithmetic mean of usage indexes assigned to interactions with mother, father and siblings (see Tab. 9-8 below).

VALUES OF THE "FTL HOME USAGE INDEX"	FOREIGN-BORN PUPILS		PUPILS BORN IN ITALY	
	N	%	N	%
ZERO (0.0)	5	*(5.8)*	3	*(3.9)*
LOW (0.1-0.3)	7	*(8.1)*	17	*(22.4)*
BALANCED (0.4-0.6)	15	*(17.4)*	10	*(13.2)*
HIGH (0.7-0.9)	31	*(36.0)*	32	*(42.1)*
FULL (1.0)	28	*(32.6)*	14	*(18.4)*
TOTAL	86	*(100.0)*	76	*(100.0)*

Tab. 9-8: Values of the "home usage index" for the family tradition languages (FTLs) spoken by pupils with foreign background: birthplace-disaggregated data

As expected, values obtained for the home usage index are lower than those obtained for family usage index: while for the latter index only 7

[12] In tables where cases do not reach the sum of 100, percentages are listed within brackets.

pupils score zero or low values (see Tab. 9-7b), for the former their number raises to 32.

On the other hand, it must also be noted that 68.6% of foreign-born pupils (59 cases out of 86) and 60.5% of native-born pupils (46 cases out of 76) score high or full values for the home usage index of family tradition languages.

As clearly indicated in the literature[13], siblings are the most active agents of innovation in language use at home, promoting secondary shift to Italian: in Tab. 9-9, where mean values of usage indexes of the family tradition languages are displayed for each interlocutor in the home domain (UI Mo = mother; UI Fa = father; UI Si = siblings), one observes that UI Si is always lower than UI Mo and UI Fa, both for foreign-born and for native-born pupils with foreign background.

USAGE INDEXES			FOREIGN-BORN PUPILS		PUPILS BORN IN ITALY	
	min.	**max.**	**N**	**Mean UI**	**N**	**Mean UI**
UI Mo	.0	1.0	86	.814	76	.755
UI Fa	.0	1.0	86	.820	76	.724
UI Si	.0	1.0	86	.526	76	.409
Home UI	.0	1.0	86	.720	76	.629

Tab. 9-9: Mean values of usage indexes of the family tradition languages for each interlocutor in the home domain: birthplace-disaggregated data

9.3.2.1. A comparison between self-reported language use of pupils and parents

The possibility to merge pupils' questionnaires with parents' questionnaires provides the opportunity to compare self-reported language use of pupils and parents in their reciprocal interaction.

The data discussed in this paragraph pertain to a subset of the 162 pupils with foreign background who have been referred to in the two preceding sections. Data concerning 124 pupils will be presented here: these are the pupils whose parents provided valid answers to the question about language use with their children (BQ52b).

In Tab. 9-10a the usage index of family tradition languages is considered in a two-way direction: "child to parent" and "parent to child":

[13] For references, see Chini (this volume, § 6.5).

VALUES OF THE "FTL USAGE INDEX"	CHILD TO PARENT		PARENT TO CHILD	
	N	%	N	%
ZERO (0.0)	10	*8.1*	20	*16.1*
BALANCED (0.5)	38	*30.6*	54	*43.5*
FULL (1.0)	76	*61.3*	50	*40.3*
TOTAL	124	*100.0*	124	*100.0*

Tab. 9-10a: Values of the usage index (UI) for the family tradition languages (FTLs) among pupils with foreign background and their parents in reciprocal interactions

Quite surprisingly, data show that children have a more conservative attitude than their parents: the percentage of children scoring full values for the usage index of family tradition languages is more than 20 points higher than the corresponding percentage of parents. Furthermore, children scoring zero values are half the number of parents behaving the same way.

This trend does not change if we disaggregate the data on the basis of pupils' birthplace (see Tab. 9-10b) or on the basis of parents' gender (see Tab. 9-10c), although it must be observed that:

1) among pupils born in Italy (as well as among their parents) the exclusive use of family tradition languages decreases considerably if compared to that characterizing foreign-born pupils (and their parents), while the opposite is true for the alternate use of family tradition languages and Italian;
2) pupils seem to adopt the exclusive use of family tradition languages preferably when talking to father, than when talking to mother.

VALUES OF THE "FTL USAGE INDEX"	FOREIGN-BORN PUPILS (AND THEIR PARENTS)		PUPILS BORN IN ITALY (AND THEIR PARENTS)	
	CH TO P	P TO CH	CH TO P	P TO CH
ZERO (0.0)	5 (*7.6%*)	5 (*7.6%*)	5 (*8.6%*)	15 (*25.9%*)
BALANCED (0.5)	15 (*22.7%*)	26 (*39.4%*)	23 (*39.7%*)	28 (*48.3%*)
FULL (1.0)	46 (*69.7%*)	35 (*53.0%*)	30 (*51.7%*)	15 (*25.9%*)
TOTAL	66 (*100.0%*)	66 (*100.0%*)	58 (*100.0%*)	58 (*100.0%*)

Tab. 9-10b: Values of the usage index (UI) for the family tradition languages (FTLs) among pupils with foreign background and their parents in reciprocal interactions: child's birthplace-disaggregated data

VALUES OF THE "FTL USAGE INDEX"	CHILDREN AND MOTHERS		CHILDREN AND FATHERS	
	CH TO M	M TO CH	CH TO F	F TO CH
ZERO (0.0)	6 (*9.8%*)	9 (*14.8%*)	4 (*6.3%*)	11 (*17.5%*)
BALANCED (0.5)	23 (*37.7%*)	30 (*49.2%*)	15 (*23.8%*)	24 (*38.1%*)
FULL (1.0)	32 (*52.5%*)	22 (*36.1%*)	44 (*69.8%*)	28 (*44.4%*)
TOTAL	61 (*100.0%*)	61 (*100.0%*)	63 (*100.0%*)	63 (*100.0%*)

Tab. 9-10c: Values of the usage index (UI) for the family tradition languages (FTLs) among pupils with foreign background and their parents in reciprocal interactions: parent's gender-disaggregated data

The more conservative attitude which characterizes pupils in comparison with their parents in our data does not tally with the results of a broader research carried out by Chini and colleagues on a sample of 414 young informants with foreign background recruited in the province of Pavia and in Turin (Chini, 2004: 152 f.)[14].

Chini reports that the monolingual use of family tradition languages is chosen a little more frequently by parents than by children (respectively, 53% *vs*. 50%), with percentages which appear considerably different from those obtained from our sample (respectively, 40.3% *vs*. 61.3%, see Tab. 9-10a). Such a divergence looks even more perplexing, if we take into account that, in Chini's sample, 90.8% of informants (376 subjects) are foreign-born pupils, a category which, in our sample, scores the highest percentages of full values for LTF usage index with parents (69.7%, see Tab. 9-10b).

Taken for granted that the results obtained by each of the two researches greatly differ in terms of significance, given the larger dimensions of Chini's sample, it may be nonetheless useful to try to account for such different results, in order to point out methodological and structural factors which may have affected them:

- *Data sources and research tools*: in Chini's research all the information about language use within the family has been elicited exclusively from children, who answered questions concerning their parents' language use as well. On the contrary, in our case children and parents self-reported their own language use. Moreover, parents involved in the MERIDIUM research received the questionnaire through schools: this could have induced them to

[14] See also Chini (this volume).

unconsciously emphasize their use of Italian with their children, underestimating at the same time the use of FTL(s).
As we shall see, indeed, many teachers have claimed that they ask parents to use Italian with their children as often as possible.

- *Structure of the sample and characteristics of informants:* as convincingly shown by Chini's study (2004: 317 ff.), as well as by the results of a transnational research reported in Yağmur and Extra (2004), language choice can be significantly affected by age, generation and family tradition language of informants. In this respects, Chini's sample and the MERIDIUM one differ considerably:
    - the age of informants in Chini's research ranges from 9 to 20 years, with a prevalence of the 13-17 age bracket (53.9%), while, in the MERIDIUM sample, only 10-11 years old pupils have been included;
    - the sample analyzed by Chini and colleagues is almost exclusively composed by "first generation immigrant children" (90.8%), or—following our terminology—foreign-born subjects with a foreign background. In the MERIDIUM sub-sample of 124 informants under study in this section, the distribution of foreign-born and native-born subjects is more balanced (53.2% vs. 46.8%);
    - in both Chini's and MERIDIUM samples, informants of Albanian, Moroccan, Romanian origin prevail, but in Chini's study hispanophone informants are also numerous, which is not the case in the MERIDIUM sample (see Tab. 9-6 above); conversely, in the MERIDIUM sample there are many informants of Serbian and Macedonian origin, as well as informants originating from the Indian sub-continent, who are scarcely represented in Chini's sample.

The above mentioned factors, and their complex interactions, may certainly account to a great extent for the different trends observed in the two studies carried out among children with foreign background in Italy; further research in this field is needed, integrating quantitative and qualitative tools. On the other hand, a greater attention should be paid also to the settlement contexts and to the conditions of integration of immigrant groups in them, as suggested by Chini herself (2004: 322 ff.). In this respect, one must take into account that informants involved in Chini's research were recruited in two quite different contexts of settlement, such as a metropolitan area (Turin) and some small-sized municipalities near the provincial capital Pavia, all situated in North-Western Italy; conversely, MERIDIUM informants have been recruited in dimensionally similar settlement contexts (small- or medium-sized municipalities), scattered in four regions, in the North-West, North-East and Centre of the Peninsula.

9.3.3. The "Social Usage Index" of the Family Tradition Languages

In the relational circle external to the family, usage indexes of family tradition languages decrease dramatically, although pupils live in municipalities where they have good chances to meet people originating from the same country. One may refer to Table 9-11, where the distribution of the values of the "social usage index" of family tradition languages is shown. These values have been obtained as the arithmetic mean of usage indexes assigned to interactions with friends (UI Fr), neighbours (UI Ne) and classmates (UI Cm). The mean value of each of these indexes is shown in Tab. 9-12 and it may be usefully compared to the mean values displayed in Tab. 9-9, concerning the usage indexes with interlocutors in the home domain.

Informants referred to in this section represent a sub-set of the 162 pupils with foreign background under study in sections §§ 9.3.1. and 9.3.2. above: as 8 subjects among them did not answer questions about extra-familiar language uses, data concerning only 154 pupils will be discussed.

VALUES OF THE "FTL SOCIAL USAGE INDEX"	FOREIGN-BORN PUPILS		PUPILS BORN IN ITALY	
	N	%	N	%
ZERO (0.0)	55	*(64.7)*	44	*(63.8)*
LOW (0.1-0.3)	26	*(30.6)*	20	*(29.0)*
BALANCED (0.4-0.6)	1	*(1.2)*	4	*(5.8)*
HIGH (0.7-0.9)	3	*(3.5)*	1	*(1.4)*
FULL (1.0)	0	-	0	-
TOTAL	85	*(100.0)*	69	*(100.0)*

Tab. 9-11: Values of the "social usage index" for the family tradition languages (FTLs) spoken by pupils with foreign background: birthplace-disaggregated data

USAGE INDEXES	min.	max.	FOREIGN-BORN PUPILS N	Mean UI	PUPILS BORN IN ITALY N	Mean UI
UI Fr	.0	1.0	85	.171	69	.159
UI Ne	.0	1.0	85	.124	69	.101
UI Cm	.0	.5	85	.006	69	.029
Social UI	.0	.7	85	.100	69	.097

Tab. 9-12: Mean values of usage indexes of the family tradition languages for each interlocutor outside the family domain: birthplace-disaggregated data

Data show that, outside the family, the language shift to Italian is almost complete, both for foreign-born informants and for native-born ones. We may further observe that, notwithstanding the fact that schools under study are characterized by significant rates of pupils with foreign background sharing the same national origin, there seem to be very sporadic occasions in which informants choose their family tradition languages in order to interact with classmates, as just 5 informants out of 154 (and 10 out of the total amount of 208) do so.

9.4. Proficiency in the Family Tradition Languages

Pupils have been asked to name the languages they are able to read (comics) and write (a letter to a friend), in order to assess their proficiency in family tradition languages. The data hereby discussed (see Tab. 9-13) pertain to 154 of the 162 pupils with foreign background under study in previous sections, as 8 of them did not answer these questions.

READING AND WRITING IN FAMILY TRADITION LANGUAGES	FOREIGN-BORN PUPILS N	%	PUPILS BORN IN ITALY N	%
Neither reading, nor writing	16	*(19.5)*	32	*(44.4)*
Reading only	8	*(9.8)*	3	*(4.2)*
Writing only	5	*(6.1)*	2	*(2.8)*
Both reading and writing	53	*(64.6)*	35	*(48.6)*
TOTAL	82	*(100.0)*	72	*(100.0)*

Tab. 9-13: Reading and writing in family tradition languages as self-reported by pupils with foreign background: birthplace-disaggregated data

Reading and writing in the family tradition language are widespread among foreign-born pupils (64.6%), but not uncommon among native-born pupils, who self-report these skills in 48.6% of the cases.

It is quite evident, however, that these results cannot be taken for granted, as pupils have not been tested, but only asked for a very general self-evaluation. Nevertheless, there are two possible ways in order to verify their answers indirectly.

In the first place, one may compare data on reading and writing skills with data concerning prior schooling in, or current learning experiences of, those languages (see Tab. 9-14). As one may observe, there are 49 cases (24 foreign-born pupils and 25 native-born pupils) of informants who have neither been schooled in the family tradition language, nor are currently learning this language in extra-school time; in spite of this, they claim that they can read and write in this language (shadowed cells in Tab. 9-14).

READING AND WRITING IN FTLS	SCHOOLING IN THE COUNTRY OF ORIGIN OR ONGOING LEARNING EXPERIENCES OF FTLS					
	FOREIGN-BORN PUPILS			PUPILS BORN IN ITALY		
	NO	YES	TOT.	NO	YES	TOT.
Not able	8	8	16	24	8	32
Can write but cannot read or viceversa	6	7	13	4	1	5
Able	24	29	53	25	10	35
TOTAL	38	44	82	53	19	72

Tab. 9-14: Cross-tabulation of data concerning reading and writing in family tradition languages (FTLs) and data on previous schooling in, or ongoing learning experiences of those languages: birthplace-disaggregated data

In order to clarify if these 49 informants could have overestimated their skills regarding reading and writing, one may check their family usage indexes of family tradition languages, in the light of the hypothesis that strong conservative language uses in the family domain could have favored basic informal learning in reading and writing.

Such a test gives positive results: among the 49 subjects, 31 score high values for family usage indexes and 11 reach full values, whilst only 7 informants score low or balanced values.

9.5. Extra-school Learning Experiences of Family Tradition Languages or Other Languages Different from Italian

We will now briefly discuss some data about ongoing extra-school learning experiences of family tradition languages or other languages different from Italian.

Informants were asked if they were learning other languages, besides those at school (AQ28): Tab. 9-15 below shows the answers provided by the whole sub-sample of pupils with foreign background (208 informants):

ONGOING LEARNING EXPERIENCES OF FTLs OR OTHER LANGUAGES DIFFERENT FROM ITALIAN	FOREIGN-BORN PUPILS		PUPILS BORN IN ITALY	
	N	%	N	%
no I'm not interested	15	*12.9*	7	*(7.6)*
no but I would like to	52	*44.8*	39	*(42.4)*
yes	46	*39.7*	46	*(50.0)*
no answer	3	*2.6*	0	-
TOTAL	116	*100.0*	92	*(100.0)*

Tab. 9-15: Answers to AQ28 ("Besides the languages you are learning at school, are you learning other languages (by yourself or with the help of someone)?"): pupils with foreign background—birthplace-disaggregated data

Pupils with foreign background—mainly the native-born ones—show a remarkable interest in extra-school language learning; on the basis of this, it could be hypothesized that their families encourage them to acquire proficiency in their family tradition languages. A closer look at the data, however, leads to a different conclusion.

If we consider the languages pupils are learning, we may observe that family tradition languages are not a priority choice (see Tab. 9-16):

TARGET LANGUAGES OF ONGOING EXTRA-SCHOOL LEARNING EXPERIENCES	FOREIGN-BORN PUPILS		PUPILS BORN IN ITALY	
	N	%	N	%
No ongoing learning experiences	67	*57.8*	46	*(50.0)*
Learn TFLs only	15	*12.9*	19	*(20.7)*
Learn TFLs and other languages	2	*1.7*	2	*(2.2)*
Learn only other languages	29	*25.0*	25	*(27.2)*
Learn a not specified language	3	*2.6*	0	-
TOTAL	116	*100.0*	92	*(100.0)*

Tab. 9-16: Target languages of ongoing extra-school learning experiences: pupils with foreign background—birthplace-disaggregated data

These data suggest that, for pupils with foreign background, learning a language after school hours is not necessarily related to their own or parents' desire to preserve their supposed "ethnic identity". On the contrary, data concerning the languages being learned by these pupils suggest that there is a preference for a few "super-central languages" (de Swaan 2001), which vary according to the different countries of origin of the family: English and Hindi are preferred by informants originating from the Indian sub-continent; French is preferred by pupils and families coming from North-Africa; French and/or English by those coming from North-Western Africa; the four major European languages—but also Greek or Russian—are preferred by pupils and families coming from South-Eastern European States. Such choices—paraphrasing Tove Skutnabb-Kangas (2000) definition—seem therefore to be based mainly on "enrichment-oriented" needs.

9.6. The Attitude of School Communities towards Language Repertoires, Language Use and "Enrichment-Oriented" Needs of Pupils with Foreign Background

Data discussed above allow us to conclude that multi-/plurilingualism characterizing pupils with foreign background enrolled in schools involved in our research is an authentic and widespread phenomenon, which is vital not only among foreign-born pupils, but also among pupils born in Italy from foreign parents.

However, the bi-/plurilingual identity of these pupils—which is often cultivated as a resource by their families—does not seem to express itself outside the family circle, or outside the narrow context of (intra-ethnic) friendship relations. In particular, as shall be illustrated in the following section, it does not have any visibility or recognition in the most important place where this should happen: the school.

9.6.1. Linguistic Diversity at School: An Unexplored World

As mentioned above (§9.2.), the MERIDIUM survey has been carried out in schools and classes with high rates of pupils with foreign background (see Tab. 9-4a).

School directors have always been able to provide quantitative data concerning these pupils; in most cases, they have been able to provide detailed data concerning pupils' nationalities; however, they have claimed that they do not have any database or archive concerning languages spoken by these pupils, and teachers do not take any systematic measure in order to collect information on language biographies of pupils and their families. Only in "welcoming protocols" for newly-arrived foreign-born pupils (if ever such protocols are put into practice)[15] questions about pupil's L1 are included, in order to make the task of linguistic mediators easier; on the contrary, language repertoires and language use of native-born pupils with foreign background are generally ignored.

Correspondingly, the data collection held every year by the Ministry of Education on pupils "with non-Italian citizenship" does not include the family tradition languages of these subjects among the relevant classification parameters.

Such an approach is highly contradictory when considered in the light of the alleged openness of the Italian educational system to diversity and cultural pluralism. An educational policy inspired by intercultural principles, but failing to require that teachers know, as precisely as possible, the components of pupils' and families' language repertoire, and that they help pupils to share this information with their classmates turns to be ineffective and, moreover, implicitly delegitimizing languages other than Italian. On the other hand, such an attitude also fails to help pupils with Italian background to recognize and understand the multilingual context where they spend most of their time.

When visiting the schools involved in the survey, MERIDIUM researchers had a chance to observe a diffuse situation of "invisibilization" of languages other than Italian within school communities, in spite of the multilingual welcome posters hanging on the corridors' walls.

---

[15] This is the case, for example, of VI11 and VI12 schools; other schools were still preparing welcoming protocols at the time of the survey.

Although many teachers have claimed that, at Christmas time, pupils write greeting-cards in different languages, and their parents are asked to prepare traditional dishes or to illustrate national customs, it is safe to affirm that the use family tradition languages of pupils with foreign background is practically absent within these classes. Out of 208 pupils with foreign background who have been involved in the research, just 13 have claimed that they use their family tradition language when talking to teachers, and 10 do so with their classmates.

Forms of collaborative learning through family tradition languages have not been found in schools under study, and teachers do not encourage any activity of presentation of the "languages of the class", even if these activities could be easily carried out by taking advantage of the reading and writing skills which many pupils with foreign background possess (see § 9.4.) and by involving foreign parents as well[16].

In such a situation, the linguistic diversity characterizing school communities is perceived by most pupils with Italian background just as an individual "problem" of some of their schoolmates, who "cannot learn Italian well" because the different language they speak constitutes an obstacle for them to learn it. Their linguistic diversity is therefore seen as a hinderance towards learning the language of schooling. At best, linguistic diversity is viewed as a motive for occasional curiosity which, more often than not, teachers are not able to take as an opportunity to stimulate metalinguistic awareness and interlinguistic comparison, or to remind their pupils of the equal dignity of all languages.

9.6.1.1. A case-study

On this issue, it is useful to discuss in some detail the data collected in a school situated in Lonigo, a municipality in the Vicenza province; in this school (VI2), all of the five fifth-year classes have been surveyed, obtaining a (sub-)sample of 114 pupils (75 pupils with Italian background and 39 pupils with foreign background).

In the school year 2009-10, 596 pupils in total were enrolled in VI2, that is 58% of the children of primary-school age residing in Lonigo

---

[16] Activities such as those presented in García *et al.* (2006), or projects such as *"Multilingual education: the use of minority languages in classrooms in primary education"* (2008–2012), coordinated by P. Van Avermaet in Belgium, are still totally extraneous to educational praxis of Italian schools.
On the other hand, school directors and teachers involved in the MERIDIUM survey did not know anything about the results achieved by projects promoted by the Council of Europe, such as EVLANG, Janua Linguarum (Candelier, 2004) o LEA (Bernaus *et al.*, 2007).

municipality; among them, 184 (almost 31%) had a foreign background and represented 73% of the non-national children of primary-school age residing in the municipality.

According to the data provided by the school director, South-Eastern European nationalities (mainly Romania, Serbia, Albania) prevail among pupils with foreign background, followed by the Indian sub-continent (India, Bangladesh); African States are less represented, with the exceptions of Ghana and Morocco. (see Tab. 8-17 below):

NATIONALITY	PUPILS WITH NON-ITALIAN CITIZENSHIP IN THE SCHOOL	
	N OF PUPILS	% ON THE TOTAL OF PUPILS WITH NON-ITALIAN CITIZENSHIP
Romania	37	*20.1*
Serbia	31	*16.8*
Albania	28	*15.2*
Ghana	25	*13.6*
Bangladesh	24	*13.0*
India	14	*7.6*
Morocco	12	*6.5*
Other	13	*7.1*
TOTAL	184	*100.0*

Tab. 9-17: Nationalities of pupils with non-Italian citizenship enrolled in VI2 school in the school year 2009-2010

The family tradition languages of the 39 informants with foreign background attending fifth classes in this school substantially fit the expectations deriving from the nationalities shown in Tab. 9-17 above, except for the under-representation of Albanian (see Tab. 9-18):

FTLs	N OF PUPILS
Serbo-Croatian	13
Romanian	9
'Ghanaian'	6
Bengali	4
Arabic	4
Albanian	2
English	2
'Indian'	1
Panjabi	1
'African'	1

Tab. 9-18: Family tradition languages (FTLs) of the 39 informants with foreign background attending fifth classes in the VI2 school[17]

Both pupils with foreign and Italian background were asked to name a maximum of 10 languages other than Italian which they considered to be the most widespread among VI2 student population ("languages of the school"); in Tab. 9-19 answers are displayed separately for pupils with Italian background and pupils with foreign background, in order to better point out possible differences in perception:

"LANGUAGES OF THE SCHOOL"	PUPILS WITH ITALIAN BACKGROUND (N OF CASES: 68 OUT OF 75)[18]		PUPILS WITH FOREIGN BACKGROUND (N OF CASES: 35 OUT OF 39)	
	N OF ANSWERS	% OF CASES	N OF ANSWERS	% OF CASES
French	40	*(58.8)*	18	*(51.4)*
ROMANIAN	34	*(50.0)*	25	*(71.4)*
'SERBIAN'	30	*(44.1)*	24	*(68.6)*
English	29	*(42.6)*	9	*(25.7)*
'BANGLADESE'/BENGALI	25	*(36.8)*	15	*(42.9)*
'MOROCCAN'/ARABIC	25	*(36.8)*	12	*(34.3)*

Tab. 9-19: "Languages of the school" perceived by VI2's informants: background-disaggregated data

[17] Pupils who speak two of these languages (e. g. "Ghanaian" and English) have been counted twice (e. g. once for "Ghanaian" and once for English).

[18] As not all the informants in each group (Italian *vs.* foreign background) answered this question, the total number of pupils who have provided valid answers ("N of cases") is specified at the top of each column. Language names are those used by informants.

"LANGUAGES OF THE SCHOOL"	PUPILS WITH ITALIAN BACKGROUND (N OF CASES: 68 OUT OF 75)		PUPILS WITH FOREIGN BACKGROUND (N OF CASES: 35 OUT OF 39)	
	N OF ANSWERS	% OF CASES	N OF ANSWERS	% OF CASES
'INDIAN'	20	*(29.4)*	16	*(45.7)*
'GHANAIAN'	17	*(25.0)*	16	*(45.7)*
Chinese	14	*(20.6)*	8	*(22.9)*
ALBANIAN	8	*(11.8)*	11	*(31.4)*
'African'	6	*(8.8)*	3	*(8.6)*
Other languages	8	*(<5.0)*	7	*(<6.0)*
TOTAL	256	*376.5*	164	*468.6*

Tab. 9-19 (cont.): "Languages of the school" perceived by VI2's informants: background-disaggregated data

Notwithstanding the inexplicable presence of Chinese (no pupils from China or with Chinese background are enrolled in VI2 school) and an overrating of French and English (probably due to the large use of these two languages as "vehicular codes" in the interaction between school personnel and newly-arrived children), we may say that the expectedly most prominent components of the language repertoire of the VI2 school community (language names in small caps in Tab. 9-19; see also Tab. 9-17)[19] are rather well perceived by both informants' groups.

However, two relevant differences among them must be noted. We may observe, in the first place, that, on average, pupils with foreign background are able to name more languages than pupils with Italian background (4.7 the former, 3.5 the latter). Secondly, the percentage of pupils with foreign background mentioning the most widespread languages of origin among the school population is remarkably higher than the one of pupils with Italian background. These differences suggest that pupils with Italian background are relatively less aware than pupils with foreign background of the remarkable diffusion of languages other than Italian (and English) among the student population in the school they attend.

[19] As a matter of fact, we may only guess—though with acceptable approximation—which these languages are, on the basis of nationality data provided by the school director (Tab. 9-17). The fact remains, however, that—for example—some Romanian VI2 pupils among those not involved in the survey may speak Romani, and not Romanian, as their family tradition language.

Such a different awareness is revealed, on the other hand, also by answers given by the informants to the question (AQ27) "Which languages are spoken throughout the world? Please, write the names of some of them (15 max.)" (see Tab. 9-20 below):

"WHICH LANGUAGES ARE SPOKEN THROUGHOUT THE WORLD?"	PUPILS WITH ITALIAN BACKGROUND (N OF CASES: 75 OUT OF 75)		PUPILS WITH FOREIGN BACKGROUND (N OF CASES: 38 OUT OF 39)	
	N OF ANSWERS	% OF CASES	N OF ANSWERS	% OF CASES
French	65	*(86.7)*	32	*(84.2)*
English	60	*(80.0)*	31	*(81.6)*
German	58	*(77.3)*	27	*(71.1)*
Spanish	51	*(68.0)*	26	*(68.4)*
Italian	43	*(57.3)*	18	*(47.4)*
Chinese	40	*(53.3)*	22	*(57.9)*
ARABIC/'MOROCCAN'	38	*(50.7)*	19	*(50.0)*
'SERBIAN'	25	*(33.3)*	21	*(55.3)*
Russian	24	*(32.0)*	9	*(23.7)*
Japanese	23	*(30.7)*	9	*(23.7)*
ROMANIAN	23	*(30.7)*	25	*(65.8)*
'INDIAN'	21	*(28.0)*	18	*(47.4)*
BENGALI/'BANGLADESE'	20	*(26.7)*	8	*(21.1)*
American	18	*(24.0)*	8	*(21.1)*
Greek	18	*(24.0)*	7	*(18.4)*
'African'	17	*(22.7)*	8	*(21.1)*
'GHANAIAN'	13	*(17.3)*	12	*(31.6)*
ALBANIAN	12	*(16.0)*	15	*(39.5)*
Other languages	129	*(≤16.0)*	47	*(≤16.0)*
TOTAL	698	*930.7*	362	*952.6*

Tab. 9-20: "Languages of the world" mentioned by VI2's informants: background-disaggregated data

The data in Tab. 9-20 clearly show that the languages which have been mentioned most frequently are the same for both groups of informants; furthermore, pupils with Italian background mentioned as many languages as their schoolmates with foreign background (on average, 9 items per informant in each group). It must be pointed out, however, that the "languages of the school" (in small caps) are named by a percentage of pupils with Italian background which is generally much lower than the corresponding percentage of the pupils with foreign background: this is the case for Romanian, 'Serbian', Albanian, 'Ghanaian' and 'Indian'. [20]

Such data seem to suggest that the two sub-groups of informants have enumerated world's languages following partially different criteria: pupils with Italian background have clearly privileged renowned international languages, while pupils with foreign background have taken into account also languages that, despite not having major importance as international languages, are nonetheless widely spoken within the school context that they come in contact with daily. One must not think that this is only due to the fact that they are themselves speakers of such languages: as a comparison between Tab. 9-20 and Tab. 9-18 may demonstrate, a language such as Romanian has been named by 25 pupils with foreign background, even if it is the family tradition language of only 9 informants.

9.6.2. The Maintenance of Family Tradition Languages as an Obstacle to Integration?

During the meetings with MERIDIUM researchers, teachers have often expressed the concern that pupils who use exclusively, or very frequently, their family tradition language with their parents not only may incur greater difficulties in order to learn Italian, but could also show—through their language use—an unconscious or parent-induced refusal to integrate themselves into the local community. For these reasons, many teachers have declared that they advise foreign parents not to use their family tradition language with their children.

---

[20] The fact that Arabic is mentioned—together with Chinese—by half of the respondents, both among pupils with Italian background and among pupils with foreign background, could probably be due to the fact that these two languages are clearly perceived by children as "prototypical" extra-European languages, also thanks to their peculiar writing systems. Moreover, it must be taken into account that, at the time of the survey, Chinese and North-African immigrant communities were targets of a bitter political campaign fostered by the Northern League ("Lega Nord"), a xenophobic party participating in the national right-wing coalition government (2008-2011), and governing Veneto region (from 2010). Among other issues, Northern League politicians have repeatedly questioned the use of Chinese and Arabic languages in notices, shop signs and advertisements: as an example, see two newspaper articles issued in 2010 (accessed September 26, 2012):
http://www.repubblica.it/cronaca/2010/04/24/news/negozi_cinese_e_arabo_cancellati_dalle_insegne-3578051/;
http://tg24.sky.it/tg24/cronaca/2010/11/24/via_padova_milano_natale_insegne_lingue_straniere_arabo_cinese_italiano.html.

The discussion of the psycho-affective damages on a child whose parents would follow such advice is beyond the scope of this paper, and this issue will not be dealt with here[21], nor will scientific evidence supporting the "interdependence hypothesis" (Cummins 2000) be elaborated upon. Suffice it to say, in this respect, that most of the teachers and school directors involved in the MERIDIUM research did not possess any basic notion about bilingual development in migration contexts.

In this section, evidence concerning the alleged link between the domestic use of family tradition languages and the (lack of) willingness to integrate will be discussed.

In the first place, it must be observed that the fact that a child uses only the family tradition language when talking to parents does not entail that s/he lives in a domestic environment where the use of Italian is totally absent; in fact, the data discussed in § 9.3.1. show that, irrespective of which language is used when talking to adult relatives, most pupils with foreign background tend to use Italian with siblings: among the 162 informants for whom family usage indexes have been calculated, 111 subjects (68.5%) use Italian monolingually (61 respondents), or in alternation with the family tradition language (50 respondents), when talking to siblings.

In the second place, a regular use of family tradition languages at home does not necessarily correspond to a situation of ethnic auto-segregation: in discussing the "social usage index" of the family tradition languages (see § 9.3.3.), Italian has clearly emerged—with very few exceptions—as the sole language of interaction outside the family domain (friends and neighbours), also for pupils who have claimed to use exclusively their family tradition languages at home.

Finally, there is some direct evidence that most pupils and parents with foreign background involved in the MERIDIUM research feel well integrated into the local community, as shown by answers to the question (AQ14 – BQ17) "How much do you feel part of the town where you live?": 79.3% of pupils (165 out of 208) and 80.6% of parents (137 out of 170)[22] gave positive answers ("just enough/very much").

In order to test more specifically the hypothesis that the degree of integration into the local community is in inverse relation with the use of family tradition languages in children/parents interactions, these data can be cross-tabulated with those concerning language use as self-reported by

[21] See the discussion of some clinical cases in Contento (2010).

[22] The total number of foreign-born parents is less than the number of children with foreign background since not all parents have filled in their questionnaire.

the 124 pupils and their parents referred to in § 9.3.2.1. The results are shown in Tabs. 9-21a e 9-21b:

PUPILS WHO:		FEEL PART OF THE TOWN WHERE THEY LIVE			
		not at all/ a little bit	just enough/ very much	do not know	Tot.
use only Italian with parents	N	3	7	0	10
	%	*(30.0)*	*(70.0)*	-	*(100.0)*
alternate Italian and FTL with parents	N	1	33	4	38
	%	*(2.6)*	*(86.8)*	*(10.5)*	*(100.0)*
use only FTL with parents	N	9	62	5	76
	%	*(11.8)*	*(81.6)*	*(6.6)*	*(100.0)*
TOTAL	**N**	13	102	9	124
	%	*10.5*	*82.3*	*7.3*	*100.0*

Tab. 9-21a: Degree of integration into the local community and use of family tradition languages (FTLs) in children/parents interactions: cross-tabulation of answers provided by pupils with foreign background

PARENTS WHO:		FEEL PART OF THE TOWN WHERE THEY LIVE			
		not at all/ a little bit	just enough/ very much	do not know	Tot.
use only Italian with pupils	N	0	19	1	20
	%	-	*(95.0)*	*(5.0)*	*(100.0)*
alternate Italian and FTL with pupils	N	8	41	5	54
	%	*(14.8)*	*(75.9)*	*(9.3)*	*(100.0)*
use only FTL with pupils	N	7	39	4	50
	%	*(14.0)*	*(78.0)*	*(8.0)*	*(100.0)*
TOTAL	**N**	15	99	10	124
	%	*12.1*	*79.8*	*8.1*	*100.0*

Tab. 9-21b: Degree of integration into the local community and use of family tradition languages (FTLs) in children/parents interactions: cross-tabulation of answers provided by foreign parents

If the hypothesis were true, the cells corresponding to informants who feel well integrated into the local community and use only FTL in pupil/parent interactions (see shadowed cells in Tabs. 9-21a and 9-21b) should be void or should collect, at least, a scant number of cases; on the contrary, in both the tables above these cells collect the great majority of cases in the row representing informants using only FTLs in pupil/parent interactions.

9.6.3. Meeting the "Enrichment-oriented" Language Needs of Pupils and Families

In the Italian schools involved in the MERIDIUM research, teachers are generally not aware of language learning activities that pupils may carry out after school hours; some of them have occasionally observed that pupils of Indian or African origin speak fluently in English, or have reported rather vaguely that some pupils with foreign background attend courses, usually run by migrants' associations, in order to learn their "languages of origin". On the other hand, school directors do not collect any information about language courses attended by pupils after school hours, be they of Italian or of foreign origin.

As shown by data discussed in §9.5., 44.2% of pupils with foreign background involved in the MERIDIUM survey claim to be learning a language which is different from Italian (92 informants out of 208). It must be pointed out that, among these informants, informal learning activities prevail: in most cases, additional languages are learned with the help of parents, siblings, relatives or friends, or in an autonomous way, by means of learning tools such as books, grammars, dictionaries, DVDs and CDRoms. The fact remains, however, that families of foreign origin seem to be inclined to invest substantially on additional linguistic competences for their children: 23 pupils attend structured language courses and 36 pupils are taught by their own parents.

It is worth noting that family tradition languages do not seem to represent a privileged target in this respect. Besides the data concerning pupils discussed in § 9.4. (Tab. 9-16), an interesting clue of this tendency comes from answers given by foreign-born parents to the question (BQ34), when asked if they were favourable or not to the possibility that pupils with foreign background could be taught their family tradition languages in Italian schools (see Tab. 9-22):

TEACHING OF FTLS AT SCHOOL	FOREIGN-BORN PARENTS OF:				TOTAL	
	FOREIGN-BORN CHILDREN		CHILDREN BORN IN ITALY			
	N	%	N	%	N	%
Unfavourable	38	*(41.3)*	22	*(28.2)*	60	*35.3*
Favourable	20	*(21.7)*	37	*(47.4)*	57	*33.5*
Do not know	29	*(31.5)*	18	*(23.1)*	47	*27.6*
Do not answer	5	*(5.4)*	1	*(1.3)*	6	*3.5*
TOTAL	**92**	***(100.0)***	**78**	***(100.0)***	**170**	***100.0***

Tab. 9-22: Answers provided by foreign-born parents to the question BQ34 ("Do you think that children of immigrants should be given the opportunity to learn their own language/s in Italian schools?"): child's birthplace-disaggregated data

Considering the whole sample, no unequivocal tendency emerges (see percentages in "Total" column in Tab. 9-22); however, results look quite different if one considers separately the answers provided by parents of children born abroad and those provided by parents of children born in Italy: most informants in the former group declare themselves unfavourable or uncertain, whilst almost a half of the latter group declares itself favourable.

The qualitative and quantitative limitations of the MERIDIUM research induce prudence in interpreting these data; nonetheless, it can be said that foreign-born parents involved in the survey are generally uncertain and confused about advantages and disadvantages related to the maintenance of family tradition languages by their children. Probably, they are worried that studying the family tradition language may interfere negatively on the learning of Italian, or may determine too heavy a workload, especially if the child is born abroad, and therefore is still learning the language of schooling.. This interpretation of the data seems to be corroborated by the fact that foreign-born parents of pupils born in Italy are more favourable to the teaching of family tradition languages at school.[23]

Though any hypothesis needs to be further investigated by means of more suitable research tools, such as interviews, it is worth noting that the observed uncertainty can be only worsened by the above-mentioned

---

[23] One should also take into account that foreign parents are often aware that the language varieties they speak may be quite different from the respective standard varieties, and, therefore, they do believe that even studying the standard varieties may pose problems for their children. For a case-study, see Carpani (2010).

tendency of teachers to "invisibilize" and delegitimize family tradition languages of pupils with foreign background. In such a situation, foreign-born parents are not helped to form a well-grounded and unbiased opinion on the advantages which their children may have through the maintenance of these languages.[24]

On the other hand, the data concerning extra-curricular learning of "additional languages" (i.e. different from Italian and family tradition languages) show that foreign families have a remarkable interest towards the possibility that their children become proficient in international languages of wider communication.

In Tab. 9-23 the additional languages that pupils with foreign background have more frequently claimed to be learning are displayed; for comparative purposes, in the same table the data pertaining to pupils with Italian background who have claimed to be learning a foreign language after school hours are also provided (118 pupils out of 451, 26.2%):

LANGUAGE	PUPILS LEARNING IT AS AN ADDITIONAL LANGUAGE:			
	WITH FOREIGN BACKGROUND (N OF CASES: 58 OUT OF 208)		WITH ITALIAN BACKGROUND (N OF CASES: 118 OUT OF 451)	
	N OF ANSWERS	% OF CASES	N OF ANSWERS	% OF CASES
French	22	*(31.0)*	40	*33.9*
Spanish	13	*(18.3)*	44	*37.3*
English	10	*(14.1)*	11	*9.3*
German	6	*(8.5)*	15	*12.7*
Other	20	*(≤6.9)*	33	*≤3.5*
TOTAL	71	*(122.4)*	143	*121.2*

Tab. 9-23: Main additional languages being learned in extra-school time by pupils with foreign background and by pupils with Italian background

[24] Analogous considerations may also apply to Italian parents, who should be helped by teachers to recognize multilingualism in their children's classroom as an asset, rather than perceiving it as a hindrance. In the absence of such an explicit positive stance from the part of the school, most Italian parents will still be wary of so-called "immigrant languages". As a matter of fact, 253 Italian parents out of 412 involved in the MERIDIUM survey (61.4%) have declared themselves as unfavourable to the teaching of family tradition languages to pupils with foreign background at school; 26.5% did not answer the question or declared themselves uncertain, while only 12.1% have expressed a favourable position.

It can be observed that French and Spanish arouse remarkable interest among both pupils' categories, as together they represent half or more of the cases in each group. These languages are perceived as important international languages, not only because they are official languages of the European Union, but also because they are official languages—or, in any case, are widely spoken as second languages—in many African or American countries.

This example can be useful to draw attention to the fact that, by means of a simple survey such as the one just mentioned, school directors could identify a small group of international languages which are of interest for pupils and families both of Italian and foreign origin: on this basis, each school could put in place experimental teaching activities or laboratories, which would meet "enrichment-oriented" language needs of all pupils, stimulating interlinguistic comparison and introducing gradually the study of a second European foreign language, which, in Italy, is compulsory from the first year of the lower secondary school (ISCED 2).

9.7. Multilingualism as a Collective Resource: Some Proposals from the MERIDIUM Project

The MERIDIUM sociolinguistic research had a mainly "explorative" and, therefore, non-generalizable character; nonetheless, the data discussed so far raise some interesting issues concerning the need of a radical rethinking of language education in the Italian educational system. The direction of such a reassessment is clearly indicated by the Council of Europe and the European Commission policy documents, where plurilingual and intercultural education is promoted.

The MERIDIUM survey in Italy has been carried out in small-medium size towns, where families of foreign origin involved in the research have been living for a few years. Data show that they have positively integrated into the social and educational local fabric; throughout the years local institutions have adopted substantial measures to support these families, notwithstanding the financial cuts in public funding.

The domestic use of family tradition languages turned out to be very vital among pupils with foreign background and their families, both in the monolingual mode, and in the bilingual mode, alternating with Italian. This does not imply, however, that these informants tend to maintain their "ethnic identity" by excluding other possible cultural influences: on the contrary, foreign-born parents declare themselves particularly satisfied with intercultural programs that their children take part in at school.

In the municipalities involved in the MERIDIUM survey, schools seems to represent the most relevant institutional agent which favors integration between "Italian citizens" and "foreign citizens": for example, schools offer Italian L2 classes both for children and adults, and carry out intercultural activities involving pupils' parents on a regular basis.

Such a commitment, however, is still based on a vision which tends to exclude the use of languages which are different from Italian and English, and pays little attention to developing language awareness in pupils. This is a noteworthy weakness, in the face of a multi- and plurilingual scenario such as the one shown by the data concerning primary-school population in Italy.

There are many and understandable reasons justifying this state of affairs: as many teachers pointed out, it is difficult to introduce any change, when school programs are already overloaded; many pupils—mainly the "newly-arrived" ones—still need to be taught basic Italian; in-service teachers do not have the time and the resources to attend training courses. However, what seems to be lacking, from the part of educational authorities, as well as among school personnel, is mainly the awareness of the benefits which would derive to all pupils by adopting a plurilingual perspective on education[25].

From such an attitude, two main consequences arise:

- In the first place, teachers are inclined to ignore or underestimate the complexity of the linguistic repertoire of pupils with foreign background, with possible negative effects on methods adopted in order to teach these pupils and assess their learning outcomes[26]. At a more general level, negative effects may also occur on the perceptions and attitudes that pupils with Italian background develop towards plurilingualism and linguistic diversity.
- In the second place, teachers may often—though involuntarily—worsen the linguistic insecurity of parents, inducing them to adopt a language use ("Italian only") with their children which is unnatural

[25] Only very recently (November 2011), the Ministry of Education has launched the project "Languages of schooling and plurilingual and intercultural curriculum" (LSCPI—*Lingue di scolarizzazione e curricolo plurilingue e interculturale:* see http://www.istruzione.it/web/istruzione/lscpi, accessed September 26, 2012) on a national scale, in order to promote the implementation of integrated methods to teach the languages of schooling in primary schools, following guidelines inspired by the Council of Europe *Platform for plurilingual and intercultural education* (see:
http://www.coe.int/t/dg4/linguistic/LangEduc/LE_PlatformIntro_en.asp, accessed September 26, 2012).

[26] On this issue, see Green (2000), Ghezzi and Grassi (2002), Cummins (2006), Contento (2010), Lüdi (2011).

> and useless—if not counterproductive—to the end of a well-balanced identity construction of the child.
> Once again, such a behavior may also be detrimental for intercultural relations and social cohesion within and outside the school-community, as it contributes to entrench the idea that languages (and, therefore, cultures) other than Italian have no recognition in the social and institutional context.

The seminars organized within the MERIDIUM project in order to disseminate the results of the sociolinguistic research provided a good occasion to discuss these problems directly with school directors and teachers. During these meetings, some major steps have been identified, as possible starting points in order to favor a gradual change of perspective.

First, teachers should gather detailed information on the linguistic repertoire of pupils and families, actively involving all the children and their parents in this task: this measure would not only allow to constitute a sort of "database" of the linguistic resources available within the school, but would also promote awareness, mutual exchange and understanding among the members of this "community of practice". To this end, an *ad hoc* modified version of MERIDIUM questionnaires could represent a useful ready-to-use tool, very similar to the one put forward in the Council of Europe *Guide for the development and implementation of curricula for plurilingual and intercultural education* (Beacco *et al.*, 2010, Appendix II) and "intended to pave the way for realistic curriculum choices" (p. 27).

Secondly, the need to discuss explicitly issues related to language diversity and plurilingualism with all the pupils has been noted by a large number of participants in the seminars. In this respect, it is worth mentioning that, in the classes involved in the MERIDIUM research, it has been found that the use of a language which is different from Italian in the family domain characterizes not only a large number of pupils with foreign background (even born in Italy), but also pupils with Italian background, whose language repertoires often include a rich variety of regional languages and Italian dialects.

On request of some school directors, and under the auspices of the Office of Schooling of the Umbria region (Ufficio Scolastico Regionale dell'Umbria), the members of the MERIDIUM research unit of the University for Foreigners of Perugia have held a 20-hours training course for primary and lower-secondary school teachers. Assuming, as a starting point, the informative materials and the teaching tools designed by the

MERIDIUM staff[27], researchers and teachers have collaborated in order to plan some teaching modules concerning plurilingualism and linguistic diversity. These modules have been subsequently tested in 12 classes of 7 primary and lower-secondary schools during the school year 2011-2012. In Tab. 9-24 below a summary of themes, goals and activities planned within the three modules, tested by all the participants of the training course, is provided:

THEMES	GOALS	ACTIVITIES
Getting to know the "languages of the school" and the "languages of the local community"	• To arouse pupils' curiosity towards the language diversity characterizing their everyday-life context • To provide teachers with basic references to web resources and books concerning the languages of the world	Interviewing school-friends; observation and documentation of the "linguistic landscape" of the town where pupils live; collection of multilingual texts
Plurilingualism in pupils' and families' histories	• To help pupils' reflect upon the complexity of individual and family linguistic repertoires; • To attract pupils' attention towards the "multifunctionality" of the linguistic resources available to every speaker; • To help pupils consider (internal or international) migration as an occasion of enrichment of the individual and collective linguistic repertoire.	Interviews with parents and relatives; "linguistic biographies" of family members; linguistic-genealogical trees; role-playing

Tab. 9-24: MERIDIUM teaching modules tested in 7 primary and lower-secondary schools (school year 2011-2012) under the supervision of the research unit of the University for Foreigners of Perugia

[27] See, especially, the multilingual brochure *Babel and languages*, Appendix C (this volume).

THEMES	GOALS	ACTIVITIES
How languages are learned	• To draw pupils' attention towards language learning strategies; • To stimulate reflection upon similarities and differences between different languages	Role-playing; "comprehension team contests" (by means of videos or cartoons in all the languages of the school); translation exercises on simple sentences

Tab. 9-24 (cont.): MERIDIUM teaching modules tested in 7 primary and lower-secondary schools (school year 2011-2012) under the supervision of the research unit of the University for Foreigners of Perugia

While a detailed report of this experience is still in preparation (Scaglione and Tusini, forthcoming), it is safe to say that this initiative has been warmly welcomed both by teachers, by pupils and by their families. The extracts quoted below are drawn from the "MERIDIUM register" of a fifth grade teacher after the end of the project:

> Children have spontaneously inferred that bilingualism is an asset. At this age, they are perfectly capable of understand its importance, and they feel admiration for a class-friend who can speak, read and write in two languages. They also became aware of the fact that knowing a language means much more than simply attending curricular classes of a foreign or second language. […]
> Conclusions which pupils have come to at the end of the project reveal a deep enrichment not so much on the cognitive side, as on the emotional side, especially for children who can speak two languages and who sometimes, in their school career, experience difficulties. Becoming aware of their ability to do something that others are not able to do, such as speaking two languages, has increased their self-confidence. On the other hand, this project has provided children born in Italy from foreign-born parents the occasion to better appreciate the value of the different cultures with which they are in contact.[28]

The class where this teacher works is composed of 19 pupils: 10 of them (8 born abroad and 2 born in Italy) have foreign-born parents, representing 7 different nationalities, while 9 pupils were born in Italy

[28] The author of the report is Monica Ercolanoni, a teacher currently serving at Primary School "E. Pestalozzi" (Perugia). The extracts have been translated from Italian by the author of this contribution.

from Italian parents. Below, some of their remarks about the project are quoted:

> Thanks to this project, I understood the meaning of "bilingual". "Bilingual" means that a child can speak more than one language, and I am one of them, as I can speak two languages: Italian and Romanian.
> (Iulian, born in Romania of Romanian parents, arrived in Italy in 2004)
>
> This project has allowed me to discover that, in the school I attend, bilingual children are more numerous than children who speak just one language.
> (Filippo, born in Italy of Italian parents)
>
> I have found out that I love my mother-tongue. For me, my mother-tongues are two: Italian and Albanian. I have understood that knowing two languages is very useful. I enjoyed this project very much.
> (Giorgia, born in Italy of Albanian parents)
> Thanks to this project, I have discovered languages I did not know and I found out that all languages are valuable.
> (Leonardo, born in Italy of Italian parents)

This example of collaboration between teachers and researchers represents a tentative answer to a third issue which has emerged from the discussion with educational officials: the need that—possibly under the supervision of the Ministry of Education—schools and universities interact in a more systematic way, exchanging data and testing new strategies to promote positive attitudes towards plurilingualism and linguistic diversity.

References

Beacco J.-C., *et al*. 2010. *Guide for the development and implementation of curricula for plurilingual and intercultural Education.* Strasbourg: Language Policy Division, Council of Europe (available at www.coe.int/lang, accessed September 26, 2012).

Bernaus M., *et al*., eds. 2007. *Plurilingual and pluricultural awareness in language teacher education: a training kit*. Strasbourg: Council of Europe (available at: http://archive.ecml.at/mtp2/publications/B2_LEA_E_internet.pdf, accessed September 26, 2012).

Candelier M., ed. 2004. *Janua Linguarum - The gateway to languages. The introduction of language awareness into the curriculum: awakening to languages*. Strasbourg: Council of Europe (available at http://archive.ecml.at/documents/pub121E2004Candelier.pdf, accessed September 26, 2012).

Carpani D. 2010. Nuovi cittadini, nuove prospettive della scuola interculturale: le ricerche sul campo a Genova. In *Lingua, identità e immigrazione. Prospettive interdisciplinari*, ed. M. V. Calvi, G. Mapelli, M. Bonomi, 119-131. Milano: FrancoAngeli.

Chini M., ed. 2004. *Plurilinguismo e immigrazione in Italia. Un'indagine sociolinguistica a Pavia e Torino*. Milano: FrancoAngeli

Contento S., ed. 2010. *Crescere nel bilinguismo. Aspetti cognitivi, linguistici ed emotivi*. Roma: Carocci.

Cummins, J. 2000. *Language, Power and Pedagogy. Bilingual children in the Crossfire*. Clevedon, Buffalo, Toronto: Multilingual Matters.

De Swaan A. 2001. *Words of the World. The Global Language System*. Cambridge (U.K.): Polity Press.

García O., T. Skutnabb-Kangas, M. E. Torres-Guzmán, eds. 2006. *Imagining Multilingual Schools. Language in Education and Glocalization*. Clevedon, Buffalo, Toronto: Multilingual Matters.

Ghezzi C., and R. Grassi. 2002. Interazione e plurilinguismo in classe. In *Comunicare nella torre di Babele. Repertori plurilingui in Italia oggi*, ed. S. Dal Negro and P. Molinelli, 95-122. Roma: Carocci..

Giovannini G., ed. 1998. *Allievi in classe stranieri in città. Una ricerca sugli insegnanti di scuola elementare di fronte all'immigrazion*e. Milano: FrancoAngeli.

Green P., ed. 2000. *Alunni immigrati nelle scuole europee. Dall'accoglienza al successo scolastico*. Trento: Edizioni Centro Studi Erickson.

Leclerc J. 2012. *L'aménagement linguistique dans le monde – Europe – Kosovo*. Last modified September 1, 2012.
http://www.tlfq.ulaval.ca/AXL/europe/Kosovo.htm.

Lüdi, G. 2011. Quale integrazione per i parlanti delle lingue di immigrazione? In *Lingue e diritti umani*, eds. S. Giannini and S. Scaglione, 81-113. Roma: Carocci.

MIUR. 2009a. *Alunni con cittadinanza non italiana. Scuole statali e non statali. Anno scolastico 2007/2008*. Roma: Ministero dell'Istruzione, dell'Università e della Ricerca, Direzione Generale per gli Studi, la Statistica e per i Sistemi Informativi (available at:
http://www.istruzione.it/web/istruzione/intercultura-pubblicazioni, accessed September 26, 2012).

—. 2009b. *Gli alunni stranieri nel sistema scolastico italiano. A.s. 2008/09*. Roma: Ministero dell'Istruzione, dell'Università e della Ricerca, Direzione Generale per gli Studi, la Statistica e per i Sistemi Informativi (available at:

http://www.istruzione.it/web/istruzione/intercultura-pubblicazioni, accessed September 26, 2012).

—. 2010. *Gli alunni stranieri nel sistema scolastico italiano. A.s. 2009/10.* Roma: Ministero dell'Istruzione, dell'Università e della Ricerca, Direzione Generale per gli Studi, la Statistica e per i Sistemi Informativi (available at: http://www.istruzione.it/web/istruzione/intercultura-pubblicazioni, accessed September 26, 2012).

MIUR-ISMU. 2011. *Alunni con cittadinanza non italiana. Verso l'adolescenza. Rapporto nazionale a.s. 2010/2011*. Milano: Fondazione ISMU (available at: http://www.ismu.org/file-download.php?id=5537, accessed September 26, 2012).

OECD. 2010. *PISA 2009 Results: Overcoming Social Background - Equity in Learning Opportunities and Outcomes* (Vol. II) (available at: http://dx.doi.org/10.1787/9789264091504-en, accessed September 26, 2012).

Scaglione S., and S. Tusini, eds. Forthcoming. *Promuovere il plurilinguismo nella scuola italiana. Il progetto MERIDIUM per la scuola primaria.*

Skutnabb-Kangas T. 2000. *Linguistic genocide in education—or worldwide diversity and human rights?* Mahwah, London: Lawrence Erlbaum Associates.

Toso F. 2006. *Lingue d'Europa*. Milano: Baldini Castoldi Dalai.

Vertovec S. 2007. Super-diversity and its Implications. *Ethnic and Racial Studies* 30/6. 1024-1054.

Yağmur K., and G. Extra, eds. 2004. *Urban Multilingualism in Europe. Immigrant Minority Languages at Home and at School*. Clevedon, Buffalo, Toronto: Multilingual Matters.

Chapter Ten

Migration and Multilingualism in Social and Educational Contexts in Spain

Vicente González Martín,
Manuel Heras García,
Paulino Matas Gil
and María Mar Soliño Pazó

The participation of our team from Universidad de Salamanca in the MERIDIUM Project is rooted in a protracted concern about the different topics regarding migration and multilingualism in Europe.

As contemporary literature scholars, we are particularly interested in exploring the impact of new literary, cultural and linguistic traditions on Spanish culture: at the University of Salamanca migrant literature is currently receiving great attention, as one of the most promising research areas within the field of literary studies. Consequently, taking part in the MERIDIUM project has given us the opportunity to consider migration and linguistic integration from a broader perspective, involving both educational and social dimensions.

10.1. Migration in the Past

The Spanish perspective about immigration has changed throughout history. We mainly perceive it today as a massive phenomenon, motivated by economic reasons, as it involves individuals in search of better prospects. This is quite a recent phenomenon in Spain, despite the fact that in the last years the country has received almost five million legal and illegal immigrants, whose level of integration and participation in the different collective projects in Spain is quite controversial, if not widely contested by many sectors.

Traditionally, Spain has been an emigration country. The migratory flows from Spain after 1492 have been mostly to America and, since the Civil War, towards the most industrialized and rich countries in West Europe: France, Germany and Switzerland. Migrants were at first political exiles; later, they travelled as labour force. In contrast, during the 16th and 17th centuries, when the Spanish presence in Italy was intense, the interchange of scholars, soldiers, courtiers between both countries was abundant.

Political emigration during the 1936-1939 Civil War involved approximately 600,000 Spaniards. As Franco's troops were approaching the north of Spain and conquering Santander, Gijon, San Sebastian or Bilbao, between August 1936 and October 1937, the first massive evacuations of civil population and soldiers took place towards France. The first move involved about 150,000 Spaniards, with a second move in February 1938 and a final one between January and April 1939. The main destinations were France and Latin America, although many headed towards the USSR, including children. Some were deported to Germany, and the rest spread to Belgium, Netherlands and Great Britain. Many of these exiled started to acknowledge that their absence would last many years; they acquired a perspective which would enable them to overcome the disasters of the Civil War. Many understood diversity as the grounds for material and intellectual wealth.

In the 1950s people moved to Europe to work, in a historical period when the Franco regime accepted a gradual political opening. Then, thousands of people from central and southern Spain moved to Germany, France or Switzerland with the intention of returning as soon as they could. They often did not succeed.

The historical immigration to Spain was usually made up by courtiers, some teachers and writers, in the years of the Spanish Empire. During the 20th century it involved writers and artists from Latin America, such as Rubén Darío, Mario Vargas Llosa or Raul Rivero. Others came from Portugal, like José Saramago, apart from the very frequent interchange of population between Spain and Portugal along the bordering areas, known as *la raya*, or "the line".

10.2. Migration Today

This historical concept of Spanish migration radically changed towards the year 2000: Spain was no longer a country from which masses emigrated and it transformed into a country which received an intense flow of immigration. This significant increase in the number of foreigners is outstanding: in the 2007 census, 9.7% of the residents were foreigners; in 2011, this figure increased to 14.1% out of a total population of 47.1 million. Immigrants have often settled in those areas in Spain were economy is more dynamic, especially in the sectors of housing, agriculture and tourism. Therefore, they are concentrated in Madrid, Catalonia, Valencia Region, Balearic Islands and Canary Islands. [1]

It should also be said that there is a relatively important number of foreign residents in areas of the Mediterranean coast and on the islands. These cannot be considered "economic" immigrants, i.e. individuals searching for better jobs and economic security as many of them are pensioners from Great Britain, Germany, Italy or Switzerland; they have a high purchasing power and seek the benign weather, good prices and effective and cheap health services.

The following are the main characteristics of the most important foreign nationals' groups.

As far as their origin is concerned, the 2011 census shows that in Spain there are 809,409 Romanians; 766,187 Moroccans; 478,894 from Ecuador; 392,577 Britons and 372,541 Colombians. Globally speaking, the highest rate of foreign nationals - 36.2% - comes from Latin America, 34.5% from the European Union, 14.8% from North Africa; 4.4% from Sub-Saharan countries; 2.7% from the Far East; 1.7% from the Indian Sub-continent; 0.7% from North America, and 0.5% from the Philippines. Only 0.5% hail from the rest of Asia and from Oceania and only 0.02% of these foreign nationals are stateless. They are mostly men, except those who come from Latin America, where women constitute 54% of the total.

Historical and cultural factors explain the origin of most immigrants and their adaptation in Spain: Latin American is clearly the most numerous, with 1,500,785 individuals, mostly from Ecuador, Colombia, Argentina, Bolivia, Peru and Brazil. The growth of the arrivals from this area started in 1998, at a rate of increase of 61% every year compared to previous figures. This led to an increase which can be quantified at 663% from 2000 until 2010. Since then, the flow decreased due to the recent deep economic crisis affecting Spain and other European nations. (Aubarrell, 2003; Consejo Económico y Social, 2004; Tornos, 2004)

The reasons for this outstanding growth of immigration from Latin America are due to different economic contexts found in each country.

---

[1] See the data of the Spanish National Institute of Statistics since 1996 (*Instituto Nacional de Estadística*, www.ine.es).

The main reason which causes a movement of population abroad is the lack of economic prospects. Political repression is also cited as one of the main reasons. It is relevant to consider too that the political situation in Spain has changed in the last twenty years, the Spanish economy has grown since the mid- Nineties and there are more permissive migratory policies and regularization processes, including the opening of the borders under the slogan *papeles para todos* ("papers for all"). Above all, there is a certain openness of the Spanish population towards the Latin American population, because of the historical, cultural and religious links with them, and especially because we share the same language. Finally, there is a decisive factor which encourages these immigrants to settle in Spain: the policies of family regrouping which have been promoted by different Spanish governments. Within this context it is relatively easy for a family to settle in Spain for a period of time or even for life, if adequate employment is found (Díaz Nicolás, 2005; Trinidad García, 2002).

An outstanding phenomenon, corroborated by the findings of our research within the MERIDIUM project, is represented by the fact that Latin American immigrants integrate very easily with the Spanish population. This is one of the reasons which explain why there is a high number of Latin American immigrants who do not regularize their position. At the beginning of 2005, before the regularization process, many individuals from America who had settled in Spain did not possess the authorization to reside legally (45%). This implies that they lacked civil rights, and were at risk of exclusion and exploitation.

One must also consider that women were the majority of this group: city councils registered a growth of 223% in the presence of Latin American women in the last ten years, although the tendency is moving towards parity in the number of male and female immigrants. The most convincing explanation for the presence of women is the active participation of Latin America women in the labour markets in their countries, and also their capacity to adapt to circumstances, and their willingness to accept domestic work of any kind. Usually these women reached Spain alone, and were often employed in domestic services. Nowadays, they are often required to take care of elderly people. Women tended to reach Spain first, and brought their husbands and children after them, helping them find a job.

The high demand of workers in the last decade in sectors like agriculture or construction required mostly men: Latin Americans are more frequently employed than nationals from other countries. There have been also active policies of Spanish governments to keep friendly ties between Spain and Latin America. For example, the Universidad de

Salamanca is frequented by more than 350 Latin American students, mostly with scholarships, especially from banking institutions like Banco Santander. Nevertheless, a growing number of Latin American young people who obtained a qualification in Spain and gained employment in Spanish companies (such as the Spain Telecommunication Company *Telefónica)*, have returned to their country of origin because of the economic crisis. Some of them, however, keep their jobs thanks to telecommunication and information technologies.

Occupations of Latin American immigrants vary greatly. 67% are occupied in services, 8% in agriculture and 5% in industry. Most of them are found in unskilled jobs, not necessarily because their educational level is lower than that of Spanish nationals. Their experience and training are therefore wasted. This also leads to the stereotype of an unskilled worker, who is badly paid and does not have a professional future (Martínez Buján, 2003).

A large number of immigrants come from Africa, but they obviously have different characteristics from those hailing from Latin America. First of all, they are mostly Muslims, who constitute about 3% of the Spanish population. 70% are immigrants: 50% from Morocco, 20% from other countries namely Senegal, Nigeria, Algeria, Mali, Pakistan, Mauritania, Gambia and Guinea. Most of these immigrants are men, and work in agriculture or construction; women work mostly in restaurants and in domestic services. Their work is generally seasonal and precarious. Spaniards usually mistrust them, especially in the cities, where they live in closed communities. This attitude changes in rural areas, where African origin immigrants are better integrated and are well considered.

They have steadily been bringing their families with them, but their wives are not visible socially. Single women are very few, although this has been changing recently.

Muslims are mostly from Morocco. By 2010, in Spain there were 7,661,897 Moroccans, although real figures are probably higher than official ones. Historical relations with Morocco have alternated good and bad moments, determined, among other factors, by the Spanish colonization until the 20th century and by the Spanish presence in the cities of Ceuta and Melilla, which caused tension between the two countries, creating occasional conflict with the Moroccan monarchs. Many Moroccan immigrants reach Spain at the risk of their life crossing the Mediterranean Sea to reach the coasts in Andalusia or the Atlantic to the Canary Islands. Spanish institutions and companies have accepted them despite the previously mentioned lack of trust towards these immigrants.

For many reasons, immigrant Muslim population in Spain values highly the society where they are living. Muslims in Spain can practice their religion openly, in a tolerant environment. 83% say that they think they have adapted to the life and costumes of their place of residence. 74% say that Spain welcomes the immigrants; 67% declares they feel comfortable hear. Only 10% says they deal only with people of their nationality, and 15% only with people of their religion. They mostly speak well Spanish, and an important number also Catalan (Metroscopia-Gobierno de España, 2011).

The number of immigrants originating from East Europe has grown since 1989. They mostly work illegally. Those who are 'legal' range mostly between 25 and 44 years old. Numbers are similar for males and females, and they are generally employed in the services sector. Statistically, between 1998 and 2011, citizens from east Europe, whether they belong to the EU or not, constituted 25% of the foreign population in Spain. The most numerous are Romanian nationals, 280,409; Bulgarians 136,504, Polish 75,050 and small numbers of Ukrainians and Russians. The exemption of the visa for Bulgarians and Romanians as from 2002 meant a high growth of these two communities, especially because many illegal residents could have access to resident permits (Pajares, 2002, 2007; Viruela Martínez, 2004).

The perception in Spain of Eastern Europe immigrants is usually negative or, at least partially so, even though it varies depending on the place they live and the work they fulfil. They are well appreciated in agriculture, especially in Andalusia, Murcia or in Eastern Spain, due to the fact that they are hard and reliable workers. In other areas, they are discriminated, often unfairly, as they tend to be prejudicially associated to illegality.

Finally, one must mention the growing Chinese community. In Spain there are more than 100,000 people from China. Most of them —85%— come from the south. A special characteristic of this group is that they are both employers and employees. They operate in economic activities that are mostly handled by them alone; they deal preferably with people of their own community, and do not necessarily integrate with others. Nevertheless, Chinese immigrants of second generation speak Spanish well and often deal with non-Chinese people in their environment, although they remain faithful to their traditions and their traditional careers, especially Economics and Business Administration, which allow them work in the family business. They constitute an example of adaptation to the country without losing the links with their country of origin. They still feel Chinese, and they work and earn money to live and to help their families in China (Beltrán, 2001, 2003).

The above considerations may be considered to be valid only until 2011 as immigration towards Spain is experiencing fast and unforeseeable transformations, also conditioned by the economic crisis which may lead to a decrease of the number of immigrants in Spain. As an example, according to the INE, in 2011 589,859 individuals left Spain, whereas 450,000 immigrants entered the country. It is thought that by 2020 the population will diminish significantly: from 46,152,925 to 45,585,572 in 2021. In any case, these are only predictions as recent history seems to back Giambattista Vico's opinions about the development of history through *corsi* and *ricorsi*, and what today seems totally consolidated may fall tomorrow to be built the day after.

10.3. The MERIDIUM Research in Spain

The methodological design of the MERIDIUM research in Spain is based on data collection from 12 different Educational Centers of the Spanish cities that have been selected in 6 regions of the country.

Questionnaires were administered in 12 Spanish provinces (Madrid, Valencia, Huelva, Almería, Murcia, Gran Canaria, Pontevedra, Gijón, Oviedo, Burgos, Segovia and Salamanca), and provided the basis of a descriptive quantitative analysis. Informants are children from 9 to 11 years old, who filled in the questionnaires in their classrooms, with the help of our staff and their school tutors (Questionnaire A). Each child took another questionnaire home to be filled in by their parents (Questionnaire B).

10.3.1. Socio-demographic Profile of Informants

A total number of 713 questionnaires has been collected: 429 are those filled in by pupils, while 284 are those filled in by parents[2].

The pupils' sample is perfectly even from the point of view of gender: 214 informants are males and 214 are females[3]. Among them, 348 (81.1%) were born in Spain, while 81 (18.9%) where born abroad: 20 (4.7%) were

---

[2] As one may observe, a remarkable number of parents did not complete the questionnaire. According to school directors and teachers, this is due to the fact that parents felt that this was an intrusion in their private life or did not feel that they were duty bound to provide the information being requested.

[3] In one case, the informant did not respond the question on gender.

born in Europe, 52 (12.1%) in South America, 5 (1.2%) in Asia and in the Middle- East, and 4 (0.9%) in African Countries.

Tab. 10-1 displays the distribution of pupils also in terms of their background (parents' birthplace):

CATEGORY OF PUPILS		N	%
Native-born with native background		293	*70.3*
Native-born with mixed background		36	*8.6*
Native-born with foreign background		8	*1.9*
Foreign-born with native background		2	*0.5*
Foreign-born with mixed background		6	*1.4*
Foreign-born with foreign background		72	*17.3*
Information not provided [4]		12	*2.8*
	TOTAL	429	*100.0*

Tab. 10-1: Pupils' sample: pupil's and parent's birthplace-disaggregated data

The 284 adult respondents are distributed as follows (Tab. 10-2 below) as to birthplace and gender[5]:

INFORMANT BIRTHPLACE		MALE	FEMALE	TOTAL
native-born	N	55	157	212
	%	*19.5*	*55.7*	*75.2*
foreign-born	N	24	46	70
	%	*8.5*	*16.3*	*24.8*
TOTAL	N	79	203	282
	%	*28.0*	*72.0*	*100.0*

Tab. 10-2: Parents' sample: cross-tabulation of data concerning birthplace and gender

The age distribution is quite different among native-born and foreign-born parents (see Tab. 10-3):

[4] 12 informants did not respond to the question concerning their parents' birthplace.

[5] In Tab. 10-2 total respondents are 282 since 2 informants did not respond the question on birthplace

AGE BRACKET	PARENTS BY BIRTHPLACE:			
	native-born		foreign-born	
	N	%	N	%[6]
<30	5	*2.4*	5	*(7.1)*
30-39	58	*27.4*	33	*(47.1)*
40-49	130	*61.3*	30	*(42.9)*
50 or more	14	*6.6*	2	*(2.9)*
No answer	5	*2.4*	0	-
TOTAL	212	*100.0*	70	*(100.0)*

Tab. 10-3: Parents' age distribution: birthplace-disaggregated data

The composition of the family unit reflects the variety of family models found in Spain; the significant numbers of respondents living with the extended family may reflect, in part, lodging arrangements brought by the current economic crisis:

FAMILY STRUCTURE	PARENTS BY BIRTHPLACE:			
	native-born		foreign-born	
	N	%	N	%
Monoparental family	23	*10.8*	5	*(7.1)*
Nuclear family	164	*77.4*	49	*(70.0)*
Extended family	25	*11.8*	16	*(22.9)*
TOTAL	212	*100.0*	70	*(100.0)*

Tab. 10-4: Family structure as self-reported by parents: birthplace-disaggregated data

The occupational situation of pupils' parents, as self-reported by adults informants, is shown in Tab. 10-5:

[6] In tables where cases do not reach the sum of 100, percentages are listed within brackets.

OCCUPATIONAL SITUATION OF PUPILS' PARENTS	PARENTS BY BIRTHPLACE:			
	native-born		foreign-born	
	N	%	N	%
both spouses unemployed	18	*8.5*	8	*(11.4)*
one spouse working	76	*35.8*	32	*(45.7)*
both spouses working	117	*55.2*	30	*(42.9)*
Information not provided	1	*0.5*	0	-
TOTAL	212	*100.0*	70	*(100.0)*

Tab. 10-5: Occupational situation of adults informants and their spouses: birthplace-disaggregated data

10.3.2. Socio-linguistic Profile and Self-ascription of Informants

If we analyze language use within the different domains (within and outside the family circle), as self-reported by children, we observe that, within the whole sample, Spanish is used with all the interlocutors by 90% or more of the informants: monolingual uses largely prevail, whilst alternation with other languages is virtually absent.

Pupils' background-related differences are displayed in Tabs. 10-6a-c (family domain) and Tabs. 10-7a-c (extra-familiar domain), where a subset of informants who have provided valid answers for each category of interlocutors (232 out of 429) is analysed:

LANGUAGE USE OF PUPILS WITH NATIVE BACKGROUND	WHEN TALKING TO: (N AND %)			
	grandpar.	mother	father	siblings
only languages different from Spanish	0 -	2 *1.2*	4 *2.4*	7 *4.2*
Spanish and other languages	1 *0.6*	4 *2.4*	2 *1.2*	8 *4.8*
only (varieties of) Spanish or regional languages	164 *99.4*	159 *96.4*	159 *96.4*	150 *90.9*
TOTAL	165 *100.0*	165 *100.0*	165 *100.0*	165 *100.0*

Tab. 10-6a: Language use of pupils with native background within the family domain

LANGUAGE USE OF PUPILS WITH MIXED BACKGROUND	WHEN TALKING TO: (N AND %)			
	grandpar.	mother	father	siblings
only languages different from Spanish	1 *(5.0)*	2 *(10.0)*	0 -	3 *(15.0)*
Spanish and other languages	2 *(10.0)*	1 *(5.0)*	1 *(5.0)*	2 *(10.0)*
only (varieties of) Spanish or regional languages	17 *(85.0)*	17 *(85.0%)*	19 *(95.0)*	15 *(75.0)*
TOTAL	20 *(100.0)*	20 *(100.0)*	20 *(100.0)*	20 *(100.0)*

Tab. 10-6b: Language use of pupils with mixed background within the family domain

LANGUAGE USE OF PUPILS WITH FOREIGN BACKGROUND	WHEN TALKING TO: (N AND %)			
	grandpar.	mother	father	siblings
only languages different from Spanish	21 *(50.0)*	18 *(42.9)*	16 *(38.1)*	13 *(31.0)*
Spanish and other languages	1 *(2.4)*	3 *(7.1)*	2 *(4.8)*	4 *(9.5)*
only (varieties of) Spanish or regional languages	20 *(47.6)*	21 *(50.0)*	24 *(57.1)*	25 *(59.5)*
TOTAL	42 *(100.0)*	42 *(100.0)*	42 *(100.0)*	42 *(100.0)*

Tab. 10-6c: Language use of pupils with foreign background within the family domain

LANGUAGE USE OF PUPILS WITH NATIVE BACKGROUND	WHEN TALKING TO: (N AND %)			
	friends	neighbs.	classmats.	teachers
only languages different from Spanish	3 *1.8*	2 *1.2*	3 *1.8*	7 *4.2*
Spanish and other languages	7 *4.2*	1 *0.6*	15 *9.1*	27 *16.4*
only (varieties of) Spanish or regional languages	155 *93.9*	162 *98.2*	147 *89.1*	131 *79.4*
TOTAL	165 *100.0*	165 *100.0*	165 *100.0*	165 *100.0*

Tab. 10-7a: Language use of pupils with native background outside the family domain

LANGUAGE USE OF PUPILS WITH MIXED BACKGROUND	WHEN TALKING TO: (N AND %)			
	friends	neighbs.	classmats.	teachers
only languages different from Spanish	0 -	0 -	0 -	0 -
Spanish and other languages	2 *(10.0)*	1 *(5.0)*	1 *(5.0)*	3 *(15.0)*
only (varieties of) Spanish or regional languages	18 *(90.0)*	19 *(95.0)*	19 *(95.0)*	17 *(85.0)*
TOTAL	20 *(100.0)*	20 *(100.0)*	20 *(100.0)*	20 *(100.0)*

Tab. 10-7b: Language use of pupils with mixed background outside the family domain

LANGUAGE USE OF PUPILS WITH FOREIGN BACKGROUND	WHEN TALKING TO: (N AND %)			
	friends	neighbs.	classmats.	teachers
only languages different from Spanish	2 *(4.8)*	2 *(4.8)*	0 -	0 -
Spanish and other langugages	3 *(7.1)*	1 *(2.4)*	1 *(2.4)*	0 -
only (varieties of) Spanish or regional languages	37 *(88.1)*	39 *(92.9)*	41 *(97.6)*	42 *(100.0)*
TOTAL	42 *(100.0)*	42 *(100.0)*	42 *(100.0)*	42 *(100.0)*

Tab. 10-7c: Language use of pupils with foreign background outside the family domain

Similar results are obtained if parents' data are taken into consideration, as shown in Tabs. 10-8a-b below, where a sub-set of 229 (out of 284) parents who have provided valid answers to relevant questions are analysed:

LANGUAGE USE OF NATIVE PARENTS	WHEN TALKING TO: (N AND %)				
	partner	children	friends	neighbs.	collgs.
only languages different from Spanish	0 -	2 *1.1*	0 -	0 -	2 *1.1*
Spanish and other languages	4 *2.3*	11 *6.3*	4 *2.3*	0 -	4 *2.3*
only (varieties of) Spanish or regional languages	171 *97.7*	162 *92.6*	171 *97.7*	175 *100.0*	169 *96.6*
TOTAL	175 *100.0*	175 *100.0*	175 *100.0*	175 *100.0*	175 *100.0*

Tab. 10-8a: Language use of native-born parents within and outside the family domain

LANGUAGE USE OF FOREIGN PARENTS	WHEN TALKING TO: (N AND %)				
	partner	children	friends	neighbs.	collgs.
only languages different from Spanish	14 *(25.9)*	9 *(16.7)*	5 *(9.3)*	1 *(1.9)*	0 -
Spanish and other languages	3 *(5.6)*	8 *(14.8)*	8 *(14.8)*	3 *(5.6)*	4 *(7.4)*
only (varieties of) Spanish or regional languages	37 *(68.5)*	37 *(68.5)*	41 *(75.9)*	50 *(92.6)*	50 *(92.6)*
TOTAL	54 *(100.0)*	54 *(100.0)*	54 *(100.0)*	54 *(100.0)*	54 *(100.0)*

Tab. 10-8b: Language use of foreign-born parents within and outside the family domain

Answers provided by pupils about their sense of belonging to social groups (their class, town of residence, Spain) display, on the whole, a general feeling of positive integration: percentages of positive answers are always around 85% or higher. When we disaggregate data by pupils' background, and consider the sub-set of 232 pupils whose language use has been analysed above, the following results are obtained (see Tabs. 10-9a-c below):

OPTIONS	"HOW MUCH DO YOU FEEL PART OF YOUR..": (N AND %)		
	class	town of residence	country of residence
Very much/just enough	151 *91.5*	153 *92.7*	162 *98.2*
A little bit/not at all	8 *4.8*	7 *4.2*	2 *1.2*
Don't know/no answer	6 *3.6*	5 *3.0*	1 *0.6*
TOTAL	165 *100.0*	165 *100.0*	165 *100.0*

Tab. 10-9a: Sense of belonging of pupils with native background to their class, town of residence, country of residence

OPTIONS	"HOW MUCH DO YOU FEEL PART OF YOUR..": (N AND %)		
	class	town of residence	country of residence
Very much/just enough	17 *(85.0)*	15 *(75.0)*	18 *(90.0)*
A little bit/not at all	3 *(5.0)*	5 *(25.0)*	1 *(5.0)*
Don't know/no answer	0 -	0 -	1 *(5.0)*
TOTAL	20 *(100.0)*	20 *(100.0)*	20 *(100.0)*

Tab. 10-9b: Sense of belonging of pupils with mixed background to their class, town of residence, country of residence

OPTIONS	"HOW MUCH DO YOU FEEL PART OF YOUR..": (N AND %)		
	class	town of residence	country of residence
Very much/just enough	33 *(78.6)*	32 *(76.2)*	24 *(57.1)*
A little bit/not at all	7 *(16.7)*	7 *(16.7)*	17 *(40.5)*
Don't know/no answer	2 *(4.8)*	3 *(7.1)*	1 *(2.4)*
TOTAL	42 *(100.0)*	42 *(100.0)*	42 *(100.0)*

Tab. 10-9c: Sense of belonging of pupils with foreign background to their class, town of residence, country of residence

These results suggest that the sense of belonging of pupils is globally very positive, even though the allegiance to the country of residence is felt by pupils with foreign background to a remarkably lower extent than the allegiance to their school-class and to the town where they live. In this respect, it must be taken into account that, for the most part, these pupils were born abroad (36 out of 42).

Children's data may be compared to those of the adults' sub-set previously analysed, which are displayed in Tabs. 10-10a-b:

OPTIONS	"HOW MUCH DO YOU FEEL PART OF YOUR..": (N AND %)	
	town of residence	country of residence
Very much/just enough	133 *76.0*	169 *96.6*
A little bit/not at all	34 *19.4*	6 *3.4*
Don't know/no answer	8 *4.6*	0 -
TOTAL	175 *100.0*	175 *100.0*

Tab. 10-10a: Sense of belonging of native-born parents to their town of residence and country of residence

OPTIONS	"HOW MUCH DO YOU FEEL PART OF YOUR..": (N AND %)	
	town of residence	country of residence
Very much/just enough	41 *(75.9)*	37 *(68.5)*
A little bit/not at all	9 *(16.7)*	14 *(25.9)*
Don't know/no answer	4 *(7.4)*	3 *(5.6)*
TOTAL	54 *(100.0)*	54 *(100.0)*

Tab. 10-10b: Sense of belonging of foreign-born parents to their town of residence and country of residence

In terms of sense of belonging to particular groups (town of residence, country of residence) the results are similar to those found in both data (children and adults): a high identification with the family group and the country of residence. However, foreign-born respondents seem to have a high sense of belonging to the town of residence (75.9%) whereas native-born parents have a high sense of belonging to the country of residence (96.6%). In the case of children with mixed background and children with foreign background there is a higher sense of belonging to one's school-class rather than to the country or town of residence (see Tabs. 10-9a-c and contrast with Tabs. 10-10a–b).

The linguistic situation observed within the MERIDIUM samples reveals a generalized knowledge of Spanish, which prevails in use, although it must be taken into account that what many foreign-born informants name as "Spanish" is not the standard variety, but the variety of Spanish spoken in Latin American countries. This diffuse situation of contact between varieties which are remarkably different from each other in many respects is worth investigating further, in order to study its possible impact on the local varieties of Spanish spoken by native-born speakers (mainly young people) in areas where relevant Latin American communities are settled, as well as, more specifically, on the learner varieties of Spanish characterizing immigrants who are native speakers of other languages.

The densest demographic groups of non-Spanish speakers are from Morocco, Romania, Bulgaria and China. There are therefore four major groups of immigrants who speak languages that belong to different families and/or branches (Semitic branch of Afro-Asiatic languages, Romance and Slavic branches of Indo-European languages, Chinese branch of Sino-Tibetan languages). This favours the use of Spanish in interethnic communication, in spite of the difficulties which native speakers of typologically diverse languages may experience in order to learn Spanish.

On the other hand, the linguistic heterogeneity of Spain has always allowed the use of other languages in areas where socioeconomic conditions have led to settlements of specific populations that do not speak Spanish. This happens, for instance, in the community of North-Europeans or Scandinavians in Balearic Islands, the Costa del Sol or the Canary Islands where communities have formed mainly due to tourism or retirement reasons. Furthermore, we must also take into account the dialect continuum[7] of some monolingual areas such as Andalucia, Extremadura, Murcia and the Canary Islands (communities represented in the MERIDIUM study).

Social integration is influenced by the linguistic abilities of the immigrant population as these abilities are used in order to acquire social

---

[7] This dialect continuum, namely the way a linguistic system makes itself manifest within the geographical area where it is spoken, is evident in the questionnaires filled in by children, in whose writings we find phonetic representations (i.e. they spell according to the way they perceive sounds) according to dialects of their place of birth. This, as stated above, is especially evident in some specific localities.

and cultural knowledge. Immigrants improve the possibilities of integration when they become reasonably proficient in the official language of the country of residence, with its styles and registers; this kind of knowledge enables them to participate in more complex communicative situations.

Therefore, sociolinguistic research on immigration in Spain should be further promoted, as one of the main sources of knowledge on the issue of integration of migrants, together with research on demography, sociology and economy. Within these fields, a notable amount of documents and reports about immigration in Spain has been published in recent years. On the other hand, statistics published by the National Institute of Statistics (www.ine.es), as well as web pages dedicated to migrants on the websites of different institutions of the Autonomous Communities of Spain (for instance the portal of integration and coexistence "*InmigraMadrid*"[8] or "*Salamanca Acoge*"[9]), or the Ministry of Employment and Social Security (www.mtin.es), are a good indication of the attention paid to the issue of integration by the most prominent public institutions in Spain.

10.4. Migration and Schooling

The concept of citizenship has become important in Spain, and it has also changed over the course of time, extending its meaning beyond the remit of monolingualism or monoculturalism to "multicultural citizenship". This suggests reconciling the political promotion of diversity and cultural autonomy with integration in an egalitarian system (similar examples of this are found in countries such as Australia, Canada, Sweden and the Netherlands). Despite the demographic increase in Spain, immigration rate is not as high as it is in countries such as Germany, the Netherlands, France or the United Kingdom, although it has grown considerably in the last two years.

Nonetheless, this growth has led to a situation where one finds many educational institutions where the percentage of foreign alumni exceeds that of the Spanish ones (examples of this are found in Lleida, the Canary Islands and Andalucia). This is fundamentally due to two reasons: firstly, obligatory schooling for immigrants, who therefore also have access to education. Secondly, the increased numbers of immigrants over the past

---

[8] See the website www.madrid.org/cs/Satellite?pagename=PortalInmigrante/Page/INMI_home&language=en, accessed September 26, 2012.

[9] See the website http://www.redvoluntariadosocial.org/entidades/salamanca-acoge/, accessed September 26, 2012.

years, which has led to classrooms with children that come from an endless variety of countries and cultures.

We must try to perceive *interculturalism* beyond the *multicultural* perspective, as it establishes a positive approach and a relationship model between cultures. Moreover, by considering cultural interaction as an educational issue it becomes essential to understand that intercultural education also ought to be given space in the curriculum, as hinted in a number of contributions to the MERIDIUM Project.

Students with socio-cultural disadvantages or pertaining to ethnic minorities frequently present interpersonal conflicts related to the existence of stereotypes and negative attitudes towards them. In this context, it is essential to foster responsibility and respect in order to develop a non-discriminatory education guided towards social justice and thereby creating possibilities of self-realization. One must keep in mind that educational institutions should not only consider these issues, but also create the opportunity for pupils to have different learning experiences which also take into account one's personal background.

Spanish schools undertake actions to involve migrants adequately in the process of learning and teaching. Hence, the educational initiative "Educational Compensation" (*Educación Compensatoria*), the main objective of which is that of family involvement in schooling projects in order to:

- lessen differences concerning values and contents that school and families transmit;
- secure family support in school projects;
- reduce feelings of low self-esteem which may be the result of being born in a disadvantaged family;
- contribute to favour families' esteem towards the school.

The access to higher level of education is the key to integration and social promotion; it is well known that formation is a fundamental element in order to combat social and economic exclusion. Hence, providing education to immigrants' children must be a priority. We are concerned that in some cases immigrants leave schooling at a very early stage, not so much because of cultural prejudices but rather because they do not consider it to be a possibility of social and economic improvement.

Education, however, does not solely include the schooling context, as the social dimension of schools, as well as its effect on each and every individual, even once school-years are over, is important. It would obviously be a serious mistake if one were to concentrate solely on schools, and on lessons held during school hours, to eradicate immigration problems. Complementary and extracurricular activities that encourage immigrant children and teenagers' to participate in leisure activities and in other non-formal environments, together with Spanish-born children, should be a priority as this can lead to better integration even in the long term. In addition, the establishment of mechanisms in order to create relationships between families and schools is also needed. In other words, intervention is needed, not only on behalf of schooling staff, but also through professional and social workers' intervention (López Sala, 2005).

School represents a microcosm of society and hence must strive to foster the existence of other languages and cultures. At the same time opportunities for the acquisition of the Spanish language should be created, thus facilitating communication and thereby enhancing the possibility of social integration of non-national students. In the schools surveyed, children start learning the language by developing their speaking skills. By using vocabulary which is often used in everyday life and based on students' interests, teaching is reinforced by means of systematic learning based on frequency of use of words and commonplace expressions, and through the employment of resources (visual, technology enhanced learning, using media, etc.). In each situation we have observed the introduction of content which matched the students' needs according to the situation which was present in the classroom. At a later stage more complex linguistic structures were taught in class. According to progress registered by students, especially in their use of vocabulary and grammar, reading and writing lessons were subsequently introduced, also on the basis of the level of competence of students and of their native tongue. The evaluation of students included both the formative aspect, that includes decision-making and redirection of processes, and the summative aspect, by means of which pupils' performance was examined.

10.5. Conclusion

The descriptive data presented here show a new landscape of Spain. Immigration in Spain has been brought about by economic or labour reasons; this has created new social complexities and a new sociolinguistic scenario for Spain in the last two decades. This type of immigration, coming from developing or underdeveloped countries, mainly seeks to improve quality of life. Of the total foreign population in the electoral register, up to the 1st January 2010, almost 80% come from Latin-American countries, Eastern countries or North-African countries.

In Spain, economic immigration has evolved in such a way that what in 1998 represented approximately 0.9% of the total population, nowadays represents almost 9%. This noticeable growth has been increasing since 2000at an accelerated rate.

It should be noted that this accelerated growth rate has not been homogenous throughout Spanish territory. For instance, amongst all the autonomous communities, Madrid on its own registers 21% of economic immigration on a national scale, which represents 626,249 individuals. In fact, in the Madrid region 9 out of 10 foreigners are originally from underdeveloped or developing countries. (Lucas, 2002)

This research has illustrated some aspects of multiculturalism and multilingualism in a selected number of Spanish Primary schools. Results reveal the importance of educational institutions in the process of teaching and learning of the immigrant population. The importance of creating more awareness towards diversity and of creating opportunities for further integration has also been highlighted, together with the necessity to involve both students and their parents in this process.

This could help to move away from stereotypes as cultural integration is not only enriching, but also has implications on the development of society.

We believe that the task of the educational institutions is fundamental together with the implementation of multicultural policies that could stretch beyond schooling thereby permeating society. An early exposition to cultural diversity and tolerance are also considered to be fundamental for the social and linguistic integration of the immigrant population in Spain.

References

Aubarrell, G. 2003. *Perspectivas de la inmigración en España*. Barcelona: Icaria.

Beltrán Antolín, J. 2003. Diáspora y comunidades asiáticas en España. *Scripta Nova. Revista electrónica de geografía y ciencias sociales*. 7/134. Accessed September 26, 2012. www.ub.es/geocrit/sn/sn-134.htm.

Beltrán Antolín, J., and A. Sáiz López. 2001. *Els xinesos a Catalunya. Familia, educació i integració*. Barcelona: Ata Fulla.

Consejo Económico y Social. 2004. *La inmigración y el mercado de trabajo en España,* Madrid: CES.

De Lucas, J. 2002a. Políticas de inmigración. 30 propuestas. *Claves de razón práctica* 121. 32-36.

—. 2002b. La dimensión política de la inmigración: una reflexión pendiente. In *La inmigración, una realidad en España, Seminario de investigación para la Paz*, ed. Centro Pignatelli, 263-286. Zaragoza: Departamento de cultura y turismo.

Díez Nicolás, J. 2005. *Las dos caras de la inmigración,* Madrid: Ministerio de Trabajo y Asuntos Sociales.

López Sala, A. M. 2005. *Inmigrante y Estados: la respuesta política ante la cuestión inmigratoria*. Madrid: Editorial Anthropos.

Martínez Buján, R. 2003. *La reciente inmigración latinoamericana a España* (CEPAL, Serie Población y Desarrollo 40). Santiago de Chile: Naciones Unidas (available at: http://www.eclac.org/publicaciones/xml/4/12614/lcl1922_p.pdf, accessed September 26, 2012)

Metroscopia-Gobierno de España. 2011. *La Comunidad Musulmana de origen inmigrante en España*. Accessed September 26, 2012. www.lamoncloa.gob.es/NR/rdonlyres/703D0352-E39F-4325-94BA-768A9BDDA98F/172156/estudio_resumen_2010.pdf.

Pajares Alonso, M. 2002. Inmigración y políticas de integración social. In *La inmigración en España: contextos y alternativas,* eds. F. J. García Castaño and C. Muriel López, 527-534. Granada: Laboratorio de Estudios Interculturales.

—. 2007. *Inmigrantes del Este. Procesos migratorios de los rumanos.* Barcelona: Icaria editorial.

Tornos, A. 2004. Nuevos movimientos migratorios en una Unión Europea ampliada. *Revista Migraciones* 16. 237-254.

Trinidad García, Mª L. 2002. Los acuerdos migratorios bilaterales concluidos por España: un complejo instrumento para unos resultados escasos. In *La inmigración en España. Contextos y alternativas*, eds. F. J. García Castaño and C. Muriel López, 493-505. Granada: Laboratorio de Estudios Interculturales.

Viruela Martínez, R. 2004. El recurso de la emigración. Balance durante la transición rumana. *Papeles del Este* 9 (available at: http://www.ucm.es/BUCM/cee/papeles/09/pape0404220011a.pdf, accessed September 26, 2012).

CHAPTER ELEVEN

MULTILINGUALISM AND IMMIGRATION IN THE PORTUGUESE LINGUISTIC LANDSCAPE

MARIA ISABEL TOMÁS

The profound socioeconomic changes of the second half of the 20th century led to the alteration of Portugal's traditional status as a supplier of emigrants to numerous countries in several continents. Portugal became, from the 1990s to the present, an immigration destination. The sharp ethno-cultural homogeneity and strong linguistic unity which have characterized European Portugal for centuries are no longer defining traits of the Portuguese landscape. But immigration is not the only external flow in the last few decades: emigration, emigrant return and returnees from former colonies have also played a role in the building up of super diversity in Portugal, cultural complexity and heterogeneity which is characteristic of most European countries as a consequence of the recent migrant flows (Vertovec, 2006; 2007). Linguistic and cultural diversity is a daily visible trait: in the streets, at the working place and, in particular, in schools, given the increasing immigration flows into the country.

The research conducted within the framework of the MERIDIUM project had, as two of its main goals, to investigate the level of awareness of (and the attitudes towards) the presence of other languages in the everyday-life context (school, work, neighbourhood, sociability networks) among both the local population and the migrants, children as well as their parents; to identify the level of perception of and the attitudes towards language and educational policies and their implementation at the local level. The data gathered will provide a "snapshot" of the growing linguistic diversity and its reflection on perceptions and attitudes towards the new linguistic landscape of each of the countries involved in the project. It also identifies perceptible trends which could later be explored and confirmed by further qualitative and quantitative studies, which may contribute to the definition and implementation of educational policies and integration measures at institutional levels, both locally and nationally.

In the following sections of this chapter an overview of the immigration phenomenon in Portugal during the last decade will be presented, followed by a description of the research study from which we draw our data. The main section will be dedicated to the analysis of the data obtained both from children and adult respondents. The relevant findings and the directions for further research will be discussed in the last sections.

11.1. Immigration in Portugal Today

Foreign population holding a residency permit by December 31st 2009[1] amounted to 454,191 individuals, a value which represents a 3.1 increase as compared to the 2008 figures. The increasing migratory flows into the country have been the major component in the country's population increase since 1993, compensating for the decreasing birth rate and contributing to the attenuation of the sharp ageing of the Portuguese population. Statistical estimates for 2009 point to an overall population of 10,637,700[2], an increase of 10,500 residents, as compared to the estimates for 2008.

According to SEF (*Serviço de Estrangeiros e Fronteiras*) estimates for 2009, the majority of immigrant citizens still come from African Countries with Portuguese as Official Language (PALOPs), representing 24% of the overall immigrant population, in spite of the sharp decrease observed in the last few years. In 2001, they represented 45.28%.

European immigrants (39.1% in 2009) exhibited a 6.3% increase compared to 2008, due to the substantial increase in the flows coming from Eastern European countries, particularly from Ukraine (11.6%), Romania (7.2%), Moldavia (4.6%) and Russia (1.4%). Two findings exemplify this trend: in 2009, Romania surpassed the United Kingdom as the most numerous group as far as EU Member States are concerned; Ukraine surpassed Cape Verde as the second most numerous nationality.

Brazil accounted for 25.6% of the foreign legal population in 2009, a 34.3% increase in relation to 2001. Brazil and PALOPs together, stand for 47% of the immigrant population.

---

[1] Residency permits and prorogations granted by SEF.

[2] The figures for the 2011 Census have not yet been published. All the statistical data referred to in this paper come from the latest available (2009) official estimates provided by INE (*Instituto Nacional de Estatística*: http://www.ine.pt/xportal/xmain?xpgid=ine_main&xpid=INE) and SEF (http://sefstat.sef.pt/).

The vast majority of immigrants are concentrated in the age groups which are normally associated to working life: 48% in the 20-39 age group (218,060 immigrants), 31.48% in the 40-60 age group.

Data concerning immigrant sex distribution display an increase in female immigrant numbers, both due to family regrouping policies and to the increase of female immigrants in the labour market. Of the total legal foreign population in 2009, 51.6% were males, while female immigrants represented, in the same year, 48.4% of the immigrant total, compared to 56.2% (males) and 43.8% (females) in 2001.

Immigrants are concentrated predominantly in the coastal areas, particularly in the districts of Lisbon (196,798), Faro (73,277) and Setúbal (49,309), areas where a significant share of national economic activities are located. The joint immigrant population of these three districts amounts to 70.3% (319,384) of a total of 454,191 immigrants in 2009.

11.1.1. Policies and Measures Related to the Migratory Phenomenon

Portuguese national policies, and their implementation[3], regarding immigration have tried to respond to the increasing social complexity and challenges posed by the migratory flows in the last few decades. The latest evaluation by the Migrant Integration Policy Index (MIPEX) 2011 (which compares national policies of the EU States, Norway, Switzerland, Canada and the USA) has ranked Portugal second, following Sweden (MIPEX 2011).

In the public school system, measures such as the offer of Portuguese classes for non-native students (PLNM) continue to be implemented in some schools. A few schools have developed specific projects on Intercultural Awareness.

Support and Integrative Policies are defined at national level. Regional and local implementation and management of measures and projects are the responsibility of local and regional administrative entities (Municipalities, Parish Councils, Regional Boards of Education, Schools, etc.), often in partnership with civil society organizations (Immigrant Associations, NGOs, churches, etc.). Municipalities in territories with high concentration of migrants have taken steps to promote economic and social integration

---

[3] For a comprehensive listing of Government bodies, policy papers and programs, key legislation, research and statistical agencies, key stakeholders, etc., consult http://ec.europa.eu/ewsi/en/info_sheet.cfm?ID_CSHEET=60, accessed September 26, 2012.

of these citizens, namely through the creation of Local Centers for Immigrant Assistance and Integration (CLAII).

11.2. The MERIDIUM Survey in Portugal

The sociolinguistic survey conducted by the Portuguese MERIDIUM team was based on the data from 632 paired questionnaires (316 adults and 316 children), that were designed as common frameworks for all the six countries involved. They were administered to 5th grade students in six public primary schools, in the three areas[4] designated for the study: districts of Lisbon, Setúbal and Faro, all of them areas of higher immigration density. The adult questionnaires were distributed to their parents. The specific urban centres chosen within those areas reflect the dynamics observed in migratory flows within the respective district. In each municipality the schools with larger contingents of foreign students were identified and contacted. Questionnaires were distributed in those schools where school boards and teachers agreed to cooperate with the researchers.

11.2.1. Characterization of the Areas Chosen

The most recent statistic data available (SEF Provisional Data 2009) confirm the choice of the relevant areas for the sociolinguistic research undertaken by Portuguese team of the MERIDIUM Project: the Districts of Lisbon, Setúbal and Faro. These three areas have the highest migratory density in the country, a concentration which mirrors the increasing population movement to the coastal areas: in 28% of Portugal's European territory there is a concentration of 75% of its population (2001).

The MERIDIUM data on immigrant employment confirm the findings of Reis *et al.* (2007) for the whole country: the patterns of geographical concentration reflect, in each of the districts and municipalities selected for the study, the dynamics of the economic vocation of each particular location.

[4] See MERIDIUM Country Report – Portugal (eng), p. 10-14 and the Portuguese longer version of the Report, p. 73-78, available at: http://meridium.unistrapg.it/?q=en/country-report, accessed September 26, 2012.

11.2.1.1. Lisbon District

Lisbon is (according to the data available for 2009) the Portuguese district with the highest number of immigrant residents: 196,798 legal foreign residents, reflecting its centrality in the country's economy. The municipalities with higher migratory concentration in this district are Lisbon, Amadora, Sintra, Cascais e Loures. Primary schools in three municipalities were selected to take part in the MERIDIUM sociolinguistic survey. These municipalities are representative of the diverse contexts we find in the district: two municipalities of medium size and strong immigrant concentration—Sintra and Amadora, and a medium size municipality—Mafra—with smaller but increasing concentration.

LOCALITY	YEAR	TOTAL POPULATION	FOREIGN LEGAL RESIDENTS	
			Total	**% of total population**
Sintra	2001	363,556	23,470	6.5
	2009	419,382	39,897	9.5
Amadora	2001	175,872	12,511	7.1
	2009	181,774	19,994	10.9
Mafra	2001	54,358	1,808	3.0
	2009	64,217	4,394	7.0

Tab. 11-1: Demographic growth in Sintra, Amadora, Mafra (2001-2009). (Source: INE and SEF)

The Municipality of Sintra integrates the Lisbon Metropolitan Area and is served by road and train networks that facilitate a fast access to Lisbon. During the last few decades the Municipality has been under a strong urbanization pressure, due to the urban expansion in the region, determined by the growth of the tertiary sector in Lisbon, the population and housing saturation of the Municipality of Amadora, located closer to Lisbon along the same transportation networks that serve Sintra. Sintra has also been acquiring a significant number of new residents, attracted by the job market in some sectors of the local economy and the favorable housing prices.

The analysis of economic activity in Sintra indicates a growing weight of the tertiary sector, responsible for 70% of the employment, in contrast with less than 30% in the secondary sector, the primary sector showing only a residual value in the economy.

Sintra has also been characterized by a strong demographic increase during the last few decades. From 1991 to 2001, the population of Sintra grew by 39.3%, contrasting with a growth of 2.3% for the Greater Lisbon Area, 4.8% for the Lisbon and Tagus Valley statistic region and 4.6% for the whole country.

Most of the demographic growth may be attributed to the migratory flows.

The largest contribution in 2001 came from the European Countries, namely from EU Member States. In 2009 Cape Verde (55.6%) is the country with the highest number of resident nationals, followed closely by Brazil (20.4%). The group which aggregates nationals from PALOP countries is, by far, the most relevant (55.6% of the total). In second place, come Eastern European citizens (14.3%).

The second municipality studied in the MERIDIUM Project is Amadora. Its location in the periphery of the nation's capital had a direct influence on its demographic, economic and social structures: during the second half of the 20th century, the progressive development of transportation infrastructures that brought it closer to Lisbon and the industrial development that took place in the 1950s and 60s led to a strong demographic increase, influenced also by the attraction of low housing prices in a municipality so close to the center of economic activity—Lisbon. Amadora had, in 2001, one of the highest population densities of the country: 7,903/Km^2. Lisbon had, for the same period, a density of 1,410 inhabitants/Km^2.

Distribution by nationality of origin of immigrants in Amadora does not show, for 2009, any substantial change: the largest group still comes from PALOP countries (61%), with a majority from Cape Verde. Cape Verde nationals, however, have been replaced as the single most numerous community by Brazilian nationals (19%). Immigrants from Eastern European countries (7%) almost doubled in comparison to 2001 figures.

The Municipality of Mafra is located on the West coast of the country and integrates the periphery of the Lisbon Metropolitan Area. It has a low population density and shows a trend towards a strong population increase, partly due to the migration flows, attracted by job opportunities in a municipality where the tertiary sector has an increasing predominance. In 2002 this sector represented 68% of the enterprises and 59% of the jobs.

The dynamics of recent migratory flows led to a substantial increase in the number of immigrant residents and to a change in the ranking by nationality. Citizens from European countries represent now only 4% of the total. Brazil is the country with the greatest number of nationals

(59.1%). Three Eastern European countries: Ukraine, Moldavia and Romania, together, rank third.

In the three municipalities studied (Sintra, Amadora and Mafra) local implementation of policies and measures, defined at the national level, is the responsibility of the local administrative institutions, namely the creation of CLAII Centers. Their mission is to support immigrant citizens in regularization procedures, to disseminate information on legislation, acquisition of Portuguese nationality, access to services (health, education, employment and professional training, etc.).

Some initiatives and projects are being developed by civil society institutions: Churches, NGOs and Immigrant Associations. Several different institutions (Churches, NGOs) also offer support and social services to the immigration communities.

The following table shows the type of services available to immigrants in these localities.

LOCALITY	CLAII CENTERS	MUNICIPAL PROJECTS	CIVIL SOCIETY PROJECTS
Sintra	yes (6)	yes	yes
Amadora	yes (3)	yes	yes
Mafra	yes (1)	yes	yes

Tab. 11-2: Integration and support measures in Sintra, Amadora and Mafra

11.2.1.2. Setúbal District

The Setúbal Peninsula is part of the Lisbon and Tagus Valley Region and has a population of 845,858 inhabitants, 797,111 of them residing in the Setúbal Peninsula. The most heavily populated municipality is Seixal (INE, 2007), followed by Almada and by Setúbal, the district capital, with 122,554 inhabitants.

The long coastal area of the district plays a decisive role in the economy, mainly through the weight of tourism: the Região de Turismo da Costa Azul covers the municipalities of Setúbal, Palmela, Sesimbra and Alcácer do Sal. Port installations in Setúbal and Sines are also relevant to the economy, attracting businesses and jobs. The primary sector (agriculture, fishing and wine production) has some weight in some municipalities. The industrial sector (cement and paper manufacture) is also present.

The district population represents 8% of the national population and has experienced a 20% increase in the last two decades, the second biggest demographic expansion among all districts. The district has also shown, since the mid-1990s, a sharp increase in the number of immigrant residents: 15,985 in 1996, 20,214 in 2000, 41,637 in 2004 and 49,309 in 2009

According to SEF's Provisional data for 2009, Brazil takes first place (28%), followed by Cape Verde (18%). If we aggregate, however, the immigrants from the PALOP countries, they become the single most representative group (37.5%). Citizens from Eastern European countries (20.2%) come third, after Brazil. China, with 1,135 immigrants in this district, has contributed increasingly to the migratory flows in the country, especially in the urban centers. The school selected for the MERIDIUM survey is located in the Municipality of Setúbal.

The municipality of Setúbal, the district capital, with a heavy concentration of social facilities and services, attracts a significant number of immigrants.

YEAR	TOTAL POPULATION	FOREIGN LEGAL RESIDENTS	
		Total	**% of total population**
2001	113,934	3,850	3.4
2009	125,293	8,322	6.6

Tab. 11-3: Demographic growth in the Municipality of Setúbal (2001-2009). (Source: INE and SEF)

The migrant population in the Setúbal Municipality exhibits a somewhat different composition from that of other municipalities in the same district, with Brazilians occupying the first place in the ranking (42.9%). Eastern European citizens come second (23%), followed by citizens from PALOP countries (18%), a less numerous presence than in the overall district where they represent 37.5% of the total foreign population.

At the local level, the Municipality has been implementing political measures defined by the central government bodies: a CLAII Center, a Municipal Office (SEI) created in 2009 to provide specific information on employment, health, education, housing and culture, in Portuguese, Russian and Creole, a Cultural Center supported by the Municipality, for the use of the diverse ethnic and migrant communities, in a low income neighbourhood, the participation of Immigrant Associations in the *Local Council for Social Action (CLASS)*—a plenary body with deliberative powers. Civil Society institutions (NGOs and Associations) often form partnerships with official organisms to develop and implement projects and initiatives.

11.2.1.3. District of Faro

Faro District coincides in its totality with the province of Algarve. Its coastline is 150 kilometers long; its average population density is 80 inhabitants/Km^2. However, the population is concentrated in the high density territories on the coast, (Albufeira, Faro, Lagoa, Lagos, Olhão, Portimão and Vila Real de Santo António), where most of the economic activity is located; the low density municipalities in the mountainous interior (Serra) are characterized by an ageing and disperse population. The transition zone (Barrocal) provides agricultural products.

The tertiary sector (commerce and services) is the most relevant sector of the economy, as the main activity in the region —tourism— represents, directly and indirectly 60% of the jobs and 66% of the regional GDP. According to data supplied by Turismo de Portugal, the region welcomes close to 10 million visitors every year. Passengers in the Faro Airport in 2009 amount to almost five million. Global revenues from the tourist industry surpassed 500 million € in 2009 (29.3% of the overall hotel revenues in the country).

In 2009, the resident population totaled 430,084 people, an increase of 3,939 since 2008, and of 9.8% in terms of the population figures for 2001 (395,218). The relevant factor in this increase was most probably the increase in the migratory flows to the district, which showed a 0.9% crude rate of net migration as compared to the previous year.

The analysis of SEF's provisional data for 2009 shows that the dynamics observed in migratory flows in Portugal in recent years find a parallel in Faro District: where in the past migratory flows came predominantly from African countries, especially from the former Portuguese colonies, one nowadays sees a sharp increase in the flows coming from Brazil and from Central and Eastern European countries. China has seen its share in the composition of the migratory landscape increase significantly in recent years. The integration of immigrants in the regional job market comes as an answer to the needs of the regional economy, an economy driven by tourism. The immigrant population works mainly in the sub-sectors related to the tourism industry: hotels, restaurants, commerce, services and construction. The two schools chosen for the MERIDIUM sociolinguistic survey are located in the Municipality of Faro.

The Municipality of Faro is located on the coast, in the central area of the Algarve. In 2001, over 80% of the active population in the municipality was occupied in the tertiary sector: commerce, services, tourism industry, and real estate. The primary sector (agriculture, animal production and fishing) occupied just 3% of the population. The growth in the sub-sectors of the tourism industry attracts increasing numbers of migrants to the Faro Municipality

YEAR	TOTAL POPULATION	FOREIGN LEGAL RESIDENTS	
		Total	% of total population
2001	58,081	3,134	5.8
2009	58,675	7,326	11.5

Tab. 11-4: Demographic growth in the Municipality of Faro (2001-2009). (Source: INE and SEF)

Eastern European countries rank first, with Ukraine surpassing Brazil as the single most represented nationality in Faro.

Reacting to the sharp increase in immigrant numbers, local administrative authorities have pursued the implementation of measures advocated in the national legislation and the political guidelines emanating from the state organisms in charge of immigrant integration and assistance: the establishment of a CLAII Center, the institution of a Protocol, signed by SEF and the Municipality, in order to provide assistance to immigrant citizens in the local Health Centers, the establishment of a Regional Health Observatory for immigrant citizens, the opening in 2009 of a CNAI (*Centro Nacional de Apoio ao Imigrante*) extension in Faro and the publication of a Resources Guide for the inclusion of immigrant citizens and distribution of informative leaflets on immigrant access to social services. Government agencies in Faro are involved in training programs targeting adult immigrants.

11.3. Data Analysis

11.3.1. Characterization of the Sample - Children

The data collected did not reveal noteworthy differences between regions, municipalities and schools. As such, we chose to describe and discuss the sample as a whole.

11.3.1.1. Socio-demographic Characterization

272 children (86.1% of the total sample) were born in Portugal and 44 children (13.9%) were born elsewhere. Of those children not born in the survey country, 12 (3.8%) were born in Europe; 16 (5.1%) in African countries and 16 (5.1%) in South America, in line with the overall

predominance of PALOP countries and Brazil in the current migration patterns observed in the country.

If we adopt a finer categorization of the student population, based on the birth country of the child and the birthplace of his/her parents ("background")[5], further discriminating among lusophone and non-lusophone countries, the following results are obtained:

BACKGROUND		PUPIL'S COUNTRY OF BIRTH (N)		TOTAL (N)
		Portugal	Other country	
Native background	Both parents from PT	194	1	195
Mixed background	One parent from PT and the other from a lusophone country	31	0	33
	One parent from PT and the other from a non-lusophone country	25	2	27
Foreign background	Both parents from foreign lusophone countries	9	30	39
	One parent from a lusophone country	3	1	4
	Both parents from non-lusophone countries	2	10	12
	TOTAL	264	44	308
	Information not provided	8	0	8
	GRAND TOTAL	272	44	316

Tab. 11-5: Pupils by background and birth country

11.3.1.2. Sociolinguistic Characterization of the Sample[6]

When we examine the children's language use within and outside the family circle (see Tabs. 11-6a-c and 11-7a-c, p. 258 ff.)[7], the data in the

[5] See §7.3, Tab. 7-1, this volume.

[6] Throughout the analysis specific questions in the Children's questionnaire will be referred to as AQ followed by the number of the question (ex. AQ10). Similarly, the questions in the Adult questionnaire will be coded as BQ…

[7] In order to obtain complete comparability among the informants, only those who have provided valid answers for all the (categories of) interlocutors in each domain

sample exhibit predictable patterns: Portuguese is the language used mostly by children with native or mixed background (Nb/Mb), in every interactional context (with parents, siblings, grand-parents, schoolmates, friends, neighbours and teachers). Foreign-born children with foreign background (FFb) interact mainly in other languages with parents, siblings and grandparents, but use Portuguese in most interactions outside the family circle.

Native-born children with foreign background (NFb), though conforming to the pattern found outside home interactions, provide intriguing results in family interactions: Portuguese use in this domain is well above the figures for FFb children and very close to the results for children with partially or totally native background. The fact that immigration flows in Portugal have always had a strong component from lusophone countries may explain these results: the inclusion (Tab. 11-5 above) in this group of children from African countries with Portuguese as Official Language (PALOP), the ambiguity (for Brazilian children) of the label "Portuguese", covering both European and Brazilian Portuguese, children of returning Portuguese emigrants who may have Portuguese as the home language.

In interactions outside the family circle, the use of Portuguese is notably higher (in all domains of interaction) for this group than the figures found for foreign-born children with foreign background. Two factors, namely, the historical colonial connection of some of the countries of origin and emigrant return, relevant both for attitude and academic achievement studies in the Portuguese context, were not taken into account in this study. Further studies in these research areas should distinguish such aspects which influence family background status, as these could have an important impact on educational aspects.

Bilingualism in family interactions (mother, siblings and grandparents) is residual for children with native or mixed background (Nb/Mb) and more relevant for children with foreign background, with a higher incidence of the use of Portuguese in the group of those born in Portugal (NFb). The bilingual mode in Portuguese data is most probably linked to the ambiguity of the label "Portuguese" for Brazilian children (covering both European and Brazilian Portuguese), for some children born in or with a PALOP (African countries with Portuguese as Official Language) family background, and for children of returning Portuguese emigrants who may have Portuguese as the home language. A finer discrimination in

(or set of domains) will be taken into account (222 subjects out of 308 for the family domain and 300 subjects for interactions outside the family circle).

the categories is therefore required if we want to thoroughly understand bilingualism in the Portuguese student population.

INTERLOCUTOR	LANGUAGE USE (N AND %)			TOTAL
	Portuguese	Port. + other lg.	Other languages	
mother	166 *92.2*	12 *6.7*	2 *1.1*	180 *100.0*
father	168 *93.3*	7 *3.9*	5 *2.8*	180 *100.0*
siblings	171 *95.0*	6 *3.3*	3 *1.7*	180 *100.0*
grandparents	174 *96.7*	4 *2.2*	2 *1.1*	180 *100.0*

Tab. 11-6a: Language use in interactions within the family domain as self-reported by children with native and mixed background (Nb/Mb)

INTERLOCUTOR	LANGUAGE USE (N AND %)[8]			TOTAL
	Portuguese	Port. + other lg.	Other languages	
mother	9 *(90,0)*	0 -	1 *(10.0)*	10 *(100.0)*
father	9 *(90.0)*	1 *(10.0)*	0 -	10 *(100.0)*
siblings	9 *(90.0)*	0 -	1 *(10.0)*	10 *(100.0)*
grandparents	7 *(70.0)*	2 *(20.0)*	1 *(10.0)*	10 *(100.0)*

Tab. 11-6b: Language use in interactions within the family domain as self-reported by native-born children with foreign background (NFb)

[8] In tables where cases do not reach the sum of 100, percentages are listed within brackets.

INTERLOCUTOR	LANGUAGE USE (N AND %)			TOTAL
	Portuguese	Port. + other lg.	Other languages	
mother	6 *(18.8)*	6 *(18.8)*	20 *(62.4)*	32 *(100.0)*
father	6 *(18.8)*	6 *(18.8)*	20 *(62.4)*	32 *(100.0)*
siblings	9 *(28.1)*	4 *(12.5)*	19 *(59.4)*	32 *(100.0)*
grandparents	5 *(15.6)*	0 -	27 *(84.4)*	32 *(100.0)*

Tab. 11-6c: Language use in interactions within the family domain as self-reported by foreign-born children with foreign background (FFb)

INTERLOCUTOR	LANGUAGE USE (N AND %)			TOTAL
	Portuguese	Port. + other lg.	Other languages	
classmates	242 *97.6*	5 *2.0*	1 *0.4*	248 *100.0*
friends	237 *95.6*	8 *3.2*	3 *1.2*	248 *100.0*
neighbours	247 *99.6*	0 -	1 *0.4*	248 *100.0*
teachers	242 *97.6*	6 *2.4*	0 -	248 *100.0*

Tab. 11-7a: Language use in interactions outside the family domain as self-reported by children with native and mixed background (Nb/Mb)

INTERLOCUTOR	LANGUAGE USE (N AND %)			TOTAL
	Portuguese	Port. + other lg.	Other languages	
classmates	13 *(92.9)*	0 -	1 *(7.1)*	14 *(100.0)*
friends	11 *(78.6)*	2 *(14.3)*	1 *(7.1)*	14 *(100.0)*
neighbours	13 *(92.9)*	1 *(7.1)*	0 -	14 *(100.0)*
teachers	14 *(100.0)*	0 -	0 -	14 *(100.0)*

Tab. 11-7b: Language use in interactions outside the family domain as self-reported by native-born children with foreign background (NFb)

INTERLOCUTOR	LANGUAGE USE (N AND %)			TOTAL
	Portuguese	Port. + other lg.	Other languages	
classmates	27 *(71.1)*	9 *(23.7)*	2 *(5.3)*	38 *(100.0)*
friends	21 *(55.3)*	10 *(26.3)*	7 *(18.4)*	38 *(100.0)*
neighbours	30 *(78.9)*	5 *(13.2)*	3 *(7.9)*	38 *(100.0)*
teachers	34 *(89.5)*	1 *(2.6)*	3 *(7.9)*	38 *(100.0)*

Tab. 11-7c: Language use in interactions outside the family domain as self-reported by foreign-born children with foreign background (FFb)

11.3.1.3. Self-ascription and Sense of Belonging

When asked to define themselves using five adjectives[9], children of all groups do not show significant differences in terms of description categories and Positive/Negative connotations of traits, even if native born children with foreign background (NFb) seem to differ slightly from the other two groups, a difference probably related to cultural differences.

Ethno-linguistic and religious terms were residual for all children though slightly higher for children with foreign background: 0.5% for children with native or mixed background (Nb/Mb), 1.7% for foreign born children with foreign background (FFb) and 2.7 % for native born children with foreign background (NFb).

When questioned about their sense of belonging and allegiance with social groups, national and transnational entities (their class, friends, town of residence, Portugal, Europe), answers in the three groups indicate a strong sense of identification with the smaller circles (family and socializing groups) and a predictable divergence in the figures related to the larger entities (see Tab. 11-8).

[9] Data related to AQ10 "Who are you? Please use five words to represent yourself"

Category of Informants	Positive sense of belonging[10] (N and %) to:				
	Class	Friends	Town	Portugal	Europe
Nb/Mb	222	233	236	245	234
(255 respondents)	*87.1*	*91.4*	*92.5*	*96.1*	*91.8*
NFb	10	12	11	10	12
(14 respondents)	*(71.4)*	*(85.7)*	*(78.6)*	*(71.4)*	*(85.7)*
FFb	28	35	28	18	20
(39 respondents)	*(71.8)*	*(89.7)*	*(71.8)*	*(46.2)*	*(51.3)*

Tab. 11-8: Positive identification with groups as self-reported by children (AQ12-AQ16)

11.3.1.4. Attitudes toward Languages and Awareness of Linguistic Diversity

Children were questioned on language attitudes towards specific languages (Portuguese, language of origin and other languages). The data show some interesting results:

A. A majority of children in the three groups consider their L1 to be as beautiful as other languages: 168 children with native or mixed background (66.1% of the category); 25 foreign-born children with foreign background (61.0% of the category); 7 native-born children with foreign background (50.0% of the category);
B. Having relatives or parents who speak a language other than Portuguese is seen as positive by 104 children with native or mixed background (52.0%); 23 foreign-born children with foreign background (57.5%); 8 native-born children with foreign background (57.1%).

Awareness of surrounding linguistic diversity does not seem to be the same among the groups, with children having a foreign background revealing a higher awareness of diversity in their school: while only 93 children with native or mixed background (36.5%) report that in their school there are “many” or “quite a few” pupils who speak other languages besides Portuguese (AQ20), these options have been chosen by 24 foreign born children with foreign background (58.5%) and 6 native born children with foreign background (42.9%).

[10] Questionnaire alternatives “very much” and “just enough” are aggregated for AQ12 to AQ16.

A similar distribution of frequencies can be observed also when pupils are asked how often they hear people speaking a language other than Portuguese in the town where they live (AQ22): also in this case, FFb and NFb are more aware of the linguistic diversity around them (56.1% and 64.3%, respectively) than children with native or mixed background (19.6%)

Attitudes towards diversity do not show striking differences in the three groups (see Tab. 11-9 below).

CATEGORY OF INFORMANTS	OPTIONS (N AND %)					
	Amused	**Curious**	**Annoyed**	**Scared**	**I do not notice**	**I don't know**
Nb/Mb (255 respondents)	39 *15.3*	169 *66.3*	10 *3.9*	4 *1.6*	11 *4.3*	22 *8.6*
NFb (14 respondents)	2 *(14.3)*	11 *(78.6)*	0 -	0 -	0 -	1 *(7.1)*
FFb (41 respondents)	6 *(14.6)*	21 *(51.2)*	1 *(2.4)*	1 *(2.4)*	7 *(17.1)*	5 *(12.2)*

Tab. 11-9: Children's attitudes towards diversity (AQ33) "How do you feel when you hear someone speaking a language other than Portuguese?"

11.3.2. Characterization of the Sample - Adults

11.3.2.1. Socio-demographic Characterization of the Sample

Among the 316 adult informants, women largely prevail (253, 80.1%), a pattern that reflects gender role assignment prevalent in the ethnic groups included in the sample: women who work at home and are child caretakers.

Age distribution was as expected, concentrated for both groups in the following age brackets:

1) 30-39 years: 113 Portuguese-born informants out of 228 (51.6%); 43 foreign-born informants out of 88 (49.4%);
2) 40-49 years: 79 Portuguese-born respondents (36.1%) and 37 foreign-born informants (49.4%).

When taking the country of origin into consideration, sample distribution reflected roughly the ethnic composition of the country for these age brackets: on the total sample, 228 informants were born in Portugal (72.2 %); 24 in other European countries (7.6 %); 17 in America (5.4%); 44 in Africa (13.9%); 1 in Asia/Middle East (0.3%); 2 in Australia (0.6%). Such a distribution mirrored the more relevant migration flows (PALOP countries, Eastern Europe, Brazil).

The composition of the family unit (see Tab. 11-10 below) reflected the variety of family models found throughout the country; the noteworthy numbers of respondents living with the extended family may reflect, in part, lodging arrangements brought about by the economic crisis.

INFORMANT'S COUNTRY OF BIRTH	TYPE OF FAMILY UNIT (N AND %)		
	monoparental	**nuclear**	**extended**
Portugal (221 respondents)	26 *11.8*	169 *76.4*	26 *11.8*
Other countries (82 respondents)	13 *(15.9)*	46 *(56.1)*	23 *(28.0)*

Tab. 11-10: Composition of adult informants' family units

Schooling figures (Tabs. 11-11a and 11-11b below) showed that the majority of both native-born respondents and adults born in other countries (as well as their partners) have 9 years or more of schooling (68.8% of Portuguese-born and 70.9% of foreign-born respondents). Data for both groups show residual illiteracy rates.

INFORMANT'S COUNTRY OF BIRTH	YEARS OF SCHOOLING (N AND %)			
	No schooling	**1-8 years**	**9-13 years**	**+ 13**
Portugal (223 respondents)	1 *0.4*	69 *30.8*	92 *41.1*	62 *27.7*
Other countries (86 respondents)	1 *(1.2)*	24 *(27.9)*	34 *(39.5)*	27 *(31.4)*

Tab. 11-11a: Years of schooling – Adult informants

INFORMANT'S PARTNER COUNTRY OF BIRTH	YEARS OF SCHOOLING (N AND %)			
	No schooling	**1-8 years**	**9-13 years**	**+ 13**
Portugal	1	82	74	28
(185 respondents)	*0.6*	*44.3*	*40.0*	*15.1*
Other countries	0	22	24	19
(65 respondents)	-	*(33.8)*	*(36.9)*	*(29.3)*

Tab. 11-11b: Years of schooling – Adult informants' partners

Employment rates of respondents point to high unemployment among the (mostly female) respondents (25.6% among native-born respondents and 18.6% for foreign-born individuals), and their (mostly male) partners (10.1% and 6.8% respectively).

Occupations declared by respondents were aggregated in 8 categories, based on the ISCO-88 classification (see Tab. 11-12):

- 1 - Legislators, senior officials, managers;
- 2/3 – Professionals; technicians and associate professionals;
- 4/5- Clerks; service workers, shop and market sales workers;
- 6/7/8 - Skilled agricultural and fishery workers; crafts and related trades; plant and machine operators and assemblers;
- 9- Elementary occupations;
- 0 - Armed forces and Security personnel;
- Others

OCCUPATIONAL GROUP	INFORMANT'S BIRTH COUNTRY (N AND %)	
	Portugal	**other countries**
1	1 *0.6*	2 *(2.9)*
2/3	51 *30.4*	15 *(21.4)*
4/5	68 *40.4*	19 *(27.1)*
6/7/8	11 *6.6*	11 *(15.7)*
9	21 *12.5*	13 *(18.6)*
0	5 *3.0*	0 -
Others	11 *6.6*	10 *(14.3)*
TOTAL RESPONDENTS	168 *100.0*	70 *(100.0)*

Tab. 11-12: Occupational categories of adult informants

Portuguese-born respondents show higher rates in groups 0 (Armed Forces and Security forces), 2/3 (professionals), 4/5 (tertiary sector); those born in other countries show preponderance in groups 1 (managers), 6/7/8 (Secondary sector) and 9 (elementary occupations).

11.3.2.2. Sociolinguistic Characterization of the Sample

Portuguese is the mother tongue for 217 native-born informants (98.6% of this group), and for 33 foreign-born informants (38.4%). Portuguese is used almost exclusively by Portuguese-born respondents within the family circle (95.8% with partner; 93.7% with children), with colleagues (86.8%), friends (87.7%) and neighbours (95.4%). Figures for foreign-born respondents are significantly lower, although Portuguese is still the dominant language (with partner —58.6%; children —67.0%; co-workers —74.5%, friends —58.8% and neighbours —80%). Portuguese is the major language in all domains of language use (see Tab. 11-13 below).

Informant's Country of Birth	Portuguese in language use domains (N and %)				
	At work	For reading	Speaking with friends or family	Writing	Watching a movie
Portugal (214 respondents)	190 *88.8*	205 *95.8*	213 *99.5*	182 *85.0*	162 *75.7*
Other (83 respondents)	75 *(90.4)*	70 *(84.3)*	79 *(95.2)*	66 *(79.5)*	55 *(66.3)*

Tab. 11-13: Portuguese in language use domains as self-reported by adult informants

11.3.2.3. Self-ascription and Sense of Belonging

The use of ethno-linguistic and religious terms in self-description is, in the case of adults as with children, residual. Only 0.5% of Portuguese-born respondents employed these descriptors, compared to 2.7% of foreign-born individuals. Such low figures and the focus of the actual descriptors in the religious sphere seem to confirm the very low incidence of ethnic and religious issues in the overall society although, since these issues were not the main focus of MERIDIUM, they deserve further investigation.

In terms of allegiance and sense of belonging to particular groups (family, friends, and town of residence, Portugal, Europe and country of origin) results are similar to those found in children's data: high identification with one's family group and country of origin. Respondents born in other countries seem to be divided between two allegiances: the new and the old country (see Tab. 11-14 below).

Informant's Country of Birth	Positive sense of belonging[11] (N and %) to:				
	Family	Friends	Town of residence	Portugal	Europe
Portugal (223 respondents)	220 *98.7*	205 *91.9*	193 *86.5*	217 *97.3*	182 *81.6*
Other (87 respondents)	84 *(96.6)*	73 *(83.9)*	65 *(74.7)*	49 *(56.3)*	43 *(49.4)*

Tab. 11-14: Positive identification with groups as self-reported by adult informants (BQ15-BQ19)

[11] Questionnaire alternatives "very much" and "just enough" are aggregated for BQ15 to BQ19.

Sociability networks differ for the two groups: 87.8% of Portuguese-born respondents assert that their friends are born in Portugal; 69.6% of them indicate that their friends speak a language other than Portuguese, while 43.7% of foreign-born individuals have friends coming from their country of origin. 78.2% of these respondents say their friends speak a language other than Portuguese.

11.3.2.4. Attitudes toward Languages and Awareness of Linguistic Diversity

Awareness of language diversity[12] is similar for both groups (98.2% and 98.8% respectively). The persistent higher awareness for linguistic diversity in the neighbourhood of residence, shown by foreign-born citizens, may be explained by a higher residential concentration of this group in areas where immigrants prevail, either for economic reasons or proximity to the community of origin.

The perception of linguistic diversity ("how many languages, besides Portuguese, are spoken in your town?" BQ28) shows slightly different results from region to region and from municipality to municipality, possibly due to variation in local and individual factors such as: local economy (relevance of tourism industry) occupation, varying characteristics of residential areas of respondents.

Overall attitudes towards linguistic diversity fall roughly within the same range, showing a positive outlook towards diversity for both groups. The majority of respondents does not agree with linguistic isolationism (BQ22: "it is better to speak with those who speak the same language"): 147 (66.5%) of those born in Portugal and 56 (64.5%) of the foreign born respondents; 149 (67.7%) Portuguese-born respondents and 56 (64.4%) born in other countries do not see linguistic diversity in neighbourhoods as a source of problems; both groups see tolerance and mutual respect as a solution (96.0% and 83.6% respectively).

Feelings towards languages other than Portuguese, heard in daily situations, are strikingly similar (see Tab. 11-15).

---

[12] The percentages aggregate two choices available for the question (BQ29) "Have you heard languages other than Portuguese spoken around you?": "it happens often" and "it happens occasionally".

INFORMANT'S COUNTRY OF BIRTH	ATTITUDES TOWARDS LANGUAGES OTHER THAN PORTUGUESE HEARD IN DAILY LIFE (N AND %)					
	amused	**curious**	**annoyed**	**scared**	**I do not notice**	**I do not know**
Portugal (224 respondents)	11 *4.9*	155 *69.2*	3 *1.3*	3 *1.3*	42 *18.8*	10 *4.5*
Other (85 respondents)	3 *(3.5)*	56 *(65.9)*	1 *(1.2)*	1 *(1.2)*	16 *(18.8)*	8 *(9.4)*

Tab. 11-15: Attitudes of adult informants towards languages other than Portuguese heard in daily life (BQ40)

Both groups consider their mother tongue as beautiful (54.4% *vs* 67.0%) and just as useful (54.3% *vs* 62.8%) as other languages.

Both groups rate the importance of knowing how to speak other languages very similarly; 56.7% (*127*) of Portuguese-born individuals and 56.3% (49) of the foreign-born rate it very positively.

11.3.2.5. Perception of the Existence of Local Measures Promoting Multilingualism

The data reveal an interesting and consistent trend in what concerns the perception of the existing measures (at the local level, by municipalities, schools etc.) targeting the promotion of multiculturalism and multi-/plurilingualism: foreign-born respondents show higher awareness rates relating to the existence of such measures in the community, in particular the promotion of other languages (as seen in the Tables 11-16 and 11-17, next page). A possible explanation is the fact that they are the target group for these measures and, as such, they are more aware of their availability in the community.

The role of schools in the promotion of bilingualism and multiculturalism was deemed to be unsatisfactory by both groups (54.3% *vs* 52.3%, respectively) [13].

---

[13] Percentages aggregate figures for "very little" and "not at all" for question BQ44: "In general, do you think that in Portugal schools create an interest among children towards people from different cultures and who speak other languages?",

OCCASIONS FOR INTERCULTURAL ENCOUNTERS	INFORMANT'S BIRTH COUNTRY (N AND %)	
	Portugal	Other countries
Many times	1 *0.4*	2 *(2.4)*
Sometimes	23 *10.3*	7 *(8.2)*
A few times	26 *11.7*	21 *(24.7)*
Never	36 *16.1*	10 *(11.8)*
I don't know	137 *61.4*	45 *(52.9)*
TOTAL RESPONDENTS	223 *100.0*	85 *(100.0)*

Tab. 11-16: Perception of local measures promoting intercultural encounters (BQ42)

PROMOTION OF OTHER LANGUAGES	INFORMANT'S BIRTH COUNTRY (N AND %)	
	Portugal	Other countries
Many times	2 *0.9*	6 *(7.1)*
Sometimes	10 *4.5*	7 *(8.2)*
A few times	41 *18.4*	16 *(18.8)*
Never	28 *12.6*	9 *(10.6)*
I don't know	142 *63.7*	47 *(55.3)*
TOTAL RESPONDENTS	223 *100.0*	85 *(100.0)*

Tab. 11-17: Perception of measures by local institutions targeting promotion of other languages (BQ43)

The cross tabulation by region (district) regarding whether schools stimulate interest in multilingualism and multiculturalism shows similar results, even if the District of Setúbal exhibits a slightly less pessimistic view (see Tab. 11-18).

	REGION (N AND %)		
EVALUATION[14]	Lisbon	Setúbal	Faro
Positive	32 *27.8*	28 *(37.3)*	34 *29.1*
Negative	62 *53.9*	39 *(52.1)*	64 *54.7*
Does not know	21 *18.3*	8 *(10.6)*	19 *16.2*
TOTAL RESPONDENTS	115 *100.0*	75 *(100.0)*	117 *100.0*

Tab. 11-18: (BQ44) "In general, do you think that in Portugal schools create an interest among children towards people from different cultures and who speak other languages?": region-disaggregated data

11.4. Discussion of the Relevant Findings

The descriptive data presented above highlight a few relevant vectors in the sociolinguistic landscape of contemporary Portugal, transformed in the last two decades by intensified migratory flows into the country: an increasing social complexity and a linguistic heterogeneity that characterizes those flows. Today, people in the towns and cities of European Portugal are confronted with ethnic, cultural and linguistic diversity, in a country accustomed to exporting labour to other countries and characterized by a strong linguistic and ethnic homogeneity.

An emergent multicultural and multilingual society such as this raises questions and concerns related to the effects of immigration in the country and on the lives of immigrants and nationals. The State, throughout successive governments, has tried to rise to the challenge by enacting key legislation, by creating agencies and by putting measures and guidelines to promote immigrant integration in place[15]. The key question is: what effects have those policies and measures had on:

a) the attitudes of the population towards immigration-induced diversity in the areas of higher immigrant density,

b) the perception of the existence of such policies and measures

[14] "Positive" answers aggregate the alternatives "very much so" and "quite a bit"; "negative" answers aggregate the alternatives "very little" and "not at all"

[15] See MERIDIUM Country Report – Portugal (eng), p. 6-9 and the Portuguese longer version of the Report, p. 34-67, available at: http://meridium.unistrapg.it/?q=en/country-report

c) the effective integration of immigrant groups, particularly at a linguistic level?

Here again, the data from the MERIDIUM survey may offer us a glimpse at the kind of multilingual and multicultural society Portugal is becoming and may offer insights regarding the type of immigrant integration and whether this has been successful or not. The data of this project, as far as the Portuguese sample is concerned, can be seen as a "real-time" observation of a specific moment in Portuguese history. It also provides an indication of areas which require further investigation and calls for a more pro-active implementation of measures, in particular the data concerning:

1) domains of language use;
2) self-ascription and sense of belonging;
3) attitude toward languages and awareness of linguistic diversity;
4) awareness of local measures and the role of schools in the promotion of integration.

If we look at the data for these categories, we find that in this sample:

- children with foreign background use mostly languages other than Portuguese within the family circle and Portuguese outside it; for foreign-born adults, Portuguese is the major language in all domains of language use, although within their family circle the use of Portuguese is significantly lower than its use by native-born informants;
- both children and adults in the sample show high identification with the family group and the country of origin. Foreign-born adult respondents seem to be divided between two allegiances: the country of origin and the new country. Children in the same group exhibit higher identification rates both with Portugal and their country of origin. Identification with Europe is significantly lower in the foreign-born group;
- social networks differ for the two groups: native-born respondents declare that most of their friends were born in Portugal while foreign-born individuals mostly have friends coming from their country of origin;
- overall attitudes towards linguistic diversity fall roughly within the same range, showing a positive outlook towards diversity for both groups: the majority does not agree with linguistic isolationism and does not see linguistic diversity in the neighbourhood as a source of problems. Tolerance and mutual respect are highly valued. Feelings

towards languages heard in daily life are similar: negative feelings are low in both groups and both groups consider learning languages as very important;
- both groups support immigrant language teaching in the public school system, although acceptance rate is higher for nationals.

These findings suggest that in the high contact areas, with a high concentration of immigrants, Portuguese nationals show a noteworthy degree of tolerance and solidarity towards non-nationals, and a positive view towards language diversity.

In a comparative study of educational achievement in 14 countries (Northern European, Southern European, United States, Canada, Australia and New Zealand), Buchmann and Parrado (2006: 366) suggest that "national-level institutional variations in the incorporation of immigrants condition the effect of immigrant status on educational achievement.". Buchmann and Parrado (2006: 350 ff.) propose three institutional "types":

1) inclusionary immigration regimes, countries with long immigrant traditions, such as the United States, Canada, New Zealand and Australia;
2) exclusionary immigration regimes, where labour immigration is seen as temporary and where there is "slight inclination to accommodate the cultural demands of minorities" such as the Northern European countries;
3) a third group of countries in Southern Europe (Spain, Portugal and Greece), with a long tradition of emigration, which have made a rapid transition from sending to receiving countries and which "have a rather neutral stance toward immigrants".

Further investigation is needed to validate the link between the strong institutional efforts towards immigrant integration that have been made in Portugal and the tolerance and relative solidarity towards immigrants suggested in the MERIDIUM study.

Furthermore, changing definitions of identity, both in native-born informants and foreign-born informants, hinted by the answers to this survey, demand further studies to investigate this identity-changing process in a complex society that is being transformed by immigration.

The efficacy of the implementation of integration measures and educational policies at a local level, in terms of awareness of the existence of those measures and of the role of schools in promoting plurilingualism and multiculturalism has also been considered in this study and requires urgent attention by the agents involved.

11.5. Suggestions for Further Research

The results of data analysis for the Portuguese sample of the sociolinguistic research conducted by the MERIDIUM project exhibit some predictable patterns and a notably unexpected, albeit positive, tendency: the strong support shown by adult respondents (in particular those born in Portugal) towards the teaching of immigrant languages in the public school system, notwithstanding the economic crisis being felt in the country and its manifestations, such as budget cuts and increasing unemployment rates. Xenophobic attitudes are not manifest, and support for plurilingual education (see Tab. 11-14 below) seems to be in line with mostly tolerant views towards linguistic diversity, as shown by respondents.

ACCEPTANCE	INFORMANT'S BIRTH COUNTRY (N and %)	
	Portugal	**other country**
Yes	157 *70.4*	58 *(67.4)*
No	21 *9.4*	14 *(16.3)*
Does not know	45 *20.2*	14 *(16.3)*
TOTAL RESPONDENTS	223 *100.0*	86 *(100.0)*

Tab. 11-19: Acceptance/rejection of immigrant language teaching in the public school system

When broken down by district, overall support is also high: Lisbon – 72.3%; Setúbal – 62.5%; Faro – 67.0%. Similar results are obtained when crosstabulated by school. The theoretical discussion on bilingual education and its advantages (both for student success and for integration) is still going on in countries with a large percentage of non-native speakers. In Portugal, a study conducted by ILTEC (*Instituto de Linguística Teórica e Computacional*) with the support of Gulbenkian Foundation[16] resulted in a pilot project (one bilingual class) on bilingual education, in a Lisbon area school[17]. However, there is no guarantee that such initiatives may continue.

[16] "Diversidade Linguística na Escola Portuguesa", 2003-2007, available at http://www.iltec.pt/divling/index.html, accessed September 26, 2012.

[17] "Bilinguismo, aprendizagem do Português L2 e sucesso educativo na escola portuguesa - 2007-2012". For details on this Project, see Mateus (2011).

Further research on language attitudes towards the teaching of immigrant languages is necessary in order to lead to other studies, possibly on the same lines with the one mentioned above. Such research could pave the way for other projects geared to the teaching of immigrant languages in public schools, especially those with a large number of non-native speakers.

Furthermore, as the recent European economic crisis develops and deepens, with severe consequences in the Portuguese case, the decrease in immigrant flows into the country, the accelerating rate of immigrant return to their countries of origin, the significant increase in the number of Portuguese nationals who resort to emigration, are rapidly changing the demographic, cultural and linguistic landscape of Portugal. Austerity measures with cuts that reverberate throughout the economy and the society are endangering the efforts towards integration and, most likely, will affect the attitudes toward multilingualism hinted in the MERIDIUM study. Whatever the outcome of this changing scenario the MERIDIUM project will serve as a useful and revealing survey which also offers the opportunity to compare multilingualism and multiculturalism in Portugal's Primary schools to the situation present in other European contexts.

References

Buchmann, C., and E. A. Parrada. 2006. Educational Achievement of Immigrant-Origin and Native Students: A Comparative Analysis Informed by Institutional Theory. In *The Impact of Comparative Education Research on Institutional Theory* (*International Perspectives on Education and Society Series)*, eds. D. P. Baker and A. W. Wiseman, 7, 345-377. Oxford: Elsevier.

Huddleston, T. *et al.* 2011. *Migrant Integration Policy Index (2011).* Brussels: British Council and Migration Policy Group.

Mateus, M. H. M. 2011. Diversidade Linguistica na Escola Portuguesa. *Revsita Lusófona de Educação* 18. 13-24 (available at: http://redalyc.uaemex.mx/redalyc/pdf/349/34922201002.pdf, accessed September 26, 2012).

Mateus, M. H. M. *et al.* eds. 2008. *Diversidade Linguística na Escola Portuguesa.* Lisbon: Fundação Calouste Gulbenkian.

MIPEX. 2011. *Migrant Integration Policy Index III*. Brussels: British Council and Migration Policy Group (available at: http://www.mipex.eu/download, accessed September 26, 2012)

Reis, J. *et al.* 2007. *Imigrantes em Portugal. Economia, Sociedade, Pessoas e Território.* Coimbra: CES (available at:

http://www.ces.uc.pt/myces/UserFiles/livros/176_relatorio_imigracao_qualificada.pdf, accessed September 26, 2012)

Vertovec, S. 2006. *The Emergence of Super-Diversity in Britain*. ESRC Centre on Migration, Policy and Society Working Papers, 25. Oxford: University of Oxford (available at: http://www.compas.ox.ac.uk/fileadmin/files/Publications/working_papers/WP_2006/WP0625_Vertovec.pdf, accessed September 26, 2012)

—. 2007. Super-diversity and its implications. *Ethnic and Racial Studies* 30/6. 1024-1054.

CHAPTER TWELVE

MIGRATORY EXPERIENCE AND ATTITUDES TOWARDS MULTILINGUALISM: THE ROMANIAN CASE STUDY

LILIANA COPOSESCU, ELENA BUJA, GABRIELA CUSEN AND LUIZA MESESAN-SCHMITZ

12.1. Introduction

The present paper is the final outcome of the LLP MERIDIUM (*Multilingualism in Europe as a Resource for Immigration—Dialogue Initiative among the Universities of the Mediterranean*) international project which aims at studying the nature of the correlations between the linguistic and educational policies and the improvement/diffusion of the attitudes toward multilingualism and linguistic diversity in the countries of the Mediterranean. Within the project coordinated by *Università per Stranieri di Perugia*, Romania had a unique status, being regarded as the "exporting" country of migrants, all the other partner countries being "importers" of migrants. Due to this position, we might be expected to provide data referring to the outbound migration phenomenon[1], but in this paper we have chosen to focus on how migratory experiences may influence individual repertoires and attitudes towards multilingualism/ plurilingualism, making special reference to migrant workers having decided to leave their temporary place of residence and return to Romania. We have called these migrants "returnees".

Our paper is structured as follows: Section 12.2 provides information on the Romanian national context, with reference to linguistic aspects,

[1] We have provided such data both in the Country Report and in the Context Analysis (http://meridium.unistrapg.it/it/country-report)

ethnic minorities, language policies, language education and migratory profile. In Section 12.3 we present our case study, starting from the criteria for the selection of the two areas in the country where the study was conducted, moving on to the research methodology and concluding with a comparative presentation of the perception and attitudes of Romanian children and adults towards linguistic diversity and multilingualism/ plurilingualism. Section 12.4 focuses on the returnees, i.e. children and their parents with migratory experience in our corpus of data. Finally we draw some conclusions and mention some directions for further research (Section 12.5).

12.2. The Romanian National Context

The first section aims at presenting the demographic and linguistic characteristics of Romania, as well as those elements that are necessary for the evaluation of the migratory profile and of the migration policies in Romania.

12.2.1. Linguistic Aspects, Ethnic Minorities and Language Policies

Romanian is a European language, first and foremost due to its geographical position. Being the only Romance language in Eastern Europe, it is of special interest to foreign specialists.

According to Avram (2001), the Romanians represent the largest nation of south-eastern Europe, the total number of speakers of Romanian being estimated to around 29 million, out of which 20 million, i.e. 90% of the country's population speak it as their mother tongue. Just like some other languages spoken within the European Union, Romanian has the privilege of not being confined within a single state. It is also both the national and the official language of the Republic of Moldova, where it is spoken by about 3 million people. Romanian is also the mother tongue of approximately 1.5 million people in the countries geographically close to Romania, some of them already part of the European Union (Bulgaria, Greece, Hungary, etc), some others aspiring to this status (Macedonia, Albania, Serbia, and Montenegro). It is also the language of many migrants who settled in various European countries (Austria, France, Sweden, Germany, etc.). Consequently, Romanian is not a European language at a regional level only, but also, to a certain extent, at a continental level.

Apart from the majority population speaking Romanian[2], 16 ethnic minorities co-exist in the country, these minorities differing in size[3], geographical distribution[4] and length of cohabitation with the majority population[5]. Irrespective of these differences, all these ethnic minorities are supported by the Romanian government in their endeavours to preserve and develop their national identity through their own cultural, religious or political organizations, with weekly or monthly periodicals published either in their mother tongue or bilingually (one of the languages being Romanian). These publications are meant to promote the cultural traditions, the literature and the history of the respective people. Moreover, children of the largest minority groups can study in their mother tongues at primary and secondary levels (Bulgarians, Serbians and Lipovan Russians), or even at tertiary level (the Hungarians, who can enrol in a number of Romanian universities that offer education programs in Hungarian). On the political arena, almost all the minority groups are represented in the Parliament or in the Senate or Chamber of Deputies. All these rights are in agreement with the international conventions and treaties[6] that Romania has ratified, as well as with the Romanian Constitution and regulations.

12.2.2. Language Education in Romania

This section gives an overview of language education in Romania at the pre-university level of the national education system. The issue is approached from two perspectives: first, that of modern/foreign language education and second, that of minority language education[7].

---

[2] Romanian is the single official and national language of Romania

[3] The largest minority is represented by Hungarians (6.6% of the total population), whereas the smallest one is represented by the Armenians (0.1% of the entire population), according to the 2001 census.

[4] The Hungarian minority live in Transilvania; the Czechs and Slovaks settled in the western part of the country, while the Roma population is scattered all over the country.

[5] Some groups came to the territory of present-day Romania as early as the 10th century (the Germans) or the 12th century (the Armenians), whereas some other minorities settled in the country more recently (the Italians started coming to Romania in the 19th century).

[6] *The Convention for the Protection of National Minorities* and *The European Charter for the Regional or Minority Languages.*

[7] The source of the information detailed here is the web-site of the Romanian Ministry of Education, Research, Youth and Sports: www.edu.ro.

Foreign/modern language learning/teaching starts at the primary level of education with some similar activities even at the pre-school level. In Romanian primary schools, children start the study of foreign languages when they are in the 3rd grade (aged 9). Occasionally, at the request of parents, schools organise foreign language courses for children aged 7 or 8 (1st or 2nd grade). The foreign languages taught in primary schools for 2 hours a week are English, French, German, Russian, Italian and Spanish. The main objectives at this level of foreign language education focus on the development of the four language skills and on the acquisition of culture and civilisation elements specific to the respective countries.

In secondary schools (grades 5 to 8) pupils study foreign languages such as English, French, German, Italian, Japanese, Portuguese, and Spanish. They study 2 foreign languages for 2 to 3 hours a week[8]. The foreign language curriculum at this level focuses on explicit and straightforwardly evaluable results of learning. This curriculum is based on the EU Recommendation (2006/962/EC) and states that compulsory education graduates will have a "European profile" consisting of key-competences. The development of a competence to communicate in a foreign language is directly aimed at academic skills and the transferability of all other key competences belonging to the same curricular area.

In Romanian high-schools, students study English, French, German, Italian, Russian, Portuguese, and Spanish. Like at the lower secondary level, students study 2 or 3 foreign languages for 2 to 6 hours a week depending on the type of high-school and class they attend. The foreign language curriculum at this level stipulates the development of general and specific academic skills focusing on the communicative function of language and on the main elements of the process of communication. Another important focus of language learning/teaching in high-schools is that of educating the students in the spirit of European values.

Secondly, minority language education in Romania is regulated by the curriculum for mother tongue languages and literatures which refers to the teaching and learning of such minority languages as Hungarian, German, Polish, Bulgarian, Croatian, Russian, Romani[9], Serbian, Slovak, Turkish and Ukrainian. The students belonging to minority language communities are encouraged to study their own language and literature in order for them

---

[8] For L1, the curriculum stipulates 2 or 3 hours per week, depending on the school's decision, whereas for L2, the number of hours is fixed to 2 per week.

[9] Much to our surprise, a participant in our May 2011 workshop, who is a member of the Roma community, mentions the fact that there is a growing trend in producing and teaching Romani literature among the approximate 2,000 Roma children in Braşov county (see presentation on the MERIDIUM website).

to develop and improve their competences in the area of both receptive and productive language skills. This allows them to acquire knowledge that is specific for the spiritual and cultural heritage of their ethnic group and offers a better understanding of intercultural issues within the Romanian space. One important aspect worth mentioning here is that of the teaching of Romanian to primary school children in contexts where the language of education is that of the minority ethnic group. The study of Romanian is regulated by a curriculum which emphasises the development of language skills that can help them understand the Romanian spiritual values and offers them the chance for a better life in a multicultural environment. This curriculum is based on the communicative-functional model of language teaching and is similar to the one for foreign languages.

Children live in a multicultural environment not necessarily in the social context of our country, but also in many foreign countries where their parents or relatives have recently migrated.

12.2.3. Migratory Profile

After 1990 an increase in the outgoing migration is recorded in Romania, the highest rate being reached in 2001. Three important waves of migration have been noticed: ethnic-based outbound migration between 1990 and 1995 accounts for the first wave; the second wave between 1995 and 2002 was characterised by study-related and work-related migration. Starting with the third emigration wave (2002), labour abroad becomes a mass phenomenon, the number of emigrants constantly growing until 2007. After Romania's accession to the European Union in 2007, a slight decrease in the number of legal emigrants is recorded (it might well be that especially because of the free accession to countries in the European Union the number of non-recorded work emigrants has actually increased).

Several forms of emigration have been identified: permanent legal emigration, temporary labour emigration, or emigrants returning to Romania (returnees), starting from 2008. Temporary labour emigration as well as illegal labour emigration is the most often encountered form of migration, and the countries preferred by Romanians adopting such forms of emigration, starting from 2002, are Italy and Spain. The same preference has been recorded among persons who intend to emigrate in the near future. The selection criteria indicated by these migrants include the number of acquaintances and relatives in the respective countries, the existence of direct or indirect (through other members) experience with foreign countries, the proficiency level in Italian and Spanish, or the ease in learning these languages.

Moldova is the Romanian geographical area with the highest number of labour emigrants, followed, at equal rates (insignificant differences) by the Transilvania and Muntenia regions. In terms of intentions to emigrate, the ranking changes, Banat being first, followed by Moldova and Transilvania. As for permanent legal emigration, Transilvania and Muntenia rank first, and Moldova second. In other words, Moldova is the origin of most illegal emigrants, also called "Euro-commuters", while Transilvania and Muntenia are the origin of most permanent legal emigrants or emigrants with work contracts. Within these geographical areas, there are differences in migratory routes. Most emigrants to Italy come from Moldova; Muntenia provides most emigrants to Italy and Spain, whereas people from Transilvania choose Italy, Spain, and Germany.

With the starting of the world economic crisis the phenomenon of emigrant families returning home has been recorded. Most emigrants that left the country in the last five years come from Moldova, and the same area has the highest number of returnees from Italy, as shown by the number of children re-enrolled in Romanian schools in 2008. According to statistics on children re-registered in Romanian schools, Transilvania ranks second. Based on these data, Moldova and Transilvania regions have been selected for the investigation of school-children' and adults' attitudes towards multilingualism.

12.3. The Case Study

The aim of this section is to report the findings of the survey conducted in Romania concerning the degree of awareness of the presence of plurilingual repertoires and the propensity to conceive of them as a resource among elementary school pupils and their parents.

12.3.1. Selection of Country Areas for the Case Study

In order to meet the main objectives of the case study, that is the evaluation of the level of awareness of the benefits of plurilingual competencies and the extent to which these competencies are perceived as resources, the following criteria have been taken into account:

- high rate of both permanent and temporary labour migration (see Tab. 12-1 below);
- a region with an urban centre with a minimum of 100,000 inhabitants and some rural centres which are significant in terms of the migration phenomenon under examination: a large number of

families having left to work abroad and a large number of school-aged children; (See Tab. 12-2 below)

- a large number of people intending to join the labour migration groups in the following years.

COUNTY	2006	2007	2006-2007
Braşov	831	557	1388
Sibiu	768	413	1181
Cluj	557	325	882
Mureş	486	277	763
Hunedoara	308	247	555
Sălaj	80	39	119
Covasna	125	78	203
Alba	239	142	381
Bistriţa-Năsăud	176	120	296
Harghita	290	103	393

Tab. 12-1: Number of permanent work migrants in Transilvania counties (Source: National Institute for Statistics)

TOWNS IN BRAŞOV COUNTY	Population (2009)	People over 18 years of age (2009)	N of migrants (2000-2008)	N of migrants per 1000 inhabitants over 18 years of age (2000-2007)
Braşov	278003	238453	3788	15.9
Făgăraş	38050	31907	1008	31.6
Codlea	24618	19283	200	10.4
Săcele	32604	24683	113	4.6

Tab. 12-2: Number of migrants in Braşov County (Source: Braşov County Statistics Department)

On the basis of these criteria, the Braşov team has selected Transilvania (as a region), and Făgăraş (as an investigation area) because the migratory flows constitute a trend in these localities since 1990. Moreover, this region comes second in point of temporary labour migration and intended migration.

"Babeş-Bolyai" University from Cluj gathered data from Moldova, because the largest number of Romanian migrants to countries like Italy and Spain come from this region.

These minimal criteria allow a comparative approach meant to identify certain significant factors influencing the opinions, attitudes and behaviour related to plurilingual competencies of both school-aged children and adults living in the area mentioned above. The selected region allowed for the analysis of at least the following situations:

- children whose parents (either only one or both) being labour migrants, are taken care of by relatives;
- families (with children) that have never left their place of residence;
- temporary labour migrant families having worked abroad for at least one year and returned to their place of residence.

12.3.2. Research Methodology

Taking into account both the theoretical criteria and the convenience of data collection, we have undertaken a case study, based on the administration and analysis of 300 questionnaires (150 given to school-aged children and 150 to their parents/guardians) for each of the two regions, Transilvania and Moldova. In the micro-region of Transilvania, the study was conducted in the urban place of residence Făgăraş and in a number of surrounding villages (Dacia, Jibert, Cuciulata, Hoghiz, Buneşti, Feldioara) which were selected according to the same criteria employed for the selection of the region: high rate of temporary labour migration, older migratory flows, large numbers of returnees (estimated according to the large number of children re-enrolled in schools in 2006-2009. (see Tabs. 12-3, 12-4 and 12-5 below)

	RE-ENROLLED RETURNEES (2006-2009)					
	PRIMARY SCHOOL	LOWER-SECONDARY AND HIGH-SCHOOL	TOTAL	RETURNEES FROM		
				Italy	**Spain**	**Other countries**
N	107	232	339	217	54	68
%	*31.3*	*68.7*	*100.0*	*65.0*	*16.0*	*19.0*

Tab. 12-3: Returnees in Braşov schools (source: Braşov County School Inspectorate)

SCHOOL	TOTAL STUDENT POPULATION	CHILDREN BORN ABROAD	NATIVE CHILDREN WITH A DIRECT MIGRATION EXPERIENCE	NATIVE CHILDREN WITH AN INDIRECT MIGRATION EXPERIENCE	TOTAL CHILDREN WITH A MIGRATION EXPERIENCE (N AND %)
Nr.1	688	12	2	16	30 *(4.4)*
Nr.2	626	20	7	40	67 *(10.7)*
Nr.3	306	4	5	40	49 *(16.0)*
Nr.5	232	-	-	15	15 *(6.5)*
Nr.7	117	3	2	25	30 *(25.6)*

Tab. 12-4: Children with migration experience in primary schools in Făgăraş (source: Braşov County School Inspectorate)

SCHOOL	TOTAL STUDENT POPULATION	CHILDREN BORN ABROAD	NATIVE CHILDREN WITH A DIRECT MIGRATION EXPERIENCE	NATIVE CHILDREN WITH AN INDIRECT MIGRATION EXPERIENCE	TOTAL CHILDREN WITH A MIGRATION EXPERIENCE (N AND %)
Buneşti	191	-	1	38	39 *(20.4)*
"Aron Pumnul" Cuciulata	175		1	71	72 *(41.1)*
Hoghiz	286	2	5	24	31 *(10.8)*
Jibert	211	4	3	10	17 *(8.0)*
Dacia	74	-	-	6	6 *(8.1)*
"Petru Rareş" Highschool Feldioara	424	-	4	100	104 *(24.5)*

Tab. 12-5: Primary-school children with migratory experience (source: Braşov County School Inspectorate)

In the micro-region of Moldova, the following settlements in Bacău County were selected: Oneşti (urban region) and Mănăstirea Caşin, Lupeşti, Ştefan cel Mare (rural region).

Prior to this, the drafted questionnaires had been pre-tested in "Axente Sever" School in Aiud (Alba County) and in School Nr. 12 in Braşov in order to see how the respondents (both children and adults) fare with the questions contained in them. This proved to be very useful in that it helped us identify some problems related to the formulation of the questions, the lexical items contained in them, or to the possible multiple answers provided for them. We realized that especially in the questionnaires meant for the children, some words were too abstract for them (e.g. *colectiv* "group"—AQ12, *cetăţean* "citizen"—AQ14), and thus the questions in which they occurred were left unanswered. We therefore tried to refine our research tool, making it as clear and accessible as possible for our respondents.

On feeding the answers provided by the Romanian subjects into the MERIDIUM database, we faced some problems related to the selection of the best variant(s) provided by this instrument, on the one hand, and to the translation of some Romanian terms, on the other hand. As we were growing accustomed with the template for the data analysis, our discussions revealed that we did not know exactly which option to select. For example, when children did not use the correct term for languages (they either indicated the name of the country where the language is spoken or they used a wrong suffix—*limba ţigăneşte* instead of *limba ţigănească* "gypsy language"), some of us tended to choose the correct term from the list. Neither was there unanimous agreement as to some translations. Thus, the adjective *deştept* encountered in the children's characterization of themselves was translated by us by the synonymic series: "clever", "smart", or "intelligent". This called for a meeting in which we came to an agreement with respect to both the translation of the terms employed by the subjects in the questionnaires and to the choices we were to make from the lists provided in the template.

In the following subsection we will report on our findings related to some of the dimensions that we considered relevant for indicating the attitude of the Romanian subjects towards multilingualism/ plurilingualism.

12.3.3. Perception and Attitude of Romanian Children and Adults towards Linguistic Diversity and Multi-/Plurilingualism

Indicators of the dimension are the respondents' perception of the existence of linguistic diversity around them and of languages spoken other than the official language of the country they live in.

Both the children and the adults in our study perceive a rather small linguistic diversity in the local context. Thus, only a small number of the children (11%) assert that they have many school mates/friends who speak other languages than Romanian. These mates/friends speak, in the respondents' opinion, one or two languages, mainly English, French, German, Hungarian, Italian, and Spanish. The languages they know are limited to those spoken in Europe, such as Italian, Spanish, French, English and German, these being the languages they would like to know when they are older. With adults, perceived nationality is rather homogenous and to a large extent indefinite: about a quarter of the overall sample could not answer the question about nationality in their neighbourhood and nearly half of them thought there are few or no non-nationals in their neighbourhood.

When it comes to language diversity at the global level, the Romanian children named between five to ten languages spoken in the world and 67% of the respondents identified mainly the Chinese writing system from among the ones given. With respect to the adults, they best recognised the Cyrillic and the Chinese writing systems (with 79% correct identifications and about 21% wrong identifications each), followed by the Arabic one (45% correct and 55% wrong answers).

The comparative analysis among countries that participated in the survey (Italy, Slovenia, Spain, Portugal and Malta) shows that Romanian children have fewer linguistic resources, but this relates to the national context. They have less personal experience of contacts with peers speaking other languages than their native language, and have fewer opportunities to hear children speaking other languages than Romanian. An explanation could be that there are very few Romanian children with parents born in other countries (5 "non-native" respondents). Comparatively, Romanian children named fewer languages which are spoken throughout the world than children from Spain or Italy.

Romania distinguishes itself from other countries in the group as being the least exposed to ethno-linguistic diversity by some indicators. The most significant difference is that the Romanian adults report less often hearing people speak other languages than Romanian and many of them have not had such an experience: about 10% of the Romanian sample report never having such an experience, while the percentage for the other countries is 0 or close to this value. Romania also scores highest for the "it happens occasionally" answers to the same question.

Perceived diversity in everyday life context is also at lowest rates with Romania. Moreover, exposure to foreign languages at a local level is lowest for Romania, as it is the Romanian sample that makes up the largest percentage of people indicating no language, other than the official language of the country, being spoken locally: nearly 50%, as compared with nearly 30% in Spain, the second largest, which is also very high when compared to percentages in the other countries in the group, where "no other language" is mentioned by only 5% of the respondents, in each case. When it comes to familiarity with different language systems, Romanian adults score second highest on correct recognition of the Cyrillic script, with only Slovenia scoring higher.

Romanians' attitude towards linguistic diversity is measured according to respondents' inclination towards learning foreign languages, the social prestige associated with multilingualism/plurilingualism, and perception of linguistic diversity as a resource or a problem. Of the overall number of children who have friends or relatives who speak other languages than Romanian, 62% feel proud, 4% feel embarrassed, and 21% do not really care. However, most children (67%) feel curious when they hear people speaking foreign languages, and only 4% have negative feelings, like being annoyed or scared. When it comes to hearing a language they do not know, the degree of acceptance drops: 21% of the respondents associate it to some noise while 42% do not know what to answer.

Tolerance towards other languages seems to be quite high, since only 34% consider their mother tongue to be the most beautiful, 55% of the sample declare the language they have learned at home to be beautiful, but accept that there are other beautiful languages as well, and only 11% consider other languages to be more beautiful than their mother tongue.

The data show that a great majority of the children (97%) would like to be able to speak foreign languages when they are older, and they list the major European languages: English, French, German, Italian, Spanish and also languages like Hungarian or Russian.

Most of the adult respondents in our study (three-fourths of the overall sample) consider it to be a good thing to have foreign friends. They also find it positive to meet people who speak one's own language. Most of the respondents (almost 80%) believe that respect and tolerance among people would make speaking different languages unproblematic. Evaluations of native language tend to be more positive on the aesthetic (or rather emotional) criterion than on an instrumental one. There are more respondents who believe their native language is the most beautiful and not other languages (40% versus 3%) than are respondents who think their native language is very useful and not other languages (22% versus 27%). Attitude towards speaking well at least one language, besides one's own native language/s, is overwhelmingly positive: almost all of the respondents (91%) consider this to be "very much" and "just enough" important.

As compared to the other countries in the study, Romanian respondents show least openness towards ethno-linguistic diversity, as they agree mostly with the idea that it is better to meet people who speak one's own language: 65%, while percentages for the other countries are below 40%. Nevertheless, Romanian subjects give the highest value to speaking foreign languages, as they make up the highest percentage (60%) of "proud" attitudes with relatives and/or friends who speak languages which are different from the official language of the country. They also show highest emotional affinity towards their mother tongue: almost 40% find it to be the most beautiful, while the correspondent percentage for Malta is nearly 30% and for the other countries, around 20%.

There is no significant difference among countries in terms of children's positive attitude towards learning foreign languages, but it is noticeable that Romanian children tend to prefer private lessons as a way of learning new languages. They feel as proud if they have friends or relatives that speak other languages than the official language of their country, and as curious when they hear people speak foreign languages as children from the other countries in the group. However, there is difference in terms of evaluation of the native language, more than 30% of the Romanian children assessing their mother tongue in emotional terms, as being the most beautiful language.

The attitude towards linguistic diversity and multilingualism/ plurilingualism should be understood in the socio-linguistic context of Romania and should be correlated with the Romanians' migratory experience. Though more than 16 ethnic groups coexist with the Romanian majority, these represent less that 10% of the country's population and are scattered over the entire territory. Consequently, ethnic Romanians are not so much confronted with speakers of other languages. A higher concentration of minority groups appears in Transilvania, which is reflected in the people's attitudes towards linguistic diversity. These people are more indifferent to linguistic diversity due to their frequent exposure to the languages of the minorities, so their experience with a multilingual environment is not something new for them. At the same time, they also think that linguistic diversity may constitute a problem and a source of conflicts, especially when members of the ethnic minorities do not speak the official language of the country, i.e. Romanian.

On the other hand, those persons who had the experience of a much larger linguistic diversity, as are the Romanians with a migratory experience, show a more positive attitude towards this issue. This may also be due to the different contexts in the host countries they have lived in, where they noticed that linguistic diversity is even larger than in Romania and that despite this, people can still communicate in the official languages of the respective countries.

When it comes to speaking more "foreign" languages, the Romanians' attitude becomes more favourable. As long as there is one official language, which could be used by all the inhabitants of a country to communicate among themselves without any problems, having a diverse/rich linguistic capital is very much appreciated, those people who master a number of foreign languages being respected. This aspect is encouraged by the educational policy of Romania: as compared to children in other EU countries, Romanian children have the possibility to learn more European languages in secondary school, in high-school, and later on at university (where, depending on the program they enroll in, they can study two foreign languages).

In the following section of our paper we pay special analytical attention to the category of respondents which we called "returnees", i.e. Romanian people having worked/lived abroad for at least one year and who returned to Romania. The reason of our selection of this particular group of respondents is that we wanted to identify whether, and to what extent, a migratory experience may influence individual repertoires and attitudes towards multilingualism. Despite the small number of returnees (32.9%, representing 96 adults, and 11.8%, representing 37 children) in our study, we have attempted to draw a profile of individuals with direct and indirect migratory experience as well.

12.4. Returnees

This section is an overview of studies on returnees in the context of the migration phenomenon, followed by a sociolinguistic profile of the returnees in our study.

12.4.1. Studies on Returnees

At present in Romania there are very few studies on returnees (adults and children). One of these studies, *Locuirea temporară în străinătate. Migraţia economică a românilor: 1990-2006* [=*Temporary Residence Abroad. Economic Migration of the Romanians: 1990-2006*] (FSD, 2006) was conducted by the Soros Foundation and reports on the migration phenomenon until 2006. It is worth mentioning that the major reason for work migration was people's discontent with the economic situation in their native regions. It seems that the migratory experience has affected both the mentality and the attitudes of the returnees with respect to the local community. This is due to the fact that they feel more attached to the European countries where they prospered economically. This was actually their main goal for emigrating.

Other studies on returnees are: *Comunităţi româneşti în Spania* [=*Romanian Communities in Spain*] (FSR, 2009), conducted by a team of specialists from the Faculty of Sociology, Bucharest University, in 2008 and funded by the Soros Foundation; the surveys *Comunitatea românească în Italia: condiţii sociale, valori, aşteptări* [=*Romanian Community in Italy: Social Conditions, Values, Expectations*] (MMT-ASG, 2007) and *Comunitatea românească în Spania: condiţii sociale, valori, aşteptări* [=*Romanian Community in Spain: Social Conditions, Values, Expectations*][10] conducted by Metro Media Transilvania and the Agency for Governmental Strategies, in 2007 and 2008 respectively; *Enquesta Nacional de Inmigrantes*, a survey conducted by the National Institute for Statistics in Spain between October 2006 and February 2007 (INE, 2009). These surveys provide some information about Romanian emigrants and a profile of those who intend to return to Romania.

Bădescu *et al.* (2009: 268-283) bring a number of new elements that can add to the profile of the returnees in 2006, based on a qualitative piece of research conducted on high-school pupils whose parents have had migratory experience. An important characteristic is that they have a larger linguistic capital (i.e. foreign languages spoken by the respondents) than respondents that had no migratory experience (this is also confirmed by our study). The study shows that in some cases returnees with high-school children have become more careful with children's schooling than they had been before the migratory experience. There are situations in which returnees have worked with people of different ethnic origins, having the same status of "immigrant" and have thus become more tolerant towards foreigners than they had been before their migratory experience. The conclusion of the study is that optimism, social confidence, political participation and tolerance are significantly higher with returnees than with people who have had no migratory experience.

Statistical data concerning the children who have returned to Romania after a migratory experience are even scarcer than those related to adults. There are two studies carried out by the Soros Foundation: *Efectele migraţiei: Copii rămaşi acasă* [=*Effects of Migration: The Children Left at Home*] (FSR, 2007) and *Şcoală şi comunitate. Model de intervenţie în comunităţile cu copii rămaşi acasă* [=*School and Community. A Model of Intervening in the Communities with Children Left at Home*] (FSR, 2011). Both studies partially tackle the situation of children who returned to Romania after having spent some time abroad.

---

[10] The report of this survey, which was available on the website of the Romanian Government until October 2011 (http://www.publicinfo.gov.ro/pagini/sondaje-de-opinie.php), has been removed recently; for a summary, see http://cauta-si-gaseste.blogspot.it/2011/06/agentia-pentru-strategii-guvernamentale.html, accessed September 26, 2012.

A special category of returnees who represent a potential vulnerable group consists of school-age migrants that have been (re-)enrolled in the Romanian educational system after arriving in the country. Until 2009, over 6,000 pupils who had studied for various time spans abroad, especially in Italy and Spain, had been enrolled in Romanian schools (FSR, 2011: 21).

According to Gmelch (1980), (quoted in FSR, 2011: 22), the reintegration of returnees is very problematic especially for females and children, in the case of the latter the effects being more severe for school-age and teen-age pupils. The study carried out by the Soros Foundation in 2011 highlights the major problems the children who returned after a migratory experience are confronted with: general problems of integration in the school system, differences between the educational systems, language problems, having been discriminated against while abroad, reasons for returning to Romania, as well as the bureaucracy related to the procedure of re-enrollment in the Romanian schools.

According to the authors of the study, there are two categories of children with migratory experience: on the one hand, there are children who come in touch with the Romanian educational system for the first time in their lives, and on the other hand there are children who, prior to going abroad, had attended (at least for one year) the classes of a Romanian school. Thus, for the latter, the following problems may occur: catching up with the subjects in order to reach the level of the grade they have been assigned to or being enrolled a second time in the same grade in order to recuperate the information they had missed while abroad.

The same problems are true of the children who had no prior contact with the Romanian education system. Moreover, they may also have difficulties in using the Romanian language (they either do not know it at all or they make grammar mistakes).

A third study conducted by the Soros Foundation in 2008 *Efectele migraţiei: Copii rămaşi acasă. Riscuri şi soluţii* [=*Effects of Migration: The Children Left at Home. Risks and Solutions*] (FSR, 2008) describes what happens to the children of the Romanian emigrants in Spain with respect to their integration in the Spanish system. The Romanians living in Spain are mainly interested in the rapid integration of their children in the Spanish society, especially by learning the language. For this reason, they prefer to use Spanish when talking to their children. Consequently, the children either do not speak Romanian at all, or they acquire a variety of Romanian different from that spoken in Romania, "spiced" with many Spanish expressions and characterized by many grammatical mistakes. It follows that the migrants' children speak Spanish better than Romanian because on entering the Spanish educational system, they have classes with native speakers of Spanish. Romanian, as a mother tongue, is acquired from their parents, whose level of education is rather low and whose Romanian language competence leaves a lot to be desired. These children seem to adapt easily to the Spanish educational system, even if, in the beginning, they might encounter some language problems. But once they return to Romania (due to the world's economic crisis), they have major problems because of their poor competence in Romanian.

Another problem these children face is the adjustment to a new educational system, with a new syllabus, with other subjects and other means/ways of teaching. Generally speaking, schooling in Romania is perceived to be more difficult than abroad. In most western European countries the teaching methods are more attractive and practical, children do not have to do so much homework, and the teacher-student relationship is less formal. Although in Romania children get high marks more easily than abroad, the subjects to be studied are more numerous and taught at a higher level.

Children have different opinions related to the Romanian versus the foreign educational system. There are Romanian pupils who performed extremely well in foreign schools, but also pupils who could not cope in the Western educational systems. The phenomenon could be determined on the one hand by the age when the child enters the new educational system (the younger the child, the easier the adaptation), and on the other hand by his/her competence in the language in which they are taught.

Unfortunately, the integration of these children in the Romanian system depends to a large extent on the goodwill and motivation of the teachers, as there are no policies in this respect. There is, nevertheless, an advantage the returnees have. According to some teachers' statements (in the press), coming back to Romania seems to have a positive effect on children's psyche: while abroad, children may have felt "foreigners", being excluded by their class-mates. This discrimination is very much present among the children who migrated to countries where the Romanian communities are quite large (as is the case of Spain and Italy). This discrimination could be the reason why they are now returning. An analysis of some Romanian newspapers identifies the economic crisis and the lack of financial stability in the host countries as major causes of the return of the Romanian migrant families. Very few newspaper articles mention the children's inadaptability to the foreign educational systems as a return cause.

As migration is a rather recent and growing phenomenon in Romania, and re-enrollment of returnee children in Romanian schools is even less frequent, the problem of granting immigrant children the right to study in their mother tongue in Romanian schools seems less relevant for our respondents (one third of the adult respondents did not provide an answer in connection with this issue). The attitude in favour and against creating opportunities for returnee children could be interpreted as reflecting a more general trend of giving linguistic minorities the opportunity to study in their mother tongues in Romanian schools.

The extent to which schools promote, among children, an interest in and an open attitude towards people of various cultures and speaking different languages seems to be of equally reduced relevance for our respondents: only one third of the respondents in the sample expressed an opinion in this respect. These respondents think that schools do not contribute enough to the creation of opportunities for diverse cultural and linguistic awareness.

12.4.2. Profile of Emigrants Intending to Return to their Country of Origin

Starting from some of the above-mentioned studies, Sandu (2010: 113-117) draws a profile of emigrants intending to return. The emigrants' intention of returning is a result of evaluation and indicates either failure or fulfilment of objectives assumed in the country of emigration. Their resources, experience, and feelings of identity are evaluated. The economic, human (education and knowledge of the language of the country of emigration) and sociocultural resources (the frequency of participation in religious services) play an important role in migrants' decision to return to their country of origin. Despite the fact that most of them were better off abroad, they decided to return to Romania due to their lack of competence in the language of the host country.

This is confirmed by our study where most of the subjects with migratory experience (returnees) state that they know the language of the country they lived in, only to contradict themselves later, by reporting that they cannot read, write, or speak in that language.

A second reason for returning to their country of origin is the desire to be with their families. Thus, family constitutes a major element in the propensity to return to the country of origin. According to the study *Locuirea temporară în străinătate. Migrația economică a românilor: 1990-2006* [=*Temporary Residence Abroad. Economic Migration of Romanians: 1990-2006*] (FSD, 2006: 69), the households with migrants or those with one family member having work experience abroad are significantly associated with the extended nuclear family. Thus, 68% of

Romanian households with migratory experience have extended families.

Our study brings further evidence in this respect, as the interviewed returnees live in Romania together with their children in an extended family. Compared to the other respondents in the sample, the returnees live in families composed of larger numbers, as they live with other members of the extended family. At present more than a half of them are unemployed.

Finally, another important factor in their intention to return is their feeling of identity. Respondents who feel to a higher degree that they belong to their town of residence decide to return to Romania but postpone the moment until they fulfill the financial objectives for which they have emigrated in the first place (Sandu, 2010: 129).

In conclusion, there seems to be a number of elements that determine the intention of emigrants to return to the country of origin and they can, indirectly, contribute to envisage a profile of returnees, on the basis of economic, human and sociocultural resources.

The following subsection draws the sociolinguistic profile of the Romanian returnees with direct and indirect migratory experience in our study, as compared to children with no migratory experience, in an attempt to bring further evidence with respect to the migration phenomenon and its effects on attitudes and perception of multilingualism/plurilingualism. We have three categories of returnees: children with direct migratory experience, children with indirect migratory experience (via their parents), and adults with direct migratory experience.

12.4.3. Children with Direct Migratory Experience in our Study

Children with direct migratory experience are those pupils who have lived with their families abroad for at least one year and have returned to Romania.

The socio-linguistic description of the sample is done in terms of family composition, the linguistic resources of the subjects, the dimensions of languages spoken at home and outside their family, perceived identity and group identification, and attitude towards linguistic diversity and learning foreign languages.

12.4.3.1. Family Composition

Children with direct migratory experience report having lived in a country other than Romania. Their main destinations were Italy, Spain and

Poland (the most common destination of Roma children). A large number of fathers of such families do not live with their children. Fathers usually work as installation operators either on car and various equipment assembly lines or as unskilled workers. Mothers, on the other hand, may work as service operators or in commerce. There are comparatively more relatives living abroad in these families, especially in Italy, Spain and Germany, than in the other families. The majority of the returnees also have relatives in Italy.

12.4.3.2. Linguistic Repertoires

Most of these children (72%) can speak the language of the country they lived in. In Romania, many continue to speak this language with their parents but some of them do not speak it with anybody at all. The majority of the children with a migratory experience feel proud to speak the language of the country they lived in. As hypothesised by the studies reviewed previously, some of these children (28%) had problems with Romanian when they re-enrolled in the Romanian schools.

When they were younger, some of these children with a migratory experience spoke a different language from the one they speak at present (German, English, Italian, Polish, Spanish or Turkish). They also have better knowledge of Italian and Spanish since they acquired these languages at home with their parents, grandparents, siblings or other relatives who also had a migratory experience.

The social network to which the returnee children belong is characterised by a larger linguistic diversity than that of children with no migratory experience. Thus, these children have a larger number of friends who speak languages other than Romanian and their parents have more acquaintances/friends who speak various foreign languages. This is confirmed by the children in our study, who reported to a great extent that they hear languages other than Romanian spoken around them.

The children with a migratory experience have a similar level of knowledge about the languages spoken throughout the world and list the same foreign languages as the children with no migratory experience. The foreign languages mentioned are either the ones they study at school (English, French and German), or the ones learned while the returnees were abroad (Spanish, Italian and Polish). Neither is there any difference in the identification of the writing systems (Cyrillic, Arabic, Chinese, and Devanagari) by returnees and children who have never been abroad. This is also obvious in the equal number of primary school children who identified the four writing systems. A possible explanation for the lack of differences registered in the answers is the fact that none of the four writing systems is being used in the European countries the Romanians mainly chose as a destination. The Chinese writing system, on the other hand, was easily identified by both groups of children due to the fact that Chinese scripts appear on products imported from China.

12.4.3.3. Attitude Towards Linguistic Diversity

Returnee children feel more indifferent to their relatives speaking other languages than Romanian, while children with no migratory experience feel prouder of this to a larger extent. In other words, children who have a migratory experience and are used to linguistic diversity do not feel this is important. Children with no migratory experience find it interesting that people in their families speak other languages than Romanian and consider that other languages are more beautiful than their mother tongue, while returnees give more importance to their mother tongue and consider it to be the most beautiful.

12.4.3.4. Perceived Identity and Group Identification

Perceived identity has been operationalised in questions in which respondents were asked to describe themselves in five words, and to express their feeling of belonging to groups of classmates/friends, place of residence, and citizenship.

Returnees, just like all the other children in the sample, describe themselves mainly in terms of personality traits, like for instance *cinstit/ă* (honest), *harnic/ă* (hard-working), *ambiţios/oasă* (ambitious), *isteţ/eaţa* (clever). These children do not define themselves in terms with ethno-linguistic connotations, so we may conclude that their migratory experience has not had any impact on this aspect of their identity, as they characterize themselves just like the respondents who have not been abroad.

Returnees feel less integrated in their class at school as compared to children with no migratory experience, but feel more integrated in their group of friends. This could be due to the fact that their friends might have also had migratory experience and speak the same foreign language. Comparatively, returnees feel less attached to the city they live in, they identify themselves less with being Romanian and they feel they are citizens of the European Union to a larger extent. The fact that returnees lived abroad accounts for their feeling of belonging rather to the European Union than to the community they live in at present.

By comparison with the other children, returnee children perceive a smaller linguistic diversity at school, as they have fewer classmates speaking other languages. This can be correlated with their considering themselves less integrated in their class. The languages they hear around them are similar to the ones reported by all the other children in the sample: English, French, Italian, Spanish and Hungarian.

12.4.3.5. Attitude Towards Learning Foreign Languages

Returnee children show greater interest than the other children in the sample in learning other languages than the major European languages when they are older. Of the major European languages they seem to favour Italian. Other major European languages they wish to learn when they grow up are English, French, German and Spanish. Just like the other children in the sample, they wish to learn these languages to be able to travel, for the job they would like to have and because they like to learn languages. The children in this category reported more than the other children that one of their reasons for learning languages is that their parents can also speak other languages. Figure 12.1 below shows the most salient features of the respondents in this category.

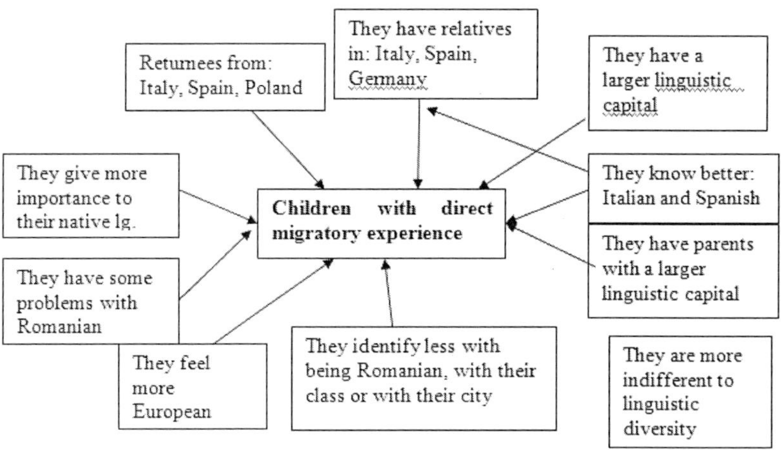

Fig. 12-1: Profile of children with direct migratory experience

12.4.4. Children with Indirect Migratory Experience (via their Parents)

Some of the interviewed children (31%) have an indirect migratory experience via their parents who worked abroad and returned, or only one of the parents returned, the other still being in a foreign country at work. These children's profile is partially similar to that of the children with a direct migratory experience. In these families there are more fathers who do not live with their children because they work. As with the returnees with direct migratory experience, the main occupations of the parents who have worked abroad are: installation operators or workers on car and various equipment assembly lines for fathers, and service operators or workers in commerce for mothers.

In the families of children with indirect migratory experience there are comparatively more relatives living outside the country than in the families of all the other children in the sample, especially in Italy, Spain and Germany. Consequently, they are more proficient in Italian, Spanish or German than the other children because they acquire these languages at home with their parents, grandparents, siblings and other relatives. They report being better at speaking and understanding these languages than at reading or writing them. The languages they wish to learn when they are older are Italian, English, French, German and Spanish. Italian is at the top of their preferences.

In terms of identity, there are no differences between these children and the rest of the sample. Both categories are identified by personality elements, but the children with indirect migratory experience do not report any aspects with an ethno-linguistic or religious connotation. They identify themselves as European citizens more than the rest of the children.

Experience with ethno-linguistic diversity is greater among these children since they mention hearing other languages to a larger extent. This is obvious when they report that their parents have friends who speak other languages than Romanian.

The indirect migratory experience, but in particular the direct one, has a great impact on the linguistic repertoire and on the attitude towards linguistic diversity, but does not have a major influence on the attitude towards foreign languages. These children have a much richer linguistic repertoire, as they know Italian and Spanish, languages that they have acquired from their parents/relatives who spent some time in the countries of Europe where these languages are spoken. Their level of competence is not necessarily a high one. Linguistic diversity (through contact with speakers of other languages from other countries or with relatives with a migratory experience) for these children is something common, so they do not have any emotional reactions when they hear people speaking other languages. However, this does not diminish their interest in learning other foreign languages, showing a propensity for those languages spoken by their relatives who have a migratory experience. The Romanian educational context encourages this attitude, as most of the foreign languages studied in the Romanian schools overlap with those spoken by the adults who lived/worked abroad (Italian, German and French).

12.4.5. Adults with Migratory Experience

An important number of respondents in the overall sample (one third) report having worked or lived abroad. For about half of them, experience outside the country lasted for only a few months, and for a quarter of them, it lasted for more than five years. The most favoured destination countries were Italy, Germany and Spain.

Most of the respondents having had migratory experience (76%) report knowing the language spoken in the host country. Many of them (about one third of the overall sample) indicate that their partners (wife/husband) have also lived or worked abroad, the favoured destinations being again Italy, Germany and Spain.

12.4.5.1. Perceived Identity and Group Identification

Migratory experience does not make a significant difference in the way people see and describe themselves: respondents who have worked or lived abroad feel part of their families just about as much as those with no such an experience and, just as in the case of the rest of the sample, they present themselves very minimally in terms of ethno-linguistic or religious connotations. Even though the respondents' views in this respect are quite similar, there is some slightly less strong identification with friends and city/town (4% and 8% less cumulated positive answers for the two questions, respectively) for adults with migratory experience, which leads to a further hypothesis that migratory experience could lower community belonging feelings. In terms of citizenship, migratory adults also feel more Romanian than European, the reports for the two subgroups being quite close for the European identification (about 59%) and slightly lower for the Romanian identification (89% cumulated "just enough" and "very much" answers for respondents with migratory experience, as compared with 92%, which represents the corresponding percentage, for non-migrants).

Significantly less respondents who have worked or lived abroad report having most of their friends from their country of origin (82% affirmative answers, as compared with 97% affirmative answers for adults with no migratory experience); instead there is no difference with respect to the plurilingual capital of their friends or relatives, which leads to the idea that the migratory experience increases the chances of belonging to an ethnically diverse social network. Nevertheless, it should be noticed that the ethnic diversity of the social network is not necessarily perceived by the respondents as being positive.

12.4.5.2. Attitude Towards Linguistic Diversity

Attitude towards linguistic diversity seems to be linked with the experience of having worked or lived abroad. A small number of the migratory adults believe that it is better to meet people who speak one's own language (57% versus 68% for the non-migratory sub-sample) and more of them feel proud of relatives and/or friends who speak languages which are different from the official language of the country (64% versus 57%). Also, they show less emotional affinity with their native language (only 33% of them believe that their native language is the most beautiful, as compared with 42% of the non-migrants), as compared to adults with no migratory experience, and give less instrumental value to their native language, attributing more utility to other languages (20% think their native language is very useful and 35% believe that other languages are more useful, while for the non-migrants sub-sample the percentages are equal: 23% in favour of the native language and 23% in favour of other languages).

Migratory adults distinguish themselves neatly from the non-migrants in terms of personal experiences with foreign languages: 37% of the adult returnees report learning another language, other than their mother tongue/s, while only 19% of the respondents with no migratory experience do the same. Migratory experience accounts for a higher interest in learning a foreign language.

In conclusion, both children and adults with migratory experience feel proud to be able to speak the language of the country they lived in, showing thus a more positive attitude towards multilingualism than those who did not experience living abroad. As far as the linguistic capital is concerned, returnees show greater interest in speaking and learning foreign languages mostly in order to travel, to have a better job or to speak the language with relatives that also had a migratory experience.

Interestingly enough, returnees have a stronger sense of belonging to the European Union than to their own country and linguistic diversity is not something exceptional for them, but rather something normal. However, paradoxically, returnee children consider their mother tongue (Romanian) as being the most beautiful language.

Thus, we can state that both adults and children with migratory experience have a much richer linguistic repertoire. But, in the case of the adults (as shown by Sandu, 2010) this does not reach advanced levels of competence, as they can speak, but cannot read or write properly. It is true, nevertheless, that returnees are more proficient in the languages of the countries they have been to than individuals with no migratory experience, and, as the studies mentioned indicate, very many of them also have basic knowledge of other foreign languages.

Just like the children, this group of adults has a more positive attitude towards linguistic diversity due to their contact with people of different races, ethnicities, and religions encountered in the host countries.

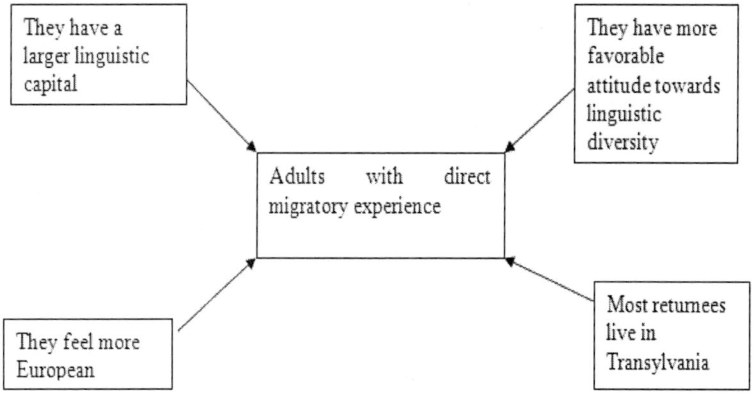

Fig. 12-2: Profile of adults with direct migratory experience

12.5. Conclusion and Directions for Further Research

Migratory experience leads to a drop in the degree to which subjects, both children and adults, feel they belong to the local community. Thus, they identify themselves less with the locality they live in and as being Romanians and define themselves more as European citizens.

There seems to be a relationship between migratory experience and the opportunity of belonging to a more ethnically diverse social network for children and adults alike. This also seems to lead to different attitudes towards their mother tongue among children versus adults. Adults tend to be less attached to their native language, considering it as the most beautiful language to a lesser degree than non-migrant adults, while for children the results are reversed (returnees consider their mother tongue as the most beautiful to a larger degree than non-migrants). Also, adults with migratory experience feel proud to have relatives and friends who speak other languages than Romanian to a higher degree than non-migrants, whereas children returnees are rather indifferent towards this aspect.

Migratory experience also appears to be related to a higher probability that children and adults alike manifest increased interest in learning a foreign language, with most of these subjects studying, at the moment of the survey, another language (besides the language studied at school, in the case of children).

Both children and adults with migratory experience are more open towards ethno-linguistic diversity than non-migrant respondents. Adults consider to a higher degree that it is positive to have friends who originate from other countries than Romania, learn more foreign languages and consider that there are other languages as beautiful as their mother tongue. Parents' attitude towards ethno-linguistic diversity seems to influence their children's attitude, returnees being more open to learning foreign languages and towards linguistic diversity than non-migrant children.

We are well aware of the fact that due to the small number of returnees our data are not representative and we want to underline that this is just a case study. However, we do consider that our study may shed light on the general picture or profile of Romanian returnees.

Since one of the problems identified with returnee children is their re-enrollment in the Romanian educational system, we suggest that one of the further research directions be that of corroborating children's reports with teachers' identification of the actual problems these children may encounter. This could be done by interviewing the primary school teachers who have returnees in their classes. Based on the key problems identified by these interviews, measures could be taken to help the returnees integrate better in school.

References

Avram, M. 2001. Vorbitori, număr de. In *Enciclopedia limbii române,* ed. M. Sala, 617. Bucureşti: Univers Enciclopedic.

Bădescu, G., O. Stoian, and A. Tănase. 2009. Efectele culturale ale migraţiei forţei de muncă din România. In *Sociologia migraţiei,* ed. R. G. Anghel and I. Horvath, 268-285. Iaşi: Polirom.

FSD. 2006. *Locuirea temporară în străinătate. Migraţia economică a românilor: 1990-2006.* Bucureşti: Fundaţiei pentru o Societate Deschisă (available at: www.soros.ro/ro/documente.php?document=354, accessed September 26, 2012).

FSR. 2007. *Efectele migraţiei: copii rămaşi acasă.* Bucureşti: Fundaţia Soros România (FSR) (available at: http://www.soros.ro/ro/comunicate_detaliu.php?comunicat=54#, accessed September 26, 2012).

—. 2008. *Efectele migraţiei: Copiii rămaşi acasă. Riscuri şi soluţii.* Bucureşti: Fundaţia Soros România (FSR) (available at: http://www.soros.ro/ro/publicatii.php?cat=15&pag=2#, accessed September 26, 2012).

—. 2009. *Comunităţi româneşti în Spania.* Bucureşti: Fundaţia Soros România (FSR) (available at: http://www.soros.ro/ro/comunicate_detaliu.php?comunicat=85#, accessed September 26, 2012).

—. 2011. *Şcoală şi comunitate. Model de intervenţie în comunităţile cu copiii rămaşi acasă.* Bucureşti: Fundaţia Soros România (FSR) (available at: http://www.soros.ro/ro/publicatii.php, accessed September 26, 2012).

INE. 2009. *Encuesta Nacional de Inmigrantes 2007: una monografía.* Madrid: Instituto Nacional de Estadistica (available at: http://www.ine.es/jaxi/menu.do?type=pcaxis&path=%2Ft20%2Fp319&file=inebase, accessed September 26, 2012).

MMT-ASG. 2007. *Comunitatea românească în Italia. Condiţii sociale, valori, aşteptări.* Accessed September 26, 2012. www.mmt.ro/cri.pdf.

Sandu, D. 2010. *Lumile sociale ale migraţiei româneşti în străinătate.* Iaşi: Polirom.

Vintilă-Rădulescu, I. 2004. *Limba romană din perspectiva integrării europene.* Accessed September 26, 2012. http://www.unibuc.ro/ro/limba_romn_din_perspectiva_integrrii_europene.

CHAPTER THIRTEEN

LANGUAGE USE, PERCEPTION AND ATTITUDES AMONGST MALTESE PRIMARY SCHOOL CHILDREN

SANDRO CARUANA, GEORGE CREMONA AND ALEXANDRA VELLA

13.1. Introduction—Language use in Malta

The Maltese Islands—area 316Km^2—are located at a distance of 93km and 288km respectively from the closest points in Sicily and Libya, a position which has often been referred to as the crossroads between East and West. The population of Malta, which currently stands at 417,617[1] (National Statistics Organisation), has, unlike that of other nearby Mediterranean islands such as Lampedusa and Pantelleria, undergone rapid growth, particularly during the period of the Hospitaller Knights of the Order of St. John, when the population increased five-fold (Brincat, 2011: 148).

The geographical location of the Islands has resulted in a history characterised by a series of dominations: the Phoenicians, Carthaginians, Romans, Byzantines, Arabs, Normans, Angevins, Aragonese, Castilians and the Order of the Knights of St. John were all in Malta for periods of time of differing durations. After a brief period of French rule which followed the departure of the Knights of St. John from the Islands, Malta became part of the British Empire. British rule lasted from 1800–1964 when Malta achieved Independence. Malta became a Republic in 1974 and a member of the European Union in 2004.

---

[1] National Statistics Office, Malta, http://nso.gov.mt/docs/sdds.html, last update September 27, 2012.

Maltese, a Semitic language, owes its origins to the period of time (870-1090 A.D.) when the Arabs took over Malta. A variety of Arabic referred to as Siculo-Arabic is generally considered to be the precursor of the Maltese language of today. Various linguists have examined Maltese in terms of its linguistic stratigraphy. Most agree that Siculo-Arabic should be considered the principal stratum in the case of Maltese. Italian and English are superimposed/added to this principal stratum in the accounts of both Mifsud (1995) and Brincat (2011), who however disagree somewhat on the details, with Mifsud suggesting Italian as a superstratum and English as an adstratum, and Brincat claiming Sicilian as the superstratum in the case of Maltese, with two additional adstrata consisting of Italian and English.

In the present-day scenario, Maltese is the national language of Malta, whilst Maltese and English are recognised as co-official languages of the Islands. Malta is therefore officially bilingual. Moreover, most Maltese can be said to be bilingual in Maltese and English (sometimes trilingual with Italian), to differing degrees. Maltese is also rich in dialects[2] so that many Maltese, apart from being bilingual in Maltese and English, are also bidialectal in Standard Maltese and a dialect of Maltese. Maltese is the mother tongue of the vast majority of the population and is spoken all over the island. However, a number of Maltese citizens also claim either English, or Maltese and English simultaneously, as their first language. It is also important to note that Maltese is not a homogenous entity because, in spite of the size of the Islands, dialectal variation exists even in this relatively small language. Moreover, as Berruto (1998: 16) claims, in a bilingual context codeswitching and codemixing are always present, whether to a greater or to a lesser extent, and Malta is no exception to this[3].

The linguistic scenario is a rich and complex one and language choices are governed by a large number of factors, non-linguistic as well as otherwise. English is the preferred choice in some domains, particularly domains where the written mode has precedence. Maltese would seem to be the preferred choice in other domains, particularly those in which the spoken mode tends to have precedence such as that involving legal

---

[2] While the so-called *djaletti* vary at the level of pronunciation (see e.g. Aquilina and Isserlin, 1981; Camilleri and Vanhove, 1994) they also vary at other levels of structure (see e.g. Borg, 1988a and 1988b; Agius, 1992). For an overview of recent work on dialects of Maltese see Borg (2011).

[3] See Camilleri (1995); Caruana (2002); Sciriha (2004); Neame (2006); Sciriha and Vassallo (2006), among others.

proceedings and parliamentary debates, as well as in ecclesiastical quarters.

In the domain of the media, use of English seems to be preferred in those media which are primarily written, such as newspapers, with Maltese being the preferred choice in local radio and television which primarily involve the use of spoken language. Apart from the more traditional media, in which the presence of Maltese can be said to be very strong, one also needs to consider the internet. Although the presence of Maltese in this domain has increased, particularly in the last decade (Rosner and Joachimsen, 2011), English is still a strong competitor to Maltese insofar as the internet is concerned. This is probably not surprising given that this medium predominantly involves use of the written rather than the spoken mode. The sub-domain of computer-mediated communication such as that used in chatting is also interesting in this respect. Patterns of usage in this sub-domain can be seen to be changing rapidly, language use being characterised by a high degree of innovation. Some very interesting patterns in the chat-speak of young Maltese bilinguals are discussed in Brincat and Caruana (2011).

The field in which English can be said to really have precedence over Maltese is that of education. In this domain, Maltese and English are both obligatory subjects from the start of primary schooling. At Secondary level, students start learning one or two other languages, and may generally choose between Arabic, French, German, Italian and Spanish. Moreover, textbooks, as well as exams, for the vast majority of (non-literary) subjects are in English. This in spite of the fact that Malta has what Fabri (2010: 811) calls a "flourishing literary and cultural scene" and one in which, in the words of Adrian Grima (2008), one of Malta's new generation of writers:

> Most Maltese literature is written in Maltese. Many would not even accept the idea that a novel written in a different language by a Maltese person in Malta or elsewhere can be considered a work of Maltese literature

And yet, English becomes increasingly indispensable as one progresses through the educational system. Proficiency in both spoken, but particularly in written English, constitutes an advantage to those students who pursue their studies beyond secondary level.

13.2. Migration in Malta

Malta has always been a meeting point at a crossroads in the centre of the Mediterranean: the presence of foreigners is widely accepted.

Furthermore, many Maltese citizens have direct experience of the social implications and difficulties faced by emigrants, as documented by Attard (1999): this is mainly due to the fact that the post-War years in Malta were characterised by massive emigration, mainly for economic reasons. Many Maltese citizens emigrated to Australia: other destinations included the US, Canada and Great Britain. This trend has practically ceased in recent years (in fact today there are also a number of returned migrants) and, with further economic development, the Maltese have become accustomed to having a number of individuals from overseas amongst them, often visiting the island for leisure or work purposes.

Recently, however, the renowned "Maltese hospitality" has been facing a severe test indeed: this is mainly due to the influx of illegal immigrants reaching the Maltese shores on a relatively regular basis. The current situation in Malta as far as foreign presence is concerned is extremely complex indeed, both from a social and from a linguistic perspective. The arrival of immigrants from North Africa to Southern Mediterranean countries is a well-known phenomenon and, given the geographical position of the Islands, these migratory movements have affected Malta greatly (see Farrugia, 2010; and Pulis, 2010). Immigration has led to considerable logistic problems and, at times, the island's migrant centres, run by the Maltese security forces, has housed over 1,000 people.

Finally, another recent phenomenon which often goes unnoticed, even in the local media, is the arrival of young adults from Eastern European countries who are employed (legally or illegally) or exploited in various sectors of the local community—these range from workers in the building and manufacturing industries, to cleaners or waiters in restaurants and hotels, to dancers or entertainers working in local establishments and also to those involved in prostitution.

Although these migratory movements largely concern adults, who do not normally come to Malta accompanied by children, schools are not unaffected by the situation. In fact, as shall be elaborated upon further below, schools in Malta are becoming increasingly multicultural and multilingual, and headteachers, teachers and administrative staff often encounter problems in communicating with students as well as with their parents or guardians. As one may note in Fig. 13-1 below (Eurydice network, 2009) Malta is the only EU state which has not put in place any official provisions intended to enhance communication between schools and immigrant families:

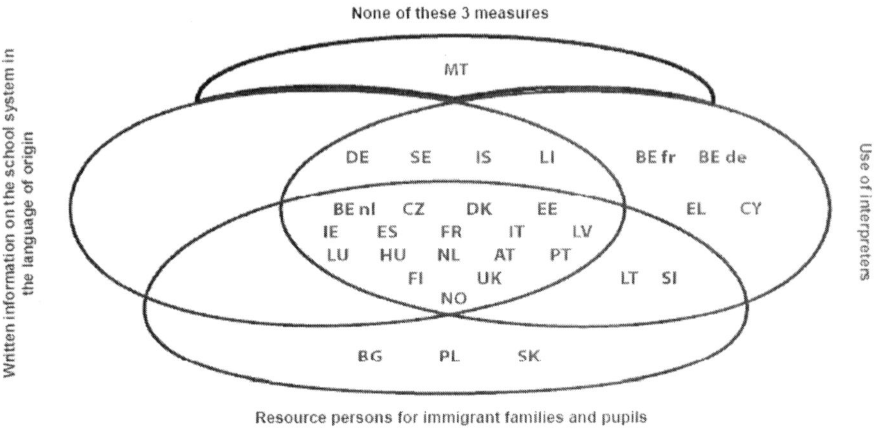

Data not available: RO

Source: Eurydice.

Fig. 13-1: Measures enhancing communication between schools and immigrant families, general education (ISCED 0-3), 2007/08

The lacunae highlighted by the data provided in the figure above are confirmed in a study carried out amongst teachers and educational leaders by Francalanza and Gauci (2009). Participants in this study, which used interviews and focus groups as its main method of data collection, clearly highlight the difficulties which are sometimes encountered in order to accommodate children who are not born in Malta in local schools. Furthermore, current teacher-training programmes do not cater sufficiently for situations that may arise when one has to face students of different nationalities. These considerations are also confirmed in a study by Valentino (2011) whose research was carried out through ethnographic interviews with a college principal, a head-teacher, teachers and learning support assistants, as well as by means of classroom observations. One of the author's most significant conclusions is effectively summarised in the words of a school headteacher:

> Jiena nħoss li għandu jkun hawn guidance kif għandi nimxi għax jiena stess lanqas naf. Jiena qatt ma kelli dawn it-tfal minn daqshekk pajjiżi differenti. ......taf kemm hi ħaġa sabiħa. There is body in the school, diversity and richness. Nixtieq ngħinhom iktar u jkun hawn għajnuna iktar għax nibża' li jkun hawn min mhux qed jitkellem. (Valentino, 2011: 48)

> *I feel there should be guidance on how to tackle this situation as I admit that I myself do not know how to deal with it. I never had children from so many different countries in my school. ...you should see how beautiful it is. There is body in the school, diversity and richness. I would like to help them more and more support should be available as I am afraid that some of them do not speak up when they need to.*

Having acknowledged the shortcomings of the Maltese educational system especially insofar as official policies and provisions regarding children of non-Maltese origin and their integration within schools, one must also state that formulating such policies is not easy, not only because of the recentness of immigration phenomena, but also because of the heterogeneity of these children's origins. In fact, in Malta there are no clear-cut ethnic groups which may warrant teaching in a minority language in schools, as is the case in the Netherlands (Dreissen, 2005) or in Germany (Gogolin, 2005). Consequently, the presence of speakers of different languages, hailing from diverse cultural milieus, poses various challenges to an educational system needing to integrate children who enter the system without Maltese, but worse still, without English. Comparing Malta to most European states, including small, multilingual states such as Luxembourg (Maurer-Hetto, 2009; Weber, 2009) is useful only to a certain extent, not only because of differences within the educational systems, but also because of the different nature and history of immigration in these contexts. Some analogies, on the other and are found when considering the situation in Cyprus:

> During the past few years, an increased number of students, coming mainly from the Soviet Union and other foreign countries, have enrolled in primary education. As a consequence Cypriot education policy has been modified to include provisions that support the language and distinctive cultural features of the various ethnic groups, while also noting that these children need to learn Greek as their second language to foster a smoother transition into the Greek Cypriot society. (Spinthourakis *et al.*, 2008: 8)

In terms of actual numbers, figures show that the number of non-Maltese students in mainstream education in Malta is in fact not very high. According to National Statistics Office figures there were 2.8% such students at primary level in the academic year 2007-2008, 2% of whom attended State schools. Further to this, data collected directly from the Education Directorate for the year 2009-2010 show that there were 259 non-Maltese students in Maltese primary State schools. Figures for 2010-2011 refer to 373 non-Maltese children attending these schools, representing an increase of 94 students. Maltese infant schools (from ages

3-4) registered a shift from 46 foreign-born students in 2009-10 to 132 in 2010-11.

One further point worth making is that, contrary to common perception, the largest group of non-Maltese students hail from the UK and the second largest group from the Balkan States and Russia. Children of illegal immigrants who have been granted permits to stay for long periods of time in Malta or who have the possibility of obtaining Maltese citizenship, while possibly constituting the most challenging group insofar as both linguistic and cultural integration is concerned, in fact constitute the smallest of the three groups.

Although the number of non-Maltese students may not be very large, the demographic distribution facts are such that these students tend to cluster in two main areas, the Buġibba/St. Paul's Bay area, and the Marsaxlokk/Birżebbuġa area. Reasons for this are various but will not be dealt with here. According to Calleja, Grech and Cauchi (2010: 19) out of 555 foreign-born students in Maltese schools in the scholastic year 2008-09, 189 students (98 in Primary, 91 in Secondary), i.e. 34% of the total, were clustered in one of the nine State colleges on the Island. Consideration of these facts was useful in helping us identify the area schools from which we collected our data.

13.3. The MERIDIUM Project – Methodology

In Malta the MERIDIUM questionnaire was distributed in three primary schools. Schools were selected from the State sector both because preliminary research in these schools revealed that they suited the purpose of the MERIDIUM project of identifying schools attended not only by students born in Malta of Maltese parents, but also by students of non-Maltese parentage. The schools included in the MERIDIUM project were also chosen according to their geographical location: one was chosen from the Centre, the other two from the Northern region and from the South respectively, with the schools chosen being those having larger than usual numbers of students of non-Maltese parentage (see Section 13.2 above). Furthermore, since the sample for Maltese schools, at the planning stage of the MERIDIUM project, was set at 300 questionnaires (150 student questionnaires; 150 adult questionnaires) it was decided to limit the study to only one of the Educational Sectors in Malta, that of State schools (the other sectors comprise Church and Independent/Private schools), rather than extending it to all three sectors since this would have meant having too small a number of participants from each sector.

The sample is therefore not representative of the Maltese population. Rather, the schools were chosen specifically in order to reach the objectives of the MERIDIUM Project. Consequently, the results obtained are descriptive in nature and should be interpreted in the light of the characteristics of the chosen sample, as described below. In the presentation of results, a factor that has been taken into consideration is whether the participants' place of birth leads to different responses. In the case of children who form part of the MERIDIUM sample this is considered in unison with their parent's/parents'[4] place of birth. For adults, place of birth of the participants' partner is also taken into consideration, where applicable. The analysis therefore takes account mainly of how the socio-demographic background of children and adults, and the possible diverse use of languages as a result of their place of birth, could shape their sociolinguistic reality, their identity, their experience of contact with ethno-linguistic diversity, their perceptions of diversity in everyday contexts and their attitudes toward language diversity. It is acknowledged that place of birth is not the sole characteristic that may influence these aspects of experience and that it may only provide limited information about an individual. Esser (2006: 13ff), for example, lists four main contexts (family and migration biography, country of origin, receiving country and ethnic group) which influence language acquisition and though one's place of birth fits within this framework, it also must be seen in the light of other factors. Finally, it must be stated that the results presented below constitute a selection of the findings from the MERIDIUM questionnaire distributed in Malta, those considered of most relevance in the context of the project as a whole.

13.4. Participants and Setting

A total of 194 questionnaires were distributed to children in Year 5 classes (attended by 10-year-olds). Participants could opt freely for a questionnaire in either one of the two official languages of Malta[5]. 163 (84%) of the children chose to answer the questionnaire in Maltese while 31 (16%) chose to complete the one in English. Every one of these questionnaires was distributed to the children's parents as parental influence is viewed as a possible predictor especially where use of

---

[4] The term parent/s will be used throughout this paper. However, this refers both to participants' biological parents as well as to adoptive parents/guardians (as per questions included in the MERIDIUM questionnaire).

[5] Malta was the only country within the MERIDIUM Project in which, due to the officially bilingual status of the nation, such a choice was offered.

languages, linguistic attitudes and issues related to identity are concerned. In all 168 parents returned the questionnaires, but four were blank.

As a result of the above, the total number of children's questionnaires which could effectively serve to obtain results for the MERIDIUM Project was 164, of which 142 (86.5%) were completed in Maltese and 22 (13.5%) in English. Out of these 164 questionnaires completed by parents, 135 (82%) were in Maltese and 29 (18%) were in English.

The total number of questionnaires therefore used for the descriptive quantitative analysis in Malta is 328 (164 children questionnaires and 164 parent questionnaires). This number represents 84.5% of the total of 388 questionnaires distributed to children in the three Maltese primary schools selected and to their parents.

13.5. Socio-demographic Data

13.5.1 Gender, Age and Background

The participants are first presented in terms of details on socio-demographic background, namely their gender, their place of birth and information regarding their personal background.

INFORMANT'S GENDER		N	%
Male		84	*51.2*
Female		80	*48.8*
	TOTAL	164	*100.0*

Tab. 13-1: Children's gender

As shown in Tab. 13-1, 84 (51.2%) children who took part in the MERIDIUM project are male, whereas 80 (48.8%) are female. 157 (95.7%) of these participants were born in 2000 and were therefore 10 years old when the questionnaire was distributed. The remaining participants were a year older, as they were born in 1999, but they still formed part of Year 5 classes.

INFORMANT'S GENDER		N	%
Male		32	*19.5*
Female		132	*80.5*
	TOTAL	164	*100.0*

Tab. 13-2: Adults' gender

As can be seen from Tab. 13-2 above, 32 (19.5%) of the parents who completed the questionnaire were male whereas 132 (80.5%) were female. 132 (80.5%) declared that they were married (or cohabitating with their partner), 26 (16%) said that they were separated (or not cohabitating with their partner). The remaining six adults did not answer this question. 14 (8.5%) of the parents were aged between 21-30 years; 98 (60%) between 31-40 years and 43 (26%) between 41-50 years. 9 (5.5%) parents were 51 years old or over.

As regards schooling, 21 (12.8%) of the adult participants attended school for a period of time ranging between 6-10 years, 86 (52%) for a period of time ranging between 11-13 years and 54 (33%) for 14 years or more. Three participants did not answer this question. As far as the participants' partners are concerned, 26 (16%) attended school for a period of time ranging between 6-10 years, 64 (39%) for a period of time ranging between 11-13 years and 40 (24%) for 14 years or more. This question was not completed by 34 (20.7%) participants.

13.5.2 Place of Birth

134 (81.7%) of the children included in the MERIDIUM Project were born in Malta whereas 13 (8%) were born elsewhere. 17 participants did not answer the question. Of the 13 participants who were not born in Malta, 11 indicated the country in which they were born. The countries are: Italy (2 participants), the UK (2 participants), Belgium, Bulgaria, Egypt, Germany, Russian Federation, Serbia and Thailand. Tab. 13-3 presents information regarding the children and their parents' place of birth (background):

CHILDREN'S PLACE OF BIRTH AND BACKGROUND	N	%
Born abroad - both parents foreign[6]	7	*4.3*
Born abroad - one parent foreign	6	*3.7*
Born in Malta - both parents foreign	8	*4.9*
Born in Malta - one parent foreign	22	*13.4*
Born in Malta - both parents Maltese	104	*63.4*
Missing data	17	*10.4*
TOTAL	164	*100.0*

Tab. 13-3: Birth status: children's birthplace and background (self-reported)

[6] The term "foreign" here implies "not born in Malta". This term is used in the tables included in this paper for the sake of conciseness.

Of the 13 participants who said that they were born in a foreign state, 7 were born of parents who were both foreign, while 6 participants had one parent who was born in Malta. In addition to the above there were 8 other participants born in Malta both of whose parents were born abroad and another 22 participants having one parent born abroad and the other in Malta. The above indicates the complexity involved in understanding children's backgrounds in Maltese schools as a number of their familial situations are intertwined[7]. While the majority of children who answered the questionnaire were born in Malta of Maltese parents, the tally of students born abroad as well as that of those with either both parents or one parent born in a foreign state, is relatively high as it amounts to 43 students (26.2% of the total). One must also consider that 23 (14%) of the participants claim to have lived for more than six months away from Malta and 12 (7%) of the participants claim to have attended primary schooling abroad.

As far as adult participants are concerned, 131 (80%) participants were born in Malta whereas 33 (20%) were born elsewhere, namely in: the UK (7 participants), Australia (6 participants), Canada, Morocco (4 participants each), Russia, Serbia (2 participants each), USA, Belgium, Bulgaria, Cyprus, Egypt, Iran, Netherlands and Thailand. 11 of the participants who were not born in Malta have been in Malta for less than 10 years, 10 of them have been in Malta between 11-20 years, 6 of them between 21 and 30 years and 6 of them for 31 years or more.

Information provided on participants' partners shows that 108 (66%) of them were born in Malta, whereas 23 (14%) were born abroad. 33 (20%) respondents did not answer this question. The 23 partners of participants who were born abroad were born in: the UK (6 participants), Italy (5 participants), Australia, Serbia (3 participants each), Bulgaria (2 participants), Canada, Egypt, Iran and Jordan. Tab. 13-4 presents the composition of the marital/partnership status of the adults in the sample.

---

[7] In addition to the complexity referred to here, mainly based on the consideration that participants or their parents were born in different countries, one must add that the terminology used in this field is sometimes problematic if not outright misleading. It is hereby acknowledged that being born in a foreign state does not automatically imply that one may not feel integrated in the society in which s/he lives in; it is also acknowledged that terms such as "foreigner", "immigrant", "non-national" etc. are laden and may be interpreted incorrectly and also, in some cases, lead to prejudice. As far as the Maltese context is concerned, further considerations regarding these terminological issues may be found in Caruana and Klein (2008). For the purpose of this paper, these terms are used neutrally, and are based on considerations resulting from the participants' birthplace and/or country of origin.

This information is deemed to be central as far as the MERIDIUM sample is concerned because it gives an indication of language use in the household by taking into account both the place of birth of respondents and (where applicable) that of their partner:

MARITAL/PARTNERSHIP STATUS		N	%
Not answered / not applicable		33	*20.1*
Both partners born in Malta		95	*57.9*
Both partners NOT born in Malta		11	*6.7*
One partner born in Malta, the other abroad		25	*15.2*
	TOTAL	164	*100.0*

Tab. 13-4: Marital/partnership status of adult informants

The category labelled as "not answered/not applicable" in Tab. 13-4 includes those participants who are separated or divorced from their partner (28 participants out of the 33 who form part of this category). 25 participants included in this category were born in Malta whereas 8 were not (3 in Morocco, 3 in USA, 1 in Holland, 1 in Canada).

13.6. Sociolinguistic Data

13.6.1 Children

The children participating in the study were asked about their language use when they communicate with relatives, peers, neighbours and teachers. Tab. 13-5 below shows results relating to language use at home, whereas those on language use in other social domains are presented in Tab. 13-6. The tally of raw scores in these tables is higher than the number of participants (n=164). This is due to the fact that in a number of cases participants made more than one choice:

INTERLOCUTOR	CHILDREN'S LANGUAGE USE AT HOME (N AND %)				
	Maltese	**English**	**Other**	**No answer**	**Total**
Mother	136	55	20	5	216
	63.0	*25.5*	*9.0*	*2.5*	*100.0*
Father	127	35	15	12	189
	67.0	*18.5*	*8.0*	*6.5*	*100.0*
Siblings	121	32	11	26	190
	64.0	*17.0*	*6.0*	*13.0*	*100.0*
Grandparents	125	28	14	21	188
	66.0	*15.0*	*7.5*	*11.5*	*100.0*

Tab. 13-5: Children's language use at home

As shown in Tab. 13-5 Maltese is the language used most frequently with close relatives, though English plays an important role in this context too[8]. These results are similar to others reported in recent studies including Sciriha and Vassallo (2006) and Peska (2009). None of the seven students who were born abroad of foreign parents use Maltese with any of their relatives. Two of them use English with their mother, their brothers/sisters and their grandparents while three of them use English with their father. In other cases languages of the participants' country of origin are mentioned and these included two varieties of Arabic, namely 'Egyptian' and 'Moroccan'. Maltese features as a language used to communicate with relatives in the case of participants' who were born abroad of whom only one parent was foreign. Two of these participants use Maltese with their mother (but not with their father), three of them use the language with their brothers/sisters and four of them with their grandparents. English also features among these participants' language use whereas other languages used pertain to the participants' birthplace and include Russian, Thai and Italian. As expected, Maltese on its own, as well as Maltese together with English, feature very prominently in the language use of participants born in Malta. This is a reflection of the country's bilingual situation but can also provide some noteworthy insights as children who are not born in Malta, besides having to gain familiarity with the language/s used locally, must also learn to adjust to the fact that their peers use more than one language and that, as a consequence of this, as explained in the introduction of this paper, code-switching and mixing may be rather natural for them[9]. In fact, when participants' birth status is taken into

[8] For further information on English in Malta see Bonnici (2009).

[9] For further examples of code-switching in Malta one may refer to Camilleri (1995) and Brincat (2011: 417-456).

consideration some differences do emerge: participants born abroad and participants born in Malta with both parents who are foreign normally only use one language at home whereas participants born in Malta use two languages with family members more often.

Results relating to language use outside the home are shown in the next table (Tab. 13-6):

INTERLOCUTOR	CHILDREN'S LANGUAGE USE OUTSIDE THE HOME (N AND %)				
	Maltese	**English**	**Other**	**No answer**	**Total**
Relatives	115 *(60.5)*	30 *(16.0)*	13 *(7.0)*	32 *(16.5)*	190 *100.0*
Classmates	129 *(64.5)*	44 *(22.0)*	1 *(0.5)*	26 *(13.0)*	200 *100.0*
Friends	124 *(63.0)*	40 *(20.0)*	4 *(2.0)*	29 *(15.0)*	197 *100.0*
Neighbours	117 *(64.0)*	25 *(14.0)*	5 *(3.0)*	35 *(19.0)*	182 *100.0*
Teachers	123 *(61.0)*	47 *(23.0)*	1 *(0.5)*	31 *(15.5)*	202 *100.0*

Tab. 13-6: Children's language use outside the home

The results shown in Tab. 13-6 generally confirm the trend already illustrated with reference to participants' use of language at home: participants born in Malta, who have at least one Maltese parent too, use more than one language quite regularly as they alternate between Maltese and English. It must also be noted that the tendency to use more than one language increases among all participants when they speak to their teachers: this is a reflection of the Maltese schooling system as English plays a very important role in this domain even though Maltese is used frequently especially for informal communication[10].

Overall these data reveal that most Maltese participants use Maltese to communicate both at home and elsewhere but also that a number of them use English alongside Maltese quite often. This is a situation which is reflected in the local schooling system, where both languages are used often. Since English plays an important role in the educational system in Malta, students whose L1 is Maltese and who communicate almost exclusively in this language may find themselves at a disadvantage in schools[11]. On the other hand, some students born abroad have to face a

[10] See Caruana (2011).

[11] See Brincat (2007).

rather arduous situation as at home they may speak a language which is not used in Maltese schools: at school they therefore must switch to English to communicate with peers and teachers. English therefore takes on the role of a lingua franca and though it may be useful in class and in order to keep in touch with one's studies it does not necessarily help children integrate fully with their Maltese peers who are inclined to use Maltese rather than English especially in informal settings (including break time and in various sorts of friendly student-student or student-teacher interaction).

In addition to the above children were also asked in which languages other than Maltese and English, they can utter a simple sentence ("I want a sandwich"), and which other languages, beside Maltese and English, they could understand, read and write. Results to these questions, reported in Tab. 13-7, show that Italian plays an important role in Malta's sociolinguistic scene[12]. However, one must also take account of the fact that the results presented here are from self-reported data (and therefore require further investigation) and that many of the participants who compiled the questionnaire had just undergone a language awareness programme at their school which happened to include some lessons in basic Italian.

LANGUAGE FUNCTION	CHILDREN'S COMPETENCE IN OTHER LANGUAGES, BESIDE MALTESE AND ENGLISH (N AND %)[13]			
	Italian	**Other**	**No answer**	**Total**
Utter a simple sentence	24 *(39.0)*	12 *(20.0)*	25 *(41.0)*	61 *(100.0)*
Read	65 *42.5*	31 *20.0*	57 *37.5*	153 *100.0*
Write	58 *38.0*	26 *17.0*	67 *45.0*	151 *100.0*
Understand	75 *44.0*	35 *20.5*	60 *35.5*	170 *100.0*

Tab. 13-7: Children's competence in other languages, beside Maltese and English

[12] A number of participants answered 'English' or 'Maltese'. These do not form part of the tally included in Tab. 13-7, which includes only languages other than Maltese and English.

[13] In tables where total cases do not reach the sum of 100, percentages are listed within brackets.

In Tab. 13-7 the 'other' category mainly includes languages indicated by participants who were either non-nationals or whose parents (or at least one of them) was born abroad. In fact answers were very much in line with the nationality of the participants or of their parents: languages mentioned included Serbian, Russian, Arabic and German. Other varieties, namely 'Iranian', 'Egyptian' and 'Belgian' were also mentioned by participants born in these countries, or whose parents are of these nationalities.

13.6.2 Adults

Of the 164 adults who took part in MERIDIUM, 117 (71.3%) participants state that Maltese is their mother tongue whereas 15 (9.1%) participants indicate English as their L1. In other cases participants' mother tongue was reported to be one of the following: Arabic, Italian (3 participants each), Russian, Serbian (2 participants each), 'Moroccan', Bulgarian, Dutch, Flemish[14], French, Thai (one participant each). 16 participants did not answer this question.

When asked about their knowledge of different languages it is interesting to note that, participants born in Malta still self-report a relatively high level of competence in Italian. In fact 35% of the participants claim that they are conversant in this language. This result is undoubtedly due to the age of the respondents: a number of them were probably exposed regularly to Italian via television when they were young[15]. Furthermore, on analysing the results, it is evident that competence in this language is much higher among those participants who were born in Malta and much less so in participants who were not (excluding, of course, those who were born in Italy). A number of participants who were not born in Malta, besides mentioning their own mother tongue/s, also claimed to be conversant in languages which are quite widespread in specific contexts (e.g. participants born in Eastern European countries included Russian among the languages they know).

Participants were asked about their language use at home and outside. Tab. 13-8 below presents results relating to language use at home. The table gives raw scores, and therefore total tallies are higher than the number of participants (164). This is due to the fact that in a number of

[14] 'Dutch' and 'Flemish' were the languages indicated by two adult participants, respectively born in the Netherlands and in Belgium. The nomenclature used by the participants is retained in the report of their responses in this section.

[15] The historical role and status of Italian has been described by Cassola (1998) and by Brincat (2003 and 2011). The acquisition of Italian via television in Malta is also extensively documented in Brincat (1998) and in Caruana (2003 and 2006).

cases participants indicated that they use more than one language in the different circumstances:

INTERLOCUTOR	ADULTS' LANGUAGE USE WITHIN THE FAMILY DOMAIN (N AND %)				
	Maltese	**English**	**Other**	**No answer**	**Total**
Partner / spouse	108 *75.5*	16 *11.0*	12 *8.0*	7 *5.5*	143 *100.0*
Children	138 *64.0*	54 *25.0*	12 *5.5*	12 *5.5*	216 *100.0*
Siblings	125 *68.0*	16 *9.0*	18 *10.0*	24 *13.0*	183 *100.0*
Parents	120 *70.0*	16 *9.0*	10 *6.0*	25 *15.0*	171 *100.0*
Grandparents	90 *52.5*	7 *4.0*	15 *9.0*	59 *34.5*	171 *100.0*

Tab. 13-8: Adults' language use within the family domain

From the results reported in the table above, one may note that participants use English more frequently with their children than they do with other members of their families. Though the majority of participants born in Malta speak to their children in Maltese, about 25% of them also use English. However, there is also the tendency to use English among participants not born in Malta, one reason for this being that 18 out of the 33 participants forming this group were born in English-speaking countries (the UK, Australia, Canada and the US). In this group there are also five participants who use say that they use both Maltese and English when speaking to their children. These are participants who have been in Malta for over twenty years.

When considering participants also in the light of their partner's birthplace, only four participants in the group 'one partner born in Malta, the other abroad' state that they speak a language other than Maltese and English to their children (Arabic and Italian, with the latter mentioned three times). In the case of the category 'both partners not born in Malta' (composed of 11 participants) foreign languages (including Arabic, Serbian, Bulgarian and Russian) are mentioned by five participants. The remaining six participants state that they speak English to their children.

Tab. 13-9 gives results on participants' language use outside the home. Even in this case, since raw scores are provided, tallies are higher than the number of participants (164).

INTERLOCUTOR	ADULTS' LANGUAGE USE OUTSIDE THE FAMILY DOMAIN (N AND %)				
	Maltese	English	Other	No answer	Total
Relatives	129	36	10	20	195
	66.0	*18.5*	*5.0*	*10.5*	*100.0*
Workmates	98	35	2	35	170
	57.0	*21.0*	*1.0*	*21.0*	*100.0*
Friends	128	44	13	22	207
	62.0	*21.0*	*6.0*	*11.0*	*100.0*
Neighbours	129	36	5	23	193
	67.0	*18.5*	*2.5*	*12.0*	*100.0*

Tab. 13-9: Adults' language use outside the family domain

Results indicate that English also plays an important role in the contexts listed in Tab. 13-9. This is especially so for the 33 participants not born in Malta (18 of whom are born in English speaking countries): 13 of the participants forming part of this group use English to speak to relatives (four use Maltese; three use Arabic, and one each Dutch, French and Russian); 15 use English in the workplace (six use Maltese and one uses Dutch); 24 use English with friends (six use Maltese, two use Arabic, Serbian and one each Dutch, French and Russian); 22 use English with neighbours (six use Maltese, two use Arabic and one uses Serbian). Participants were also asked about their use of official and foreign languages. Tab. 13-10 below reports results relating to the use of Maltese and English, while Tab. 13-11 describes the use of foreign language/s:

LANGUAGE FUNCTION	ADULTS' USE OF THE OFFICIAL LANGUAGE TO... (N AND %)			
	Yes	No	No answer	Total
Work	94	36	34	164
	57.3	*22.0*	*20.7*	*100.0*
Read	132	16	16	164
	80.5	*9.8*	*9.8*	*100.0*
Discuss with friends/relatives	127	14	23	164
	77.4	*8.5*	*14.0*	*100.0*
Write	102	40	22	164
	62.2	*24.4*	*13.4*	*100.0*
Watch films	141	8	15	164
	86.0	*4.9*	*9.1*	*100.0*

Tab. 13-10: Adults' use of the official languages to…

LANGUAGE FUNCTION	ADULTS' USE OF FOREIGN LANGUAGE/S TO... (N AND %)			
	Yes	No	No answer	Total
Work	33 *20.1*	92 *56.1*	39 *23.8*	164 *100.0*
Read	50 *30.5*	81 *49.4*	33 *20.1*	164 *100.0*
Discuss with friends/relatives	49 *29.9*	81 *49.4*	34 *20.7*	164 *100.0*
Write	40 *24.4*	87 *53.0*	37 *22.6*	164 *100.0*
Watch films	89 *54.3*	51 *31.1*	24 *14.6*	164 *100.0*

Tab. 13-11: Adults' use of foreign language/s to...

In the case of the results reported in the two tables above, the differences registered are compounded by the fact that those who responded "no" also include a number of individuals who responded in this way either because they are unemployed or because they are housewives. The percentages relating to the use of Maltese and English are highest for the activities of reading and watching films, very much in line with considerations included in Brincat (2011: 418). Foreign languages are also used often (54.3%, as reported in Table 13-11) in order to watch films, undoubtedly because of the easy accessto the Italian media, particularly television, in Malta (see Caruana 2003 and 2006 as well as Borg *et al.* 2009).

These variables do not vary much when measured against marital/partnership status except in the case of the response to the question regarding the use of foreign languages in discussions with friends or relatives, as illustrated in Tab. 13-12: from these data one can observe that, as one might expect, a wider use of foreign languages (i.e. languages other than Maltese/English) is reported in the groups in which participants' and/or their partners were not born in Malta.

MARITAL/PARTNERSHIP STATUS	"DURING THE LAST WEEK DID YOU USE A LANGUAGE, OTHER THAN MALTESE AND/OR ENGLISH, TO DISCUSS WITH FRIENDS/RELATIVES?" (N AND %)		
	No	**Yes**	**Total**
Not answered / not applicable	12 *(50.0)*	12 *(50.0)*	24 *(100.0)*
Both partners born in Malta	55 *(73.3)*	20 *(26.7)*	75 *(100.0)*
Both partners NOT born in Malta	5 *(50.0)*	5 *(50.0)*	10 *(100.0)*
One partner born in Malta, the other abroad	9 *(43.0)*	12 *(57.0)*	21 *(100.0)*
TOTAL	81 *62.3*	49 *37.7*	130 *100.0*

Tab. 13-12: (BQ51c) "During the last week did you use a language, other than Maltese and/or English, to discuss with friends/relatives?": marital/partnership status-disaggregated data

Overall, the picture that emerges regarding use of different languages by adult participants who participated in the MERIDIUM survey is somewhat less clear-cut than that of the children. Whereas most of the 14 children who were born abroad use only one language quite often, in the case of adults born abroad there is the tendency to use both English and their mother tongue (with the exception, of course, of participants whose first language is English itself). One must consider that 24 out of the 33 adult participants have been in Malta for over ten years and this will undoubtedly have contributed to "shaping" their habits of language given the local context. In this regard, Esser (2006: 23) refers to several studies which indicate that duration of stay in a country has significant effects on L2 acquisition. English and Maltese, on the other hand, are used simultaneously by around 25% of adult participants born in Malta and choosing one language rather than the other depends on the context and on the social network in which one is involved.

13.7. Identity

13.7.1 Children

When children were asked to describe themselves in five words, only two participants (one is a national with Maltese parents and another is a non-national with both parents being non-Maltese) used terms to denote ethno-linguistic or religious identity. In most cases adjectives were used to describe their personality, a physical quality as well as some activity they enjoy. In this respect, therefore, nationality and ethnic features did not affect the way the participants in Malta described themselves.

The participants were also asked questions in order to determine the extent to which they associate their identity with the narrower and broader context they live in. They were therefore asked to what extent they feel part of their class, their group of friends, the city/town/village in which they live. They were also asked to what extent they feel Maltese or European. Results are reported in percentages in Tab. 13-13:

"How much do you feel … ?"	Options (%)					
	Very much	**Just enough**	**A little bit**	**Not at all**	**I don't know**	**No answer**
Part of your class	*60.5*	*26.9*	*6.6*	*3.0*	*2.4*	*0.6*
Part of your group of friends	*70.1*	*16.2*	*10.8*	*1.8*	*0.6*	*0.6*
Part of your city/town/village	*59.3*	*21.0*	*7.2*	*7.8*	*4.2*	*0.6*
Maltese	*62.3*	*16.2*	*15.0*	*4.8*	*1.8*	*0.0*
European	*34.7*	*24.0*	*10.2*	*9.0*	*22.2*	*0.0*

Tab. 13-13: (AQ12-16) "How much do you feel … ?"

Results indicate that the country of birth has an effect on the responses given: generally Maltese children whose parents are both Maltese feel more part of the contexts presented in Tab. 13-13[16]. Children born in Malta (even of foreign parents) generally show a higher degree of integration than children born abroad. This is especially evident in the results registered when participants were asked, "How much do you feel Maltese?" as shown in Tab. 13-14:

[16] A similar consideration, albeit in a totally different context, is reported in Golan and Olshtain (2011).

INFORMANT'S BIRTH STATUS	"HOW MUCH DO YOU FEEL MALTESE?" (N AND %)					
	Very much	**Just enough**	**A little bit**	**Not at all**	**I don't know**	**Total**
Born abroad - both parents foreign	0 -	1 *(14.3)*	5 *(71.4)*	1 *(14.3)*	0 -	7 *(100.0)*
Born abroad - one parent foreign	0 -	3 *(50.0)*	1 *(16.7)*	2 *(33.3)*	0 -	7 *(100.0)*
Born in Malta - both parents foreign	5 *(62.5)*	0 -	2 *(25.0)*	1 *(12.5)*	0 -	8 *(100.0)*
Born in Malta - one parent foreign	9 *(40.9)*	9 *(40.9)*	2 *(9.1)*	0 -	2 *(9.1)*	22 *(100.0)*
Born in Malta - both parents Maltese	81 *78.6*	11 *10.6*	11 *10.6*	0 -	1 *1.2*	103 *100.0*
Missing data	7 *(77.9)*	2 *(11.8)*	4 *(23.5)*	4 *(23.5)*	0 -	17 *(100.0)*
TOTAL	102 *62.2*	26 *15.9*	25 *15.2*	8 *4.9*	3 *1.8*	164 *100.0*

Tab. 13-14: (AQ15) "How much do you feel Maltese?": children's birthplace and background-disaggregated data

In this case, as can be seen from Tab. 13-14, children born in Malta (most notably those whose parents are Maltese) feel much more "Maltese" than others born elsewhere. Although further research is clearly necessary given the small numbers in the various cells, these data nonetheless provide an indication that, at least in the case of the MERIDIUM sample, there seems to be a link between birthplace and "feeling Maltese", which is an aspect of one's identity.

Participants were also asked which country they feel that they are citizens of: 110 (67%) participants state that they feel that they are Maltese citizens. The number of participants, however, who feel that they are citizens of another country is quite high, especially when one considers that only 13 participants were not born in Malta. In fact a total of 43 (26%) participants stated that they felt that they were citizens of a foreign state. 11 (7%) participants did not answer this question. In this case the influence of participants' place of birth is evident: 11 of the 13 participants not born in Malta state that they do not feel that they are Maltese citizens. Conversely, of the 8 participants born in Malta of both a foreign mother and father, only 2 state that they felt that they are citizens of a foreign state. Parental influence is manifest in the answer of some participants born in Malta with at least one foreign parent, as 7 out of 22 state their citizenship to be the same as that of their foreign mother/father.

13.7.2 Adults

As in the case of the children who formed part of the MERIDIUM sample, adults were also asked to what extent they associate their identity with the contexts they live in. Results are reported in percentages in Tab. 13-15:

"HOW MUCH DO YOU FEEL … ?"	OPTIONS (%)					
	Very much	Just enough	A little bit	Not at all	I don't know	No answer
Part of your family	*85.4*	*9.1*	*2.4*	*0.6*	*1.8*	*0.6*
Part of your group of friends	*38.4*	*32.9*	*14.0*	*4.3*	*9.1*	*1.2*
Part of your city/town/village	*27.4*	*46.3*	*18.9*	*4.3*	*3.0*	*0.0*
Maltese	*51.8*	*34.8*	*7.3*	*3.0*	*3.0*	*0.0*
European	*20.1*	*29.9*	*25.6*	*12.2*	*10.4*	*1.8*

Tab. 13-15: (BQ15-19) "How much do you feel … ?"

Though the adults' results follow a similar pattern to those provided by children, there is a considerable decrease in the numbers of those who choose the "very much" option. Whereas children feel very much part of their group of friends, this trend is not so strong in the responses provided by adults. Results indicate that marital/partnership status can yield effects on the response to the question: "How much do you feel Maltese?" as shown in the table below:

INFORMANT'S MARITAL/ PARTNERSHIP STATUS	"HOW MUCH DO YOU FEEL MALTESE?" (N AND %)					
	Very much	Just enough	A little bit	Not at all	I don't know	Total
Not answered / not applicable	17 *(51.5)*	8 *(24.2)*	4 *(12.1)*	3 *(9.1)*	1 *(3.0)*	33 *(100.0)*
Both partners born in Malta	53 *(55.8)*	35 *(36.8)*	5 *(5.3)*	0 -	2 *(2.1)*	95 *(100.0)*
Both partners NOT born in Malta	4 *(36.4)*	3 *(27.3)*	2 *(18.2)*	2 *(18.2)*	0 -	11 *(100.0)*
One partner born in Malta, the other abroad	11 *(44.0)*	11 *(44.0)*	1 *(4.0)*	0 -	2 *(8.0)*	25 *(100.0)*
TOTAL	85 *51.8*	57 *34.8*	12 *7.3*	5 *3.0*	5 *3.0*	164 *100.0*

Tab. 13-16: (BQ18) "How much do you feel Maltese?": marital/partnership status-disaggregated data

The data reported in Tab. 13-16 are not as clear-cut as those reported for the children's sample (Tab. 13-14). This may be due to the fact that (as reported in Section 13.5.2) a number of the participants and/or their partner have been in Malta for a considerable amount of time, despite having been born abroad. The percentage of adults whose partner is also Maltese who chose the "very much" option is higher than that registered in the other groups. It is also noteworthy that only 2 participants out of the 11 who form part of the category "both partners not born in Malta" state that they do not feel Maltese at all and another 2 state that they only feel "a little bit" Maltese. This suggests that most of the participants who are part of this small group feel that they are integrated within Maltese society. However data regarding the "not answered/not applicable" group (which include 8 participants who were born abroad) show that one should not make this claim too strongly as 7 participants who were born abroad (out of a total of 33 who form part of this group) state that they do not feel Maltese at all or that they only feel "a little bit" Maltese.

13.8. Experience of Contact with Ethno-linguistic Diversity

13.8.1 Children

Participants were asked how often they hear other languages, besides Maltese and English, being spoken. 56.7% claim that they sometimes hear people speaking languages other than English or Maltese. 32.3% say it happens often whereas 9.8% say it never happens. 37.8% of the children who form part of the MERIDIUM sample claim that they have friends who do not attend their same school who speak a language other than English or Maltese. Most of these state that they speak Italian. A very similar number (37.2%) of this participant group claims that their parents have friends who speak a language other than English or Maltese. Yet again Italian is indicated as the most widespread language, followed, somewhat surprisingly by German and then by Russian. 36% claim that they have relatives who speak a language other than English or Maltese. Again Italian is indicated to be the most widespread language, followed by 'Australian' [this may be due to the children having experience of visiting relatives who form part of Maltese communities in Australia] and then by French, Russian and Spanish.

13.8.2 Adults

More than half of the adults who formed part of the MERIDIUM sample (52.4%) state that they hear people speaking languages other than Maltese and English "occasionally". 42.7% state that this happens often and only a mere 3% say that it never happens. This result is quite heavily conditioned by one's marital / partnership status, as adult participants who form part of the "both partners not born in Malta" and the "one partner born in Malta, the other abroad" groups are more likely to hear foreign vernaculars being spoken when compared to the category "both partners born in Malta". This is probably due to the fact that since one or both partners were not born in Malta they may have relatives or friends who speak other languages, besides Maltese and/or English. In fact, the percentage of adult participants who state that they have foreign relatives or friends who speak languages other than Maltese and English amounts to 56% of the total of the sample: the language which is cited more often is overwhelmingly Italian in the case of Maltese nationals while participants born abroad mention a number of other languages including Russian, German, Serbian and French.

13.9. Perceptions about Diversity in the Everyday Life Context

13.9.1 Children

When the children who form part of the MERIDIUM sample were asked how many pupils in their school speak languages other than Maltese and English, the response was as follows: 22 (13.4%) participants stated that they believe that many children do so, 30 (18.3%) participants opted for "quite a few" whereas 56 participants (34.1%) stated that only a few children spoke languages other than Maltese and English. Only 13 (7.9%) participants chose the "no one" option. The remaining 43 participants either gave "I don't know" as an answer, or did not provide a reply. Once again the language mentioned most frequently when students were asked to report the language/s which, according to them, their peers spoke (besides Maltese and English) was Italian, followed quite closely by French. However, in the case of the answers to this question, one also observes how students' perception of languages probably differs quite considerably from what occurs in reality: in fact, among the participants born in Malta, 16 mentioned Arabic as a language their peers speak, another 16 mentioned Russian and another 18 mentioned Chinese. The nature of the MERIDIUM sample renders it quite unlikely that these languages are spoken to the extent suggested and it is quite probable that our participants equated languages they do not comprehend with the languages they included in their reply to this question. Arabic and Chinese, in fact are often perceived as incomprehensible and "difficult". The frequent mention of Russian, on the other hand, could also be a reflection of the current situation in Malta which has, in recent years, experienced a considerable increase in the number of foreigners from Eastern European countries. Some differences also emerge in the response of children born abroad or whose parents are foreign, undoubtedly because of their contact with family members of foreign nationality: in fact languages such as Serbian and Bulgarian are mentioned by these participants but not by participants who were born in Malta of Maltese parents.

One of the questions which the participants responded to with most interest was the one in which they were asked to identify four languages which are not written using Latin characters, namely Cyrillic, Arabic, Chinese and Devanagari. The following table summarises the answers provided:

SCRIPT	ANSWERS (N AND %)				
	Correct	Wrong	No answer	I don't know	Total
Cyrillic	19	57	83	5	164
	11.6	*34.7*	*50.6*	*3.1*	*100.0*
Arabic	87	34	41	2	164
	53.0	*20.7*	*25.0*	*1.3*	*100.0*
Chinese	121	18	23	2	164
	73.8	*10.9*	*14.0*	*1.3*	*100.0*
Devanagari	1	78	79	6	164
	0.6	*47.6*	*48.1*	*3.7*	*100.0*

Tab. 13-17: (AQ35) "Which language is it?"

As one may notice, participants are very familiar with Chinese script, quite familiar with Arabic characters, but much less so with Cyrillic and Devanagari. Whilst the lack of familiarity with Cyrillic and Devanagari was to be expected, one could have imagined a higher degree of familiarity with Arabic script when considering the proximity of Malta with Arabic speaking countries and the fact that Maltese is a Semitic language. In the results there are only very marginal differences in the amount of correct responses provided in answers to this question by children born in Malta as compared to children born abroad: however, it must be said that informants born in Eastern European countries or in Arabic-speaking territories, or those with one or both parents born in these regions, were obviously among those who recognised Cyrillic or Arabic scripts more promptly.

13.9.2 Adults

When the adults who formed part of the MERIDIUM sample were asked, in their opinion, how many people in their neighbourhood are not Maltese nationals, the response was as follows: 36% answered "many"; 23.2% answered "quite a few"; 22% answered "a few" and 7.3% said "none". 19 participants either did not answer this question or gave "I don't know" as an answer. Results differed when participants were asked how many people in their neighbourhood speak languages other than Maltese and English. In this case 21.3% answered "many"; 17.7% answered "quite a few"; 37.2% answered "a few" and 9.8% said "none". 23 participants either did not answer this question or stated "I don't know". The language which featured most frequently in the response to this question was Arabic, which was mentioned 34 times. In addition to this, other varieties which are related to Arabic were mentioned, namely 'Moroccan' (3 times),

'Tunisian' (twice) and 'Libyan' (once). Somewhat surprisingly, Russian and 'African' (both mentioned 17 times) were also included in the response to this question. These were followed by Italian (mentioned 16 times). The response to this question, as already hinted when referring to answers given by the children included in the sample, gives another indication of some changing aspects of the Maltese linguistic scene. In fact, it is clear that Russian is perceived as being present in Malta today as a result of recent migratory flows and that there is also a considerable perception of the presence of Arabic and African languages. Whether such perceptions do indeed correspond to the extent to which these languages are really present in Malta is an issue which merits investigation.

As in the case of the children's sample, adults were required to name four languages which are not written using Latin characters, namely Cyrillic, Arabic, Chinese and Devanagari. The following table summarises the answers provided:

SCRIPT	ANSWERS (N AND %)				
	Correct	**Wrong**	**No answer**	**I don't know**	**Total**
Cyrillic	65	49	45	5	164
	39.6	*29.8*	*27.4*	*3.2*	*100.0*
Arabic	142	5	16	1	164
	86.6	*3.0*	*9.7*	*0.7*	*100.0*
Chinese	131	13	20	0	164
	79.9	*7.9*	*12.2*	-	*100.0*
Devanagari	17	60	77	10	164
	10.4	*36.6*	*47.0*	*6.0*	*100.0*

Tab. 13-18: (BQ41) "Which language is it?"

When compared to the children's results one notes that, in the case of adults, the amount of correct responses is considerably higher as compared to the children's responses. Also, Arabic script surpasses Chinese as the most recognisable one. Furthermore the fact that almost 40% of the sample identified Cyrillic script correctly is a possible further indication of the presence of Eastern European languages in Malta today as a result of recent migration from the regions where these languages are spoken.

13.10. Opinions and Attitudes about Ethno-linguistic Diversity

13.10.1 Children

When participants' were asked to rate to what extent they think of their mother tongue as "beautiful", most of the results (64%) clustered in the option "it's beautiful, but there are other beautiful languages as well" which is the most neutral response of the three options provided, the other two being: "I think that the language/s that I have learnt at home is/are the most beautiful" and "I think other languages are more beautiful". In this case no noteworthy differences were noted when this response was examined against the birth status of the respondents. Participants were asked to describe their reactions when they hear languages which are unfamiliar to them:

OPTIONS	N	%
Amused (nieħu pjaċir)	71	*43.3*
Curious	49	*29.9*
Annoyed	4	*2.4*
Scared	4	*2.4*
I don't take any notice	17	*10.4*
I don't know	18	*11.0*
Missing data	1	*0.6*
TOTAL	**164**	***100.0***

Tab. 13-19: (AQ33) "When I hear someone speaking a language which is different from Maltese/English in the place where I live, I feel …"

A rather high percentage (43.3%) answered 'amused' to this question. However, in this case it must be pointed out that the term "amused" was translated into Maltese by "nieħu pjaċir", which literally means "I enjoy it". The choice of this option can therefore possibly be explained by the fact that the Maltese translation has much more positive connotations than the English equivalent. This result should therefore be interpreted in the light of the fact that most participants completed the questionnaire in Maltese. Again, in this case no noteworthy differences were noted when this response was examined against the birth status of the respondents.

Participants were asked to indicate whether, when they are older, they would like to know how to speak other languages besides those they already know or are studying. An overwhelming number of 156 (95.1%) participants responded positively to this question. This result augurs well in view of the fact that one of the goals of EU language policies is that of encouraging citizens to be able to communicate in two languages over and above their mother tongue (Commission of the European Communities, 2008: 5)[17]. The reasons given to accompany this response are as follows: 110 (67.1%) stated that they would like to learn languages in order to travel; 87 (53%) because they would like to follow TV programmes in foreign languages; 84 (51.2%) because languages could be important for their future occupation; 64 (39%) because they like studying languages; 41 (25%) because one or both of their parents know how to speak other languages and 29 (17.7%) participants because they have friends who speak other languages. The trend that emerges from the response to this question is that friends and parents have considerably less influence on the participants' desire to learn new languages when compared to travel opportunities, the influence of television (once again, in this case one must keep in mind that Italian television is quite popular in Malta) and opportunities that languages might offer for future employment. The languages mentioned most frequently are those studied in Maltese schools as foreign languages: Italian (mentioned 71 times); French (58); Spanish (47); German (31); Arabic (8). Other languages were mentioned only sporadically. Again, in this case there are no noteworthy differences when this response was examined against the birth status of the respondents.

13.10.2 Adults

Generally, positive opinions were expressed regarding having friends who are from a country which is not one's own. This is evident both in the response of participants whose partner is Maltese as well as in those of participants who are not Maltese or who are in a mixed-nationality relationship. In all categories over 80% agreed that it is positive to have foreign friends and no major differences emerge between the groups. There was also general consensus that it is not necessarily better to meet people who speak one's own languages. However, approximately one-third of the participants expressed the view that meeting people with whom one may communicate without having to surmount language barriers is an advantage. Some differences emerged between the groups when asked whether having people who speak different languages in the same neighbourhood may lead to problems:

[17] See also Camilleri (2007).

INFORMANT'S MARITAL/PARTNERSHIP STATUS	OPTIONS (N AND %)				
	I do not agree	I agree	I don't know	Not answered	Total
Not answered / not applicable	15 *(45.5)*	9 *(27.3)*	9 *(27.3)*	0 -	33 *(100.0)*
Both partners born in Malta	43 *(45.3)*	27 *(28.4)*	24 *(25.3)*	1 *(1.1)*	95 *(100.0)*
Both partners NOT born in Malta	9 *(81.8)*	1 *(9.1)*	0 -	1 *(9.1)*	11 *(100.0)*
One partner born in Malta, the other abroad	17 *(68.0)*	4 *(16.0)*	4 *(16.0)*	0 -	25 *(100.0)*
TOTAL	84 *51.2*	41 *25.0*	37 *22.6*	2 *1.2*	164 *100.0*

Tab. 13-20: (BQ23) "When there are people who speak different languages living in the same neighbourhood there may be problems": marital/partnership status-disaggregated data

As indicated from the results included in the table above, 81.8% of the participants in the "both partners not born in Malta" group and 68% of the participants in the "one partner born in Malta, the other abroad" group, did not agree with the statement for which results are presented in Tab. 13-20. On the other hand this percentage was considerably lower (45.3%) in the "both partners born in Malta" group.

Differences between groups were also registered for participants' reaction to the statement, "If there is respect and tolerance among people, speaking different languages is not a problem":

Informant's marital/partnership status	Options (N and %)				
	I do not agree	**I agree**	**I don't know**	**Not answered**	**Total**
Not answered / not applicable	8 *(24.2)*	21 *(63.6)*	3 *(9.1)*	1 *(3.0)*	33 *(100.0)*
Both partners born in Malta	5 *(5.3)*	69 *(72.6)*	19 *(20)*	2 *(2.1)*	95 *(100.0)*
Both partners NOT born in Malta	0 -	10 *(90.9)*	0 -	1 *(9.1)*	11 *(100.0)*
One partner born in Malta, the other abroad	3 *(12.0)*	20 *(80.0)*	2 *(8.0)*	0 -	25 *(100.0)*
Total	16 *9.8*	120 *73.2*	24 *14.6*	4 *2.4*	164 *100.0*

Tab. 13-21: (BQ24) "If there is respect and tolerance among people, speaking different languages is not a problem": marital/partnership status-disaggregated data

Though the results outlined in the table above indicate that there is an overwhelming majority of participants who agreed with the above-mentioned statement, the percentages are highest in the case of the "both partners not born in Malta" group (90.9%) followed by the "one partner born in Malta, the other abroad" group (80%).

13.11. Conclusion

Despite the fact that the number of foreign students in Maltese primary classrooms is not very large, this number has risen in the recent years. This situation presents a number of challenges and information gathered while collecting data in schools for the MERIDIUM Project, as well as results of recent research (e.g. Francalanza and Gauci, 2009; Calleja, Grech and Cauchi, 2010; Valentino, 2011), show that these students are still relatively "invisible" within the local schooling system, especially where policies and planning are concerned. Issues concerning these students are sometimes considered within the theoretical and practical framework of "diversity" (Bartolo, Mol Lous and Hofsäss, 2007), in which various pedagogical suggestions are put forward in order to respond to their needs. Yet, this is a broad area within the field of Education whereas, also in consideration of today's situation in the Mediterranean area, school integration issues related to immigrant students may require further specialisation as:

> the benefits of multilingualism and multilingual education have been advocated during the last decade although multilingualism presents a phenomenon difficult to grasp in its complexity and therefore posing a number of problems to scholars working in the field. (Cenoz and Jessner, 2009: 121)

Such specialisation would certainly be useful especially where teacher education is concerned, as research carried out in Malta clearly highlights that presently schoolteachers do not feel adequately prepared to face the challenges of the multilingual and multicultural classroom.

It is clear that integrating children with a migrant background into Maltese schools is not an easy task: these children are faced with a diversified language context in which the patterns of interplay of the two languages, Maltese and English, in different domains are not easily discernible to those who have not been born in Malta or who have lived in the country for a relatively short time. Foreign students in primary schools not only have to cope with learning the context languages, but also need to gain awareness of the specific requirements of language use in the local bilingual situation. This implies that they must become familiar with the different contexts and ways in which Maltese and English are intermingled, as well as with the sociolinguistic implications of their alternate use. Knowing English is certainly an advantage, but it does not necessarily solve all possible problems as knowledge of Maltese is also an important prerequisite to fuller integration within local classrooms and school communities:

> what matters is that language proficiency meets the formal and informal requirements in the *relevant* everyday areas and functional systems, such as school, training and labour market. Thus, a 'functionally differentiated' multilingualism – and not just any kind – is important (Maas and Mehlem, 2003: 30f.), so that partly very specific requirements are set, whose (non) fulfilment can have clear consequences for success in the relevant functional areas. To this is added an often neglected and self-evident fact: analogous to any kind of multiple inclusion in the process of immigrants' social integration, linguistic assimilation is a *necessary* condition for any *competent* bilingualism or multilingualism (Esser, 2006: 15, italics as in the original).

The analysis of the data collected from children attending Maltese primary schools and their parents indicates that students who were not born in Malta (or whose parents were born abroad) originate from a number of different countries and possess heterogenous social and personal backgrounds. Some aspects highlighted in this research, such as their lack of knowledge of the Maltese language and the fact that they feel less "Maltese" than their fellow students, sometimes cause difficulties when they are placed in local schools. Furthermore, their problems may be compounded because, as stated repeatedly in the course of this report on the analysis of the MERIDIUM data, the number of these children is still relatively small. Due to practical constraints it is therefore often very difficult for local schools to implement programmes through which they could help these children maintain their mother tongue by teaching it to them during school hours, as may occur in schools in other European countries attended by groups of students with similar linguistic and cultural backgrounds. On the other hand, however, there is quite a clear indication that English is used widely even when adults born abroad speak to their children, even in cases where these do not originate from English-speaking countries. This is spurred both by the importance of English within the local educational system and by the status of the language as an international lingua franca.

Compared to the past, where Malta's linguistic situation was almost exclusively characterised by the use of context languages (Maltese, English and, in some cases, Italian), today many adults and children have regular experience of contact with linguistic diversity. It is worth highlighting the presence of Eastern European languages, especially Russian and Serbian, in Malta today as a result of recent migratory flows. In the past these languages were totally absent from the Maltese linguistic scene. Although there is reasonably regular contact with other languages and positive attitudes are registered towards multilingualism (Caruana and Lasagabaster, in press), there is a rather poor recognition of Arabic script among children who formed part of the MERIDIUM sample, despite the fact that Maltese is a Semitic language.

The data collected in the context of MERIDIUM provide further insight into Malta's present day sociolinguistic and socio-cultural situation. Dissemination of results has been met favourably both in local schools and in the wider community. During the discussions held as part of the dissemination it emerged clearly that educators view schools and classrooms as places which offer opportunities to students with different backgrounds to reflect on linguistic and cultural diversity. The presence of foreign students is considered to be enriching, despite the challenges it creates. Although the body of research in the field has increased recently, head-teachers, teachers and school staff still lament the fact of the limited availability of practical resources necessary to address problems which arise, for example, when dealing with newcomers who start attending school in the course of, rather than at the beginning, of the year, or with students who have difficulty understanding both Maltese and English. A question which features regularly is whether didactic tools are readily available for the needs of today's multicultural classrooms. Such queries clearly spell out the urgency of devising educational policies and teaching materials which address these needs and take into consideration practical experiences in different settings (as outlined in Kenner and Hickey, 2008) and an "adjusted" curriculum (Olshtain and Nissim-Amitai, 2004). Although this is a situation which Malta is still coming to terms with, the sooner measures are put in place to deal with its consequences the better, especially in view of the likelihood that there will continue to be an increase in the number of students with foreign backgrounds in Maltese schools in the future.

References

Agius, D. 1992. Morphological alternatives in the Gozitan dialects of Maltese. *Materiaux Arabes et Sudarabiques (MAS-Gellas), Nouvelle Série*, 4.111-161.

Aquilina, J., and Isserlin, B. 1981. *A survey of contemporary dialectal Maltese, vol. 1 - Gozo*, Leeds: University of Leeds.

Attard, L. 1999. *L-emigrazzjoni Maltija: is-seklu dsatax u għoxrin*. Malta: Pubblikazzjonijiet Indipendenza.

Bartolo, P., A. Mol Lous and T. Hofsäss, eds. 2007. *Responding to student diversity. Teacher education and classroom practice*, Malta: University of Malta.

Berruto, G. 1998. *Situazioni di plurilinguismo, commutazione di codice e mescolanza di sistemi. Babylonia* 6.16-21.

Bonnici, L. 2009. Maltese English: History of use, structural variation and sociolinguistic status. In *Introducing Maltese Linguistics*, eds. B. Comrie, R. Fabri, E. Hume, M. Mifsud, T. Stolz and M. Vanhove, 393-414. Amsterdam: Benjamins.

Borg, A. 1988a. The maintenance of Maltese as a language: What chances? In *European workshop on multicultural studies in higher education,* 89-106. Strasbourg: Directorate of Education, Culture and Sport, Division for Higher Education and Research.

—. 1988b. *Ilsienna*. Ħas-Sajjied: Malta.

—. 2011. Lectal variation in Maltese. In *Variation and Change: The dynamics of Maltese in space, time, and society*, eds. S. Caruana, R. Fabri, and T. Stolz, 11-32. Berlin: Akademie Verlag.

Borg, J., M. Lauri and A. Hillman. 2009. *Exploring the Maltese Media Landscape*. Valletta: Allied Newspapers Ltd.

Brincat, G. 1998. A Malta l'italiano lo insegna la televisione. *Italiano e Oltre* 13. 52-58.

—. 2003. *Malta. Una storia linguistica.* Genova: Le Mani.

Brincat, J. 2011. *Maltese and other languages. A linguistic history of Malta.* Malta: Midsea.

Brincat, L. 2007. *Do our students have an attitude problem towards English? A sociolinguistic study.* Unpublished B.Ed. (Hons) dissertation, University of Malta.

Brincat, L. and S. Caruana. 2011. Il-Malti Mgħaġġel: Maltese in computer-mediated chat conversations. In *Variation and Change: The dynamics of Maltese in space, time, and society*, eds. S. Caruana, R. Fabri, and T. Stolz, 65-89.Berlin: Akademie Verlag.

Calleja, C., M. Grech, and B. Cauchi. 2010. *Education and ethnic minorities in Malta*, Malta: The e-SPICES Learning Partnership.

Camilleri, A. 1995. *Bilingualism in education, the Maltese experience.* Heidelberg: Julius Groos Verlag.

—. ed. 2007. *Promoting linguistic diversity and whole-school development*, Strasbourg: Council of Europe.

Camilleri, A., and M. Vanhove. 1994. A phonetic and phonological inventory of the Maltese dialect of Mġarr. *Zeitschrift für Arabische Linguistik* 28. 87-110.

Caruana, M. 2002. *Attitudes towards code switching in Malta: a sociolinguistic study*. Unpublished B.A. (Hons) dissertation, University of Malta.

Caruana, S. 2003. *Mezzi di comunicazione e input linguistico, L'acquisizione dell'italiano L2 a Malta*. Milano: Franco Angeli.

—. 2006. Trilingualism in Malta—Maltese, English and italiano televisivo. *International Journal of Multilingualism* 3/3. 159-172.

—. 2007. Language use and language attitudes in Malta. In *Language use and attitudes towards multilingualism in bilingual European contexts*, eds. A. Huguet and D. Lasagabaster, 184-207. London, Cleveland: Multilingual Matters.

—. 2011. Bilingualism and language policy in Malta. In *Language contact and language decay. Socio-political and linguistic perspectives*, eds. P. Ramat and E. Miola, 11-46. Pavia: IUSS.

Caruana. S., and G. B. Klein, eds. 2008. *Intercultural communication in bureaucratic and institutional contexts.* Perugia: Guerra.

Caruana, S., and D. Lasagabaster. In press. *Faraway, so close: multilingualism in the Basque Country and in Malta from a socio-*

educational perspective. In *Current Multilingualism: A New Linguistic Dispensation*, eds. D. Singleton, J. Fishman, L. Aronin and M. Ó Laoire. Berlin: Mouton de Gruyter.

Cassola, A. 1998. *L'italiano a Malta*. Malta: MUP.

Cenoz, J., and U. Jessner. 2009. *The study of multilingualism in educational contexts*. In *The exploration of multilingualism*, eds. L. Aronin and B. Hufeisen, 121-138. Amsterdam, Philadelphia: John Benjamins.

Commission of European Communities. 2008. *Multilingualism: an asset for Europe and a shared commitment*. Accessed September 26, 2012. http://ec.europa.eu/education/languages/pdf/com/2008_0566_en.pdf.

Driessen, G. 2005. From Cure to Curse: The Rise and Fall of Bilingual Education Programs in the Netherlands. In *The effectiveness of bilingual school programs for immigrant children*, ed. J. Söhn, 77-107. Berlin: Wissenschaftszentrum Berlin für Sozialforschung.

Eurydice Network. 2009. *Integrating immigrant children in school in Europe*. European Commission: Education, Audiovisual and Culture Executive Agency (available at:
http://eacea.ec.europa.eu/education/eurydice/documents/thematic_reports/101EN.pdf, accessed September 26, 2012).

Esser, H. 2006. *Migration, language and integration, AKI Research Review 4*. Berlin: Wissenschaftszentrum Berlin für Sozialforschung.

Fabri, R. 2010. Maltese. *Revue Belge de Philogie de d'Histoire* 88/3. 791-813.

Farrugia, K. 2010. *The economic and social implications of irregular immigration in Malta*. Unpublished Master of Arts dissertation, University of Malta.

Francalanza, J., and B. Gauci, 2009. *The colours of Malta*. Unpublished Post Graduate Certificate in Education Long Essay, University of Malta.

Golan, C. P., and E. Olshtain. 2011. A model of identity and language orientations: the case of immigrant students from the Former Soviet Union in Israel. *Journal of Multilingual and Multicultural Development* 32/4. 361-376.

Gogolin, I. 2005. Bilingual Education—the German Experience and Debate. In *The effectiveness of bilingual school programs for immigrant children*, ed. J. Söhn, 133-145. Berlin: Wissenschaftszentrum Berlin für Sozialforschung.

Grima, A. 2008. *Living life in a language*. Accessed September 26, 2012. http://www.adriangrima.com/adrian-grima_living-life-in-a-language.pdf.

Kenner, C., and T. Hickey, eds. 2008. *Multilingual Europe: diversity and learning*, Staffordshire: Trentham Books Limited.

Maas, U., and U. Mehlem. 2003. Klärung der begrifflichen Grundlagen. In *Qualitätsanforderungen für die Sprachförderung im Rahmen der Integration von Zuwanderern*, eds. U. Maas and U. Mehlem, 17-39. IMIS-Beiträge Themenheft 21. Osnabrück: IMIS.

Maurer-Hetto, M. 2009. Struggling with the languages of the 'legitimate market' and the 'islets of liberty' (Bourdieu). A case study of pupils with immigrational background in the trilingual school-system of Luxembourg. *International Journal of Multilingualism*, 6/1. 68-84.

Mifsud, M. 1995. *Loan verbs in Maltese: A descriptive and comparative study*. Leiden, New York, Köln: Brill.

Neame, J. 2006. *Code-switching in Sliema*. Unpublished B.A. (Hons) dissertation, University of Malta.

Olshtain, E., and F. Nissim-Amitai. 2004. Curriculum decision-making in a multilingual context. *International Journal of Multilingualism*, 1/1. 53-64.

Peska, S. 2009. *Attitudes towards English among Bi- and Multilingual Adolescents in Malta*. Unpublished diplomarbeit Magistra der Philosophie, University of Innsbruck.

Pulis, K. 2010. *The phenomenon of irregular immigration the central issues as perceived by Maltese political parties*. Unpublished Master of Arts dissertation, University of Malta.

Rosner, M., and J. Joachimsen. 2011. *Languages in the European Information Society—Maltese* (META-NET white paper series). Berlin: META-NET DFKI Projektbüro Berlin (available at: http://www.meta-net.eu/whitepapers/download/meta-net-languagewhitepaper-maltese.pdf, accessed September 26, 2012).

Söhn, J., ed. 2005. *The effectiveness of bilingual school programs for immigrant children*. Berlin: Wissenschaftszentrum Berlin für Sozialforschung (available at: http://www2000.wzb.eu/alt/aki/files/aki_bilingual_school_programs.pdf, accessed September 26, 2012).

Sciriha, L. 2004. *Keeping in touch. The sociolinguistics of mobile telephony in Malta*. Malta: Agenda.

Sciriha, L., and Vassallo, M. 2006. *Living languages in Malta*. Malta: Vassallo & Sciriha.

Spinthourakis, J., E. Karatzia-Stavlioti, G. Lempesi, I. Papadimitriou and C. Giannaka. 2008. *Educational policies that address social inequality. Cyprus: Country Report*. Accessed September 26, 2012. http://www.epasi.eu/CountryReportCY.pdf.

Valentino, N. 2011. *Language Learning Policies for minority children in the Primary School*, unpublished B.Ed. (Hons) dissertation, University of Malta.

Weber, J. 2009. *Multilingualism, education and change*. Frankfurt am Main: Peter Lang.

CHAPTER FOURTEEN

LINGUISTIC PLURALITY IN EUROPEAN COUNTRIES: SLOVENIAN ISTRIA BETWEEN A POLICY OF COEXISTENCE AND THE ISSUE OF IMMIGRATION

LUCIJA ČOK AND MAJA ZADEL

14.1. Introduction

As human beings, we live between the subjective world and social reality, which is a reflection of our adaptation to it. Within this reality, an individual uses linguistic means of communication, actions and behaviours and exchanges, opinions and judgments with others to unconsciously create his or her idea of the objective world. No two languages can truly and fully express the same objective reality. Through this interpretation (Sapir, 1972:57), we can think of language as the symbolic basis of the culture of an individual environment where the language is being used. An individual is also and above all a constituent part of a group, a society, a nation. Due to the cultural intertwinement and linguistic diversity of the modern world society and its age-long tradition to preserve itself in this way, its functioning cannot be imagined without the ethnic awareness of individuals and groups. This also means that there are differences and similarities that are intertwined within society. Therefore, only through understanding, are various national communities able to comprehend the specifics of other communities and mutually interact without prejudice.

The democratic management of cultural diversity in Europe, which is rooted in the history of the old continent and further emphasized by globalization, sets out postulates with the objective to enable the existence of a European reality involving the active participation of all nations and societies. These postulates are: the respect for diversity (linguistic, cultural, ethnic, etc.), creating bases for the coexistence of diversity, the respect for the rights of individuals and social groups, eliminating all forms of discrimination and promoting social inclusion and equal opportunities for every individual. The Council of Europe's White Paper[1] on Intercultural Dialogue offers an intercultural approach in the development of a multilingual and multicultural Europe based on the dignity of the individual (subject to our common humanity and common destiny). In order to achieve a European identity, the latter should be based on our shared core values, the respect for our common heritage and cultural diversity and the respect for the dignity of each individual. Intercultural dialogue plays an important role here, as it can be used to prevent ethnic, religious, linguistic and cultural differences.

Slovenia has been and still remains an area of contact between nations and languages. From Roman, Byzantine, Venetian, Napoleonic or Austro-Hungarian dominance to this day, the territory of Slovenian Istria has preserved and accepted linguistic and cultural diversity throughout changing political and social currents. During the first, monarchic, and even more so, during the second, Federal Yugoslavia, what was at that time the former Republic of Slovenia, has created conditions for the tolerant coexistence of the autochthonous minorities (Italian and Hungarian) on democratic legal provisions. In Slovenia as an independent country, the relationship between the majority and the minorities has been strengthened even further. In the Slovenian legal system, the prohibition of discrimination is a constitutional category, since Article 14 of the Constitution states that in Slovenia everyone shall be guaranteed equal human rights and fundamental freedoms. Any incitement to national, racial, religious or other discrimination and to kindle national, racial, religious or other hatred and intolerance is unconstitutional (Article 63 of the Constitution). Nevertheless, the new Slovenian legislation devoted less attention to immigrants, mostly citizens of the former Yugoslav republics, some of whom have lost their status of citizens and were then marked as the "Erased" (*Izbrisani*) overnight, namely people who have lost their civil rights after the Federation had dissolved.

The subject of our studies and research is focused on a narrower spectrum of the regulation of immigrants' rights, i.e. the integration of children of immigrants in the Slovenian educational system. The treatment

[1] The White Paper on Intercultural Dialogue, "Living together as equals in dignity", CM (2008) 30 final version, 2 May 2008, 118th Session of the Committee of Ministers (Strasbourg, 7 May 2008), available at http://www.coe.int/t/dg4/intercultural/whitepaper_interculturaldialogue_2_EN.asp, accessed September 26, 2012.

and formation of a culturally and linguistically diverse community is a particularly sensitive task for the democratic cultural and educational policies of an individual country. The integration of children into the school system is directly related to their indirect integration into the wider social environment. Within the school population, much like within society as a whole, there is a lack of a legal basis which would allow for a more effective planning of the integration processes of children of immigrants into the Slovenian educational system. Some results of the analysis of the current situation conducted by government offices[2] point to an underdeveloped integration strategy for children of immigrants into the educational system, professionals lacking the knowledge and skills necessary to ensure effective and permanent cooperation with parents, poor knowledge of key elements of their language and culture necessary to avoid potential misunderstandings or to facilitate communication with parents and encourage them to participate and, lastly, teachers lacking the knowledge and skills needed to promote the intercultural communication between Slovenian and immigrant parents.

The unfinished strategy of including immigrants' children in schooling based on universal human and democratic principles, the lack of appropriate expert knowledge and know-how of professionals for quality cooperation with their parents, overly modest knowledge of key elements of the language and culture of immigrants (which could avoid possible misunderstandings and establish channels of contacts with parents, thus encouraging them to cooperate), overly modest knowledge and skills of teachers necessary to stimulate intercultural communication between parents of Slovenian children and parents of immigrants: these are only some findings of situation analyses[3] carried out by governmental offices.

What further aggravates the situation, on the other hand, is the children of immigrants' lack of knowledge of the Slovene language and the underestimation of the importance of preserving their mother tongue. Furthermore, they sometimes regard their cultures and their languages as inferior in comparison with the Slovenian language and culture. As a result of such shortcomings, there is a lack of integration of children of immigrants and their parents into the school environment and the wider

---

[2] Strategija vključevanja otrok, učencev in dijakov migrantov v sistem vzgoje in izobraževanja v Republiki Sloveniji. Poročilo komisije za pripravo koncepta vključevanja učencev migrantov v sistem vzgoje in izobraževanja (Strategy of inclusion of migrant children, pupils and students into the education system in the Republic of Slovenia. Report of the Commission for the preparation of the concept of integration of migrant pupils into the educational system), MES - May 2007.

[3] *Ibidem.*

Slovenian environment. In recent years, the results of analyses mentioned above have prompted the government and those in charge of school policies to formulate measures necessary to remedy the situation.

Within the monograph entitled: *Slovenska Istra med politiko sožitja in priseljeništvom* (The Slovenian Istria between a Policy of Coexistence and the Immigration Issue), edited by Annales Publishing House of the Science and Research Centre (SRC), the researchers Lucija Čok and Maja Zadel collected some of data obtained from MERIDIUM project and presented them to the Slovenian public. A much more extensive database than that, which was used in the comparative analysis of seven universities in six countries included in the project, offered the opportunity for some additional analyses, particularly in terms of the involvement of Slovenian Istria in the issue of immigration.

14.2. Slovenia: Country Context

Slovenia has always been an area of contact among people where the language was frequently regarded as the only means of connection between the inhabitants, thereby a major aspect of Slovene identity. Slovenia is a small European nation which was under the rule of foreigners for several eras and which, consequently had to fight for the recognition of its rights. During the Napoleonic era, the Slovene national spirit was consolidated with the establishment of the Illyrian provinces and the capital of Ljubljana. However, only four years later, with the Vienna Congress, the whole territory was once again annexed to Austria. In 1918, following the defeat of the Austrian Empire, Slovenia became a part of the Reign of Serbs, Croats and Slovenes proclaimed in Belgrade by Alexander Karadjordjević.

After WWII, when Slovenia became part of the Socialist Federative Republic of Yugoslavia, Slovene communist leaders were faithful interpreters of the socialist reforms including the promotion of the self-management, the brotherhood and the unity of the southern Slavic peoples. In the eighties of the last century, after the death of Tito, the will for pluralism and opening towards the West became stronger and stronger until it finally resulted in the secession of Slovenia from the rest of the former Yugoslavia. At the plebiscite that took place on the Christmas Day of 1990, 90% of the Slovene population voted in favour of the independence, which led to the proclamation of sovereignty on June 26, 1991.

In March 2003, 89.6% of Slovenes voted in favour of the State's entrance into the European Union. Relationships between the Republic of

Slovenia and the rest of Europe are considered to be fundamental in order to move forward by the majority of the Slovenes, although Europe is not perceived as some sort of "promised land".

Today, Slovenia remains one of the smallest members of the European Union with a fully autonomous economic development, in spite of its territorial dimensions and the current economic crisis. With accession to European Union, the Republic of Slovenia witnessed alterations in almost every area of society: legislation was reformed, the financial market was liberalized, and foreign investments were facilitated by means of a stable currency guarantee. In the space of a few years, more than 500 kilometres of superhighways were opened, extending on the whole national territory (20,256 square kilometres). In the first quarter of 2011, there were 73% of households, and 69% of people from age of 10 to 74 years who had access to the Internet (Statistical Office of the Republic of Slovenia[4]).

Many Slovenes still live across the borders of the Slovene Republic. Slovenia is therefore especially active in regulating the status of the minorities and very sensitive when it comes to their protection. According to the Population, Households and Housing Census 2002, the Slovene part of the population amounted to 1,631,363, whereas the Hungarian and Italian national minorities amounted to 6,243 and 2,258 inhabitants respectively. Other ethnic communities, who did not have this status–officially recognized rights (only groups with more than 1,000 declared Slovene citizens were taken into account), were: 38,964 Serbs, 35,642 Croats, 21,542 Bosnians, 6,186 Albanians, 3,972 Macedonians, etc. In the Census, there was also the possibility to choose the category "Yugoslavian", which was mostly selected by the second generation of ethnically mixed marriages, immigrants from Bosnia and Herzegovina and possibly also by military cadre from other republics. (Kržišnik Bukić, 2010: 509–510)

A special group of non-Slovene inhabitants is composed of 3,246 Romanis. Due to their social disjunction, a different way of life and tradition, they need special assistance whenever there is the need and their will to be incorporated into mainstream living and working conditions.

Special rights, designed for Italian and Hungarian national minorities (autochthonous minorities) are of dual nature, being collective and individual rights simultaneously. The recognition of dual nature of minority rights and the implementation of the "positive concept of protection of minorities" is defined in the Article 64 of the Constitution of

[4] See: http://www.stat.si/eng/novica_prikazi.aspx?id=4240, accessed September 26, 2012. For the website of the Statistical Office of the Republic of Slovenia, see: http://www.stat.si/eng/index.asp.

the Republic of Slovenia[5] which establishes also the obligation of the State to ensure the realization of these special rights, morally and materially.

The Constitution of the Republic of Slovenia also guarantees expression of ethnic affiliation to the inhabitants of non-Slovene ethnic origin. According to the Article 61 of the Constitution, they may establish their ethnic organizations and associations, use their language and script, express and develop their specific ethnic culture and, for their activities, receive funds from the republic budget on the basis of the public tender of the Ministry for culture.

The non-Slovene inhabitants can be classified into the following groups:

- the "classical" (territorial) minorities: Italian and Hungarian minorities, living in the border areas; and a small number of autochthonous ethnic groups: Jews and German speaking ethnic group;
- Roma;
- the newly-formed ethnic communities (comprising mostly members of the nations of the former Yugoslavia: Croats, Muslims, Macedonians, Montenegrins), which emerged as a result of contemporary processes of economic immigration and accepted the citizenship of Slovenia.

Migration in the 20th century is mostly related to former states of the Socialist Federal Republic of Yugoslavia (SFRY), from where intensive migratory movements were registered. These units are now Bosnia and Herzegovina, Montenegro, Croatia, FRY Macedonia, Slovenia and Serbia. Slovenia, as the most economically developed federal unit of the SFRY, was also a prominent immigration area. Even though the immigrants' main reason for immigration was the

> aspiration to employment in the economically most developed Yugoslav Republic, the Slovenian economy itself has always expressed a great interest for the inflow of labour force from other Yugoslav republics (Kržišnik Bukić, 2010: 518).

[5]Article 64 of the Constitution of Slovenia (*Ustava Republike Slovenije*). Special Rights of the Autochthonous Italian and Hungarian Ethnic Communities in Slovenia. See: http://www.uradni-list.si/_pdf/1991/Ur/u1991033.pdf, accessed September 26, 2012.

MUNICIPALITY		IMMIGRANTS TO SLOVENIA BY YEAR OF FIRST IMMIGRATION (N AND %)							
		1952 or earlier	**1953-1960**	**1961-1970**	**1971-1980**	**1981-1991**	**1992-1996**	**1997-2001**	**Total**
Izola	N	188	500	601	921	584	213	246	3,253
	%	*5.78*	*15.37*	*18.48*	*28.31*	*17.95*	*6.55*	*7.56*	*100.0*
Koper	N	641	1287	2166	2359	1731	582	580	9,346
	%	*6.86*	*13.77*	*23.18*	*25.24*	*18.52*	*6.23*	*6.21*	*100.0*
Piran	N	282	631	598	874	618	335	255	3,593
	%	*7.85*	*17.56*	*16.64*	*24.33*	*17.20*	*9.32*	*7.10*	*100.0*
SLOVENIA	N	14930	12877	26121	53653	35594	13540	12890	169,605
	%	***8.80***	*7.59*	***15.40***	***31.63***	***20.99***	*7.98*	*7.60*	***100.0***

Tab. 14-1: Immigrants to Slovenia by the year of first immigration (municipalities) (Source: Statistical Office of the RS, 2002 Population, Households and Housings Census)

MUNICIPALITY		IMMIGRANTS TO SLOVENIA BY COUNTRY OF FIRST RESIDENCE (N AND %)						
		Bosnia-Herzegovina	**Croatia**	**Macedonia**	**Yugoslavia**	**EU**	**Other**	**Total**
Izola	N	1114	1322	157	400	204	56	3,253
	%	*34.25*	*40.64*	*4.83*	*12.30*	*6.27*	*1.72*	*100.0*
Koper	N	3250	3827	293	1156	647	173	9,346
	%	*34.77*	*40.95*	*3.14*	*12.37*	*6.92*	*1.85*	*100.0*
Piran	N	908	1671	129	472	314	99	3,593
	%	*25.27*	*46.51*	*3.59*	*13.14*	*8.74*	*2.76*	*100.0*
SLOVENIA	N	69279	48609	6593	26951	13287	4886	169,605
	%	***40.85***	***28.66***	***3.89***	***15.89***	***7.83***	***2.88***	***100.0***

Tab. 14-2: Immigrants to Slovenia according to the country of primary residence (municipalities) (Source: Statistical Office of the RS, 2002 Population, Households and Housings Census)

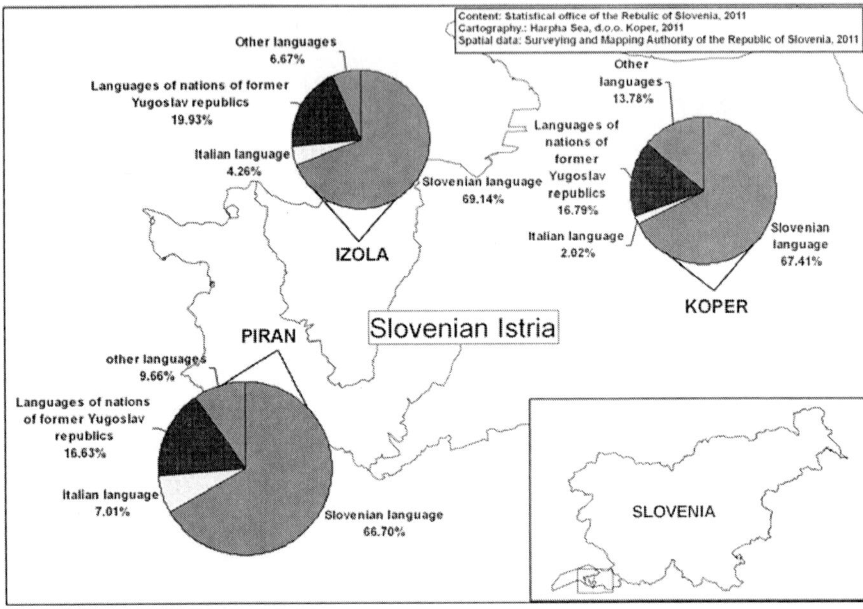

Fig. 14-1: The percentages of residents by their mother tongue (Koper, Izola, Piran) (Source: Statistical Office of the RS, 2002 Population, Households and Housings Census)

According to the data from census surveys, it can be established that immigration was most extensive in the 1970s, since almost a third (31.63 per cent) of all immigrants immigrated to Slovenia between 1971 and 1980, as referred to in Tab. 14-1 (p. 349).

The municipalities with the highest share of persons who declared themselves as Albanians, Bosniacs, Bosnians, Montenegrins, Croats, Macedonians, Muslims or Serbians (according to alphabetical order) are Izola, Jesenice and Velenje (Kržišnik Bukić, 2010: 514), although the region with the highest population share of non-Slovenian national affiliation is the Coast-Karst region, of which Slovenian Istria is part (Vertot *et al.*, 2001: 18).

If we examine migration from the Yugoslavian territory to Slovenia considering the number of immigrants according to the mother tongue criterion, we can establish that the municipalities with more than 15 percent share of individuals who speak Albanian, Montenegrin, Bosnian, Croatian, Croatian-Serbian, Serbian or Serbo-Croatian, in the alphabetical order, are: Izola, Jesenice, Koper, Ljubljana, Piran, Postojna and Velenje (Kržišnik Bukić, 2010: 515).

The region of Slovenian Istria is the largest area–as it is composed of three municipalities: Koper, Izola and Piran–in the Republic of Slovenia, with immigrants from the former Yugoslav republics and is consequently also interesting for research work. The officially recognised indigenous Italian minority also lives on this territory, meaning that this is a region where various languages and cultures mix.

14.3. MERIDIUM Research and Project Methodology

14.3.1 Objectives and Indicators

Among the objectives of the MERIDIUM, the most relevant for the Slovene context were:

- to investigate the level of awareness (among local population and migrants) of other languages present in the everyday life context
- to consider the linguistic diversity as a resource
- to investigate to what extent both awareness and attitudes vary between childhood and adulthood
- to investigate how the interviewees perceive the institutions and the working world attitudes towards linguistic diversity and multilingualism

The selected area for case study is characterised by immigration density from former Yugoslav countries to Mediterranean Slovenia. Research data was collected on the basis of:

a. context analysis (identifying and analysing local linguistic policies, the presence of significant projects in the field, and the presence of ethnic and/or intercultural associations operating in the area, etc.)
b. surveys by way of questionnaires to reveal the degree of awareness of the presence or multilingual repertoires and the propensity to conceive them as a resource.

The objective was to carry out an integrated evaluation and to determine the following:

- How do linguistic and educational policies affect (as carried out in a local circle) the perception and the attitude of the citizens (natives and immigrants) towards linguistic diversity and to multilingualism?

- How does living in a highly dense centre of immigration/ emigration affect these perceptions/attitudes?
- How do these perceptions/attitudes change when considering both children and adults?
- How is multilingualism perceived within educational institutions, especially primary schools?

The following primary schools were involved in the Slovenian study:

- Osnovna šola Cirila Kosmača Piran/Scuola elementare Ciril Kosmač Pirano (Ciril Kosmač Primary School Piran)
- Osnovna šola Koper/ Scuola elementare Capodistria (Koper Primary School)
- Osnovna šola Antona Ukmarja Koper/ Scuola Elementare Anton Ukmar Capodistria (Anton Ukmar Primary School Koper)
- Osnovna šola Elvire Vatovec Prade/ Scuola elementare Elvira Vatovec Prade (Elvira Vatovec Primary School Prade)

14.3.2. The Sample

The sample included pupils and parents. A questionnaire was distributed among 156 pupils in four primary schools. The pilot class was the 5th grade of Koper Primary School, where 24 children responded to the questionnaire in April 2010. The research was implemented in two municipalities of the Slovenian Istria, namely in three schools in the Koper Municipality, and in one school in the Piran Municipality, in May and June 2010. The first questionnaire was carried out at Piran Primary School in May 2010 the second took place at the Elvira Vatovec Primary School, always in May 2010, the third at the Koper Primary School also in May 2010. The final part of the data collection was held at the Anton Ukmar Primary School in June 2010.

a) Research sample: pupils

117 pupils from the Koper Municipality were included in the research, representing 75% of the total, whereas 39 pupils were from the Piran Municipality, representing the remaining 25%. The majority of participants in the research attended the Anton Ukmar Primary School (41 pupils), followed by those attending the Ciril Kosmač Primary School (39 pupils), the Koper Primary School (38 pupils) and the Elvira Vatovec Primary School (38 pupils). Roughly, each school represented 25% of the total of the participants. All pupils were learning Italian and English and three pupils were also learning French.

b) Research sample: parents

137 parents of pupils participated in the research, 101 (74%) of which came from the Koper Municipality and 36 (26%) from the Piran Municipality. 36 are parents of children who attend the Ciril Kosmač Primary School 35 parents of children from the Anton Ukmar Primary School and from the Koper Primary School and, finally 33 parents of children attending the Elvira Vatovec Primary School.

14.4. Data Analysis

In the following analysis of the children's and parents' sample, the responses will be presented in descriptive statistics.

14.4.1. Socio-demographic and Sociolinguistic Characteristics of the Sample

a) Pupils

In our case, there were 66 boys (42.3%) and 90 girls (57.7%) included in the research. The age of interviewed children is almost equally distributed, since there were 75 10-year olds, representing 48.1%, and 81 11-year olds, representing 51.9%. Only one child was born in 1998, all other children (155 pupils) were born in 1999.

In the analysis, children will be stratified in groups according to their country of birth and their parents' country of birth ("background").

Informant's country of birth		Informant's background: native	mixed	foreign	Total
Native-born	N	98	28	14	140
	%	*70.0*	*20.0*	*10.0*	*100.0*
Foreign-born	N	1	3	7	11
	%	*(9.1)*	*(27.3)*	*(63.6)*	*(100.0)*
Valid total	N	99	31	21	151
	%	*65.6*	*20.5*	*13.9*	*100.0*
				Information not provided	5
				Grand total	156

Tab. 14-3: Pupils stratified by country of birth of informants and of their parents ("background")[6]

From these data, three groups of children are to be taken into consideration: children with partially or totally native background (Nb/Mb: children with at least one parent born in the survey country), native-born children with foreign background (NFb: children born in the country of survey to foreign-born parents) and foreign-born children with foreign background (FFb: foreign-born children to foreign-born parents).

As can be seen in Tab. 14-4, the two groups of children with foreign background are small, composed of only 14 and 7 interviewees. For this reason data will be presented in numbers of respondents.

	Children with partially or totally native background (Nb/Mb)	Native-born children with foreign background (NFb)	Foreign-born children with foreign background (FFb)	Total
N	130	14	7	151
%	*86.1*	*9.3*	*4.6*	*100.0*

Tab. 14-4: Pupils stratified by their country of birth and their parents' country of birth

[6] In tables where cases do not reach the sum of 100, percentages are listed within brackets.

b) Parents

In the sample of parents, there were 36 male participants, namely fathers (26.3%), 101 women, namely mothers (73.7%). Almost one half of the parents (47.4%) included in the research were between 40 and 49 years of age, 45.3% of them were between 30 and 39 years of age, 2.9% of them were between 50 and 59 years of age.

In the analysis, parents will be stratified in two groups according to their place of birth.

	NATIVE-BORN INFORMANTS	FOREIGN-BORN INFORMANTS	VALID TOTAL	INFORMATION NOT PROVIDED	GRAND TOTAL
N	111	25	136	1	137
%	*81.6*	*18.4*	*100.0*	-	-

Tab. 14-5: Parents stratified by their country of birth

The majority of the interviewees were born in Slovenia, almost a fifth was born abroad, and one interviewee (0.7 per cent) did not fill in his/her birthplace.

Most of the parents (72.8% or 99 respondents) live in two-parent families, a fifth (19.1% or 26 respondents) lives in extended families and 8.1% (11 respondents) of them live in single-parent families.

Two thirds (67% or 91 respondents) of interviewees have a partner born in Slovenia, a fifth (20.6% or 28 respondents) has a partner born abroad, 15 respondents or 11% of the parents do not have a partner. According to the distribution regarding the country of interviewees' birth it can be seen that 11 interviewees born in Slovenia have a partner born abroad (9.9%) and four interviewees born abroad have a partner born in Slovenia (16%), meaning that these are potentially ethnically mixed families including Slovenians and members of other nations.

The majority of the foreign-born parents came to Slovenia more than 20 years ago (76% or 19 respondents), quite a smaller percentage of them came from 11 to 20 years ago (16% or 4 respondents), or less than 5 years ago (8% or 2 respondents). These data are in accordance with those obtained from the Population, Households and Housings Census, where it can be seen that the largest number of immigrants came to Slovenia and to Slovenian Istria prior to 1990s.

The majority (58.2% or 64 respondents) of parents, born in Slovenia, attended schooling for more than 13 years, a third (35.5% or 39 respondents) between 9 and 13 years, 6.4% or 7 respondents attended schooling for less than 9 years. Parents, born in other countries, mostly attended schooling between 9 to 13 years (52.2% or 12 respondents), 6 respondents (26.1%) attended schooling for 8 years or less, only 5 respondents (21.7%) attended schooling for more than 13 years.

An analogous pattern is visible with interviewees' partners, as 52.7% (49 respondents) of partners of interviewees born in Slovenia attended schooling for more than 13 years, 43% (40 respondents) of them attended schooling from 9 to 13 years, 4.3% (4 respondents) of them attended schooling for 8 years or less. 11 (55%) partners of parents born abroad attended schooling from 9 to 13 years, 25% (5 respondents) of them attended schooling for more than 13 years, 20% (4 respondents) of them for less than 9 years.

Differences between parents born in Slovenia and those born abroad can also be seen from the vocational aspect. Interviewees born in Slovenia most often work in employments that are classified[7] as professionals (40.4% or 38 respondents), technicians and other associate professionals (21.3% or 20 respondents), service workers and shop and market sales workers (10.6% or 10 respondents), clerks (9.6% or 9 respondents), legislators, senior officials and managers, and other (6.4% or 6 respondents in each category). Each of the other professions is listed in less than 5% of cases. On the other hand, foreign-born interviewees most often work as service workers and shop and market sales workers (30% or 6 respondents), craft and related trade workers (25% or 5 respondents), elementary workers (20% or 4 respondents), technicians and other associate professionals (15% or 3 respondents), professionals and clerks (5% or one respondent respectively). It seems that foreign-born parents, in comparison with interviewees born in Slovenia, to a greater extent are employed in occupations that are classified within lower brackets. Conversely, they are less frequently engaged in higher classified professions (there were no legislators, senior officials or managers in the

[7] ISCO88 classification:

1. Legislators, senior officials, managers
2. Professionals
3. Technicians and other associate professionals
4. Clerks
5. Service workers and shop and market sales workers
6. Skilled agricultural and fishery workers
7. Craft and related trade workers
8. Plant and machine operators and assemblers
9. Elementary workers
0. Armed forces

sample, and this group only constituted 5% of professionals, which present the largest group of interviewees born in Slovenia).

Differences are smaller in the case of partners of interviewees. Partners of interviewees born in Slovenia are mostly professionals (28.4% or 23 partners), technicians and other associate professionals (12.3% or 10 partners), service workers and shop and market sales workers, persons employed in craft and related trade sector, and other non-classified occupations (11.1% or 9 partners respectively). Other occupations (plant and machine operators and assemblers, legislators, senior officials and managers, clerks, elementary workers and skilled agricultural and fishery workers) emerge in less than 10% of this group. Most of the partners of foreign-born interviewees are technicians and other associate professionals, sellers and persons employed in the service sector (21.1% or 4 partners in each category), there are less persons working as professionals and clerks (15.8% or 3 partners respectively) and approximately the same percentage working as craft and related trade workers (10.5%) or other non-classified occupations (10.5% or 2 partners respectively). There is one employed as an elementary worker. Also in this case, the higher ranking vocations are mostly performed by partners of interviewees born in Slovenia, although the percentages are more equally distributed than in the case of the interviewees themselves.

14.4.2. Experience of Contacts with Ethno-linguistic Diversity

The results indicate that learning languages, the mediation of cultures and educational processes may have an impact on the perception of linguistic diversity and multilingualism of pupils and their parents. It must be pointed out that the following analysis and discussion, in the absence of a statistically representative sample, presents data at a descriptive level.

When most children hear someone speaking a language that is different to Slovene, they are "amused" or "curious": 107 children with native background, 12 native-born children with foreign background and 4 foreign-born children with foreign background. In both cases, we can perceive a positive attitude to foreign or unknown languages. Another example is when children state that they are "proud" to have friends or relatives who speak languages that are different than Slovene: two thirds of children with partially or totally native background (66 pupils) feel "proud". In the answers of foreign-born children, the percentage is even higher (11 pupils born in Slovenia and 6 born abroad), which, again, confirms the positive attitude to the foreign language. When asked, which language they find most beautiful—their native language or other languages—the majority of children answered that their native language is as beautiful as other languages: 84 children with native background, 10 native born children with foreign background and 5 foreign born children with foreign background.

This shows the openness and positive attitude of children towards foreign languages and cultures, although they are still foreign to them. This outcome could possibly be related to their everyday contacts with multilingualism and to the diverse cultural environment in which they are living, where special significance is given to education for multilingualism in schools with Slovenian and schools with Italian language of instruction[8], as well as to the importance of bilingualism. This, consequently, may affect their attitude towards language diversity.

In the recognition and naming of various writings, in which the Latin alphabet is not used, the demographic traits of Slovenian Istria emerge. Almost half (64 pupils) of the children with partially or totally native background and the large majority of children with foreign background (12 native-born pupils and 6-foreign born pupils) recognised the Cyrillic script. This shows the specific features of the Slovenian Istria, where a large percentage of immigrants come from former Yugoslav countries, a number of them being Serbs. This means that almost half of interviewed children were in contact with the Cyrillic alphabet, although the majority of them do not speak Serbian.

The number of informants who identified correctly the Arabic script was smaller: 43 children with native background, 7 native-born children with foreign background and 3 foreign-born children with foreign background correctly identified this script. These results are not surprising, since the Arabic script is geographically and culturally more remote than the Cyrillic one. This confirms the demographic specifics of the Slovenian Istria, where we can find a high percentage of children whose parents are from former Yugoslav countries, among others also the children of Bosnian parents who are Muslim or Christian. This is why the percentage of those who recognised the Arabic alphabet is higher among children with foreign background, since this writing is present in the Islamic religion and the written tradition.

In the case of the Chinese script, the percentage of correct answers was again high: 92 children with native background, 10 native born children with foreign background and 6 foreign-born children with foreign

[8] Due to the presence of an Italian minority, there are elementary and secondary schools where Italian and Slovene are both taught at school. Apart from members of the Italian ethnic community, these schools are attended also by Slovenes and members of immigrant ethnic communities.

background recognised this writing, thereby proving that they possess a satisfactory recognition of this language, as Chinese characters strongly differ from other writing systems present in the Asian culture.

However, in the case of the Devanagari script the percentage of correct answers of children was very low: namely only one child (with native background) of the entire sample answered correctly. This proves that the large majority of the children have not been in contact with this writing and culture, so they could not have recognised it.

These answers show that children who were included in the research carried out in Slovene primary schools possess an awareness of the concept of multilingualism and that a number of them can identify the characters used in writing non-European languages.

14.4.3. Perception of Linguistic Diversity in the Global and Local Context

Children's response indicated that they are aware that some pupils speak other languages than Slovene: 56 children with native background, 11 native-born children with foreign background and 3 foreign-born children with foreign background stated that "many" or "quite a few" children speak languages other than Slovene.

The children were also asked how often they hear people speaking other languages than Slovene. There were 33 children with partially or totally native background who stated that that hear other languages being spoken "often" and 94 "sometimes"; whereas 7 native-born children with foreign background hear other languages being spoken "often" and 6 "sometimes"; 4 foreign-born children with foreign background hear other languages being spoken "often" and 3 hear them "sometimes".

In the answers to questions on awareness of the presence of multilingualism in schools differences between the groups of informants emerge. More than one half of the children of native-born parents did not perceive the presence of fellow pupils who speak languages other than Slovene, mostly because there are not many of them or they are dispersed in various classes. On the other hand, children with foreign background noticed many more pupils who speak languages other than Slovene. However, these differences between groups of informants are not so evident when children were asked whether people who speak languages other than Slovene are present in their environment, including contexts outside school.

The affiliation to the close environment is very strong: 122 children with native background, 11 native-born children with foreign background and 5 foreign-born children with foreign background feel “very much” and “just enough” part of the town where they live. Considering the differences between the three groups (bearing in mind that they are not very large), we can establish that children with native background identify with the place where they live to a greater extent than the children with foreign background (either born in Slovenia or not), who probably still feel affiliated to another place.

The differences between children with native background and foreign background are mostly visible with the affiliation to the wider environment, i.e. the state. There are 124 children with native background that feel Slovenian “very much” and “just enough”. On the other hand, 4 native-born children with foreign background feel Slovenian “very much” and “just enough” and 7 feel “a little bit” or “not at all”. Among the foreign-born children with foreign background, there are 2 who feel Slovene “very much” and “just enough”, 4 who feel Slovenian “a little bit” or “not at all”. The high number of children with native background who feel Slovene is typical of the relatively recent declaration of independence of Slovenia and it is also probably the reflection of civil education in schools. The fact that figures of children with foreign background (including those who are foreign-born) are not as high, always within the terms of the small sample being analysed, is also worth considering.

A detailed analysis is presented in Tab. 14-6 (p. 361), where it can be seen that children with native background are more affiliated to Slovenia than children with foreign background (either native-born or foreign-born).

The affiliation to the larger environment is more evenly distributed among the three groups than affiliation to the state, but less than the affiliation to the place of residence. Here again, children with native background feel “European” (112 children responded by stating that they feel “very much” and “just enough” European, while for children with foreign background this affiliation is not so strong; 7 native-born children and 4 foreign-born feel “very much” and “just enough” European).

It seems that all three groups of children are most affiliated to the close environment, namely to the city/town where they live; this is mostly evident in responses from children with foreign background (either native-born or foreign-born).

Category of informants		How much do you feel Slovenian?					Total
		very much	just enough	a little bit	not at all	I don't know	
Nb/Mb	**N**	100	22	7	1	0	130
	%	*76.9*	*16.9*	*5.4*	*0.8*	-	*100.0*
NFb	**N**	2	2	2	5	3	14
	%	*(14.3)*	*(14.3)*	*(14.3)*	*(35.7)*	*(21.4)*	*(100.0)*
FFb	**N**	1	1	1	3	1	7
	%	*(14.3)*	*(14.3)*	*(14.3)*	*(42.9)*	*(14.3)*	*(100.0)*
Total	**N**	104	26	10	9	4	153
	%	*68.0*	*17.0*	*6.5*	*5.9*	*2.6*	*100.0*

Tab. 14-6: Affiliation of children to the State

Category of informants		How much do you feel Slovenian?					Total
		very much	just enough	a little bit	not at all	I don't know	
Native born	**N**	74	28	6	2	1	111
	%	*66.7*	*25.2*	*5.4*	*1.8*	*0.9*	*100.0*
Foreign born	**N**	9	7	5	3	1	25
	%	*(36.0)*	*(28.0)*	*(20.0)*	*(12.0)*	*(4.0)*	*(100.0)*
Total	**N**	83	35	11	5	2	136
	%	*61.0*	*25.7*	*8.1*	*3.7*	*1.5*	*100.0*

Tab. 14-7: Affiliation of parents to the State

Similar questions were posed to their parents in order to investigate their perception towards multilingualism in the context in which they live. Parents stated that they are in favour of socialising with individuals of different nationalities: both, native (81 respondents) and foreign-born parents (20 respondents) think that it is positive to have friends who originate from a country which is not their own. Similarly, parents do not think it is necessarily better to meet with people who speak their own language (71 native and 16 foreign-born parents). This shows that there is a degree of acceptance of diversity of languages and nationalities.

The issue of tolerance was also addressed with the majority of respondents stating that they disagree that problems may arise where there is the presence of people who speak different languages (65 native and 15 foreign-born parents). Though not in the majority, a number of respondents agreed that in some cases problems may indeed be the result of the presence of individuals who speak different languages within the same environment. However, when respect and tolerance are present, speaking different languages is not perceived to be a problem according to 101 native-born and 23 foreign-born parents.

Parents perceive the presence of people of different origins in their neighbourhood: there are 96 out of 109 native-born parents and 21 out of 25 foreign-born parents that perceive that "many" or "quite a few" individuals that are not of Slovenian nationality live in their neighbourhood.

Similarly, parents notice people who speak other languages in their environment: the majority in both groups perceives "many" and "quite a few" people who live in their neighbourhood and speak languages other than Slovene (83 native-born parents and 16 foreign-born parents).

When asked, which languages other than Slovene are spoken in their town[9], native-born parents listed the following languages (most frequently selected): Italian (27.8%), Croatian (22.4%), Albanian (13.6%), Serbian (11.2%), Serbo-Croatian (9.5%); while foreign born parents listed the following languages: Croatian (25.0%), Italian (18.8%), Serbian (14.1%), Albanian (10.9%), and Bosnian (7.8%).

In addition to this, approximately two thirds of both groups, native-born (71 respondents) and foreign-born parents (16 respondents), "often" hear people speaking other languages than Slovene.

It is typical of the demographic composition of the area where data were collected that parents born in Slovenia, as well as parents born

[9] This was an open question (BQ28), where informants could list a maximum of 10 languages.

abroad, perceive the presence of inhabitants that are not Slovenian in their local and work environment. The number of those who selected the language that is heard most often by parents born in Slovenia corresponds to the ethnically mixed environment of the Slovenian Istria, where the Italian minority lives together with a large number of immigrants. In fact native-born parents mention Italian as the language (other than Slovene) that they here spoken most often. On the other hand foreign-born parents mention Croatian as the language they hear most frequently.

The perception of linguistic diversity in the global context was the subject investigation in the parents' questionnaires. Approximately half of the parents feel part of the local environment: 57 native-born and 13 foreign-born parents feel "very much" and "just enough" part of the town where they live.

Interestingly, the majority of native-born (102 respondents) and also of foreign born-parents (16 respondents) feel "very much" and "just enough" Slovenian.

Respondents feel European, but to a smaller degree (especially the native-born parents) than they feel Slovenian or part of their town: 67 native-born and 15 foreign-born parents state that they feel European "very much" and "just enough".

The question of the affiliation to their country of origin was posed just to foreign-born parents: 12 parents feel "very much" and "just enough" part of their country of origin, 11 feel "a little bit" part of their country of origin and one informant that does not feel part of his/her country of origin at all.

As shown in Tab. 14-7 (p. 361), parents who are born in Slovenia have a higher degree of affiliation to Slovenia than parents born abroad.

Comparing the answers to the questions analysed above, we can observe many differences between the groups. Parents (native and foreign-born) have a much lower degree of affiliation to their town/city of residence than their children. Interestingly, foreign-born parents feel more Slovenian than children with foreign background. Similarly, children with foreign background—who feel less affiliated to the local environment than their peers with native background—on the other hand, feel mostly affiliated to their local environment, when compared to how much they feel part of Slovenia or of Europe. The difference between native and foreign-born parents can be seen in the degree of affiliation to the State, since parents born in Slovenia have comparably higher affiliation to this country than parents born abroad. On the other hand, children state that they feel a slightly higher degree of affiliation to Europe (except in the case of native-born children with foreign background, since there are 7 that feel European "very much" and "just enough") than their parents. This difference, however, is mostly evident in the case of children with native background and native-born parents.

14.4.4. Perceptions and Experiences with Institutions

Only 37 of the children included in the sample are learning foreign languages outside school, whereas 41 parents are learning another language, other than their native language/s. Children learn languages at home or by attending foreign languages courses against payment; parents, however, learn languages through their own personal initiative. Schools offer additional classes of Slovene for pupils who are children of immigrants. In nationally mixed areas as Slovenian Istria, they attend classes of English as an obligatory first foreign language and classes of Italian as the second/minority language. It is quite understandable that children of immigrants do not attend additional classes of foreign languages, since they are already are exposed to three languages besides their own mother tongue when integrating into the educational community.

The work of institutions and local authorities was considered through some questions included in the parents' questionnaire. In their response they stated that local authorities do not promote many meetings between people of various nationalities, since only 44 native-born and 12 foreign-born parents perceive that this happens "many times" or "sometimes". On the other hand, there is a large share of those who say that local authorities "never" (11 native-born and 4 foreign-born parents) promote such meetings or that they do not know about them (36 native- born and 7 foreign-born parents).

Local authorities are more active in providing opportunities for learning foreign language: 58 native-born parents and 14 foreign-born parents perceive that this happens "often" or "quite a lot". There is a large share of people who are not aware of the possibilities of learning languages in the local environment (31 native born and 10 foreign born parents).

More than one half of the parents believe that schools in Slovenia stimulate the children's curiosity to meet people of different languages and cultures; 66 native-born and 15 foreign-born parents believe that this is "very much so" and "quite a bit". There are 31 native-born and 7 foreign-born parents who believe that schools in Slovenia stimulate the children's curiosity regarding foreign languages and cultures "very little". There are also 6 native-born parents who believe there is no stimulation at all, while some parents stated that they did not know the answer to this question: 5 parents born in Slovenia and 3 parents born abroad.

14.4.5. Discussion

The data collected reveal that children generally have a positive attitude towards languages: the education of multilingualism in minority and majority communities, and functional bilingualism of the environment in which these children live, seem to have positive impact on their attitudes to language and language diversity. Slovenian Istria includes the presence of the indigenous Italian minority and a large percentage of children of immigrants from former Yugoslav countries, especially Bosnians. Consequently, almost one half of the children included in the MERIDIUM sample recognise the Cyrillic alphabet, although the majority of them do not speak Serbian. Children of Bosnian parents may also recognise the Arabic alphabet, which is present in Islam written tradition. The level of recognition of Chinese script indicates that these children are aware of linguistic diversity, a concept which may also favour a positive attitude towards multilingualism as well as stimulating the knowledge about non-European languages and cultures. Since this is an area of immigration, almost half of immigrant children also use Slovene outside school as a second language. However, answers of native-born children with foreign background also indicate that children of immigrants adapt in time to the language and culture of the context that they are living in and that, possibly, they slowly lose contact with their original environment or with their parents' country of origin.

The data on tolerance to linguistic diversity, socialising of various nationalities and recognising ethnically mixed environment confirm the impact of linguistic and cultural diversity on the conduct of individuals and the society. In these categories there were no noteworthy differences between answers given by native-born and foreign-born respondents and the answers provided do not present the separation of the social community based on their ethnic origin.

Considering the differences between children with native and foreign background and among the latter, between native-born and foreign-born informants, we can establish that children with native background identify themselves with their place of residence in a higher percentage than the children with foreign background. However, children with foreign background have the highest degree of affiliation to their town of residence, considering the three options (local, state and European environment). Children with native background have a slightly higher degree of affiliation to Slovenia than to the town where they live or European environment, although all three affiliations are very high. It seems that being European is quite a more extended phenomenon, therefore it is less identifying than being Slovenian, and that is possibly why foreign-born children with foreign background declare affiliation to a wider environment as they feel less part of one given state than their native-born counterparts, although it must be noted that the sample size is small and this consideration definitely merits more investigation.

Children with native background recognise the language of the minority (Italian) more than the children with foreign background. However, the environment accepts immigrants and their languages as the level of respect of other languages is reportedly very high.

The school is the most active institution involved in providing education for tolerant and efficient co-habitation of languages and cultures and integrating children of immigrants into the social community. One half of the parents believe that schools in Slovenia stimulate the children's curiosity to learn about people of different languages and cultures. Even if it is stated that local authorities do not promote meetings among people of various nationalities, they occasionally offer the possibility to learn languages. However, almost one third of all interviewed parents do not know about such opportunities and not much has been done to promote these initiatives.

14.5. Conclusion

Each year, the Slovene educational system witnesses the inclusion of children of immigrants, refugees, asylum seekers and temporarily protected persons. Past experiences have revealed that these migrant children, primary school pupils and secondary school students, find it more difficult not only to participate in classes and other activities organized by schools and kindergartens, but also to integrate into the wider social environment. This often results from their lack of knowledge of Slovene (for them, Slovene is mostly a foreign/second language), lack of strategies and instruments for the inclusion of migrant children in the Slovene systems of upbringing and schooling, and inadequate inclusion of these children and their parents in the school system and the wider Slovene environment. The possible discrimination that they face in everyday life is often rooted in discrimination at institutional level. The *Strategy of the inclusion of children and pupils in the system of education in the Republic of Slovenia*, adopted by the Ministry for Education and Sport of RS in May 2007 marks a turning point in the social inclusion history of migrant children in Slovenia and, hopefully, data collected through the MERIDIUM Project could also shed further light on a complex and dynamic phenomenon.

References

Čok, L. 2001. The role of the minority languages in Slovene education policy: the case of Slovene Istria. *Geographica Slovenica* 34/1. 253-266.

Čok, L. *et al.* 2009. *MERIDIUM. Nacionalno poročilo – Slovenija. Country Report–Slovenia*. Accessed September 26, 2012. http://meridium.unistrapg.it/sites/meridium.unistrapg.internal/files/slovenia_report_slo.final_.pdf.

Kržišnik Bukić, V. 2010. Migracije iz drugih jugoslovanskih republik v Slovenijo po 2. svetovni vojni. In *Migracije in slovenski prostor od antike do danes*, eds. P. Štih and B. Balkovec, 502–525. Ljubljana: Zveza zgodovinskih društev Slovenije.

Sapir, E. 1972. *Cultura, linguaggio e personalità.* Torino: Einaudi.

Vertot, N. *et al.* 2001. *Popisi na Slovenskem 1848–1991 in Popis 2002.* Ljubljana: Statistični urad Republike Slovenije (available at: http://www.stat.si/popis2002/gradivo/popisna.pdf, accessed September 26, 2012).

CHAPTER FIFTEEN

CONCLUSIONS

SANDRO CARUANA, LILIANA COPOSESCU AND STEFANIA SCAGLIONE

The MERIDIUM research focused its attention mainly on situations related to linguistic diversity, perceptions and attitudes towards languages, in 57 primary schools, chosen specifically to participate in the survey, in six Southern European countries. These issues were dealt with by considering school environments and parents' role, as well as their influence on the language/s children acquire and learn in addition to the way they perceive linguistic diversity and form language attitudes. The research was therefore based on the consideration that schooling and parental influence can have an impact not only on the formation of children's linguistic repertoire, but also on the possibility that one may benefit from a multilingual and multicultural environment. In fact, over the past years, migration patterns in Southern European countries have changed considerably and in many contexts documented by the MERIDIUM research the number of immigrants/emigrants has increased considerably. Furthermore, these individuals originate from many different countries and have varied backgrounds. This diversity is also present in schools, thereby in a context where, on the one hand one must proceed with extreme caution because of the delicacy and susceptibility involved when dealing with children and where, on the other hand, one can exploit and capitalise on children's creativity and, in many cases, also on their readiness to accept quite unquestioningly whoever may not share their origins and background.

The nature of the MERIDIUM research was mainly exploratory, with one of the goals being that of providing further insight regarding linguistic diversity in Southern Europe, especially in areas where, up till now, a relatively limited amount of research has been carried out. Wherever possible, some comparative considerations where also put forward, always taking into account the diverse sociolinguistic situations of the countries under study and the specificity of the various primary schools which were selected to participate in the research. The very nature of the study is therefore descriptive and results are not representative of the national contexts from which they were obtained. However, the research methodology based on questionnaires has been considered to be a strong point of the research, and has been qualified as "innovative and worth to be presented to other institutions in Europe" in the Lifelong Learning Programme (LLP) Final Report Assessment sheet by the Education, Audiovisual & Culture Executive Agency (EACEA). In this regard, it must be observed that the main conceptual dimensions on which MERIDIUM questionnaires have been constructed during the first year of the project (2009) largely coincide with those that were subsequently suggested in the *Guide for the development and implementation of curricula for plurilingual and intercultural education* (Beacco *et al.* 2010, Appendix II) in order to collect data which «are intended to pave the way for realistic curriculum choices» (p. 27).

The questionnaires used in the Project enabled researchers to obtain data from a relatively large number of subjects. They were designed mainly with the intention of providing a common framework for all the six countries involved in the research. However, for Romania, a country subject to outbound migratory fluxes, specific questions targeted for returned migrants were also used. Future research, possibly also based on qualitative instruments, could provide further insight in order to complement the results obtained by the MERIDIUM research. Such forms of research—including ethnographic studies and action research—could lead to critical analyses of specific situations which the MERIDIUM survey investigated through the use of questionnaires.

As expected, even in the light of considerations included in the literature in the field, the results obtained were noticeably characterised by a high degree of diversity, thereby confirming that even in the case of the MERIDIUM Project data, the notion of super-diversity (Vertovec, 2007) is relevant. In countries like Italy, Spain and Portugal, many languages are present in the primary schools in which the MERIDIUM research took place. In Spain and Portugal, however, one does find some clustering, as immigrants hailing from Hispanophone or Lusophone contexts form relatively large groups within the schools. In Malta, Romania and Slovenia different sociolinguistic conditions (together with dissimilar historical and geographical characteristics) lead to less heterogeneous forms of language diversity when compared to findings registered in the primary schools that participated in the MERIDIUM survey in Italy, Spain and Portugal.

A further difference regards the family background of children who participated in the MERIDIUM research (see Tab. 15-1).

SURVEY COUNTRY		NATIVE-BORN INFORMANTS			FOREIGN-BORN INFORMANTS			TOT.
		NNb	NMb	NFb	FNb	FMb	FFb	
IT	N	450	31	92	4	3	116	696
	%	*64.7*	*4.5*	*13.2*	*.6*	*.4*	*16.7*	*100.0*
ES	N	293	36	8	2	6	72	417
	%	*70.3*	*8.6*	*1.9*	*.5*	*1.4*	*17.3*	*100.0*
PT	N	194	58	14	1	2	41	310
	%	*62.6*	*18.7*	*4.5*	*.3*	*.6*	*13.2*	*100.0*
RO	N	276	8	0	8	3	0	295
	%	*90.5*	*2.7*	-	*2.7*	*1.0*	-	*100.0*
MT	N	104	22	8	0	6	7	147
	%	*70.7*	*15.0*	*5.4*	-	*3.7*	*4.3*	*100.0*
SI	N	98	28	14	1	3	7	151
	%	*64.9*	*18.5*	*9.3*	*.7*	*2.0*	*4.6*	*100.0*
TOT	N	1415	183	136	16	23	243	2016
	%	*70.2*	*9.1*	*6.7*	*.8*	*1.1*	*12.1*	*100.0*

Key: NNb = native-born with native background; NMb = native-born with mixed background, NFb = native-born with foreign background; FNb = foreign-born with native background; FMb = foreign-born with mixed background, FFb = foreign-born with foreign background.

Tab. 15–1: MERIDIUM sample A (pupils) stratified by survey country, birth country of informants and of their parents ("background")

In Italy and in Spain, for example, respectively, both parents of 29.4% and 19.2% of the pupils involved in the research are foreign-born[1]. In Portugal, children with foreign background amount to 17.8%, but another 19.5% have one foreign-born parent. The situation in Malta and in Slovenia is similar to that of Portugal (more children with mixed background than children with foreign background), but on a much smaller scale.

On the other hand, in the Italian sub-sample we have a considerable number of children with foreign background who are born in Italy (so-

[1] As explained throughout the research, one must take account of the problems related to terminology in this field. The term "foreign" is therefore used solely with reference to the place of birth of subjects, meaning that they were not born in the context in which the research was carried.

called "second generation immigrants"), while data from Spanish and Portuguese schools reveal that most children with foreign background have arrived recently to these countries. These situations, present both within and across contexts, provide an indication of the complexity of immigration conditions and clearly point to the fact that in schools (and often even in single classrooms) there are multiple issues to deal with. It is therefore legitimate to ask whether educational authorities, policy-makers, heads of schools and teachers are adequately prepared in order to deal with such super-diverse situations. Results of the MERIDIUM project clearly show that in these contexts there still is the need to create adequate policies for cultural and linguistic integration, which is to be implemented by suitably qualified staff and through appropriate teaching materials. Within the MERIDIUM project some didactic materials were also developed[2]. These teaching tools are described as being "excellent and worth to be introduced more broadly" in the Lifelong Learning Programme (LLP) Final Report Assessment sheet by the EACEA. Prominence must therefore also be given to develop practical skills and to create more teaching tools which are relevant to individuals who have different backgrounds, culture, values and beliefs.

With the exception of Portugal and Romania, adult subjects (both native-born and foreign-born) participating in the MERIDIUM Project show a certain resistance to the proposal that home-languages of immigrant children should be taught in schools (see Tab. 15-2, next page):

The reasons behind the positive and, especially, the negative responses presented in Tab. 15-2 require further investigation, also through the use of qualitative instruments. Furthermore, it will be possible to interpret the data comparatively to a greater degree of reliability, when statistically representative samples are chosen, according to the different countries' realities. At this point, however, we can state that these data deserve great attention, even on the grounds that the number of informants who did not answer this question, or stated that they are not able to answer it, is rather high both in the "native-born" and in the "foreign-born" categories. This may indicate that, despite awareness of language diversity as a result of migration, for many of our informants the role of schools as possible agents in order to maintain linguistic diversity is not necessarily taken into consideration.

[2] See Appendix C, this volume.

SURVEY COUNTRY	INFORMANTS BY BIRTHPLACE	"DO YOU THINK THAT CHILDREN OF IMMIGRANT ORIGIN SHOULD BE GIVEN THE OPPORTUNITY TO LEARN THEIR OWN LANGUAGE/S IN [THIS COUNTRY'S] SCHOOLS?" (N AND %)			TOTAL
		Yes	No	Idk/NA	
IT	foreign born	59 *33.0*	72 *40.2*	48 *26.8*	179 *100.0*
	native born	52 *12.4*	258 *61.7*	108 *25.8*	418 *100.0*
	TOTAL	111 *18.6*	330 *55.3*	156 *26.1*	597 *100.0*
ES	foreign born	24 *(35.3)*	26 *(38.2)*	18 *(26.5)*	68 *(100,0)*
	native born	43 *20.5*	114 *54.3*	53 *25.2*	210 *100,0*
	TOTAL	67 *24.1*	140 *50.4*	71 *25.5*	278 *100,0*
PT	foreign born	58 *(67.4)*	14 *(16.3)*	14 *(16.3)*	86 *(100.0)*
	native born	157 *70.4*	21 *9.4*	45 *20.2*	223 *100.0*
	TOTAL	215 *69.6*	35 *11.3*	59 *19.1*	309 *100.0*
RO	foreign born	3 *(75.0)*	1 *(25.0)*	0 -	4 *(100.0)*
	native born	133 *47.8*	44 *15.8*	101 *36.3*	278 *100.0*
	TOTAL	136 *48.2*	45 *16.0*	101 *35.8*	282 *100.0*
MT	foreign born	14 *(45.2)*	10 *(32.3)*	7 *(22.6)*	31 *(100.0)*
	native born	36 *28.6*	48 *38.1*	42 *33.3*	126 *100.0*
	TOTAL	50 *31.8*	58 *36.9*	49 *31.2*	157 *100.0*
SI	foreign born	4 *(16.0)*	12 *(48.0)*	9 *(36.0)*	25 *(100.0)*
	native born	29 *26.6*	55 *50.5*	25 *22.9*	109 *100.0*
	TOTAL	33 *24.6*	67 *50.0*	34 *25.4*	134 *100.0*

Tab. 15-2: Sample B (parents): answers to BQ34 by survey country and birthplace of informants

Although, as stated above, the sociolinguistic situation in the six countries involved in the MERIDIUM Project is complex and highly diverse, some interesting analogies were noted. First of all, the presence of students with different backgrounds is increasing at primary level thereby giving rise to challenges that schools must be equipped to face, both in terms of teacher education and at practical levels. It is encouraging to note, however, that although schools are more multiethnic and multicultural when compared to the past, this is also often seen as a potential source in order to create an enriching experience and as an opportunity to broaden the horizons of all students. Such considerations emerge especially when researchers who were collecting the MERIDIUM data were given direct feedback by teachers. Secondly, it was noted that, in most contexts, place of birth (both of children and of parents) may play a significant role in the formation of identity. Clearly, one's identity is influenced and shaped by other factors, but one's place of birth plays a noteworthy role in this respect, as it may condition the manner in which one perceives oneself and the way one is perceived by others. Thirdly, children who are born in one of the six countries included in the MERIDIUM project, of parents also born in the same country, generally show an interest towards foreign languages, towards language learning and also towards language diversity although, as stated earlier, there is hesitancy when one is asked whether migrants' languages should be taught in schools. However, interest towards foreign language learning is still largely directed towards European languages which are traditionally taught in schools (especially towards English), rather than towards "new" languages present, due to migration, in the contexts investigated. Finally, the enthusiasm and promptness by which children, in particular, filled in the MERIDIUM questionnaire, irrespective of their nationality, is another indication of their eagerness to express themselves and their willingness to participate in research involving the use of languages.

The results obtained in the MERIDIUM project, despite their limitations which were repeatedly outlined in the contributions to the second part of this volume, certainly set the scene for further research and provide a basis for educational authorities and teachers to reflect upon when implementing measures aimed at giving value to multicultural and plurilingual situations which are very much the reality in many schools in Southern Europe today. Furthermore, while highlighting the diversity and complexity of the issues which were investigated, the considerations put forward by the contributors to this volume also confirm the importance of having realistic and goal-oriented policies both at a national level, and also on a European scale.

Through MERIDIUM a cross-section of the reality found in schools in various areas in Southern Europe has been presented. This research must be also considered in view of its attempt to shed further light on situations present in previously relatively unexplored areas, thereby creating the basis for further inter and intra-national research and networking. In this sense, one observes that understanding more fully linguistic diversity and multiculturalism in schools is indeed necessary in order to address issues that are encountered in these institutions in Southern Europe today, thereby moving towards more inclusive systems which are vital to create reflection, acceptance and involvement while putting aside prejudice and fear.

References

Beacco J.-C., *et al.* 2010. *Guide for the development and implementation of curricula for plurilingual and intercultural Education.* Strasbourg: Language Policy Division, Council of Europe (available at www.coe.int/lang, accessed September 26, 2012).

Vertovec, S. 2007. Super-diversity and its Implications. *Ethnic and Racial Studies* 30/6. 1024-1054.

CONTRIBUTORS

Román Álvarez Rodríguez is Professor of English Studies at the University of Salamanca and former Dean of the Faculty of Philology. He was Head of the English Department and Director of the British Council Centre in Salamanca. He has been teaching English Literature for many years, and has published books and essays on diverse aspects of English and American Literature, Literary Theory and Criticism, and Cultural and Translation Studies.

Elena Buja is Associate Professor at Transilvania University in Braşov (Romania) where she teaches subjects related to Linguistics, such as phonetics and phonology, lexicology and semantics. Her main research topics are first language acquisition, multilingualism and cultural differences in non-verbal communication. She obtained her PhD from Eotvos-Lorand University in Budapest with a thesis on the acquisition of tense and aspect in Romanian L1.

Antoinette Camilleri Grima is Professor of Languages in Education at the University of Malta. She has published widely in the areas of Bilingualism in Education, Intercultural competence, Maltese Sociolinguistics and Learner Autonomy. She was engaged as an expert in several Council of Europe projects and co-ordinated workshops on whole-school policies for diversity and bilingual education. In Malta she developed an innovative methodology for the teaching of Maltese as a first language, and published several books and interactive courses for the teaching of Maltese as a foreign language.

Sandro Caruana is Associate Professor and Head of the Department of Arts & Languages in Education, University of Malta, where he holds courses on Italian language teaching methodology. He also lectures within the Department of Italian (Faculty of Arts) where he holds courses on General Linguistics and Sociolinguistics. He has been guest lecturer at several Italian universities and has published extensively on language teaching and learning, on the role and status of Italian in Malta and on intercultural communication He is the coordinator of the MERIDIUM research unit of the University of Malta. His publications include *Mezzi di* *comunicazione e input linguistico* (2003); *Intercultural communication in bureaucratic and institutional contexts* (2008), edited with Gabriella B. Klein; *'Letter to a teacher': Lorenzo Milani's contribution to critical citizenship* (2009), with Carmel Borg and Mario Cardona (translated into Spanish and Valencian) and *Variation and Change. The dynamics of Maltese in Space, Time and Society* (2011), edited with Ray Fabri and Thomas Stolz.

Marina Chini is Professor of Linguistics at the University of Pavia, Italy. She also taught at the Universities of Trento (1995-96) and Vercelli-Turin (1996-2000). She obtained her PhD from the University of Pavia in 1992 with a thesis on the acquisition of gender in Italian L1 and L2. Since 1989, she has been participating in the Pavia Project on L2 Italian and, since 1994, she has cooperated on European projects concerning learner varieties. She currently lectures on Sociolinguistics and Second Language Acquisition and her main research topics are Second Language Acquisition, Bilingualism and the Sociolinguistics of migration, on which she published a book in 2004, as well as several articles. Her latest article in this field of research has been published in the *International Journal of the Sociology of Language* 210/2011. She also edited a monographic issue of the journal *Studi Italiani di Linguistica Teorica e Applicata*, XXXVIII, 1/2009 on Italian sociolinguistics, including issues related to migration.

Liliana Coposescu is Associate Professor at the Faculty of Languages and Literatures, Transilvania University of Braşov, Romania. She obtained a PhD from Lancaster University, UK, and currently teaches Pragmatics, Discourse analysis, and Research methods in Applied Linguistics. She is the coordinator of the MERIDIUM research unit of the University of Braşov. Her research interests and publications are in the field of intercultural communication and discourse analysis, among others.

George Cremona is Assistant Lecturer in German language teaching methodology within the Department of Arts & Languages in Education, University of Malta. His main areas of interest include the analysis of texts as tools to teach Modern Foreign Languages, the role of the media (with special attention to the Internet), as well as Multimodality and its effects on Foreign Language teachers and learners. In 2007 he was awarded a Masters in Comparative Education from the University of Malta. He collaborates actively with various German and Maltese schools on a number of projects related to Comparative Education and Foreign

Language teaching and he is currently reading for a PhD in the field of Multimodality and Language learning.

Gabriela Cusen is Associate Professor at Transilvania University of Braşov. She obtained her PhD in Linguistics from Lancaster University, U.K. and her area of expertise includes Applied Linguistics and Second Language Acquisition (SLA). She has published about 15 research articles on Second Language Acquisition, and has been a research team member in Research Project 4GR/28.05.2007 *Institutional Talk and Intercultural Communication in International Companies in Braşov*. Her interest in SLA finds its practical applicability in her activity as the director of the Centre for Modern Languages which is a university department acting as an interface between this tertiary education institution and the local community to meet the language learning needs of an evergrowing number of citizens.

Lucija Čok, Professor and scientific counsellor in the field of Multilingualism and Interculturalism, was the first Rector of the University of Primorska. Furthermore, as Minister of Education, Science and Sport (2000-2002), she contributed to the reforms in the field of educational system in Slovenia and participated in the national strategies leading to the integration of Slovenia in the European Research Area and the European Higher Education Area. In her research she has dealt with the social, psycho-linguistic and didactic aspects of teaching and studying foreign languages; her research findings have been published in numerous papers in French, Italian and English. She has lectured at foreign universities, has been responsible for national development projects, coordinated international projects, as well as headed projects at the European Centre for Modern Languages in Graz. She is a member of numerous boards of experts that have prepared the research and education policy in Slovenia as well as a member of High Assessment panels within the directorates of the European Commission and the EUA Institutional Evaluation Program; within the MERIDIUM Project, she coordinates the MERIDIUM research unit of the University of Primorska. She has received the prestigious award from the President of France (Légion d'honneur) for her promotion of the French language and culture and the strategies for the encouragement of linguistic diversity. She was also awarded the title of Cavaliere della Repubblica d'Italia from the President of Italy.

Joana Duarte is a post-doctoral assistant at the Institute for International Comparative and Intercultural Education of the University of Hamburg. Her main research interests are multilingualism and its consequences on educational systems, bilingual school models and language assessment tools. She has conducted her research in Lisbon, Athens and Cologne, where she coordinated the EU-Comenius project "EUCIM-TE: European Core Curriculum for Inclusive Academic Language Instruction". In her current position in Hamburg she works in the LiMA research cluster (Linguistic Diversity Management in Urban Areas) and coordinates language assessment of multilingual speakers in a panel study on language development. Her most recent publications include: "Global students for global education research?" (with Ian Menter and Radhica Gorur), in *The Routledge doctoral student's companion* (2010), *Bilingual language proficiency. A comparative study*, Waxmann (2011) and "Migrants' educational success through innovation: The case of the Hamburg bilingual schools", *International Review of Education* (2011).

Vicente González Martín is Professor of Italian Literature at the University of Salamanca, where he is currently Dean of the Faculty of Philology. He has been Head Researcher in various projects financed by the European Union over the past years, such as: *European Youth and Reading*; *European Network for the promotion of books, reading and tradition*, and *Hacia la unidad en la diversidad: Difusión de las lenguas europeas*. He is also in charge of the Doctorate Course *Thinking, religion and woman in Mediterranean literature* (at the University of Salamanca) and collaborates with the Doctorate Courses concerning themes of Mediterranean culture with the University Federico II of Naples and the University of Catania. He is the coordinator of the MERIDIUM research unit of the University of Salamanca. He has published various articles on the literature of emigration, and has participated in international congresses on this topic and in the creation of the "Network of Mediterranean universities". He currently is the director of the "Cátedra Sicilia" and also of the publication "RSEI. Revista de la Sociedad Española de Italianistas".

Manuel Heras García is Assistant Professor at the University of Salamanca. His main lecturing duties regard the Foreign Language teaching. This includes language teaching to immigrants in a Master Degree course in Spanish as a Second Language and also in a Master Degree in Spanish Language and Culture for American Teachers in Atlanta (United States). He also lectures on the Doctorate Course

Thinking, religion and woman in Mediterranean literature at the University of Salamanca and has an extensive experience in the organization of international conventions, scientific meetings, seminars, etc. He is also an expert in educational technologies, heading the website of the Department of Modern Philology. His publications are essentially on the linguistic aspect and the processing of methods for contrastive teaching of languages.

Cornelia Ilie is Professor of English Linguistics at Malmö University, Sweden. She has coordinated international research projects and published extensively on political discourse, media practices and intercultural rhetoric. She is the coordinator of GENPARDIS (*Gender and Parliamentary Discourse practices*), the president of ESTIDIA (European Society for Transcultural and Interdisciplinary Dialogue) and member of the IAU (International Association of Universities) Reference Group of Experts.

Ana Kralj is Research Associate at the Science and Research Centre and assistant professor at the Faculty of Humanities, University of Primorska. Her research is focused on globalization processes, nationalism, undocumented migration, policies on immigration, asylum and integration, and analysis of the status of marginalized social groups.

Paulino Matas Gil is Professor of Italian Literature at the University of Salamanca. He has been a member of the research group headed by Prof. Vicente González, participating in various European Projects as well as in the Doctorate Course *Thinking, religion and woman in Mediterranean literature* at the University of Salamanca. He is also a member of the Doctorate School in Sciences of text, edition, analysis, reading and communication at the University of Siena. Likewise he is coordinator of the Erasmus—Socrates program with different Italian universities and is an expert in literature on travelling (member of CIRVI) and in Italian—Spanish comparative studies, as he has published numerous essays on this topic, such as *The reception of Italian literature from the 1900s in Spain: approach to journalistic language through books on newspaper style in Italy and Spain,* etc.

Luiza Mesesan Schmitz is Senior Lecturer at the Faculty of Sociology and Communication, Transilvania University of Braşov. Her PhD is in the Sociology of Health and Illness and her areas of specialisation also include Demography and Social Statistics. She has participated in research projects with the Sociology department on educational services for children (financed by Medina Association, Italy), on social representations, perceptions and images constructed at Braşov community level, and on *European Community Integration Effects Acknowledged at Braşov Community Level and Implications on The Quality of Life and Lifestyle.*

Stefania Scaglione is Associate Professor of Linguistics at the University for Foreigners of Perugia, where she holds courses on Sociolinguistics and Language Policy and Planning. She is the coordinator of the MERIDIUM Project and of the MERIDIUM research unit of the University for Foreigners of Perugia. Her main areas of research include sociolinguistic aspects of migration and linguistic rights. On these topics she has published *Attrition. Mutamenti sociolinguistici nel lucchese di San Francisco* (2000), *Italiano e Italiani nel mondo* (2004), *Lingue e diritti umani* (2011, edited with Stefania Giannini).

María Mar Soliño Pazó, PhD, is lecturer in German Linguistics and Language at the University of Salamanca. Her main research is in Applied Linguistics (Teaching of Foreign Languages, Acquisition of Foreign Languages in different contexts and Contrastive Linguistics) and in children's as well as young people's literature. She has participated in various research projects with the Spanish Ministry of Science and Technology, which relate to the translation and study of linguistic pluralism in multicultural societies, having analyzed the importance of cultural and linguistic pluralism in the world today. Her fields of interest are German as a foreign language, German semantics, children's literature in the classroom (intercultural aspects and children's literature in foreign language learning and teaching). She is author of several articles in these research fields. She has been Research Fellow at the University of Lisbon (Portugal), Postdoctoral Fellow at Frankfurt University (Germany) and Visiting Scholar at Leipzig University (Germany).

Maria Isabel Tomás is Assistant Professor in the Linguistics Department at the Faculty of Social and Human Sciences (FCSH) UNL, since 2005, where she holds courses in the areas of Sociolinguistics, Research Methods in Linguistics, Teaching Portuguese as L2, Language and Identity in Creole Communities. She is the coordinator of the MERIDIUM research unit of the Universidade Nova of Lisbon. Her research work and publications have focused on Portuguese based Creoles as minority languages, in particular on Linguistic Processes and Social Contexts in Language Obsolescence. Current research interests cover Multilinguism and Interaction Analysis in Social Work.

Stefania Tusini is Researcher of General Sociology at the University for Foreigners of Perugia. She specialized in Social Sciences Methodology with a PhD at the University "La Sapienza" of Rome. Her main interests concern empirical social research, both quantitative and qualitative. She carried out research in Florence, Rome and Perugia, coordinating several working teams as project manager. Her main publications are on methodology of empirical social research, mostly interview techniques, relational dynamics of interviewing, question wording bias and semantic issues.

Alexandra Vella is a Senior Lecturer in Phonetics and Phonology, at the Institute of Linguistics, University of Malta. Her specialization is in Phonetics and Phonology, particularly Intonational Phonology, and her research focuses on Maltese prosody and intonation, and on the influence of these on the intonational structure of Maltese English. She is also interested in interlanguage phonology and in accent and dialect variation. She is currently working on a project aimed at archiving material from a Survey of Maltese Dialects carried out in the 1960s, and in creating a searchable database using samples from the data. She also heads the SPAN Project on the prosodic annotation of data from a spoken corpus of Maltese.

Maja Zadel is Early Stage Researcher at the Institute for Mediterranean Humanities and Social Studies at the Science and Research Centre, University of Primorska. In her doctoral studies she is focusing on ethnic and transcultural studies in relation to mass media.

APPENDICES

APPENDIX A

QUESTIONNAIRES A (PUPILS) AND B (PARENTS)

The questionnaires hereby reproduced are the English versions of the data-collection tool used by each one of the MERIDIUM research units in order to carry out the sociolinguistic survey in their respective countries. The questionnaires have been translated into Italian, Spanish, Portuguese, Slovene, Maltese and Romanian.

MERIDIUM
Multilingualism in Europe as a Resource for Immigration
Dialogue Initiative among the Universities of the Mediterranean

University of Malta
L-Università ta' Malta

Questionnaire A

City / Town ____________________

School ____________________

Class ____________

Serial number
(to be copied on parent's questionnaire)

____

Date __/__/____

Researcher ______________________

Lifelong Learning Programme

This project has been funded with support from the European Commission.
This publication [communication] reflects the views only of the author, and the Commission cannot be held responsible for any use which may be made of the information contained therein.

HELLO! WE ARE A TEAM OF UNIVERSITY RESEARCHERS. WE WOULD LIKE YOU TO ANSWER THESE QUESTIONS WITH US. WILL YOU PLEASE HELP US?

1) You are....
   - □ male
   - □ female

2) How old are you? ______________________

3) In which year were you born? ________________

4) In which country are we now? ______________________

5) Were you born in Malta?
   - □ no. Where?______________________
   - □ yes
   - □ I don't know

6) If you were not born in Malta, how old were you when you came to Malta?

____

7) Have you ever lived in a different country than Malta (for more than six months)?

- ☐ no
- ☐ yes . Where?____________________
- ☐ I don't know

8) Did you ever attend school (from Year 1 to Year 5) in a different country from Malta?

- ☐ no
- ☐ yes. Where? ____________________
- ☐ I don't know

9) If you answered YES, please tell us for how long you went to this school.

- ☐ for a few months
- ☐ 1 or 2 years
- ☐ 3 or 4 years
- ☐ 5 years or more
- ☐ I don't know

10) Who are you? Please use five words to define yourself:

1. ________________
2. ________________
3. ________________
4. ________________
5. ________________

11) What job would you like to do when you are older?

- ☐ I would like to be ____________________
- ☐ I don't know

12) How much do you feel part of your class?

□ very much □ just enough □ a little bit □ not at all □ I don't know

13) How much do you feel part of your group of friends?

□ very much □ just enough □ a little bit □ not at all □ I don't know

14) How much do you feel a citizen of the city/town where you live?

□ very much □ just enough □ a little bit □ not at all □ I don't know

15) How much do you feel Maltese?

□ very much □ just enough □ a little bit □ not at all □ I don't know

16) How much do you feel European?

□ very much □ just enough □ a little bit □ not at all □ I don't know

17) Which country do you feel a citizen of? ______________________

18) According to you, how many Maltese children are there in your class? (also count those who are absent)

____

19) Which is/are the language/s which most people normally use in Malta?

____

20) According to you, how many children in your school speak other languages besides Maltese and/or English?

□ many □ quite a few □ a few □ no one □ I don't know

21) If there are children speaking other languages, which language/s do they speak?____________________________________

____

22) How often do you hear people speaking other languages than Maltese and/or English?

□ it has never happened to me
□ it happens sometimes
□ it happens often

23) Do you have friends, who do not attend your school, who speak other languages, besides Maltese and/or English?

□ no
□ yes. Please tell us which languages they speak ______________________
□ I don't know

24) Do your parents have friends who speak other languages, besides Maltese and/or English?

□ no
□ yes. Please tell us which languages they speak ______________________
□ I don't know

25) Do you have relatives who speak any other languages besides Maltese and/or English?

□ no
□ yes. Please tell us which languages they speak ______________________
□ I don't know

26) If you have friends or relatives who speak languages which are different from Maltese and/or English how do you feel about this?

□ proud
□ I do not really care
□ embarrassed
□ I don't know

27) Which languages are spoken throughout the world? Please, write the names of some of them.

____
____
____
____

28) Besides Maltese and/or English, are you learning other languages (by yourself or with the help of someone)?

- □ no, I'm not interested
- □ no, but I would like to
- □ yes. Please tell us which languages you study ______________________

29) If yes, how are you learning this language?

- □ through private lessons / private tuition
- □ I attend a language school
- □ I am attending a course at an institution / a course organised by the Local Council
- □ other: ______________________________

30) When you are older, would you like to know how to speak other languages, besides those you already know or you are studying? (max. 3 answers, to be ordered by adding a number)

- □ no
- □ yes, to travel
- □ yes, because it is important for the job I'd like to have when I'm older
- □ yes, because some of my friends already know how to speak other languages
- □ yes, because my mother / father know how to speak other languages
- □ yes, because I like studying languages
- □ yes, because there are TV programmes in which foreign languages are spoken
- □ other reasons. Which ones? ______________________________

____

31) Tell us which languages you'd like to speak when you are older:

____

____

32) Do you think that the language/s you have learnt at home is/are beautiful? Or do you think that other languages are more beautiful? (only one answer)

□ I think that the language/s that I have learnt at home is/are the most beautiful
□ it's beautiful, but there are other beautiful languages as well
□ I think other languages are more beautiful. Which ones?____________________
____

33) When I hear someone speaking a language which is different from Maltese and/or English in the place where I live, I feel: (only one answer)

□ amused
□ curious
□ annoyed
□ scared
□ I don't take any notice
□ I don't know

34) When you hear someone speaking a language you do not know, do you think that it sounds like ...

□ music
□ noise
□ something else, that is ______________________________________
□ I do not know

35) Here you will read some sentences written in unusual alphabets. Try to guess which languages they are.

	Which language is it?
Всички хора се раждат свободни и равни по достойнство и права. Те са надарени с разум и съвест и следва да се отнасят помежду си в дух на братство	
يولد جميع الناس أحراراً متساوين في الكرامة والحقوق، وقد وهبوا عقلاً وضميراً، وعليهم أن يعامل بعضهم بعضاً بروح الإخاء.	
人人生而自由,在尊严和权利上一律平等。他们赋有理性和良心,并应以兄弟关系的精神相对待。	
अनुच्छेद १. सभी मनुष्यों को गौरव और अधिकारों के मामले में जन्मजात स्वतन्त्रता और समानता प्राप्त है। उन्हें बुद्धि और अन्तरात्मा की देन प्राप्त है और परस्पर उन्हें भाईचारे के भाव से बर्ताव करना चाहिए।	

36) Which language/s do you usually speak <u>at home</u> with your:

mother ____________________
father ____________________
brothers/sisters ____________________
grandparents ____________________

37) Which language/s do you usually speak <u>outside</u> with your:
relatives ____________________
classmates____ ____________________
friends (your age) ____________________
neighbours (adults) ____________________
teachers (on the whole)____________________

38) Do you remember which language/s you used to speak when you were young?
□ the same one/s I speak now
□ a different language, that is ____________________
□ I do not remember

39) In which languages do you know how to say "I want a sandwich"?

____

40) Besides Maltese and/or English, which languages do you know how to read in (e.g. comics)?

____

41) Besides Maltese and/or English, which languages do you know how to write in (e.g. a letter to a friend)?

____

42) Besides Maltese and/or English, which languages do you understand (e.g. a song or a cartoon)?

____

43) **Who lives permanently with you in the same house? Underline YES or NO below:**

My mother	YES	NO
My father	YES	NO
Younger brothers / sisters	YES	NO
Brothers / sisters of the same age	YES	NO
Older brothers / sisters	YES	NO
Grandparents	YES	NO
Other relatives	YES	NO
(your or your parents') Friends	YES	NO

44) **Do your grandparents, uncles/aunts and cousins live in Malta?**

□ yes, they all live here

□ some live here; some live in other countries. Where? ____________________

____

□ they all live in other countries. Where? ____________________

____

45) **In which country was your father born?** ____________________

46) **In which country was your mother born?** ____________________

47) What is your father's job?

☐ he is (e. g. a mechanic, a teacher etc.)

____

☐ at the moment, he doesn't work
☐ I have no father
☐ I don't know

48) What is your mother's job?

☐ she is (e. g. a hairdresser, a teacher etc.)

____

☐ at the moment, she doesn't work
☐ I have no mother
☐ I don't know

MERIDIUM

Multilingualism in Europe as a Resource for Immigration
Dialogue Initiative among the Universities of the Mediterranean

Now you are a member of our team!
This is "Babel", our mascot:
Tear off this page and, if you like, use it as a badge.

MERIDIUM
Multilingualism in Europe as a Resource for Immigration
Dialogue Initiative among the Universities of the Mediterranean

University of Malta
L-Università ta' Malta

Questionnaire B

City / town ______________

School _________________

Class ___________

Serial number ___________

Date __/__/___

Researcher _____________

Lifelong Learning Programme
Education and Culture DG

This project has been funded with support from the European Commission.
This publication [communication] reflects the views only of the author, and the Commission cannot be held responsible for any use which may be made of the information contained therein.

INSTRUCTIONS

We are a team of researchers from the University of Malta and we are carrying out a study on how people living in Malta perceive and judge languages. We have obtained permission from the Department of Education to ask some questions on this issue to your child at school, in a completely anonymous manner. Now we would like to know your opinion too.
Therefore we kindly ask you to answer these questions.

Your answers will be treated in a completely anonymous way. All the data you will provide will be treated in strictest confidentiality, only for the purposes of this research, and will be used in order to provide statistical data.
We have tried to formulate the questions in a straightforward way, also taking into consideration the fact that some of you may be foreigners. Some questions may therefore not be perfectly applicable to your situation. However, we would like to ask you to read all questions carefully and answer those related to you.
We kindly ask you to send the questionnaire to us by using the self-addressed envelope which we have provided.
Thank you!

1) **You are:**
□ male □ female

2) **Age:** ______________

3) **You are:**
□ Married / Living with your partner
□ Divorced or separated / Single / Widow or widower (if you mark this option you may not answer questions in which we ask information regarding husband / wife / partner)

4) **In which country were you born?** ______________________

5) **In which country was your husband / wife / partner born?**______________________

6) **How long have you been in Malta?**
□ I was born here □ I arrived here __________ years ago

7) **For how many years did you attend school?**
□ Total number of years _________ (please count all the years you have attended school, from the first year of Primary school to the last year you attended, including University)
□ I never attended school (go to number 9)

8) **Where did you attend school?**
□ in Malta
□ in another country. Which one? ____

9) **For how many years did your wife / husband attend school?**
□ Total number of years _________ (please count all the years you have attended school, from the first year of Primary school to the last year you attended, including University)
□ She/he never attended school (go to number 11)

10) **Where did your wife / husband attend school?**
□ in Malta
□ in another country. Which one?____

11) Who lives with you at home? Please mark YES or NO.

husband / wife / partner	YES	NO
children	YES	NO
father / mother	YES	NO
father in-law / mother in-law	YES	NO
brothers / sisters	YES	NO
grandparents	YES	NO
other relatives	YES	NO
friends or acquaintances	YES	NO

12) What is your job?
□ I do not work / I am unemployed
□ I am a / I work at ______________________________

13) What is your husband's / wife's job?
□ He/she does not work / He/she is unemployed
□ He/she is a / He/she works at ______________________________

14) Who are you? Please write 5 words to define yourself

1. ____________________
2. ____________________
3. ____________________
4. ____________________
5. ____________________

15) How much do you feel part of your family?
□ very much □ just enough □ a little bit □ not at all □ I don't know

16) How much do you feel part of your group of friends?
□ very much □ just enough □ a little bit □ not at all □ I don't know

17) How much do you feel part of the city/town in which you live?
□ very much □ just enough □ a little bit □ not at all □ I don't know

18) How much do you feel Maltese?
□ very much □ just enough □ a little bit □ not at all □ I don't know

19) How much do you feel European?
□ very much □ just enough □ a little bit □ not at all □ I don't know

20) If you weren't born in Malta, how much do you feel part of your country of origin?
□ very much □ just enough □ a little bit □ not at all □ I don't know

21) It is positive to have friends who originate from a country which is not your own
□ I do not agree □ I agree □ I don't know

22) I think that it's better to meet up with people who speak my own language
□ I do not agree □ I agree □ I don't know

23) When there are people who speak different languages living in the neighbourhood there may be problems
□ I do not agree □ I agree □ I don't know

24) If there is respect and tolerance among people, speaking different languages is not a problem
□ I do not agree □ I agree □ I don't know

25) Do most of your friends come from your country of origin?
□ no □ yes □ I don't know

26) According to you how many people who are not of Maltese origins live in your neighbourhood?
□ many □ quite a few □ a few □ none □ I don't know

27) According to you how many people who live in your neighbourhood speak languages which are different from Maltese and/or English?

□ many □ quite a few □ a few □ none □ I don't know

28) According to you, which languages, other than Maltese and/or English are spoken in your town/city/area?
□ ____
□ I don't know

29) How often do you hear people speaking different languages, other than Maltese and/or English?
□ it never happened
□ it happens occasionally
□ it happens often

30) Do you have relatives or friends who speak any other languages besides Maltese and/or English?

- □ no
- □ yes. Which languages? ______________________________
- □ I don't know

31) Having relatives and/or friends who speak languages which are different from Maltese and/or English makes you feel:

□ proud □ indifferent □ embarrassed □ I don't know

32) Are you learning another language, other than your native language/s?

- □ no, I'm not interested (go to question 34)
- □ no, but I would like to (go to question 34)
- □ yes. Which language? __________

33) How are you learning this language?

- □ through private lessons / private tuition
- □ I attend a language school
- □ I am following a course at an institution or a course organised by the Local Council
- □ by myself
- □ other. How? ______________________________

34) Do you think that children of immigrants should be given the opportunity to learn their own language/s in Maltese schools?

- □ no
- □ yes. At what age should they be given this opportunity? __________
- □ I don't know

35) Do you think your native language/s is/are beautiful? Or do you think that other languages are more beautiful? (just one answer)

- □ I think that my native language/s is/are the most beautiful
- □ it's beautiful, but other are just as beautiful
- □ I think other languages are more beautiful. Which ones? __________

36) Do you think your native language/s is/are useful? Or do you think that other languages are more useful?

- □ I think that it is very useful (go to question 38)
- □ it is just as useful as others (go to question 38)
- □ I think other languages are more useful. Which ones? __________

37) Why do you believe this/these language/s is/are more useful? __________

____

38) **Which language do you think is more useful in order to: (please, fill in each section)**

have a good job	
make many friends	
earn more money	
be more respected	

39) **According to you, how important is it to speak well at least one language, besides your native language/s?**

□ very much □ just enough □ a little bit □ not at all □ I don't know

40) **When I hear someone speaking a language which is different from my own, in the town/city/area where I live, I feel: (just one answer)**

□ amused
□ curious
□ annoyed
□ scared
□ I don't take any notice
□ I don't know

41) **Here there are some languages which are written differently from Maltese and/or English. Try to guess which languages are:**

	Which language is it?
Всички хора се раждат свободни и равни по достойнство и права. Те са надарени с разум и съвест и следва да се отнасят помежду си в дух на братство	
يولد جميع الناس أحراراً متساوين في الكرامة والحقوق، وقد وهبوا عقلاً وضميراً، وعليهم أن يعامل بعضهم بعضاً بروح الإخاء.	
人人生而自由,在尊严和权利上一律平等。他们赋有理性和良心,并应以兄弟关系的精神相对待。	
अनुच्छेद १. सभी मनुष्यों को गौरव और अधिकारों के मामले में जन्मजात स्वतन्त्रता और समानता प्राप्त है। उन्हें बुद्धि और अन्तरात्मा की देन प्राप्त है और परस्पर उन्हें भाईचारे के भाव से बर्ताव करना चाहिए।	

42) In your city/town/area, do local institutions (e.g. your Local Council) create occasions where people from different cultures, and who speak different languages, can meet?

□ many times □ sometimes □ few times □ never □ I don't know

43) In your city/town/area, do local institutions (e.g. your Local Council) create opportunities to learn other languages?

□ many □ quite a lot □ a few □ none □ I don't know

44) In general, do you think that in Malta schools create an interest among children towards people from different cultures and who speak other languages?

□ very much so □ quite a bit □ very little □ not at all □ I don't know

45) Which is your native language? ______________________

46) Which <u>other languages</u> do you know how to speak (e.g. to have a conversation)?______________________

47) Which languages do you know how to read in (ex. a newspaper)? (please include your native language)

□______________________

□ none

48) Which languages do you know how to write in (ex. a letter)? (please include your native language)

□______________________

□ none

49) Which languages do you understand, ex. listening to a song or to the radio? (include your native language) ______________________

50) During the last week you used Maltese and/or English to:

work	YES	NO
read newspapers and/or books	YES	NO
speak to friends or relatives	YES	NO
write a letter or some other form of correspondence	YES	NO
watch a film	YES	NO

51) During the last week you used a language, other than Maltese and/or English to:

work	YES	NO
read newspapers and/or books	YES	NO
speak to friends or relatives	YES	NO
write a letter or some other form of correspondence	YES	NO
watch a film	YES	NO

52) Which language or languages do you use <u>at home</u> to speak to your: (please, fill in each section)

wife/husband/partner ____
children ____
brothers/sisters ____
parents ____
grandparents ____

53) Which language or languages do you use <u>outside</u> to speak to your: (please, fill in each section)

relatives ____
colleagues at work ____
friends ____
neighbours ____

That's all! We would just like to remind you that this questionnaire is anonymous.

All information provided will be treated in full respect of privacy laws and all results will be produced collectively, not individually.

For further information, please contact Dr. Sandro Caruana (tel: / email:).

Thank you very much!

APPENDIX B

ADDITIONAL QUESTIONS IN THE ROMANIAN VERSION OF QUESTIONNAIRES A AND B

Questionnaire A

7a) How old were you when you returned to Romania? _________

9a) Can you speak the language of the country you lived in?

□ no □ yes □ I don't know

9b) If yes, where and with whom do you speak this language?

□ At home with parents □ At home with brothers/sisters
□ With friends □ With relatives
□ At school □ On the internet
□ With nobody

9c) When you speak this language you feel:

□ Proud □ Indifferent □ Embarrassed
□ I don't know

9d) Have you had problems in school because you do not speak Romanian well?

□ no □ yes □ I don't know

9e) Has it ever happened that your schoolmates laugh at you because you do not speak Romanian well?

□ no □ yes □ I don't know

Questionnaire B

13a) Have you ever had experience of working/living abroad?

□ No (go to question 13d)

□ Yes. Where? ______________________________

13b) For how long have you worked/lived abroad?

□ a few months □ 1-2 years □ 3-4 years

□ more than 5 years

13c) Can you speak the language of the country you worked/lived in?

□ No □ Yes

13d) Has your spouse ever had experience of working/living abroad?

□ No (go to question 14)

□ Yes. Where? ______________________________

13e) For how long has he/she worked/lived abroad?

□ a few months □ 1-2 years □ 3-4 years

□ more than 5 years

APPENDIX C

BABEL AND LANGUAGES

The booklet hereby reproduced has been prepared as part of the MERIDIUM European research on multilingualism in Southern European countries and countries of the Mediterranean. It has been conceived as a tool to stimulate children's curiosity on language diversity. At the same time, it is addressed both to primary school teachers and to parents: the former may use it as part of their teaching materials and as a stimulus to prepare similar resources, whereas the latter may consider it to represent an opportunity to reflect with their children on the language history of their family as well as on their language use.

MERIDIUM
Multilingualism in Europe as a Resource for Immigration
Dialogue Initiative among the Universities of the Mediterranean
BABEL AND LANGUAGES
BABEL E LE LINGUE
BABEL E AS LÍNGUAS
BABEL ŞI LIMBILE
BABEL IN JEZIKI
BABEL Y LAS LENGUAS

Notes for teachers and parents

This booklet has been prepared as part of the MERIDIUM European research on multilingualism in European Countries of the Mediterranean. It is a useful tool to stimulate children's curiosity on this subject, and at the same time, it is addressed to primary school teachers as teaching material and to parents as an opportunity to reflect with their children about language history of their family as well as their language use.

Nota per gli insegnanti e i genitori

Questo opuscolo è stato redatto nell'ambito della ricerca europea MERIDIUM sul multilinguismo nell'Europa mediterranea. Nasce come strumento utile a stimolare la curiosità dei bambini su questo tema; al tempo stesso, si propone agli insegnanti di scuola primaria come spunto didattico e ai genitori come occasione per riflettere insieme ai propri figli sulla storia e le abitudini linguistiche della famiglia.

Nota para os professores e pais

Este livrete foi preparado no âmbito do projecto europeu de investigação MERIDIUM sobre o multilinguismo na Europa Mediterrânica.. É seu objectivo ser um instrumento útil para estimular a curiosidade das crianças em relação a este tema; simultaneamente, poderá ser utilizado pelos professores do Ensino Básico como material de ensino e pelos pais como uma oportunidade para reflectiram em conjunto com os filhos sobre a história e os hábitos linguísticos da sua própria família.

Notą pentru profesori i părinţi

Această brourǎ a fost realizatǎ ca parte a proiectului european MERIDIUM, proiect de cercetare a multilingvismului în Europa Mediteraneană. Este un instrument util pentru stimularea curiozităţii copiilor in legătură cu acest subiect, adresându-se, in acelaşi timp, profesorilor din ciclul primar pentru a o folosi ca material didactic, şi părinţilor ca oportunitate de a reflecta, alături de copiii lor, asupra istoriei utilizǎrii limbii in familie.

Opomba za učitelje in starše

Ta knjižica je nastala v okviru evropskega raziskovanja večjezičnosti Sredozemlja MERIDIUM. Ponuja se kot uporabno sredstvo, ki naj spodbuja radovednost učencev za to tematiko, obenem pa naj ponudi didaktično pomoč učiteljem osnovne šole, staršem pa priložnost, da razmislijo skupaj s svojimi otroki o družinski zgodovini in domačih jezikovnih navadah.

Nota para profesores y padres

Este cuadernillo ha sido redactado dentro de la investigación europea MERIDIUM sobre el multilingüismo en los países europeos del Mediterráneo. Nace como instrumento útil para estimular la curiosidad de los niños sobre este tema; al mismo tiempo, se dirige a los profesores de la escuela primaria como sugerencia didáctica y a los padres como una oportunidad para reflexionar junto a sus hijos sobre la historia y los hábitos lingüísticos de la familia.

Agreement number – 2008 – 4286 / 001 – 001

Education and Culture DG

Lifelong Learning Programme

This project has been funded with support from the European Commission. This publication reflects the views only of the author, and the Commission cannot be held responsible for any use which may be made of the information contained therein.

Hi!
My name is Babel and I come from the planet Multilingua, where we study the languages of the universe in order to communicate with the inhabitants of other planets. On Multilingua, knowing many languages is important, because when we have problems, doubts or curiosities, we can turn to the inhabitants of all the planets in the universe to know what we need.
I made a trip to Earth to learn the languages of this planet, and I discovered that there are so many! Now, with the help of researchers at the MERIDIUM European Centre, who come from Italy, Malta, Portugal, Romania, Slovenia and Spain, I wrote my diary in six terrestrial languages to tell the inhabitants of my planet what I have discovered. However, I am still missing some information: could you help me to find it?

Ciao!
Il mio nome è Babel e vengo dal pianeta Multilingua, dove ci occupiamo di studiare le lingue dell'universo, per entrare in comunicazione con gli abitanti degli altri pianeti. Su Multilingua, sapere tante lingue è importante, perché, quando abbiamo un problema, un dubbio o una curiosità, possiamo rivolgerci agli abitanti di tutti i pianeti dell'universo per sapere quello che ci serve.
Ho fatto un viaggio sulla Terra, per conoscere le lingue di questo pianeta, e ho scoperto che ce ne sono tantissime! Adesso, con l'aiuto dei ricercatori del Centro Europeo MERIDIUM, che vengono dall'Italia, da Malta, dal Portogallo, dalla Romania, dalla Slovenia e dalla Spagna, ho scritto il mio diario di viaggio in sei lingue terrestri, per raccontare agli abitanti del mio pianeta quello che ho scoperto. Però mi mancano ancora alcune informazioni: vorresti aiutarmi a raccoglierle?

Olá!
O meu nome é Babel e venho do planeta Multilingua onde me entretenho a estudar as línguas do Universo para poder comunicar com os habitantes de outros planetas. No meu planeta, conhecer muitas línguas é muito importante porque, quando temos um problema, uma dúvida ou uma curiosidade, podemos falar com os habitantes de todos os planetas para saber aquilo que precisamos.
Fiz uma viagem à Terra para conhecer as línguas deste planeta e descobri que são imensas! Por isso, com a ajuda dos investigadores do Centro Europeu MERIDIUM, que vêm da Itália, de Malta, de Portugal, da Roménia, da Eslovénia e de Espanha, escrevi o meu diário de viagem em seis línguas terráqueas para poder contar aos habitantes do meu planeta o que descobri aqui. Mas faltam-me ainda algumas informações: podes ajudar-me a recolhê-las?

Bună!
Numele meu este Babel și vin de pe planeta „Multilingua", unde studiem limbile universului, pentru a putea comunica cu locuitorii altor planete. Pe Multilingua, cunoașterea multor limbi este importantă, deoarece când avem o problemă, o îndoială sau o curiozitate, ne putem adresa locuitorilor tuturor planetelor din univers pentru a afla ceea ce avem nevoie.
Am făcut o călătorie pe Pământ, pentru a învăța limbile acestei planete, și am descoperit că sunt foarte multe! Acum, cu ajutorul cercetătorilor de la Centrul European MERIDIUM, care vin din Italia, Malta, Portugalia, România, Slovenia și Spania, mi-am scris jurnalul în șase limbi terestre, pentru a le spune locuitorilor de pe planeta mea ce am descoperit. Însă, încă îmi lipsesc câteva informații: vrei să mă ajuți să le strâng?

Pozdravljeni!
Moje ime je Babel in prihajam s planeta Multilingva. Tam se učimo vesoljske jezike, da bi se lahko sporazumevali s prebivalci ostalih planetov. Na Multilingvi je pomembno znati jezike, ker se s prebivalci drugih planetov vesolja dogovarjamo, kako rešiti posamezen problem ali odpraviti dvom.
Potoval sem že na Zemljo, da bi spoznal jezike tega planeta, vendar sem ugotovil, da jih je zelo veliko. Zdaj bom s pomočjo raziskovalcev Evropskega središča MERIDIUM, ki prihajajo iz Italije, Malte, Portugalske, Romunije, Slovenije in Španije pisal v svoj dnevnik potovanj v šestih zemeljskih jezikih in tako pripovedoval prebivalcem svojega planeta, kar bom odkrival. Potrebujem pa nekaj več informacij: mi jih lahko pomagaš zbrati?

¡Hola!
Me llamo Babel y vengo del planeta Multilengua, donde nos ocupamos de estudiar las lenguas del universo para comunicarnos con los habitantes de otros planetas. En Multilengua saber muchas lenguas es importante, porque, cuando tenemos un problema, una duda, una curiosidad, podemos dirigirnos a los habitantes de todos los planetas del universo para saber lo que necesitamos.
He hecho un viaje a la Tierra, para conocer las lenguas de este planeta, y he descubierto que ¡hay muchísimas! Ahora, con la ayuda de investigadores del Centro Europeo MERIDIUM, de Italia, Malta, Portugal, Rumanía, Eslovenia y España he escrito mi diario de viaje en seis lenguas terrestres para contar a los habitantes de mi planeta lo que he descubierto. Pero me falta todavía alguna información: ¿querrías ayudarme a recogerla?

2

1

On Earth, some 6000 languages are spoken! Some of these languages are also used to write textbooks, comic books, laws, scientific treaties etc; others are hardly ever written, but this does not mean that they are less valuable than the others! People use them to communicate with each other every day, or to give a special name to people and things that are particularly significant in the local community.

Sulla Terra si parlano circa 6000 lingue! Alcune di queste lingue si usano anche per scrivere libri scolastici, fumetti, leggi, trattati scientifici; altre non vengono scritte quasi mai, ma questo non vuol dire che siano meno utili! Le persone le usano per comunicare tra loro quotidianamente, o per dare un nome speciale a persone e cose particolarmente significative per la comunità in cui vivono.

Na Terra falam-se cerca de 6000 línguas! Algumas destas línguas também são usadas para escrever livros escolares, histórias aos quadradinhos, leis, tratados científicos, etc.; outras línguas quase nunca são escritas, o que não quer dizer que sejam menos úteis do que as outras! As pessoas usam-nas para comunicar com os outros no dia a dia ou para dar um nome especial às pessoas e às coisas que são particularmente importantes na comunidade em que vivem.

Pe Pământ se vorbesc cam 6000 de limbi! Unele dintre acestea sunt folosite pentru scrierea manualelor, cărţilor de benzi desenate, legilor, tratatelor stiinţifice, etc.; altele nu se scriu aproape niciodată, însă asta nu înseamnă că sunt mai puţin valoroase! Oamenii le folosesc pentru a comunica şi pentru a numi persoanele şi obiectele care au o semnificaţie aparte pentru comunitatea locală.

Na Zemlji govorimo okoli 6000 jezikov in veliko govorov! V jezikih pišemo knjige, stripe, zakone, znanstvene razprave. Mnogi govori pa ne poznajo pisane besede. To pa ne pomeni, da so manj uporabni! Ljudje jih uporabljajo vsak dan, da se sporazumevajo, ali da poimenujejo ljudi in stvari, posebej pomembne za njihovo skupnost.

¡En la Tierra se hablan alrededor de 6000 lenguas! Algunas de ellas se usan también para escribir libros de texto, tebeos, leyes, tratados científicos; otras no se escriben casi nunca, pero esto no quiere decir que sean menos útiles que las otras. Las personas las usan para comunicarse entre ellos cotidianamente, o para darle un nombre especial a personas y cosas que son particularmente importantes para la comunidad en la que viven.

List, in a column, the names of languages that are both written and spoken, and the name of languages or dialects that are only spoken. Show your parents, or your teachers and school-friends, what you have written. Ask them if they agree with you in order to see whether they agree or if other languages come to mind:

Prova a elencare in una colonna i nomi di lingue che si parlano e si scrivono, e nell'altra i nomi di quelle che si parlano soltanto, e poi mostra ciò che hai scritto ai tuoi genitori, o ai compagni e agli insegnanti, per vedere se condividono le tue scelte e se a loro vengono in mente altre lingue:

Escreve numa das colunas o nome de algumas línguas de que te lembres e depois mostra a lista aos teus pais, ou aos teus colegas e professores, para ver se eles também já ouviram falar das línguas que escreveste ou se se lembram de outras, e lista-as na outra coluna:

Scrie într-o coloană numele limbilor vorbite şi scrise şi numele limbilor (sau dialectelor) doar vorbite. Arată ce ai scris părinţilor sau colegilor şi profesorilor, să vezi dacă sunt de aceeaşi părere şi dacă pot adăuga şi alte limbi:

Zapiši imena jezikov in govorov, ki ti pridejo na misel, nato pokaži svojim staršem, ali svojim sošolcem, ali svojim učiteljem, kar si napisal. Ugotovil boš, če delijo s teboj tvoj nabor ali se spomnijo še drugih jezikov:

Intenta escribir en una columna las lenguas que se hablan y que se escriben, y en la otra el nombre de las que sólo se hablan y luego enséñales lo que has escrito a tus padres o a tus compañeros y a los profesores, para ver si comparten tus opciones y si a ellos se le ocurre alguna lengua más:

1)	2)

4

2

Many people who live on Earth think that speaking or understanding many languages is something rare and difficult. On the other hand, in the world 1 person out of every 3, uses two or more languages everyday: at school, at home, at work, with friends... People who do so ("bilinguals") normally would have learnt the languages they know through their parents or friend, but also by studying or by living among people who speak them.

Molti terrestri pensano che saper parlare e capire lingue diverse sia una cosa rara e difficile. Al contrario, nel mondo 1 persona su 3 usa ogni giorno due o più lingue diverse, a scuola, a casa, al lavoro, con gli amici. Le persone che si comportano in questo modo ("bilingui") di solito hanno imparato le lingue che sanno dai loro genitori, parenti o amici, ma anche studiandole e vivendo tra persone che le parlano.

Muitos terráqueos pensam que falar e compreender várias línguas é uma coisa rara e muito difícil. Pelo contrário, no mundo 1 em cada 3 pessoas usa diariamente duas ou mais línguas diferentes, na escola, em casa, no trabalho, com os amigos. As pessoas que o fazem (os "bilingues") aprenderam normalmente essas línguas com os pais, os familiares e os amigos, mas também por andarem na escola e por viverem no meio de pessoas que falam essas línguas

Mulţi pământeni cred că a vorbi şi a înţelege multe limbi este ceva rar şi greu. Pe de altă parte, în lume 1 din 3 oameni foloseşte zilnic două sau mai multe limbi: la şcoală, acasă, la muncă, cu prietenii... Aceşti oameni („bilingvi") au învăţat de obicei aceste limbi de la părinţi, rude sau prieteni dar şi studiind şi trăind printre oameni care le vorbesc.

Mnogi zemljani še vedno menijo, da znati različne jezike je težko. Vendar ni tako, 1 človek od 3 uporablja dnevno v šoli, doma, na delu ali s prijatelji dva jezika ali več. Te osebe so dvojezični govorci in so se običajno naučili jezike od svojih staršev, sorodnikov ali prijateljev, ali pa so se jih naučili v šoli in v življenju z ljudmi, ki jih govorijo.

Muchos terrestres piensan que saber hablar distintas lenguas es una cosa rara y difícil. Al contrario, en el mundo 1 persona de cada 3 usa a diario dos o más lenguas diferentes, en la escuela, en casa, en el trabajo, con los amigos. Las personas que actúan así ("bilingües") habitualmente han aprendido las lenguas propias de sus padres, parientes o amigos, pero también estudiándolas y viviendo entre personas que las hablan.

Write down the languages that you use to speak about daily things: are you bilingual? Then, write the languages that your parents and your grandparents speak: are they the same ones that you speak?

Scrivi qui sotto le lingue che sai parlare per conversare normalmente di cose quotidiane: sei bilingue? Scrivi anche le lingue che sanno parlare i tuoi genitori e i tuoi nonni: sono le stesse che sai tu?

Indica a língua (ou línguas) que usas para falares no dia a dia: és bilingue? Em seguida, indica as línguas que os teus pais e os teus avós falam normalmente: são as mesmas que tu falas?

Scrie limbile pe care le foloseşti de obicei pentru a vorbi despre activităţile zilnice: eşti bilingv? Apoi, scrie limbile pe care le vorbesc părinţii şi bunicii tăi: sunt aceleaşi pe care le vorbeşti tu?

Spodaj zapiši jezike, ki jih znaš, da se lahko gladko pogovarjaš o vsakodnevnih stvareh: si dvojezičen? Napiši tudi jezike, ki jih govorijo tvoji starši, tvoji stari starši: so isti kot tisti, ki jih znaš ti?

Escribe más abajo las lenguas que sabes hablar para conversar normalmente de cosas cotidianas: ¿eres bilingüe? Escribe también las lenguas que saben hablar tus padres y tus abuelos: ¿son las mismas que sabes tú?

3

Thanks to the presence of people who are bilinguals, or who speak more than one language, in every country in the world many different languages are spoken. The languages spoken by most people in a population can be chosen as "official" languages and are very useful for people who live in their country. However, people speak other languages, that may also be typical of certain regions in a country, or languages that are normally spoken in other countries.

Grazie alla presenza dei bilingui, in ogni Stato del mondo si parlano molte lingue diverse. Le lingue che sono usate dalla maggioranza della popolazione possono essere proclamate lingue "ufficiali" e sono molto utili per vivere in quello Stato. Ma le persone parlano anche altre lingue, che possono essere tipiche di particolari regioni del Paese, oppure lingue parlate soprattutto in altri Stati.

Graças aos falantes bilingues, falam-se várias línguas em cada um dos países do mundo. As línguas usadas pela maioria da população num determinado país podem ser escolhidas como "línguas oficiais" e são muito úteis para quem vive nesse país. Nalguns países, as pessoas podem também falar outras línguas, típicas de determinadas regiões desse país, ou mesmo línguas faladas sobretudo noutros países.

Datorită prezenţei persoanelor bilingve, adică a celor care vorbesc mai mult decât o singură limbă, în fiecare ţară din lume se vorbesc mai multe limbi. Limbile folosite de majoritatea populaţiei pot fi alese ca limbi „oficiale" şi sunt foarte utile pentru a trăi în acea ţară. Totuşi, oamenii vorbesc şi alte limbi, tipice pentru anumite regiuni ale ţării respective, sau limbi vorbite în mod normal în alte ţări.

Pristnosti dvojezičnih govorcev gre zahvala, da se v vsaki med državami govorijo različni jeziki. Jeziki, ki jih uporablja večina govorcev so "uradni" jeziki in omogočajo skupno življenje. V posameznih pokrajinah pa ljudje govorijo tudi druge jezike, značilne za tisto okolje ali pa jezike drugih sosednih držav.

Gracias a los bilingües, en todos los países del mundo se hablan diferentes lenguas. Las lenguas que son utilizadas por la mayoría de la población pueden considerarse como "oficiales" y son muy útiles para vivir en ese país. Las personas pueden hablar también otras lenguas, que pueden ser las típicas de regiones específicas del país o que se hablan en otros países.

Imagine planning a journey with your friends in which you would visit all those places where a language you know is spoken: which areas of your country would you be able to visit? Which other countries would you go to?

Immagina di progettare con i tuoi compagni un viaggio che tocchi tutti i posti dei quali almeno uno di voi conosce la lingua: in quali regioni del tuo Paese potreste soggiornare? Quali altri Stati potreste visitare?

Imagina-te a planear uma viagem com os teus colegas. Nessa viagem, irão visitar todos os lugares onde se fale uma língua que seja conhecida por, pelo menos, um dos alunos da tua turma: que outros países irias visitar?

Imaginează-ţi că planifici o călătorie cu prietenii în toate locurile în care se vorbeşte o limbă pe care o ştiti: care regiuni ale ţării le-aţi putea vizita? Aţi putea merge şi în alte ţări?

Zamisli si načrt potovanja s svojimi sošolci tja, kjer se govori jezik vsaj enega med vami: v katero pokrajino tvoje države bi šel? Bi lahko obiskal tudi druge države?

Imagina planear un viaje con tus compañeros que pase por todos los sitios de los que por lo menos uno de vosotros conoce la lengua: ¿qué regiones de tu país podríais visitar? ¿Qué otros países podríais visitar?

4

There are some languages that are similar to each other and there are others that do not resemble each other at all. If they are similar, they are said to belong to the same family, just like brothers, sisters and cousins. This happens because they descend from the same ancient language, that is the same "ancestor language". Sometimes this can be seen also by comparing certain words.

Tra le lingue, ce ne sono alcune che tra loro si assomigliano molto o abbastanza e quelle che non si assomigliano per niente. Se si assomigliano, si dice che appartengono alla stessa famiglia, proprio come i fratelli e i cugini, perché discendono dalla stessa lingua antica, cioè dalla stessa "lingua progenitrice". A volte questo si può vedere anche confrontando alcuni tipi di parole.

Há algumas línguas que são muito parecidas com outras e há também línguas que não são nada parecidas entre si. Se são parecidas, diz-se que pertencem à mesma família, como se fossem irmãs ou primas, por descenderem de uma mesma língua antiga, um "antepassado" comum. Por vezes, podemos verificar esse facto comparando certo tipo de palavras nas diversas línguas.

Sunt unele limbi care se aseamănă foarte mult între ele, dar sunt şi limbi care nu seamănă deloc una cu alta. Dacă sunt asemănătoare, se spune despre ele că fac parte din aceeaşi familie, ca fraţii, surorile şi verişorii; aceasta pentru că provin din aceeaşi limbă veche, adică aceeaşi „limbă strămoşească". Uneori asta se poate vedea comparând anumite cuvinte.

Med jeziki so si nekateri med seboj zelo ali še kar podobni, spet drugi pa so si popolnoma različni. Kadar so sorodni, pravimo, da pripadajo isti jezikovni družini, tako kot bratje ali bratranci, saj izhajajo iz istega starega jezika,torej iz istega "prajezika". To včasih spoznamo, če primerjamo nekatere besede med seboj.

Entre las lenguas, hay algunas que se parecen mucho o bastante entre sí y otras que no se parecen en nada. Si se parecen, se dice que pertenecen a la misma familia, como los hermanos o los primos, porque vienen de la misma lengua antigua, es decir, de la misma "lengua madre". A veces esto se puede comprobar comparando ciertas palabras.

This is how numbers "1" and "2" are called in several languages. Under each one of them write the name of the language you recognize and use the same colour for those which look similar. Get help from parents, classmates and teachers!

Questi sono i nomi dei numeri "1" e "2" in diverse lingue: scrivi sotto ciascuna coppia le lingue che riconosci e colora in modo simile quelle che ti sembrano più somiglianti tra loro. Chiedi aiuto ai genitori, ai compagni e agli insegnanti!

Estes são os nomes dos números "1" e "2" escritos em várias línguas. Por baixo de cada uma das palavras que reconheceres escreve o nome da língua em que está escrita e usa a mesma cor para colorires as outras palavras que achas mais parecidas com essas. Pede ajuda aos teus pais, colegas e professores!

Iată cum sunt numite cifrele "1" şi "2" în diferite limbi. Scrie sub fiecare dintre ele limbile pe care le recunoşti şi foloseşte aceeaşi culoare pentru cele care seamănă între ele. Cere ajutorul părinţilor, colegilor şi învăţătorului/învăţătoarei!

Spodaj so imena v različnih jezikih za številko "ena" in "dva". Zapiši pod besedami jezik, ki ti je znan in pobarvaj v isti barvi tiste, ki se ti zdijo najbolj podobne med seboj. Prosi starše, ali sošolce, ali učitelje za pomoč!

Estos son los nombres del número "1" y "2" en varias lenguas: escribe debajo de cada pareja las lenguas que reconoces y colorea del mismo color las que te parecen más parecidas entre ellas. Pide ayuda a tus padres, compañeros y profesores.

uno - due		eden - dva		yī – èr
	one - two		ek - do	
unus - duo		edin - dve		ichi - ni
	eins - zwei		ikk - do	
unu - doi		jeden - dva		otu - abua
	ena - dve		jekh - duj	
um - dois		jedan - dva		wieħed - tnejn
	un - deux		bir - iki	
uno - dos		një - dy		wāħid – 'ithnān

5

On Multilingua we speak 'Multilanguage'. To express our ideas and feelings, we use a writing system called 'multi-symbolism'. I have found out that on Planet Earth people use a variety of writing systems: from top to bottom, from left to right, and viceversa. The beauty of each writing system is that each one of them has something unique.

Sul pianeta Multilingua parliamo la "multilingua". Per esprimere idee e sensazioni usiamo un sistema di scrittura che chiamiamo "multisimbolo". Ho scoperto che sulla Terra le persone usano vari sistemi di scrittura, disponendo i segni dall'alto in basso, da sinistra a destra e viceversa. La bellezza dei sistemi di scrittura è che ciascuno di essi ha in sé qualcosa di unico.

No Planeta Multilingua falamos "Multilinguês". Para expressar ideias e sentimentos usamos um sistema de escrita chamado "multi-simbolismo". Descobri que no Planeta Terra as pessoas escrevem de maneiras muito diferentes, de cima para baixo, da esquerda para a direita e mesmo da direita para a esquerda. O que torna os sistemas de escrita mais belos é que cada um deles tem algo de único.

Pe Planeta Multilingua noi vorbim „multilingua". Pentru a ne exprima ideile şi sentimentele folosim un sistem de scriere denumit „multisimbolism". Am aflat că pământenii vorbesc multe limbi şi că utilizează diferite sisteme de scriere, unele de sus în jos, altele de la stânga la dreapta sau invers. Frumuseţea fiecărui sistem de scriere este că are ceva unic.

Na planetu Multilingva govorimo "multilingvalščino". Svoje misli in čustva izražamo v pisavi, ki ji pravimo "večsimbolščina". Spoznal sem, da na Zemlji ljudje uporabljajo različne načine pisanja: od zgoraj navzdol, od leve proti desni in obrnjeno. Lepota vseh sistemov je v tem, da ima vsak med njimi nekaj povsem edinstvenega.

En el planeta Multilengua hablamos la "multilengua". Para expresar ideas y sensaciones usamos un sistema de escritura que llamamos "multisímbolo". He descubierto que en la Tierra las personas usan varios sistemas de escritura: de arriba a abajo, de izquierda a derecha y viceversa. La belleza de los sistemas de escritura es que cada uno de ellos tiene en sí algo único.

Can you figure out which writing system is associated with the following languages? Match the writing system with the corresponding languages. For each writing system the word for 'friendship' has been given.

Sai dire quale sistema di scrittura è associato alle lingue elencate? Abbina il sistema di scrittura con la lingua corrispondente. Tutte le parole che vedi scritte con sistemi diversi significano "amicizia".

Consegues descobrir que sistema de escrita está associado a cada uma das seguintes línguas? A palavra escrita em cada um dos sistemas de escrita significa "amizade".

Stii care sistem de scriere este folosit in următoarele limbi? Asociază fiecare sistem de scriere cu limbile corespunzătoare. Pentru fiecare sistem de scriere ai ca exemplu cuvântul „prietenie".

Prepoznaš pisave, ki bi naj pripadale k naštetim jezikom? Poveži pisavo z odgovarjajočim jezikom! Vse besede, ki jih vidiš, pomenijo "prijateljstvo".

¿Sabrías decir qué sistema de escritura corresponde a las lenguas enumeradas? Une el sistema de escritura con las lenguas correspondientes. Todas las palabras que ves escritas significan "amistad"

1.	Japanese / giapponese / japonês / japoneză / japonščina / Japonés	a.	Дружба
2.	Greek / greco/ grego /greaca / grščina / Griego	b.	miqësi
3.	Hindi / hindi / híndi / hindi / hindijščina / Hindi	c.	우정
4.	Chinese / cinese / chinês / chineză / kitajščina / Chino	d.	φιλία
5.	Arabic/ arabo / árabe / araba / arabščina / Árabe	e.	दोस्ती
6.	Albanian / albanese / língua albanesa / albaneză / albánščina / Albanés	f.	友誼
7.	Ukrainian /ucraino / ucraniano / ucrainiană / ukrajinščina / Ucraniano	g.	友情
8.	Korean / coreano / coreano / coreeană / korejščina / Coreano	h.	الصداقة

6

You learn languages at school, by listening to songs, by watching cartoon and films, by surfing the Internet. During your holidays you may meet children of your age and as you play with them you try your best to communicate too: with your hands, using gestures and with all your senses. We can learn languages everywhere and at every moment of our lives - from when we are very young till when we grow much older.

Impari le lingue a scuola, ascoltando canzoni, guardando cartoni animati e film, navigando in Internet.
Durante le vacanze incontri coetanei e giocando con loro comunichi in molti modi: con i gesti, con le espressioni e con tutti i sensi.
Possiamo imparare le lingue ovunque e in ogni momento - dall'infanzia alla vecchiaia.

Podes aprender línguas de muitas maneiras: na escola, a ouvir canções, a ver filmes e desenhos animados, a navegar na Internet. Durante as férias podes encontrar crianças da tua idade e enquanto brincas com elas tentas também comunicar: com as mãos, usando gestos e todos os outros sentidos. Podemos aprender outras línguas em qualquer lugar e em qualquer momento da nossa vida - desde muito pequenos até sermos velhos.

Limbile străine pot fi învăţate în şcoală, ascultând melodii, vizionând filme şi desene animate, navigând pe internet. În timpul vacanţelor, când te întâlneşti cu prietenii ca să vă jucaţi, încerci să comunici cum poţi: cu mâinile, gesticulând, şi cu toate simţurile. Putem învăţa o limbă oriunde, oricând în viaţă - din copilărie până la bătâneţe.

Jezikov se učiš v šoli, pa tudi ob poslušanju pesmi, gledanju risank in filmov, brskanju po svetovnem spletu. Med počitnicami srečaš sovrstnike in ob igri z žogo se sporazumevaš kot pač znaš: z rokami in vsemi tvojimi čutili.
Jezike se lahko učimo povsod in vedno - od malih nog do pozne starosti.

Aprendes las lenguas en la escuela, escuchando canciones, viendo dibujos animados y películas o navegando por Internet. Durante las vacaciones encuetras chicos de tu edad y jugando con ellos te comunicas con ellos como puedes: con las manos y con todos los sentidos. Podemos aprender las lenguas en cualquier parte y en cualquier momento - desde la infancia hasta la vejez.

You can surely remember a song that you have learnt, the name of a monument, of a typical dish or of traditional clothing in another language than yours. Think about these and write down what you remember:

Certamente ricordi se hai imparato una canzone, il nome di un monumento, il nome di un piatto tipico o di un abito tradizionale in una lingua diversa dalla tua. Pensaci e scrivi:

Lembras-te com certeza onde e como aprendeste uma canção, o nome de um monumento, de um prato típico ou de um traje tradicional, numa língua diferente da tua. Pensa nisso e escreve esses títulos e nomes:

Cu siguranţă îţi aminteşti un cântec pe care l-ai învăţat, numele unui monument, numele unui fel de mâncare sau al unei îmbrăcăminţi tradiţionale, într-o altă limbă decât a ta. Gândeşte-te la acestea şi scrie:

Prav gotovo se spomniš, kje in kako si se naučil pesem, si videl nove in zanimive stvari, si izvedel več o drugem narodu, v drugem jeziku od tvojega lastnega. Pomisli in zapiši:

Sin duda te acuerdas si has aprendido una canción, el nombre de un monumento, el nombre de un plato típico o de un traje tradicional en otra lengua diferente de la tuya. Piénsalo y escribe:

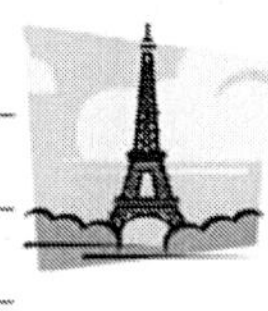

7

Let's do about a game with languages now! Please say whether you agree or disagree with the statements that you find below. At the end of this game you will know if you are an ideal citizen of the planet Multilingua!

Adesso faremo un test sulle lingue: rispondi se sei d'accordo o no con ognuna delle frasi che troverai nelle prossime pagine. Alla fine, saprai se sei un cittadino ideale del pianeta Multilingua!

Agora vamos fazer um teste sobre línguas. Responde, por favor, se estás de acordo ou não com cada uma das afirmações que vais encontrar na página seguinte. No fim do teste, poderás saber se és ou não o cidadão ideal do planeta Multilingua!

Acum haide să jucăm un joc despre limbi! Te rog spune dacă eşti de acord sau eşti împotriva afirmaţiilor de mai jos. La sfârşitul jocului vei şti dacă eşti cetăţean ideal al planetei Mulitilingua!

Še preizkus o jezikih: odgovori, če soglašaš ali ne soglašaš s povedmi, ki so na spodnjih straneh. Izvedel boš, če si vzoren državljan planeta Multilingva!

Ahora haremos un test sobre las lenguas: responde si estás de acuerdo o no con cada una de las frases que encontrarás en las páginas siguientes. Al final, sabrás si eres un ciudadano ideal del planeta Multilengua!

Agree / D'accordo / Concordo / De acord / Soglašam / De acuerdo

Neither agree nor disagree / Né d'accordo, né in disaccordo / Não concordo nem discordo / Nici de acord nici împotrivă / Niti soglašam, niti ne soglašam / Ni de acuerdo ni en desacuerdo

Disagree / In disaccordo / Discordo / Impotrivă / Ne soglašam / En desacuerdo

1. Learning new languages is useful and exciting
   Imparare nuove lingue è utile e divertente
   Aprender novas línguas é útil e divertido
   Este util şi palpitant să înveţi limbi străine
   Učiti se novih jezikov je koristno in zabavno.
   Aprender nuevas lenguas es útil y emocionante.
2. Children who know more than one language are lucky!
   I ragazzi che sanno più di una lingua sono fortunati!
   As crianças que sabem mais do que uma língua têm muita sorte!
   Copiii care ştiu mai multe limbi sunt norocoşi!
   Otroci, ki zanjo več jezikov so srečni!
   ¡Los niños que saben más de una lengua son afortunados!
3. Languages are like shoes! Without them you cannot go far in life!
   Le lingue sono come le scarpe: senza, non si può fare molta strada nella vita!
   As línguas são como os sapatos! Na vida não se pode ir longe sem elas!
   Limbile sunt precum pantofii! Fără ele nu poţi ajunge prea departe în lume!
   Jeziki so kot čevlji: brez njih v življenju ne moreš daleč priti!
   Las lenguas son como los zapatos. ¡Sin ellos no puedes ir por la vida!
4. Learning a new language helps me know more about the other languages that I know already
   Imparare una nuova lingua mi aiuta a conoscere meglio anche le lingue che so già
   Aprender uma língua nova ajuda-me a saber mais sobre as outras línguas que eu já conheço
   Faptul că învăt o nouă limbă mă ajută să ştiu mai multe despre celelalte limbi pe care le cunosc deja
   Naučiti se novega jezika mi pomaga pri boljšem poznavanju jezikov, ki jih že znam.
   Aprender una nueva lengua me ayuda a saber más sobre las otras lenguas que ya sé.

5. I admire people who try to communicate with others whose language they do not know
Ammiro le persone che cercano di comunicare anche con gente di cui non conoscono la lingua
Admiro as pessoas que tentam comunicar com outras que falam línguas que elas não conhecem
Îi admir pe acei oameni care încearcă să comunice cu persoane a căror limbă nu o cunosc
Občudujem tiste, ki se poskušajo sporazumevati tudi z ljudmi, katerih jezika ne poznajo.
Admiro a la gente que intenta comunicarse con otros cuyas lenguas no sabe.

6. Learning languages helps me grow and become a better person
Imparare le lingue mi aiuta a crescere e a diventare una persona migliore
Aprender línguas ajuda-me a crescer e a tornar-me uma pessoa melhor
Învăţarea limbilor mă ajută să cresc şi să devin o persoană mai bună
Učiti se jezike pomaga odrasti v boljšega človeka.
Aprender otras lenguas me ayuda a crecer y a hacerme mejor persona.

7. I still do not know enough languages. As I grow older I will surely learn more!
Non conosco ancora abbastanza lingue. Da grande ne imparerò certamente di più!
Ainda não sei línguas em número suficiente. Irei certamente aprender mais à medida que for crescendo!
Încă nu ştiu suficient de multe limbi. Dar pe măsură ce voi creşte, voi învăţa cu siguranţă mai multe!
Še vedno ne znam dovolj jezikov. Ko odrastem se jih bom prav gotovo učil več!
No sé todavía bastantes lenguas. ¡Cuando sea mayor sin duda aprenderé más!

mostly	**Result**
maggioranza di	**Risultato**
maioria de	**Resultado**
majoritatea	**Rezultat**
večina odgovorov	**Rezultat**
mayoría de	**Resultado**

You can make more of an effort to learn more about new languages and you might also one day learn how to become more interested in them than you are today: you are at the beginning of your voyage towards Multilingua!

Puoi sforzarti un po' per imparare qualcosa di nuovo su lingue che non conosci e magari troverai il modo per appassionarti di più a questo argomento: in partenza per Multilingua!

Podes fazer um esforço maior para aprender mais sobre novas línguas e um dia poderás vir a interessar-te mais por elas: Boa viagem para Multilingua!

Ai putea depune mai mult efort pentru a afla mai multe lucruri despre alte limbi şi vei putea ajunge să fii mai interesat de ele decât eşti azi: la punctul de plecare spre Multilingua!

Prav gotovo bi se lahko malo potrudil, da bi izvedel več o jezikih, ki jih ne znaš. Morda pa se boš navdušil nad tem: Odhod na Multilingvo!

Puedes esforzarte un poco para aprender algo nuevo sobre lenguas que no sabes y quizás encuentres la forma de apasionarte más en este tema: ¡saliendo hacia Multilengua!

18

You do love languages and you wish to learn more about them, and you certainly can find the time to develop these qualities: you are travelling towards Multilingua!

Ami le lingue, vuoi saperne di più e troverai certamente il tempo per sviluppare queste tue qualità: in viaggio per Multilingua!

Gostas de línguas e gostarias de aprender mais sobre elas. E vais de certeza encontrar tempo para desenvolver essas tuas qualidades: Boa viagem para Multilingua!

Iţi plac limbile şi doreşti să afli mai multe despre ele şi cu siguranţă îţi vei face timp să-ţi perfecţionezi aceste calităţi: eşti în drum spre Multilingua!

Jeziki so ti všeč in želiš vedeti več o njih. Prav gotovo boš našel čas, da razviješ svoje sposobnosti: Na pot na Multilingvo!

Te gustan las lenguas, quieres saber más de ellas y sin duda encontrarás el tiempo para desarrollar estas cualidades tuyas: ¡de viaje a Multilengua!

You love languages, you find them useful and you wish to learn more: YOU ARE AN IDEAL CITIZEN OF MULTILINGUA!

Ami le lingue, le trovi utili e vuoi impararne altre: CITTADINO IDEALE DI MULTILINGUA!

Gostas de línguas, achas que elas são úteis e queres aprender mais: CIDADÃO IDEAL DE MULTILINGUA!

Iubeşti limbile, le consideri utile şi doreşti să înveţi mai multe: EŞTI UN CETĂŢEAN IDEAL AL PLANETEI MULTILINGUA!

Rad imaš jezike, zdijo se ti koristni in želiš se učiti več: IDEALEN DRŽAVLJAN MULTILINGVE!

Te gustan las lenguas, las consideras útiles y quieres aprender otras: ¡CIUDADANO IDEAL DE MULTILENGUA!

19

That was great! I am now returning to my planet and I thank you for your help. I hope that even you enjoyed yourself as much as I have in this journey among languages. We would be very pleased to receive more information from Earth on Mulilingua: write to the addresses of the MERIDIUM universities and send me questions, stories, pictures, your own work, tasks you may have carried out at school, with your friends and teachers, Anything which concerns languages would be fine. If you visit the MERIDIUM website you will find a competition for you! Goodbye!

Bene! Io sto per tornare sul mio pianeta e ti ringrazio per avermi aiutato. Spero che anche tu ti sia divertito quanto me, in questo viaggio attraverso le lingue. Su Multilingua saremmo molto felici di ricevere altre notizie dalla Terra: scrivi agli indirizzi delle università MERIDIUM e mandami domande, racconti, disegni, lavori fatti da te, oppure realizzati a scuola, con i tuoi compagni e gli insegnanti. Qualsiasi cosa, insomma, purché riguardi le lingue. Se visiti il sito MERIDIUM, troverai anche un concorso per te! Arrivederci!

Ora bem! Vou regressar ao meu planeta e agradeço-te teres-me ajudado. Espero que te tenhas divertido nesta viagem pelas línguas. No meu planeta, Multilingua, gostaríamos muito de continuar a receber notícias da Terra: escreve para um dos endereços das Universidades MERIDIUM e envia-nos perguntas, histórias, desenhos, trabalhos feitos por ti, projectos realizados na tua escola com os teus colegas e professores, em resumo, tudo o que tenha a ver com as línguas. Se visitares o sítio MERIDIUM na Internet poderás encontrar um concurso em que podes participar! Até à próxima!

Excelent! Acum mă întorc pe planeta mea şi îţi mulţumesc pentru ajutor. Sper că te-ai distrat tot atât de bine ca şi mine în această călătorie în lumea limbilor. Pe Multilingua vom fi foarte fericiţi să primim şi alte ştiri de pe Pământ: scrie-ne pe adresa universităţilor MERIDIUM şi trimite-ne întrebări, povestiri, desene, lucrări de-ale tale sau realizate la şcoală împreună cu prietenii şi cu profesorii. Orice are legătură cu limbile este bine primit. Dacă vizitezi site-ul MERDIIUM, vei găsi un concurs pentru tine! La revedere!

Dobro! Vračam se na svoj planet in se ti zahvaljujem za pomoč. Upam, da si se zabaval z menoj na tem potovanju z jeziki. Na Multilingvi bomo zelo srečni, če se nam boš kaj oglasil z Zemlje: piši na naslove univerz MERIDIUM in pošlji mi vprašanja, zgodbe, risbe, svoje izdelke, ali pa tiste, ki jih boste naredili v šoli s sošolci in učitelji. Pošlji karkoli, kar se tiče jezikov. Če obiščeš spletno stran MERIDIUM, boš našel tudi natečaj, ki ti je namenjen. Na svidenje!

¡Bien! Yo estoy a punto de volver a mi planeta y te doy las gracias por haberme ayudado. Espero que tú también te hayas divertido tanto como yo, en este viaje a través de las lenguas. En Multilengua seremos felices si recibimos más noticias de la Tierra: escribe a las direcciones de las Universidades MERIDIUM y envíame preguntas, cuentos, dibujos, trabajos hechos por ti, o hechos en la escuela, con tus compañeros y los profesores. En definitiva, cualquier cosa con tal de que esté relacionada con las lenguas. Si visitas el sitio web de MERIDIUM, podrás encontrar también un concurso para ti. ¡Hasta la vista!

20

Partners

University for Foreigners of Perugia
Website: www.unistrapg.it
coordinator: Stefania Scaglione
mail: meridium@unistrapg.it

University of Malta
Website: www.um.edu.mt
coordinator: Sandro Caruana
mail: sandro.caruana@um.edu.mt

Faculty of Social Sciences and Humanities
Nova University of Lisbon
Website: www.fcsh.unl.pt
coordinator: Maria Isabel Tomás
mail: pimeridium@fcsh.unl.pt

Babeş-Bolyai University
Website: www.ubbcluj.ro
coordinator: Dan Chiribuca
mail: meridiumcluj@yahoo.fr

TransilvaniaUniversity of Brasov
Website: www.unitbv.ro
coordinator: LilianaCoposescu
mail: lili_coposescu@yahoo.com

University of Primorska
Website: www.upr.si
coordinator: Lucija Çok
mail: lucija.cok@upr.si

University of Salamanca
Website: www.usal.es/webusal/
coordinator: Vicente González Martin
mail: vgm@usal.es

MERIDIUM

Multilingualism in Europe as a Resource for Immigration
Dialogue Initiative among the Universities of the Mediterranean

Study and Documentation Centre on Multilingualism in European Countries of the Mediterranean
http://meridium.unistrapg.it/

Published by MERIDIUM partners
May 2011
Printers in Italy

The New Economics of Technology Policy

The New Economics of Technology Policy

Edited by

Dominique Foray

Professor and Director, Chair in Economics and Management of Innovation (CEMI), College of Management of Technology (CDM), Ecole Polytechnique Fédérale de Lausanne (EPFL), Switzerland

Edward Elgar

Cheltenham, UK • Northampton, MA, USA

Published by
Edward Elgar Publishing Limited
The Lypiatts
15 Lansdown Road
Cheltenham
Glos GL50 2JA
UK

Edward Elgar Publishing, Inc.
William Pratt House
9 Dewey Court
Northampton
Massachusetts 01060
USA

A catalogue record for this book is available from the British Library

Library of Congress Control Number: 2009925927

Mixed Sources
Product group from well-managed forests and other controlled sources
www.fsc.org Cert no. SA-COC-1565
© 1996 Forest Stewardship Council
FSC

ISBN 978 1 84844 349 5 (cased)

Printed and bound by MPG Books Group, UK

Contents

Contributors

Philippe Aghion, Department of Economics, Harvard University, USA

Spyros Arvanitis, KOF Swiss Economic Institute, Eidgenössische Technische Hochschule Zürich, Switzerland

Yochai Benkler, Harvard Law School, Harvard University, USA

Iain M. Cockburn, School of Management, Boston University, USA

Dirk Czarnitzki, K.U. Leuven, Belgium/ZEW, Germany

Paul A. David, Oxford University, UK/University of Stanford, USA

David Encaoua, Paris School of Economics (PSE), Centre Economie Sorbonne (CES), Université Paris I, France

Irwin Feller, Department of Economics, Pennsylvania State University, USA

Dominique Foray, CEMI, College of Management of Technology, Ecole Polytechnique Fédérale de Lausanne, Switzerland

Hans Gersbach, CER-ETH – Center of Economic Research, Eidgenössische Technische Hochschule Zürich, Switzerland

Bronwyn H. Hall, University of California, Berkeley, USA/University of Maastricht, The Netherlands/NBER

Dietmar Harhoff, INNO-tec Ludwig-Maximilians-Universität München, Germany

Heinz Hollenstein, KOF Swiss Economic Institute, Eidgenössische Technische Hochschule Zürich, Switzerland/Austrian Institute of Economic Research (WIFO), Vienna, Austria

Beat Hotz-Hart, Socioeconomic Institute, University of Zurich, Switzerland

Jacques Mairesse, CREST-INSEE, France/University of Maastricht, The Netherlands/UNU-MERIT/NBER

Franco Malerba, KITeS, Bocconi University, Italy

Pierre Mohnen, University of Maastricht, The Netherlands/UNU-MERIT/ CIRANO

David C. Mowery, Walter A. Haas School of Business, University of California, Berkeley, USA/NBER

Richard R. Nelson, Columbia University, USA/University of Manchester, UK

Nathan Rosenberg, Stanford Institute for Economic Policy Research, University of Stanford, USA

Bhaven N. Sampat, Department of Health Policy and Management, Columbia University, USA

Mark Schankerman, Department of Economics, London School of Economics, UK

Luc Soete, University of Maastricht, The Netherlands/UNU-MERIT

W. Edward Steinmueller, SPRU – Science and Technology Policy Research, University of Sussex, UK

Nora Sydow, KOF Swiss Economic Institute, Eidgenössische Technische Hochschule Zürich, Switzerland

Andrew A. Toole, Rutgers University, USA/ZEW, Germany

Manuel Trajtenberg, Eitan Berglas School of Economics, Tel Aviv University, Israel/Head of the National Economic Council at the Prime Minister's Office, Israel

Reinhilde Veugelers, K.U. Leuven, Belgium/Bruegel/CEPR

Eric von Hippel, Sloan School of Management, Massachusetts Institute of Technology, USA

Acknowledgements

This volume consists of papers and discussions presented at a conference organized by the Ecole Polytechnique Fédérale de Lausanne (CEMI, Collège du Management de la Technologie), which took place at Monte Verità (Switzerland).

We are grateful for the financial support received for this event from the Centro Stefano Franscini, the Swiss National Science Foundation and the DIME Network of Excellence.

We would also like to thank the Innovation Promotion Agency CTI of Switzerland for sponsoring this volume.

A special thank you goes to all the people who contributed to the production of this volume, and in particular to Tea Danelutti for her very appreciated help and supervision.

1. General introduction

Dominique Foray

This book focuses on technological policies, in other words all public interventions intended to influence the intensity, composition and direction of technological innovations within a given entity (region, country or group of countries).[1]

This book explores numerous avenues and pathways in its attempt to shed light on the theory and practice of technological policies, as they can be analysed and documented using modern tools of economic analysis:

- It examines relatively conventional themes in a subtle way (the questions of research and development subsidies and the financing of innovative firms).
- It tackles subjects yet to be investigated (such as policies adapted to innovation by users and/or applied within the framework of communities of practice).
- It takes another look at questions and debates that remain unsettled after decades of academic work (how useful and rational is a so-called mission policy; is there such a thing as a policy adapted to different stages of development?).
- It opens up new perspectives (for example the selection of priorities and the maintaining of a good balance in the allocation of resources between disciplines or fields of research).
- It reviews the ranges of indicators available for the development of an economy of innovation and technology on its way to becoming a discipline primarily oriented towards the production of 'evidence', intended to inform policy-making and allow its accurate evaluation.
- It presents case studies, on Switzerland (the homeland of Monte Verità[2]) and Europe.

The 'fashionable' themes of the globalization of innovation, the role and effects of intellectual property, and the place of academic research in technological policy recur to a greater or lesser extent in every chapter.

Beyond all these topics and beyond the infinite variations that the most talented members of our profession may envisage regarding the question of the effectiveness of tools and instruments, this work also invites us to re-examine the very foundations of this area of research and the practices that ensue from them, fundamentals that are still insufficiently questioned:

- What is the pertinent level of aggregation, the most favourable unit of analysis that will produce original and interesting results? Rather than pondering on these questions, we are usually content to continue the tradition of 'national' studies without considering the nonetheless very disrupting phenomenon of the globalization of the knowledge economy.
- What are the objectives of technological policy? Rather than debating this subject, we continue to seek the best way of pushing countries to step up their research and development (R&D) intensity and to distinguish the best performers with the help of extremely simplifying indices and indicators, which can only provide a very partial, or perhaps even inaccurate, vision of reality.

These two questions are thus still usually little discussed, whereas they are in fact essential. This results in an enormous conformity among economists doing technology policy research, to paraphrase a famous article by Stigler (1982) devoted precisely to the role of economists with regard to public policies. This enormous conformity can, in our opinion, only serve to delay the inevitable and obviously beneficial arrival of a paradigm shift in our way of tackling the problems and assessing the results of technological policies. The paradigm shift predicted in this work, particularly in the concluding chapters, encompasses the unit of analysis and objectives attributed to technological policy. It would radically disrupt the instruments and empirical practices forming the basis of the evidence-based policy research that economists strive to develop in order to clarify policy-making and evaluate policies.

Today we find ourselves in the fairly typical situation of 'pre-revolutionary' times – that of no longer knowing whether it is better to adopt a pessimistic or an optimistic view of the way in which economists deal with these problems. The pessimist would say that what we observe relatively well today and what we are capable of meticulously analysing in terms of causal relationships concerns factors that hardly matter. What does really count (for example drive and ambition as human qualities leading to innovation and entrepreneurship) remains far beyond the scope of the instruments of observation and theoretical tools of economists, while the way in which these factors can be activated remains to a large extent unknown.

The optimist, on the other hand, would retort that a tremendous amount has already been accomplished and that our knowledge base henceforth permits a far keener understanding of the importance of a wide range of factors looked upon as 'decisive', and even of their sensitivity to different degrees of intervention (with regard to intellectual property or research tax credit for example).

Whatever happens, do not choose between the pessimistic and optimistic visions but rather turn the former into a challenge that can be successfully assumed with the help of the latter. This will only be achieved, though, if the economist community collectively accepts, with full knowledge of the facts and with wisdom (in other words realizing that it is the only way), the prospect of a paradigm shift, as prophesied in the final pages of this volume.

It is this process that the Monte Verità Conference and the book derived from it have endeavoured to follow. The basic principle was exceedingly simple: gather the biggest names in our field on Ascona's 'Mountain of Truth', a magical place and cradle of many revolutions in thought. Over 100 years have gone by since the first meetings held on Monte Verità, the hill overlooking Ascona and Lake Maggiore, assembled anarchists, psychoanalysts, followers of the sexual revolution and other partisans of the Monte Verità Art of Life School (Folini, 2000). We hope we have captured a little of the spirit of this place in deciding to orchestrate a sort of small revolution in thought in a domain that in our view lies at the core of the issues of the knowledge economy, and of growth and development for our societies of tomorrow.

In conclusion, I would like to express my very sincere thanks to all the authors who agreed to write original contributions on these subjects, while conforming to a certain number of restricting editorial guidelines, and doing so within a very acceptable time limit. My thanks also go to the discussants who accepted the difficult task of writing brief comments on one or several chapters in the book.

I wish you happy reading!

NOTES

1. The term 'technological innovation' must be understood in a very broad sense. It essentially includes technical changes (products and processes) and organizational changes. Both types of change are either considered separately (a change in technique, a change in organization) or in association with larger-scale projects. The innovations take effect at all levels of aggregation, large-scale technological innovations themselves consisting of multitudes of innovations at lower levels of aggregation. Consequently the domain of technological policy is a very wide one. It includes interventions aimed at assisting firms, directly or indirectly, in innovation activities, those aimed at directly achieving innovations generally considered as being 'out of reach' for private companies, those that

concern the environment, institutions and specific infrastructures – all factors that can greatly influence the motivation and performance of firms.

2. Monte Verità is a seminar centre located in Switzerland on the hills overlooking Ascona and Lake Maggiore.

REFERENCES

Folini, M. (2000), *Monte Verità: Ascona's Mountain of Truth, Guide to Swiss Monuments*, Berne: SHSA.

Stigler, G. (1982), 'Economists and public policy', in *Ideas, their Origins and their Consequences: Lectures to Commemorate the Life and Work of G. Warren Nutter*, Washington DC: American Enterprise Institute for Public Policy Research (for Thomas Jefferson Center Foundation), pp. 85–97.

PART I

Frameworks and Rationales for Technology Policy

2. Building effective 'innovation systems' versus dealing with 'market failures' as ways of thinking about technology policy

Richard R. Nelson

In this chapter I compare two different theoretical frameworks in economics for orienting analysis of issues in technology policy. One is a neoclassical framework that sees appropriate policies as dealing with 'market failures'. The other framework is provided by an evolutionary and institutional approach to economic analysis that sees appropriate policies as building or maintaining an effective 'innovation system'. It should be no surprise that I believe the latter framework is the more useful one.

I begin by laying out the key general differences between the two broad theoretical frameworks, and how they lead to different perspectives on technology policy. Then I turn to a particular case: technology policy regarding pharmaceuticals. Finally, I comment on the general question of the role of economic theories in framing policy analysis.

2.1 DIFFERENCES IN THE PERSPECTIVES

At the broadest level, and possibly the deepest, the difference between the neoclassical theory that has dominated microeconomic theorizing over the last half century, and the evolutionary economic theory that is taking shape, concerns their assumptions about the economic context for action. Neoclassical economics sees the economy as in an equilibrium configuration, at rest, or undergoing well-anticipated change. In such a context the action best suited to the context can be assumed to be one that decision-makers have learned through relevant experience, or can calculate based on what they know securely. In contrast, evolutionary theory sees the economy as always in the process of change, with economic activity proceeding in a context that never is completely familiar to the actors, or perfectly understood by them. (For a discussion see Nelson and Winter, 1982.)

The difference here corresponds to the distinction Schumpeter drew, in his *Theory of Economic Development* (1934), between the context for action set in a continuing circular flow of economic activity, and the context set by an economic environment where innovation is going on. We modern evolutionary economic theorists, like Schumpeter, believe that the latter context is a much better characterization than the former of conditions in modern capitalist economies. And it would seem that it certainly is the context that should be assumed in analysis concerned with the design or evaluation of technology policies.

This difference in the assumed context of action leads the two theories to very different conceptions of what is meant by 'rational' behavior. Both theories assume that individual and organizational economic actors pursue objectives, usually in a reasonably intelligent way. Rational behavior in neoclassical theory means that economic actors can and do choose the course of action from all possible ones that, in fact, maximizes their expected utility. In contrast, the 'rationality' of actors in evolutionary theory is bounded, in the sense of Herbert Simon (see for example his *Models of Man*, 1957). There is no way they can understand fully the context in which they are operating, yet they have to cope, somehow. To a considerable extent the coping involves the use of routines that have in the past yielded satisfactory results. But the actors in evolutionary theory also have the capability to try something new, for example when they judge what they have been doing as inadequate in a changed context, or more generally where they think they see an opportunity to do better.

A related difference between the two theories is in how they conceive good economic performance. Neoclassical theory proposes that the performance of an economy should be judged in terms of how close it is to a theoretical optimum. In evolutionary theory there is no theoretical optimum, since the range of possibilities for economic action is always changing, generally growing, but in a way that cannot be predicted or specified in detail. Economic performance is seen in terms of the rate and nature of progress. Enhancing these clearly is what technology policy is all about.

I want to note – highlight – that most of what is valuable in the standard contemporary tool kit of concepts and understandings is not tied to the assumptions of neoclassical theory. I include here such concepts as 'public goods' and 'externalities'. These concepts surely are extremely valuable in organizing thinking about issues of technology policy. So also is the proposition that for the most part competition is an important vehicle for advancing the public interest, and monopoly or collusion something to be avoided if possible. The argument that 'incentives matter' and that, in many cases, designing policies to shape incentives appropriately is a more effective strategy than trying directly to mandate behavior, is built deep within the traditions of today's standard economics, and almost surely generally provides good guidance.

But these concepts and maxims are not logically tied to a structure of modern neoclassical economic theory. They are perfectly at home within an economic analysis structured by evolutionary theory, although in some cases they are seen then in a somewhat different light.

I want to turn now to another important difference between neoclassical economics and the evolutionary-institutional approach that I espouse. It regards how one should look at the institutional complexity of modern capitalist economies.

I believe that the deep incorporation in modern neoclassical economics of the theory that, under particular conditions, the operation of a pure market yields outcomes that are Pareto optimal, leads to a way of recognizing actual institutional complexity that is awkward and potentially biased. In particular, non-market elements in an economy, for example elements of an active technology policy, tend to be analyzed and rationalized as possible responses to 'market failures'. From my point of view, there are three different (but related) major problems with this orientation.

First of all, it gives pure market organization a privileged standing, as the default structure. The implicit presumption is that one should go with market organization, and leave market organization strictly alone, unless one can develop a case that there is something wrong with doing that. Supplements to market organization, or quite different forms of finance and organization of an activity, are placed in a position of being a 'second-best' solution, justified only because markets 'fail' in some sense.

But it seems to me intellectually strained to rationalize that government agencies are in charge of managing the air traffic control system, or matters relating to public health, or (to get to technology policy) for funding a good portion of a nation's basic research, with universities doing much of that work, because of 'market failures'. It is much more balanced, much less biased, to see different types of funding and organization as being good for different kinds of things, than to see markets as the preferred general-purpose mode of operation, except when they 'fail'. This certainly seems a better way of thinking about a variety of possible technology policies, from the generally accepted one of funding basic research, to more controversial ones like supporting certain kinds of industrial applied research. (For a more extended argument, see Nelson, 2002.)

An important reason, and the second problem with the market-failure theory point of view, is that pure market organization always fails, at least to some extent. The conditions for a pure market organization to result in a 'Pareto optimal' equilibrium never are fully met. This is recognized, implicitly, in serious policy discussion, where the argument about policy is almost never about whether the situation actually is 'optimal', but rather about whether the problems with the existing regime are sufficiently severe to warrant active new policy measures. That is, analysis of active government policies, like technology policies, inevitably involves a comparison of different ways of doing things. My argument is that the comparative mode of analysis should be theoretically explicit, and that the analysis of different ways of organizing, governing and funding an activity should proceed without bias.

Thus it is clear that virtually all research and development (R&D) yields externalities, in the sense that some parties not involved in R&D decision-making will be able to learn something useful from the results. It also is true that the understandings won from any R&D effort have public good properties, at least in the sense that use by one party does not reduce the stock of understanding that might be used by another.

But there are good reasons for leaving decisions and investments in R&D aimed to advance commercial product lines and process technologies mostly to commercial firms. Among other things, that is where the relevant expertise resides. And various special institutional devices, like a patent system, can help support incentives of firms to do this kind of R&D, even though allowing patents generates economic inefficiencies (market failures under a neoclassical perspective) of their own. The institutional 'call' here, that is endorsed by most knowledgeable economists, is that balancing the pluses and minuses of different ways of getting commercial product and process development done, society is better off leaving it mostly to business firms and paying the price of allowing patent protection of new product and process technology. However, as I will consider in a moment, in some areas the consensus here is not sharp, for example regarding certain classes of pharmaceuticals.

Regarding basic research, the results of which are likely to be far upstream from something commercial, the situation is different. Here university researchers often have a better knowledge of what is going on in a field than do most researchers in commercial firms. While if one allows patents on research outputs far upstream from direct practical application one can provide firms with a profit incentive to do such work, as in fact has been done in biotech, the economic costs of allowing basic scientific discoveries to become private property can be very considerable. The comparative institutional call here is widely agreed to support funding basic research with public monies, and having it undertaken in institutions that have an interest in open science.

My argument is that in both of these cases, the important analysis is not so much whether markets 'fail' to some degree or not. Rather, the issue is how best to get the work done.

The third problem with the market-failure orientation to questions of public policy is that, as the examples above indicate, just as there is no such thing as a perfect market, there is no such thing as a pure market, or from another point of view, markets are always supported and complemented by a wide range of non-market apparatus. A patent system is a complex and expensive legal structure put in place (among other reasons) to enhance the expectations of potential private inventors that they can profit from their market-oriented work. The R&D of for-profit pharmaceutical companies aimed at developing new drugs draws from the public funding of biomedical research and training at universities.

Which brings me to the concept of an innovation system. I have used the term (Nelson, 1993) to recognize and refer to the complex and varied set of actors and arrangements that, through the actions and interactions they engender and mold, influence the pace and pattern of technological innovation in a field. Innovation systems – I use the term flexibly to fit the particular subject matter under analysis – come in a variety of sizes and shapes: national, regional, sectoral and technology-specific. The advantage of the concept, at least in my view, is that it focuses attention on the variety of institutions and institutional actors that are involved in innovation in a field, and it does so without invoking the notion of 'market failure' to rationalize the non-market parts of the system.

From this point of view, government programs, policies and special legal structures are part of the system. This does not mean that technology policies do not require careful scrutiny, evaluation and continuing efforts to adjust them to changing circumstances, to make them better. But policies to support, for example, biomedical research at universities, and proposals to modify those policies, are considered in their own right. Thus the question of whether to provide more public money for research at universities and public labs for the purpose of developing drugs for diseases that mainly plague poor countries clearly is a difficult one. But within a perspective that sees an 'innovation system' as a natural concept, it can be addressed without a background notion that the market obviously could do the whole job in the best possible way, if it were not for the market failure problem.

My brand of evolutionary economics sees institutional evolution as a central part of the dynamic processes of economic change. Institutions evolve, along with technologies. The institutions, and the way they evolve, involve both private and public actors. An important consequence of this point of view is that policy-making is seen as a continuing process. Existing institutional structures, including bodies of relevant law, and particular government policies and programs, can never be regarded as optimal. They are, and should be, always subject to scrutiny. While the intensity of political debate about whether reforms are needed in a particular sector or industry, and if so, the appropriate reforms, tends to wax and wane, the policy process is a continuing one.

In some cases the policy dialogue cuts across a wide swath of economic sectors, as with the current discussion regarding whether patent reform is necessary. But much of the discussion, as well as the policies, are technology- or sectoral-specific. Below I have chosen to do a relatively extensive discussion of present policy issues regarding pharmaceuticals, rather than touching more lightly on several cases.

2.2 TECHNOLOGY POLICY AND PHARMACEUTICALS

A major advantage of the innovation system orientation to technology policy, at least in my view, is that it induces a broad view of the various forces and actors whose actions are determining the pace and character of technological advance in a field, and thus wards off the analyzing of a particular policy issue as if it were the only one of concern. In many sectors, and broad technologies, a number of policy debates are going on at the same time. Pharmaceuticals is a fine case in point. I focus below on the US, but much of the policy debate I describe is also going on in other countries.

The innovation system in pharmaceuticals contains many actors and many aspects. The discovery or creation of new pharmaceuticals, their production and their marketing, is largely today the business of for-profit private enterprise. However, since the 1950s the introduction of new pharmaceuticals to the market, and modes of production of pharmaceuticals, have been under tight regulatory restraints in the United States, and in most other advanced industrial nations. While pharmaceutical companies do the greater share of the work on the development and testing of new pharmaceuticals, since shortly after World War II, the National Institutes of Health have taken broad responsibility for the funding of basic biomedical research in the United States. Most of that research goes on at universities. An important portion of the testing of new pharmaceuticals, while funded by industry, goes on at university-affiliated medical centers. In some cases a government agency has funded and guided aspects of the testing of a new pharmaceutical.

Although to a lesser degree than in most high-income countries, a large portion of the purchases of pharmaceuticals in the United States is covered by insurance. A growing portion of that insurance is public. While in other countries particularly the public part of the health insurance system has negotiated pharmaceuticals prices with companies, this is happening to a lesser degree in the United States.

Patent protection is particularly important for pharmaceutical companies. And pharmaceutical companies have a strong influence on the shape of patent policy in the United States.

None of these features stays constant for very long. The whole structure is almost always changing in one way or another, and the appropriate direction of change is a continuing matter of public policy debate. Let me parse various aspects of the current policy debates regarding pharmaceuticals going on in the US. Some of these do not relate directly to matters bearing on technological innovation, but all of them set the context for the technology policy debates.

In the US the most visible and probably most important policy debate concerns proposals for public policies to extend the range of people covered by health insurance. This debate has been strongly influenced by technological advances in pharmaceuticals. Today the accepted medical treatments for a wide range of diseases involves the use of pharmaceuticals that were not available ten or twenty years ago, and these drugs are expensive. The rising price of medical care is a major factor behind the growing pressures for widening insurance coverage. And how the issue gets resolved will have strong influences on pharmaceutical development. Almost surely there will be a significant expansion in publicly supported health insurance coverage, and with that new pressures and mechanisms to put ceilings on or bargain down the price of pharmaceuticals. This will affect both the profits of pharmaceutical companies, and their incentives as well as their funding for new drug development.

The concern in the US about the high prices of pharmaceuticals is also behind a continuing debate about whether current patent law overly curtails competition. Here an important part of the argument is about whether companies with patents are extending their monopoly, holding off the rise of generic competition, through a set of mechanisms that have been given the name 'evergreening'.

The issue of pharmaceutical prices is also involved in the growing political pressures in the US to try to do something about the high prices of pharmaceuticals in poor countries. The issue of high pharmaceutical prices facing developing countries is tangled up with whether those countries are justified in buying, or encouraging the production of, generic versions of those pharmaceuticals under the terms of TRIPS (Trade-Related Intellectual Property Rights). It would appear that a major diplomatic battle is pending between some of the larger and more powerful developing countries, and the United States.

The pharmaceutical companies have expressed their concern, and with good reason, that the advent of price controls or stronger downward pressure on prices in the US, and a reduction in the strength of patent protection, will erode their revenues, and hence their capacity to do research and development. They have made similar arguments against policies aimed to reduce prices in less developed countries, although the stakes for them there are less.

In contrast, a number of voices have been arguing that most of the R&D done by pharmaceutical companies is either oriented to developing 'me too' drugs that add little of therapeutic value to what already is available, or involves picking up embryonic new drugs that that have come out of publicly funded university research, and establishing a patent-based monopoly on what the public has largely paid for. While still vague, there are clearly some arguments afoot that a significant change in the way pharmaceutical R&D is done is in order, and that in particular government support should move beyond the funding of basic research, and start to encompass drug development.

In particular, there is advocacy for the public support of pharmaceuticals development in contexts where it can be argued that company expectations of profit potential are low, while the social, and even the broad economic, benefits of the development of new medication would be high. Here there are separate discussions about three different areas: the development of drugs for diseases prevalent in poor countries but not rich countries; so-called 'orphan' drugs for life-threatening or debilitating diseases where the affected group is relatively small; and vaccines. Proposals for programs in these areas face the challenge of designating appropriately the kind of organization that would do the publicly financed work; what would be done about any resulting intellectual property rights; whether the inducement should be in the form of a guaranteed market, or prize, or whether the program should work through contracts and grants; and so on.

And then there are a variety of issues relating to possible reform of the intellectual property rights system bearing on pharmaceuticals. A number of studies have shown that, compared with most other industries, the ability of a company in the pharmaceuticals industry to profit from its innovations is strongly dependent on patent protection. At the same time, it is clear that pharmaceutical companies are able to use their patent protection to support very large margins between production costs and the prices they charge. This fact is prominent in many of the debates about high pharmaceuticals prices, and what to do about that problem.

As mentioned earlier, one contentious matter is whether, and if so how, to rein in the current proclivity of pharmaceutical firms holding patents on a particular drug to delay generic competition on the expiration of the original patent through practices called 'evergreening'. The issue of whether governments of low-income countries should have the right to purchase pharmaceuticals from generic producers, in effect voiding the legal power of the patent in such cases, has also been mentioned above. One of the arguments for government funding of pharmaceuticals development as well as research is that then the patent rights could be controlled by government, and licensed on terms that would encourage competitive pricing.

But there also are issues relating to what should be patentable in the broad area of pharmaceutical research, including the upstream science. For example, should genes, or gene fragments, or receptors, be patentable? A related issue stems from the fact that, in the period since 1980, when the Bayh–Dole Act was passed, universities have been active participants in patenting. Should Bayh–Dole be amended, and should there be some restrictions placed on university patenting and licensing?

There are a number of other issues under discussion that I could mention here. However, I think I have described enough of what is going on so that it is clear that the various technology policy issues relating to pharmaceuticals need to be seen in the context of the overall 'innovation system' – the wide variety of forces and actors that influence technological innovation in this area. And the context needs to be seen in the light of evolutionary theory. It is change that is driving the policy discussion. Analysis based on the assumption that the problem is to move from one unhappy neoclassical equilibrium position to another better one, and that the key to getting to a better equilibrium is the understanding of present market failures and the design of policies to fix or cope with them, is at best not very helpful, and in my view misses much of what is going on.

2.3 HOW DOES ECONOMIC THEORY INFLUENCE POLICY ANALYSIS?

But should understanding that externalities are almost always generated by R&D, that scientific and technological knowledge is non-rivalrous in use, and that monopoly tends to lead to and support large gaps between price and costs, play a role in thinking about the kinds of technology policy issues I have sketched above? Obviously yes. But as I argued earlier, working with these kinds of concepts and maxims does not require accepting the whole baggage of neoclassical theory. We evolutionary economists feel perfectly at home working with them when considering how to make innovation systems work better. In the particular case being considered, these understandings certainly weigh against allowing broad patents on research results that have a wide range of potential applications and, more generally, against relying heavily on for-profit enterprise to fund and undertake this kind of research. But they equally warn against encouraging, or allowing, universities to patent these kinds of things. The nature and relevance of these kinds of understandings extends well beyond their signaling of 'market failure'.

I think it useful to reflect a little on the question: 'What kind of policy guidance can be drawn from any kind of a broad economic framework?' Certainly not the kind of guidance that a basic knowledge of constants and relationships that physics, or aeronautical engineering, gives to the designers of a new aircraft wing. The guidance there is to a considerable extent in the form of established quantitative knowledge that enables reasonably reliable calculation of the relationships between wing shape and drag, the ability of different materials to withstand pressure and heat, and so on.

Econometricians sometimes propose that estimated econometric models provide quantitative relationships and constraints to guide the development of economic policy, but this proposal should be taken with a grain of salt. While econometric models can provide some 'ballpark' numbers to help locate the policy analysis, no economic policy-maker that I know treats these numbers with anything like the respect that aeronautical engineers treat numbers regarding the strength of materials. Also, the econometrician's argument should not be taken as a case for neoclassical theory. As I suggested earlier, most of the (reduced form) equations calculated by econometricians are as compatible with an evolutionary theoretic rationale as with a neoclassical theoretic rationale.

Rather, what an economic theory provides for policy analysis is a framework for interpretation. My argument in this chapter is that the most useful framework for analysis of issues of technology policy that economists now have is an evolutionary theory of economic change that recognizes the complex institutional structures supporting and molding innovation that is signaled by the concept of an 'innovation system'.

REFERENCES

Nelson, R. (ed.) (1993), *National Innovation Systems*, Oxford: Oxford University Press.

Nelson, R. (2002), 'The problem of market bias in modern capitalist economies', *Industrial and Corporate Change*, **11**, 207–44.

Nelson, R. and S. Winter (1982), *An Evolutionary Theory of Economic Change*, Cambridge, MA: Harvard University Press.

Schumpeter, J. (1934), *The Theory of Economic Development*, Cambridge, MA: Harvard University Press, first published 1911.

Simon, H. (1957), *Models of Man*, New York: Wiley.

3. Technology policy: the roles of industrial analysis and innovation studies[1]

W. Edward Steinmueller

3.1 INTRODUCTION

The rationales put forward for technology policy shape the potential for policy-making. Traditionally, a limited number of rationales have been available. The most familiar are those of

- market failure (Nelson, 1959; Arrow, 1962);
- infant industry development (Shafaeddin, 2000);
- coordination failure, for example in the case of compatibility standards (David and Greenstein, 1990; Tassey, 2000)

In addition, and of particular relevance to developing economies, the development of demand and its effects in inducing innovation have been offered as a rationale within both development (Binswanger and Ruttan, 1978; Ruttan, 2001) and evolutionary economics (Metcalfe, 1995). A rationale that is less popular among economists, but frequently suggested by policy-makers, is imperfect capital markets (see Hall, Chapter 15 in this volume). For example, the hypothesis is that financial institutions may be too risk-averse to invest in new technology-based firms and hence there is a need for bolstering 'risk capital'.[2] Finally, relatively neglected, but still salient, rationales include the role of procurement (Flamm, 1987), and mission-oriented research (Mowery, 1995 and Chapter 12 in this volume), including defence and other social needs such as health, safety and environmental protection.

The relative weight of these rationales has waxed and waned over time but the policy discourse has, until relatively recently, almost universally relied on one or more of these rationales. The goals of employing technology policy have been similarly constrained. In the developing countries, these have fluctuated between growth and employment on the one hand,

and competitiveness (sometimes verging on mercantilism) on the other (European Commission, 1993). In the middle-income countries, the focus is on the issue of how to employ technology policy to address the problems of late industrialization, among which the prospect of leapfrogging is one of persistent interest (Soete, 1985; Steinmueller, 2001).

The aim of this chapter is to discuss the contributions and shortcomings of the economics of technological change research programme as an evidence base for the practice of technology policy, where these rationales and goals are beginning to be enlarged.[3] As well as practice having its own dynamic, it is increasingly drawing upon a set of ideas from the more experience-based[4] areas of economic research. I highlight three lines of thought – systems of innovation, evolutionary economics and the localization of innovative activities – that complement (and also reflect) the efforts of policy-makers to operate outside the constraints imposed by the existing frameworks of rationales and goals. The necessary disclaimer here is that technology policy is always a risky business, more prone to failure than to success, but ultimately seen as necessary by those charged with 'doing something' to meet a growing array of challenges to growth, employment and sustainability. It is apparent to most that there is a wide gap between what is practised and what is preached concerning the effectiveness of laissez-faire economic policy in the area of technology – not least in those countries advancing the strongest rhetoric of market liberalism.

The concern that gives rise to this chapter is that there are two important missing links in the evidence base that academic research is offering to policy-makers. Their existence, in my view, reduces both the power and the effectiveness of the above lines of thought for policy-making. These links are, in brief, the capacity to make effective analysis of technological performance at the level of individual industries, and the research foundation for understanding the motivations to innovate. If these links are strengthened, there remain important problems in bringing them and the related lines of thought into more effective practice, which deserve additional consideration. The plan of this chapter is therefore to highlight the contributions and limitations of the above three lines of thought in making technology policy, and to make the case for both the significance of the two missing links and the tractability of making progress in developing them further.

My basic theses are that it is inevitable that the politics of technology policy will produce targeted industrial policy and that these policies could be improved if scholars of science, technology and innovation were willing to take an active role in outlining and critiquing future as well as past policies. In explaining the inevitability of technology policy, laissez-faire agnosticism is a lean diet for politicians and a challenge to both politicians and civil servants, who are often motivated by the need to take action to meet the changing fortunes of industries, regions and citizens. Even the slightly more substantial diet offered by economists who argue that the unpredictability of technological progress demands a policy of facilitation and horizontal structural support (that is, competition across a broad set of areas) is unlikely to satisfy the demand for a policy 'action plan'. Regarding doing better, scholars of science, technology and innovation do have more to offer than the retrospective analysis of the rate and direction of technological change. In the vacuum of logic and evidence concerning technology policies which are targeted toward specific industries and lines of technological advance, other approaches to stock-taking and direction-setting are being taken up.

In Europe, the role of the current melange of approaches often labelled as Foresight and including Delphi studies, scientometric and bibliometric analysis, and various tools of facilitated deliberation and consensus-making, are filling the vacuum created by the absence of researchers with specific claims to industrial and technological expertise. Often these processes are subject to opportunistic capture, a process that is often aided by the lack of transparency of policy-making process. In the US, it would appear that a new era of the military industrial complex is directing one branch of progress, an enormous medical research establishment is directing a second branch, and other branches are being ceded to purely commercial interests. As we confront a new generation of moral and ethical challenges in areas of poverty reduction, biotechnology, weapons development and climate change, neither the European nor the American system seem to be developing either the theory or the evidence base needed to confront these challenges.

3.2 WHERE HAVE ECONOMISTS GOT TO IN UNDERSTANDING TECHNOLOGY POLICY?

From the perspective of 1968, the issue of technology policy was largely conceived in terms of the linear model in which technology was seen as applied science, suggesting that the stimulation of the science base would suffice to provide the tools to settle the technological frontier, and that technology transfer – the exchange of information – would serve to bring about a world of converging living standards. In this framework, the rationales and goals of technology policy were essentially to provide for open markets and vigorous competition so that the most effective technological solutions would be widely applied. This message remains a central tenet of many economists who subscribe to Karl Popper's views on the unpredictability of scientific advance. The set of rationales and goals outlined above was seen as more or less sufficient to this task and thus, a significant share of economists have little new to offer the policy debate.

In the intervening period, however, those economists who have been most active in studying processes of technological change have learned that technology transfer is problematic, that science is the product, as well as the source, of technological development, and that markets often produce technologies that seem less than fit for purpose or downright harmful. Moreover, they have learned that the consequences of liberal free trade policies are not only that trade improves living standards but also that trade raises concerns that trading partners, with whom almost all countries are increasingly interdependent, will be more competitive, leaving some countries with catering and retail sales as the primary employment opportunities for the next generation. During the 1980s and 1990s, the competitiveness agenda emerged as the single greatest impetus for technology policy and it continues to be highly influential. To some extent, however, the more strident features of the competitiveness agenda have begun to be muted by the recognition that a global division of labour continues to support the growth of specializations and intra-industry trade which, in turn, supports economic growth and employment. In addition, developments such as global climate change and the infirmities of ageing populations have moved forward in the priorities for technology policy. In short, much of policy practice is based upon pragmatic and issue-driven responses to a shifting collection of priorities cast up by economic growth and the political process.

The emergence over the past 30 years of research on systems of innovation, evolutionary economics and the localization of innovative activities and the evidence base that they provide offers a number of new perspectives on technology policy.[5] Each has enriched the academic debate concerning both the rationale and the goals of technology policy, and each has demonstrated some practical shortcomings for policy practice.

The concept of national systems of innovation (NSI) as pioneered by Freeman (1987) and Lundvall (1992) and further developed by Nelson (1993) opened up the area of comparative institutional analysis as a new foundation for policy-making. The NSI approach was an extension of the pre-existing rationale of coordination failure, but also drew upon contemporaneous debates about the sources of comparative advantage, or 'varieties of capitalism'[6] investigations that addressed concerns with national competitiveness and the shortcomings in earlier hopes for technology transfer to reshape the opportunities for catching-up and convergence. Perhaps the most influential contribution of the NSI approach has been its combination with a more systemic view of the innovation process (Kline and Rosenberg, 1986) in order to create a method for diagnosing systemic dysfunction – for example the possibility that public research laboratories or universities were disconnected from or dysfunctionally connected to the industries with which they were associated.

Despite its value in diagnosing dysfunction, those seeking prescriptive policy from the NSI approach have often been disappointed. Institutions are situated within the entire historical and cultural framework of particular countries and therefore cannot usually be reliably transferred, adapted or translated into other contexts. Having confronted a generation of students eager to find prescriptive technology policy for purposes of growth and development in this theory is a 'learning experience' in its own right, an experience that is often reproduced in discussions with policy-makers who have similar expectations.

The NSI approach is also plagued by the problem that when one approaches the practicalities of policy directed at specific industries, national boundaries become restrictive. This is particularly true in the case of new technology based firms (NTBFs), where knowledge is increasingly distributed on a global basis with local specialization inherently interdependent with complementary expertise elsewhere in the world. Recognition of these problems has enlarged the NSI approach to a more general consideration of systems of innovation (Edquist, 1997) with technological, geographic or organizational similarities spanning national boundaries or, at the level of specific industries, the idea of sectoral systems of innovation (Malerba, 2004).

These amendments to the NSI approach are promising and provide one of the bases for addressing the first missing link – the problem of industrial analysis capability – that motivates this chapter.

A second major source of insights into technology policy has come from evolutionary economics. Indeed, the origins of modern applications of evolutionary theory to economics arose, in part, from reflections on the inadequacy of viewing technological change as an exogenous feature of economic systems[7] or science as independent of technology (Rosenberg, 1982). One of the contributions of evolutionary economics to technology policy is the association of value with variety. Evolutionary economics rejects the neoclassical limitations on variety arising from tight market selection processes, which leads to the sidelining of variety as mere product differentiation. Instead, evolutionary economics indicates that variety may generate value by increasing the fitness of a collection of actors facing unanticipated challenges – without it, larger adjustment costs and structural crises appear more likely. A complementary idea, path-dependence, indicates that variety may provide a basis for avoiding lock-in to a stable and inferior equilibrium (David, 1993). These ideas have been joined by similar thinking in environmental economics aimed at disrupting the dominance of particular patterns of urban transport and energy use.[8]

When applied to industrial innovation, however, it is possible to raise the concern that evolutionary economics is uncomfortably close to an expansive argument for infant industries – if variety is sought as a matter of policy, it may require additional measures to preserve this variety long enough for it to gain a market following. For example, the US effort to stimulate a domestic flat panel display industry, in part for military security reasons, involved restricting cooperation with foreign companies and, in part, due to this 'variety-preserving' restriction, ultimately failed in its stated purpose (Hart et al., 2000). While evolutionary economics does create the presumption of a value in variety, it offers little guidance as to either how much variety is enough or when to stop in its creation.

Perhaps of even greater importance, however, evolutionary economics has raised the level of attention devoted to the cognition and learning capacities of actors. By explicitly rejecting the more aggressive models of individual rationality and in enriching the iron law governing firm decision-making for profit maximization, evolutionary economics has inspired researchers to ask hard questions about the composition of motives that underlie the choice to innovate, the nature and reproducibility of routines, and the means by which individuals and companies become aware of technological opportunities. It has also provided a basis for understanding the interdependent process by which technological opportunities and demand are negotiated in both the character of goods and services and the nature of supporting institutions – a process that is often characterized as co-evolutionary. The fact that this linkage is mediated by a variety of other processes than market exchange is of particular significance for dynamic efficiency – a topic to which I will return.

The third idea, the localization of innovative activities, is expressed in studies of regional innovation systems (Cooke and Morgan, 1998; Cooke, 2001) and in specific studies of clustering and the co-location of research and productive activities, particularly in high-technology industries (Saxenian, 1994). At the centre of these approaches is a pragmatic accommodation to the finding that knowledge does not travel so freely as the term 'technology transfer' seems to promise. Knowledge-related activities appear to localize because of a mixture of Marshallian district features, the localized accumulation of specialized inputs (including skilled labour), and the related creation of collective knowledge. This knowledge is assembled rather than shared – that is, the 'community' knows more, in the sense of having a greater diversity of capabilities for fruitful recombination and reconfiguration, than its individual human or organizational components. These approaches have also given rise to a multifaceted understanding of 'proximity' – with geographic, cognitive and socio-cultural elements (Granovetter, 1973, 1974; Powell et al., 1996; Amin and Cohendet, 2004).

Studies of the localization of innovative activities have helped provide some indication of the major changes that are under way in both the internationalization of knowledge sourcing and the increasing specialization within countries. For example, localization appears to lead to a new kind of unbalanced economic development in which activities within countries are becoming centralized at the same time as industries develop more extensive international links and interdependencies (Cantwell and Iammarino, 2003).

Whether studies of localization have improved the evidence base for making regional policy is more debatable. One possible defence is that policy-makers have been much more excited about the possibility of creating new clusters of innovative activity than the literature on this topic would give them any reason to be. To cite one example, the construction of regional advantage is often of a time scale incommensurate with the operation of specific programmes or the tenure of particular governments.

In sum, these three sets of ideas provide the foundation for a more situated understanding of the process of innovation – rather than being a universal, it is situated in terms of national and sectoral institutions, the accumulation of variety and learning, and in terms of location. It would seem to be a reasonable expectation that with this many degrees of freedom, improvement might be made in the design of technology policy. Unfortunately, this expectation remains largely unfulfilled.

3.3 WHAT MIGHT BE USEFUL FURTHER DEVELOPMENTS?

What is missing? The two areas where academic research seems to provide too little guidance (or it arrives too late) are in the assessment of industrial technological performance and in a deeper understanding of the processes governing the decision to innovate. I will treat each of these issues by first arguing that these are shortcomings and then exploring the reasons that these shortcomings exist and how they might be addressed.

In order to proceed beyond a generic set of policies designed to hasten the production or dissemination of new knowledge that might be of commercial relevance (the linear model approach to technology policy) it is necessary to create relevant knowledge about the paths or trajectories (Dosi, 1982) along which technology might develop within a specific industry. In economics, we often discount the pursuit of such knowledge as second-guessing the market or attempting to 'pick winners', a kind of hubris that befalls those who would replace market outcomes produced by an industry full of diverse profit-seeking actors with judgements about what would be desirable. Nonetheless, if the ideas derived from systems of innovation, evolutionary economics and localization are to be more than *ex post* interpretations of the technological and economic development of industry, they must be coupled with some means of setting priorities.

The basic thesis of Dosi (1982) was that corresponding to scientific paradigms, it is possible to distinguish technological paradigms, configurations of complementary technological features that define artefacts and systems, and trajectories of improvements of these features. In effect, nature provides a set of opportunities for progress along these trajectories that humans explore through search and experimentation processes that are cumulative. The tension between the apparent regularity of the idea of a trajectory and the fundamental uncertainty of technology is embedded in Dosi's text. In introducing the idea of the technological paradigm that underlies trajectories, Dosi (p. 152) states:

> if the hypothesis of technological paradigm is to be of some use, one must be able to assess also in the field of technology the existence of something similar to a 'positive heuristic' and a 'negative heuristic'. In other words a technological paradigm (or research programme) embodies strong prescriptions on the *directions* of technical change to pursue and those to neglect.

Later, however, Dosi (p. 154) says: 'it is doubtful whether it is possible *a priori* to compare and assess the superiority of one technological path over another'. The paradox remains.

There are two points to be made here. First, there is obviously some conflict between maintaining that trajectories are cumulative and positing that they are subject to fundamental uncertainty – cumulativeness provides some indication of the rate and direction of change. Moreover firms disclose through their behaviour what their technical managers believe to be the best bets for moving forward, as well as the most troubling bottlenecks blocking advance in physical productivity and revenue growth. Among the ways in which they do this is the allocation of funds and the establishment of claims (through publications and patents) to specific directions of search.[9] Second, as recognized by Rosenberg (1976), the qualities or performance attributes defining trajectories serve as focusing devices for organizing the process of cumulative advance. Indeed, in some industries, such as the semiconductor industry, expected technological progress is 'road-mapped'[10] in order to solve coordination problems among the many different technologies that must be developed in parallel to achieve the next cumulative step in industrial capability. In an important sense, trajectories are observable because they are constructed – both in the responses made to other firms' technological claims and activities and through cooperative efforts to solve coordination problems spanning different organizations within industries. These are both areas in which the sectoral system of innovation approach sheds some light, but where research needs more specifically to unite the indicators that we have concerning technological activity and the characterizations and interpretations of paths of technological advance. This, in short, is what I mean by being able to assess the technological performance of industries.

There are several levels at which one may pursue the knowledge needed for understanding the paths of industrial technological development, each of which involves a different sort of observational platform. Indeed, some of the materials for remedying the missing link of more appropriate industrial analysis are emerging from the study of patterns of innovative behaviour at an industry level. Despite their shortcomings, indicators derived from patents and publications are providing a much more focused understanding about the dynamics of knowledge creation in specific industries. In many cases, what has been missing is the expertise to understand and classify evidence of progress along or changes in technological trajectory. Moreover, such studies would greatly benefit from being linked to studies of industrial dynamics (construed here as the demography of firms comprising an industry), product life cycles, and the decomposition of industries into relevant units of competitive analysis.

Much of this analysis is hindered by the unavailability of indicators or the long delay in constructing them. With respect to industrial dynamics, however, many countries have created the necessary procedures for preserving confidentiality in the reuse of national statistical office, taxation and other company-level data. In addition, in the areas of product life cycles and competitive analysis, the opportunities are improving as well due to the deepening of financial analysis and investor information services. While the quality of data accessible to researchers often falls below that available to national statistical offices and large market consulting firms, substantial improvements are being made. In addition, further knowledge can be gained by more situated case study analysis in the area of 'capabilities' development – the creation of heuristics for understanding the cumulative nature of learning as it applies to specific industries that are situated in a historical context (Bell and Pavitt, 1993, 1995).[11]

Much of the research suggested in the previous several paragraphs is under way in one form or another. To make it more relevant for policymaking, however, there is one more step that is needed, linking interindustry comparison to national or regional growth accounts. As Kuznets

(1966) observed, a basic feature distinguishing the growth performance of individual economies is the presence of a handful of sectors that grow at a more rapid rate than the average for the country. In the 1960s, it was only possible to speak of industries as broad aggregates, and in most cases the ability to associate an industry with a collection of technological trajectories was limited. Today, it is possible to observe industries at a much finer level of aggregation and thus to come much closer to the associating specific technological trajectories with growth rates and other indicia of performance. There are important and policy-relevant lessons to be learned from studies of individual industries. However, it is only when these studies provide a basis for the answer to 'Compared to what?' type questions about recent and expected rates of technological improvement that a set of priorities and mechanisms for a more specific technological policy can be made. This is a feasible task, but it is not one for which current academic incentives or social science research priorities are well adapted. This is unfortunate, because it leaves policy deliberation at the mercy of ad hoc consultancy and industry-led studies, which have been subject to opportunistic capture.

The second area of research that would better link systems of innovation, evolutionary economics and studies of the localization of inventive activities is a deeper understanding of the motives to innovate. In this area, there are two major problems. The first is achieving a more successful transmission of existing research findings from the innovation studies field to the policy-level discussion of economic theory. In other words, there are important things we already know about the motivations and processes of innovation that are simply not taken into account in the policy discourse. The second major problem is that basic economic reasoning has led, in many contexts, to a focus on an overly simplified connection between profit-seeking behaviour and the choice to pursue innovation.

Regarding things that we already know that are not getting connected to policy, perhaps the single most important area involves intellectual property rights. Indeed the economics of technological change field is today having a love affair with patent indicators, which leads some younger researchers and many policy-makers to conclude that patents and innovation are synonymous. They are not. As useful as patent counts may be as instrumental variables for the rate and direction of technological change, they remain (with the ever-present exception of the pharmaceuticals industry) only one element of the process by which knowledge is commercialized as products and services. Even a superficial reading of the empirical findings concerning the range of appropriation mechanisms discovered in pioneering research (for example Levin et al., 1987; Cohen et al., 2000), will disclose the limited strategic significance of patents compared to other means of appropriation that these studies found. These findings, and their reinforcement by subsequent studies, have not however prevented a headlong rush in policy-making towards making the filing of patents a criteria for the success of publicly funded research, or the assignment of patent ownership a central feature in the negotiation of publicly funded cooperative research. Despite sober academic assessments (for example Mowery et al., 2001) of the limits and dubious consequences of such policies, they are becoming ever more deeply embedded in policy-making and the public imagination.

By contrast, much of what we know about the motives for innovation is linked to the dynamics of market growth and development. Most often, firms innovate under pressure – either the pressure of competition or the pressure of falling behind in relative growth. Innovation is most often not the search for the quiet life of the monopolist, but an effort to survive in an increasingly turbulent and uncertain market environment. This has led to a long discourse about Schumpeterian dynamics and the role of creative destruction and related efforts to reproduce patterns of industrial structure and financing in other parts of the world bearing some resemblance to the Silicon Valley phenomenon.

In many respects, what is proving to be successful bears very little resemblance to some of the basic features of Silicon Valley such as high labour mobility and the governance of new firms by activist venture capitalists.[12] Instead, we may observe that some industries develop a dynamic based upon a variety of structures ranging from large enterprises governing a network of specialized suppliers to flatter and more networked structures examined in the 'complex products and systems' literature (Prencipe et al., 2003). These and other empirical observations concerning the nature and incidence of strategic technology development partnerships, the division of innovative labour and the emergence of markets for technology, suggest that the dynamics of firm and industry growth may provide a more adequate guide to innovative activity and its performance consequences than the traditional measures based on inputs to research or commercialization activities. Of course, it may be said that this line of reasoning risks equating firm growth with innovation, and there are clearly sources of firm growth that are incidental such as rises in general income supporting increases in income-elastic goods. These risks are, however, augmented by the possibility that existing measures of innovation, even with the elaborations offered by the various Organisation for Economic Co-operation and Development (OECD) *Frascati* and *Oslo* manuals and the Community Innovation Surveys based upon them, are failing to capture the more pervasive and subtle effects of innovation stemming from market and organizational change.

The primary value of expanding the examination of the motives for innovation is to escape the rather closed orbit provided by an oversimplified economic reasoning in which innovation is seen as an investment, administered by a research and development unit of the firm, that brings new processes forward into productive use. While scholars engaged in the study of innovation do not generally hold this view except when teaching elementary economic theory courses, the links in reasoning between investment and innovation, forward-looking planning for innovation, and the idea of 'return on innovative investment' all contribute to distract attention from the experiential and learning features of innovation, the role of customers as innovation advocates, the role of information scanning and searching, the investment in knowledge as an option and tool of risk management, and many other facets of the practice of innovative firms.

3.4 CONCLUSION

To understand the implications from a policy perspective, we have only to consider the Lisbon Agenda, which, in its current incarnation, focuses on four priority areas, the first two of which are 'investing in knowledge and innovation' and 'unlocking business potential, especially of SMEs'.[13] Here, as in many translations of the economic logic of knowledge investment into policy, the focus is on raising the level of investment and stimulating the level of entrepreneurship (particularly in smaller companies). The actions proposed to deal with these goals are diverse, ranging from the controversial establishment of a European Institute of Technology and large-scale Joint Technology Initiatives to lowering the administrative costs and speeding the time for establishing new businesses. These may well be beneficial actions.

However, in the context of the current discussion, two points stand out as being particularly vague and disconcerting with respect to the issue of dynamic markets. First, in 'follow-up' actions, the report notes: 'The assessment of the national implementation reports shows that a lack of competition remains a concern, hampering innovation and productivity growth.' A report is proposed. Second, also in follow-up actions, it is noted that Europe needs: 'a lead markets strategy, i.e. public authorities must try to ensure that markets are, as far as possible, ready for emerging technologies and business models so helping European enterprises to become global leaders in these sectors'. In short, there is some intimation that all is not well with respect to dynamism, but there is by no means any consensus as to what is to be done about it other than write reports and try harder.

The Lisbon Agenda presents an unusual opportunity to see how the messages from academic research are translated into policy practice. The view is not a very encouraging one, even though some of the ideas are getting through – there are loose connections between the idea of the European Research Area and systems of innovation; there is increasing talk of variety and experimentation; and a growing concern with the issues of localization. In terms of policy practice, however, the focus remains on the earlier generation of innovation and technological change – where mobilizing investment for research and development, translating science into technology, and attempting to a create a population of new technology-based firms were the centre of attention. To move beyond this, in my view, the focus must shift towards specific industries and the forces governing their innovative performance or lack of it. As researchers, we should be building the foundation for this more detailed policy practice.

NOTES

1. I am grateful to Professor Robin Mansell for ideas regarding a better explanation of the motivation for this chapter.
2. In practice, the term 'venture capital' is often used without due consideration of other institutional features accompanying venture capital such as strong corporate governance or high-level managerial decision by investors.
3. For reasons of length, this chapter is considerably less than comprehensive as a taxonomy of the variety of practices – a more comprehensive critical treatment is Mowery (1995).
4. This is meant as a contrast to axiom-based regions of economics, which remain dominant in academic economic literature.
5. Each of these concepts has a connection with one or more of the contributors to this volume and I hope they will forgive me for the rather schematic treatment with which I will treat them for present purposes.
6. Some of these arguments are synthesised in Hall and Soskice (2001).
7. Evolutionary economics is, of course, a broad canvas for remapping the theory of economic behaviour, only a part of which is directly connected to technology policy. Nonetheless, in Nelson and Winter (1982) the features of organizational learning and routine provide a part of the answer to the questions posed by their earlier queries posed in Nelson and Winter (1977).
8. One such approach involves the creation and management of 'niche' technologies (Schot, 1992; Verheul and Vergragt, 1995).
9. Other behavioural indications include their pattern of alliances (Hagedoorn et al., 2000), acquisitions or equity stake taking and licensing.
10. See http://www.itrs.net/ (accessed 19 May 2007).
11. Among the examples of situated capabilities studies see Figueiredo (2002).
12. Even these generalizations are somewhat facile in the light of the experience of some major Silicon Valley firms such as Hewlett-Packard or Cisco.
13. See Commission of the European Communities (2006), pp. 10–11. The other two priorities are employment – in particular, employment flexibility, and energy and climate change.

REFERENCES

Amin, A. and P. Cohendet (2004), *Architectures of Knowledge: Firms, Capabilities and Communities*, Oxford: Oxford University Press.

Arrow, K.J. (1962), 'Economic welfare and the allocation of resources for invention', in NBER (ed.), *The Rate and Direction of Inventive Activity: Economic and Social Factors*, Princeton, NJ: Princeton University Press, pp. 609–25.

Bell, M. and K. Pavitt (1993), 'Technological accumulation and industrial growth: contrasts between developed and developing countries', *Industrial and Corporate Change*, **2** (2): 157–211.

Bell, M. and K. Pavitt (1995), 'The development of technological capabilities', in I. ul Haque (ed.), *Trade, Technology, and International Competitiveness*, Washington, DC: World Bank, pp. 69–101.

Binswanger, H.P. and V.W. Ruttan (1978), *Induced Innovation: Technology, Institutions and Development*, Baltimore, MD: Johns Hopkins University Press.

Cantwell, J. and S. Iammarino (2003), *Multinational Coporations and European Regional Systems of Innovation*, London: Routledge.

Cohen, W.M., R.R. Nelson and J.P. Walsh (2000), 'Protecting their intellectual assets: appropriability conditions and why US manufacturing firms patent (or not)', NBER Working Paper, 7552.

Commission of the European Communities (2006), 'Implementing the Renewed Lisbon Strategy for Growth and Jobs: "A year of delivery"', Communication from the Commission to the Spring European Council, Brussels, COM (2006) 816 final Part I.

Cooke, P. (2001), 'Regional innovation systems, clusters and the knowledge economy', *Industrial and Corporate Change*, **10** (4), 945–74.

Cooke, P. and K. Morgan (1998), *The Associational Economy, Firms, Regions and Innovation*, Oxford: Oxford University Press.

David, P.A. (1993), 'Path dependence and predictability in dynamic systems with local network externalities: a paradigm for historical economics', in D. Foray and C. Freeman (eds), *Technology and the Wealth of Nations*, London: Pinter Publishers, pp. 209–31.

David, P.A. and S. Greenstein (1990), 'The economics of compatibility standards: an introduction to recent research', *Economics of Innovation and New Technology*, **1** (1), 3–41.

Dosi, G. (1982), 'Technological paradigms and technological trajectories', *Research Policy*, **11** (3), 147–62.

Edquist, C. (ed.) (1997), *Systems of Innovation: Technologies, Institutions and Organizations*, London: Pinter.

European Commission (1993), 'Growth, competitiveness, employment: the challenges and ways forward into the 21st century', White Paper, Brussels, European Commission, COM (93)700 final.

Figueiredo, P.N. (2002), 'Does technological learning pay off? Inter-firm differences in technological capability-accumulation paths and operational performance improvement', *Research Policy*, **31** (1), 73–94.

Flamm, K. (1987), *Targeting the Computer: Government Support and International Competition*, Washington, DC: Brookings Institution.

Freeman, C. (1987), *Technology and Economic Performance: Lessons from Japan*, London: Pinter.

Granovetter, M.S. (1973), 'The strength of weak ties', *American Journal of Sociology*, **78** (6), 1360–80.

Granovetter, M.S. (1974), *Getting a Job: A Study of Contacts and Careers*, Chicago: University of Chicago Press.

Hagedoorn, J., A.N. Link and N. Vonortas (2000), 'Research partnerships', *Research Policy*, **29**, 567–86.

Hall, P.A. and D.W. Soskice (2001), *Varities of Capitalism: The Institutional Foundations of Comparative Advantage*, Oxford: Oxford University Press.

Hart, J.A., S.A. Lenway and T.P. Murtha (2000), 'Technonationalism and cooperation in a globalized industry: the case of flat panel displays', in A. Prakash and J. Hart (eds), *Coping with Globalization*, London: Routledge, pp. 117–47.

Kline, S.J. and N. Rosenberg (1986), 'An overview of innovation', in R. Landau and N. Rosenberg (eds), *The Positive Sum Strategy: Harnessing Technology for Economic Growth*, Washington, DC: National Academic Press, pp. 275–305.

Kuznets, S. (1966), *Modern Economic Growth: Rate, Structure and Spread*, New Haven, CT and London: Yale University Press.

Levin, R.C., A.K. Klevorick, R.R. Nelson and S.G. Winter (1987), 'Appropriating the returns from industrial R&D', *Brookings Papers on Economic Activity* (Special Issue), 783–820.

Lundvall, B.-Å. (ed.) (1992), *National Systems of Innovation: Towards a Theory of Innovation and Interactive Learning*, London: Pinter.

Malerba, F. (ed.) (2004), *Sectoral Systems of Innovation*, Cambridge: Cambridge University Press.

Metcalfe, S. (1995), 'The economic foundations of technology policy: equlibrium and evolutionary perspectives', in P. Stoneman (ed.), *Handbook of the Economics of Innovation and Technological Change*, Oxford: Blackwell, pp. 409–512.

Mowery, D.C. (1995), 'The practice of technology policy', in P. Stoneman (ed.), *Handbook of the Economics of Innovation and Technological Change*, Oxford: Blackwell, pp. 513–57.

Mowery, D.C., R.R. Nelson, B.N. Sampat and A.A. Ziedonis (2001), 'The growth of patenting and licensing by US universities: an assessment of the effects of the Bayh–Dole Act of 1980', *Research Policy*, **30** (1), 99–119.

Nelson, R.R. (1959), 'The simple economics of basic scientific research', *Journal of Political Economy*, **67** (3), 297–306.

Nelson, R.R. (ed.) (1993), *National Systems of Innovation*, Oxford: Oxford University Press.

Nelson, R.R. and S.G. Winter (1977), 'In search of useful theory of innovation', *Research Policy*, **6** (1), 36–76.

Nelson, R.R. and S.G. Winter (1982), *An Evolutionary Theory of Economic Change*, Cambridge, MA: Harvard University Press.

Powell, W.W., K.W. Koput and L. Smith-Doerr (1996), 'Interorganizational collaboration and the locus of innovation: networks of learning in biotechnology', *Administrative Science Quarterly*, **41** (1), 116–45.

Prencipe, A., A. Davies and M. Hobday (eds) (2003), *The Business of Systems Integration*, Oxford: Oxford University Press.

Rosenberg, N. (1976), 'The direction of technical change: inducement mechanisms and focusing devices', in N. Rosenberg (ed.), *Perspectives on Technology*, Cambridge: Cambridge University Press, pp. 108–25.

Rosenberg, N. (1982), 'How exogenous is science', in N. Rosenberg (ed.), *Inside the Black Box: Technology and Economics*, Cambridge: Cambridge University Press, pp. 141–59.

Ruttan, V.W. (2001), *Technology, Growth and Development*, Oxford: Oxford University Press.

Saxenian, A. (1994), *Regional Advantage: Culture and Competition in Silicon Valley and Route 128*, Cambridge, MA: Harvard University Press.

Schot, J. (1992), 'The policy relevance of the quasi-evolutionary model', in R. Coombs, P. Saviotti and V. Walsh (eds), *Technological Change and Company Strategies: Economic and Sociological Perspectives*, London: Academic Press, pp. 185–200.

Shafaeddin, M. (2000), 'What did Frederick List actually say? Some clarifications on the infant industry argument', UNCTAD Discussion Paper Series #149, Geneva.

Soete, L. (1985), 'International diffusion of technology, industrial development and technological leapfrogging', *World Development*, **13** (3), 409–22.

Steinmueller, W.E. (2001), 'ICTs and the possibilities for leapfrogging by developing countries', *International Labour Review*, **140** (2), 194–210.

Tassey, G. (2000), 'Standardization in technology-based markets', *Research Policy*, **29** (4–5), 587–602.

Verheul, H. and P. Vergragt (1995), 'Social experiments in the development of environmental technology: a bottom-up perspective', *Technology Analysis and Strategic Management*, **7** (3), 315–26.

4. Increase learning, break knowledge lock-ins and foster dynamic complementarities: evolutionary and system perspectives on technology policy in industrial dynamics

Franco Malerba

4.1 INTRODUCTION

Which is the basic rationale for technology policy put forward by evolutionary theory and the innovation system perspective? In this chapter, I will focus on industrial dynamics and I will concentrate on the basic points of the two approaches. Given the limited space, I will not discuss the market failure approach, already done very effectively by Metcalfe (1995). I will discuss mainly technology policy, although innovation policies will also be examined.

Evolutionary theory emphasizes learning, problem-solving activities and the competences of heterogeneous actors in uncertain and changing environments. The innovation system literature highlights interdependencies and complementarities among a wide set of different agents. Both approaches have several common aspects: the relevant effects of institutions on innovation, the differences in the sectoral and technological contexts and the role of interaction among heterogeneous actors in affecting the rate of technological change.

In terms of public policies, evolutionary theory and the innovation system approach concentrate on dynamics, processes, relationships and interdependencies. The focus is on four key dimensions: why intervene, how, where and when. The why and how to intervene are also basic issues of the traditional approach to public policy. In an evolutionary and system view when to intervene (the timing) and where (in which part of the system) become crucial for policy. In fact policy intervention could take place too soon or too late. And policy needs to consider how established the technological trajectory is, the role of increasing returns, the stage of industry life cycle and the presence or not of all the potential players. Also the side-effects of policies become important in a system view. Policies on specific actors may directly or indirectly affect other actors in the innovation system or actors in horizontally or vertically related sectors, with indirect consequences which are hard to predict and often surprising. These unintended consequences of policies may be relevant. For example, policies targeted to foster technical change in an upstream industry may create such a change in the market structure that downstream industries, in terms of the vertical integration of producers or the monopolization of the technology, may be severely affected. Finally, in a system perspective, a specific policy does not usually work in isolation. Thinking in terms of systems of policies is more appropriate. Specific policies work effectively together with other policies: this is so in terms of the targets and effects.

Given this introductory discussion, in the following pages I will concentrate on technology and innovation policies aiming at generating a satisfactory performance in terms of technological change and rate of innovation.

The starting point is that in evolutionary and system perspectives, public policy emerges because evolutionary and system failures are present, or trade-offs and lock-ins impair the unfolding of the dynamics of new technologies or the rate of innovation in industries. Please note that the term 'failure' here is not used with respect to any optimality situation. From this starting point, the following discussion is centered mainly on learning and competences. Incentives will not be examined in depth.

I will first identify some key evolutionary failures (section 4.2). Then I will discuss system failures (section 4.3). I will then conclude with some considerations on the failures of the policy-makers who operate in changing and interdependent contexts (section 4.4).

4.2 EVOLUTIONARY FAILURES

From evolutionary theory it is possible to identify some key problems, failures and trade-offs that form the basic rationale for policy intervention. These problems, failures and trade-offs refer to key drivers of innovation: technological opportunity conditions, learning, the dynamic interplay between technology and competences, and appropriability. Let us examine each of them briefly.

The first failure regards the failure in the generation of high technological opportunity conditions. This problem affects the rate of innovation in an industry in various ways by affecting the research and development (R&D) of established firms and the entry of new innovators in industry, as has been widely discussed in the literature, from Nelson and Winter (1982), to Metcalfe (1995), to Cimoli et al. (2006). In this situation the government may want to increase opportunity conditions in various ways. Two come up as obvious ones: the support for basic research, and the development of a common knowledge infrastructure (Dosi et al., 2006).

A second failure regards failure in the learning by firms and in the accumulation of capabilities. This issue has also been widely discussed by the evolutionary literature. The basic rationale for policy intervention here is that learning and capabilities are at the root of innovation and technology diffusion, but in several instances learning may not be able to take off and capability accumulation may be severely impaired. One reason refers to the lack of a sufficient level of R&D able to trigger dynamic processes of learning and competencies accumulation. Another reason is due to the presence of an inadequate level and range of advanced human capital. A third reason is related to the lack of diffusion of technical and market knowledge in the population of firms.

In these cases public policy may intervene in various ways. First, the government may support the formation of advanced human capital through the support of the education system, through university training in new emerging scientific fields and technologies, and through continuous retraining. For example, the United States has been an example of a country in which at the university level the educational system has been able to move rapidly to new fields and to create new academic disciplines. In this respect, the support of basic research may also develop tacit capabilities in solving complex problems in various scientific and technological realms, and train advanced human capital. In addition, the government may decide to support R&D in industry in various ways, particularly in uncertain and complex technologies. Finally, diffusion policies regarding information, technical dissemination and problem-solving can be quite useful for the population of small and medium-sized firms, as has been the case in various European countries (see the classic work by Ergas, 1987).

A third issue regards the presence of evolutionary lock-ins and trade-offs such as the exploration–exploitation trade-off in firms' search process, and the basic tension between variety creation and selection in industrial dynamics (Malerba, 1996). These aspects are closely related, and are quite common in sectors and countries. Let us start from the case in which the policy-maker confronts a situation in which firms remain locked into an inferior technology as a consequence of a 'competence trap'. This may be the result of a situation in which firms with accumulated capabilities in certain products and technologies are driven by their very success to remain in the existing technologies and products, thus disregarding radical new alternatives. In a sense, as the evolutionary and the management tradition forcefully point out, learning may indeed lead firms to specialization and success, but by itself it contains the seeds of possible future failures. In this case public policy may help the industrial system to try to move out of lock-ins in various ways: by supporting basic research in universities (with the effects of opening windows on new technologies, increasing the problem-solving abilities of researchers and developing networks of knowledge); by upgrading the level of advanced human capital; and by using public procurement as a way to trigger firms' learning in new technologies (see Mowery, Chapter 12 in this volume, for the cases of military technologies in the United States and energy and telecommunications in Sweden).

Competence traps may be related to the broader discussion regarding the exploration–exploitation trade-off faced by companies, and the tension between variety generation and selection in industrial dynamics. The basic trade-off between exploration and exploitation is well known in the managerial and economic literature. Firms may be characterized by a drive for too much exploitation (that is, small modifications in existing technologies and a focus only on incremental innovations) at the expense of some exploration. Or in the opposite case (more rare, however) they can be driven by too much exploration at the expense of the full exploitation of what has been explored. The tension between variety generation and selection is at the base of the evolutionary process (Nelson and Winter, 1982; Metcalfe, 1995). The generation of variety through innovation, firms' entry, new knowledge and behavior introduces novelties in an industry. Market selection restricts the range of variety through the elimination of unsuccessful firms, technologies, products and behavior, and changes the relative weights of the established entities, through the growth of some of them and the decline of others. Variety generation and selection processes may also concern non-market contexts, which play as important a role for innovation and diffusion as market contexts. In sum, industries may be characterized by a lot of variety generation with weak selection processes, or by too tough selection with little variety generation (Malerba, 1996).

The rationale for policy intervention is that situations of very tough selection combined with very low variety eliminate trial and error processes, and may at the extreme produce lack of progress and innovation because the industry may become rapidly dominated by one firm and end up being characterized by only one view – that of the monopolist. Moreover in these situations the working of path-dependency, global or local positive feedbacks and network externalities may lead an industry to be locked into an inferior technology. Potentially superior technologies may not take off and the generation of diversity may be reduced or blocked. On the other hand, situations with weak selection combined with very high variety may lead to too much experimentation and exploration, with the presence of slack behavior, wasted resources, the survival of too many ineffective firms and limited industry growth. What are the policy options here?

In a situation of an industry with too much exploitation and with processes of path-dependency, increasing returns and positive network feedbacks that may end up locking an industry into a given technology or standard, one policy option is to keep technological rivalry open. This is not an easy task however, due to the 'Narrow Policy Window Paradox' (David, 1987): the government has a very short time scale for intervention, usually rather early in the competition among technologies or standards. The government may intervene by favoring experimentation and by using public procurement and R&D subsidies for the support of possible alternatives to the winning technologies. However, a related issue is how the government can choose which technologies to support. This is the 'Blind Giant Quandary' (David, 1987). It regards the lack of knowledge by public agencies on the features and potentialities of alternatives very early in the technological competition and industry life cycle. In this respect the government may do three things. First, it may support public or private organizations which have the specific task of exploration and experimentation, such as universities. Second, it may support an alternative, so that some degree of competition is present in the system. Third, it may try to develop a 'vision' about potentially new interesting technological alternatives, or set up some 'anticipatory policies', so that research by public organizations and domestic firms may be focused in new directions. Here the concerted 'vision' of Japanese government policy with respect to new electronics technologies comes to the forefront (Fransman, 1995). But as discussed later on in the chapter, a 'vision' by the government is not easy to develop in dynamic settings. Government policy could be (but is not necessarily) effective when it picks among established technologies or trajectories, but it may face a high risk of failure when it tries to select and support completely new technologies in a changing, uncertain and complex world.

Another policy is the creation of conditions that favor an increase in variety through the entry and survival of new firms. Compared to incumbents, entrants in fact are often characterized by different capabilities, cognitive frames and approaches, and bring into an industry new ideas, products and technologies. However this reasoning only holds for the top tier of entrants. Most entrants in fact are not innovative, remain quite marginal and exit a short time after entry. So the direct support of all entrants could be a very wasteful policy. On the contrary, the government may create a context favorable to the entry of new firms – in particular small enterprises – and to the working of an effective selection process that allows for the emergence and growth of the most successful ones. As it has been shown in several studies, the most critical stage for a new firm is not entry as such, but the subsequent stage of growth, transformation and consolidation of the new organization. It is this specific stage that may eventually need some kind of indirect or direct policy support.

Public policy may support the generation of variety through a common infrastructure (standard and gateway technologies). In a way, public policy may create the conditions for the generation of diversity by increasing modularity and reducing the incompatibility among competing approaches, thus providing a common base upon which variety may be increased. This is the role of norms, standards and open interfaces, which create platforms upon which new products and technologies may be developed, and reduce the risk of introducing incompatible innovations. When competing approaches have progressed significantly and have established a rather large user base, the government may push for gateway technologies, which connect often previously incompatible technologies. In both cases, variety is reduced at the level of basic technologies, but it is potentially increased in terms of ranges of product and process innovations. Another way to support a common infrastructure upon which variety of products and processes can be developed is the diffusion of codified information about various competing technologies, so that firms themselves may try to develop gateway technologies. This can be done through the widespread and intensive use of information technologies. Examples of the role of standards in the innovation process are the establishment of the European Telecommunications Standards Institute (ETSI) and the role played by the National Institute of Standards and Technology (NIST) in the initial development of the semiconductor and computer industries in the United States.

Finally, a more controversial and less explored trade-off is the one between tight appropriability and distributed competences. The trade-off could be phrased in the following way. A very tight appropriability regime (that is, in terms of intellectual property rights – IPR) may increase the incentive to innovate and induce more R&D spending in the short run, but it reduces the exploration of alternative approaches, the pursue of complementary paths and the long-run creation of distributed competencies in an industry. The opposite holds for a less stringent appropriability regime. This trade-off so simply stated, however, faces several critiques. First, there is no clear evidence that tight degrees of appropriability in terms of patent regimes have a monotonic positive effect on R&D expenditure (and therefore on the rate of innovation). And this is particularly true in the case of firms with low levels of competences. Second, an evolutionary perspective stresses that the association of appropriability with patents is too reductive. For companies, patents are not the only means of appropriability nor the most relevant one: secrecy, lead times, complementary assets and idiosyncratic competences are other means used by firms. These means have different relevance according to the size of the firm or the type of sector, as Levin et al., 1987, and many others after them have clearly shown. Therefore complementarity and substitutability among various appropriability means with respect to both protection and the process of competence creation, accumulation and distribution within an industry have to be fully assessed and specified. Keeping these remarks aside for a moment, Winter (1993) has shown that in the long run tight patent protection may have negative effects on the variety of approaches and distribution of firms' competencies within a sector by increasing expensive innovative R&D, restricting competition and limiting cheap imitative R&D. As a consequence, in the long run tight patent protection decreases the total R&D done in an industry and the total number of firms doing R&D, and thus reduces the creation of distributed capabilities.

In terms of policy, this trade-off calls for policies that design a patent system that has two features: it provides some degree of protection and therefore incentives for innovation; and also it does not narrow too much the variety of exploratory paths, nor block the development of diverse and distributed competencies in industry. In other words, this means an appropriability regime that is not excessively stringent, allows for experimentation of alternative approaches and limits the appropriation of public scientific knowledge.

4.3 SYSTEM FAILURES

A system perspective is quite complementary to an evolutionary approach, because it links the learning, competences and heterogeneity of actors to the relations and interactions among them. In this way, both static and dynamic complementarities become key for understanding the effects of systems on technological change and the rate of innovation. These complementarities are at the base of the burgeoning literature on innovation systems in its various dimensions: national systems, sectoral systems, local systems and technological systems. From this literature, it is possible to identify some basic system failures that call for public policy intervention.

Failures may take place because a key element – a node in the system – necessary for the working of the complementarities is missing, or has limited competences or has low absorptive capabilities. As a consequence, virtuous cycles related to the workings of dynamic complementarities cannot take place. Rather, agents remain trapped in vicious cycles of low interaction and low learning. Examples may range from vicious cycles in vertical relations between producers and users (or in networks of firms and other organizations) to innovation blocks in some national innovation systems. Here policies are similar to the ones related to failures in learning and the accumulation of capabilities (discussed above), and concern the increase in the effectiveness of learning and the development of the capabilities of agents. Within this view, the government may decide to strengthen the capabilities of a specific public organization (or firm) located in a key node within the structure of the network (such as the university or some government laboratories) with the basic aim of trying to get into motion co-evolutionary processes of innovation and growth.

Failures may also occur because connections among heterogeneous agents and complementary activities are not present. This may be due to lack of information about the presence of other actors or because of bounded rationality which constraints the actions of agents. In this case an innovation system cannot fully develop, and the overall level of exploration and exploitation of the system may be limited. In this respect, policies have to facilitate connectivity, by facilitating the access of firms and other organizations to complementary assets and capabilities. In order to do that, government policy may try to open linkages among previously isolated system elements. There are several examples of this kind of public intervention. One regards EU policies of cooperation and knowledge diffusion. These policies have connected previously unconnected heterogeneous agents which had different competencies and knowledge. In addition, the government may facilitate the mobility of scientists and corporate employees, thus allowing for a deeper and faster exchange of tacit knowledge and skills. Finally, in some countries – such as Germany and the Netherlands – public policy has supported specific bridging organizations that aim to connect actors in the scientific and technological realm with small and medium-sized firms.

Finally, failures may occur in the change of existing innovation systems or in the emergence of new ones. Here the policy may intervene because there are mismatches or misalignments among actors within an established system which is undergoing transformation, or because a new innovation system may fail to emerge and develop (as has been the case for biotechnology in several countries). Here policies may create the conditions that help the effective working and development of innovation systems. Examples of this kind are standard-setting policies. On the other hand, policies of top-down central coordination of the emergence and the transition processes may prove problematic in systems that evolve in dynamic and uncertain settings, because the knowledge and capability requirements for the central coordination that the policy-maker needs to have are often widely distributed across the system. Think for example of the failure of the *dirigiste* attempt at central system coordination – the French 'national champion policy' of the 1960s and 1970s in mainframes (Mowery, 1995; Ergas, 1987). This issue will be examined in more depth in the next section.

4.4 POLICY-MAKERS IN CHANGING AND UNCERTAIN ENVIRONMENTS: INSIGHTS FROM EVOLUTIONARY THEORY AND THE INNOVATION SYSTEM APPROACH

What about policy-makers who operate in contexts examined by evolutionary theory and the innovation system approach, characterized by changing and uncertain environments and by linkages and interdependencies of various kinds? With respect to the technologies and industries in which they want to intervene, policy-makers present several of the features that evolutionary theory has discussed for firms: bounded rationality, learning processes and competences. Therefore, it is possible to identify some failures that impair the launching or implementing of successful technology policies. They are related to the lack of learning from failures; the limited competencies in carrying on tasks; the misrepresentation of the specificity of the context; the absence of a proper 'vision' on new technologies; and the inability to coordinate complementarities among the various actors. Let us examine them briefly.

4.4.1 No Learning from Mistakes and Lack of Competences

As mentioned above, public agencies and government officials are characterized by routines and competencies accumulated over time in the course of their activities. As there are competent and incompetent firms, so there are competent and incompetent public agencies and government officials. They may or may not learn from their policy mistakes. The lack of competences may create serious problems in the selection, launch and implementation of policies. For example, in Italy during the 1970s and 1980s national public policy with respect to technology and innovation was carried out by rather incompetent public agencies and government officials.

4.4.2 Lack of Flexibility and Adaptability in the Course of the Program

Public policy may not be flexible enough in the face of unpredicted changes in industry evolution. Flexibility is required because in an uncertain and evolving environment policies that are launched in order to address specific failures or trade-offs and that use certain types of tools may be confronted later on with a change in the technological, competitive or institutional setting. A famous example of that is Japan and its successful catching-up process with the United States in computers. Here a policy designed to catch up with IBM in mainframes was indeed successful in reaching its goal, but it was discovered at the end of the process that the target – IBM and mainframes – was no longer the relevant one for Japan because during the 1980s the market had changed, moving from mainframes to personal computers (where Japanese firms had major disadvantages).

4.4.3 Misrepresentation of Sectoral Systems, Technologies or Institutional Frameworks

Another problem that the policy-maker may face is the inability to understand the specificity of a sectoral system, a technology or the institutional setting in which policy has to take place. For example, sectoral systems differ considerably in their knowledge base, actors relevant for innovation, networks and institutions, and in terms of co-evolutionary processes. Therefore, the policy-maker has to be aware of the major differences that exist between sectors and of the differential impact that horizontal policies have on sectors.

4.4.4 No Vision or Inappropriate Vision

Given that industrial evolution takes place in a changing and uncertain environment and that abundant scientific and technological opportunities play a major role in fostering industrial dynamics, governments may want to support new or emerging fields of science and technology. However they often do not have the proper vision of the future opportunities. Moreover, contrary to firms and managers, most of the knowledge by the government on new opportunities is not 'direct', because government officials are not directly involved in the generation and adoption of new technologies (remember the 'Blind Giant Quandary' discussed by David, 1987). Pavitt (1987) has labeled 'myopic' those public policies that focus on the short run and privilege only existing large firms and their current technologies (and are also subject to their pressure). When the government is able to construct a 'long-term vision', public policy has the possibility to bring into the industrial realm a view that is different – more general, more related to the public interest and sometimes with a longer time horizon – from that of firms, which is specific, local and private. Therefore sometimes the government vision has proved quite useful in focusing firms'

R&D policies in certain broad directions, in technologies or scientific fields which have been considered relevant for a country's industrial development, innovation or competitiveness. This is the case of Japanese public policy in the electronics industry during the 1970s and 1980s and its ability to transmit its long-term vision to firms' R&D policies.

4.4.5 Coordination Failures

Finally, governments may fail in activating the appropriate connections or in aligning the different actors in an innovation system. In the previous section the failures of top-down centralized coordination policies in industries where technical change is rapid, and uncertainty is high, have been discussed. However, decentralized and bottom-up coordination policies also did not always prove to be successful in cases of drastic changes in the context, because of governments' inability to redirect complex networks, to respond rapidly to major transformations or to answer rapidly to new bottom-up problems. The now burgeoning literature on national systems of innovation is rich in cases of government failures of this kind.

4.5 CONCLUSIONS

This chapter has discussed the evolutionary and innovation system approaches to technology and innovation policies in industrial dynamics. Some key evolutionary traps and trade-offs and some system failures have been identified: learning failures, competence lock-ins, and trade-offs regarding exploration and exploitation, variety generation and selection, appropriability and the distribution of competences. In addition, static and dynamic complementarities failures have been examined. The chapter has also pointed out that the policy-maker may also face failures, due to: the lack of competencies in carrying out tasks; absence of flexibility to adapt to new problems and changing environments; misrepresentation of the specificity of a sectoral system, technology or institutional framework; lack of or inappropriate long-term vision; and inability to coordinate dynamic complementarities within a system of innovation.

In sum, an evolutionary and a system view does not vindicate an 'optimal' intervention or 'optimal' timing and instruments. In a changing and uncertain world governments cannot identify the 'best' policy. They have to engage in problem-solving processes, be aware of the type of environment in which they operate and understand the dynamics of the technology and industry they intervene upon. Evolutionary and innovation system approaches point to the role of systems of policies, in which various policies are used together for innovation and technology diffusion. This focus on systems of policies rather than on one single traditional tool becomes relevant if one recognizes (as in this chapter) the interdependent and articulated contexts in which policy takes place.

This remark leads to one last point. As emphasized by some authors in a different context (Aghion et al., Chapter 5 in this volume), simulation models are quite useful as a policy evaluation tool. They are even more so when an evolutionary and system view is adopted, and industrial dynamics is examined. Here history-friendly models seem quite appropriate. These models allow us to examine the joint effects of different types of public policies on the co-evolution actors and related industries in changing and uncertain technological and market environments. History-friendly models that have examined public policies (for example Malerba et al., 2001, 2008) have shown: that different policies have quite different effects – or no effect at all – on some key policy targets; that the side-effects of policies might be extremely relevant; that there are major inter-industry effects of policies, transmitted vertically and horizontally across markets; that the unintended consequences of policies may be significant; and that the degrees of efficacy of policies depend on the specific nature of the dynamic processes driving industry evolution.

REFERENCES

Cimoli, M., G. Dosi, R. Nelson and J. Stiglitz (2006), 'Institutions and policies shaping industrial development: an introductory note', LEM working paper series, 2.

David, P. (1987), 'Some new standards for the economics of standardization in the information age', in P. Dasgupta and P. Stoneman (eds), *Economic Policy and Technological Performance*, Cambridge: Cambridge University Press, pp. 206–39.

Dosi, G., P. Llerena and M. Sylos Labini (2006), 'The relationships between science, technologies and their industrial exploitation: an illustration through the myths and realities of the so-called "European Paradox"', *Research Policy*, **35** (10), 1450–64.

Ergas, H. (1987), 'Does technology policy matter?', in B.R. Guile and H. Brooks (eds), *Technology and Global Industry Companies and Nations in the World Economy*, Washington, DC: National Academies Press, pp. 191–245.

Fransman, M. (1995), 'Is national technology policy obsolete in a globalized world? The Japanese response', *Cambridge Journal of Economics*, **19** (1), 95–119.

Levin, R., A. Klevorick, R. Nelson and S. Winter (1987), 'Appropriating the returns from industrial R&D', *Brookings Papers on Economic Activity*, 783–820.

Malerba, F. (1996), 'Public policy and industrial dynamics: an evolutionary perspective', ISE report TSER/4thFP, DGXII/EC, contract SOE1-CT95-1004.

Malerba, F., R. Nelson, L. Orsenigo and S. Winter (2001), 'Competition and industrial policy in a history friendly model of the evolution of the computer industry', *International Journal of Industrial Organization*, **19** (5), 635–64.

Malerba, F., R. Nelson, L. Orsenigo and S. Winter (2008), 'Public policies and changing boundaries of firms in a "history friendly" model of the coevolution of the computer and semiconductor industries', *Journal of Economic Behavior and Organization*, **67**, 335–80.

Metcalfe, S. (1995), 'The economic foundations of technology policy equilibrium and evolutionary perspectives', in P. Stoneman (eds), *Handbook of the Economics of Innovation and Technological Change*, Oxford: Basil Blackwell, pp. 513–57.

Mowery, D. (1995), 'The practice of technology policy', in P. Stoneman (ed.), *Handbook of the Economics of Innovation and Technological Change Basil Blackwell*, Oxford: Oxford University Press, pp. 513–57.

Nelson, R. and S. Winter (1982), *An Evolutionary Theory of Economic Change*, Boston, MA: Belknap Press.

Pavitt, K. (1987), 'The objective of technology policy', *Science and Public Policy*, **14** (3), 182–8.

Winter, S. (1993), 'Patent and welfare in an evolutionary model', *Industrial and Corporate Change*, **2**, 211–31.

5. Can we link policy practice with research on 'STIG systems'? Toward connecting the analysis of science, technology and innovation policy with realistic programs for economic development and growth[1]

Philippe Aghion, Paul A. David and Dominique Foray

5.1 INTRODUCTION: AN OVERVIEW OF THE ARGUMENT

The conceptualization of science, technology and innovation (STI) systems has gained acceptance among social scientists and other policy analysts. The appeal of this perspective has grown with the widening recognition of the existence of a multiplicity of interdependencies among the processes of scientific discovery and invention, technological change and innovative economic activities, and the intricate connections that the former have with specific features of any given society's political, legal and social institutions. Behind much of the interest that presently focuses upon that intricate and still far from thoroughly understood nexus of dynamic interrelationships is the supposition that its structural properties play a powerful role among the determinants of the nature, pace and direction of macroeconomic growth. The processes of long-run growth and development, however, are themselves complex and no less intricately entangled with institutions affecting the growth of knowledge and the distribution of information that touch many aspects of human creative activity besides the advancement of scientific and technological knowledge.

It cannot reasonably be imagined, even for theoretical exercises, that resource investments in the 'STI subsystem' will automatically yield steady flows of innovation that somehow immediately 'plug into' economic production systems to yield growth – even if that is what is depicted simplistically by many of the still fashionable macroeconomic growth models. What is called for, instead, is a more concerted effort to articulate explicitly the multiplicity of dynamic linkages characterizing institutionally grounded science, technology, innovation and (economic) growth systems – STIGS, and thus to focus policy-oriented studies and proscriptive analyses upon the complex realities of seeking to stimulate development and improve long-run macroeconomic performance through those channels of influence. To begin thereby breaking down the conceptual walls that still compartmentalize STI policy discussions, on the one hand, and economic growth and development policy analyses, on the other, and which unfortunately inhibit those areas of subdisciplinary specialization from more fully informed and fruitful discourse with each other, forms the larger purpose towards which this chapter is directed.

In order to have any realistic hope of achieving that objective it is necessary to seek a suitably detailed yet manageable integrating framework of analysis, and that exploratory search forms the second and more immediate objective that occupies much of the following discussion. Alternative candidates are available as analytical platforms upon which to begin constructing the sort of expanded conceptual framework that is required. The two starting points that spring most readily to mind here are, firstly, the familiar class macroeconomic growth models and the associated growth accounting calculus that draw upon neoclassical production and capital theory; and, secondly, the variety of non-neoclassical models that are more accommodating to Schumpeterian and explicitly evolutionary insights into the dynamics of complex, non-linear systems. Certainly it can be argued that each can be commended – albeit on somewhat different grounds – for further adaptation as vehicles of analysis that are logically consistent with the pursuit of enlightened public policies aimed at managing elements of a STIG system that is beset by poorly performing markets.

Whether that constitutes a compelling recommendation is an issue that will resurface from time to time in the following text, but should be initially broached here. The traditional preoccupation of contributors to the literature on the economics of 'technology policy' has been with market-mediated behaviors and competitive interactions among business firms affecting aggregate or sectoral levels of investment in research and development (R&D). Those entities are depicted typically as responding to market-generated signals of profitability, and also to exogenously imposed regulatory incentives and constraints that alter market conditions; firms are thus represented as being predictably and passively responsive to the application of a variety of fiscal and institutional instruments that can be wielded by government policy-makers. Conventional usage refers to the latter as 'interventions' in the market for R&D investment, thereby reinforcing a general proposition that each public policy action should be regarded as a discrete departure from some norm, and therefore warranted only where the outcomes of resource allocation directed by untrammeled market processes have been found to be in some sense 'socially inefficient'. Like other bold abstractions from reality, this one has its uses and its drawbacks, and the intention throughout this chapter is to keep both properties more or less continuously in view.

Since holding two seemingly conflicting viewpoints in one's head concurrently generally poses something of a challenge, it perhaps will prove helpful to emphasis at the outset the less frequently stated drawbacks of the foregoing all too familiar abstractions. One may start by noticing that while public policy actions are quite often precipitated by specific events, only rarely do they emerge as unheralded isolated responses, and more typically they find justifications as extensions of previously established policy precedents. The specific instrumentalities employed, and the domains of their application, are likely to be interrelated, both politically and administratively. As a practical matter, therefore, the latter are difficult to design freely to be 'fit for purpose' despite the urgings of economic advisers; instead, they are constrained by the capabilities of existing government agencies and public institutions, while often reflecting the aspirations of the leaders of those organizations to alter their future capabilities, their sphere of influence and, if nothing else, the size of their budgets.

Such recognition and acceptance of the continuing roles and extensive involvement of those public sector agencies in the economy lends some force to Nelson's (Chapter 2, this volume) critique of the habit of referring to government actions in support of innovation as interventions justified by particular 'market failures'; and likewise to his contention that the appropriate orienting question of innovation systems theory should concern the identification of the modes of interaction between the array of public and private entities that would best promote innovation, rather than focusing attention on the question 'what do markets not do well'.

Turning then to the other element of bold abstraction, the 'black-boxing' of the firm for purposes of analytical convenience, clearly it is pertinent to recognize that the strategies of the large firms that are collectively responsible for the bulk of private expenditure on R&D (and nowadays for the larger portion of national R&D outlays in the major Organisation for Economic Co-operation and Development, OECD economies) are far from passive. Their strategies evolve endogenously, being shaped in part by the ways in which they deal internally with the problems of coordination and informational asymmetries – some of which impart a lack of plasticity and path-dependent momentum that render these organizations less than perfectly responsive to market signals and government-initiated incentives which (optimistically) are expected to alter their behavior. Indeed, by acting alone or in concert these firms frequently attempt and sometimes succeed in reshaping both their markets and their regulatory environments, thereby invalidating the supposition that would-be designers of innovation policies have a free hand to plot and steer an optimal course for the industry and the economy at large.

Greater acceptance of these fundamental realities would also have the desirable effect of containing one of the unfortunate consequences of economic theorists' readiness to gloss over the 'internal life of the firm' when specifying models of the R&D–innovation–growth connection: the progressive relegation of studies of the nexus of decision-making involving business innovation strategies, R&D investment commitments and research management practices to specialists working in the sister disciplines of economics – management studies, sociology of knowledge and organizational science. As Steinmueller (Chapter 3 in this volume) points out, as much as has been learned thereby, a side-effect of this now advanced trend has been to confine these socially significant decision processes within the firm to being explicitly examined and evaluated primarily, if not exclusively, in reference to the private objectives of business enterprise. What has been lost in this 'division of intellectual labor' is the important broader social welfare-analytic perspective that industrial organization and growth economics would more naturally introduce as prominent topics for discussion.

The foregoing prefatory remarks should suffice to make it evident that an appropriate framework within which to link STIG policy research and practices would not only transgress the unmarked present boundary between macroeconomic growth policy and science, technology and innovation policy analysis; it also would call for explicit integration of insights from the genre of political economy research that is now being undertaken in the field of development economics, and the perspectives formed by organizational science and sociological studies of company management affecting research and innovation. To reach beyond those lines of disciplinary demarcation will be quite a challenge, especially while trying to keep a foot on one or the other of the two established conceptual platforms that presently are available as initial bases for systems analysis in this area.

We are aware, and so should emphasize, that to meet even that challenge will not be enough. Quite obviously it would leave open the question of whether or not the resultant expanded framework for empirical and theoretical analysis would be one within which it is feasible to design and evaluate appropriate policy measures that harness the economic and political resources of particular societies to support a creative STI subsystem, and then mobilize the individual agents and organizations of the economy to exploit that creativity effectively for welfare-enhancing economic growth. Raising this practical question in concrete ways constitutes the modest third aim of this chapter, for we cannot suppose that we are capable of providing any suitable answer from a priori considerations. To approach that objective, however, we can at least attempt to indicate both the difficulties and the importance of the issues involved. This requires revisiting several familiar science and technology policy themes and introducing some of the specific complications that typically are put to one side, but which will be seen to belong within any 'STIG system perspective' that makes even minimal contact with some of the awkward realities that face the policy practitioner in this field.

5.1.1 Organization of the Discussion

The discussion directed towards those three main goals is organized in the following four main sections of the chapter. Section 5.2 begins with an overview of the thrust of contemporary science, technology and innovation policy discussions – informed by applying the familiar 'market failure' rationale for public policy actions to the sphere of knowledge production and distribution. This takes account of a larger, and rather more complicated system perspective than was contemplated by the seminal formations of Nelson (1959) and Arrow (1962), because 'market failure' justifications now are offered in connection with a variety of research and diffusion problems that involve innovation complementarities, coordination system failures and phenomena such as system lock-in to suboptimal configurations – associated with the economics of path-dependent processes of technological and institutional evolution.

Each of those specific expressions of the modern 'market failure' calls for a corresponding search in section 5.3 for appropriate policy designs and instruments, including fiscal tools and institutional mechanisms. When the complex nature of the problems arising from informational externalities and asymmetries in the context of research investments are adequately acknowledged, it is seen (in section 5.3.2) that a number of basic guidelines for public policy offered by the existing literature turn out to be rather less useful than would appear at first sight.

Further complications are confronted in section 5.4, which begins by explicitly recognizing a number of critical interdependencies between the subjects of narrowly focused STIG policies and other important spheres of public sector action. These are conceived of primarily from the standpoints of their impacts upon education and training, the distribution of economic opportunity, the efficiency and flexibility of labor markets, the stability and responsiveness of financial markets, and effective product market competition. That they may impinge indirectly upon long-run macroeconomic performance is certainly acknowledged in a general way, but section 5.4.1 makes the point that their relevance for STIG policy-making warrants greater attention that it typically receives. The potential limitations of narrow growth strategies of 'technologically driven innovation' are especially likely to be exposed where insufficient consideration is given to policies that would concurrently address those complementary components of the larger dynamic system. To avoid such errors it seems essential to escape the confines of conventional 'market failure' analysis and try (in section 5.4.2) to take into account the reality that market processes in modern economies are powerfully shaped by, and embedded in particular institutions and organizations. Those structures exhibit distinctive evolutionary dynamics that may lead to their having dysfunctional interactions with other parts of the economy system's organizational ecology, as well as in inefficiencies in their purely internal operations. Exploring that perspective brings the morphology of 'institutional failures', and the logic of institutional reform as a development and growth policy tool, within the ambit of the broader STIG system perspective.

Section 5.5 then confronts the practicalities and costs of actual policy design and its implementation. Understanding the basic principles of market failures does not carry one very far in the direction of deriving practical recommendations about the construction of effective policy 'interventions' (or decisions to defer intervention), particular as these have to be executed in real time, and sometimes in particular sequences if they are to be effective. The difficulties in designing 'interventions' for a system of such complexity pose formidable challenges, because at least some of the conditions that call for government policy interventions also imply that important aspects of the system's behavior may be 'emergent properties' that cannot reliably be deduced from a knowledge of the properties of its constituent parts. An attractive path of escape from this conundrum is indicated (in section 5.5.2), where it is suggested that greater recourse should be made to the approach and tools that are being developed and deployed in the field of system dynamics, particularly the methods of 'virtual experimentation' using agent-based stochastic simulation models.

The chapter concludes (in section 5.6) with a number of cautionary words for those, ourselves included, who may hope to become visibly effective in 'directing' the processes of scientific advance, technological change and innovative activity along trajectories that improve the economic welfare and material well-being of whole societies and regions of the world. The 'would-be-managers' here do not stand outside the game, they are inevitably a part, and at best a small and transiently influential part, of these proceedings. We suggest why hoping to do more than avert particularly wasteful or pernicious policy errors that arise from the neglect of empirical evidence in favor of ideological pre-commitments, and from disregard for long-run systemic thinking in the enthusiasm for politically expedient short-run policy impacts, seems extraordinarily ambitious; and that claiming to have been able to do more than that is quite likely to be a risky exercise in professional hubris.

5.2 TOWARD A LARGER DYNAMIC SYSTEM PERSPECTIVE FOR POLICY ANALYSIS

The modern economic case for policy intervention in this area (as in others) rests first on establishing persuasive grounds for concluding that in its absence the outcomes would be suboptimal. That step, which is necessary but not quite sufficient for practical policy purposes, is rooted in the now classical formal statements about the problematic functioning of competitive market processes when they deal with information, itself both an input and an output of 'research', as an economic commodity.

5.2.1 The Market Failure Rationale for Policy: Public Goods and Appropriability Problems

Modern economists have followed Nelson (1959) and Arrow (1962) in arguing that the potential value of an idea to any individual buyer generally would not match its value to the social multitude, since the latter would be the sum of the incremental benefits that members of society derived from their individual use of the idea. Those private benefits, however, will not readily be revealed in a willingness to pay on the part of everyone who would gain thereby; once a new bit of knowledge is revealed by its discoverer(s), some benefits will instantly spill over to others who are therefore able to share in its possession at little incremental cost. Why should they then offer to bear any of the initial sunk costs incurred in bringing the original thought to fruition?

Commodities that allow themselves to be used simultaneously for the benefit of a number of agents are sometimes described as being non-rival in use (see Romer, 1990), or as having the property of unbounded 'expansibility' (see David, 1993, p. 217), or to generate 'intertemporal knowledge spillovers' (see, for example, Dasgupta and David, 1994; Aghion and Howitt, 1998). This characteristic is a form of non-convexity, or an extreme form of decreasing marginal costs as the scale of use is increased: although the cost of the first instance of use of new information may be large, in that it includes the cost of its generation, further instances of its use impose at most a negligibly small incremental cost. Sometimes this formulation is thought to be defective in ignoring the costs of training potential users to be able to find, or to grasp the import of information, or to know what to do with it. But, although it is correct to recognize that developing the human capability (knowledge) to make use of data and information are processes that entail fixed costs, the existence of the latter does not vitiate the proposition that reuse of the information will neither deplete it nor impose significant further (marginal) costs. A second peculiar property of ideas that deserves to be underscored here is the difficulty and cost entailed in trying to retain exclusive possession of them when, at the same time, undertaking to put them to use. Although it is possible to keep secret a new bit of information or a novel idea, the production of visible results that were not otherwise achievable will reveal (at very least) that a method exists for obtaining that effect.

The dual properties of non-rival usage and costly exclusion of others from possession of ideas (or other commodities) define what economists mean when they speak of 'pure public goods'. While the term has become familiar, confusion lingers around its meaning and implications. It does not imply that such commodities cannot be privately supplied, nor does it mean that a government agency should or must produce it, nor does it identify 'public goods' with *res publica*, the set of things that remain in the public domain. What does follow from the nature of pure public goods is the proposition that competitive market processes will not do an efficient job of allocating resources for their production and distribution. Where such markets yield efficient resource allocations, they do so because the incremental costs and benefits of using the commodity are assigned to the users. In the case of public goods, however, such assignments are not automatic and they are especially difficult to arrange under conditions of competition. The disclosure even of a novel commodity's general nature and significance (let alone its exact specifications) in the course of negotiations for a market transaction can yield valuable transactional spillovers to the potential purchaser, who would remain free to then walk away. Complex conditional provisions in the contracts and a considerable measure of trust are required for successfully marketing an idea, and both of these are far from costless to arrange especially in arm's-length negotiations among parties that do not have symmetrical access to all the pertinent information. Contracting for the creation of information goods whose specifications may be stipulated but which do not yet exist is fraught with still greater risks; and, a fortiori, fundamental uncertainties surround transactional arrangements involving efforts to produce truly novel discoveries and inventions. This leads to the conclusion that the findings of scientific research, being new information, could be seriously undervalued were they sold directly through perfectly competitive markets, and the latter would therefore fail to provide sufficient incentives to elicit a socially desirable level of investment in their production.

5.3 STIG POLICIES AND THE APPROPRIABILITY PROBLEM IN COMPLEX DYNAMICAL SYSTEM CONTEXTS

The foregoing describes what has come to be referred to as the 'appropriability problem', the existence of which is invoked ubiquitously in the mainstream economics literature as the primary rationale for government 'interventions' to correct the suboptimal provision of public goods of widely disparate sorts, ranging from airline safety, to control of infectious disease, to protection from nuclear attack, to scientific discoveries. The recommended policy response to the specific diagnosis of chronic under-investment in scientific and technological research by the private sector is that the public sector should first undertake to increase R&D expenditure, using general tax revenues for the purpose, and then have recourse to subsidies that would have the effect of altering the relative prices and private rates of return so as to create incentives for increased private investments.

5.3.1 The Limits of Generic Guidelines for Public Policy Action

A number of principles are advanced as guidance for such interventions, some of which turn out to be less compelling than would appear at first sight. The prescription to act so as to bring marginal social rates of return into equality in all lines of investment (public and private) can be helpful in knowing when to stop, but less so if one cannot decide where to start. Should one begin by trying to boost research investments where the positive gap between social and private discounted expected rates of return are largest, accepting private time discount rates or uniformly imposing a social discount rate? And what rate? – for that can matter for the policy choice when the investment pay-off streams are not monotonic. That these are well-known issues in public finance does not make them any the easier to resolve (as evidenced in the recent heated debates provoked by the Stern Report's recommendations regarding the appropriate way to value the benefits that future generations will derive from present expenditure to halt global warming (Stern, 2006)). More troubling still is the absence of any theoretical warrant for the presupposition that the public good properties of information, and therefore of research outputs, imply that socially inadequate levels of R&D investment will be found everywhere, in all lines of business, firms and branches of industry throughout the private sector. Quite the contrary: inefficient overinvestment in R&D is likely to be the condition that emerges where there are 'common pool problems' (arising from failures of firms adequately to take into account the likely consequences of others' investments on their own rates of return); or there are tournament-like pay-off structures ('winners taking all', or nearly all, in patent races and slaloms down the industrial learning curve); or when imperfect inferences from the observable behaviors of potential rivals induces 'herding' in the selection of R&D projects and consequent excess correlation of firms' research portfolios (on which see, for example, Dasgupta and Maskin, 1987; Dasgupta and David, 1994).

Taking complications of the foregoing sort into account leads this discussion to a significant but sobering pair of conclusions. First, although there may be good reason to suppose that the aggregate level of private R&D expenditure will be socially suboptimal, intermingled regions of excess and deficient levels of expenditure may characterize large zones of the research landscape, making it hard to justify reliance upon any uniform, generic guidelines when allocating public research subsidies to stimulate private investment further. Good public policy in this area cannot be constructed without detailed analysis of specific industrial conditions. Second, and possibly still more discouraging, for government programs to take their cues from the intensity of private sector research interest in favoring particular areas of scientific discovery and technological activity is especially likely to result in further augmenting the tendencies toward social overinvestment that, as was just pointed out, are prone to arise endogenously from the interactions of business decisions among rival firms seeking competitive advantage through innovation.

The latter proposition is just a particular instance of the more general need to listen with a skeptical ear to the advocates of 'neutral' implementations of pro-innovation policies, who maintain that the proper policy course is for governments to fix the aggregate-level market failures by providing generic research subsidies, but then back off and leave it to private agents to be guided by local technical knowledge and market signals in making the best use of the resources placed at their disposal. The internal contradiction in that position is apparent: since it is granted that competitive markets can not be relied upon to get the economy to an appropriate aggregate level of investment, by what magic will those same processes manage to allocate a 'policy-corrected total' in ways that will turn out to be socially optimal?

Of course, the problem of achieving the right distribution of research expenditures among different kinds of projects has not passed unnoticed, even in theoretical discussions of optimal R&D policy. Part of the conventional 'market failure' justification offered for government intervention in the sphere of scientific and technological research and development recognizes a difference between exploratory, fundamental investigations, sometime labeled 'basic research', on one side, and 'applied' or 'commercially oriented' R&D on the other. Following Arrow (1962) a special need to subsidize research of the first kind has been found in its greater uncertainties and the longer time horizons that are typical in exploratory ('blue skies') projects. That rationale, however, abstracts from the existence of two quite different organizational and incentive mechanisms that have become thoroughly institutionalized, and through which modern governments have tended to furnish economic support for different classes of research activity.

The distinct institutionalized regimes of 'open science' and 'proprietary R&D' each address the same appropriability problem, but they do so in contrasting ways that serve quite different purposes that can be complementary in their effects, and hence interact at super-institutional macroeconomic level to sustain long-term innovative capabilities and a country's potential for economic growth. Open science, a cooperative mode of research that treats new findings as tantamount to being in the public domain, is able fully to exploit the 'public goods' properties of data and information, permitting these to be concurrently shared in use and reused indefinitely. This is an efficient and effective recipe for promoting faster growth of the stock of knowledge. Maintenance of the key 'open science' norm of information disclosure within publicly funded universities and research organizations works in conjunction with tying researchers' rewards to the achievement of 'priority' in new discoveries; by inducing more rapid and complete disclosures, the collegiate reputational reward system abets faster validation of findings, reduces excess duplication of research effort, and enlarges the domain of complementarities. It thus yields positive spillovers among research programs in the public sector, as well as externalities that enhance the rate of return on private sector R&D investments. The evident limitations of this mode of advancing knowledge are twofold. Firstly, because rapidly disclosing what you have discovered makes it very difficult to appropriate directly any of the economic benefits that are derived from the newly generated knowledge, the enterprise of open science is completely dependent upon material support from the public purse (and the patronage of private foundations, especially those exempted from taxation). But, secondly, the research programs pursued in open science communities, being funded ultimately by political and administrative mechanisms, to that extent remain less closely tied and responsive to the market signals arising from the utility that producers and consumers derive when new knowledge is exploited for commercial ends. Taxpayers may be prepared to tolerate a certain level of 'science for science's sake', but the conduct of research at the frontiers of science has grown to be an increasingly expensive proposition and the indulgence of even the most enlightened of taxpayers can be exhausted.

Proprietary R&D is the mode of pursuing research that can be seen as the answer to the problems posed by open science. Inasmuch as the unlimited entry of imitative rivals would tend to erode the private profitability of investing in commercially oriented applications research, discoveries and inventions made by researchers in proprietary R&D labs need either to be kept secret, or be exploited under the 'protected' provided intellectual property (IP) rights monopolies. But this is not a perfect solution: although the prospective award of exclusive exploitation rights is conducive to the maximization of private wealth stocks that reflect current and expected future flows of economic rents (extra-normal profits) gained by responding innovatively to perceived market demands, the restrictions that IP monopolies impose on the actual utilization of innovations have a perverse consequence. They curtail both the immediate social benefits and the externalities that wider diffusion could create for future innovative activity. Whereas the proprietary model of research operating in isolation is likely soon to exhaust profitability from exploitable discoveries and inventions and run in to declining rates of return and shrinking R&D budgets, the contributions of the open science sector, by contrast, are particularly conducive to maximization of the rate of growth of society's stocks of reliable knowledge, and thereby to supporting both the social and private marginal rates of return from current and prospective innovation-oriented research investments.

This functional juxtaposition suggests a logical explanation for the coexistence and perpetuation of institutional and cultural separations between the two organizational regimes: the publicly supported research pursued in 'the Republic of (Open) Science' and the commercially oriented R&D conducted under proprietary rules in the private business sector. Maintaining these subsystems in a productive balance with each other, therefore, is one of the central tasks, if not the central task, towards which informed science and technology policies should be directed. Implicit in the foregoing is the important point that balancing the allocation of resources at the macro-institutional level is a very different undertaking than trying to combine key features of the two regimes within a single public institution or private organization. These alternative resource allocation mechanisms are not fully compatible with one another when conjoined within a common institutional setting, because they require different organizational policies regarding the control of information, and they involve distinct and conflicting incentive structure affecting the behaviors of those engaged in research at the micro-level. A fortiori, within same research groups and institutes an unstable competitive tension tends to emerge between the conflicting organizational norms, and the likely outcome is that if the groups adhering to distinct norms do not break apart, the more fragile micro-level structures of cooperation and the informal peer esteem-based incentives that support those behaviors will be undermined (see, for example Owen-Smith and Powell, 2001; David and Hall, 2006).

5.3.2 Positioning Policy between Responses to Coordination Failure and Excess Momentum

The inability of private agents to coordinate their investment plans in order to create mutual positive externalities, and thereby to increase both private and social returns from their respective innovations, has been recognized historically as a feature of periods of profound technological transition in capitalist economies – such as the dawning of the canal and the railway-building eras in the economies of the West. A rather newer perception is that such inabilities reflect a generic source of 'market failure' that calls for corrective policy responses. This reflects a conceptualization of the economy as an evolving complex system, exhibiting properties of increasing returns and self-reinforcing mechanisms in which the management of innovational complementarities plays a major role in determining the motivation for and the performance of decentralized private investments, including those in R&D. It is attractive therefore to consider using the structure of micro-level incentives created by complementarities in technical systems and organizational mechanisms as a means of amplifying the effects of key policy interventions. In that way it might be feasible, with a smaller expenditure of public resources to propel the economy, or some large sectors thereof, toward development along a new techno-economic trajectory that would shift resources away from lower productivity uses and expand the future opportunity set of still higher productivity investments.

This vision encourages the view that STIG policy should seek to identify and encourage certain classes of technology that provide 'natural levers' to lift the economy's rate of economic growth. The recent popularity of the concept of a 'general purpose technology' (GPT), and its relationship to innovation, productivity improvement and acceleration of economic growth (David, 1991; Bresnahan and Trajtenberg, 1995; Helpman, 1998; David and Wright, 2003) could then be seen as an attractive ground upon which to build support for governmentally initiated programs of that kind. It will be seen, however, that there are some pitfalls awaiting incautious travelers along this particular policy route.

The aspect of GPTs that should render them attractive for public policy planners is that they often give rise to noticeably 'hot' areas of private technological research, where those engaged are enthusiastic about investing in commercialization opportunities that they believe soon to be within reach (biotech, nanotech, synthetic biology, and so on). If the GPT rationale for focused programs of public investment is to be invoked persuasively, one should be able to make the case that the dynamics of development and diffusion of the new class of technologies is likely to be characterized by strong innovation complementarities between inventions and the 'co-invention of applications'. Thus, in examining the mechanisms through which a GPT in the shape of information technology has contributed to late twentieth-century economic growth, Bresnahan (2003) stresses that the phenomenon of socially increasing returns of scale that is manifested at the economy-wide level rests upon the complementarity of quite different forms of innovative activity. Positive feedbacks between the invention of new information technologies and co-invention of applications in new domains appear concurrently in many particular markets. Where there are innovative opportunities in two domains of invention, the process is one resembling 'cross-catalysis', with positive feedback flowing back and forth and sustaining a temporally extended flow of advances. The development of very general scientific and technological knowledge, emerging from explorations of certain fundamental physical phenomena in a number of distinct domains where their potential applicability is recognized, in turn, forms a common foundation for specialized engineering advances in distinct industrial clusters. Opportunities are thereby created for further innovations that realize new functionalities and technological affordances from the design of products and systems that entail the convergence of previously distinct technological clusters, sometimes exploiting the complementarities between older and newer clusters.

But these are just the conditions in which dynamic coordination failures are likely to arise from the very structure of complementarities in which the social increasing returns associated with the GPT-based development are rooted. 'Chicken and egg' situations do not automatically resolve themselves into action; excess inertia and the inability of the system to exploit fully the potentialities of the GPT can create an important policy problem. Appropriate policy responses in such complex settings are correspondingly more difficult to prescribe than those discussed in connection with cases involving essentially isolated 'market failures' (see section 5.2.1). They are closer in nature to the strategies for designing coordinated policies interventions in product and factor input markets that are closely coupled with scientific research and market-oriented R&D. The emphasis there fell upon the importance of devising an integrated set of mutually compatible and preferably mutual reinforcing policy actions to reinforce the impact of such a program. But, in addition, it is likely to be necessary for government interventions to be coordinated not only on the supply side, but also to align the development of demands for complementary innovations with the development of supply capacities that will allow them to come to the market concurrently, so that their diffusion into use can be mutually reinforcing. (This was Ragnar Nurske's seminal contribution to the 'big push' strategy of development, which in the 1950s and early 1960s was a popular rationale for development policies featuring complementary import-substitution investment.)

The policy design problem we are considering is thus especially tricky, both because the issues of timing are more delicate and the dynamic processes themselves are fraught with uncertainties, and because one cannot ignore the intricacies of constructing a technically interrelated system through the self-coordinated actions of decentralized innovators and producers of system components. This challenge for policy-making is a particularly critical one where network externality effects are a dominant source of positive feedbacks. Special attention has to be given to the timely creation of conditions of interoperability or technical compatibility, as these permit the realization of economic complementarities and fruitful market and non-market interactions among organizationally and temporally distributed researchers, inventors, innovators, and end-users.

5.4 POLICY COMPLEMENTARITIES AND INSTITUTIONAL DYNAMICS – AND BROADENED SYSTEMS PERSPECTIVE

The economic pay-offs from public programs that aim to promote innovation by supporting private R&D investments are more likely to be disappointing, if indeed they materialize at all, when program design and implementation decision fail to take account of the interdependence of the STIG subsystem with the economy as a whole. There is evidently a need to focus on the more 'tightly coupled' elements and give priority to identifying the ones that are strong complements of the activities or institutional structures that the policy intervention seeks to affect. Complements call for complementary policy interventions in order to promote positive feedback responses in the tightly coupled parts of the economy, or at least to mitigate the force of negative feedbacks that can dampen, or effectively counteract, the intended effects of the policy intervention targets to improve the performance in the STIG subsystem.

5.4.1 Crossing Some Boundaries of Intra-Disciplinary Specialization

We must therefore take note of the need for some coordination across well-defended boundaries of specialization within the economic policy community, inasmuch as R&D subsidies strategies have been found to be rather ineffective when attention fails to be paid to the context that is set by policies for education and training, labour market policies, competition policy and macroeconomic stabilization policies (see Aghion and Howitt, 2005). In respect to each of those distinct domains of policy formation, it would be a signal error to concentrate on detailing a single policy measure while ignoring others that could be in conflict with its contributions toward the objectives that particular science and technology policies are intended to secure.

Thus, in conceiving of an integrated program to leverage the positive feedbacks of an emerging general purpose technology (along the lines considered in the previous section), it would be appropriate to examine how it would fit within, or require alterations in government-sponsored research and public funding of basic research in university and government labs, with the criteria used in awarding R&D subsidies and tax credit incentives, and how it could be reinforced by institutionally grounded policies that train researchers in new specialities, or by adjustments in visa and immigration regulations to recruit those with required skills from abroad. If it were anticipated that the emerging technological systems would significantly alter production and distribution organizations, attention to the measures that would render labor markets more responsive and industrial relations more accommodating of the adjustments in occupational ladders and working conditions that the introduction of new innovations would be likely to set in motion. Setting out to effect 'policy complementarities' of these kinds, however, raises non-trivial problems of coordination among different policy objectives, and the concerns of different policy audiences, a subject that calls for the more institutionally based discussion that is undertaken in the following subsection.

5.4.2 Institutional Mechanisms: Autonomously Evolving Structures or Policy Instruments – or Both?

Institutions and organizations engaged in the creation and transmission of technological knowledge, like institutions for other purposes, are neither fixed nor exogenously determined. They emerge and evolve endogenously, shaped by the nature and the economic and social significance of the type of knowledge with which they are concerned, the interests they serve and the resources they are able to command through both market and political processes. But because institutional and organizational structure are less plastic and incrementally adaptable than technologies, they mobilize and deploy resources to stabilize those parts of their environment in which changes would otherwise be likely to undermine the economic rents being enjoyed by agents within them, although not necessarily by all the agents (see David, 1994). Auto-protective responses of this kind may reinforce the stasis of other complementary elements of the institutional structure and so can work to impede beneficial innovation elsewhere in the system. Conglomeration is another strategy that may serve similarly defensive purposes: institutions sometimes find it attractive to take on new functions that actually do not have strong complementarities with the core functionalities and deeply embedded routines of the organization, yet provide additional access to resources, including coalitions of convenience with other entities.

Yet, being resistant to disruption of their learned internal routines, and on that account less plastic, it is also the case that formal institutions that seek to stabilize their external environments may become blind to the strength of the forces against which they are working. They are consequently vulnerable to drifting perilously close to the boundaries of their continued viability; becoming dysfunctional in devoting their resources to resisting forces that are driving transformations in the system around them, they are subject to abrupt and catastrophic alteration: subjected to politically imposed 'reforms', captured and absorbed by other organizations, or dissolved and supplanted by newly created institutions.

The economic case for 'reforms' of institutions that directly affect the performance of the STIG system therefore may be developed along two separate branches: 'interventions' to change institutions that are seen to be contributing to inefficient outcomes of market-directed processes, and reforms in the internal organizational structures and incentives of public institutions that perform badly in delivering services through non-market channels. 'Market failures' may be traced to obsolete institutions or perversely functioning procedures. Non-market institutions and organizations, that is, those whose resource support is not drawn from their ability to sell goods and products to private parties on competitive markets in order to fund their own operations, nonetheless are not free from pressures that may transform and even extinguish them. Obviously, the same may be said for specific government organs and agencies.

Inasmuch as the research and training 'products' of public sector research organizations, including government institutes, universities, polytechnics and the like, are not priced and distributed through market channels, the criteria for determining where and when to make targeted interventions are vague, and tend to be arrived at ad hoc. Being readily tied to the appropriation of public funding, the policy analysis tends to be framed in terms of tactical choices between decentralized guidance with well-defined incentives and performance targets, or centralized 'command and control'. General theoretical insights from the economics literature on organizational design (see, for example, Sah and Stiglitz, 1988) suggest that where the program involves high inputs of specialized expertise, where information on which resource allocation should be based is not symmetrically distributed, and where activity planning is highly contingent on the uncertain outcome of sequential production stages, decentralization of agenda control and flat organizations are preferable.

This principle seems a reasonable rationale for large, focused national programs that seek to mobilize the efforts of multiple public (and subsidized private) research and training organizations, including research universities, to create a knowledge infrastructure supporting innovation in a new research domain – nanotechnologies, for example. But, by the same token, it invites substantial coordination problems and inertial drag in the responsiveness of the system to sudden shifts that may occur in the external scientific and intellectual environments, or in the conditions affecting governmental or private sector investment support.

There are many instances where a case can be made for internal institutional 'reforms' because the performance of private R&D labs and public sector research organizations is being adversely affected by the 'rent-protecting' behaviors of agents with vested interests. Another chapter would be needed to develop fully and present the genesis and possible solution approaches to such situations, especially where the organizations in question are buffered against the pressures of market competition or external takeovers; or where such extreme remedies are likely to disrupt functionally effective subunits that are trapped within a larger dysfunctional system. 'Reforming' macro-institutional arrangements, such as the legal regime of intellectual property rights, the legislative and administrative law frameworks that structure government university industry R&D programs and projects, and the financing of research training in science and engineering, is generally an undertaking beset by formidable difficulties. These are structures (perhaps 'systems' implies too much in the way of order and intentionality) that have evolved in an incremental, path-dependent fashion, responding at the margins to current pressures and opportunities to garner external support by taking on new missions for which they may not be particularly well suited. The modern patent and copyright systems offer a striking case of legal institutions whose role in the economy has evolved far from their initial historical purposes, and to which other organizations have become adapted even to the point of utilizing them for strategic ends quite inimical to the ostensible purposes on which their claim to legitimacy rests.

'Institutional policy' is surely as important as other classes of government interventions that have figured more prominently in the preceding discussion (section 5.2, especially), but institutions are neither technologies nor commodities, and although economists have much to contribute by analyzing the internal incentives and rule structures of specific existing organizations and institutions, and have developed techniques for evaluating alternative mechanism designs in similarly concrete situations, the present state of economic research on institutional dynamics offers few if any general, a priori points of guidance for policy reformers. Those who seek to stimulate innovation, say, by reforming intellectual property law, or the workings of patent offices, or the organization of research universities, are well advised to study closely the organizations' histories and professional cultures, as these shape individual behaviors and institutional performance, as well as the specifics of the material incentive structures that have evolved (endogenously) within them. In other words, development policy experiences, which involve some immersion in the local culture and a grasp of the inherited constraints on the melioration of dysfunctional performance (without disrupting the routines that permit continuing fulfillment of vital functions upon which external agents and agencies rely), seem a no less promising practical route to success in addressing needs for institutional reform in developed economies.

5.5 FROM THEORY TO PRACTICE: TOWARD A MORE LIMITED ROLE FOR GOVERNMENTS?

The general concept of market failure is no longer a controversial issue and the various generic causes of market failures provide a theoretical framework to identify circumstances – indeed, in some respects, too many circumstances – warranting the provision of public assistance to R&D and other innovation-related activities. While in theory some cases of market failures are obvious, there is a second issue to be considered: the practicality and cost of the policy intervention, because it may well be the case that there are some forms of 'market failure' that, however serious they may be, are just too costly (or too difficult) to try to correct.

5.5.1 The Challenges of Practical Implementation

A prime example of this is the case of a bad coordination equilibrium involving the selection of technical artifacts or organizational practices characterized by strong network externality effects. Such a situation may come into being as a result of some particular sequencing of events in the incremental evolution of a complex technological system, leaving a majority of those affected wishing they could free themselves to adopt an alternative that now appeared to have offered a better choice. But, having got into the existing position along with all the other users, and thus benefitting from the externalities that coordination affords, everyone wants to remain where they are rather than bear the burden of attempting an uncoordinated escape to an alternative technical system. The end result: a system that remains 'locked in' to technically dominated practices that individuals find costly simply to abandon and replace.

Of course, there are situations where the problem is intractable, because even if it was politically possible to organize and execute a collective escape to a new and better position, the prospective collective gains would not be of sufficient magnitude to justify undertaking the entailed social costs of the migration to a better technology. Some bad technological outcomes might have been avoidable, but regrettable as their existence may be, they are not necessarily worth undoing. This is more likely to be the case once a decentralized system has been allowed to become entangled with organizational and institutional practices that have adapted to it, and correspondingly reshaped business practices, and other technologies that form to accommodate or exploit its special properties. The end-to-end architecture of the Internet, a key technical feature of its design that has posed innumerable problems for previously elaborated free-for-service business models and forms of contracting, may be a good case in point (see, for example, David, 2007a); in the end even businesses that are not taking full advantage of the accommodation to innovative applications that the Internet's 'connectionless' system offers will have entrenched themselves in viable niches that they will resist seeing disturbed by a radically reconfigured high-speed network design.

The lesson for thinking about STIG policies in an historical framework is that one is led away from a static analysis of whether or not to intervene, on the evidence that there is market failure and a better arrangement is conceivable if one could start again with a clean slate. Policy decisions will look different when the options are evaluated at different points in time, that is to say, at different moments in the development of a new scientific field, or in the diffusion of a novel technology. In general, thinking ahead and exercising some leverage on the process in its early stages entails smaller resource costs than will be required for corrective actions subsequently. The only problem with acting on advice is the comparative dearth of information about what one should do at the moments when policy actions would have greatest potency. But it is interesting to observe that it is in just such situations, where public policy-makers are most inclined to hesitate, that business entrepreneurs infused with robust motivations will be inclined to plunge into risky innovative ventures – especially when they have the use of other people's money to do it.

Another important practical challenge concerns the correction of coordination failures, which was identified above as an important potential obstacle to the full deployment of a GPT (Klette and Moen, 2000). Understanding the basic principles of coordination problems does not lead directly to useful conclusions about how to construct a suitable technology policy response. The practical implementation of a policy involves answering more than a simple set of questions: what activities in what firms need to be coordinated, and in what way? The appropriate choice of policy tools also requires a detailed technical grasp of the externalities and the innovative complementarities involved. Some economists have emphasized that the informational requirements at a practical level raise serious questions about the feasibility of government policy to correct coordination failures in the real world. For instance, Matsuyama (1998) argues that coordination problems are pervasive phenomena, and that economists' articulation of these problems by means of simplistic game-theoretic models tends to trivialize the coordination difficulties that face policy-makers. In real coordination problems, the nature of the 'game', the pay-off structure, the identity of the players and even their number are often unknown to the policy-maker.

But while policy-makers are seen to face immense difficulties in the course of the practical program implementation, it is not at all obvious that managers of large firms are always better situated; they may be unable to implement cooperative solutions through negotiations and contractual relationships. The latter is the Coasean route to solving such coordination problems through market mechanisms. As a result, the appreciation of the costs of practical implementation and the appreciation of a possibility of a solution provided through market mechanisms point to a similar conclusion about the limited role for governments to act effectively to overcome coordination failures that diminish the returns on public and private investments in science, technology and innovation.

The US government role as a successful coordinator in the case of information technology (IT) is often taken as an example of what government should do in other fields. That case, however, involved a very particular context characterized by a strong identification of R&D investments in computer and computer networking technologies with a specific, high-priority government mission (national security). It seems that the US government has had difficulties replicating that performance in other areas. Perhaps the repeated failures in energy technology R&D and diffusion policy (see, for example, Jaffe et al., 2003) are attributable to the absence of a strong link between R&D public spending and a government mission that can mobilize broad political support (Mowery, 2006).

5.5.2 Some Tools to Enhance the Art of Managing the Complex System Dynamics of Innovation

The theory of technology policy is pretty good. Unfortunately, understanding the basic principles of market failures, coordination failures and policy complementarities does not take one very far in the direction of useful, practical conclusions about how to construct technology policy. There is a broad open research agenda which has to address such implementation issues.

'System dynamics' theory offers a method for understanding the dynamic behavior of complex systems. The basis of the method is the recognition that the structure of any system, the many circular, interlocking, sometimes time-delayed relationships among its components, is often just as important in determining its behavior as the individual components themselves. It has been pointed out that there are some features that are especially prominent in STIG and other tightly coupled subsystems of modern economies, particularly non-convexities due to indivisibilities and externalities that create a multiplicity of 'attractors' or local equilibrium states (or paths in a dynamical system). In addition, the amplifying effects of positive feedback can produce strong non-linearities in the responses of agents, or whole subsystems, making it possible that the instabilities created by these feedbacks result in unexpectedly abrupt and discontinuous transitions, formal mathematical 'catastrophes', between markedly different states of the system. Thus, it would be reckless to ignore the potential for surprising and perverse outcomes to emerge from what may appear to the unschooled policy-planner to be smooth, incremental adjustments in incentives, or local targets, or a program of gradual modification of regulatory constraints intended to improve the performance of a particular regional market or institutions.

Recognizing the possibility that things may go badly awry, without being able to explore how sensitive the system is to modifications in one or several of its structures, may not be such a good thing as it sounds at first. The problem is that a 'little bit of knowledge' is likely to encourage policy inaction. Yet, as business decision-makers understand, or come to be taught, inaction is itself a strategy that can be punished severely by unfolding events that are driven by forces outside the decision-maker's control. Suspending action in a battle requires suspending time, as Joshua's command ('Sun stand thou still') sought to do; but without being able to halt time and others' actions, inaction can be far more dangerous than experimenting with policies, and especially if one acts in ways that are reversible, or subject to subsequent corrective modifications. So we might conclude that an options-theoretic approach is called for: the expected costs of deferring irreversible investments that would seize the gains from existing knowledge (in order to collect more information) should continually be weighed against the expected costs of prematurely making commitments that will turn out to be mistaken.

This sounds reassuring; but how to assess those costs, and how to identify those situations in which a policy commitment that can be effectively reversed at reasonable costs becomes essentially infeasible to undo? The area of environmental policy is fraught with such traps: lakes that become so polluted that they cannot clean themselves, and so on. The policy can be reversed, perhaps, but by then the action will be ineffectual, or will entail far greater resource costs than were sunk when it was first introduced. It was relatively costless to remove the system of institutional patent agreements whereby US universities could obtain patents on the results of federally funded research, as was done in 1980 by the passage of the Bayh–Dole Act. A proposal today to modify the terms of the Act, let alone undo it, is likely to encounter fierce lobbying resistance, if not from the administrators of some of the universities that were lucky and smart enough to learn how to benefit from the new regime, then from an entire new profession of university technology managers who have their own professional association (AUTM), complete with a newsletter, offices in Washington, DC, and plans to open branches in Europe (see David 2007b, for further discussion).

Clearly, some among these effects can be modeled in anticipation, and simulation exercises would provide a framework in which to assemble and integrate empirical information about the behavior of various parts of the institutional, environmental, demographic and governmental systems that will interact. Moreover, the construction of the apparatus for such modeling exercises will force researchers to pay attention not only to how subsystems are linked with one another, but also to the vital question of the time lags and adjustment speeds that govern the propagation of responses throughout the system. This will expose many of the worst conceits and delusions of policy advocacy that involve abstracting from the question of how long it would take before the promised effects are realized. That will not make getting government ministers and legislators to adopt sound STIG policies any easier, because most of the policies' results will emerge much too far in the future to be of immediate political interest. But, at least, it would contribute to clearing the air of the promises that this or this particular legal, institutional reform, administrative rule or tax measure affecting the funding of academic science or corporate R&D, or both, will combat current unemployment, stimulate new firm growth, or reduce infant mortality in time for the next election campaign.

5.6 CONCLUDING CAUTIONS ABOUT THE AMBITIONS OF STIG POLICY RESEARCH AND PRACTICE

Technology and innovation policy for growth is widely accepted, but it immediately becomes politically controversial when its implementation goes beyond the support of exploratory and 'far-from-commercialization' research, and enters into specific details that are perceived to have differential effects on particular markets, institutions and industries. There are good reasons for caution in entering those realms, but the growth potential of R&D and innovation is too clear to abandon policy efforts simply because they are difficult to implement, or politically too charged. It is thus critical to try different ways of structuring policy in this area so as to minimize the array of conceptual and practical policy challenges that are entailed. This chapter has sought to confront these challenges by addressing the issue of practical implementation of correcting market failures, and policy coordination failures, by finding an appropriate systems paradigm and (simulation) tools to work within it to assess the dynamics of interactions among policy initiatives, and finally, by addressing the problems of practical policy evaluation.

The last words are saved for those who aspire to become visibly effective agents in directing the processes of scientific advance, technological change and innovation along trajectories so as to contribute to improving the economic welfare and material well-being of whole societies and nations. Palpable effects of public agency interventions in STIG processes are not likely to translate into political credits within the time frame within which practical politicians and public servants in representative democracies have to function, except if their objectives are confined to redistributing claims of resources gathered by taxation among their respective constituencies. In the realms where creating new scientific and technological knowledge and finding ways to use it are essential, the advances are incremental and cumulative, and the assignment of responsibilities for significant successes are retrospective rather than contemporaneous. Moreover, in complex, contingent and at best partially understood dynamical processes, individuals who hope to claim responsibility for changing the system's 'performance' for the better are all too likely to find that they are the targets of blame (albeit in many instances equally unjustified) for outcomes that were unanticipated and unwanted.

NOTE

1. This chapter draws upon the authors' longer article, 'Science, technology and innovation policy for economic growth: linking policy research and practice in "STIG systems"', forthcoming in *Research Policy* (Special Issue from the SPRU 40th Anniversary Conference on The Future of Science, Technology and Innovation Policy). (Preprint available as SIEPR Policy Paper No. 06-039, July 2007, at: http://siepr.stanford.edu/papers/pdf/06-039.html.) Comments and suggestions received from W. Edward Steinmueller, Nick von Tunzelmann, Giovani Dosi and others participant on the occasion of the SPRU conference, and further useful commentaries on subsequent drafts from Olivier Goddard, Lawrence Goulder, Ben Martin, Richard Nelson and Luc Soete are acknowledged gratefully. Not all of this help could be absorbed, and those who kindly offered it should not be implicated in the views expressed herein.

REFERENCES

Aghion, P. and P. Howitt (1998), *Endogenous Growth Theory*, Cambridge, MA: MIT Press.

Aghion, P. and P. Howitt (2005), 'Appropriate growth policy: a unifying framework', the 2005 J.A. Schumpeter lecture, 20th Annual Congress of the European Economic Association, Amsterdam.

Arrow, K.J. (1962), 'Economic welfare and the allocation of resources for inventions', in NBER (ed.), *The Rate and Direction of Inventive Activity: Economic and Social Factors*, Princeton, NJ: Princeton University Press, pp. 609–25.

Bresnahan, T.F. (2003), 'The mechanisms of information technology's contribution to economic growth', in J.-P. Touffut (ed.), *Institutions, Innovation and Growth*, Cheltenham, UK and Northampton, MA, USA: Edward Elgar, pp. 116–41.

Bresnahan, T.F. and M. Trajtenberg (1995), 'General purpose technologies: engines of growth', *Journal of Econometrics*, **65**, 83–108.

Dasgupta, P. and P.A. David (1994), 'Toward a new economics of science', *Research Policy*, **23** (5), 487–521.

Dasgupta, P. and E. Maskin (1987), 'The simple economics of research portfolios', *Economic Journal*, **97** (387), 581–95.

David, P.A. (1991), 'General purpose engines, investment, and productivity growth: from the dynamo revolution to the computer revolution', in E. Deiaco, E. Hörnel and G. Vickery (eds), *Technology and Investment: Crucial Issues for the 90s*, London: Pinter Publishers, pp. 141–54.

David, P.A. (1993), 'Knowledge, property and the system dynamics of technological change', in L. Summers and S. Shah (eds), *Proceedings of the World Bank Annual Conference on Development Economics: 1992*, (Supplement to the *World Bank Economic Review*), Washington, DC: International Bank for Reconstruction and Development, pp. 215–48.

David, P.A. (1994), 'Why are institutions the "carriers of history"? Path-dependence and the evolution of conventions, organisations and institutions', *Structural Change and Economic Dynamics*, **5** (2), 205–20.

David, P.A. (2007a), 'Economic policy analysis and the Internet: coming to terms with a telecommunications anomaly', in C. Ciborra, R.E. Mansell, D. Quah and R. Silverstone (eds), *Oxford Handbook on Information and Communication Technologies*, Oxford: Oxford University Press, pp. 148–67.

David, P.A. (2007b), 'Innovation and Europe's academic institutions: second thoughts about embracing the Bayh–Dole Regime', in F. Malerba and S. Brusoni (eds), *Perspectives on Innovation*, Cambridge: Cambridge University Press, pp. 251–78. (Preprint available as SIEPR Policy Paper 04-027 at: http://siepr.stanford.edu/papers/pdf/04-27.html.)

David, P.A. and B.H. Hall (2006), 'Property and the pursuit of knowledge: IPR issues affecting scientific research', *Research Policy*, **35** (6), (Special Issue, Guest-edited by P.A. David and B.H. Hall), 767–71.

David, P.A. and G. Wright (2003), 'General purpose technologies and surges in productivity: historical reflections on the future of the ICT revolution', in P.A. David and M. Thomas (eds), *The Economic Future in Historical Perspective*, Oxford: Oxford University Press for the British Academy, pp. 135–66.

Helpman, E. (ed.) (1998), *General Purpose Technologies and Economic Growth*, Cambridge, MA: MIT Press.

Jaffe, A.B., R.G. Newell and R.N. Stavins (2003), 'Technology policy for energy and the environment', Paper from the NBER Meeting on Innovation Policy and the Economy, April.

Klette, J. and J. Moen (2000), 'From growth theory to technology policy: coordination problems in theory and practice', University of Oslo, draft.

Matsuyama, K. (1998), 'Economic development as coordination problems', in M. Aoki, H.-K. Kim and M. Okuno-Fujiwara (eds), *The Role of Government in East Asian Economic Development: Comparative Institutional Analysis*, Oxford: Oxford University Press, pp. 134–60.

Mowery, D.C. (2006), 'Lessons from the history of federal R&D policy for an "Energy Arpa"', Committee on Science, US House of Representatives.

Nelson, R.R. (1959), 'The simple economics of basic scientific research', *Journal of Political Economy*, **67**, 297–306.

Owen-Smith, J. and W.W. Powell (2001), 'Careers and contradictions: faculty responses to the transformation of knowledge and its uses in the life sciences', *Research in the Sociology of Work*, **10** (Special Issue on 'The Transformation of Work', ed. Steven Vallas), 109–140.

Romer, P.M. (1990), 'Endogenous technological change', *Journal of Political Economy*, **98** (5), S71–S102.

Sah, R.K. and J.E. Stiglitz (1988), 'Committees, hierarchies and polyarchies', *The Economic Journal*, **98** (39), 451–70.

Stern, N. (2006), *The Economics of Climate Change: The Stern Review*, HM Treasury, Cambridge: Cambridge University Press.

6. Comments[1]

Dietmar Harhoff

Thank you for allowing me to comment on the topic of Part I of the book and on three of the contributions. Our colleagues have contributed interesting and thought-provoking chapters. Some of the results they have discussed are based on long-standing and very fertile research programmes that they have initiated over the last decades. Some of the concepts have even become household names in innovation research: evolutionary theories of innovation and national systems of innovation, to name the two most prominent ones. These concepts have received considerable attention, both in the scientific community and in policy debates, and sometimes more in the latter than in the former. As researchers in economics, we are sometimes troubled by the fact that our theories and results are not being taken up by policy-makers. One can interpret this either as a response driven by academic vanity, or as a justified critique of the ignorance that some policy-makers portray. The observation may also demonstrate how badly we as researchers communicate our concepts to the policy community. But one of my concerns is the case in which a theory or concept is more cheerfully embraced by policy-makers than by other scientists – and not for the sake of its clarity and other virtues, but because of its flexibility in use. I will come back to this point later on.

Advice from innovation researchers is currently very much sought after by policy-makers. There appears to be a real need or at least a desire in policy circles to hear some guidance as to what measures should be undertaken in the realm of technology policy. Since I think that this is too narrow a term, I will refer to it as 'innovation policy' (as most policy-makers do in these days), and even if it is just for the reason that the term 'technology' may divert our attention from the fact that knowledge-driven services are nowadays the most important and dynamic sector in industrialized economies.

To simplify somewhat, let us assume that our policy-maker's first and foremost problem is to determine what measures should be undertaken (if any) to support science and innovation, and then, of course, to administer them effectively. That should resonate with some of the policy objectives discussed by the authors of Chapters 2, 3 and 4. A related question is of course 'how much' of these measures to provide as public support. In other words: can we do too much of a good thing? The latter question is usually neglected in policy circles – budget constraints take care of it. But it is an important normative question, and hence we need a framework that allows us to make normative statements when we want to deliver guidance to policy-makers. A kind of a policy repair shop (repair a little here, cut a little there) would not be satisfactory. As Dick Nelson points out in his conclusions to Chapter 2, an economic theory should deliver frameworks. I would like to add: not just patchwork.

This is of course the very positive, idealistic interpretation of what policy-makers would like to see and what economic theory can or should deliver. Along these lines we can discuss (and the authors do that) which framework is particularly well suited for the job. All three have preferences for thinking in terms of innovation systems and for using the concept of evolutionary change. I will quarrel with some of their propositions below, but many of their statements have my sympathy. However, a black-and-white juxtaposition of neoclassical versus evolutionary theories does not strike me as helpful.

As I pointed out before, one way of framing the decision-maker's question is to ask how overall innovation performance could best be supported by the public sector. There is a second type of question that sometimes comes up: how can I best argue as an ambitious employee in, say, the German Ministry for Education and Research, that a particular measure should be undertaken? And how can I prevent another, competing measure from being adopted? Speaking more directly: how can I make sure that my interventionist career-promoting idea will be funded? For concreteness, please imagine that our employee meets the minister in the morning in the lift (not everyone can meet a venture capitalist), and the minister comes in and says: 'What should we do today?' And the employee says: 'Nothing, everything is fine. The complementarities are in place, learning occurs, markets are working, spillovers are being internalized, everything is truly fine.' And the minister retorts: 'And upon what dimension of merit should I promote you?'

Incentives matter, not just for the people who undertake innovation but also for policy-makers, and we should acknowledge that. It is a part of the competitive life in a policy environment, just as there are career concerns in academia, universities, and so forth which do not always generate optimal outcomes. Franco Malerba points to this aspect in Chapter 4, and I applaud him for putting this topic on the agenda. Too little is known about the political economy of science and innovation policies. In particular, it leads us to the question of whether we should be concerned about the ease with which particular theory can be put to strategic use by our career-driven public sector employee. My answers are short: the potential for abuse increases as the theory gets more complex, since it offers more room for interpretation; as the theory becomes more qualitative, since it can be formed and moulded to the problem at hand; and as the theory has less and less content that can be tested empirically, since a reality check may stand in the way of the strategic purpose described before. Of course, all types of theories and concepts can be abused in various ways – the number of market failures that have been dreamt up by the policy consulting industry is enormous. But I remind you that one key element in the success of economics lies in abstracting from highly complex real-world situations to a set of important, first-order effects. Certainly one can overdo the simplification. But I am currently more worried about the impact of the opposite: complexification.

Let me comment on Chapters 2, 3 and 4, without being able to address them in detail. I do not need to elaborate on Dick Nelson's contributions to our field – they are awesome and inspiring at the same time. Yet Dick Nelson is a self-proclaimed heretic. Heresy is quite nicely accepted among the contributors to this volume, and I ask myself: why is that? Is the neoclassical inquisition asleep? Or is the juxtaposition of neoclassical versus evolutionary not all that provoking any more? Maybe, with the advent and surge of interest in behavioural economics, evolutionary game theory and other fields of inquiry, we have become much more pragmatic than we used to be. There may be several reasons for this pragmatism and for the acceptance of what used to be heresy. First of all, economists dealing with the phenomenon of innovation have been forced to pay more attention to reality than researchers in other subfields of the discipline. Innovation is a key force in bringing about change and disequilibrium. How strongly can you tie your own views to static situations if you study the very opposite of it? Second, in economics at large we have had a renaissance of institutional considerations, witnessed for example by the Nobel award to Douglass North. The notion that institutions are of primary importance, in particular when we study the emergence of new industries or technologies, is not at all controversial or heretic. Nor is the presumption that there are serious 'deviations' from our very simplistic behavioural assumptions. It seems to me that it has become awfully hard to be a heretic – and people like Dick Nelson are responsible for it. Please read this statement as nothing else but a compliment and expression of deep intellectual respect.

Dick Nelson may not be as heretic as he claims, but he is certainly very pragmatic in a way. He embraces some concepts developed in neoclassical circles very nicely – he likes the concepts of non-rivalry, public goods, incentives, externalities, monopoly distortions, asymmetric information and others. There is a place for them in evolutionary theories, he says.

And he is right. But he does not say that the virtues of non-market organizations have been embraced in the mechanism design literature – a mainstream topic, by the way – that institutions have been modelled successfully in many subfields of economics, and that sometimes these models look awfully neoclassical. Moreover, deviations from so-called rational behaviour are attracting a lot of attention in experimental economics and other areas. When evolutionary theory embraces concepts it likes, what should keep 'neoclassicals' from doing the same with other aspects that they like? The lines of delineation have become blurred. Let us not contemplate them for too long.

Let me use the language of trademarks in order to appreciate and acknowledge Dick Nelson's contributions. You all know the expression 'I will xerox this page.' When a trademark becomes so successful that it is being used as a verb, the trademark is no longer valid, because it has become generic. In a sense, we all have been 'Nelsoned'. Dick Nelson's success is measured by the lack of reaction to the heresy claim. Yes, there are probably very few researchers in this audience who would call themselves card carrying members of the NRA, the neoclassical revolutionary army. But many of Dick Nelson's concepts have been taken up by 'neoclassicals', and there is less heresy nowadays about them than the (former) heretic suggests.

Pragmatism seems to be a character trait of researchers dealing with innovation, as I pointed out before. But before I praise pragmatism too much, let me return to the juxtaposition of the two job descriptions for our policy-maker. Is the market failure view or the systems building view better in either educating people upon what could be done prospectively, or preventing them from putting interventionist ideas into reality that better should not have been undertaken? I cannot answer that question in general terms, although – as I pointed out – I think that complex, qualitative concepts can be abused more easily than simple, formalized ones. Let me give you one example, associated with the biotechnology debate in Germany (this relates to what Franco Malerba calls system failures – the dysfunctional perpetuation of an established innovation system). In this debate there is a basic assumption that Germany is a country in which a specialization on incremental R&D and innovation has developed over time and prevails. References to long-term employment relationships, close house bank lending relationships and patterns of industrial specialization on improvement rather than radical change have been used to argue that Germany should continue to specialize in this form. Please note a creeping transition from the positive to the normative analysis. The theory of national systems has been used (in my view, abused, in this case) in order to proclaim the perpetuation of established ways of thinking. In my perception, the theory was so heartily embraced by the policy-makers because it gave them uncontested freedom in interpretation and explanation, because it allowed them to defend the status quo, and because the theory was extremely flexible – for opportunistic purposes. This does not mean that I do not recognize the virtue of using the concept of systems of innovation for particular forms of analysis and research questions. But I also see huge dangers when a complex theory is being used and interpreted rather freely. And I am not at all in favour of dropping one of the strengths of economic analysis – the attempt to develop a normative perspective. The latter aspect is neglected in the literature on national systems of innovation, I think.

Let me turn now to two other contributions. Ed Steinmueller (Chapter 3) contrasts three 'classical' rationales for innovation policy (market failures, infant industry development and coordination failures) with three other lines of thought – systems of innovation, evolutionary economics and the localization of innovation. I am a bit hesitant to follow him swiftly into the realm where policy-makers wish to 'operate outside the constraints imposed by the existing frameworks of rationales and goals'. While I happily agree that innovation policy is challenging and that we have to overcome all too narrow concepts, I am also very much a friend of concepts that do impose limits and do not let the policy-maker wander off according to his or her own preferences. Again – the normative element in economic analysis is powerful and productive. And lean diets (alluded to by Ed Steinmueller in his chapter) are good for policy-makers.

Ed Steinmueller is concerned with two shortcomings in the economist's evidence base: first, the lack of effective analysis of industrial performance; and second, our inadequate understanding of why individuals or firms pursue innovation. I share his general concerns – in these areas, there are weaknesses. We can neither measure nor assess innovation performance with superb precision (although, I argue, we can do that with decent precision) and we have only a muddled understanding of the motivational forces. On the latter point, I can see considerable progress that has been made since the mid-1990s, for example, coming with the exploration of motives for innovation in open source communities, to name just one field. All in all, while I accept his analysis of current weaknesses, I do not share his assessment that progress on these two fronts would automatically lead to better innovation policies. Without a normative element, we may just improve the toolbox for the aforementioned ambitious policy-maker.

Let me turn to Franco Malerba's chapter. As he points out, a major contribution of the evolutionary approach has been to highlight the importance of learning, competence acquisition and heterogeneity of actors in uncertain environments. The innovation system literature contributes to our understanding the notion that elements of innovation systems exert complementary effects and interdependencies on each other. Franco Malerba complements these aspects with a number of interesting observations. He points to the question of when to intervene, and he is right in pointing out that that question only emerges seriously when you adopt a dynamic view of technical change. Since it is an important question, this point in favour of a dynamic, evolutionary view is well taken. He systematically explores failures that can be addressed by innovation policies. Generally speaking, his failure types capture situations in which the underlying potential of an economic system to achieve 'a satisfactory performance in terms of technological change and rate of innovation' is not being exploited fully. But my hope that this focus would lead to a return to an analysis of normative issues is not fulfilled – these are explicitly excluded. That leaves me with an uncomfortable question: if policy-makers find themselves in a complex, interdependent world, with multiple trade-offs, with various forms of failures and, of course, with different costs associated with overcoming those failures – how do they make decisions unless they systematically evaluate options, presumably with some normative guidance? Do they not engage in some form of cost–benefit analysis? Economic welfare analysis and associated concepts may be crude tools, but they are not worse than the heuristics engineers use to build bridges. For all the emphasis that the three authors have put on the decision-making situation of the policy-maker – what is the poor person supposed to do when it comes to making decisions?

I apologize for the provocation. The concepts and frameworks promoted by our three colleagues surely have value. Research along their lines will help to expand our understanding of innovation processes. But the research approach one adopts is also determined by the research question one tackles. Can we meaningfully analyse the evolution of industries without an evolutionary approach? No. Is there anybody who would negate the existence of complementarities between institutions when focusing on the role of such institutions for innovation processes? No. But in a model of patent litigation and its impact on R&D incentives, valuable insights can be generated using a game-theoretical model. There is no reason to despise simplicity and normative approaches unless they get in the way of our research objective.

There may be little need to point that out – I have already praised the pragmatism of this group of researchers. Maybe by now, there is too much of that. In the course of the last decades, the various schools have adopted important elements of the respective frameworks and methodologies. Is there a truly shocking, novel idea in our field that we would call heretic? I cannot detect any at this point. Maybe we are in desperate need of new heresy.

NOTE

1. This chapter is an extended version of the comments delivered at the conference, covering Chapters 2, 3 and 4.

PART II

How Much and Where?

7. Critical episodes in the progress of medical innovation

Nathan Rosenberg

7.1 US PERSPECTIVES ON THE LIFE SCIENCES

There seems to be widespread agreement in the United States that the twenty-first century will be dominated by the so-called 'life sciences'. Indeed, if one examines the contribution of federal monies to research budgets, broken down by academic disciplines (Figure 7.1), it is easy to draw the conclusion that the transition to the life sciences has already been completed. Obviously, I have no crystal ball, but we all have access to data for the past 40 years or so, and the trend is perfectly unambiguous.

If we turn to a more detailed breakdown of research and development (R&D) expenditure at academic institutions for a single year (2001) there may be some surprises (Table 7.1). The surprises that I have in mind (at least to someone who has never looked at a detailed breakdown of R&D expenditure at US universities) is that the physical sciences amounted to less than 9 percent of the total for the year 2001 (8.6 percent). On the other hand, the life sciences for the same year were approaching 60 percent of the total (58.6 percent). If we look at the components of the life sciences it appears that the medical sciences alone account for more than 30 percent of the total (31.1 percent).

I do not know how many readers will be surprised by these numbers, but I can only report to you that, when I travel around the US academic world and ask the question: 'Where does most of the university research money go in the USA?' more often than not the response is that the physical sciences receive more than 50 percent. To which I am tempted to reply: wake up and smell the coffee.

In view of these numbers, it should not be surprising to be told that, if one ranks Organisation for Economic Co-operation and Development (OECD) countries by publications in what is called 'basic life sciences', the US is, far and away, the dominant country[1] (US, 32.8 percent; Japan, 8.8 percent; UK, 8.2 percent).

It is tempting – but also facile – to say that the US is a very rich country,

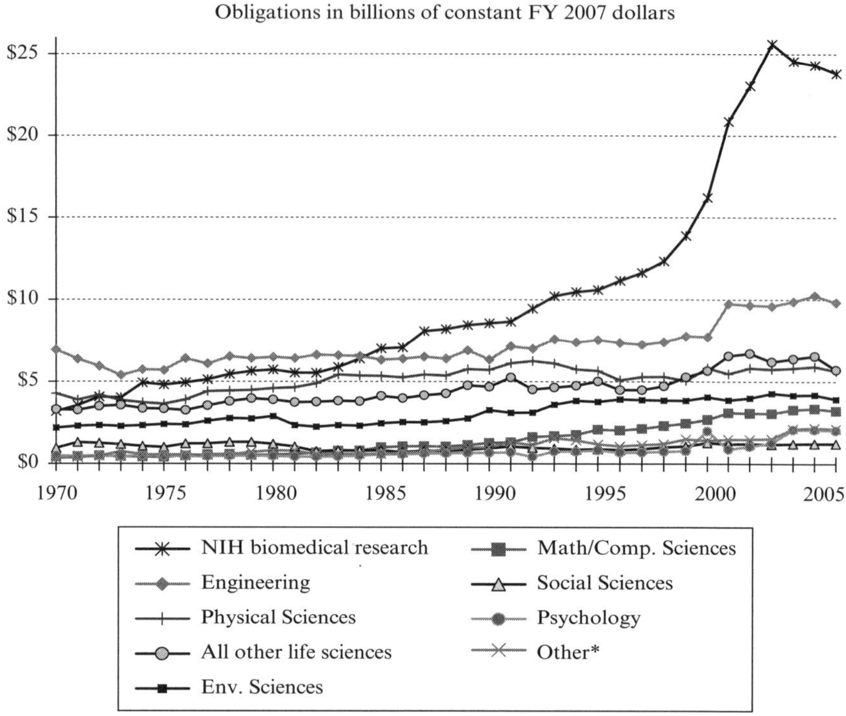

Notes: Life sciences – split into NIH support for biomedical research and all other agencies' support for life sciences. * Other includes research not classified (includes basic research and applied research; excludes development and R&D facilities). FY 2005 and 2006 data are preliminary. Constant-dollar conversions based on OMB's GDP deflators.

Source: American Association for the Advancement of Science (2007).

Figure 7.1 Trends in federal research by discipline, FY 1970–2006

and that this accounts for US leadership, but it also needs to be observed that the European Union countries, and Japan, have drastically reduced the gap in terms of aggregate gross domestic product (GDP). It is also true that the US has the highest share, among all the OECD countries, of the percentage of its active population that is in possession of a university degree. In 1996 26 percent of the US population, ages 25–64, had a university-level education. Canada, which was second, was far below (Canada, 17 percent; UK and Sweden, 13 percent; France, 10 percent).

Having said this, US expenditure on biomedical research remains very high compared to the rest of the world. The National Institutes of Health (NIH) R&D budget experienced a remarkable doubling in the five years

Table 7.1 R&D expenditure at US universities (2001)

Field	All R&D expenditure		Federal expenditure		Non-Federal expenditure	
	Millions of dollars	% distribution	Millions of dollars	%	Millions of dollars	%
All fields	32723.1	100.0	19190.9	58.6	13532.2	41.4
Sciences	27723.4	84.7	16347.1	59.0	11376.3	41.0
Physical sciences	2800.4	8.6	1971.5	70.4	828.9	29.6
Astronomy	378.0	1.2	259.7	68.7	118.3	31.3
Chemistry	1007.1	3.1	660.3	65.6	346.8	34.4
Physics	1236.5	3.8	925.6	74.9	310.9	25.1
Other	178.7	0.5	125.9	70.5	52.8	29.5
Mathematics	357.3	1.1	241.3	67.5	115.9	32.5
Computer sciences	953.8	2.9	643.2	67.4	310.6	32.6
Earth, atmospheric, and ocean sciences	1826.8	5.6	1182.6	64.7	644.2	35.3
Atmospheric sciences	300.4	0.9	232.1	77.3	68.3	22.7
Earth sciences	552.5	1.7	328.1	59.4	224.4	40.6
Ocean sciences	674.4	2.1	447.9	66.4	226.5	33.6
Other	299.5	0.9	174.5	58.3	125.0	41.7
Life sciences	19189.1	58.6	11178.7	58.3	8010.4	41.7
Agricultural sciences	2318.1	7.1	613.4	26.5	1704.7	73.5
Biological sciences	5943.6	18.2	3872.2	65.1	2071.4	34.9
Medical sciences	10176.7	31.1	6248.7	61.4	3928.1	38.6
Other	750.7	2.3	444.5	59.2	306.2	40.8
Psychology	581.9	1.8	398.1	68.4	183.8	31.6
Social sciences	1435.5	4.4	544.5	37.9	891.1	62.1
Economics	270.9	0.8	89.9	33.2	181.0	66.8
Political science	252.2	0.8	71.9	28.5	180.3	71.5
Sociology	327.2	1.0	148.2	45.3	179.0	54.7
Other	585.2	1.8	234.4	40.1	350.8	59.9
Other sciences	578.7	1.8	187.1	32.3	391.5	67.7
Engineering	4999.6	15.3	2843.8	56.9	2155.9	43.1
Aeronautical/astronautical	338.6	1.0	254.5	75.2	84.1	24.8
Bioengineering/biomedical	211.3	0.6	120.7	57.1	90.6	42.9
Chemical	413.5	1.3	214.8	51.9	198.7	48.1
Civil	666.7	2.0	270.6	40.6	396.1	59.4

Table 7.1 (continued)

Field	All R&D expenditure		Federal expenditure		Non-Federal expenditure	
	Millions of dollars	% distribution	Millions of dollars	%	Millions of dollars	%
Civil	666.7	2.0	270.6	40.6	396.1	59.4
Electrical/electronic	1 160.4	3.5	725.2	62.5	435.2	37.5
Mechanical	685.4	2.1	415.8	60.7	269.6	39.3
Materials	450.9	1.4	240.3	53.3	210.7	46.7
Other	1 072.7	3.3	601.9	56.1	470.9	43.9

Notes: Details may not add to totals because of rounding.

Source: National Science Board (2004).

1998 to 2003.[2] There has been no increase in the last few years, so that it has remained roughly stable at around $29 billion. For the sake of comparison, the UK has performed brilliantly in the realm of biomedical research, even though this brilliance has been achieved with only a small fraction of the US NIH budget. The MRC (Medical Research Council) has reported that: 'In 2005/06 the MRC spent more than 224 million pounds on research and training support in universities and teaching hospitals, and nearly 238 million pounds in our own units and institutes' (Medical Research Council, 2007). We could round off the sum of these two numbers to £500 million and, at the current exchange rate say, very crudely, that the MRC R&D budget amounts to $1 billion, compared to the NIH R&D budget of $29 billion.

US leadership in basic research publications certainly appears to be connected to the high percentages of spending on life sciences. But I want to suggest that, in the longer run, this may be the basis for excessively narrow and inappropriate policy recommendations – so many of the really fundamental breakthroughs have come from outside of what we call the life sciences; to be specific, some of the biggest breakthroughs have come from the realm of physics.

A great strength of the US Academic Medical Centers (AMCs) is that they have vastly facilitated interdisciplinary research – along two dimensions: (1) much greater opportunities for joint research, such as between medical schools on the one hand, and physics and electrical engineering on the other; and (2) the AMCs brought, under the same roof, clinicians and disciplines that were becoming more directly relevant to the medical world, such as genetics and biochemistry.

7.2 IN THE BEGINNING WAS CAMBRIDGE

The great breakthrough in the emergence of the life sciences was intimately connected with a methodology that made it possible to examine the structure of very large protein molecules. Such examinations were at the center of the new science of molecular biology. What was involved was the crossing of certain disciplinary boundaries in the scientific world – or at least in the academic world – that were widely regarded as impenetrable. In much of the academic world, boundaries have frequently been barriers.

Erwin Schrödinger, an Austrian physicist, threw down the gauntlet in a book published in 1945, called *What is Life?* Moreover, in the early 1930s, Niels Bohr had suggested that physicists undertake an 'epistemological transfer' in order 'to try to see how the new vision of the physical world changed perceptions of the biological world' (Morange, 1998, p. 72). By 'changed perceptions', of course, Bohr was referring to quantum theory. In the new physics, 'A given object, such as a photon could, indeed, should, be studied both as a wave and as a particle' (Morange, 1998, p. 72).[3] Although the origins of the new science of molecular biology are, with good reason, associated with Cambridge (UK), the more specific institutional location in Cambridge was quite remarkable, that is, Cavendish Laboratory. What made the location remarkable is that, at the time, the Cavendish Laboratory was regarded as the world's most distinguished center for research in the realm of physics.

Before proceeding further with some of the specifics of the emergence of molecular biology, I would like to introduce a perspective that is central to my argument, that is, in looking upon the growth of the life sciences through the longer course of the twentieth century, we should no longer be surprised to find that the life sciences had their critical beginnings in the realm of physics. In fact, such dependency goes as far back in time to the beginning of the X-ray machine in the middle of the 1890s. It should be recalled that X-rays were (serendipitously) discovered by Röntgen, who was a professor of physics at Würzburg at the time.[4] X-rays have, of course, remained the most widely used diagnostic devices throughout the twentieth century. Their discovery created an entirely new medical specialty: radiology.

The list of new medical technologies that emerged from the realm of physics is both long and very impressive. Let me simply remind you by going beyond X-rays:

- Electronic microscopy.
- Computerized tomography (CT) scanner.
- Endoscopy.

- Magnetic resonance imaging (MRI).
- Isotope tracer techniques.
- Linear accelerators.
- Lasers.
- Spectroscopies.

Note that all of these new technological capabilities drew directly upon the growing stocks of knowledge that have accrued in the realms of theoretical and applied physics as well as electronic engineering and, of course, chemistry. Several of these instruments also came to play crucial roles in therapeutic devices as well as diagnostic instruments. I would insist only that the growth of knowledge in physics played a prominent role in the development of new forms of medical instrumentation.

Furthermore, the X-ray machine would shortly provide a platform for a powerful new, complex research tool: X-ray crystallography.

7.2.1 X-Ray Crystallography

X-ray diffraction is a method for establishing the structure of a protein:

> The protein Perutz decided to study was hemoglobin. The work involved purifying it, obtaining crystals, then directing a beam of x-rays at the crystals. The diffraction of the beam and its decomposition into a number of different beams left a trace on a photographic plate placed behind the crystals, forming a diffraction pattern. The theory of diffraction, developed by Lawrence Bragg and his father, explained that the distribution and intensity of the diffraction pattern were a consequence of the structure of the molecules present in the crystal. (Morange, 1998, pp. 105–6)

X-ray crystallography had its origins in Germany, where Max von Laue discovered the phenomenon of X-ray diffraction in 1912. Its applications were, in the early years, employed by William Bragg and his son, Lawrence, in the new field of solid-state physics, but also, later on, in developing the discipline of molecular biology. The main center of the methodology of X-ray diffraction was, for many years, in the Cavendish Laboratory, presided over by Lawrence Bragg. Numerous scientists went there in order to learn how to exploit the technique, including Max Perutz and John Kendrew who shared a Nobel Prize in Chemistry. Another was James Watson, a young PhD. in zoology from Indiana University, who was heavily influenced there by the geneticist H.J. Muller and whose dissertation was supervised by Luria, the microbiologist. Francis Crick, a graduate student who had not yet finished his graduate work in physics, and James Watson, shared the Nobel Prize in Physiology or Medicine.

(Lawrence Bragg had already received a Nobel Prize in Physics in 1915, which he shared with his father, for their work in applying X-rays in the study of crystal structure. He was 25 years old when he received the prize.)

Thus, the life sciences were born in a remarkably unexpected location: the Cavendish Laboratory which was, at the time, widely regarded as the world's most distinguished physics research center. Establishing a 'branch' of the Medical Research Council at the Cavendish Laboratory was an extremely bold decision, which turned out to be a marvelously successful exercise in interdisciplinary research (although it should be noted that there were a number of disgruntled young men who complained that they had come to the Cavendish as the most reliable stepping stone into the world of nuclear physics . . .).

It should be emphasized that inferring the three-dimensional structure of very large-molecule proteins by the new technique of X-ray crystallography, which offered only two-dimensional photographs of very large molecules, appears to have been remarkably difficult. However, it provided much of the basis for the blooming of the new discipline of molecular biology.[5]

There seems to have been a unanimity among the participants during the 1950s that no one could deliver three-dimensional pictures as good as those of Rosalind Franklin, who died very early. Her crystallographic data were the most powerful confirmation of the double helix structure of DNA. Morange has called her an 'exceptional experimentalist' (Morange, 1998, p. 108). She certainly was that.

A primary concern for me is that success or failure of technological progress, in the course of the twentieth century, has involved the ability to accommodate the changing institutional requirements of newly emerging technologies. More specifically, these requirements involved the intimate connection of disciplines that had previously involved few connections or, in many cases, none at all. Since there existed at the time virtually no direct institutional connections between the worlds of physics and biology, bold leadership and indefatigable energy were required.

Bold leadership was especially necessary in the case of Bragg's position as the 'number one man' of a research institution dedicated to progress in nuclear physics under the earlier leadership of the great Rutherford. Perutz recounted his first meeting with Bragg in the following terms:

> I waited from day to day, hoping for Bragg to come round the Crystallographic Laboratory to find out what was going on there. After about six weeks of this I plucked up courage and called on him in Rutherford's Victorian office in Free School Lane, When I showed him my x-ray pictures of hemoglobin his face lit

> up. He realized at once the challenge of extending x-ray analysis to the giant molecules of the living cell. Within less than three months he obtained a grant from the Rockefeller Foundation and appointed me his research assistant. Bragg's action saved my scientific career and enabled me to bring my parents to Britain [as refugees from Hitler's invasions of Austria and Czechoslovakia]. (Morange, 1998, p. 37)

Why did Germans fail to exploit von Laue's brilliant breakthrough? I confess that I cannot offer a cogent explanation; although I can suggest some poorly informed speculations: Germany at that time (in the early years of the twentieth century) still had a cultural posture in the realm of science that emphasized 'pure' science – in the tradition of Kant, Hegel, and so on, a culture that separated the engineering disciplines from the universities. The creation of the Hochschulen in the second half of the nineteenth century reflected the intention of cleansing German higher education of merely 'practical' knowledge. By contrast the British have long had a much more empirical and experimental tradition, as well as a strong utilitarian philosophy, that shaped the direction of scientific research, which attached a high priority to finding and exploiting potentially useful knowledge. It is worth recalling that Lawrence Bragg carried the title Cavendish Professor of Experimental Physics, just like his predecessor, Rutherford.

Some insight into von Laue's strength of character and professional integrity is illuminated by his behavior after Hitler and the Nazis took power, post 1933. Von Laue:

> defended, even at the risk of reprimand or personal injury, scientific views, such as the theory of relativity, which were not approved by the Party or by strong adherents to it . . . When Einstein resigned from the Berlin Academy and the Vice-President of this Academy stated that this was no loss, von Laue was the only member of the Academy who protested. (Nobel Foundation, 1914)

As Crowther has observed:

> The object of von Laue's original work was to discover the nature of x-rays. He and his colleagues demonstrated that x-rays were diffracted by the atoms in a crystal of zinc blende, proving that x-rays possessed wave properties. Bragg saw that the spots in the Laue diffraction pattern could be regarded very simply as due to the partial reflection of the incident beam of x-rays by the principal planes formed by the atoms within the crystals.
>
> The atomic structure of the crystals might easily be deduced from appropriate x-ray pictures. Bragg directed attention to the *use* of x-rays rather than a consideration of their *nature* (my emphasis). He discovered that they might provide an extraordinarily powerful method of elucidating the atomic structure of crystalline substances.

> He first published this discovery in November 1912. The structures of crystals of potassium chloride and sodium chloride were determined, and the new branch of physics splendidly launched. (Crowther, 1974)

Max Perutz, an Austrian refugee, has been often described as the founding father of modern X-ray protein crystallography. Perutz determined the three-dimensional structure of hemoglobin, an exercise that lasted fully 22 years (hemoglobin has a molecular weight of 70 000). On this basis Bragg obtained a research grant for Perutz from the Rockefeller Foundation. Perutz's scientific achievement was referred to by a distinguished contemporary as entering into the 'secret of life'.[6] Bernal was a hugely influential figure in the early days of protein crystallography who has received far too little attention. As a teacher of crystallography at Cambridge, his students included Max Perutz, Maurice Wilkins and Dorothy Hodgkin – three Nobel Laureates.

The Medical Research Council set up the MRC Unit for the Study of Molecular Structure of Biological Systems to be headed by Perutz. The unit was relocated and renamed the Laboratory of Molecular Biology. Perutz presided over the MRC Unit Laboratory for 32 years (1947 to 1979) a period that included the work of Watson, Crick, Wilkins and Franklin which revealed that the molecular structure of DNA takes the form of a double helix.

At an earlier date, when Bragg was reporting on his own professional interests at the Cavendish, he once stated:

> The department which we call crystallography would perhaps be better described as the department for discovery of the structure of the solid state . . . Mainly by x-rays we seek to discover the way the atoms are arranged in crystals and in other forms of solids. The scope of the work is very considerable. At one end we are investigating such substances as minerals and alloys in the inorganic field; other researchers are examining complex organic compounds . . . finally at the other extreme we have a little group which is financed by the Medical Research Council under the direction of Perutz, which is engaged in a gallant attempt to work out the structure of the highly complex molecules which build up living matter, the proteins.[7]

Bragg's leadership was obviously subjected to considerable criticism from the young scientists who wanted to achieve stardom by achieving important breakthroughs in 'mainstream' nuclear physics. 'Bragg was under criticism from the nuclear physicists for not supporting their own subject more strongly in a laboratory world-famous for its reputation in nuclear physics under J.J. Thomson and Rutherford – and indeed for not being a nuclear physicist himself' (Thomas and Philips, 1990, p. 88). These complaints were, of course, swamped when the intense protein work of the period 1951–3 led to the announcement of the double helix structure of DNA. As Watson saw it:

> The solution to the structure was bringing genuine happiness to Bragg. That the result came out of the Cavendish and not Pasadena was obviously a factor. More important was the unexpectedly marvelous nature of the answer, and the fact that the x-ray method he had developed forty years before was at the heart of a profound insight into the nature of life itself. (Thomas and Philips, 1990, p. 48)

7.3 US ACADEMIC MEDICAL CENTERS (AMCS)

Beginning in the early 1950s, medical research in the US could be observed to be moving more and more closely to university communities. Medically related research activities were increasingly integrated into the structures of both research and teaching at the medical schools (Table 7.2). As Ginzberg and Dutka (1989, p. 36) have observed:

> the external funding by the NIH went far to alter the orientation of the nation's leading medical schools in the direction of laboratory research, vastly increased the number of investigators, and by contributing greatly to the specialization that came to characterize the medical profession, resulted in the dominance of high tech medicine.

The contrast with the European continent was quite substantial. The American AMCs brought about a confluence of increasingly relevant disciplines, in a way that did not occur nearly as readily in European contexts. European medical schools trained Doctors of Medicine (MDs) without much exposure to these newly emerging disciplines.[8]

Table 7.2 Growth of US academic medicine, 1960–92 (1992 $)

	1960	1970	1980	1992
Support from NIH (millions of $)	1320	3028	5419	8407
Average Medical School budget (millions of $)	24.1	64.6	91.9	200.4
Full-time Medical School faculty (no.)				
Basic	4023	8283	12816	15579
Clinical	7201	19256	37716	65913
Matriculated medical students (no.)	30288	40487	65189	66142

Source: Gelijns and Rosenberg (1999).

I will draw heavily here upon the Stanford experience, not necessarily because it is typical of American AMCs in general, although many of the trends are widely shared, but rather because I know more about the specifics of the Stanford experience than that of any other AMC.

Before the 1950s, the Stanford Medical School had been located for several decades in San Francisco. The obvious advantage of a sizeable urban location was access to a pool of people bearing a variety of diseases or disabilities. At the same time there was a growing awareness of an expanding body of scientific knowledge of great potential value to the medical world. The decision-makers eventually concluded that the benefits of early access to this growing knowledge outweighed the benefits to the training of future medical doctors of a large human population. The conclusion was the decision to relocate the medical school in Palo Alto, adjacent to the Stanford University campus.

Stanford's new Medical Center (including its new Medical School) was opened on the Stanford campus in 1959:[9]

> The move of the Medical School to the main campus was accompanied by a complete revision of the medical curriculum in which more basic science was introduced. The Stanford Program, as it was called, lengthened the period of medical education from four to five years and included substantial work in basic science as well as a significant exposure to laboratory training. In addition, the medical faculty became a so-called 'full-time' faculty, shifting its base of support from clinical fees to funds provided by the University. Thus in moving to the main campus the Medical School faculty became essentially university faculty just like faculty in the Engineering School or the Humanities and Sciences, and along with this the emphasis of the new Medical Center was to shift in the direction of scientific medical research . . . Two new departments were to be created in the medical school along with this move, the Department of Biochemistry and the Department of Genetics.

In the midst of this major transition of the Medical School, Fred Terman had become Provost in 1955. Terman simply has to be described as a charismatic, energetic academic entrepreneur who had achieved considerable success in raising the status of Stanford's School of Engineering. Terman's style of encouraging entrepreneurial academic activity meshed well with the initiatives that had already been started by President Sterling, Dean Alway and Professor Kaplan in reshaping the Medical School. Terman wasted no time in encouraging the Medical School faculty to adopt his strategies for building programs with government funds.

Terman thought an opportunity was being missed for expanding the Medical School research faculty through government funds in just the same way he had built the Department of Electrical Engineering and other parts of the Engineering School. As Terman wrote to Dean Greulich:

> When in my office, you stated that teaching duties in the Medical School normally took about half the time of a faculty member, and that the other half of his time was available for research. If one could have 50% of this research time charged against research contracts and grants, rather than carried by the regular budget, it would free enough salary money in the Medical School budget to raise all salaries by 33%. If all of the research time could be charged to research contract (which is probably an impossibility although nearly true in Engineering) it would free enough salary money to double salaries . . . I suggest this method of aiding the finances of the Medical School be taken advantage of whenever possible . . .

Perhaps the most striking success of Terman's efforts at building an entrepreneurial culture during his Provost years was in building the new science departments of the Medical School.

Acting on the advice of Henry Kaplan, Terman's first move in expanding the new research orientation of the Medical School was in hiring Arthur Kornberg. Negotiations began with Kornberg in 1957. Kornberg was the Director of the Department of Microbiology at Washington University, St Louis, where he had been since 1953 following a move from the NIH. At Washington University Kornberg had already assembled a stellar cast of young biochemists and molecular biologists . . . Kornberg and his colleagues also had an extremely impressive track record of Public Health Service grants for supporting their research. Kornberg negotiated with Terman and Alway to move the entire department to Stanford beginning in 1959. This was a major coup for the new Medical School, for in the months following his initial acceptance of the Stanford offer, Kornberg received the Nobel Prize for his work on the replication of DNA. Kornberg not only moved most of his staff to Stanford but was also successful in being awarded more than $500 000 in Public Health Service grants to equip his new laboratories at Stanford. Among the group who came to Stanford from Washington University was Paul Berg who later (1980) won a Nobel Prize in Chemistry '. . . for his fundamental studies of the biochemistry of nucleic acids, with particular regard to recombinant-DNA' (Nobel announcement).

As part of his negotiations for building biochemistry, Terman encouraged Kornberg to propose potential faculty for other departments that would complement the strengths in biochemistry, and he invited Kornberg to serve on the search committee for the chairmanship of the Chemistry Department. Kornberg immediately proposed bringing Joshua Lederberg to Stanford. Lederberg, who had been awarded the Nobel Prize in 1958, accepted the offer and left Wisconsin to form the new Genetics Department at the Stanford Medical Center in 1959. At Stanford Lederberg wasted no time in building a program in molecular medicine with matching grants of $1 million each from the Rockefeller and the Kennedy Foundations to support construction of facilities for the Kennedy Center for Molecular

Medicine in 1962. Lederberg also received a $500 000 grant from NASA in support of work on planetary biology that year, a project that eventuated in the ACME computing facility and then the SUMEX computing facility.

From their inception the Departments of Biochemistry and Genetics have been hotbeds of innovation in the field of molecular genetics and molecular medicine, and they have been major sources of the biotech revolution in the Bay Area from the 1980s to the present. This movement has been so important that it is worth considering it as a new phenomenon parallel to the Silicon Valley phenomenon that we might call 'Biotech Valley'. Aggressive pursuit of federal funding combined with careful cultivation of relationships to industry have been key elements of the entrepreneurial strategy of both departments. I should add here that Kornberg also made a very different sort of contribution to Stanford's pre-eminence in biochemistry: his son, Roger Kornberg, won the 2006 Nobel Prize in chemistry. 'Much of his work has focused on an enzyme called RNA polymerase, which makes messenger RNA and controls the process of selecting certain genes from the thousands that make up DNA to duplicate at any one time.'[10] His research made extensive use of X-ray crystallography.

Clearly Terman was working with a model of a medical school that would be in a position to readily exploit a wide range of scientific and engineering disciplines wherever those disciplines might be located within the entire structure of Stanford University. At the same time, Kornberg's biochemistry department and Lederberg's genetics department were exemplary cases of what Terman often referred to as 'steeples of excellence through entrepreneurship'. Kornberg, Kaplan, Lederberg and Berg did come to constitute a new form of entrepreneurship, an academic entrepreneurship whose source of capital lay in the huge, and rising, budgets of federal agencies, primarily the growing budgets of the NIH.

The federal budgets also supported a competitive process among research universities – a process in which Stanford University unmistakably defeated Washington University at St Louis. With respect to the medical school, Terman's strategy for success was to attract (and to retain) the most talented researchers in the academic medical world.

A final footnote on a very different sort of innovation that developed in the Genetics Department: a complex piece of hardware was conceived in the Herzenberg Laboratory, where it was brought to the working prototype stage, and then to numerous performance improvements.

A remarkable research device emerged from the Herzenberg Lab that has had a profound effect upon the research process in medicine and closely-related fields of biology. The device is a cell sorter – FACS, that is, fluorescence activated cell sorter. The primary conceptualization and subsequent redesign were the work of Leonard and Leonore Herzenberg.

The FACS machine is essentially a cell-sorting instrument that can sort cells into subsets according to the proteins they contain, many times faster than was ever possible before.

It is widely accepted that FACS has transformed the field of flow cytometry. By the late 1990s it was estimated that there were approximately 30 000 FACS in use throughout the world.[11]

Leonard Herzenberg received the Kyoto Prize, Japan's equivalent to the Nobel Prize, in 2006, for his development of the FACS machine.

7.3.1 Magnetic Resonance Imaging

Magnetic resonance is, arguably, the most powerful new diagnostic technology of the second half of the twentieth century, which built upon no antecedent technology, as in the case of the CT scanner. Its origins were, as was true of so many scientific instruments, found as the unexpected by-product of research activities within the larger university community. Nuclear magnetic resonance (NMR) had its origins in fundamental research that was originally undertaken in order to acquire some highly specific pieces of scientific knowledge. In the case of NMR, two university scientists, Felix Bloch at Stanford and E.M. Purcell at Harvard, shared the Nobel Prize in Physics in 1952, for research leading to a deeper understanding of the magnetic properties of atomic nuclei that, in turn, provided the basis for powerful instrumentation, especially in chemistry, for determining the structure of certain molecules, and medical diagnostic technologies.[12]

Instrumentation and techniques have moved from one scientific discipline to another in ways that have been full of consequences for the progress of science. In fact, it can be argued that an understanding of the progress of individual disciplines is generally unattainable in the absence of an examination of how different areas of science have influenced one another through technology transfer. This understanding is frequently tied directly to the timing, and the mode of transfer, of scientific instruments as well as useful new knowledge. What is obviously true is that opportunities for such transfers have been considerably strengthened as medical schools have been located, geographically and organizationally, closer to the universities.[13]

7.3.2 Radiotherapy

When Kaplan first arrived at the Stanford Medical School, it was still at its old location in San Francisco, and it would be true to say that faculty in its clinical departments performed very little or no basic research. When the Medical School moved to Palo Alto, Kaplan, who came to the Stanford

Medical School as head of the Department of Radiology, found himself living cheek by jowl with departments of physics, engineering and biology.

In the years immediately after World War II there was a sharp focus among academic physicists on the subject of nuclear research, and this pervasive interest also prevailed at Stanford. This interest led in turn to the construction of the first microwave linear accelerators.

Stanford's ambitions became conspicuous in 1957 when Professor Wolfgang Panofsky, of the Stanford Physics Department, presented a proposal to the Atomic Energy Commission for the construction of a giant linear accelerator – 'it would run for two miles straight through the hills near Palo Alto – at a cost of $100 000 000' (Kevles, 1978, p. 386). The construction costs were to be borne primarily by the Federal Department of Energy.

Kaplan, on the other hand, saw the possibilities for medical applications, especially in the treatment of cancer.[14] This prospect was considerably strengthened when Kaplan came to know Ed Ginzton who, at the time, was the director of Stanford's Microwave Laboratory. Their collaborations soon led to the design and development of a range of clinical linear accelerators (linacs) with the qualities that Kaplan believed would be most effective for therapeutic purposes.[15]

> Whereas the Medical Research Council and the British Ministry of Health led the way by planning and funding the application of this newly discovered linac technology to medical use in England, Henry Kaplan led the way in the United States. His persistence resulted in grants in mid-1952 from the National Institutes of Health and the American Cancer Society to start machine construction and later from the Irvine Foundation to build the treatment room. (Kelves, 1978, pp. 208–9)

Kaplan and his clinical associates introduced scientific discipline to supervoltage radiotherapy techniques with their linac. However, there were two major obstacles to proliferation of their work. Their linac had been built by graduate students and an industrial source of radiotherapy linacs in the United States was needed. Kaplan envisaged his disciplined techniques being used throughout the medical community to treat cancer patients, but there were only a very few full-time specialists in radiotherapy. Kaplan's enthusiasm and energy were immensely important in helping to remove these obstacles, through influencing the government to fund the training of radiotherapy specialists and through influencing industry to make the investment in development and production of reliable high-performance machines.

In the memorial resolution commemorating Kaplan's death in 1984, it was recorded that his group 'developed an aggressive treatment program to treat Hodgkin's disease, converting a disease that was almost invariably fatal within 10 years into one which can now be permanently cured in more than 80% of the cases' (Stanford Historical Society, n.d.).

7.4 CLOSING OBSERVATIONS

It is tempting to say that the Cambridge–Cavendish achievement was primarily a matter of the development of instrumentation that opened up an entirely new window into the realm of molecular biology. Achieving this involved a drastic shift in the direction of research of a famous research institution. The dominant force seems to have been the forceful leadership of Lawrence Bragg, a remarkable applied physicist whose wide-ranging knowledge, energy, curiosity and willingness to take high risks led to one of the great scientific breakthroughs of the twentieth century. Lawrence won his Nobel Prize in 1915 when he was 25 years old, and for research that he had completed in his early twenties.

The most important single fact about the growth of the US academic medical centers is precisely that they became part of the academic community, that is, a community that, in addition to students and teaching faculty, contained a wide range of research capabilities in fields that possessed potential complementarities to the medical world.

The Anglo-American experience suggests the great value of locating medical research and medical education inside (or at least very close to) an academic community. I say this in spite of the fact that universities have not always provided exemplary models for how research ought to be organized and carried out.

A great strength of the US AMCs is that they have vastly facilitated interdisciplinary research – along two dimensions: (1) much greater opportunities for joint research, such as between medical schools on the one hand, and physics and electrical engineering on the other; and (2) the AMCs brought, under the same roof, clinicians and disciplines that were becoming more directly relevant to the medical world: genetics and biochemistry.

Moreover, a most effective way of diffusing the findings of new biomedical research is through the most recent graduates of the universities who go off to employment in the private or public sectors of the economy.

Finally, US leadership in basic research publications certainly appears to be connected to the high percentages of spending on the life sciences. But I would like to suggest that, in the longer run, this may prove to be the basis for an inappropriate allocation of research money – in view of the evidence that so many of the really fundamental breakthroughs have come from outside of what we have come to call the life sciences. Many of the largest breakthroughs have come from the realm of the physical sciences, and especially physics.

NOTES

1. European Commission (2003), p. 299.
2. Of course, what was 'remarkable' was the NIH's ability to mobilize political support in both Congress and the White House for this object, which was very carefully promoted and received bipartisan support.
3. For some insightful treatments of some of the leading figures of the 'new physics', see Fleming and Bailyn (1969). See in particular, Szilard, 'Reminiscences' (Chapter 2), and Fleming, 'Émigré physicists and the biological revolution' (Chapter 3).
4. He was also the first recipient of the Nobel Prize in Physics, in 1901.
5. For an early formulation see Klug and Crowther (1972).
6. See the recent biography of J.D. Bernal by Andrew Brown (2005).
7. See Thomas and Philips (1990) pp. 44, 48; also p. 54, where they state: 'This rapid build up was made possible by the support of the Medical Research Council and the Rockefeller Foundation.'
8. See Braun (1994). Braun's main concern, writing as a European, is with the high degree of mobility of US scientists, both among universities and, to some extent, between universities and industry, compared with the immobility of their continental European counterparts. Such immobility, he asserts, has had the effect of reducing competition among European universities.
9. The following draws upon a report that was prepared at the request of Professor Charles Kruger at a time when he was Stanford's Dean of Research. The report was completed in 2003. The three senior faculty consisted of Professors Timothy Lenoir, Nathan Rosenberg and Henry Rowen, with considerable assistance from Christophe Lecuyer, Jeannette Colyvas and Brent Goldfarb. The final report was 'Inventing the Entrepreneurial University: Stanford and the Co-Evolution of Silicon Valley' (Lenoir et al., 2003).
10. *New York Times*, 5 October 2006.
11. See Herzenberg et al. (2000).
12. 'The history of NMR spectroscopy begins just before World War II in the Stanford Physics Department, which Felix Bloch had joined in 1934.' (NSF, 2000, p. 3). This is a useful report on the intermediate steps between NMR and MRI, and it also includes the important roles played by a number of UK universities.
13. Of course, it is also true that more recent improvements in the technology of electronic communications have rendered mere distance much less of an obstacle to joint research. See Woody Powell's impressive recent studies on networking.
14. Kaplan may have been influenced by the ongoing experimentation with Lawrence's cyclotron at the University of California, Berkeley. Kevles (1978), pp. 271–3.
15. See Ginzton and Nunan (1985), pp. 205–16. For a more technical coverage, see Ginzton et al. (1957).

REFERENCES

American Association for the Advancement of Science (2007), 'Trends in federal research by discipline, FY 1970–2006', available at: http://www.aaas.org/spp/rd/discip06.pdf, accessed December 2008.

Braun, D. (1994), *Structure and Dynamics of Health Research and Public Funding: An International Institutional Comparison*, Dordrecht: Kluwer Academic Publishers.

Brown, A. (2005), *J.D. Bernal: The Sage of Science*, Oxford: Oxford University Press.

Crowther, J.G. (1974), *The Cavendish Laboratory, 1874–1974*, New York: Science History Publications.

European Commission (2003), *Third European Report on Science and Technology Indicators 2003*, Luxembourg: Office for Official Publications of the European Communities.

Fleming, D. and B. Bailyn (eds) (1969), *The Intellectual Migration: Europe and America, 1930–1960*, Cambridge, MA: Belknap Press of Harvard University Press.

Gelijns, A. and N. Rosenberg (1999), 'Diagnostic devices: an analysis of comparative advantages', in D.C. Mowery and R.R. Nelson (eds), *Sources of Industrial Leadership*, Cambridge and New York: Cambridge University Press, pp. 346–58.

Ginzberg, E. and A.B. Dutka (1989), *The Financing of Biomedical Research*, Baltimore, MD: Johns Hopkins University Press.

Ginzton, E.L., K.B. Mallory and H.S. Kaplan (1957), 'The Stanford medical linear accelerator', *Stanford Medical Bulletin*, **15** (3), 123–40.

Ginzton, E.L. and C.S. Nunan (1985), 'History of microwave electron linear accelerators for radiotherapy', *International Journal of Radiation Oncology, Biology, Physics*, **11** (2), 205–16.

Herzenberg, L., S.C. De Rosa and L. Herzenberg (2000), 'Monoclonal antibodies and the FACS: complementary tools for immunobiology and medicine', *Immunology Today*, **21** (8), 383–90.

Kevles, D.J. (1978), *The Physicists: The History of a Scientific Community in Modern America*, New York: Knopf.

Klug, A. and R.A. Crowther (1972), 'Three-dimensional image reconstruction from the viewpoint of information theory', *Nature*, **238** (25), 435–440.

Lenoir, T., N. Rosenberg, H. Rowen, C. Lécuyer, J. Colyvas and B. Goldfarb (2003), 'Inventing the entrepreneurial University: Stanford and the co-evolution of Silicon Valley', draft accessible at: http://siepr.stanford.edu/programs/SST_Seminars/Lenoir.pdf.

Medical Research Council (2007), 'Facts and figures about the MRC', www.mrc.ac.uk/AboutUs/FactsFigures/index.htm, accessed 2007.

Morange, M. (1998), *A History of Molecular Biology*, Cambridge, MA: Harvard University Press.

National Science Board (2004), *Science and Engineering Indicators 2004*, 2 vols, Arlington, VA: National Science Foundation.

National Science Foundation (NSF) (2000), 'Magnetic Resonance Imaging III', SRI Policy Division, 27 March.

Nobel Foundation (1914), 'Max von Laue: The Nobel Prize in Physics 1914 – Biography', available at http://nobelprize.org/nobel-prizes/physics/laureates/1914/laue-bio.html.

Schrodinger, E. (1945), *What is Life? The Physical Aspect of the Living Cell*, New York: The Macmillan Company.

Stanford Historical Society (n.d.), 'Memorial resolution – Henry S. Kaplan (1918–84)', available at: http://histsoc.stanford.edu/pdfmem/KaplanH.pdf.

Thomas, J.M. and D. Philips (1990), *Selections and Reflections: The Legacy of Sir Lawrence Bragg*, Northwood: Science Reviews.

8. A policy-shaped research agenda on the economics of science and technology[1]

Irwin Feller

8.1 PROBLEM STATEMENT

Sometime during the 1970s, the late United States Congressman George Brown, California, chair of the House of Representatives' science committee and a stellar congressional supporter of federal government support of basic research, observed that economists had made significant contributions to national policies for science and technology. Specifically citing the work of Solow and Mansfield, if I recall correctly, he said they had done this by demonstrating that research and development (R&D) had made significant contributions to the American economy's long-term growth and that social rates of return to R&D could exceed private rates of return. In particular, the latter finding was indicative of market failures in private sector investments in non-defense-related R&D; it thus provided a generic case for combating then politically powerful opposition to public sector support of fundamental science and pre-competitive technology. He also remarked however that these findings provided little guidance to policymakers with respect to the optimal total level of support for R&D or its allocation among competing uses, agencies or programs as budget proposals ran the gauntlets of executive and legislative branch appropriations processes.

Fast forward to recent years, and we find in the Salter and Martin review of the economics benefits of publicly funded basic research, the observation: 'the research reviewed in this paper does not suggest how much public support should be provided nor in what areas it should be invested' (Salter and Martin, 2001, p. 529).

This chapter is based on these two observations. It is an academic economist's effort to overlay a map of leading-edge science and technology policy issues atop one of research on the economics of science and technology.

The chapter takes as given ongoing research on the hardy perennials of the field of the economics of technology policy, such as whether public sector funding of R&D complements or substitutes for private sector R&D, whether specific public sector R&D programs have generated effective and efficient increments in any of a set of economic outputs, for example, jobs, sales, profits, productivity, and the extent and channels through which basic science contributes to technological innovation. It also assumes that program-specific evaluations, as represented in the United States by studies of the Manufacturing Extension Partnership (MEP) program and the Advanced Technology Program (ATP), and in Europe by studies of the impacts of the several EU Framework programs and national innovation policies, will continue, with these evaluations employing ever more sophisticated analytical frameworks, databases and statistical techniques.

The chapter is organized instead about the questions and challenges I have heard policy-makers pose in recent years to economists, as well as to other social scientists. It is thus less about program evaluation methodology and findings, per se, than about the contours, and possibly outer limits, of economic research related to assisting policy-makers form and evaluate science and technology policies.

There is a threefold rationale for organizing my contribution in this way. First, the questions pose formidable analytical and empirical challenges that spotlight the outer limits of the state of economic knowledge and program evaluation practice. Second, speaking pragmatically from experience as an occasional participant in US budget battles over the funding of economics and related social science research, a juxtaposition of questions and current or prospective answers may judiciously serve to modulate expectations about what the US's new 'science of science policy' initiative can or will produce, especially along the lines of generating new econometric investment models for public sector R&D. This modulation in turn may help avoid a backlash against future funding for the social sciences in case less is produced, or at times promised, from the current surge in research support.

Third, the approach increases the prospects – or at least one hopes it will – that answers to the type of questions listed below will create openings in what Reeve has termed the 'boundary layer' between policy-makers and evaluators that is seen as impeding the utilization of research findings (Reeve, 2005, p. 37). This boundary layer is not necessarily created by obtuseness, political imbroglios, or ideological resistance and rejection, although each of these elements may be present. Rather, as indicated by interviews I conducted recently with US science policy officials in preparing this chapter, the disquiet and dissatisfaction reflects the complexity, limited explanatory power and limited policy relevance of even the best and brightest of the science and technology evaluation work which they have commissioned or otherwise have set before them.[2]

One necessary caveat and one minor qualifier must be added to what follows. The caveat is that the use of policy-maker questions to organize this chapter is not to suggest that research on the economics of science and technology policy is to become the handmaiden of policy-maker interests. Quite the contrary. Speaking truth to power is as much our obligation as speaking truth to one another. Indeed, much of the substance of what we have come to know about processes of scientific discovery and technological innovation, as well as the individual and collective legitimacy that leads policy-makers to turn occasionally to us for information and recommendations, derives from a sequence of independently initiated research questions and externally reviewed and validated answers.[3]

The qualifier is that the list of questions below, not surprisingly, derives primarily from the US setting and experiences. A modest degree of participation in evaluations of EU Framework programs and interaction with EU and European science policy and program evaluation officials encourages me, though, to believe that the analysis presented here has enough transoceanic applicability to avoid charges of parochialism.

8.2 CONTEMPORARY QUESTIONS SHAPING THE SCIENCE AND TECHNOLOGY EVALUATION AGENDA

With keen awareness that the following does not encompass the field of the economics of science and technology policy, much less address critiques about the emphasis given to economic perspectives and methods in setting national R&D priorities or evaluating related programs (Bozeman and Sarewitz, 2005), below are some of the policy questions that I have recently been involved in providing answers to in one capacity or another.

What criteria or metrics should be used to determine the optimal level of funding for an agency (in contrast say to the use of compound formula increases followed by flatline funding, as has happened for the National Institutes of Health, and which has now been recognized as destabilizing to the scientific enterprise)? (Marburger, 2006; Sperling, 2007.) What metrics should to be used to assess the merit or worth of federal agency basic and applied research programs in light of increased demands for accountability and performance measurement, as in the Office of Management and Budget's Performance Assessment Rating Tool (PART) procedures?

What criteria and procedures should be used to reallocate funds among 'fertile' and 'less fertile' fields of science, even as proposals within each field are peer reviewed? (National Academies-National Research Council, 2007b.) What criteria should be used first to establish and then to evaluate large-scale research centers? (National Academies-Institute of Medicine, 2004.) Given the proposition that competitive, merit review processes for selecting research proposals are preferable to most other allocation arrangements (for example, formulae earmarks), are such processes 'biased' against radical, transformative and/or interdisciplinary research? If so, what alternative mechanisms, including modifications to existing merit review processes, might lead to improved outcomes? How 'innovative' is the US economy, given the absence of a national innovation survey, as administered in many other OECD countries?[4]

Each of these questions can be related to a separate set of concerns and/or events. Each, likewise, is the subject of a stream of analysis and commentary, by economists and others. But they also represent something more than a set of discrete, disconnected queries. In effect, they constitute a conceptually linked set of decisions and assessments across a science and technology policy cycle, beginning with strategic planning and ending with outcome measurement. The questions encompass the need to project relative rates of return for long-term, risky science initiatives; the premise that the frontiers of scientific inquiry increasingly lie at the interstices of existing disciplinary boundaries; assessments that the roles and relationships of traditional knowledge-generating and knowledge-using sectors within national innovation systems are evolving; and an emerging willingness to conduct a critical rethinking of existing mechanisms for setting scientific priorities and selecting among competing proposals within but especially among fields of scientific inquiry.

Several unifying themes are also evident across these questions. These include: (1) a shift away from *ex post* questions about the effectiveness or efficiency of technology development and deployment programs towards a concentration on *ex ante* investment decisions in fundamental science, especially those requiring upfront outlays of hundreds of millions, as in the case of elementary particle physics; and (2) an uneasy sense about the productivity and international competitiveness of the US science and innovation system, even as its most hallowed elements – single investigator-initiated proposals, competitively based merit review, and delegation to universities of the performance of federally funded basic research – continue to be extolled, and indeed increasingly emulated by other countries.

The following sections offer brief observations on the role of economic research in providing answers to each of these questions.

8.3 ECONOMIC ASPECTS OF THE EMERGING AGENDA

8.3.1 Setting Research Priorities (and More)

The development of allocation criteria and related methodologies for assembling and analyzing data is a long-standing, well-recognized and ever-present task of science and technology policy (Weinberg, 1963, 1964). The several presentations by Dr John Marburger, Director, Office of Science and Technology Policy, including his 2002 call for a new science of science policy (Marburger, 2002), in effect are variations on the core proposition that: 'From the government perspective, the policy issue in the short run is how to allocate the science funds in an optimal way' (Marburger, 2006, p. 5). Each of the analytical and quantitative techniques of recent years, such as bibliometrics and patent citation analysis, described for example in the *Handbook of Quantitative Science and Technology Research* (Moed et al., 2004), may be seen as efforts to provide systematic quantitative evidence of past and current performance and relationships better to inform prospective actions.

Even with these and other methodological advances, uncertainty remains the core challenge in setting priorities for fundamental science. The uncertainties are of two basic types: first, determining which lines of inquiry will yield the most important advances in an understanding of natural and social phenomena; second, lack of consensus at times about onward directions suggested by initial sightings at the frontier. As S. Cole has described these challenges, whereas the 'core' of science 'contains a relatively small number of theories or exemplars, the frontier contains a much broader and more loosely woven web of knowledge' (Cole, 1992, p. 135). At the frontiers of research, 'there are substantial levels of disagreement about who is doing important work, what are important problems, and what research should be funded' (1992, p. 135; see also Cohen, 1985). Relatedly, elsewhere, drawing upon histories of scientific and technological discoveries, Gamota and I have argued that mainstream science indicators are of modest value in responding to these challenges because they can either overpredict or underpredict the scientific or technological importance of seminal, disruptive findings (Feller and Gamota, 2007).

For economics, part of the challenge posed by these two forms of uncertainty is that the core techniques currently used to evaluate public sector technology programs have questionable applicability.[5] Audtretsch et al's (2002) review of the economics of science and technology, for example, highlights two primary approaches to the evaluation of technology-based programs: a counterfactual method and a spillover method. In practice, as applied to R&D programs, the counterfactual translates into some variant of the construction of control or comparison groups. For basic science, it becomes the less analytically compelling and politically convincing technique of writing 'what if' history, either retrospectively contemplating the consequences of certain discoveries not being made (or made at a later date), or prospectively in futurist scenarios, at times in Cassandra-like terms, of tracing the implications of having rivals make the breakthroughs first. Spillovers, especially knowledge spillovers, constitute one of the basic justifications for public sector support of basic research. Leaving aside issues such as the need for complementary assets or investments to exploit latent spillovers, the relevant issue in decision-making is not the conceptual or historically measured importance of spillovers but their predictability, form, magnitude and location, given the specific resource allocation decision at hand. Indeed, I interpret much of the writings by economists on the history of technological innovation as pointing to the wide, variable, and to a large degree unpredictable character of spillovers. Posing the question this way however is only to return to the initial state of uncertainty or ignorance concerning which of several alternative fields of science to support.

The employment of econometric models in setting science priorities also entails snares. Such models have been characterized by Salter and Martin as involving 'simplistic and often unrealistic assumptions', at least with respect to innovation (Salter and Martin, 2001, p. 513). Leamer's (1983) classic critique on the use of econometrics provides the more general case for this criticism. Addressing what he termed the Sherlock Holmes inference problem of whether theorizing should proceed before all the evidence is in, Leamer discusses the value of extending the horizon of possibilities (of model specification or sampling properties of the data) reasonably far. But in a manner that echoes all classic statements about the unpredictable nature of scientific revolutions, he then cautions that even this procedure still limits one's ability to foresee the future:

> Within the limits of a horizon, no revolutionary inferences can be made, since all possible inferences are predicted in advance (admittedly, some with low probabilities). Within the horizon, inference and decision can be turned over completely to a computer. But the great human revolutionary discoveries are made when the horizon is extended for reasons that cannot be predicted in advance and cannot be computerized. If you wish to make such discoveries, you will have to poke at the horizon, and poke again. (Leamer, 1983, p. 40)

This austere analysis however is not intended as a complete forecast about the limited utility of future research on the economics of science and technology to policy-makers. Rather it suggests that the value may lie elsewhere than in econometric models directed at generating prospective rates of returns, the putative objective advanced in initial calls for a new science of science policy. Instead, the value more likely will be found in conditioning expectations about the types of returns likely to flow from public investments in R&D, especially fundamental science, and in guiding budget-makers and policy-makers to ask the correct questions in evaluating programs. A fuller and more accurate understanding of processes of scientific discovery and technological innovation and the relationships between the two may assist policy-makers to understand better what not to expect, expect too soon, expect along specific technological or industry lines, or expect in the absence of support of complementary private sector and public sector investments. Moving backwards along the theoretical pathways subsumed in the program's logic model, it can help them set operationally correct conditions for eligibility and performance in the design, project selection and evaluation feasibility stages of launching a program. These are not trivial contributions.

8.3.2 Selection Mechanisms

A distinctive feature of the US science system is its extensive employment of scientific experts to set broad, long-term research priorities (for example, National Academies-National Research Council, 2007a), and the use of competitive, merit review processes to allocate federal research funds. These mechanisms are widely viewed as ensuring that within the penumbras of the two types of uncertainty described above, the most significant scientific questions are addressed by the individuals and institutions deemed most qualified to search for answers. Indeed, in international benchmarking exercises, members of the US scientific community have cited this comparatively greater emphasis on competitive merit review as a factor contributing to the nation's international scientific leadership (in selected fields) (National Academies-National Research Council, 2000, pp. 3–20).

The cautionary tone sounded above about modest prospects for new conceptual or methodological breakthroughs in how science and generic technology priorities are set implies that the priority-setting and allocation decisions questions cited above will likely continue to be made on the basis of these mechanisms. Even a surface comparison of the use of these mechanisms across federal science agencies however, say as between the National Institutes of Health and the National Science Foundation, highlights that the nominally homogenous concept of competitive merit review processes quickly gives way to heterogeneous implementation across agencies and programs. Study sections employing formal scoring mechanisms clearly operate within a different assessment evaluation than reviewers working independently and submitting mail reviews that employ Likert-like scales. In fact, recent paeans to the merits of expert panels and competitive, merit review procedures as selection mechanisms may have had the unintended consequence of making them the new 'black box' of science policy decision-making.

More recently, advancing beyond earlier classic studies of the peer review system (for example, Chubin and Hackett, 1990), observations by participants in these processes, buttressed by an emerging body of empirical research (for example, Brenneis, 1994; Lamont and Mallard, 2005; Laudel, 2006), have probed inside this black box. These probes have highlighted the dependence of the outcomes generated by expert and merit review panels on its internal workings. The inside-the-box cogs and gears include panelist attitudes towards scientific risk; cognitive and epistemic maps of panelists about the structure of knowledge; small-group dynamics; the number and ordering of selection criteria; voting rules; the roles and discretionary authorities of the program managers overseeing the review process; the authorities and traditions of review boards organizationally above review panels; and other factors.

Three specific issues concerning the use of expert panels and peer review processes have moved to the fore in recent science and technology policy debates: (1) the ability to forecast important trends in fundamental research, not only within but across fields of science; (2) the ability adequately to support discontinuous, radical, transformative research; (3) bias in support of interdisciplinary research.

The first issue relates to the need at national or supra-national policy levels to make comparisons across fields of science. Expert panels typically are charged with providing 'retrospective and forward-looking assessments of the status of and outlook for a research field', and providing 'broadly based recommendations for explicit scientific and programmatic priorities for future investments in the field' (National Academies-National Research Council, 2007b, p. vii). The mechanism, though, is less well suited to make comparisons across fields. Scientific communities are generally presented as loathe to set priorities among fields. The concern of some US science agency program managers is that continuous organization of panels and review processes about disciplines or fields (for example, National Institutes of Health study sections) institutionalizes support for a particular field: its best and brightest practitioners are seen as ever ready to point to important work yet to be done, without considering the field's future fertility relative to other fields, and indeed whether or not it has fertility remaining at all.

The second issue relates to whether there are systematic propensities or biases built into existing procedures that constrain the selection of high-risk, or transformative, research proposals. This issue arises from an increasingly voiced sentiment that existing merit review processes tend to be unduly conservative: that is, they reward, indeed demand, adherence to existing theoretical and methodological paradigms while penalizing 'out-of-the box' thinking.

The third issue is the more familiar one of the goodness-of-fit of interdisciplinary research within established selection systems organized in large part about existing disciplines. At all points in the production of new knowledge, extending from the submission of proposals to having findings accepted in leading journals, questions and reservations about quality are the weak spots in claims made on behalf of interdisciplinary research (Feller, 2006).

An extended description of existing expert judgment and peer review mechanisms and treatment of several possible modifications or variants is beyond the scope of this chapter (see Zinoecker and Stampfer, 2006). Many proposed revisions relate to organizational changes – for example, recruiting individuals with track records in collaborative, interdisciplinary research, or restructuring committee voting rules. Among economists who have proposed specific revisions, Jaffe (2002) has suggested that a modicum of randomness be allowed in the selection or rejection for a subset of proposals that exceed a given standard, with the hypothesized differential performance of recipients and non-recipients being studied via a regression discontinuity evaluation design. More broadly, the field is ripe for economists to design and evaluate alternative program and proposal selection mechanisms with respect to the characteristics of performers, the characteristics of the R&D they undertake, and the relationships between these two outcomes and science and technology outcome variables.

8.3.3 National Innovation Systems

The most comfortable fit between the above policy-shaped set of questions and existing economic research likely relates to reconsideration of the conceptual and empirical foundations of the national innovation system model. Even as it continues to be widely used, increased dissatisfaction is emerging about the model's analytical underpinnings, as well as the content and structure of the surveys used to gather the data upon which characterizations of such systems are based.

Conceptually, the national innovation system framework has begun to resemble earlier approaches to industrial organization wherein market processes were shaped by a set of institutions, each with sharply defined roles, that related to one another in given, historically determined ways. Structure determined conduct, which in turn determined performance. As Mazzoleni and Nelson have recently expressed this criticism:

> The National Innovation System concept focuses attention on the range of institutions that are involved in the process of innovation. While business firms play an undeniably crucial role, it is a flawed concept of innovation that which neglects other kinds of institutions involved in the processes that support and mold innovation in many modern industries. (Mazzoleni and Nelson 2007, p. 1516)

Relatedly, two recent National Academies reports, *Measuring Research and Development Expenditures in the US Economy* (2005), and *Understanding Business Dynamics* (2007c) have noted that: 'the structure of the data collection is tied to models of R&D performance that are increasingly unrepresentative of the whole of the R&D enterprise' (National Academies-National Research Council p. 2). Many of the same criticisms about the adequacy of existing data series and associated underlying structural relationships could be levied against other federal (and state) science and technology policies and programs.

As an example of the limited contemporary explanatory value of the national innovation systems model, and implicitly therefore program evaluations tied to assumptions embedded in its characterization of roles and relationships, consider the following interrelationships. Interviews with US high-tech firms conducted during my research on the effects of the Bayh–Dole Act indicate that some such firms are considering substituting university and institute researchers in other countries for US faculty and universities, in part because of lower costs but also because of what they perceive to be unrealistic financial demands by US universities for use of their intellectual property. Another stream of ongoing economic research, by Freeman, Ehrenberg and Stephan, for example, on the place of US universities in the US national innovation system, focuses on the role of graduate students in higher education and technological innovation. Yet another stream, identified with the work of Darby and Zucker, focuses on the role of star scientists in the birth and location of high-tech industries. Yet other than passing observations, no single stream addresses the possible long-term effects on the performance of the US science and innovation system of having US firms, for the above-cited reasons, substitute support of foreign universities for US universities, thus strengthening the academic research infrastructure of these countries, thereby reducing the flow of foreign nationals to US universities for graduate degree training, followed in turn by the loss to the US of the contribution these individuals make as entrepreneurs or faculty.[6]

In effect, most R&D program evaluations are forms of partial equilibrium analysis; in general, single programs are seen as too small to affect the larger economic or social system. Existing evaluations of R&D programs touch only lightly, however, on how the strategies, behavior and performance of the sectors or actors described in the national innovation system change as a result of the cumulative, long-term impact of a cluster of science and technology programs. To track and thus evaluate the sequential effects outlined above requires updated, contemporary, more general equilibrium models of national systems that 'sew together the disparate evidence', and allows for the 'conduct of policy experiments' (Kortum, 2006).

8.4 CONCLUDING COMMENTS

Tracking longer-term structural changes in the workings of national innovation systems induced by the interaction of an aggregation of specific science and technology policies represents, I believe, a highly productive way in which economists can contribute to the design and conduct of evaluations of science and technology programs. The underlying generic questions are: which organizations should be selected to perform a nation's publicly funded R&D; what mechanisms should be used to fund these organizations; and how should the relative (and competitive) performance of these organizations be evaluated?

I am not sure, nor do I think it makes any difference, whether this research is called program evaluation, economics of science and technology, economic growth, or what. It will entail, though, a shift in intellectual grounding. The shift will be from program evaluations, conceived of and defined in terms of demonstrating cause–effect relationships for single programs, to larger, more aggregated and dynamic (or historical) studies that capture both spillover effects and changing behavior on the part of key sectors and actors.

NOTES

1. This chapter draws freely in places on I. Feller (2007) 'Mapping the frontiers of evaluation of public-sector R&D programs', *Science and Public Policy*, **34** (10), 681–90.
2. The National Science Foundation's initial prospectus for its recently established Science of Science and Innovation Policy program, for example, states as follows: 'Traditional models available for informing investment programs are often static, unidirectional and not developed for domain-specific applications . . . (T)here is modest capability of predicting how future investments will yield the most promising and important opportunities'

(September 2006). Similar disenchantment among European science policy-makers with the predictive utility of several mainstream analytical techniques is reported in Gassler et al. (2007). After first observing that 'A major problem inherently of every priority setting process is to find a feasible methodology for the identification, selection and definition of thematic priorities or specific technologies' (2007, p. 14), they conclude that: 'At least until now, technocratic approaches using sophisticated methodologies (e.g. technology foresight, technology monitoring, SWOT-analyses) did not meet the high expectations, which they received at least for some time. Almost by definition, in this area, policy is confronted with "true uncertainty", i.e, the impossibility to foresee the speed and direction of future technological developments' (p. 17).
3. Indeed, it was familiarity with basic findings on the diffusion of technological innovations that many years ago led me to question the validity of a state R&D program's claims that it had generated a sizeable increase in new jobs within an astonishingly short period of time. In a sequence that can only be described as path-dependent, this event led to subsequent economic evaluations of federal and state technology programs that is the basis for my contribution to this volume.
4. It also is instructive to consider what questions are not being asked. Conspicuously absent from the list in the US setting is the question whether it is appropriate or necessary for the federal government to support basic research. Reversing positions on the legitimacy of support for basic and applied research characteristic of much of US history, federal government provision of such support is now not only viewed as appropriate, but is seen as essential, at least for long-term economic growth and competitiveness as suggested by bipartisan congressional proposals for FY 2008 to support the American Competitiveness Initiative, which provides for increased funding for basic research in National Science Foundation, the Department of Energy, and the National Institute of Standards and Technology. Support for civilian-oriented technology however currently remains politically contested.
5. The following section draws directly on Feller (2007).
6. Referring to the relationship between the location and migration of star scientists and the geographic concentration of high-tech industries, Zucker and Darby have noted: 'Overlaying this pattern (of the agglomeration of star scientists), however, are movements of many US trained foreign students who build successful careers in American academe perhaps moving from lower to higher ranked US universities but choose to return home when their native countries develop sufficient strength in their disciplines to both seek them out and to be attractive' (Zucker and Darby, 2007, p. 16).

REFERENCES

Audretsch, D., B. Bozeman, K. Combs, M. Feldman, A. Link, S. Siegel, P. Stephan and C. Wessner (2002), 'The economics of science and technology', *Journal of Technology Transfer*, **27** (2), 155–203.

Bozeman, B. and D. Sarewitz (2005), 'Public values and public failure in US science policy', *Science and Public Policy*, **32**, 119–36.

Brenneis, D. (1994), 'Discourse and discipline at the National Research Council: a bureaucratic Bildungsroman', *Cultural Anthropology*, **9**, 23–36.

Chubin, D. and E. Hackett (1990), *Peerless Science*, Albany, NY: State University of New York Press.

Cohen, I. (1985), *Revolution in Science*, Cambridge, MA: Harvard University Press.

Cole, S. (1992), *Making Science*, Chicago, IL: University of Chicago Press.

Feller, I. (2006), 'Multiple actors, multiple settings, multiple criteria: issues in assessing interdisciplinary research', *Research Evaluation*, **15**, 5–15.

Feller, I. (2007), 'Mapping the frontiers of evaluation of public-sector R&D programs', *Science and Public Policy*, **34** (10), 681–90.
Feller, I. and G. Gamota (2007), 'Science indicators as reliable evidence', *Minerva*, **45**, 17–30.
Gassler, H., W. Polt and C. Rammer (2007), 'Priority setting in research and technology policy: historical developments and recent trends', Joanneum Research, Institute of Technology and Regional Policy, Working Paper No. 36-2007.
Jaffe, A. (2002), 'Building programme evaluation into the design of public research-support programmes', *Oxford Review of Economic Policy*, **18** (1), 22–34.
Kortum, S. (2006), 'Innovation and the world economy: thoughts on measurement, theory and policy', Presentation at the NSF/SRS Workshop on Advancing Measures of Innovations: Knowledge Flows, Business Metrics, and Measurement Strategies, Arlington, VA, 6–7 June.
Lamont, M. and G. Mallard (2005), 'Peer evaluation in the social sciences and humanities compared: the United States, the United Kingdom, and France', Report prepared for the Social Sciences and Humanities Research Council of Canada.
Laudel, G. (2006), 'Conclave in the Tower of Babel: how peers review interdisciplinary research proposals', *Research Evaluation*, **15** (1), 57–68.
Leamer, E. (1983), 'Lets take the con out of econometrics', *American Economic Review*, **73**, 31–43.
Marburger, J. (2002), 'Science based science policy', American Association for the Advancement of Science, Annual Meeting.
Marburger, J. (2006), 'Emerging issues in science and technology policy', Presentation to the Council on Governmental Relations, Washington, DC, 26 October.
Mazzoleni, R. and R. Nelson (2007), 'Public research institutions and economic catch-up', *Research Policy*, **36**, 1512–28.
Moed, H., W. Glanzel and U. Schmoch (eds) (2004), *Handbook of Quantitative Science and Technology Research*, Dordrecht: Kluwer Academic Publishers.
National Academies (1999), *Evaluating Federal Research Programs*, Washington, DC: National Academies Press.
National Academies-Institute of Medicine (2004), *NIH Extramural Research Centers*, F. Manning, M. McGeary and R. Estabrook (eds), Washington, DC: National Academies Press.
National Academies-National Research Council (2000), *Experiments in International Benchmarking of US Research Fields*, Washington, DC: National Academies Press.
National Academies-National Research Council (2005), *Measuring Research and Development Expenditures in the US Economy*, Lawrence Brown, Thomas Plewes and Marisa Gerstein (eds), Washington, DC: National Academies Press.
National Academies-National Research Council (2007a), *Decadal Science Strategy Surveys*, J. Alexander (ed.), Washington, DC: National Academies Press.
National Academies-National Research Council (2007b), *A Strategy for Assessing Science*, I. Feller and P. Stern (eds), Washington, DC: National Academies Press.
National Academies-National Research Council (2007c), *Understanding Business Dynamics*, John Haltiwanger, Lisa Lynch and Christopher Mackie (eds), Washington, DC: National Academies Press.

Reeve, N. (2005), 'On the evaluation of European Union research: the 2004 five-year assessment', *Science and Public Policy*, **32**, 335–8.
Salter, A. and B. Martin (2001), 'The economic benefits of publicly funded basic research: a critical review', *Research Policy*, **30**, 509–32 .
Sperling, G. (2007), 'How to get fewer scientists', *Washington Post*, 24 July, A15.
Weinberg, A. (1963), 'Criteria for scientific choice', *Minerva*, **1**, 159–71.
Weinberg, A. (1964), 'Criteria for scientific choice II: the two cultures', *Minerva*, **3**, 3–14.
Zinoecker, K. and M. Stampfer (2006), 'Peer review and beyond?', Presentation at the conference Peer Review: Its Present and Future State, Prague, 12–13 October.
Zucker, L. and M. Darby (2007), 'Star scientists, innovation and regional and national immigration', NBER Working Paper 13547, Cambridge, MA: National Bureau of Economic Research.

9. Basic research and growth policy[1]

Hans Gersbach

9.1 INTRODUCTION

The design of appropriate growth policies is arguably the most important policy area of any government. While simple blueprints for such a policy design are not available, even for industrial countries, the workhorses of the new growth theory have generated new insights as to which policy areas are potentially relevant for growth. While at a deep level, institutional conditions are important, the following policy areas have been identified as growth-enhancing: competition and entry policy, education policy and macroeconomic policies.[2] However, their concrete configuration depends on the characteristics of a country, such as the distance to the technological frontier or the country's level of financial development. Basic research policy[3] has been neglected so far. In this short chapter, I address the key issues regarding the policy towards basic research and how these policies depend on a country's characteristics.

In the next section, I briefly review the macroeconomic significance of basic research around the world. Then, I address the nature of the public good 'basic research' and the question why a country may not want to rely solely on foreign direct investment (FDI) (or trade) as a mechanism to obtain leading-edge production techniques. In section 9.4, I employ Schumpeterian growth thinking to identify the usefulness of basic research for an individual country and address the issue how a country's level of basic research depends on its degree of globalization and on its distance to the technological frontier. In section 9.5, I address the issue of which schemes might be best suited to finance basic research. In section 9.6, I conclude with open issues.

9.2 THE IMPORTANCE OF BASIC RESEARCH

The empirical pattern of basic research shown in Tables 9.1 and 9.2 can be described as follows.

Table 9.1 Basic research expenditure

Country	Basic research expenditure as a percentage of GDP		Basic research as a percentage of R&D	
	1993	2004	1993	2004
United States	0.44	0.50	17.5	18.7
Austria	0.31	0.39	21.5	17.5
France	0.52	0.52	21.9	24.3
Germany	0.43	–	18.9	–
Norway	0.25	0.28*	14.5	16.2*
Portugal	0.14	0.19*	24.1	25.7*
Switzerland	0.80†	0.84	30.0†	28.7
Japan	0.39	0.38	13.7	11.9
China	0.03	0.07	4.3	5.3

Notes:
* Data from 2003.
† Data from 1996.

Source: OECD (2006).

Table 9.2 Basic research expenditure by sector (in million current PPP $)

Country	Business enterprise		Government & higher education		Total	
	1993	2003	1993	2003	1993	2003
United States	6427	8585	19781	40296	28741	55103
Austria	59	151*	457	741*	520	898*
France	730	1205	5008	7751	5901	9185
Germany	1127	1642	5957	–	7085	–
Norway	12	52	214	426	227	479
Portugal	1	11	141	284	174	369
Switzerland	352‡	445†	1040‡	1040†	1500‡	1573†
Japan	3292	5044	6165	8770	10075	14216

Notes:
* Data from 2002.
† Data from 2000.
‡ Data from 1996.

Source: OECD Research and Development Statistics Database.

First, large industrial countries like Germany, France, the US and Japan spend about 0.5 percent of their gross domestic product (GDP) on basic research, while smaller countries like Austria and Norway invest a somewhat smaller share. In the case of Switzerland, it is at 0.84 percent, that is, significantly higher.

Second, as illustrated by Tables 9.1 and 9.3,[4] basic research is mainly undertaken by the industrialized countries. Countries such as Portugal and China which are far away from the technological frontier invest little in basic research.[5]

Third, the amount of basic research, measured as a percentage of total research and development (R&D) expenditure for industrial countries, scatters around 20, with Switzerland (28.7) and Japan (11.9) representing the polar cases in Table 9.1.

Table 9.3 Productivity indicators

Country	(1)	(2)	(3)	(4)	(5)
	GDP per person employed, in 1990 US$ (converted at Geary Khamis PPPs)	GDP per person employed, in 2006 US$ (converted to 2006 price level with updated 2002 EKS PPPs)	GDP per hour, in 1990 US$ (converted at Geary Khamis PPPs)	GDP per hour, in 2006 US$ (converted to 2006 price level with updated 2002 EKS PPPs)	Value added per hour worked, in 1997 US$ (manufacturing sector)
United States	63942	90112	35.70	50.30	40.6
Austria	48309	76253	31.80	50.20	32.4
France	54634	81151	35.72	53.06	41.4
Germany	42321	66631	29.44	46.36	33.6
Norway	53929	85051	39.66	62.54	–
Portugal	29485	45999	17.25	26.91	14.5
Switzerland	42093	67797	27.44	44.20	–
Japan	45454	65628	25.61	36.97	–
China	10378	–	–	–	–

Notes: Columns (1)–(4): Year 2006; Column (5): Year 2001.

Sources: Columns (1)–(4): Groningen Growth and Development Centre and the Conference Board, Total Economy Database, January 2007. Column (5): Groningen Growth and Development Centre, ICOP Database 1997 Benchmark.

Fourth, a structural change is well documented for the US and may be at work in other countries, too: while most of the funding of basic research is still provided by the federal government, the amount of basic research financed by the industry has risen over the last decades.[6]

9.3 ECONOMIC VIEWS ON BASIC RESEARCH

There are different ways to conceptualize basic research in economic terms. We differentiate between four perspectives:[7]

- *Basic research as a global public good*
  The early literature on basic research has focused on basic research as a global public good (Arrow, 1962; Nelson, 1959). The output of basic research is freely available and its consumption is non-rivalrous and non-excludable. Basic research increases the world knowledge pool and helps firms to develop new products and processes.
- *Basic research as access to knowledge*
  Basic research investment can be viewed as building absorbtive capacity, that is, as investment in the capacity to absorb knowledge in the world. Cohen and Levinthal (1989) have developed this line of reasoning and Kealey (1996) has pushed it to the point where basic research is a by-product of investments into access to knowledge. Hence, private incentives to undertake basic research may be sufficiently strong to sustain a socially desirable level of basic research.
- *Basic research as a regional or national public good for domestic firms*
  Basic research has important positive side-effects for the firms of the region or the country in which it is conducted. Basic research investments provide trained scientists and problem-solvers to the industry (Nelson, 1987; Zellner, 2003) and generate further local or regional spillovers to firms (Acs et al., 1992; Jaffe et al., 1993). Hence, basic research investments constitute a regional public good for firms.[8]
- *Basic research as a regional or national public good for firms with cross-country spillovers*
  This perspective is a combination of the regional or national good perspective and international research spillovers. International research spillovers can occur directly, since knowledge is publicly available (the global public good perspective) or indirectly through productivity-improvement effects of foreign direct investment and trade.

It is useful to take a closer look at the background of the existence of international research spillovers. They have been a prominent theme in the empirical literature (see Coe and Helpman, 1995; Coe et al., 1997; Keller, 2002; Lichtenberg and van Pottelsberghe de la Potterie, 1998). Recently, Funk (2002) suggested that basic research generates much larger international spillovers than developmental research.

A common theme in another strand of the empirical literature is the focus on indirect international spillovers. In particular, foreign direct investment by leading-edge companies is a powerful mechanism to raise productivity in host countries (see Gersbach, 2002; Baily and Gersbach, 1995). FDI can contribute directly to higher levels of productivity by transferring the best production techniques to the host country and by putting pressure on the host's domestic producers to improve. The most prominent examples are the US transplants of automotive companies headquartered in Japan. Recent econometric studies (Keller and Yeaple, 2003; Alfaro et al., 2007) have confirmed the existence of such positive productivity externalities.[9] Hence, when basic research fosters innovation and thus raises productivity for operations in a country, these productivity improvements may be transferred to other countries over time and tend to increase the benefits from investing in basic research in the country of origin.

Of course, these views are not mutually exclusive and focus on particular aspects of basic research. Three conclusions emerge from this discussion:

- First, unilateral investment in basic research by individual countries is rational, as there are a variety of regional or national public good aspects. The data tend to suggest that the regional public good aspect has been constant or has increased over the last decades.
- Second, international spillovers of basic research are important among industrialized countries. In particular, exposure of a country's domestic operations to competition with operations of leading productivity through FDI (or trade) represents a separate channel, beyond domestic investment, to increase domestic productivity. This channel, however, takes time.
- Third, uncoordinated investment decisions by countries are likely to result in a considerable underinvestment in basic research.

9.4 HOW MUCH BASIC RESEARCH?

How much a country should invest into basic research can only be answered within a (new) growth concept. However, some key issues are obvious:

- Should a country that is highly exposed to competition with productivity leaders invest more in basic research than a country that is less exposed? There are plausible arguments for both answers. A highly exposed country might benefit more from induced productivity improvements (for example through FDI) and thus needs to invest less in basic research than a country sheltered from competition with productivity leaders. A highly exposed country might invest more in basic research than a sheltered country because this is the only way to ensure that domestic firms continue to earn innovation rents.
- Should a country that is close to the technological frontier invest more in basic research than a country that is lagging behind in productivity? Again, there are plausible arguments for both answers. A country with many industries close to the productivity frontier may invest more in basic research in order to allow these industries to escape competition from foreign operations. A country with many industries that are lagging in productivity might invest more in basic research in order to accelerate the catch-up of domestic industries.

Of course, both points are linked. In Gersbach et al. (2008), we tackle these interrelated issues and incorporate basic research into Schumpeterian growth models with exit and entry by foreign firms. We find that the more technologically advanced a country is, the more the amount of optimal basic research expenditure increases. For a country with a high share of technologically backward sectors, it is optimal to renounce investing in basic research. The relationship between openness and optimal basic research is somewhat ambiguous. As discussed in detail in Gersbach et al. (2008), these results might explain why, for example, Ireland invests little in basic research, and others, like France, invest much more, although both countries have approximately the same level of labor productivity.

9.5 HOW TO FINANCE BASIC RESEARCH

If basic research is interpreted as a public good, the determination of the optimal financing scheme is a public finance issue. At first sight, this issue has similarities with the financing problem of public infrastructure (see Barro and Sala-i-Martin, 1992), which is the subject of a lively policy debate among economists and politicians regarding fiscal competition (see Bénassy-Quéré et al., 2007 for a recent contribution).[10]

The financing issue of basic research is complicated by specific features. First, the subset of domestic firms that are beneficiaries of the public good is determined endogenously, as the innovation prospects are private information and potential entrepreneurs must decide whether to belong to the class of beneficiaries or not. Second, there are important equilibrium feedback effects on wages if the government increases the innovation prospects of firms. Hence, equilibrium feedback effects create a second class of beneficiaries. Third, the resource balance between innovating entrepreneurs and the supply of labor is of particular importance. Individuals who decide not to benefit from the government investment in basic research (those whose benefits are rather small) supply their labor to the entrepreneurs who decide to innovate, and this allows them to reap the benefits. Fourth, investments in basic research affect the entry decisions of foreign firms, as the innovation activities and success of domestic firms are affected.

The particular financing problem of basic research has been examined in Gersbach and Schneider (2007), where we interpret basic research as a public good.

9.6 OPEN ISSUES AND CONCLUSION

The insights generated so far suggest that basic research is an important policy area. Obviously, the next step is to integrate basic research into a growth policy framework that is adapted to a country's characteristics.

A lot of further issues related to basic research wait to be explored. Let us mention a few:

- Are higher education and basic research complementary?
- Should basic research be (more) targeted at specific technologies or industries?
- Should democratic procedures, expert groups, or bureaucratic procedures using macro-indicators determine the amount and mix of basic research?
- How should countries design their basic research strategy?

A more complete picture regarding growth policy frameworks involving basic research thus has to wait until the work has progressed.

NOTES

1. We would like to thank Maik Schneider and Olivier Schneller for helpful comments.
2. See in particular Aghion and Howitt (2006).
3. A standard definition of basic research is given by the Organisation for Economic

Co-operation and Development (OECD): 'Basic research is experimental or theoretical work undertaken primarily to acquire new knowledge of the underlying foundation of phenomena and observable facts, without any particular application or use in view' (OECD, 2003, p. 30).
4. For more empirical evidence see Gersbach et al. (2007).
5. Table 9.3 provides labor productivity levels which are a measure for the technological backwardness of a country. The level of labor productivity is usually measured as value added per hour worked and is notoriously difficult to compare across countries.
6. For example, see National Science Board (2006).
7. Schneller (2006) provides a detailed survey of basic research effects and an overview of growth models involving basic research.
8. However, non-rivalry does not hold any more in a strict sense, as the hiring of a problem-solver by one firm precludes his employment by other firms. Moreover, when basic research induces the creation of new firms, as argued by Zucker et al. (1998) and Bania et al. (1993), the group of beneficiaries might be quite small.
9. A variety of positive and negative externalities in the host country occur, which on balance tend to be positive.
10. A particular concern in this debate among economists and politicians is a possible 'race to the bottom' if governments competitively lower their tax rates in order to attract private investments. Such a race may undermine the ability of the government to finance public projects and the welfare state.

REFERENCES

Acs, Z.J., D. Audretsch and M. Feldmann (1992), 'Real effects of academic research: comment', *American Economic Review*, **82** (1), 363–7.

Aghion, P. and P. Howitt (2006), 'Appropriate growth policy: a unifying framework', *Journal of the European Economic Association*, **4** (2–3), 269–314.

Alfaro, L., A. Chanda, S. Kalemli-Ozcan and S. Sayek (2007), 'How does foreign direct investment promote economic growth? Exploring the effects of financial markets on linkages', mimeo.

Arrow, K.J. (1962), 'Economic welfare and the allocation of resources for invention', in NBER (ed.), *The Rate and Direction of Inventive Activity: Economic and Social Factors*, Princeton, NJ: Princeton University Press, pp. 609–25.

Baily, M. and H. Gersbach (1995), 'Efficiency in manufacturing and the need for global competition', *Brookings Papers on Economic Activity: Microeconomics*, **1995**, pp. 307–58.

Bania, N., R. Eberts and M. Fogarty (1993), 'Universities and the startup of new companies: can we generalize from Route 128 and Silicon Valley?', *Review of Economics and Statistics*, **75** (4), 761–6.

Barro, R. and X. Sala-i-Martin (1992), 'Public finance in models of economic growth', *Review of Economic Studies*, **59** (4), 645–61.

Bénassy-Quéré, A., N. Gobalraja and A. Trannoy (2007), 'Tax and public input competition', *Economic Policy*, **22** (50), 385–430.

Coe, D.T. and E. Helpman (1995), 'International R&D spillovers', *European Economic Review*, **39** (5), 859–87.

Coe, D.T., E. Helpman and A.W. Hoffmaister (1997), 'North–South R&D spillovers', *Economic Journal*, **107** (440), 134–49.

Cohen, W. and D. Levinthal (1989), 'Innovation and learning: the two faces of R&D', *Economic Journal*, **99** (397), 569–96.

Funk, M. (2002), 'Basic research and international spillovers', *International Review of Applied Economics*, **16** (2), 217–26.

Gersbach, H. (2002), 'Globalization at the industry level', *World Economy*, **25** (2), 209–29.

Gersbach, H. and M. Schneider (2007), 'Financing basic research in a globalized world', mimeo.

Gersbach, H., M. Schneider and O. Schneller (2008), 'On the design of basic research policy', CER-ETH – Center of Economic Research at ETH Zurich Working Paper No. 08/79.

Jaffe, A.B., M. Trajtenberg and R. Henderson (1993), 'Geographic localization of knowledge spillovers as evidenced by patent citations', *Quarterly Journal of Economics*, **108** (3), 577–98.

Kealey, T. (1996), *The Economic Laws of Scientific Research*, London: McMillan.

Keller, W. (2002), 'Trade and the transmission of technology', *Journal of Economic Growth*, **7** (1), 5–24.

Keller, W. and S.R. Yeaple (2003), 'Multinational entreprises, international trade, and productivity growth: firm-level evidence from the United States', IMF Working Paper No. WP/03/248.

Lichtenberg, F. and B. van Pottelsberghe de la Potterie (1998), 'International R&D spillovers: a comment', *European Economic Review*, **42** (8), 1483–91.

National Science Board (2006), *Science and Engineering Indicators 2006*, vols 1–2, Arlington, VA: National Science Foundation (volume 1: NSB 06-01; volume 2: NSB 06-01A).

Nelson, R.R. (1959), 'The simple economics of basic scientific research', *Journal of Political Economy*, **67** (3), 297–306.

Nelson, R.R. (1987), *Understanding Technical Change as an Evolutionary Process*, Amsterdam: North-Holland.

OECD (2003), *Frascati Manual 2002: Proposed Standard Practice for Surveys on Research and Experimental Development*, The measurement of Scientific and Technological Activities Paris: OECD Publishing.

OECD (2006), *Main Science and Technology Indicators (MSTI)*, edition 2006/2, Paris: OECD Publishing.

Schneller, O. (2006), 'Basic research and economic growth: an overview', mimeo.

Zellner, C. (2003), 'The economic effects of basic research: evidence for embodied knowledge transfer via scientists' migration', *Research Policy*, **32** (10), 1881–95.

Zucker, L.G., M.R. Darby and M.B. Brewer (1998), 'Intellectual human capital and the birth of US biotechnology enterprises', *American Economic Review*, **88** (1), 290–306.

10. Comments[1]

Mark Schankerman

The starting point in Irwin Feller's thought-provoking Chapter 8 is that the overlap between the real needs of policy-makers and the research questions addressed by academic scholars is distressingly low. In particular, he says that the 'disquiet and dissatisfaction [of policy-makers] reflects the complexity, limited explanatory power and limited policy relevance of even the best and brightest of the science and technology evaluation work'. Moreover, Feller argues that the really important questions in science and technology policy involve making *ex ante* choices about government budget allocations both across broad scientific fields, and within specific areas, rather than *ex post* policy evaluation, but it is on the latter that economists have largely focused.

Can anything be done to make ourselves (scholars) more useful to policy-makers, while at the same time maintaining scientific standards and credibility? Or is there a genuine trade-off between credibility and relevance? Do we really have to make a choice between answering narrower questions well and broader questions poorly?

Let me start with program evaluation. There have been major advances in this area over the last 20 years which have enabled economists to be much more rigorous in assessing the impact of government programs. These techniques have been applied widely in many areas, including research and development (R&D) subsidy policies, innovation incubators and many other technology support programs. We are now much more attuned to, and sophisticated in dealing with, program application and selection issues. But despite the progress that has been made, there are ways to make ourselves more useful.

One way is do much more comparative policy evaluation. The idea is not to ask whether the program was effective, but to try to understand which specific features of program design are the most effective, and in what circumstances (for example, what else is needed to make specific designs effective). In particular, we need to pay attention to how design features affect participation in the program ('adverse selection') and the effort levels of participants ('moral hazard'). To illustrate with a simple example, requiring co-payments as a condition of receiving an R&D

subsidy provides a demand-driven element which should help weed out bad projects, and incentivize greater effort by participants. Assessing a range of programs with, and some without, this feature would help identify the effectiveness of this design feature. Typically, program evaluation is done by empirical economists, with little input from applied theorists. If we are to take a more comparative design approach, I think we would benefit from more input from applied theory, especially contract theory.[2] At the end of the day, policy-makers need to know not only whether to do something, but how to do it.

How can we do this? In the absence of natural experiments that allow us to compare policy (program) designs, we need to conduct such policy experiments, ideally using randomized assignment of economic agents to the different policies. This could be done across different geographic areas at the subnational level or across countries. Of course doing this might raise serious legal issues, especially if applied to firms. For example, randomized assignment to different R&D subsidy programs could put some firms at an *ex post* competitive disadvantage, even if one could argue that there is no competitive disadvantage *ex ante* – since we do not know the more effective program design at the start. For this rcason, it is probably easier to implement this approach with households (for example welfare or education experiments). But for technology policy, we really must use firms, so we may need to think of ways to compensate participants who end up having been assigned to 'inferior' program designs.

Second, as Feller emphasizes, applications of program evaluation methodology are always conducted in a partial equilibrium context. We typically analyze programs in isolation. This can be seriously misleading in contexts where complementary institutions and/or policies are important in making the program under evaluation successful. Success often requires a bundle of policies, or environmental features.[3] When this is so, we should be looking at the bundle, and failure to do so can lead us to misleading, or wrong, recommendations. This is especially so when the recommendation involves 'replicating' the policy in quite different contexts. In theory, there is nothing preventing program evaluation techniques from being applied to policy–program bundles. There are serious obstacles to doing this in practice, but I think we should be trying to move in that direction.

What is the alternative? Feller seems to favor more use of general equilibrium simulation models. The basic idea is that, since reality is complicated, we need complicated models that incorporate interactions and feedback effects which we think might be important. And since such complicated models cannot be econometrically estimated in practice, we need to utilize simulation analysis as an alternative to estimation. As he puts it:

> Existing evaluations of R&D programs touch only lightly, however, on how the strategies, behavior and performance of the sectors or actors described in the national innovation system change as a result of the cumulative, long-term impact of a cluster of science and technology programs. To track and thus evaluate the sequential effects outlined above requires updated, contemporary, more general equilibrium models of national systems . . .

I am deeply skeptical about the usefulness of this approach. First, there is the danger of specious precision in interpreting the 'empirical results'. How can the analyst or the policy-maker validate the structure of the model and the parameterization used to simulate it? It would be very difficult (if not impossible) to calibrate such models sensibly. The conventional approach – originating in highly stylized macroeconomic models – is to calibrate parameters of the model by matching the second moments and other characteristics (for example dynamics) of endogenous variables implied by the model to their observed counterparts in the data. This approach works there precisely because those models are relatively simple and the endogenous outcomes are measurable. But it is hard to imagine how this can be done meaningfully in a very complicated model in which many of the key outcomes are not easily measurable – for example the pace and direction of innovation, what Feller refers to as 'transformative research'. If we cannot calibrate the models sensibly, how can we have any confidence in the predictions that the models generate? While superficially seductive, I think this approach is unlikely to deliver credible guidance to policy-makers, and is very likely to be misused.

But I think that there are other ways to enrich, or redirect, our analysis of technology policies. Perhaps the most important is to pay more attention to the institutional context and structures within which policies are implemented. It is not just that we need to consider potentially important complementarities, as I pointed out before. There are important issues where the main focus should be to understand the incentives, constraints and political economy of decision-making over the allocation of resources, and how these are shaped in turn by organizational structure. A good example is how federal money is allocated across scientific fields and even within disciplines such as biomedical research (by the National Institutes of Health). For this we need to enlist applied theorists – economists and others – to think carefully about both the positive, and normative, questions regarding the structure of policy-making institutions and rules. We should not take existing structures as immutable. I think research along these lines could yield important guidance in this critical area.

In emphasizing the need for economic analysis of organizational structures and incentives in science and technology policy, I am not alone.

In his historical analysis in chapter 7, Nate Rosenberg highlights the importance of 'the changing institutional requirements of newly emerging technologies'. I also think that this perspective is compatible with Feller's own view. As he says:

> More broadly, the field is ripe for economists to design and evaluate alternative program and proposal selection mechanisms with respect to the characteristics of performers, the characteristics of the R&D they undertake, and the relationships between these two outcomes and science and technology outcome variables.

In thinking about the allocation of resources to different scientific fields, it is important to retain a historical perspective. As in all things, there are fads in science, and they bring about political as well as academic pressure to redirect research budgets. But it is important not to overreact. In particular, I want to emphasize the importance of steady and balanced research budgets. First, research is an experimental, cumulative and interactive process, and it is very costly to adjust the level of effort over time. These large adjustment costs make multi-year funding horizons crucial. Second, there are strong complementarities among scientific fields, and these are hard to predict in advance. This is nicely illustrated by Nate Rosenberg's illuminating chapter on the historical links between invention in physics and life sciences. It was Nobel Prize-winning physics research that led to the development of key research instruments that made advances in molecular biology possible. Rosenberg provides a number of such examples pertaining to the life sciences. And beyond that, many research efforts are intrinsically multidisciplinary in nature. For both reasons, it is important to preserve a large measure of balance across fields, resisting any faddish focus on single scientific areas or technological trajectories. Admittedly, this does not provide policy-makers with detailed investment guidance – much as they may wish it – but it does provide a useful caution and a longer range perspective than they otherwise take.

Joan Robinson once said: 'In order to know anything it is necessary to know everything, but in order to talk about anything it is necessary to neglect a great deal' (Robinson, 1941). There are many interactions in the real world, and it is impossible for economic researchers (or anyone else) to take them all into account. The key is to abstract in an intelligent way. This is a real problem and it cannot be wished away. We should always try to be as helpful as possible in informing the policy-making process – and I have suggested a few ways to do that. But we also need to be frank in reminding policy-makers that there are limits to what we can say confidently, and no virtue in pretending otherwise.

NOTES

1. These comments only cover Chapters 7 and 8.
2. For a nice example of how contract theory is relevant to practical contract design, see the empirical analysis of the structure of venture capital contracts in Kaplan and Strömberg (2000).
3. For interesting evidence of policy complementarities in the R&D context, see Mohnen and Roller (2005). There is also a growing literature on the importance of complementarities in policy and institutions in emerging economies.

REFERENCES

Kaplan, S.N. and P. Strömberg (2000), 'Financial contracting theory meets the real world: an empirical analysis of venture capital contracts', *Review of Economic Studies*, **70** (2), 281–315.

Mohnen, P. and L.H. Roller (2005), 'Complementarities in innovation policy', *European Economic Review*, **49** (6), 1431–50.

Robinson, J. (1941), 'Rising supply price', *Economica*, **8**, 1–8.

11. Comments on Nathan Rosenberg's 'Critical episodes in the progress of medical innovation'

Iain M. Cockburn

In the past 50 years biomedical research has been both extraordinarily successful in developing our understanding of the fundamental science of living organisms and their diseases, and an extraordinary beneficiary of taxpayer largesse, particularly in the USA. Professor Rosenberg reminds us in chapter 7 – with characteristic grace and insight – of several important aspects of the development of modern biomedical science. First, the historical roots of modern molecular biology lie in the interaction between scientific disciplines, with particularly significant contributions from physics in the form of enabling ideas, technologies, methods and instruments. To paraphrase, no scientific discipline is an island unto itself, and particularly for empirical work, progress is spurred and constrained by the supply of tools and instruments that enable collection and analysis of data. The cases of X-ray crystallography, magnetic resonance imaging (MRI) and fluorescence activated cell sorting discussed by Professor Rosenberg are compelling examples of this phenomenon.

Second, institutions matter, and in several significant ways. The physical co-location of individuals in places like the Cavendish Laboratory appears to have been an important factor in a number of critical discoveries. The significance of organizational norms, incentives and governance is also evident in the central role played by US academic medical centers (AMCs) in more recent scientific progress. The distinctive governance, structure and financing of AMCs continues to encourage interdisciplinary inquiry and cross-fertilization of fields, and is enabled by a high degree of flexibility and entrepreneurialism that allows researchers to work with many different organizations and communities of practice, and to assimilate and contribute to new fields. In recent years AMCs have come under serious financial pressure as industry-sponsored clinical research has increasingly been conducted by specialist commercial entities. This may prove very costly if it forces AMCs to limit the scope of their activity.

Third, biomedical sciences have come to dominate publicly financed research, most obviously in the USA, but increasingly so in other countries. The underlying causes are far from clear, though interest-group politics ('disease advocacy') and very strong public support of the mission of the National Institutes of Health (NIH) have surely played a major role.

These observations raise some very interesting policy issues. Recognizing the contributions of physics, and physicists, to the development of molecular biology, Professor Rosenberg argues that the comparative budgetary neglect of this discipline may have very substantial long-run costs, which are presumably not confined to the biomedical arena. Should we therefore increase support for academic physics? Perhaps so, but it is far from clear that the contributions and linkages of an earlier era apply today. For example, molecular biology is an increasingly digital enterprise, with 'wet science' complemented, if not supplanted, by *in silico* research. Here, key enabling technologies and 'instruments' are software, computer networks, and the ability to integrate, 'curate' and administer huge databases of genetic, epidemiological and structural information. Professor Rosenberg's general point – that these technologies were initially developed outside the biomedical field – is thus very clear, but the specific policy prescription of supporting physics *per se* is less obviously supported by this example. It is particularly provocative that while public or military support of research has indeed played an important role in the early development of some of these technologies, much of the subsequent development of information technology (IT) has been driven by commercial actors and commercial incentives. Another enabling technology for leading-edge biomedical research is nanotech, which promises to create entirely new therapeutic paradigms operating at the subcellular level. Again, this is a field that has enjoyed significant public support, but like IT is also driven by venture capital investment and other commercial interests.

Disproportionate emphasis in the public research budget on funding biomedical disciplines may well be counterproductive (if intended to accelerate progress in these fields) if it crowds out, or starves, other disciplines. But it is far from clear *ex ante* where any reallocation of resources should go. Furthermore, the examples of bioinformatics and nanotech suggest that other, often for-profit, institutions supporting technical advance can drive the development of enabling technologies. Looking to the future, Professor Rosenberg's observations also point to a 'reverse effect' – the current levels of support of biomedical science are presumably generating ideas and tools that will be important inputs and complements to progress in as yet unanticipated fields.

PART III

Rationales for and Modes of Mission-Oriented Policies

12. What does economic theory tell us about mission-oriented R&D?[1]

David C. Mowery

12.1 INTRODUCTION: THE ELEPHANT IN THE ROOM

The economic rationale for public funding of research and development (R&D) has remained largely unchanged since its articulation in seminal work by Nelson (1959) and Arrow (1962). Both scholars argued that the difficulties of appropriating the returns from investment in research and innovation lead private firms to underinvest in these activities, creating a 'market failure' that can be addressed by (among other things) public investment in R&D. In a number of respects, this theoretical rationale echoed the policy arguments laid out by Vannevar Bush in his 1945 report, *Science: The Endless Frontier*. The market failure rationale remains central to the economic analysis of science and technology policy.

Although the market failure rationale retains great rhetorical influence as a justification for public R&D investments, casual empiricism suggests that its influence over such public investments is modest. Most Organisation for Economic Co-operation and Development (OECD) nations' R&D investment budgets are dominated by programs that serve specific government missions, such as defense, agriculture, health, energy, and other activities. The 'market failure' rationale underpins less than 50 percent of public R&D spending in most of these economies.

The dominance of government R&D spending by mission-oriented programs is hardly a new discovery.[2] But the apparent failure of the primary theoretical justification for public R&D investment to explain the allocation of these funds has some important implications. Among other things, obeisance to the market failure rationale means that policy-makers frequently apply 'lessons' from mission-oriented programs to very different contexts. In fact, however, the economic effects of many mission-oriented R&D programs often are linked to complementary policies or broader structural elements of the sponsoring agencies' missions. Apparently similar programs of public R&D investment may produce very different outcomes in different contexts.

This chapter surveys the inadequacies of the market failure framework for policy analysis of the mission-oriented programs that account for the majority of most industrial economies' public R&D investment. I begin with a summary of the evidence on the dominance of public R&D spending by mission-oriented programs, and then discuss some of the policy tools associated with mission-oriented R&D programs that are rarely included in the market failure justifications. The penultimate section of the chapter examines some of the problems for policy analysis that result from the failure of scholars and policy-makers to appreciate the differences in context between mission-oriented R&D programs and those justified by market failure arguments. Conclusions follow.

12.2 DEFINING AND MEASURING 'MISSION-ORIENTED R&D' INVESTMENT

The R&D investments of OECD member state governments typically are categorized by 'socio-economic objective', based on the purpose (mission) of the funding agency, rather than the content of the R&D program per se (OECD, 2002, p. 143). Thus, as the *Frascati Manual* (OECD, 2002) notes, health-related R&D supported by government defense agencies is classified as 'defense-related', rather than 'health' R&D. As this example suggests, the emphasis on government objectives obscures the distinctions among 'basic', 'applied' and 'development' categories within R&D budgets. Moreover, R&D program goals and agency missions are likely to be more closely linked in applied and development programs than in basic research. The relative importance of basic, applied and development spending within any government's mission-oriented R&D spending within a given category, for example health, also varies considerably among OECD member states.

Keeping in mind that similarities in agency missions may obscure significant differences in R&D program structure, a comparison of member state government R&D spending data highlights the dominance of mission-oriented programs. Figures 12.1 and 12.2 display data from the National Science Foundation (NSF) (National Science Board, 2006) on 'mission-oriented' and 'non-mission-oriented' R&D spending for six industrial economies and one middle-income industrializing economy (South Korea) for the 2003–04 period. The 'mission-oriented' categories of R&D spending, chosen to make these national data as comparable as possible, are defense, space exploration, energy, agriculture, industrial

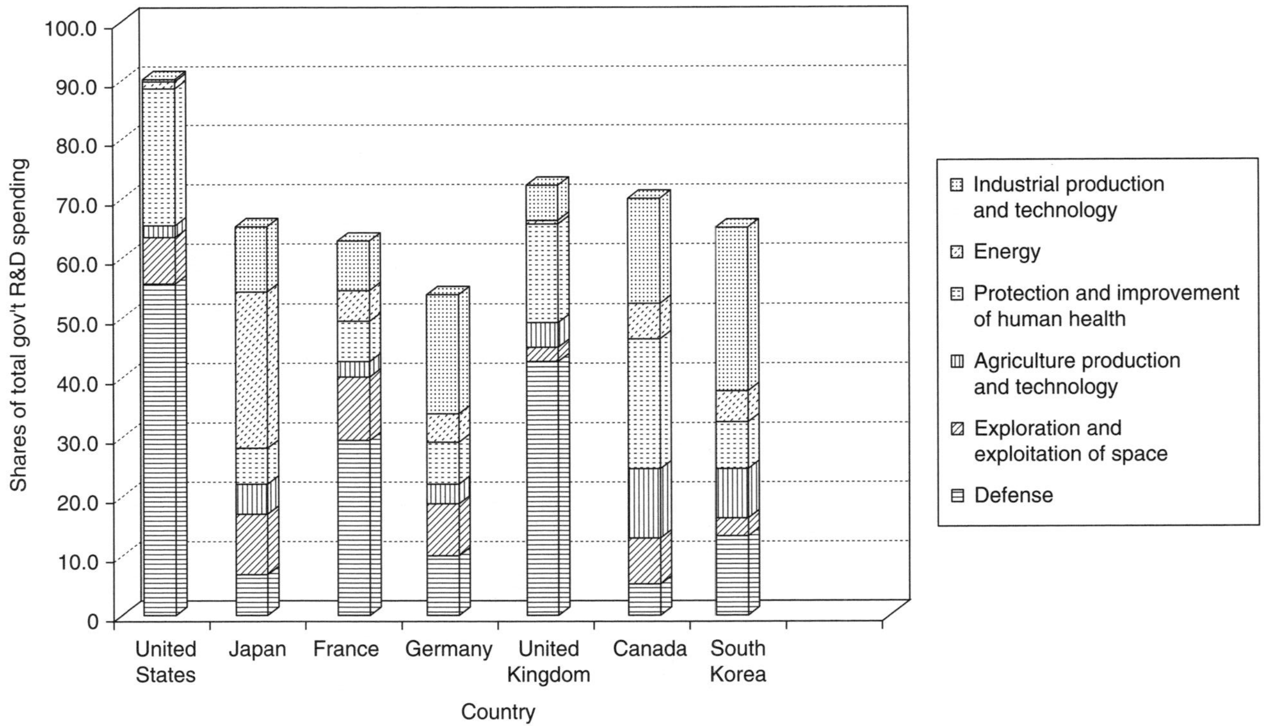

Source: National Science Board (2006).

Figure 12.1 Government R&D spending by 'socioeconomic objective', 2003–04

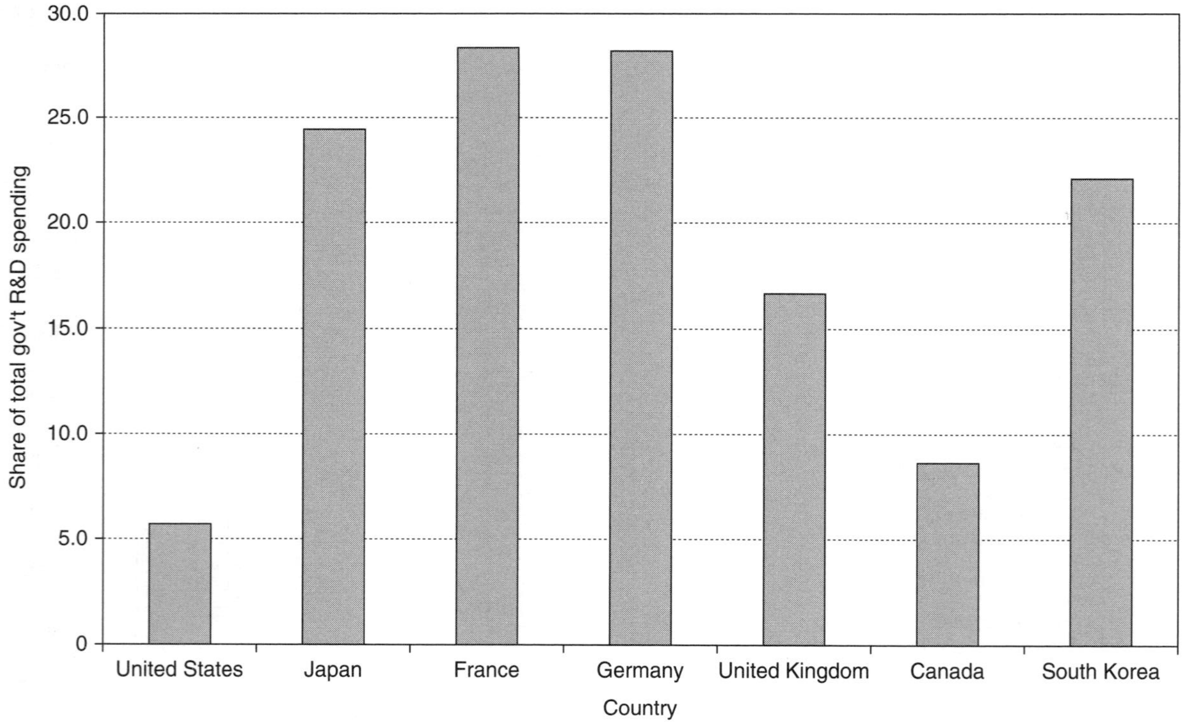

Source: National Science Board (2006).

Figure 12.2 Government spending on 'non-mission-oriented' R&D, 2003–04

technology development and health.[3] As Figure 12.1 points out, in none of these nations does 'non-mission' R&D account for as much as 50 percent of central government R&D spending, and in most of the countries included in Figure 12.1, 'mission-oriented' R&D spending accounts for more than 60 percent of the public R&D budget. The United States is an outlier, with large R&D programs in defense and health bringing the total 'mission-oriented' R&D budget to well over 90 percent of federal government R&D spending.

Also noteworthy in Figure 12.2 is the relatively small share of central government R&D spending accounted for by the 'Bush–Arrow' form of R&D spending, non-mission-oriented R&D. This class of public R&D investment accounts for nearly 30 percent of reported central government R&D spending in France and Germany, but is well below 20 percent in the United Kingdom and Canada, and barely exceeds 5 percent in the United States.

The structure of mission-oriented R&D programs differs among agencies and missions nearly as much as the structure of such programs differs from that of 'Bush–Arrow' R&D programs. The different mix of performers and funding vehicles in the R&D programs of different mission agencies has important implications for knowledge spillovers and personnel training, among other externalities supported by R&D funding. Figures 12.3 and 12.4 highlight the contrasts between US defense-related and biomedical research (the two leading fields of mission-oriented R&D in the US federal budget) in the mix of basic, applied and development spending, as well as the differences in importance of different institutional performers of R&D. The distribution among performers and R&D categories of biomedical R&D resembles that of the National Science Foundation's R&D spending more closely than it does the Department of Defense R&D programs. Although these features of publicly funded biomedical R&D are similar to those of the leading 'Bush–Arrow' public R&D program in the United States, the rationale for the enormous US investment of public funds in biomedical research has little to do with market failure – after all, biomedical research is characterized by relatively strong intellectual property rights, and industry-financed R&D spending has outstripped public R&D funding since the 1960s.

The governance of many of these large public investments in mission-oriented R&D also bears little resemblance to the idealized portrait of the '[Vannevar] Bush social contract'[4] articulated in Guston and Keniston (1994). Rather than 'scientists' controlling the allocation of public R&D funds, allocation decisions in these R&D programs were based on assessments of the research needs of specific agency missions ranging from national defense to agriculture. Indeed, in at least one important post-war

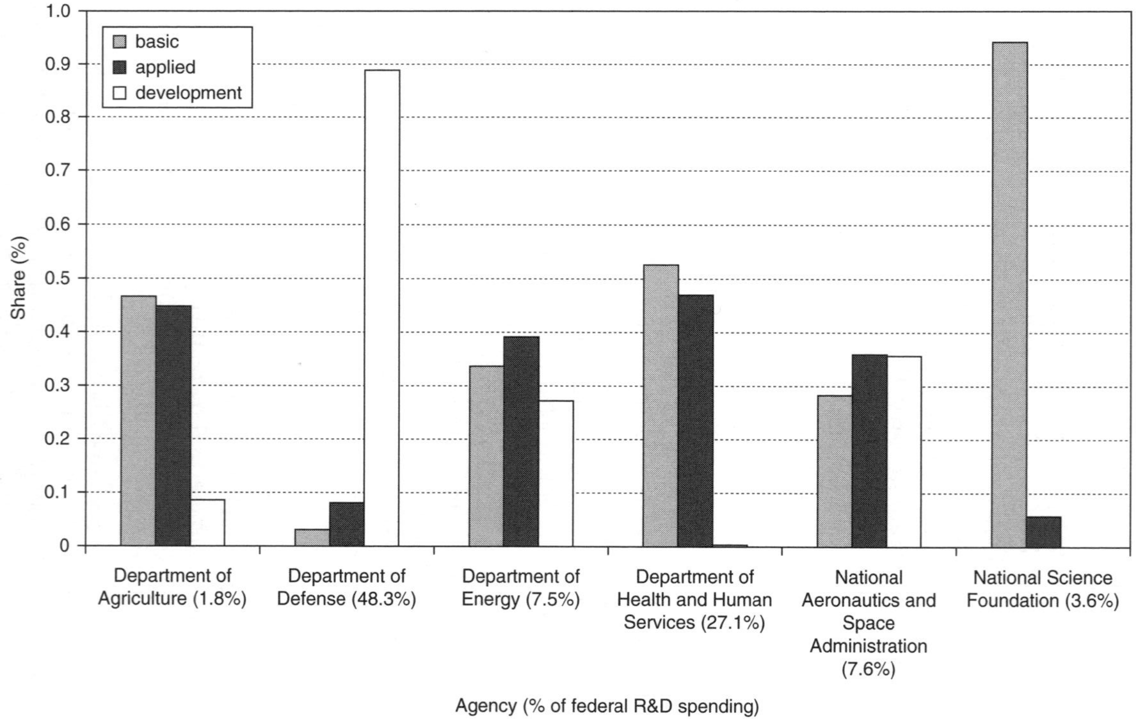

Source: National Science Board (2006).

Figure 12.3 Composition of R&D spending by agency, FY 2005

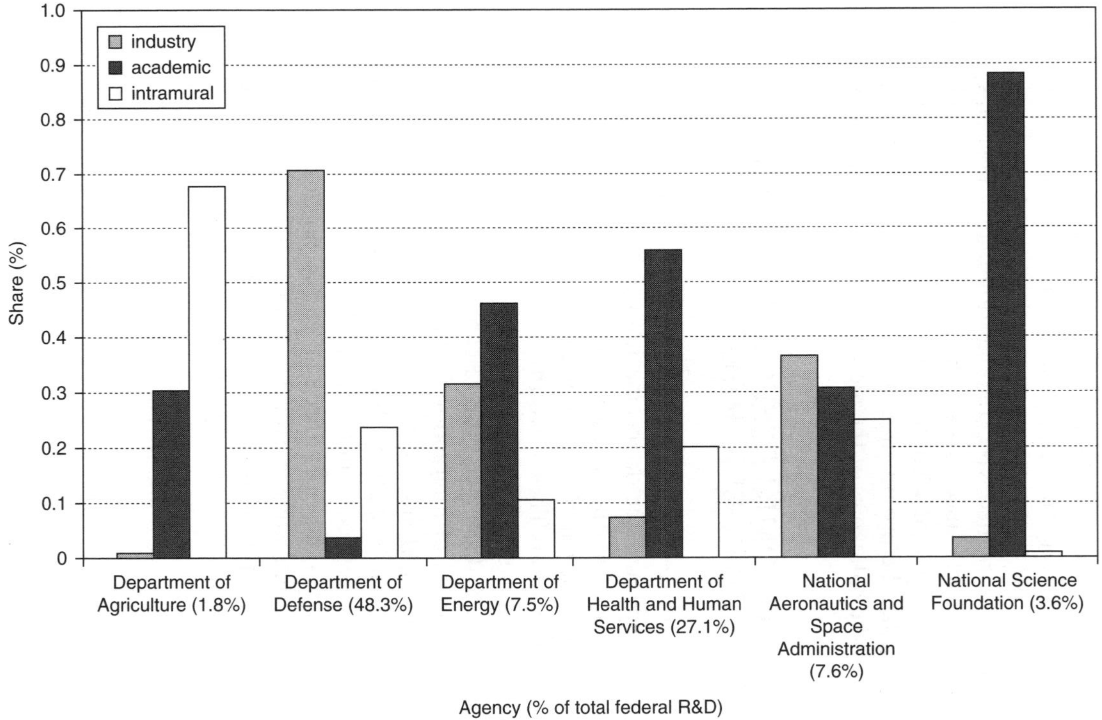

Source: National Science Board (2006).

Figure 12.4 Industry, academic and intramural performer shares of agency R&D, FY 2005

program of defense-related R&D, the US Defense Advanced Research Projects Agency's (DARPA) initiative to create academic 'centers of excellence' in the embryonic field of computer science, peer review played a minimal role (see Langlois and Mowery, 1996). Although Gibbons et al. (1994) have proclaimed the rise of a new type of publicly funded R&D ('Mode 2'), which is multidisciplinary, motivated by societal needs, and accountable to public funding agencies, in fact 'Mode 2' appears to resemble the mission-oriented R&D that has dominated most OECD governments' R&D budgets since at least the 1950s. To a surprising extent, scholarly analysis of the 'new context' of science and technology policy fails to acknowledge the prominence of mission-oriented R&D programs that have few of the hallmarks of the idealized 'Bush social contract'.

12.3 THE ECONOMIC EFFECTS OF MISSION-ORIENTED PUBLIC R&D

There are at least three channels through which mission R&D programs affect economy-wide and sector-specific innovation. Similarly to public R&D support based on the 'market failure' analysis, mission-agency R&D investments can expand the scientific or engineering knowledge that supports innovation. These investments also may create or expand institutional components of national innovation systems, such as university-based research, that provide both research and trained scientists and engineers. This channel of interaction is likely to be most responsive to mission-agency R&D spending on basic and applied research, rather than development, as well as a relatively high share of universities among the research performers (defined as in Figure 12.4).

A second important channel through which mission-agency R&D investment affects innovative performance are 'spinoffs', technologies developed with the support of these public R&D programs that have applications in both civilian and agency-mission fields. This channel of interaction has been observed most commonly in defense-related investments in technology development. The civilian 'spinoffs' associated with these defense-related investments appear to be most significant in the early development of new technologies, since these early phases of a technology's evolution often exhibit substantial overlap between defense and non-defense applications. As technologies mature, civilian and military requirements frequently diverge, and the scope for civilian benefit from such 'spinoffs' declines.

A third channel through which mission-agency R&D spending can advance civilian innovation is public procurement. Mission-agency R&D

investments, particularly in defense, are often complemented by substantial agency purchases of products embodying new technologies. Moreover, procurement competitions can themselves influence private firms' R&D spending. Lichtenberg (1984) shows that US defense contractors frequently expand privately funded R&D investment in order to compete for large military orders.

In addition to this direct link between procurement and industry-funded R&D investment, however, defense procurement has affected the development and diffusion of new technologies. The US military services, whose requirements typically emphasize performance above all other characteristics (including cost), have on a number of occasions functioned as a 'lead purchaser', placing large orders for early versions of new technologies. In some celebrated cases (for example, integrated circuits), procurement programs have enabled supplier firms to reduce the costs of their products and improve their reliability and functionality. New technologies undergo a prolonged period of 'debugging', performance and reliability improvement, cost reduction, and learning on the part of users and producers about applications and maintenance (Mowery and Rosenberg, 1999). The pace and pattern of such progressive improvement affect the rate of adoption, and the rate of adoption in turn affects the development of these innovations. Government procurement also may allow innovators to benefit from learning by increasing the scale of production for early versions of the technology. The presence or absence of procurement policies complementing their R&D investments is an important (and frequently overlooked) factor influencing the broader economic effects of mission-oriented R&D programs, and underscores the heterogeneity associated with these programs.[5]

The scope for 'pure' knowledge-based benefits from mission-agency R&D is limited by the composition of these R&D programs. For example, development spending historically has accounted for at least 85 percent of the US defense R&D budget, in contrast to its share of less than 1 percent in the R&D budget of the Department of Health and Human Services (HHS, parent agency of the National Institutes of Health).[6] 'Basic' and 'applied' research together accounted for only slightly more than 10 percent of defense-related R&D spending during the fiscal year 2005. But the sheer size of the Department of Defense (DoD) R&D budget, as well as the concentration of DoD academic research support on the physical sciences, means that defense-related investments in research (including basic and applied research activities as defined by the US Department of Defense) account for a significant share of federally funded R&D in such fields as computer science (more than 35 percent in the fiscal year 2001) or engineering (more than 30 percent; all figures from the American Association for the Advancement of Science, 2000).

Mission-agency R&D spending contributed to the growth of the US 'research infrastructure' before 1940 (primarily in agricultural R&D) and during the post-war period. The restructuring of the US 'national innovation system' that began during the 1940s increased the scale and importance of university-based research, relying on a large federal defense-related research budget in basic and applied fields of science and engineering to create the 'Cold War University' (Lowen, 1997; Leslie, 1993). Declines in defense-related investments in academic R&D in the late 1960s and early 1970s were gradually offset by growth in federally funded biomedical R&D in US universities. By the early twenty-first century (fiscal year 2003), roughly 70 percent of federally funded academic R&D in the United States came from a single agency, the National Institutes of Health.

12.3.1 Case Study of a Commercial 'Spinoff' from Mission-Oriented R&D: The Internet

The development of the Internet in the United States illustrates the ways in which the scale and structure of defense-related R&D spending generated a significant commercial spinoff. This brief case study should not be interpreted to be representative of the vast array of defense-related R&D projects sponsored during the post-1945 period by the US government, many of which generated no commercial pay-offs (consistent with their intent) and at least some of which (as in numerically controlled machine tools and civilian nuclear power) arguably damaged the economic prospects of the firms that sought to exploit potential commercial applications of defense-funded innovations. Nevertheless, the case of the Internet illustrates the ways in which mission-oriented R&D programs can influence the broad pattern of civilian innovation in a given technological field, and highlights as well the breadth of policy instruments (many of which are not present in non-mission R&D programs) that underpins this influence.

The development of both computer networking technology and the Internet in the United States benefited significantly from defense-related R&D and procurement funding (see Mowery and Simcoe, 2002, for additional detail), and the structure of this mission-oriented R&D program enhanced its commercial spinoffs. The Internet was invented and commercialized primarily in the United States, although scientists and engineers in other industrial economies (especially France and the United Kingdom) made important contributions to computer networking technologies during the 1970s. Indeed, the key inventions behind the creation of the World Wide Web came from CERN, the European nuclear physics research facility. Nonetheless, US entrepreneurs and firms led the transformation of these inventions into components of a national and global network of networks, and were early adopters of new applications.

During the early 1960s, several researchers, including Leonard Kleinrock at Massachusetts Institute of Technology (MIT) and Paul Baran of the RAND Corporation, developed various aspects of the theory of packet switching.[7] The work of Baran, Kleinrock and others led DARPA to fund the construction of a prototype network in 1968. The resulting ARPANET is widely recognized as the earliest forerunner of the Internet (National Research Council, 1999, Chapter 7). By 1975, as universities and other major defense research sites were linked to the network, ARPANET had grown to more than 100 nodes.

US dominance in commercial applications of computer networking did not result from a first-mover advantage in the invention or the early development of a packet-switched network. French and British computer scientists contributed important technical advances to packet-switching and computer-networking technologies and protocols during this period, and publicly supported prototype computer networks were established in both France and the UK by the early 1970s. But the investment by DARPA in the early deployment of computer networking technology on a large scale, as well as the ARPANET's inclusion of a diverse array of institutions as members, distinguished the US prototype national network from its British and French counterparts, and accelerated the development of supporting technologies and applications. In this and other fields of defense-related R&D, the sheer scale of the US investment (something that reflected the national-security mission of its sponsor agency) contrast with that of defense-related R&D efforts in other industrial economies during this period.[8] The combination of basic, applied and development objectives in this and other defense-related programs also would have been difficult to defend politically in other fields of mission-oriented or 'market-failure' R&D programs. The scale and impact (if not the cost-efficiency) of at least some fields of 'mission-oriented' R&D investment thus reflect the political saliency of the missions to which they are directed.

In addition to their scale, the structure of these substantial federal R&D investments enhanced their effectiveness. In its efforts to encourage exploration of a variety of technical approaches to research priorities, DARPA frequently funded similar projects in several different universities and private R&D laboratories. Moreover, the Department of Defense's procurement policy complemented DARPA's broad-based approach to R&D funding. As had been true of semiconductors, the award by DARPA of development and procurement contracts to small firms such as BBN helped foster entry by new firms into the emerging Internet industry, supporting intense competition and rapid innovation.

12.4 POLICY IMPLICATIONS

Although the mission-oriented programs that dominate the public R&D budgets of most OECD economies share a common justification (supporting agency missions) that contrasts with the market failure rationale, the contrasts among different mission-oriented R&D programs are considerable. The data in Figures 12.3 and 12.4 underscore the extent of these structural contrasts among US mission-agency R&D programs. Similar data on other OECD economies' mission-agency R&D programs are lacking, and would facilitate a more informed comparative analysis of public R&D programs. This emphasis on the contrasting institutional structure of public R&D programs is an important contribution of the 'innovation systems' approach to R&D policy, and it deserves to be incorporated more fully into the collection of indicators and R&D data. Among other things, better data on these characteristics of mission-oriented R&D programs could support a more rigorous analysis of the economic effects of such programs.

As I noted earlier, the presence or absence of complementary procurement policies is another important factor mediating the economic effects of mission-oriented R&D programs. It seems clear, for example, that many of the widely cited 'spinoff' benefits of post-war US defense-related R&D spending have as much to do with the scale and structure of the procurement programs that accompanied them as with the structure of the R&D programs themselves. The lack of such procurement programs in other mission areas, such as energy, arguably has reduced the effectiveness of US mission-oriented R&D programs in the field. Recent proposals by expert panels convened by the US National Academy of Sciences (NAS) for energy R&D programs that are modeled on DARPA fail to recognize the important role of procurement in DARPA's successful programs.[9] In the absence of a comparably ambitious procurement policy to complement the R&D investment program discussed by the NAS panel, the near-term effects of high R&D expenditure are likely to be modest.

More generally, the importance of procurement policy for the economic effects of mission-oriented R&D programs underscores the importance of demand-related policies. One reason for the economic effects of mission-oriented R&D spending by the US National Institutes of Health is the large, price-insensitive market for pharmaceuticals and medical devices created by the unusual (cost-insensitive) structure of the US healthcare delivery and reimbursement system. In the absence of a procurement policy, other policies affecting the demand for alternative energy technologies (for example, carbon taxes) are needed to support the adoption of innovations flowing from alternative-energy R&D initiatives.[10]

Still another way in which failure to attend to the characteristics of the R&D and the market (or lack of) for the results of mission-oriented R&D programs has distorted policy debate can be found in the references during congressional debate of the Bayh–Dole Act of 1980 to the 'commercialization failure' associated with the large stock of pre-1980 patents owned by the federal government. Proponents of the Act pointed to the small share (fewer than 5 percent) of the 28 000 patents owned by the federal government as of 1976 that were licensed to private firms, arguing that giving patent rights to universities and federal laboratories would create incentives for development and commercialization that were lacking under the current system. But as Eisenberg (1996) has pointed out, the majority of these 28 000 patents originated in R&D programs funded by the US Defense Department, which readily granted patent rights to research performers. A more fundamental reason for the lack of commercial exploitation of the patents was the fact that they covered technologies with limited civilian applications. Regardless of the merits of the Bayh–Dole Act, this important justification for its passage was founded on a failure to recognize the unusual (and commercially limited) content of mission-oriented R&D in the defense area. As in the case of energy R&D, political actors highlighted 'analogies' among fields of public R&D that in fact differed considerably, reflecting the mission orientation of their sponsoring agencies.

Yet another example of the unusual tensions between ends and means that results from the dominance within the US federal R&D budget of mission-oriented agencies is the Small Business Innovation Research (SBIR) program. The SBIR program was created in 1982 to mandate a 'set-aside' of a fixed share of agency R&D budgets for small-firm R&D projects, based on the arguments that small firms are more innovative than large firms, yet face significant obstacles in winning federal R&D contracts. The share of federal agency R&D budgets dedicated to small-firm R&D support has grown since the program's creation, and now stands at 2.5 percent, accounting for well over $1 billion in annual spending. During fiscal years 1982–2004, total spending by the SBIR program amounted to roughly $17 billion, dwarfing the size of other federal 'precommercial industrial R&D' programs such as the Advanced Technology Program. The SBIR program involves competitive awards of R&D contracts that require reviews of projects' technical and commercial possibilities, and one indicator of program 'success' employed by such evaluators as the US Government Accountability Office (GAO) is the commercial success of projects funded from the SBIR.

The wisdom of using public funds to subsidize commercially promising projects that might well obtain financing in the private capital markets obviously is questionable, but the role of mission agencies in financing

SBIR projects raises other problems. The SBIR award criteria create a tension between the mission requirements of federal agencies such as NASA and the Defense Department (reflecting the percentage formula for funding SBIR and the Defense Department's prominence within the federal R&D budget, this agency alone accounts for roughly one-half of annual SBIR spending) and the feasibility of commercializing technologies developed for these agency needs. As one commentator noted at a 1999 conference on the SBIR program:

> Awards are required to support research that meets the needs of the awarding agencies, yet products developed under the program are expected to be successful in the commercial marketplace. Thus, there may be a conflict between the goals of procurement and innovation. (Turner, 1999, p. 49)[11]

The dominance of mission-oriented investments within most governments' public R&D programs also has implications for the allocation of resources among scientific disciplines and research fields. Rather than originating in a 'scientific' or 'peer-review' assessment of the opportunities and needs of different research fields, the dominance of mission agencies within central government R&D spending means that agency missions drive such allocation decisions. Change in the political saliency of these agency missions, rather than an assessment of the technological or scientific merits of different R&D areas, accordingly influences shifts in the allocation of public R&D budgets. For example, the end of the Cold War and the associated declines in defense spending led to cuts in defense-related R&D spending, a key source of support for scientific and engineering R&D in US universities, and inflation-adjusted funding for the physical sciences and engineering has grown slowly or not at all since the early 1990s. Similarly, the rapid growth in the National Institutes of Health budget began in the 1970s as a result of the political decisions of the Nixon administration and Congress to pursue the 'War on Cancer'. The dominance of mission-oriented R&D, combined with a lack of good data on the implications of shifting mission priorities for balance in the overall public R&D 'portfolio', have produced significant imbalances in the financial underpinnings of US research universities and the overall national R&D infrastructure.

12.5 CONCLUSION

Economic analysis of public R&D investment has been hampered by its reliance on an intellectual framework that is fundamentally at variance with the majority of nearly all industrial economies' public R&D

investment programs. The failure to differentiate between 'market failure' and 'mission-agency' R&D programs has led to a number of ill-conceived analogies and distortions in policy debates. Rather than continued reliance on such a distorted analytic framework, a more disaggregated analytic framework that acknowledges differences among the missions accounting for more than 50 percent of most industrial-economy public R&D budgets, that more clearly and effectively distinguishes among the structural components of these mission-R&D programs, and that recognizes the role of complementary agency policies, is a more robust framework for the economic analysis of public R&D investment. This framework builds on a large body of policy analysis and scholarship in the field of 'national innovation systems'.

NOTES

1. A previous draft of this chapter was presented at the Technology Policy Conference, Monte Verità, Switzerland, 18–21 June 2007. I am grateful to conference participants for useful comments. Research for this paper was supported in part by the US National Science Foundation (Cooperative Agreement #0531184).
2. In his classic 1987 paper, Ergas drew a distinction between 'mission-oriented' and 'diffusion-oriented' national innovation systems (without using the 'innovation systems' term), highlighting the dominant role of defense-related R&D in government R&D spending in the United States, the United Kingdom and France, in contrast to other industrial economies such as Sweden or Germany. But Ergas did not focus on the role of non-defense-mission R&D funding, nor did he emphasize the gap between the Arrow–Nelson economic rationale for public R&D funding and the actual mix of publicly funded R&D in most industrial economies.
3. The data are normalized to exclude central government funding for universities, a category of government R&D spending that accounts for significant shares of the German, Canadian, Japanese and French government R&D budgets in the NSF data. In some of these nations, central government spending on universities may include significant 'non-mission-oriented' R&D programs.
4. Martin (2003, p. 9) highlights 'several essential characteristics of the [Vannevar] Bush social contract. First, it implied a high level of autonomy for science. Second, decisions on which areas of science should be funded should be left to scientists. It therefore brought about the institutionalization of the peer-review system to allocate resources, a system used before the Second World War by private foundations that supported research. Third, it was premised on the belief that basic research was best done in universities (rather than government or company laboratories).'
5. The structure of these procurement policies also is important. The US Defense Department's procurement programs in semiconductor components and numerous fields of computer technology often favored new firms (Flamm, 1988), and thereby supported the growth of entrants in industries whose structure might otherwise have become more highly concentrated. In addition, the reliance on entrant-firm suppliers led military agencies to insist on a 'second source' for critical semiconductor components, accelerating inter-firm diffusion of key product and process technologies.
6. The development share of the HHS R&D budget only slightly exceeds that of the 'Bush–Arrow' agency, the National Science Foundation (Figure 12.3).

7. On a packet-switched network, information is broken up into a series of discrete 'packets' that are sent individually, and reassembled into a complete message at the receiving end. A single circuit may carry packets from multiple connections, and the packets for a single communication may take different routes from source to destination.
8. The political saliency of the 'national security' mission assigned to the Department of Defense and related agencies (for example, the Atomic Energy Commission, forerunner of the Department of Energy and responsible for nuclear weapons development) during the post-1945 period in the United States supported investments in R&D and related activities on an unprecedented scale, underscoring the political importance of the links between R&D investments and specific program missions. The scale of US investments in biomedical R&D reflect the political attractiveness of the stated goals of curing diseases that are endemic to a high-income society (cancer, heart disease), and a similar argument applies to the size of the R&D budget and the saliency of the goals of the large programs in agricultural research funded by the federal and state governments in the United States.
9. See Mowery (2006) for additional discussion of the validity of the 'DARPA model' for federally funded energy R&D.
10. The characteristics of (or lack of) markets for the outputs of many mission-oriented R&D programs also complicate statistical analysis of these programs' productivity or economic effects. Much of this statistical analysis is predicated on the identification of consumer welfare gains and knowledge spillovers that are based on the price behavior of the improved goods incorporating the results of R&D investment. Where conventional markets do not exist for the 'goods' flowing from R&D programs, as is often the case in defense-related and other mission-oriented R&D programs, it is much more difficult to measure these economic gains, as Griliches (1979) pointed out.
11. A similar tension developed within the Technology Reinvestment Program of the early Clinton administration that sought to use defense-related R&D investments to support innovation in 'dual-use technologies' for civilian applications.

REFERENCES

American Association for the Advancement of Science (2000), *Research and Development in the FY2001 Budget*, Washington, DC: American Association for the Advancement of Science.

Arrow, K.J. (1962), 'Economic welfare and the allocation of resources for R&D', in NBER (ed.), *The Rate and Direction of Inventive Activity: Economic and Social Factors*, Princeton, NJ: Princeton University Press, pp. 609–25.

Bush, V. (1945), *Science: The Endless Frontier*, Washington, DC: US Government Printing Office.

Eisenberg, R.S. (1996), 'Public research and private development: patents and technology transfer in government-sponsored research', *Virginia Law Review*, **82**, 1663–1727.

Ergas, H. (1987), 'Does technology policy matter?', in B.R. Guile and H. Brooks (eds), *Technology and Global Industry*, Washington, DC: National Academy Press, pp. 191–245.

Flamm, K.J. (1988), *Creating the Computer*, Washington, DC: Brookings Institution.

Gibbons, M., C. Limoges, H. Nowotny, S. Schwartzman, P. Scott and M. Trow (1994), *The New Production of Knowledge*, New York: Sage.

Griliches, Z. (1979), 'Issues in assessing the contribution of R&D to productivity growth', *Bell Journal of Economics*, **10**, 92–116.

Guston, D.H. and K. Keniston (1994), 'Introduction: the social contract for science', in D.H. Guston and K. Keniston (eds), *The Fragile Contract*, Cambridge, MA: MIT Press, pp. 1–41.

Langlois, R.N. and D.C. Mowery (1996), 'The federal government role in the development of the US software industry', in D.C. Mowery (ed.), *The International Computer Software Industry: A Comparative Study of Industry Evolution and Structure*; New York: Oxford University Press, pp. 53–85.

Leslie, S.W. (1993), *The Cold War and American Science*, New York: Columbia University Press.

Lichtenberg, F. (1984), 'The relationship between between federal contract R&D and company R&D', *American Economic Review: Papers and Proceedings of the Annual Meeting of the American Economic Association*, **74**, 73–8.

Lowen, R.S. (1997), *Creating the Cold War University*, Berkeley, CA: University of California Press.

Martin, B.R. (2003), 'The changing social contract for science and the evolution of the university', in A. Geuna, A.J. Salter and W.E. Steinmueller (eds), *Science and Innovation: Rethinking the Rationales for Funding and Governance*, Cheltenham, UK and Northampton, MA, USA: Edward Elgar, pp. 7–29.

Mowery, D.C. (2006), 'Lessons from the history of federal R&D policy for an "Energy ARPA"', Testimony before the Committee on Science and Technology, US House of Representatives, 9 March.

Mowery, D.C. and N. Rosenberg (1999), *Paths of Innovation*, New York: Oxford University Press.

Mowery, D.C. and T. Simcoe (2002), 'Is the Internet a US invention? An economic and technological history of computer networking', *Research Policy*, **31**, 1369–87.

National Research Council (1999), *Funding a Revolution: Government Support for Computing Research*, Washington, DC: National Academy Press.

National Science Board (2006), *Science and Engineering Indicators: 2006*, Washington, DC: National Science Board.

Nelson, R.R. (1959), 'The simple economics of basic research', *Journal of Political Economy*, **67**, 297–306.

OECD (2002), *Frascati Manual: Proposed Standard Practice for Surveys on Research and Experimental Development*, Paris: OECD.

Turner, J. (1999), 'Discussant comments', in C. Wessner (ed.), *The Small Business Innovation Research Program: Challenges and Opportunities*, Washington, DC: National Academies Press, pp. 47–50.

13. The dismal science, the crown jewel and the endless frontier

Bhaven N. Sampat

13.1 BACKGROUND

The National Institutes of Health (NIH) is the biggest funder of biomedical research in the world, and the largest supporter of research (excluding development) in the US federal government (AAAS, 2007). It is the premier 'mission-oriented' research agency in the US, dedicated to 'science in pursuit of fundamental knowledge about the nature and behavior of living systems and the application of that knowledge to extend healthy life and reduce the burdens of illness and disability' (NIH, 2009).

According to NIH definitions, the bulk of its funding is for 'basic' research, or 'systematic study directed toward fuller knowledge or understanding of the fundamental aspects of phenomena and of observable facts without specific applications towards processes or products in mind' (Institute of Medicine, 1998, p. 20). While there is some disagreement on the actual proportions, between 55 and 70 percent of NIH research funding is focused on basic research (US Government Accountability Office (GAO), 2002; Moses et al., 2005).[1]

The lines between 'basic' and 'applied' research are blurry, and Stokes (1997), among others, has argued that much of what the NIH funds is 'use-oriented' basic research, simultaneously concerned with pushing back the frontiers of knowledge and attacking practical problems. Though Stokes does not emphasize this point, research can also be 'practical' from a patron's perspective and 'fundamental' from a performer's perspective. Indeed, in response to early concerns that the establishment of a mission-oriented health research funding agency would interfere with scientific freedom, an NIH spokesperson argued that: 'in the sense that the new knowledge is sought for the purpose of improving human health this program is one of applied research, but many of the grantees consider their projects basic' (quoted in Strickland 1972, p. 30).

A central tension permeating the history of the NIH is that the scientific community has traditionally emphasized the 'fundamental knowledge' aspect of the NIH's mission, but taxpayers ultimately are interested in the health benefits from this research (Strickland, 1972). In this chapter, I take the taxpayer perspective, that is, I view 'fundamental knowledge' as useful not for its consumption value, but rather only because of its potential impact on human health.

From this perspective, I assess the economic rationale for funding basic research at the NIH. The economic rationale for such funding rests on two pillars: first, that the health returns from NIH-funded basic research are high; in particular, that NIH funding yields significant health benefits. And second, that these benefits are not appropriable by private sector actors. Together, these compose the well-known 'market failure' argument for funding basic research. In the following two sections of the chapter, I discuss the evidence for these arguments in the context of basic biomedical research. Next, I assess the extent to which NIH allocation patterns in practice actually conform to prescriptions from economic theory. I conclude with ruminations on theory, practice and suggestions for future research.

13.2 SOCIAL RETURNS

The first pillar supporting the economic argument in support of NIH research is that there are high social returns, in the form of health benefits, from basic research funded by the NIH. Evaluating the impacts of basic research is hard, because of difficulties in measuring outputs and outcomes, lags between inputs and effects, and a lack of useful control samples to assess causality (David et al., 1992; Jaffe, 2002; Jaffe, 1998). This is true even for the NIH, where the main intended outcome – improved health – is relatively well defined (at least at a high level).

One common approach has been to relate broad patterns of NIH funding to data on improvements in health. In his March 2006 testimony before the Senate subcommittee responsible for NIH funding, NIH Director Elias Zerhouni argued:

> [T]hanks to the Nation's investment in biomedical research, we have learned to diminish the harmful impact of many diseases and disabilities for all Americans. The estimated total cumulative investment at the NIH per American over the past 30 years – including the doubling period – is about $1334, or about $44 per American per year over the entire period. Over the same time period, Americans have gained over six years of life expectancy and are aging healthier than ever before . . . The American people's return on their investment in NIH is truly spectacular.[2]

Another common approach is the 'greatest hits' approach, listing a range of specific success stories and arguing that NIH funding was essential for their fruition. For example, the NIH also generally publishes 'Selective Research Highlights' on its web page.[3]

But from an evaluation perspective, these approaches suffer from two deficiencies. The first suffers from the *post hoc ergo propter hoc* fallacy: just because we see a changes in health outcomes and changes in NIH inputs, we cannot conclude that the NIH inputs caused these changes. The second suffers from selecting on the dependent variable: examining only success stories provides little useful information on the average or marginal health returns to NIH funding.

What does empirical work in economics tell us? While there is some dissent about whether biomedical research per se, as opposed to broader socio-economic factors (like economic growth, improved nutrition, and better sanitation and public health) are the key sources of health improvements, there is an emerging consensus that while these other factors were historically more important, biomedical research was the key driver of health improvements in the second half of the twentieth century (Cutler et al., 2006). But there has been remarkably little research examining the specific role of the NIH in these improvements.

One exception is recent work in the cardiovascular arena by Cutler and Kadiyala (2003) and Heidenreich and McClellan (2003). This is an important area to study, since the bulk of improvement in mortality over the post-war era – to which Zerhouni's statement above refers – reflects progress against cardiovascular disease. Indeed, as Figure 13.1 from Cutler and Kadiyala shows, while mortality from cardiovascular disease dropped by two-thirds over the 1950–94 period, in most other areas mortality remained stagnant.

While the cardiovascular arena may not be representative, a focus on what roles NIH research played in the cardiovascular arena can provide a good idea of its overall impact in general.

What were the sources of this improvement? The authors estimate that one-third of this reduction in mortality resulted from better treatment of acute conditions (in particular, heart attacks), one-third from better medications (to manage hypertension and high cholesterol), and one-third from behavioral changes (including reduced smoking and better diets). Combining estimates of the benefits of this reduction with those on costs of these interventions, the authors conclude that the rates of return on new treatments and knowledge are high, that is, in the cardiovascular arena, technical change over the past half-century was 'worth it'. Interestingly, the highest rates of returns according to their calculations were from behavioral knowledge, which induced behavioral changes.

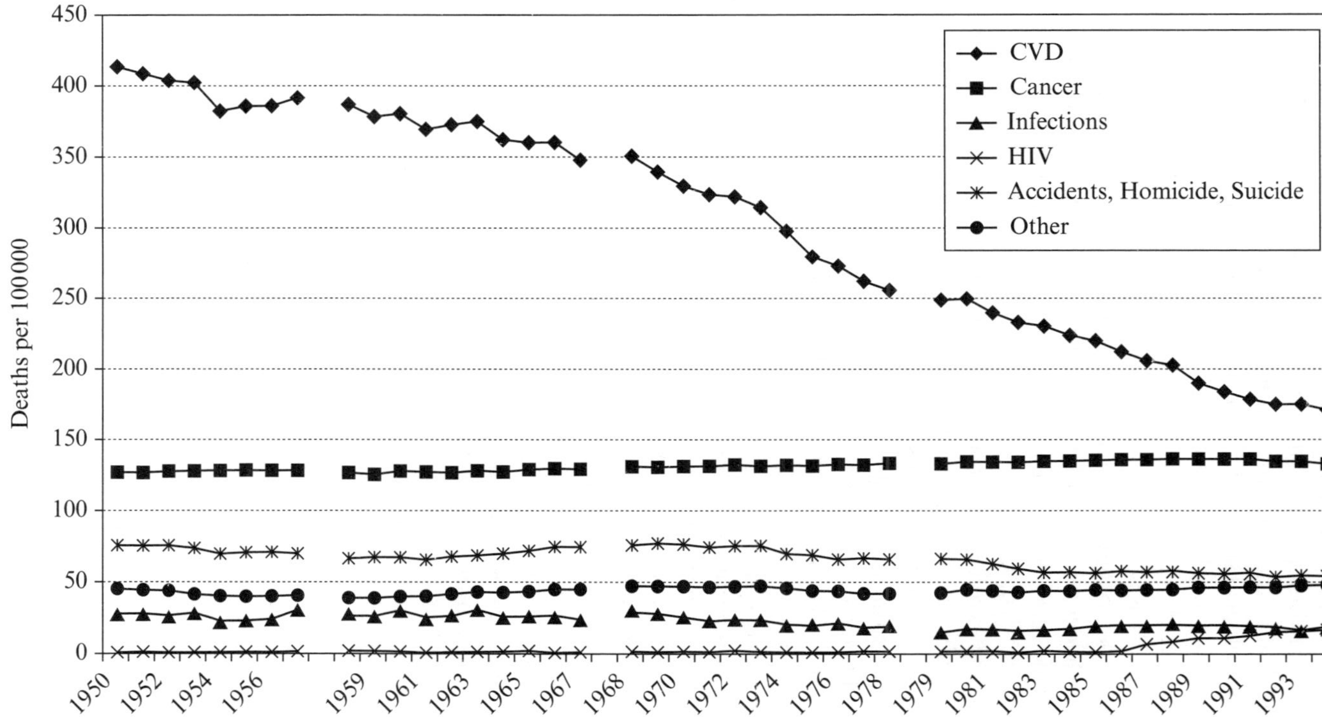

Source: Cutler and Kadiyala (2003).

Figure 13.1 Mortality by cause of death, 1950–94

While Cutler and Kadiyala do not focus primarily on this question, their historical account does point to various instances where the NIH played a critical role. But in these instances, it was not 'basic' research but rather NIH-sponsored clinical studies that were important, by generating evidence on which therapies worked, and on risk factors that induced behavioral change. Similarly, Heidenreich and McClellan (2003) highlight the importance of informal R&D by clinicians in leading to improved heart attack treatment; here too, to the extent that the NIH played a role, it was in funding clinical trials (Heidenreich and McClellan, 2003). (Indeed, Heidenreich and McClellan argue that there may be underinvestment in NIH funding for trials of off-patent drugs, a point to which I return below.)

Overall, in the cardiovascular arena, the main area where society has seen the most substantial improvements in health outcomes over the past half-century, these studies demonstrate little direct evidence of the impact of NIH-funded 'basic' research. However, this was not their main focus; it is possible that closer scrutiny may have revealed a more prominent role for such research. Also interesting is that they do find an important role of NIH-funded clinical research, a point to which I return below.

More indirect evidence on the role of public funding comes in the context of pharmaceutical innovation. A series of studies by Frank Lichtenberg argue that pharmaceutical innovation has been an important source of health improvements: in particular, disease areas where we have seen more new drugs tend to be those where we see better improvements in health outcomes (Lichtenberg, 2003). And there is some evidence that publicly funded research is an important driver of pharmaceutical innovation (Toole, 2000; Mansfield, 1995; Sampat and Lichtenberg, 2007). Based on these arguments, one could argue, by transitivity, that publicly funded basic research is an important source of health improvements.

But in general, there is little econometric evidence supporting the assertion that NIH-funded basic research has played an important role in improvement in health outcomes over the past half-century. One cannot conclude from this that such research did not play a role, given the various measurement and evaluation difficulties cited above – but it is important to recognize the lack of firm evidence supporting the proposition that NIH-funded basic research has been an important source of health improvements. Clearly, more work is needed on this front.

13.3 APPROPRIABILITY

The second pillar underlying the economic rationale for public support of 'basic' research at the NIH is the 'market failure' rationale, that firms will underinvest in basic biomedical research. Central to this argument is the notion that there is a 'spillover gap' between private and social returns from research and development (R&D), and this gap is likely greatest for 'basic' research. Thus Nelson (1959) argues that: 'basic research efforts are likely to generate substantial external economies . . . Private-profit opportunities alone are not likely to draw as large a quantity of resources into basic research as is socially desirable.'

Interestingly, the key reason Nelson offers for limited appropriability is difficulty in patenting basic research, noting that: 'significant advances in scientific knowledge are often not directly and immediately applicable to the solutions of practical problems and hence do not quickly result in patents'. Similarly, Arrow (1962) notes that: 'actual patent laws sharply restrict the range of appropriable information and thereby reduce the incentives to engage in inventive and research activities' (p. 617).

Thus the key factor underlying the 'market failure' argument for basic research is difficulty in patenting it. But in the nearly half century since Nelson and Arrow developed this theory, changes in patent law and practice weaken their rationale. A range of court decisions have broadly expanded patentable subject matter, including the Supreme Court's *Diamond* v. *Diehr* decision which opined that 'anything under the sun made by man' could be patented. Even the 'made by man' caveat can generally be avoided by careful claim drafting (Eisenberg, 2002). At the same time, rulings from the Federal Circuit have weakened the utility standard for patentability (Rai and Eisenberg, 2003) and the doctrine of reverse equivalents has increased the 'scope' of issued patents (Merges and Nelson, 1990), which respectively made it easier to patent upstream research and to enforce these patents against downstream users and inventors. As a result of these developments, firms can appropriate significantly more of the outputs of basic research than they once could.

If the non-patentability of basic research (and presumed high social returns from it) was the only reason Nelson and Arrow offered for public funding, it would seem that these changes to the patent system severely weaken the case. But a less recognized argument from both authors – perhaps because it was less explicit – is that public funding is useful precisely because we would not want inventors to patent results of basic research; because basic research results can spill over to numerous applications, the welfare losses from patenting them could be significant:

> Often the new knowledge is of greatest value as a key input of other research projects which, in turn, may yield results of practical and patentable value. For this reason scientists have long argued for free and wide communication of

research results, and for this reason natural laws and facts are not patentable (Nelson, 1959)

> Basic research, the output of which is used only as an informational input into other inventive activities, is especially unlikely to be rewarded. In fact, it is likely to be of commercial value to the firm undertaking it only if other firms are prevented from using the information obtained. But such restriction on the transmittal of information will reduce the efficiency of inventive activity in general and will therefore reduce its quantity also. (Arrow, 1962, p. 618)

However, this second argument for supporting basic research may also stand on less firm ground today than it once did. A range of developments, including passage of the Bayh–Dole Act of 1980, has led academic institutions to patent the results of NIH-funded research (Mowery et al., 2004; Azoulay et al., 2007). It is unclear whether academic institutions are less aggressive in enforcing these patents than their private counterparts would be (Rai and Eisenberg, 2003; Walsh et al., 2003). But in an era where basic biomedical research is increasingly patentable, the positive argument for public funding of NIH research rests centrally on the notion that they manage their patents with a view towards facilitating diffusion, rather than appropriating rents.

13.4 ARE NIH ALLOCATION PROCESSES RESPONSIVE TO SOCIAL RETURNS OR APPROPRIABILITY?

The previous sections examined the bases for the main economic rationale for public support of NIH funded basic research. In this section, I consider the problem from the bottom up, examining the extent to which NIH actually does consider social returns from basic research and the appropriability environment in making its allocation decisions. Evidence on this issue can help assess both the extent to which economic theory reflects institutional practice, and whether institutional practice can be improved by conforming more closely to the normative prescriptions from economic theory.

13.4.1 Social Returns

In the context of NIH research, the main social returns society expects are improved health outcomes. Accordingly, allocation patterns should be responsive to social needs in various disease areas. At the same time, not all important problems are tractable. Accordingly, scientific opportunity should also play a role. Together, scientific opportunity and disease burden define the expected social benefits from research in a disease area (Lichtenberg, 2000). From an economic perspective, NIH allocations should be responsive to each.[4]

But in the real world, there has been a sharp divide between those arguing for allocation based on disease-based criteria and those arguing for allocation based on 'scientific' criteria. This debate predates World War II, and was a recurring theme in debates about the establishment of disease-specific institutes throughout the post-war era (Strickland, 1972; Rettig, 1977; Cook-Deegan and McGeary, 2006). On the one hand, politicians and disease advocates have pushed the NIH to allocate its funds according to various measures of expected social benefits from progress in a disease area. On the other, members of the scientific community have resisted political planning of research and asserted that allocations should be made on the basis of scientific opportunity, of which scientific peers are the best judges.

These debates intensified in the mid-1990s, following increased concern by Congress and the media that there was a mismatch between NIH funding patterns and the social costs and burdens of diseases. Several influential members of Congress used these numbers to criticize the NIH for being more interested in funding scientifically interesting research than in meeting the nation's health needs and priorities (Institute of Medicine, 1998). While representatives of the biomedical research community initially dismissed statistics on disease-specific allocations as 'body count budgeting' and emphasized the roles of serendipity in scientific discovery, NIH officials later suggested that 'public health needs' are, and should be, one of the several criteria considered in allocating NIH funds (Varmus, 1999).

Surprisingly little is known about the extent to which NIH allocations are responsive to 'health needs'. An exception is the important study by Gross et al. (1999), which compared NIH funding for 29 diseases to six measures of disease burden, and found that allocations were correlated with some of the measures but not others.[5] As Cook-Deegan and McGeary (2006) have noted, the results from this study were 'grist for the mill of both NIH critics, who urge stronger weight for social need guiding scientific priorities, and NIH supporters, who note that generally positive correlations above chance suggest NIH spending does respond to the biggest health needs'.

Once funds are appropriated by Congress to individual institutes, it is unclear how the allocation process would be responsive to considerations of 'health needs'. After all, once the NIH receives its annual allocations, the primary mode of allocation is via peer review, with 'scientific merit' of a research proposal the primary determining criterion.[6] Political actors have stronger incentives to tie allocations to health benefits. And throughout the NIH's history, Congress has also been active in directing funds for particular diseases, via the creation of disease-specific institutes and via 'earmarking' allocations in reports accompanying the legislation from the House and Senate appropriations subcommittees overseeing the NIH. Both of these activities have been the subject of considerable controversy. On the one hand, some argue that they are the only channel through which considerations of 'public needs' can be injected into the allocation process, which (they contend) is otherwise narrow-mindedly oriented towards scientific merit. On the other hand, there is concern that these political directives often target diseases without concern for the scientific feasibility of research, and that this low-quality research crowds out funds for higher-quality peer-reviewed research (Greenberg, 1998).

Given the incentives of the various actors in the system described above, is unclear whether, when and how the allocation process as currently structured is responsive to the expected social returns of research. The determinants of NIH allocation patterns across disease areas remains an important empirical question.

13.4.2 Appropriability

In addition to expected social returns, economic theory suggests that a second factor the NIH should consider in its allocation decisions is appropriability, that is, the extent to which private sector actors could appropriate benefits if they were to do work in the field. In contexts where appropriability is high, the pure market failure argument for funding is less salient.

As a historical matter, the political impetus for establishing the NIH stemmed not from any recognition of 'market failure' in basic biomedical research, but from broader interest in health-related policies. When powerful forces (including the American Medical Association) opposed other government initiatives to intervene in the health arena, including national health insurance, physician training and the support of teaching in medical schools, health advocates turned their attention to federal efforts in supporting medical research, which were seen as less of a threat to physician autonomy (Strickland, 1972). And Sapolsky (1990) argues that the NIH's 'period of most rapid growth occurred during the 1950s and early 1960s when the support of biomedical research became identified as the most acceptable alternative politically to national health and other direct financing schemes for expressing the federal government's concern about the nation's health' (pp. 92–3).

Moreover, a central concern of Vannevar Bush and others in developing a post-war medical research policy was 'to ensure against government interference of research in the private sector' (Kleinman, 1994). Industry generally supported government involvement in 'basic' research mainly because they feared 'unwarranted Government competition' from government involvement in other research arenas (ibid.). Thus the logic was not, 'We value health; basic research is important for health; but the market underinvests', à la 'market failure' rationale, but rather, 'We value health; we believe basic research is one way to yield improvements in health; and the only one where we won't face substantial political opposition' (ibid.).

More importantly, there is little attention in the NIH allocation process today to the extent of private appropriability. A review of testimony in the Senate and House Labor–Department of Health and Human Services–Education subcommittees over the 1960–2005 period shows some evidence of invoking 'market failure' logic at a broad level. But there are few instances where a congressperson, representative of the scientific community, or disease advocate pointed to limited private sector appropriability as a reason for supporting (or not supporting) a particular line of basic research. Once funds are distributed to institutes, they are distributed via peer review, as described above. But NIH study section members have neither the capability nor the mandate to assess the extent of private sector appropriability for particular lines of research. Aside for its general justification as part of the *raison d'être* for the NIH, the 'market failure' logic plays little role in NIH funding decisions.

Indeed, one of the few cases when the NIH does appear to have paid attention to the appropriability environment is instructive: in sequencing the human genome (Eisenberg and Nelson, 2002). There, publicly funded researchers raced the private sector to sequence the human genome, precisely because it was concerned that the private sector would patent aggressively and limit downstream benefits from genomic research. Public funding to race the private sector is difficult to rationalize via the traditional market failure argument; it only makes sense if we believe that an important comparative advantage of public funding is that research results can be placed in the public domain.

13.5 CONCLUSION

This chapter has raised two challenges to the economic rationale for public funding of basic biomedical research. First, that there is limited information on social returns from NIH-funded basic research. Second, the presumption that the patent system creates limited appropriability of private sector investments in such research, and that public sector researchers themselves will not patent this research, is weaker today than it once was. It has also provided evidence that the current system of allocation of public funds for basic research does not appear to consider the main factors that would be needed to make allocation choices via the 'market failure' rationale, the social benefits from and appropriability of particular research endeavors. I leave it to the reader to decide whether this means that we need develop theory that better fits the real world, or that we need to fix the real world to correspond better with the normative prescriptions from theory.

What is the road forward? One point of view with which I have considerable sympathy is that more empirical research is needed to bolster the positive argument for public funding, including the health benefits from NIH basic research and the notion that private firms lack incentives to conduct this research. Another, with which I also sympathize, is that the problem may be with the 'market failure' theory itself (Nelson, 1997; Mowery, 1997). From this perspective, rather than try to justify the funding of basic biomedical research via the 'market failure' logic, economists need to recognize that the NIH is a useful institution in the US biomedical research system in its own right, with distinct capabilities, incentives and norms compared to those existing in the private sector. But if this is the case, we need to think carefully about what those capabilities, incentives and norms are, to develop a stronger argument for public funding. As I have hinted above, I believe that one of the main potential comparative advantages of public sector funding of basic research is that it can incentivize basic research without incurring the deadweight losses created by the patent system. If NIH-funded institutions start to act too much like firms with respect to their patenting and licensing activities, this would seriously undercut the economic argument for public support, from either a 'market failure' or a more heterodox perspective.

While the bulk of this chapter has focused on 'basic' research at the NIH, I conclude with some observations about clinical research and health services research, which traditionally have not been supported as generously by the NIH.

As the discussion of progress in cardiovascular disease suggested, there is some evidence that NIH-funded clinical research has been important in improving of health outcomes. Together with debates about the extent to which NIH funds should be allocated according to health priorities or scientific criteria, another perennial tension in the politics of the NIH has focused on whether there is 'enough' funding for basic versus clinical research at the NIH (Nathan and Schechter, 2006), with advocates of basic research arguing that it lays the foundations of future discovery, and advocates of clinical research, which historically has been less generously supported, arguing that major health gains result from practical testing and application.

It is interesting that the 'market failure' rationale may be more relevant for clinical research than basic research. Its output – data – is generally more akin to the pure informational goods of economic theory than are the outputs of 'basic' biological research. Moreover, data from clinical trials, including those on the efficacy of different types of treatments, are more difficult to appropriate using patent protection. This is especially true for drugs that are off-patent (Heidenreich and McClellan, 2003; Eisenberg, 2005) but also more generally. In addition, private firms often lack incentives to conduct certain types of clinical research, including head-to-head trials comparing the efficiency of drugs (Angell, 2004).

Clinical research is not only important for facilitating the introduction of new medical techniques and practices, but also in spurring the diffusion of those already in practice that work, and stopping the diffusion of those which do not (Heidenreich and McClellan, 2003). This raises another important point about the allocation of funds for biomedical research: as in other areas of science and technology policy, major welfare gains reflect not only the creation of new technologies, but also their diffusion. Yet the US health care market is characterized by haphazard diffusion patterns, with wide disparities in the uses of medical technologies and techniques. More research on the individual and organizational characteristics that spur the adoption and diffusion of effective medical technologies, and information on healthy behaviors, could yield significant health benefits. But this too remains relatively underfunded by the NIH, perhaps because it is not scientifically interesting or exciting.

I conclude by noting that this chapter is most certainly not an indictment of the NIH. Nor is it an argument that the returns to NIH are low, or that current allocation patterns are necessarily suboptimal. As suggested above, much more research is needed on each of these fronts. Rather, the discussion above is an invitation to economists (and others) to step back and re-evaluate why we fund research at the National Institutes of Health, how we do and how we should, and what we as a society want from the NIH. Such an examination may promote changes in both theory and practice.

NOTES

1. By contrast, 32 percent of pharmaceutical industry funding is for pre-human and pre-clinical research, including basic research.
2. http://www.nih.gov/about/director/budgetrequest/fy2008directorssenatebudgetrequest.htm.
3. http://www.nih.gov/about/researchhighlights/index.htm.

4. In the simple model developed by Lichtenberg, an optimal allocation would equalize marginal products of research per dollar across disease areas, where marginal products are scientific opportunity (which he defines as the probability that a research endeavor is successful) multiplied by disease burden.
5. Lichtenberg (2000) offers similar evidence.
6. One possible channel through which the NIH may respond to 'health needs' is via choices made by the NIH director and heads of individual institutes and centers, who have some discretionary funds available to emphasize particular areas of research in any given year (for example, via issuing requests for proposals) and, occasionally, can fund 'important' projects which received low merit scores during the peer review process (Dresser, 2001). But this discretionary authority likely only applies to a small share of grants, and thus funds.

REFERENCES

American Association for the Advancement of Science (AAAS) (2007), 'NIH Funding Falls in 2008 Budget', available at: http://www.aaas.org/spp/rd/nih08p.pdf.

Angell, M. (2004), *The Truth About Drug Companies: How They Deceive Us and What to do About It*, New York: Random House.

Arrow, K. (1962), 'Economic welfare and the allocation of resources for invention', in NBER (ed.), *The Rate and Direction of Inventive Activity: Economic and Social Factors*, Princeton, NJ: Princeton University Press, pp. 609–25.

Azoulay, P., R. Michigan and B. Sampat (2007), 'The anatomy of medical school patenting', Working Paper.

Cook-Deegan, R. and M. McGeary (2006), 'The jewel in the federal crown? History, politics, and the National Institutes of Health', in R.A. Stevens, C.E. Rosenberg and L.R. Burns, *History and Health Policy: Putting the Past Back In*, New Brunswick, NJ: Rutgers University Press.

Cutler, D., A. Deaton and A. Lleras-Muney (2006), 'The determinants of mortality', NBER Working Paper 11963.

Cutler, D.M. and S. Kadiyala (2003), 'The return to biomedical research: treatment and behavioral effects', in K.M. Murphy and R.H. Topel (eds), *Measuring the Gains from Medical Research: An Economic Approach*, Chicago: University of Chicago Press, pp. 110–62.

David, P.A., D.C. Mowery and W.E. Steinmueller (1992), 'Analyzing the economic payoffs from basic research', *Economics of Innovation and New Technology*, **2** (4), 73–90.

Dresser, R. (2001), *When Science Offers Salvation: Patient Advocacy and Research Ethics*, New York: Oxford University Press.

Eisenberg, R.S. (2002), 'How can you patent genes?', *American Journal of Bioethics*, **2** (3), 3–11.

Eisenberg, R.S. (2005), 'The problem of new uses', *Yale Journal of Health Policy Law Ethics*, **5** (2), 717–39.

Eisenberg, R.S. and R.R. Nelson (2002), 'Public vs. proprietary science: a fruitful tension', *Daedalus*, **131** (2), 89–101.

Greenberg, D. (1998), 'Disease lobbies', *Washington Post*, 27 October.

Gross, C.P., G.F. Anderson and N.R. Powe (1999), 'The relation between funding by the National Institutes of Health and the burden of disease', *New England Journal of Medicine*, **340** (24), 1881–7.

Heidenreich, P. and M. McClellan (2003), 'Biomedical research and then some: the causes of technological change in heart attack treatment', in K.M. Murphy and R.H. Topel (eds), *Measuring the Gains from Medical Research: An Economic Approach*, Chicago: University of Chicago Press pp. 163–205.

Institute of Medicine (1998), *Scientific Opportunities and Public Needs: Improving Priority Setting and Public Input at the National Institutes of Health*, Washington, DC: National Academy, Press.

Jaffe, A. (1998), 'Measurement issues', in L. Branscomb and J. Keller, *Investing in Innovation: Creating a Research and Innovation Policy That Works*, Cambridge, MA: MIT Press, pp. 64–84.

Jaffe, A. (2002), 'Building program evaluation into the design of public research support programs', *Oxford Review of Economic Policy*, **18** (1), 22–34.

Kleinman, D.L. (1994), 'Layers of interests, layers of influence: business and the genesis of the National Science Foundation', *Science, Technology, and Human Values*, **19**, 259–82.

Lichtenberg, F. (2000), *The Allocation of Funds for Biomedical R&D*, Washington, DC: AEI Press.

Lichtenberg, F.R. (2003), 'Pharmaceutical innovation, mortality reduction, and economic growth', in K.M. Murphy and R.H. Topel, *Measuring the Gains from Medical Research: An Economic Approach*, Chicago: University of Chicago Press, pp. 74–109.

Mansfield, E. (1995), 'Academic research underlying industrial innovations: sources, characteristics, and financing', *Review of Economics and Statistics*, **77** (1), 55–65.

Merges, R. and R.R. Nelson (1990), 'On the complex economics of patent scope', *Columbia Law Review*, **90** (4), 839–916.

Moses, H., R. Dorsey, D. Matheson and S. Thier (2005), 'Financial anatomy of biomedical research', *Journal of the American Medical Association*, **294** (11), 1333–42.

Mowery, D.C. (1997), 'What does economic theory tell us about mission-oriented R&D?', Paper prepared for Monte Verità conference on The Economics of Technology Policy.

Mowery, D., R. Nelson, B. Sampat and A. Ziedonis (2004), *Ivory Tower and Industrial Innovation*, Stanford, CA: Stanford University Press.

Nathan, D.G. and A.N. Schechter (2006), 'NIH support for basic and clinical research', *Journal of the American Medical Association*, **295** (22), 2656–8.

National Institutes of Health (NIH) (2009), 'About NIH: NIH mission', available at: http://www.nih.gov/about.

Nelson, R.R. (1997), 'Building effective innovation systems versus dealing with market failures as ways of thinking about technology policy', Paper prepared for Monte Verità conference The Economics of Technology Policy.

Nelson, R. (1959), 'The simple economics of basic scientific research', *Journal of Political Economy*, **67** (3), 297–306.

Rai, A. and R. Eisenberg (2003), 'Bayh–Dole reform and the progress of biomedicine', *Law and Contemporary Problems*, **66** (1), 289–314.

Rettig, R. (1977), *Cancer Crusade: The Story of the National Cancer Act of 1971*, Washington, DC: Joseph Henry Press.

Sampat, B. and F. Lichtenberg (2007), 'The roles of the public and private sectors in new drug development', Working Paper, Columbia University.

Sapolsky, H. (1990), *Science and the Navy: The History of the Office of Naval Resarch*, Princeton, NJ: Princeton University Press.

Stokes, D. (1997), *Pasteur's Quadrant: Basic Science and Technological Innovation*, Washington, DC: Brookings.

Strickland, S.P. (1972), *Politics, Science, and Dread Disease: A Short History of United States Medical Research Policy*, Cambridge, MA: Harvard University Press.

Toole, A.A. (2000), 'The impact of public basic research on industrial innovation: evidence from the pharmaceutical industry', SIEPR Discussion Paper No. 00-07, Stanford, CA.

US Government Accountability Office (GAO) (2002), *Clinical Research: NIH has Implemented Key Provisions of the Clinical Research Enhancement Act: Report to Congressional Committees*, Washington, DC: US Government Accountability Office, 18 September.

Varmus, H. (1999), 'Evaluating the burden of disease and spending the research dollars of the National Institutes of Health', *New England Journal of Medicine*, **340** (24), 1914–15.

Walsh, J., A. Arora and W. Cohen (2003), 'Effects of research tool patents and licensing on biomedical innovation', in W. Cohen and S. Merrill (eds), *Patents in the Knowledge-Based Economy*, Washington, DC: National Academies Press, pp. 285–340.

14. Comments

W. Edward Steinmueller

In his contribution in chapter 12, David Mowery has answered the provocative question of what economic theory has to tell us about mission-oriented research with a sensible answer – not much. Indeed, the term 'mission-oriented' research already presupposes the necessity and the utility of the national government's involvement in planning and commissioning the research. The term also serves to suppress consideration of alternative processes by which knowledge might be created or spread – an inherent contradiction of the social science devoted to examining the roles of competition and substitution. Yet, as Mowery observes, on those occasions when a rationale is offered it is likely to be one of market failure, a formulaic response that obfuscates rather than clarifies the rationale and implementation of government mission-oriented research efforts – no small matter, as such investments constitute over half of all government research expenditure in Organisation for Economic Co-operation and Development (OECD) countries and well over 90 per cent of the US federal research budget.

Mowery's argument that we should start with the dominance of mission-oriented research as a fact of life leads to useful insights into the effects or consequences of the political determination of research agendas. In particular, he observes that mission priorities quickly dictate the abandonment of the peer review of research or Vannevar Bush's injunction that scientists should determine the agenda for exploring the endless frontier. Moreover, Mowery observes that once a mission has achieved its political backing, further confusion arises by pursuing other political ends such as research support for universities or small business within the mission. These observations set the stage for Mowery to conclude that a more systematic examination of the effects of mission-oriented research in shaping the research infrastructure, in the expectations and realization of commercial 'spinoffs' from mission-led research and the complementary, and often dominant, effects of procurement on the outcomes that mission-oriented research produces.

These are all very useful points with which I am in full agreement. My view is that one can go somewhat further with the facts at hand.

The vast increase in the biomedical research mission that has occupied the US for the last twenty years is having important effects. Universities can no longer expect to receive substantial increases in the research funding afforded to many of their faculties. In universities, as in many other organizations, growth and vitality are linked. Slow or no growth means a sapping of vitality and attractiveness, sending those students not destined to be doctors off to business school rather than engaging them with science and engineering quests. Thus, the priority afforded the biomedical mission has important consequences for shaping the future of the US research infrastructure. What is happening in the skewing of human resource development also has implications for the physical research infrastructure. Building the enormous research establishments called university research hospitals threatens the atrophy of other laboratories and the contribution that they might make to the economy. In particular, the growing monoculture implied by this expansion of biomedical research limits the spinoffs that might be expected from university research and, in the US context, this is exacerbated by the relatively small procurement leverage offered by the military-related health system, which is the only segment of the US national health system directly administered by the federal government.[1]

One lesson to be taken from Mowery's line of analysis is that the portion of economic theory concerned with substitution and complementation turns out to be relevant after all, not in providing the rationale for mission-oriented research, but for assessing its consequences. Looking towards the future, one can see new missions emerging at the horizon that might, in turn, restore some balance to funding allocation. Some of them are rather frightening. It is clear, for example, that the impetus in military funding will be battlefields without soldiers. While this is likely to restore some of the historical vitality of the physical sciences and mechanical engineering, the end product may be the encouragement of further military intervention. A prominent area at the frontier of biomedical science is the brain, and we may expect the current research trajectory to produce much more powerful pharmaceutical tools for regulating how people think and feel and perhaps how they learn and remember. More optimistic, perhaps, is the urgent need to produce energy without emissions and this, like the battlefield without soldiers, offers some hope for restoring the role of the physical sciences and mechanical engineering. There is a real risk for the United States, however, that leadership in the area of energy will pass to those countries (for example Germany) that have already begun the mission. In this, as well as other possible missions, it would be useful to ask the question, how might the missions that nations undertake influence the missions that they are capable of undertaking?

From the universe of mission-oriented research that David Mowery identifies, Bhaven Sampat in chapter 13 focuses on the one receiving the greatest resources, the biomedical quest, and specifically the activities of the National Institutes of Health. Like Mowery, Sampat is concerned that the Nelson–Arrow market failure rationale for research provides an inadequate framework for either the allocation of research funds or its administration. He observes that missions are defined without any specific regard for the questions of appropriability that are central to Arrow and Nelson's arguments. He also questions whether, in an era of 'markets for knowledge' (the extension of patentability and the active stewardship of intellectual property arising from government-funded research), the Nelson–Arrow market failure framework remains relevant.

This line of argument leads to a search for other criteria by which we might judge the performance of research funding allocation. Sampat argues that 'health outcomes' should be a central criterion for such allocations and that, by this criterion, the extent of measured success is rather narrow. Despite annual research investments of $44 for every US citizen, the principal improvement in health outcomes has been the reduction in cardiovascular disease (CVD), but the highest payback activity in achieving this reduction has stemmed not from research but from behavioural change. Sampat's evidence on this point is a bit problematic. While annual CVD death rates per 100000 US citizens have fallen from the vicinity of 400 to 150, other causes of death have remained stable (despite huge investments, as in cancer) or increased by a small fraction of the CVD death rate reduction (as in the case of Acquired Immune Deficiency Syndrome – AIDS). As death remains inevitable, the most prominent health outcome is the creation of greater numbers of elderly US citizens – raising questions about the quality of life and the capacity of medical interventions to improve this quality.

Thus, looking at the health outcome consequences of research investment, we might conclude that getting to be elderly and dying of some other cause was preferred to dying of CVD. It is reasonable to suspect that this is not the explicit choice made by the political process. Instead, it is the fear of death that motivates the $44 annual expenditure and this fear is not likely to be translated very rationally into research allocation guidelines. Some diseases make better 'poster children' – they are more capable of crystallizing the fear and tragedy of death, particularly at a youthful age. Other diseases or medical conditions are stigmatized, and in some cases this may result in fewer resources being available to address them – bariatric medicine (the treatment of obesity) is an example. Still other diseases, including CVD, are ones in which drama wins over routine – the deployment of defibrillation equipment in public venues that permits occasional success in restarting hearts may receive greater funding than programmes aimed at behavioural change (diet and exercise) that have much larger payoffs in averting premature death. While these forces may predominate in the political process, Sampat argues that a more rational set of criteria can and should be applied to research allocation. It is not clear, however, that the contest between fear and rationality will favour rationality. Does rational health research policy mean 'let the technocrats decide' or, more cynically, is health research policy a modern variant of bread and circuses?

NOTE

1. The armed services health system and Veterans Administration hospitals are the only healthcare establishments where procurement is actually managed by federal agencies. Of course, the federal government does have some further ability to influence procurement through the terms in which health care costs are financed by Medicare and Medicaid.

PART IV

The Use of Models and Surveys for Technology Policy

15. The 'funding gap': financial markets and investment in innovation*

Bronwyn H. Hall

15.1 INTRODUCTION

An important problem in the managing of technology is the financing of technological development and innovation. Even in large firms, technology managers often report that they have more projects they would like to undertake than funds to spend on them.[1] There are a number of reasons for this phenomenon: low expected returns due to an inability to capture the profits from an invention, the uncertainty and risk associated with the project, and overoptimism on the part of managers. This chapter reviews these arguments in more detail and considers the evidence, both theoretical and empirical, on the extent of the problem.

Economists have long held the view that innovative activities are difficult to finance in a freely competitive marketplace. Support for this view in the form of economic-theoretic modeling is not difficult to find and probably begins with the classic articles of Nelson (1959) and Arrow (1962), although the idea itself was alluded to by Schumpeter (1942 [1960]).[2] The argument goes as follows: the primary output of innovation investment is the knowledge of how to make new goods and services, and this knowledge is nonrival: use by one firm does not preclude its use by another. To the extent that knowledge cannot be kept secret, the returns to the investment in it cannot be appropriated by the firm undertaking the investment, and therefore such firms will be reluctant to invest, leading to the underprovision of research and development (R&D) and other innovation investments in the economy.

Since the time when this argument was fully articulated by Arrow, it has of course been developed, tested, modified and extended in many ways. For example, Levin et al. (1987) and Mansfield et al. (1981) found using survey evidence that imitating a new invention was not costless, but could cost as much as 50 to 75 percent of the cost of the original invention. This fact will mitigate but not eliminate the underinvestment problem.

Empirical support for the basic point concerning the positive externalities created by research that was made by Arrow is widespread, mostly in the form of studies that document a social return to R&D that is higher than the private level (Griliches, 1992; Hall, 1996).

This line of reasoning is already widely used by policy-makers to justify such interventions as the intellectual property system, government support of innovative activities, R&D tax incentives and the encouragement of research partnerships of various kinds. In general, these incentive programs can be warranted even when the firm or individual undertaking the research is the same as the entity that finances it. However, Arrow's influential paper also contains another argument, again one which was foreshadowed by Schumpeter and which has been addressed by subsequent researchers in economics and finance: the argument that an additional gap exists between the private rate of return and the cost of capital when the innovation investor and financier are different entities.

This chapter concerns itself with this second aspect of the market failure for innovation investment: even if problems associated with incomplete appropriability of the returns to R&D are solved using intellectual property protection, subsidies or tax incentives, it may still be difficult or costly to finance R&D and other innovative activities using capital from sources external to the firm or entrepreneur. That is, there is often a wedge, sometimes large, between the rate of return required by an entrepreneur investing his own funds and that required by external investors. By this argument, unless an inventor is already wealthy, or firms already profitable, some innovations will fail to be provided purely because the cost of external capital is too high, even when they would pass the private returns hurdle if funds were available at a 'normal' interest rate.

In the following, I begin by describing some of the unique features of R&D investment. Many of these features also characterize innovative activity when it is more broadly defined to include the marketing, product development and employee training associated with an innovation. Then I discuss the various theoretical arguments why external finance for R&D might be more expensive than internal finance, going on to review the empirical evidence on the validity of this hypothesis and the solutions that have been developed and adopted by the market and some governments.

15.2 RESEARCH AND DEVELOPMENT AS INVESTMENT

From the perspective of investment theory, innovation investment has a number of characteristics that make it different from ordinary investment.

First and most importantly, in practice 50 per cent or more of the R&D portion of this investment is the wages and salaries of highly educated scientists and engineers. Their efforts create an intangible asset, the firm's knowledge base, from which profits in future years will be generated. To the extent that this knowledge is 'tacit' rather than codified, it is embedded in the human capital of the firm's employees, and is therefore lost if they leave or are fired.

This fact has an important implication for the conduct of R&D investment. Because part of the resource base of the firm itself disappears when such workers leave or are fired, firms tend to smooth their R&D spending over time, in order to avoid having to lay off knowledge workers. This implies that R&D spending at the firm level typically behaves as though it has high adjustment costs (Hall et al., 1986; Lach and Schankerman, 1988), with two consequences, one substantive and one that affects empirical work in this area. First, the equilibrium required rate of return to R&D may be quite high, simply to cover the adjustment costs. Second, and related to the first, is that it will be difficult for empirical studies to measure the impact of changes in the costs of capital on such investment, because such effects can be weak in the short run due to the sluggish response of R&D to any changes in its cost.

A second important feature of R&D investment is the degree of uncertainty associated with its output. This uncertainty tends to be greatest at the beginning of a research program or project, which implies that an optimal R&D strategy has an options-like character and should not really be analyzed in a static framework. R&D projects with small probabilities of great success in the future may be worth continuing even if they do not pass an expected rate of return test. The uncertainty here can be extreme and not a simple matter of a well-specified distribution with a mean and variance. There is evidence such as that in Scherer (1998) that the distribution of profits from innovation sometimes takes the form of a Pareto distribution where the variance does not exist. When this is the case, standard risk-adjustment methods will not work well.

An important characteristic of uncertainty for the financing of investment in innovation is the fact that as investments are made over time, new information arrives which reduces or changes the uncertainty. The consequence of this fact is that the decision to invest in any particular project is not a once and for all decision, but has to be reassessed throughout the life of the project. In addition to making such investment a real option, the sequence of decisions complicates the analysis by introducing dynamic elements into the interaction of the financier (either within or outside the firm) and the innovator. I discuss the implications for the source of financing of innovation in the next section of the chapter.

The natural starting point for the analysis of any type of investment financing is the 'neoclassical' marginal profit condition, suitably modified to take the special features of R&D into account. This condition sets the marginal product of capital equal to the pre-tax rate of return on investment in that capital. Because the financial markets supply capital at an interest rate that is evaluated after corporation tax is paid, the investment decision will depend on the depreciation rate and tax treatment of the particular capital asset. The user cost formulation directs attention to the following determinants of R&D financing:

1. Tax treatment such as tax credits, which are clearly amenable to intervention by policy-makers.
2. Economic depreciation, which in the case of R&D is more properly termed obsolescence. This quantity is sensitive to the realized rate of technical change in the industry, which is in turn determined by such things as market structure and the rate of imitation. Thus it is difficult to treat as an invariant parameter in this setting.
3. The marginal costs of adjusting the level of the R&D program.
4. The investor's required rate of return.

The last item has been the subject of considerable theoretical and empirical interest, on the part of both industrial organization and corporate finance economists. Two broad strands of investigation can be observed: one focuses on the role of asymmetric information and moral hazard in raising the required rate of return above that normally used for conventional investment; and the other focuses on the requirements of different sources of financing and their differing tax treatments for the rate of return. The next section of the chapter discusses these factors.

15.3 THEORETICAL BACKGROUND

This section of the chapter reviews in more detail the reasons why the impact of financial considerations on the investment decision may vary with the type of investment and with the source of funds. To do this, I distinguish between those factors that arise from various kinds of market failures in this setting and the purely financial (or tax-oriented) considerations that affect the cost of different sources of funds.

One of the implications of the well-known Modigliani–Miller theorem (Modigliani and Miller, 1958; Miller and Modigliani, 1961) is that a firm choosing the optimal levels of investment should be indifferent to its capital structure, and should face the same price for all types of investment (including investments in creating new products and processes) on the margin. The last dollar spent on each type of investment should yield the same expected rate of return (after adjustment for non-diversifiable risk). A large literature, both theoretical and empirical, has questioned the bases for this theorem, but it remains a useful starting point.

There are several reasons why the theorem might fail to hold in practice: (1) uncertainty coupled with incomplete markets may make a real options approach to the R&D investment decision more appropriate; (2) the cost of capital may differ by source of funds for non-tax reasons; (3) the cost of capital may differ by source of funds for tax reasons; and (4) the cost of capital may also differ across types of investments (tangible and intangible) for both tax and other reasons.

With respect to innovation investment, economic theory advances a plethora of reasons why there might be a gap between the external and internal costs of capital; these can be divided into three main types:

1. Asymmetric information between innovator and investor.
2. Moral hazard on the part of the innovator or arising from the separation of ownership and management.
3. Tax considerations that drive a wedge between external finance and finance by retained earnings.

15.3.1 Asymmetric Information Problems

In the R&D setting, the asymmetric information problem refers to the fact that an inventor frequently has better information about the likelihood of success and the nature of the contemplated innovation project than potential investors. Therefore, the marketplace for financing the development of innovative ideas looks like the 'lemons' market modeled by Akerlof (1970). The lemons premium for R&D will be higher than that for ordinary investment, because investors have more difficulty distinguishing good projects from bad when the projects are long-term R&D investments than when they are more short-term or low-risk projects (Leland and Pyle, 1977). When the level of R&D expenditure is a highly observable signal, as it is under current US and UK rules, we might expect that the lemons problem is somewhat mitigated, but certainly not eliminated.[3]

In the most extreme version of the lemons model, the market for R&D projects may disappear entirely if the asymmetric information problem is too great. Informal evidence suggests that some potential innovators believe this to be the case in fact. And as will be discussed below, venture capital systems are viewed by some as a solution to this 'missing markets' problem.

Reducing information asymmetry via fuller disclosure is of limited effectiveness in this arena, due to the ease of imitation of inventive ideas. Firms are reluctant to reveal their innovative ideas to the marketplace and the fact that there could be a substantial cost to revealing information to their competitors reduces the quality of the signal they can make about a potential project (Bhattacharya and Ritter, 1985; Anton and Yao, 1998). Thus the implication of asymmetric information coupled with the costliness of mitigating the problem is that firms and inventors will face a higher cost of external than internal capital for R&D due to the lemons premium.

Some empirical support for this proposition exists, mostly in the form of event studies that measure the market response to announcements of new debt or share issues. Both Alam and Walton (1995) and Zantout (1997) find higher abnormal returns to firm shares following new debt issues when the firm is more R&D-intensive. The argument is that the acquisition of new sources of financing is good news when the firm has an asymmetric information problem because of its R&D strategy. Similarly, Szewczyk et al. (1996) find that investment opportunities (as proxied by Tobin's q) explain R&D-associated abnormal returns, and that these returns are higher when the firm is highly leveraged, implying a higher required rate of return for debt finance in equilibrium.

15.3.2 Moral Hazard Problems

Moral hazard in R&D investing arises in the usual way: modern industrial firms normally have separation of ownership and management. This leads to a principal–agent problem when the goals of the two conflict, which can result in investment strategies that are not share value-maximizing. Two possible scenarios may coexist: one is the usual tendency of managers to spend on activities that benefit them (growing the firm beyond efficient scale, nicer offices, and so on) and the second is a reluctance of risk-averse managers to invest in uncertain R&D projects. Agency costs of the first type may be avoided by reducing the amount of free cash flow available to the managers by leveraging the firm, but this in turn forces them to use the higher-cost external funds to finance R&D (Jensen and Meckling, 1976). Empirically, there seem to be limits to the use of the leveraging strategy in R&D-intensive sectors. See Hall (1990, 1994) for evidence that the leveraged buyout (LBO) and restructuring wave of the 1980s, viewed by most researchers as driven by the need to reduce free cash flow in sectors where investment opportunities were poor, was almost entirely confined to industries and firms where R&D was of no consequence.

According to the second type of principal–agent conflict, managers are more risk averse than shareholders and avoid innovation projects that will increase the riskiness of the firm. If bankruptcy is a possibility, managers whose opportunity cost is lower than their present earnings and potential bondholders may both wish to avoid variance-increasing projects which shareholders would like to undertake. The argument of the theory is that long-term investments can suffer in this case. The optimal solution to this type of agency cost would be to increase the long-term incentives faced by the managers rather than reducing free cash flow.

Evidence on the importance of agency costs as they relate to R&D takes several forms. Several researchers have studied the impact of anti-takeover amendments (which arguably increase managerial security and willingness to take on risk while reducing managerial discipline) on R&D investment and firm value. Johnston and Rao (1997) find that such amendments are not followed by cuts in R&D, while Pugh et al. (1999) find that adoption of an employee stock ownership plan (ESOP), which is a form of anti-takeover protection, is followed by R&D increases. Cho (1992) finds that R&D intensity increases with the share that managerial shareholdings represent of the manager's wealth, and interprets this as incentive pay mitigating agency costs and inducing long-term investment.

Some have argued that institutional ownership of the managerial firm can reduce the agency costs due to free-riding by owners that is a feature of the governance of firms with diffuse ownership structure, while others have held that such ownership pays too much attention to short-term earnings and therefore discourages long-term investments. Institutions such as mutual and pension funds often control somewhat larger blocks of shares than individuals, making monitoring firm and manager behavior a more effective and more rewarding activity for these organizations.

There is some limited evidence that this may indeed be the case. Eng and Shackell (2001) find that firms adopting long-term performance plans for their managers do not increase their R&D spending, but that institutional ownership is associated with higher R&D; R&D firms tend not to be held by banks and insurance companies. Majumdar and Nagarajan (1997) find that high institutional investor ownership does not lead to short-term behavior on the part of the firm; in particular, it does not lead to cuts in R&D spending. Francis and Smith (1995) find that diffusely held firms are less innovative, implying that monitoring alleviates agency costs and enables investment in innovation. Although the evidence summarized above is fairly clear and indicates that long-term incentives for managers can encourage R&D and that institutional ownership does not necessarily discourage R&D investment, it is fairly silent on the magnitude of these effects, and whether these governance features truly close the agency cost-induced gap between the cost of capital and the return to R&D.

In the presence of uncertainty and the revelation of innovation success probability over time, the possibility of asymmetric information and moral hazard in the investor–innovator relationship creates further problems for achieving the optimal contract. For example, it is often observed that entrepreneurs or R&D managers wish to continue projects that investors would like to terminate (Cornelli and Yosha, 2003), presumably because the possibility of an ultimate benefit to them looms large and they do not face the investment cost in the case of failure. If they are also overconfident, they will be even more biased toward continuation. Asymmetric information about the project will imply that the investor has relatively more difficulty than the innovator even in determining the probability of success. The combination of information rents and agency costs will lead to inefficient funding of projects over time as well as inefficient (too low) levels of funding.

In a recent paper, Bergemann and Hege (2005) have analyzed these trade-offs in a multistage investment financing decision under changing uncertainty, with renegotiation allowed. They look at the choice between relationship financing (where the investor is able to monitor the progress of the project accurately) and arm's-length financing (where the investor must rely on the innovator for information). The investor is able to speed up or slow down the rate of financing, depending on the progress of the project and his expectations of success. In general, Bergemann and Hege find that agency costs will lead to non-optimal stopping rules for projects, stopping them too soon on average. Surprisingly, arm's-length contracts can lead to higher project values, because in these the investor can precommit to a stopping rule, which eliminates any benefit to the entrepreneur from attempts to prolong the project.

15.3.3 Capital Structure and R&D

In the view of some observers, the leveraged buyout (LBO) wave of the 1980s in the United States and the United Kingdom arose partly because high real interest rates meant that there were strong pressures to eliminate free cash flow within firms (Blair and Litan, 1990). For firms in industries where R&D is an important form of investment, such pressure should have been reduced by the need for internal funds to undertake such investment, and indeed Hall (1993, 1994) and Opler and Titman (1993) find that firms with high R&D intensity were much less likely to do an LBO. Opler and Titman (1994) find that R&D firms that were leveraged suffered more than other firms when facing economic distress, presumably because leverage meant that they were unable to sustain R&D programs in the fact of reduced cash flow.

In related work using data on Israeli firms, Blass and Yosha (2003) report that R&D-intensive firms listed on the United States stock exchanges use highly equity-based sources of financing, whereas those listed only in Israel rely more on bank financing and government funding. The former are more profitable and faster-growing, which suggests that the choice of where to list the shares and whether to finance with new equity is indeed sensitive to the expected rate of return to the R&D being undertaken. That is, investors supplying arm's-length finance require higher returns to compensate them for the risk of a 'lemon'.

Although leverage may be a useful tool for reducing agency costs in the firm, it is of limited value for R&D-intensive firms. Because the knowledge asset created by R&D investment is intangible, partly embedded in human capital, and ordinarily very specialized to the particular firm in which it resides, the capital structure of R&D-intensive firms customarily exhibits considerably less leverage than that of other firms. Banks and other debt-holders prefer to use physical assets to secure loans and are reluctant to lend when the project involves substantial R&D investment rather than investment in plant and equipment. In the words of Williamson (1988), 'redeployable' assets (that is, assets whose value in an alternative use is almost as high as in their current use) are more suited to the governance structures associated with debt. Empirical support for this idea is provided by Alderson and Betker (1996), who find that liquidation costs and R&D are positively related across firms. The implication is that the sunk costs associated with R&D investment are higher than that for ordinary investment.

In addition, servicing debt usually requires a stable source of cash flow, which makes it more difficult to find the funds for an R&D investment program that must be sustained at a certain level in order to be productive. For both these reasons, firms are either unable or reluctant to use debt finance for R&D investment, which may raise the cost of capital, depending on the precise tax treatment of debt versus equity.[4] Confirming empirical evidence for the idea that limiting free cash flow in R&D firms is a less desirable method of reducing agency costs is provided by Chung and Wright (1998), who find that financial slack and R&D spending are correlated with the value of growth firms positively, but not correlated with that of other firms. Czarnitzki and Kraft (2004) find that more leveraged German firms have lower innovation output (measured by patents), especially when ownership of the firm is dispersed.

15.3.4 Taxes and the Source of Funds

Tax considerations that yield variations in the cost of capital across source of finance have been well articulated by Auerbach (1984) among others. He argued that under the US tax system during most of its history the cost of financing new investment by debt has been less than that of financing it by retained earnings, which is in turn less than that of issuing new shares. If dividends are taxed, financing with new shares is more expensive than financing with retained earnings because the alternative use of such earnings is paying out as taxable dividends. And except for the unlikely case where the personal income tax rate is much higher than the sum of the corporate and capital gains rates, debt financing will be the least expensive source of funds because the interest is deductible at the corporate level. Shareholders normally pay tax at a higher rate on retained earnings that are paid out than on those retained by the firm and invested.[5] This analysis implicitly assumes that the returns from the investment made will be retained by the firm and eventually taxed at the capital gains rate rather than the rate on ordinary income.

It is also true that the tax treatment of R&D and other innovation investments in most OECD economies is very different from that of other kinds of investment: because R&D, marketing costs, training costs, and so on are expensed as they are incurred, the effective tax rate on the corresponding assets is lower than that on either plant or equipment, with or without an R&D tax credit in place. This effectively means that the economic depreciation of innovation assets is considerably less than the depreciation allowed for tax purposes – which is 100 percent – so that the required rate of return for such investment would be lower. In addition some countries offer a tax credit or subsidy on R&D spending, which can reduce the after-tax cost of capital even further.[6]

The conclusion from this section of the chapter is that the presence of either asymmetric information or a principal–agent conflict implies that new debt or equity finance will be relatively more expensive for R&D than for ordinary investment, and that considerations such as lack of collateral further reduce the possibility of debt finance. Together, these arguments suggest an important role for retained earnings in the R&D investment decision, independent of their value as a signal of future profitability. In fact, as has been argued by both Hall (1992) and Himmelberg and Petersen (1994), there is good reason to think that positive cash flow may be more important for R&D than for ordinary investment. The next section reports on a series of empirical tests for this proposition.

15.4 TESTING FOR FINANCIAL CONSTRAINTS

The usual way to examine the empirical relevance of the arguments that R&D investment in established firms can be disadvantaged when internal funds are not available and recourse to external capital markets required is to estimate R&D investment equations and test for the presence of 'liquidity' constraints, or excess sensitivity to cash flow shocks. This approach builds on the extensive literature developed for testing ordinary investment equations for liquidity constraints (Fazzari et al., 1988; Arellano and Bond, 1991). It suffers from many of the same difficulties as the estimates in the investment literature, plus one additional problem that arises from the tendency of firms to smooth R&D spending over time.

The ideal experiment for identifying the effects of liquidity constraints on investment is to give firms additional cash exogenously, and observe whether they pass it on to shareholders or use it for investment and/or R&D. If they choose the first alternative, either the cost of capital to the firm has not fallen, or it has fallen but they still have no good investment opportunities. If they choose the second, then the firm must have had some unexploited investment opportunities that were not profitable using more costly external finance. A finding that investment is sensitive to cash flow shocks that are not signals of future demand increases would reject the hypothesis that the cost of external funds is the same as the cost of internal funds. However, lack of true experiments of this kind forces researchers to use econometric techniques such as instrumental variables to attempt to control for demand shocks when estimating the investment demand equation, with varying degrees of success.

Econometric work that tests the hypothesis that financing constraints matter for R&D investment has largely been done using standard investment equation methodology. Two main approaches can be identified: one uses a neoclassical accelerator model with ad hoc dynamics to allow for the presence of adjustment costs, and the other an Euler equation derived from the forward-looking dynamic program of a profit-maximizing firm that faces adjustment costs for capital.[7]

The accelerator model begins with the marginal product equal to the cost or rate of return for capital and adds lags to the equation to reflect the fact that it takes time to adjust capital to its optimal level. Time dummies are generally included in the equation to capture the conventional cost of capital, assumed to be the same for all firms and firm-specific costs related to financing constraints are included by adding current and lagged values of the cash flow–capital ratio to this equation.

The Euler equation approach is based on the idea that firms will shift investment between periods until the cost of capital in each period is equalized. When the firm changes its financial position (that is, the shadow value of additional funds for investment changes) between one period and the next, it will invest as though it is facing a cost of capital greater than the market interest rate (when the shadow value falls between periods) or less than the market interest rate (when the shadow value rises between periods). When estimating the model, the changes in financial position are modeled in a number of different ways: (1) as a function of such things as dividend behavior, new share or debt issues; (2) as a function of the cash flow–capital ratio; (3) by stratifying the firms into two groups, financially constrained and financially unconstrained. This last was the method used by Fazzari et al. (1988) in the paper that originated this literature.

During the past few years, various versions of the methodologies described above have been applied to data on the R&D investment of US, UK, French, German, Irish and Japanese firms. The firms examined are typically the largest and most important manufacturing firms in their economy. For example, Hall (1992) found a large positive elasticity between R&D and cash flow, using an accelerator-type model and a very large sample of US manufacturing firms. The estimation methodology here controlled for both firm effects and simultaneity. Similarly, and using some of the same data, Himmelberg and Petersen (1994) looked at a panel of 179 US small firms in high-tech industries and found an economically large and statistically significant relationship between R&D investment and internal finance.

Harhoff (1998) found weak but significant cash flow effects on R&D for both small and large German firms, although Euler equation estimates for R&D investment were uninformative due to the smoothness of R&D and the small sample size. Combining limited survey evidence with his regression results, he concludes that R&D investment in small German firms may be constrained by the availability of finance. Bond et al. (1999) find significant differences between the cash flow impacts on R&D and investment for large manufacturing firms in the United Kingdom and Germany. German firms in their sample are insensitive to cash flow shocks, whereas the investment of non-R&D-doing UK firms does respond. Cash flow helps to predict whether a UK firm does R&D, but not the level of that R&D. They interpret their findings to mean that financial constraints are important for British firms, but that those which do R&D are a self-selected group that face fewer constraints. This is consistent with the view that the desire of firms to smooth R&D over time combines with the relatively high cost of financing it to reduce R&D well below the level that would obtain in a frictionless world.

Mulkay et al. (2001) perform a similar exercise using large French and US manufacturing firms, finding that cash flow impacts are much larger in the US than in France, both for R&D and for ordinary investment. Except for the well-known fact that R&D exhibits higher serial correlation than investment (presumably because of higher adjustment costs), differences in behavior are between countries, not between investment types. This result is consistent with evidence reported in Hall et al. (1999) for the US,

France and Japan during an earlier time period, which basically finds that R&D and investment on the one hand, and sales and cash flow on the other, are simultaneously determined in the United States (neither one 'Granger-causes' the other), whereas in the other countries there is little feedback from sales and cash flows to the two investments. Using a non-structural R&D investment equation together with data for the US, the UK, Canada, Europe and Japan, Bhagat and Welch (1995) found similar results for the 1985–90 period, with stock returns predicting changes in R&D more strongly for the US and UK firms.

Recently, Bougheas et al. (2001) examined the effects of liquidity constraints on R&D investment using firm-level data for manufacturing firms in Ireland and also found evidence that R&D investment in these firms is financially constrained, in line with the previous studies of US and UK firms.

Brown (1997) argues that existing tests of the impact of capital market imperfections on innovative firms cannot distinguish between two possibilities: (1) capital markets are perfect and different factors drive the firm's different types of expenditures or (2) capital markets are imperfect and different types of expenditure react differently to a common factor (shocks to the supply of internal finance). He then compares the sensitivity of investment to cash flow for innovative and non-innovative firms. The results support the hypothesis that capital markets are imperfect, finding that the investment of innovative firms is more sensitive to cash flow.

The conclusions from this body of empirical work are several: first, there is solid evidence that debt is a disfavored source of finance for R&D investment; second, the 'Anglo-Saxon' economies, with their thick and highly developed stock markets and relatively transparent ownership structures, typically exhibit more sensitivity and responsiveness of R&D to cash flow than Continental economies; third, and much more speculatively, this greater responsiveness may arise because they are financially constrained, in the sense that they view external sources of finance as much more costly than internal, and therefore require a considerably higher rate of return to investments done on the margin when they are tapping these sources. However, it is perhaps equally likely that this responsiveness occurs because firms are more sensitive to demand signals in thick financial equity markets; a definitive explanation of the 'excess sensitivity' result awaits further research.[8] In addition to these results, the evidence from Germany and some other countries suggests that small firms are more likely to face this difficulty than large established firms (not surpisingly, if the source of the problem is a 'lemons' premium).

From a policy perspective, these results point to another reason why it may be socially beneficial to offer tax incentives to companies in order to reduce the cost of capital they face for R&D investment, especially to small and new firms. Many governments, including those in the United States and the United Kingdom, currently have such programs. Such a policy approach simply observes that the cost of capital is relatively high for R&D and tries to close the gap via a tax subsidy. However, there is an alternative approach, relying on the private sector, that attempts to close the financing gap by reducing the degree of asymmetric information and moral hazard rather than simply subsidizing the investment. I turn to this topic in the next section.

15.5 SMALL FIRMS, START-UP FINANCE AND VENTURE CAPITAL

As should be apparent from much of the preceding discussion, any problems associated with financing investments in new technology will be most apparent for new entrants and start-up firms. For this reason, many governments already provide some form of assistance for such firms, and in many countries, especially the United States, there exists a private sector 'venture capital' industry that is focused on solving the problem of financing innovation for new and young firms. This section of the chapter reviews what we know about these alternative funding mechanisms, beginning with a brief look at government funding for start-ups and then discussing the venture capital solution.

15.5.1 Government Funding for Start-Up Firms

Examples of such programs are the US Small Business Investment Company (SBIC) and Small Business Innovation Research (SBIR) programs. Together, these programs disbursed $2.4 billion in 1995, more than 60 percent of the amount from venture capital in that year (Lerner, 1998a, 1998b). In Germany, more than 800 federal and state government financing programs have been established for new firms in the recent past (OECD, 1995). In 1980, the Swedish established the first of a series of investment companies (along with instituting a series of measures such as reduced capital gains taxes to encourage private investments in start-ups), partly on the United States model. By 1987, the government share of venture capital funding was 43 percent (Karaomerliolu and Jacobsson, 1999). Recently, the UK has instituted a series of government programs under the Enterprise Fund umbrella which allocate funds to small and medium-sized firms in high technology and certain regions, as well as guaranteeing some loans to small businesses (Bank of England, 2001). There are also programs at the European level.

A considerable body of evidence exists as to the effectiveness and 'additionality' of these programs. In most cases, evaluating the success of the programs is difficult due to the lack of a 'control' group of similar firms that do not receive funding.[9] Therefore most of the available studies are based on retrospective survey data provided by the recipients; few attempt to address the question of performance under the counterfactual seriously. A notable exception is the study by Lerner (1999), who looks at 1435 SBIR awardees and a matched sample of firms that did not receive awards, over a ten-year post-award period. Because most of the firms are privately held, he is unable to analyze the resulting valuation or profitability of the firms, but he does find that firms receiving SBIR grants grow significantly faster than the others after receipt of the grant. He attributes some of this effect to 'quality certification' by the government that enables the firm to raise funds from private sources as well.[10]

A number of recent studies have looked more closely at the twin questions of whether such subsidies displace R&D investments that would have been made anyway and whether they lead to increased innovation output. David et al. (2000) survey those done earlier and Hall (2005) looks at the recent analyses. Although the results are mixed, the usual finding is that firms receiving subsidies do perform more R&D, but that the additional amount is not quite as large as the subsidy, and that they patent slightly more. That is, there is some replacement of the firm's own R&D, and the productivity in terms of innovation is slightly lower, as one might have expected given the multiple goals of such subsidies.

15.5.2 Venture Capital

Many observers view the rise of the venture capital (VC) industry, especially that in the United States, as a 'free market' solution to the problems of financing innovation. In fact, many of the European programs described above have as some of their goals the provision of seed capital and the encouragement of a venture capital industry that addresses the needs of high-technology start-ups. Table 15.1 shows why this has been of some concern to European policy-makers: the amount of venture capital available to firms in the United States and Europe was roughly comparable in 1996, but the relative allocation to new firms (seed money and start-ups) in Europe was much less, below 10 percent of the funds as opposed to 27 percent. A correspondingly greater amount was used to finance buyouts of various kinds.

In the United States, the VC industry consists of fairly specialized pools of funds (usually from private investors) that are managed and invested in companies by individuals knowledgeable about the industry in which they

Table 15.1 Venture capital disbursements by stage of financing (1996)

	United States	Europe
Total VC disbursements (millions $1996)	9420.6	8572.0
Share seed and start-ups	27.1%	6.5%
Share for expansion	41.6%	39.3%
Share other (incl. buyouts)	31.3%	54.2%

Source: Rausch (1998) and author's calculations.

are investing. In principle, the idea is that the lemons premium is reduced because the investment managers are better informed, and moral hazard is minimized because a higher level of monitoring than that used in conventional arm's-length investments is the norm. But the story is more complex than that: the combination of high uncertainty, asymmetric information and the fact that R&D investment typically does not yield results instantaneously not only implies option-like behavior for the investment decision but also has implications for the form of the VC contract and the choice of decision-maker. That is, there are situations in which it is optimal for the investor to have the right to shut down a project and there are other situations in which optimal performance is achieved when the innovator has control.

A number of studies have documented the characteristics and performance of the VC industry in the United States. The most detailed look at the actual operation of the industry is that by Kaplan and Stromberg (2000), who examine 200 venture capital contracts and compare their provisions to the predictions of the economic theory of financial contracting under uncertainty. They find that the contracts often provide for separate allocation of cash flow rights, control rights, voting rights, board positions and liquidation rights, and that the rights are frequently contingent on performance measures. If performance is poor, the venture capitalists often gain full control of the firm. Provisions such as delayed vesting are often included to mitigate hold-up by the entrepreneur as suggested by Anand and Galetovic (2000).

Kaplan and Stromberg conclude that these contracts are most consistent with the predictions of Aghion and Bolton (1992) and Dewatripont and Tirole (1994), all of whom study the incomplete contracts that arise when cash flows can be observed but not verified in sufficient detail to be used for contract enforcement. Put simply, the modal VC contract is a complex debt–equity hybrid (and in fact, frequently contains convertible preferred securities and other such instruments) that looks more like debt when the firm does poorly (giving control to the investor) and more like equity when the firm does well (by handing control to the entrepreneur, which is incentive-compatible).

In a series of papers, Lerner (1992, 1995) studied a sample of VC-financed start-ups in detail, highlighting the important role that investing and monitoring experience has in this industry. He found that the amount of funds provided and the share of equity retained by the managers are sensitive to the experience and ability of the capital providers and the maturity of the firm being funded. Venture Capitalists do increase the value of the firms they fund, especially when they are experienced investors. Firms backed by seasoned VC financiers are more likely to time the market successfully when they go public, and to employ the most reputable underwriters.

At a macroeconomic level, VC funding tends to be procyclical, but it is difficult to disentangle whether the supply of funding causes growth or productivity growth encourages funding (Kortum and Lerner, 2000; Gompers and Lerner 1999a, 1999b; Ueda, 2001). The problem here is very similar to the identification problem for R&D investment in general: because of feedback effects, there is a chicken–egg simultaneity in the relationship. Some evidence exists (Majewski, 1997) that new and/or small biotechnology firms turn to other sources of funding in downturns, but that such placements are typically less successful (Lerner and Tsai, 2000) due to the misallocation of control rights (when the start-up firm is in a weak bargaining position, control tends to be allocated to the more powerful corporate partner, but this has negative consequences for incentives).

The limited evidence from Europe on the performance of VC-funded firms tends to confirm that from the US. Engel (2001) compares a matched sample of German firms founded between 1991 and 1998 and finds that the VC-backed firms grew faster than the non-VC-backed firms. Lumme et al. (1993) compare the financing and growth of small UK and Finnish firms. This approach permits a comparison between a financial market-based and a bank-centered economy, and indeed, they find that small UK firms rely more on equity and less on loan finance and grow faster than small Finnish firms. Further evidence on small UK high-technology firms is provided by Moore (1993), who looks at 300 such firms, finding that the availability and cost of finance is the most important constraint facing these firms, but that they are affected only marginally more than other types of small firms. That is, the financing 'gap' in the UK may be more related to size than to R&D intensity.

For Japan, Hamao et al. (1998) find that the long-run performance of VC-backed initial public offerings (IPOs) are no better than that for other IPOs, unlike Lerner's evidence for the United States. However, many venture capitalists in Japan are subsidiaries of major securities firms rather than specialists as in the United States. Only these venture capitalists have low returns, whereas those that are independent have returns more similar to the US. Hamao et al. attribute the low returns to conflicts of interest between the VC subsidiary and the securities firm that owns it, which affects the price at which the IPO is offered. This result highlights the importance of the institutions in which the venture capital industry is embedded for the creation of entrepreneurial incentives.

Black and Gilson (1998) and Rajan and Zingales (2001) take the institutional argument further. Both pairs of authors emphasize the contrast between arm's-length market-based financial systems (for example, the US and the UK) and bank-centered capital market systems (for example, much of continental Europe and Japan), and view venture capital as combining the strengths of the two systems, in that it provides both the strong incentives for the manager-entrepreneur characteristic of the stock market system and the monitoring by an informed investor characteristic of the bank-centered system. They emphasize the importance of an active stock market, especially for newer and younger firms, in order to provide an exit strategy for VC investors, and allow them to move on to financing new start-ups. Thus having a VC industry that contributes to innovation and growth requires the existence of an active IPO market to permit successful entrepreneurs to regain control of their firms (and incidentally to provide powerful incentives for undertaking the start-up in the first place) and also to ensure that the venture capitalists themselves are able to use their expertise to help to establish new endeavors.

15.6 CONCLUSIONS

Based on the literature surveyed here, what do we know about the costs of financing innovation investments and the possibility that some kind of market failure exists in this area? Several main points emerge:

1. There is fairly clear evidence, based on theory, surveys, and empirical estimation, that small and start-up firms in R&D-intensive and high-technology industries face a higher cost of capital than their larger competitors and than firms in other industries. In addition to compelling theoretical arguments and empirical evidence, the mere existence of the VC industry and the fact that it is concentrated precisely where these start-ups are most active suggests that this is so.
2. The evidence for a financing gap for large and established R&D firms is harder to establish. It is certainly the case that these firms prefer to

use internally generated funds for financing investment, but less clear that there is an argument for intervention, beyond the favorable tax treatment that currently exists in many countries.[11]

3. The VC solution to the problem of financing innovation has its limits. First, it does tend to focus on only a few sectors at a time, and to make investment with a minimum size that is too large for start-ups in some fields. Second, good performance of the VC sector requires a thick market in small and new firm stocks (such as NASDAQ or EASDAQ) in order to provide an exit strategy for early-stage investors.
4. The effectiveness of government incubators, seed funding, loan guarantees, and other such policies for funding R&D deserves further study, ideally in an experimental or quasi-experimental setting. In particular, studying the cross-country variation in the performance of such programs would be desirable, because the outcomes may depend to a great extent on institutional factors that are difficult to control for using data from within a single country.

NOTES

* This is a revised and shortened version of a paper entitled 'The financing of research and development' published in the *Oxford Review of Economic Policy*, **18** (1), 35–51, 2002. This version is reprinted by permission of the publisher, Oxford University Press.

1. See, for example, Peeters and van Pottelsberghe (2003). The author has also heard this claim in conversations with the R&D managers of a variety of firms.
2. See, for example, footnote 1, Chapter 8 of *Capitalism, Socialism and Democracy* (Schumpeter, 1942 [1960]).
3. Since 1974, publicly traded firms in the United States have been required to report their total R&D expenditure in their annual reports and 10-K filings (required balance sheets and income statement filings with the SEC) with the US Securities and Exchange Commission (SEC), under Financial Accounting Standards Board (FSAB) rule No. 2, issued October 1974, if such expenditure is 'material'. In 1989, a new accounting standard, SSAP 13, obligated similar disclosures in the UK. Most continental European countries do not have such a requirement, although they may evolve in that direction due to international harmonization of accounting standards, at least for publicly traded firms.
4. There is also considerable cross-sectional evidence for the United States that R&D intensity and leverage are negatively correlated across firms. See Friend and Lang (1988), Hall (1992) and Bhagat and Welch (1995).
5. A detailed discussion of tax regimes in different countries is beyond the scope of this survey, but it is quite common in several countries for long-term capital gains on funds that remain with a firm for more than one year to be taxed at a lower rate than ordinary income. Of course, even if the tax rates on the two kinds of income are equal, the inequalities will hold. Only in the case where dividends are not taxed at the corporate level (which was formerly the case in the UK) will the ranking given above not hold.
6. See Hall and Van Reenen (2000) for details.
7. A detailed consideration of the econometric estimation of these models can be found in Mairesse et al. (1999). See also Hall (1991).
8. It is also true that much of the literature here has tended to downplay the role of measurement error in drawing conclusions from the results. Measurement error in Tobin's q,

cash flow, or output is likely to be sizable and will ensure that all variables will enter any specification of the R&D investment equation significantly, regardless of whether they truly belong or not. Instrumental variables estimation is a partial solution, but only if all the errors are serially uncorrelated, which is unlikely.

9. See Jaffe (2002) for a review of methodologies for evaluation such government programs. For a complete review of the SBIR Program, including some case studies, see the National Research Council (1998).
10. Also see Spivack (2001) for further studies of such programs, including European studies, and David et al. (2000) and Klette et al. (2000) for surveys of the evaluation of government R&D programs in general.
11. It is important to remind the reader of the premise of this chapter: I am focusing only on the financing gap arguments for favorable treatment of R&D and ignoring (for the present) the arguments based on R&D spillovers and externalities. There is good reason to believe that the latter is a much more important consideration for large established firms, especially if we wish those firms to undertake basic research that is close to industry but with unknown applications (the Bell Labs model).

REFERENCES

Aghion, Phillippe and Patrick Bolton (1992), 'An incomplete contracts approach to financial contracting', *Review of Economic Studies*, **59** (3), 473–94.

Akerlof, George A. (1970), 'The market for "lemons": quality, uncertainty, and the market mechanism', *Quarterly Journal of Economics*, **84** (3), 488–500.

Alam, Pervaiz and Karen Schuele Walton (1995), 'Information asymmetry and valuation effects of debt financing', *Financial Review*, **30** (2), 289–311.

Alderson, Michael J. and Brian L. Betker (1996), 'Liquidation costs and accounting data', *Financial Management*, **25** (2), 25–36.

Anand, Bharat N. and Alexander Galetovic (2000), 'Weak property rights and holdup in R&D', *Journal of Economics and Management Strategy*, **9** (4), 615–42.

Anton, James J. and Dennis A. Yao (1998), 'The sale of intellectual property: strategic disclosure, property rights, and incomplete contracts', Wharton School, University of Pennsylvania, Working Paper.

Arellano, Manuel and Stephen Bond (1991), 'Some tests of specification for panel data: Monte Carlo evidence and an application to employment equations', *Review of Economic Studies*, **58** (2), 277–97.

Arrow, Kenneth J. (1962), 'Economic welfare and the allocation of resources for invention', In NBER (ed.), *The Rate and Direction of Inventive Activity: Economic and Social Factors*, Princeton, NJ: Princeton University Press, pp. 609–25.

Auerbach, Alan J. (1984), 'Taxes, firm financial policy, and the cost of capital: an empirical analysis', *Journal of Public Economics*, **23** (1–2), 27–57.

Bank of England (2001), *Finance for Small Firms: An Eighth Report*, London: Domestic Finance Division, Bank of England.

Bergemann, Dirk and Ulrich Hege (2005), 'The financing of innovation: learning and stopping', *RAND Journal of Economics*, **70** (3), 719–52.

Bhagat, Sanjai and Ivo Welch (1995), 'Corporate research and development investments: international comparisons', *Journal of Accounting and Economics*, **19** (2), 443–70.

Bhattacharya, Sudipto and Jay R. Ritter (1985), 'Innovation and communication: signaling with partial disclosure', *Review of Economic Studies*, **50** (2), 331–46.

Black, Bernard S. and Ronald J. Gilson (1998), 'Venture capital and the structure of capital markets: banks versus stock markets', *Journal of Financial Economics*, **47** (3), 243–77.

Blair, Margaret M. and Robert E. Litan (1990), *Corporate Leverage and Leveraged Buyouts in the Eighties*, Washington, DC: Brookings Institution.

Blass, Asher A. and Oved Yosha (2003), 'Financing R&D in mature companies: an empirical analysis', *Economics of Innovation and New Technology*, **12** (5), 425–48.

Bond, Stephen, Dietmar Harhoff and John Van Reenen (1999), 'Investment, R&D, and financial constraints in Britain and Germany', London: Institute of Fiscal Studies Working Paper No. 99/5.

Bougheas, Spiros, Holger Georg and Eric Strobl (2001), 'Is R&D financially constrained? Theory and evidence from Irish manufacturing', Nottingham: University of Nottingham.

Brown, Ward (1997), 'R&D intensity and finance: are innovative firms financially constrained?', London: London School of Economics Financial Market Group.

Cho, Shin (1992), 'Agency costs, management stockholding, and research and development expenditures', *Seoul Journal of Economics*, **5** (2), 127–52.

Chung, Kee H. and Peter Wright (1998), 'Corporate policy and market value: a q theory approach', *Review of Quantitative Finance and Accounting*, **11** (3), 293–310.

Cornelli, F. and O. Yosha (2003), 'Stage financing and convertible debt', *Review of Economic Studies*, **70** (1), 1–32.

Czarnitzki, D. and K. Kraft (2004), 'Innovation indicators and corporate credit ratings: evidence from German firms', *Economics Letters*, **82** (3), 377–84.

David, Paul A., Bronwyn H. Hall and Andrew A. Toole (2000), 'Is public R&D a complement or a substitute for private R&D? A review of the econometric evidence', *Research Policy*, **29** (4–5), 497–529.

Dewatripont, Matthias and Jean Tirole (1994), 'A theory of debt and equity: diversity of securities and manager–shareholder congruence', *Quarterly Journal of Economics*, **109** (4), 1027–54.

Eng, Li and Margaret Shackell (2001), 'The implications of long term performance plans and institutional ownership for firms' research and development investments', *Journal of Accounting, Auditing and Finance*, **16** (2), 117–39.

Engel, Dirk (2001), 'Hoeheres Beschaeftigungswachstum Durch Venture Capital?', Mannheim: ZEW Discussion Paper No. 01-34.

Fazzari, Steven M., R. Glenn Hubbard and Bruce C. Petersen (1988), 'Financing constraints and corporate investment', *Brookings Papers on Economic Activity*, **1**, 141–205.

Francis, Jennifer and Abbie Smith (1995), 'Agency costs and innovation: some empirical evidence', *Journal of Accounting and Economics*, **19** (2–3), 383–409.

Friend, Irwin and Harry H.P. Lang (1988), 'An empirical test of the impact of managerial self-interest on corporate capital structure', *Journal of Finance*, **43** (2), 271–81.

Gompers, Paul A. and Josh Lerner (1999a), 'What drives venture capital fundraising?', Cambridge, MA: NBER Working Paper No. 6906.

Gompers, Paul A. and Josh Lerner (1999b), *Capital Formation and Investment in Venture Markets: Implications for the Advanced Technology Program*, Washington, DC: Advanced Technology Program, NIST, US Dept. of Commerce.

Griliches, Zvi (1992), 'The search for R&D spillovers', *Scandinavian Journal of Economics*, **94**, S29–S47.

Hall, Bronwyn H. (1990), 'The impact of corporate restructuring on industrial research and development', *Brookings Papers on Economic Activity*, **1**, 85–136.

Hall, Bronwyn H. (1991), 'Firm-level investment with liquidity constraints: what can the Euler equations tell us?', University of California at Berkeley and the National Bureau of Economic Research.

Hall, Bronwyn H. (1992), 'Research and development at the firm level: does the source of financing matter?', NBER Working Paper No. 4096 (June).

Hall, Bronwyn H. (1993), 'R&D tax policy during the eighties: success or failure?', *Tax Policy and the Economy*, **7**, 1–36.

Hall, Bronwyn H. (1994), 'Corporate restructuring and investment horizons in the United States, 1976–1987', *Business History Review*, **68** (1), 110–43.

Hall, Bronwyn H. (1996), 'The private and social returns to research and development', in B.L.R. Smith and C.E. Barfield (eds.), *Technology, R&D, and the Economy*, Washington, DC: Brookings Institution and the American Enterprise Institute, pp. 140–83.

Hall, Bronwyn H. (2005), 'Government policy for innovation in Latin America', Report to the World Bank, at http://www.econ.berkeley.edu/~bhhall/bhpapers.html.

Hall, Bronwyn H., Zvi Griliches and Jerry A. Hausman (1986), 'Patents and R&D: is there a lag?', *International Economic Review*, **27** (2), 265–83.

Hall, Bronwyn H., Jacques Mairesse, Lee Branstetter and Bruno Crepon (1999), 'Does cash flow cause investment and R&D: an exploration using panel data for French, Japanese, and United States firms in the scientific sector', in D. Audretsch and A.R. Thurik (eds), *Innovation, Industry Evolution and Employment*, Cambridge: Cambridge University Press, pp. 129–56.

Hall, Bronwyn H. and John van Reenen (2000), 'How effective are fiscal incentives for R&D? A review of the evidence', *Research Policy*, **29** (4), 449–69.

Hamao, Yasushi, Frank Packer and Jay R. Ritter (1998), 'Institutional affiliation and the role of venture capital: evidence from initial public offerings in Japan', FRB of New York Staff Report No. 52, New York.

Harhoff, Dietmar (1998), 'Are there financing constraints for R&D and investment in German manufacturing firms?' *Annales d'Economie et de Statistique*, **49–50**, 421–56.

Himmelberg, Charles P. and Bruce C. Petersen (1994), 'R&D and internal finance: a panel study of small firms in high-tech industries', *Review of Economics and Statistics*, **76** (1), 38–51.

Jaffe, Adam (2002), 'Building programme evaluation into the design of public research-support programmes', *Oxford Review of Economic Policy*, **18** (1), 22–34.

Jensen, Michael C. and William Meckling (1976), 'Theory of the firm: managerial behavior, agency costs, and ownership structure', *Journal of Financial Economics*, **3** (4), 305–60.

Johnson, Mark S. and Rajesh P. Rao (1997), 'The impact of antitakeover amendments on corporate financial performance', *Financial Review*, **32** (4), 659–89.

Kaplan, Steven N. and Per Stromberg (2000), 'Financial contracting theory meets the real world: an empirical analysis of venture capital contracts', NBER Working Paper No. 7660, Cambridge, MA.

Karaomerliolu, Dilek Cetindamar and Staffan Jacobsson (1999), 'The Swedish venture capital industry: an infant, adolescent, or grown-up?', Goteborg, Sweden: Chalmers Institute of Technology.

Klette, Tor Jakob, Jarle Moen and Zvi Griliches (2000), 'Do subsidies to commercial R&D reduce market failures? Microeconometric evaluation studies', *Research Policy*, **29** (4–5), 471–95.

Kortum, Samuel and Josh Lerner (2000), 'Assessing the contribution of venture capital to innovation', *RAND Journal of Economics*, **31** (4), 674–92.

Lach, Saul and Mark Schankerman (1988), 'Dynamics of R&D and investment in the scientific sector', *Journal of Political Economy*, **97** (4), 880–904.

Leland, Haynes E. and David H. Pyle (1977), 'Informational asymmetries, financial structure, and financial intermediation', *Journal of Finance*, **32** (2), 371–87.

Lerner, Josh (1992), 'Venture capitalists and the decision to go public', Harvard Business School Working Paper No. 93-002.

Lerner, Josh (1995), 'Venture capitalists and the oversight of private firms', *Journal of Finance*, **50** (1), 301–18.

Lerner, Josh (1998a), '"Angel" financing and public policy: an overview', *Journal of Banking and Finance*, **22** (6), 773–83.

Lerner, Josh (1998b), '"Public venture capital": rationale and evaluation', in National Research Council (ed.), *The Small Business Innovation Program: Challenges and Opportunities*, Washington, DC: Board on Science, Technology, and Economic Policy, NRC, pp. 113–28.

Lerner, Josh (1999), 'The government as venture capitalist: the long-run effects of the SBIR Program', *Journal of Business*, **72** (3), 285–318.

Lerner, Josh and Alexander Tsai (2000), 'Do equity financing cycles matter? Evidence from biotechnology alliances', NBER Working Paper No. 7464 (January).

Levin, Richard C., Alvin K. Klevorick, Richard R. Nelson and Sidney G. Winter (1987), 'Appropriating the returns from industrial research and development', *Brookings Papers on Economic Activity*, **18**, 783–832.

Lumme, A., I. Kavrenen, E. Autio and M.M. Kaila (1993), 'New, technology-based companies in Cambridge in an international perspective', University of Cambridge Small Business Research Centre Working Papers 35 (September).

Mairesse, Jacques, Bronwyn H. Hall and Benoit Mulkay (1999), 'Firm-Level Investment in France and the United States: an exploration of what we have learned in twenty years', *Annales d'Economie et de Statistique*, 55–56, 27-69.

Majewski, Suzanne E. (1997), 'Using strategic alliance formation as a financing mechanism in the biotechnology industry', University of California, Berkeley.

Majumdar, Summit K. and Anuradha Nagarajan (1997), 'The impact of changing stock ownership patterns in the United States: theoretical implications and some evidence', *Revue d'Economie Industrielle*, **82**, 39–54.

Mansfield, Edwin, Mark Schwartz and Samuel Wagner (1981), 'Imitation costs and patents: an empirical study', *Economic Journal*, **91** (364), 907–18.

Miller, Merton H. and Franco Modigliani (1961), 'Dividend policy, growth, and the valuation of shares', *Journal of Business*, **34** (4), 411–33.

Modigliani, Franco and Merton H. Miller (1958), 'The cost of capital, corporation finance and the theory of investment', *American Economic Review*, **48** (3), 261–97.

Moore, Barry (1993), 'Financial constraints to the growth and development of small high-technology firms', University of Cambridge Small Business Research Centre Working Paper 31 (July).

Mulkay, Benoit, Bronwyn H. Hall and Jacques Mairesse (2001), 'Investment and R&D in France and in the United States', in Deutsche Bundesbank (ed.), *Investing Today for the World of Tomorrow*, Frankfurt am Main: Springer Verlag, pp. 229–73.

National Research Council (1998), *SBIR: Challenges and Opportunities*, Washington, DC: Board on Science, Technology, and Economic Policy, NRC.

Nelson, Richard R. (1959), 'The Simple Economics of Basic Scientific Research', *Journal of Political Economy*, **67** (3), 297–306.

OECD (1995), *Venture Capital in OECD Countries*, Paris: Organisation for Economic Co-operation and Development.

Opler, Tim C. and Sheridan Titman (1993), 'The determinants of leveraged buyout activity: free cash flow vs. financial distress costs', *Journal of Finance*, **48** (5), 1985–99.

Opler, Tim C. and Sheridan Titman (1994), 'Financial distress and corporate performance', *Journal of Finance*, **49** (3), 1015–40.

Peeters, Carinne and Bruno van Pottelsberghe de la Potterie (2003), 'Measuring innovation competencies and performances: a survey of large firms in Belgium', Institute of Innovation Research, Hitotsubashi University, Japan, Working Paper 03-16.

Pugh, William N., John S. Jahera, Jr. and Sharon Oswald (1999), 'ESOPs, takeover protection, and corporate decision making', *Journal of Economics and Finance*, **23** (2), 170–83.

Rajan, Raghuram G. and Luigi Zingales (2001), 'Financial systems, industrial structure, and growth', *Oxford Review of Economic Policy*, **17** (4), 467–82.

Rausch, Lawrence M. (1998), 'Venture capital investment trends in the United States and Europe', Washington, DC: National Science Foundation Division of Science Resource Studies Issues Brief 99-303.

Scherer, F. M. (1998), 'The size distribution of profits from innovation', *Annales d'Economie et de Statistique*, **49–50**, 495–516.

Schumpeter, Joseph (1942), *Capitalism, Socialism, and Democracy*, New York: Harper and Row (reprinted 1960).

Spivack, Richard N. (2001), *The Economic Evaluation of Technological Change*, Washington, DC: Conference Proceedings of the Advanced Technology Program, National Institute of Standards and Technology.

Szewczyk, Samuel H., George P. Tsetsekos and Zaher Z. Zantout (1996), 'The valuation of corporate R&D expenditures: evidence from investment opportunities and free cash flow', *Financial Management*, **25** (1), 105–10.

Ueda, Masako (2001), 'Does innovation spur venture capital?', Barcelona: Universitat Pompeu Fabra.

Williamson, Oliver E. (1988), 'Corporate finance and corporate governance', *Journal of Finance*, **43** (3), 567–91.

Zantout, Zaher Z. (1997), 'A test of the debt monitoring hypothesis: The case of corporate R&D expenditures', *Financial Review*, **32** (1), 21–48.

16. R&D investment under uncertainty: the role of R&D subsidies and patent policy

Dirk Czarnitzki and Andrew A. Toole

16.1 INTRODUCTION

Since business investment in research and development (R&D) is a critical factor driving innovation and economic growth, it is important to understand how public policies like R&D subsidies and intellectual property protection influence private incentives for R&D investment. There is now a sizable literature on how public R&D policies might 'correct' for underinvestment in business R&D resulting from market failures or various capital market imperfections leading to financing constraints.

The seminal papers are Nelson (1959) and Arrow (1962). One theoretical argument suggests that market failures in R&D occur due to positive externalities in knowledge-generating processes. For instance, Arrow (1962, p. 615) states that:

> No amount of legal protection can make a thoroughly appropriable commodity of something as intangible as information. The very use of the information in any productive way is bound to reveal it, at least in part. Mobility of personnel among firms provides a way of spreading information. Legally imposed property rights can provide only a partial barrier, since there are obviously enormous difficulties in defining in any sharp way an item of information and differentiating it from similar sounding items.

The public character of information leads to incomplete appropriability of investments aimed at creating knowledge. Knowledge cannot be kept proprietary, instead newly created knowledge will always leak out to competitors or others, and thus the social benefit will be higher than the private return. Under the assumption that companies intend to maximize profits, it will occur that some R&D projects would have a high social return, but they would never be carried out as private costs are higher than the private expected return. This leads to an underinvestment in R&D from the social point of view. This argument justifies governmental intervention, as it is present nowadays in most industrialized countries.

As Arrow points out, even patent systems (legally imposed property rights) that grant a temporary monopoly to the inventor for exploiting the economic returns of new technologies may only constitute an imperfect appropriation of returns, as it is difficult to define the claim of a patent and all its related applications. Therefore, it is common practice in industrialized countries to supplement patent policy with direct public grants for R&D conducted in the business sector in order to overcome the gap between private and social equilibrium of R&D in the economy.

Another argument in favor of private underinvestment in innovation activities refers to financing difficulties for R&D projects due to asymmetric information among borrowers and lenders. Unlike investment in tangible capital, R&D investment is sunk and inherently uncertain. This leads lenders to be reluctant about financing R&D and can result in financial constraints for R&D investment in the business sector (see Hall, 2002 for a recent survey on such studies).

16.1.1 How Does this Chapter Contribute to our Understanding of such Policies?

Drawing on the theory of investment under uncertainty, we argue that both government subsidy programs and patent policies are a means to purchase, albeit indirectly, a portion of the firm's option value to wait. The real options approach to investment under uncertainty predicts that firms invest less in irreversible capital as uncertainty in expected returns increases (Pindyck, 1991; Dixit, 1992; Dixit and Pindyck, 1994; Novy-Marx, 2007). R&D investment is highlighted in this literature as a particularly relevant example of irreversible capital since a large proportion of R&D supports the salaries of research personnel and cannot be recouped if projects fail. In light of the fact that the output of R&D is inherently uncertain, firms can avoid large losses by waiting for new information about future market demand or competition, and forgoing investment when this information is unfavorable. Hence, the incentive to invest in R&D today is lower because it involves exercising or 'killing' the option to invest productively at any time in the future.

The basic contribution of this chapter is to draw attention to the real options mechanism of subsidy and patent policies and to explore the importance of this mechanism empirically. Although subsidy and patent policies do not act directly to reduce uncertainties in the innovative process or potential market returns, they can offset (at least partially) the negative effect of uncertainty on the incentive to invest in R&D by increasing the firm's expected return. One implication from our analysis is that public policies intended to increase R&D investment can achieve this objective by focusing on reducing various forms of uncertainty in the innovative process or market for new products. It is important to note, however, that government intervention is not justified by a real options argument. Firms are responding in a socially efficient manner to uncertainties and government intervention is only justified by market failure arguments such as the presence of knowledge externalities or capital market imperfections as described below.

16.2 BRIEF SURVEY OF THE ISSUES AND LITERATURE

16.2.1 Incomplete R&D Appropriability and Financing Constraints

The incomplete R&D appropriability argument outlined above is the most famous rationale for government involvement in knowledge creation activities (Nelson, 1959; Arrow, 1962). Public patent policy and R&D subsidies are seen as alternative ways to increase overall investment in R&D in order to compensate for underinvestment due to incomplete appropriability stemming from knowledge externalities. However, because researchers and policy-makers are still trying to identify and understand the varieties of knowledge-creating activities and how these activities interact across performers and time, each of these policy approaches are controversial and challenging to implement.

The idea that patent protection increases a firm's ability to appropriate the returns from their innovations is commonplace in the literature.[1] The question that has received the most attention is how effective patent protection is as a means for appropriating returns. This observation is the starting point for a large theoretical and empirical literature that cannot be summarized in this chapter. Scotchmer (2004) provides a clear presentation of the issues and theory. The empirical literature uses either survey data or patent renewal data to shed light on differences in patent effectiveness or patent value (see, for instance, the literature spawned by Pakes, 1986). The literature examining the relationship between patents and firm value is surveyed in Czarnitzki et al. (2006). Also, since patenting involves the disclosure of information, the firm's decision to patent represents a trade-off between monopoly rents and disclosure. Thus, patents do not unambiguously induce R&D investment. Arora et al. (2008) discuss this issue and Cohen (2005) surveys the arguments and evidence on appropriation.

The design and implementation of effective R&D subsidy policies is also difficult. Ideally, public agencies would only grant subsidies for projects in which the private return is insufficient to induce investment but the social return exceeds the R&D cost of investment. Two main problems are identified: first, it is unclear whether the government can select those projects with high social returns but insufficient private returns. Second, once public support programs are in place, each firm has an incentive to apply for grants for any kind of R&D project because the marginal cost of a subsidy is zero (aside from its application cost). Thus firms might simply substitute public financing for private investment. This potential crowding-out effect has been the subject of numerous empirical studies. David et al. (2000) and Klette et al. (2000) surveyed the literature and find that micro-econometric studies yield mixed results. For instance, David et al. report nine out of 19 studies find crowding-out effects. With the availability of better micro firm-level databases and new econometric methods, scholars tend to find that crowding-out effects are rejected in more recent studies (see, for instance, Almus and Czarnitzki, 2003; Duguet, 2004; Czarnitzki and Licht, 2006; Czarnitzki et al., 2007; González et al., 2005; Hussinger, 2008; Toole, 2007). Lach (2002) and Görg and Strobl (2007), however, still find mixed evidence.[2]

In addition to the incomplete appropriability argument, the literature on financial constraints points out that capital market imperfections also lead to private underinvestment in R&D.[3] A survey by Hall (2002) summarizes the findings as follows. Due to asymmetric information between borrowers and lenders, a financing gap for R&D emerges. Potential lenders like banks are reluctant to fund R&D due to the inherent risk, even if the borrower has argued that there are high expected returns. Unlike investment in physical capital, R&D is treated as a current expense and there is no capitalized value on firms' balance sheets to use as collateral in credit negotiations. Thus R&D must be supported predominantly by internal financial resources. This causes a financing gap for small and medium-sized firms that do not have sufficient cash flow to fund R&D. Surprisingly the financial constraints literature attempts to test for the existence of financial constraints but typically ignores the presence of R&D subsidies. Two exceptions are Hyytinen and Toivanen (2005) and Czarnitzki (2006), who find that R&D subsidies reduce the underinvestment problem stemming from financial constraints.

16.2.2 Uncertainty and Investment

In the theoretical literature, Abel et al. (1996) show that investment decisions involve the acquisition or exercise of 'reversibility' and 'expandability' options. The reversibility option captures the value of opportunities and costs associated with disinvestment at some point in the future. The reversibility option increases the incentive for current investment when future returns are uncertain, since the firm acquires this option by purchasing capital. On the other hand, the expandability option captures the value of opportunities and costs associated with investment at some point in the future. This option decreases the incentive for current investment when future returns are uncertain, since the firm acquires this option by delaying the purchase of capital. Since these options have offsetting effects on the incentive to invest, their model shows that the net effect of uncertainty on current investment is theoretically ambiguous. Butzen and Fuss (2002), Carruth et al. (2000) and Lensink et al. (2001) provide reviews of the theoretical and empirical literatures emphasizing physical capital investment.

The type of the capital being considered for purchase will partly determine the nature of the options facing the firm and potentially resolve some of the theoretical ambiguity. For instance, research and development is typically considered in the literature as an investment that has no (or an extremely small) reversibility option but has a significant expandability option. R&D investment is often characterized as completely irreversible (see, for instance, Dixit and Pindyck, 1994, p. 424) since this expenditure is directed toward the salaries of research personnel and the purchase of task-specific equipment and materials. When irreversibility is combined with uncertainty over future returns and the opportunity to delay investment, only a positive expandability option exists and this implies that the optimal investment trigger is greater than the trigger given by the traditional net present value rule. Since the value of the expandability option increases with the level of uncertainty, the incentive for current investment is lower at higher levels of uncertainty. This suggests a negative relationship between the current level of R&D investment and uncertainty.[4]

The type of capital investment also influences the nature of the uncertainty relevant to the investment decision. Private R&D is generally regarded as investment in knowledge-producing activities aimed at the discovery and introduction into use of new products and processes. Uncertainty about future market returns to innovation will play a critical role in the decision to invest in R&D.[5] For instance, when new products are introduced into the marketplace, firms are uncertain about their acceptance by potential customers, the reliability of suppliers and production operations, and the reaction by rival firms. When these uncertainties are high, expandability options suggest R&D investment will be delayed.

Our literature search found only one published empirical analysis focused on the relationship between uncertainty and R&D investment. Using annual data for nine Organisation for Economic Co-operation and Development (OECD) countries over the period 1982–92, Goel and Ram

(2001) relate the share of R&D and non-R&D investment in gross domestic product (GDP) to indicators of aggregate inflation uncertainty, real interest rates and the growth of GDP. The separate categories of investment, R&D and non-R&D, are intended to capture differences in the degree of irreversibility of the underlying investment decisions. They measure uncertainty using five-year moving averages of each country's inflation rate in both standard deviation and level form. The results show that both versions of uncertainty reduce the share of R&D in GDP, but have no significant impact on the share of non-R&D investment in GDP. Since irreversibility is one of the required characteristics for creating a positive option value for waiting, their results are consistent with real options investment behavior.[6]

Before leaving this section, it is important to note that a negative relationship between uncertainty and investment can result from other factors aside from real options behavior. Some of these alternatives include reducing investment in response to industry-level uncertainty, systematic economy-wide uncertainty, financial constraints and firm risk-aversion. Given these other possible explanations, we are careful to include control variables in our empirical analyses that address each of these possibilities.

16.2.3 Uncertainty and Public Innovation Policy

The main contribution of this chapter is to point out that patent policy and public R&D subsidies can mitigate the incentive effect of uncertainty on firm-level R&D investment. While these policies do not act directly to reduce uncertainties, they can offset the incentive to delay investment by increasing the expected return to the firm's R&D investment, an indirect means of purchasing part of the firm's option value of waiting. If this real options mechanism is present, firms with R&D subsidies or patent protection should be less sensitive to uncertainties in the innovative process and the product market, respectively. Therefore, firms taking advantage of these policies should invest more in R&D today than those firms that do not make use of these policies.

The interesting difference between the patent system and direct subsidies is that they influence different stages of the innovative process. While patents only protect inventions after substantial investments and are conditional on successful outcomes, R&D subsidies affect firm behavior in the discovery or development phases. Therefore, these two policies may have different effects on R&D conducted in the economy. In two empirical papers, Czarnitzki and Toole (2006, 2007) analyze how uncertainty affects firm-level R&D investment. In particular, these studies explore whether R&D subsidies and patents influence firm R&D investment through a 'real options mechanism' in addition to their more traditional direct effects on

R&D investment. The next section reports their basic results and shows how uncertainty can be modeled with common innovation survey data.

16.3 DATA AND EMPIRICAL STUDY

16.3.1 Data

The data source of the analyses of Czarnitzki and Toole (2006, 2007) is the Mannheim Innovation Panel (MIP) which is an annual German innovation survey conducted by the Centre for European Economic Research (ZEW). It represents the German part of the Community Innovation Survey which is part of the harmonized innovation survey conducted by EU member states. The sample consists of product-innovating firms, as the focus of their approach is uncertainty in the product market, that is, the expected success of innovations.

The dependent variable is current R&D investment at the firm level (RD_i) in millions of DM (1.95583 DM = 1 Euro). There are two aspects of R&D investment data that need to be addressed for the regression models presented in the next section. First, the distribution of R&D investment across firms is skewed as there are many firms with moderate investment levels and some firms with high investment levels. To address this skewness, we use the natural log of current R&D in the empirical models. Second, there are a number of firms that perform R&D only intermittently. This creates some firm observations with zero current R&D investment even though they had positive R&D investment in the past.[7] Because we cannot take the log of a zero R&D observation, we set the value of current R&D for these firms to the minimum positive value for R&D observed in the sample and treat this as the censoring point in the Tobit models presented below.

One important component of our empirical model is the measure of firm-specific uncertainty about future market returns to innovation. To be completely consistent with theory, one would like a forward-looking measure of firm-specific uncertainty.[8] Because past experience is one of the most important mechanisms for learning, a reasonable proxy can be constructed based on the firm's past market experience as innovators. We use revenue volatility from past market introductions as our proxy for firm-specific uncertainty. Consequently, we assume that past market experience is informative about how firms perceive uncertainty going forward. Their market experience as innovators, however, is not the same as their market experience with established products, which rely on more stable demand and supply relationships. Thus, we generate two firm-specific uncertainty measures using the coefficient of variation of past sales revenue, one capturing uncertainty related to innovation (*UNC_NEW*) and the other capturing uncertainty related to established products (*UNC_OLD*). This allows for two separate sources of uncertainty to affect R&D investment.[9]

Our uncertainty measures are calculated as coefficients of variation of past sales revenues at the firm level. In order to adjust sales volume for firm size effects, we rescale past sales revenues by the number of employees. The number of observations available for calculating the coefficients of variation for each firm depends on available pre-sample data for which we have three to nine years available ($s = 1,\ldots,S$, with S ranging between 3 and 9):

$$UNC_{it} = \frac{\sqrt{\frac{1}{S}\sum_{s=1}^{S}\left[\frac{R_{i,t-s}}{L_{i,t-s}} - \left(\frac{1}{S}\sum_{s=1}^{S}\frac{R_{i,t-s}}{L_{i,t-s}}\right)\right]^2}}{\frac{1}{S}\sum_{s=1}^{S}\frac{R_{i,t-s}}{L_{i,t-s}}}, \tag{16.1}$$

where R denotes the value of new or established product sales of firm i in year t and L refers to the number of employees. Consistent with the real options theory, higher expected product market uncertainty should delay R&D investment and thereby have a negative impact on the level of current R&D investment.

Before discussing the regression results of Czarnitzki and Toole (2006, 2007), we illustrate the distribution of uncertainty related to innovation, (*UNC_NEW*), for firms with and without public R&D subsidies and patents. The histograms in Figure 16.1 show that the distribution of uncertainty is skewed across firms. While our measure of uncertainty is never equal to zero, it can be quite small when firms do not experience much volatility on their past sales of new products. These firms perceive a relatively stable environment in their product markets. It is clear from the top panel of Figure 16.1 that subsidized firms generally face less uncertainty than non-subsidized firms. In the patent case, seen in the lower panel, we find that firms using patents as means of protection for their inventions (considering the same time period as for the uncertainty measure) also experienced less uncertainty, on average. This result is also supported by t-tests on mean differences across groups. We also performed tests on differences at the median across groups to account for skewness of the distribution and results are robust: patenting and subsidized firms experience less volatility of new product sales than non-patenting and non-subsidized firms. Thus, it appears that these policies are associated with more predicable market performance.

Since the histograms do not clearly illustrate the differences between the two policies, we also show cumulative distribution functions of the two groupings. These are depicted in Figure 16.2. Looking at the top panel, it

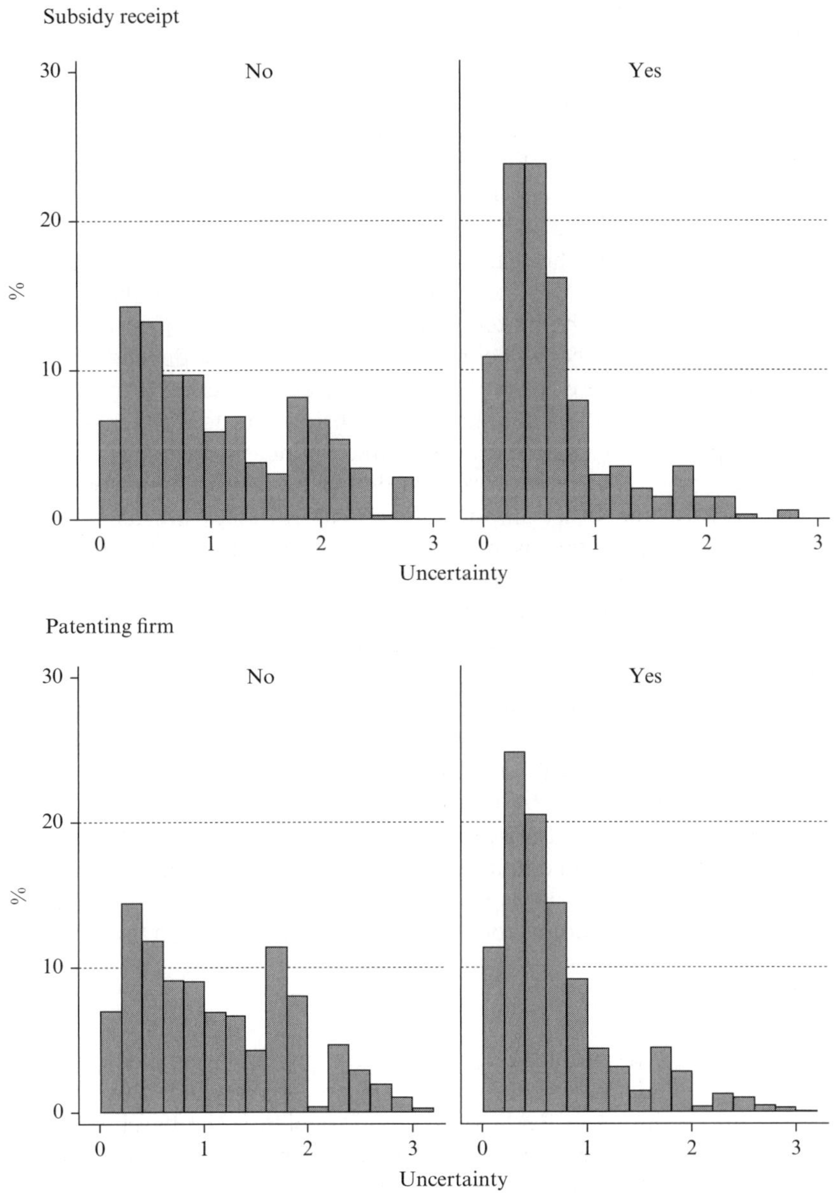

Figure 16.1 *Uncertainty at the firm level grouped by subsidy receipt and patentees*

is clear that the distributions of uncertainty among subsidized firms and non-subsidized firms are quite different, with subsidized firms experiencing less market volatility. The lower panel in Figure 16.2 shows a similar situation for patenting versus non-patenting firms.

To examine how R&D subsidies and patents influence the R&D investment–uncertainty relationship, we use interaction variables. First, we will show baseline regression specifications that examine the R&D investment–uncertainty relationship. This specification holds any past R&D subsidies or patent received by the firm constant (as well as many other control variables). Then we introduce interaction variables into the baseline model. Compared to the baseline model, these allow the firm's response to uncertainty to depend on being a subsidy recipient or depend on being a patent holder. If there is a real options mechanism acting through these innovation policies, the firms that have subsidies or hold patents should be less responsive to any given level of uncertainty in the market for new products compared to those firms that do not have subsidies or patents.

Very briefly, the other important control variables are as follows.[10] Industry-level uncertainty is measured as the coefficient of variation in industry sales per firm at the three-digit NACE level.[11] We also use a full set of industry dummy variables to capture shocks to R&D. Systematic economy-wide uncertainty shocks are captured using a full set of annual time dummy variables. Controls for internal and external access to financial capital address potential financial constraints. The firms' risk preferences are captured by the 'aggressiveness' of their recent innovation strategy with the most risk-averse firms postulated to follow a less aggressive approach to the market. There are controls for industry concentration, firm size and location in Eastern Germany. For the regressions related to patenting we also include the firms' patent stock per employee to control for existing R&D capabilities. Note that these controls are lagged in the regressions to guarantee they are predetermined and do not introduce any simultaneity issues in the analysis.

16.3.2 Empirical Results

Table 16.1 presents modified versions of the regression results appearing in Czarnitzki and Toole (2007) which analyze the relation between firm-specific uncertainty and R&D subsidies. Model A is the baseline regression and model B introduces the interaction term between new product market uncertainty and receipt of an R&D subsidy. In Models A and B, new product market uncertainty (*UNC_NEW*) is negative and highly significant. This finding indicates that firms reduce current R&D investment as perceived uncertainty in the market for innovations increases. Recall that these regressions hold constant other sources of uncertainty

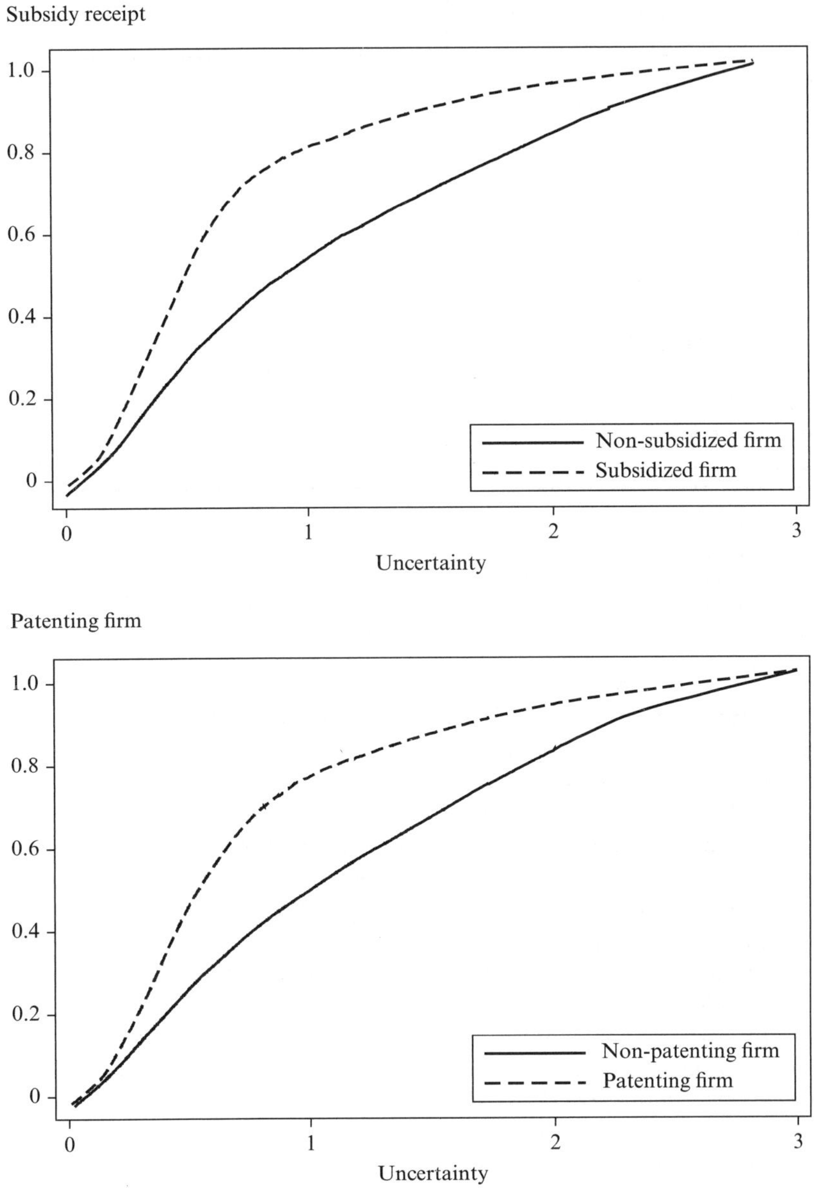

Figure 16.2 Cumulative distribution functions of uncertainty among firm groups

Table 16.1 Pooled cross-sectional Tobit regressions: subsidy policy

Dependent Variable: Ln(R&D)it		
Variable	Model A	Model B
$UNC\_NEW_{i,t-1}$	−2.295***	−2.817***
	(0.242)	(0.275)
$UNC\_NEW_{i,t-1}$*SUBSIDY DUMMY		2.538***
		(0.318)
$UNC\_OLD_{i,t-1}$	−0.356	−0.342
	(0.297)	(0.286)
SUBSIDY DUMMY	2.431***	0.603**
	(0.234)	(0.297)
# of firm-year observations	1115	1115
Log-Likelihood	−1967.32	−1941.61
McFadden-R^2	0.199	0.209

Notes: Standard errors in parentheses.
*** (**,*) indicate a significance level of 1% (5%, 10%).
The models also include: intercept, industry-level uncertainty, innovation strategy, price-cost margin, financial credit rating, location dummy for Eastern Germany, firm size, Herfindahl index of industry concentration, ten industry dummy variables, one time dummy.

and include our proxy capturing the firm's risk preferences. Revenue volatility in the firm's established product markets (*UNC_OLD*) is negatively related to current R&D investment, but is not statistically significant. The R&D subsidy dummy variable is strongly significant and positive suggesting that receipt of a government subsidy increases firm R&D investment.[12] This is consistent with the findings of prior research using German data by Almus and Czarnitzki (2003) and Hussinger (2008).

Table 16.2 presents modified versions of the regression results appearing in Czarnitzki and Toole (2006) which analyze the relation between firm-specific uncertainty and patenting.[13] Model A is the baseline regression and model B introduces the interaction term between new product market uncertainty and patenting by the firm. Once again, new product market uncertainty (*UNC_NEW*) is negative and highly significant in both models. Firms reduce current investment in response to higher levels of uncertainty. This is consistent with real options investment behavior, particularly since our regressions include controls for other potential reasons for a negative relationship between investment and uncertainty. The coefficient estimate for uncertainty in established product markets is negative but insignificant. The firm's patent stock per employee has the expected positive impact on current R&D investment.

Table 16.2 Pooled cross-sectional Tobit regressions: patent policy

Variable	Model A Pooled cross-sectional Tobit[a]	Model B Pooled cross-sectional Tobit[a]
$UNC\_NEW_{i,t\text{-}1}$	−4.106***	−4.273***
	(0.334)	(0.350)
$UNC\_NEW_{i,t\text{-}1}$*PATENT DUMMY		0.710**
		(0.355)
$UNC\_OLD_{i,t\text{-}1}$	−0.659	−0.708
	(0.421)	(0.420)
$PSTOCK_{i,t\text{-}1}/EMP_{i,t\text{-}1}$	9.579***	7.750***
	(2.024)	(2.100)
# of firm-year observations	2974	2974
Log-Likelihood	−6160.16	−6154.64
McFadden-R^2	0.146	0.146

Notes: Standard errors in parentheses.
*** (**,*) indicate a significance level of 1% (5%, 10%).
[a] Standard errors are clustered at the firm-level (881 clusters).
The models also include: intercept, industry-level uncertainty, innovation strategy, price-cost margin, financial credit rating, location dummy for Eastern Germany, firm size, Herfindahl index of industry concentration, ten industry dummy variables, six time dummies.

Model B in Table 16.2 includes the interaction between uncertainty and patenting. The patent dummy variable takes the value of one if the firm patented at least once in the past and zero otherwise. The interaction term is positive and significant at a 5 percent level. This result can be interpreted as: holding the level of patenting per employee constant (and the other covariates as well), the decision to invest in R&D for firms that hold patents is not as sensitive to uncertainty in the market for new products relative to those firms that do not patent. This is a fairly significant finding since it provides empirical evidence supporting patent protection as a means to stimulate R&D investment. That is to say, this evidence suggests legal protection from rivals in the product market works to stimulate R&D by reducing the patenting firm's sensitivity to uncertainty – a 'real options mechanism' for intellectual property protection.

When faced with a result such as this, there are two natural questions that come to mind. First, does the fact that firms choose to patent introduce a self-selection issue that might bias our result? This line of reasoning suggests there might be some unobservable difference between firms that causes those firms choosing to patent to be less sensitive to uncertainty

Dirk Czarnitzki

Jacques Mairesse

Bronwyn Hall

Manuel Trajtenberg

Luc Soete

David Mowery

Eric von Hippel

Bhaven Sampat

than those firms choosing not to patent. Czarnitzki and Toole (2006) performed two robustness checks to address this issue. First, exploiting firm-level panel data, we include a firm-specific effect in the model. The results are robust. Second, if selection into patenting is truly driving our result, then looking within the group of firms with patents should wipe out our finding. In fact, within the group of patenting firms there appears to be a monotonic relationship between patenting and their reaction to uncertainty so that firms holding more and more patents are less and less sensitive to uncertainty. Thus, the difference does not only appear between non-patentees and patentees, but also within the group of patentees.

A second question asks: if patenting actually does protect firms from rivalry and reduce uncertainty in the market for new products, then why don't all firms patent? The value or effectiveness of patenting varies by industry and technology (Lanjouw, 1998; Schankerman, 1998). Our analysis finds an average effect across firms, controlling for industry and other factors, that patenting reduces the firms' sensitivity to uncertainty and increases current R&D investment. In general, firms will choose to protect their competitive advantages through a variety of behaviors, and patenting is only one such mechanism (see Cohen et al., 2000 for important information on how firms protect knowledge). Further, our finding does not suggest or imply that patenting is a 'cure-all' or 'panacea' type policy which is applicable to all firms in all circumstances.

Finally, the regression results presented in Tables 16.1 and 16.2 are about the mitigating effects of R&D subsidies and patenting on the firm's investment response to uncertainty. In this regard, it is informative to illustrate visually the estimated differences in the firms' marginal responses on the expected R&D investment, as Tobit models result in non-linear marginal effects depending on the value of the covariates. Figure 16.3 shows the R&D investment–uncertainty response curves for some interesting groups of firms in our sample. These curves are drawn holding the other characteristics of the firms at their median values (that is, a 'median' firm). The top panel of Figure 16.3 shows how expected R&D investment level (on the vertical axis) changes as uncertainty in the market for new products (on the horizontal axis) increases. The solid curve shows the response for firms with R&D subsidies while the dotted curve shows the response of those firms without R&D subsidies. Clearly, the dotted curve falls quite quickly and shows that expected current investment falls more quickly in response to uncertainty when firms do not have R&D subsidies. Similarly, the bottom panel illustrates the responsiveness of expected current R&D investment across the groups of firm with and without patent protection. Those firms without patent protection (the dotted curve) reduce their expected levels of R&D investment more quickly as uncertainty increases.

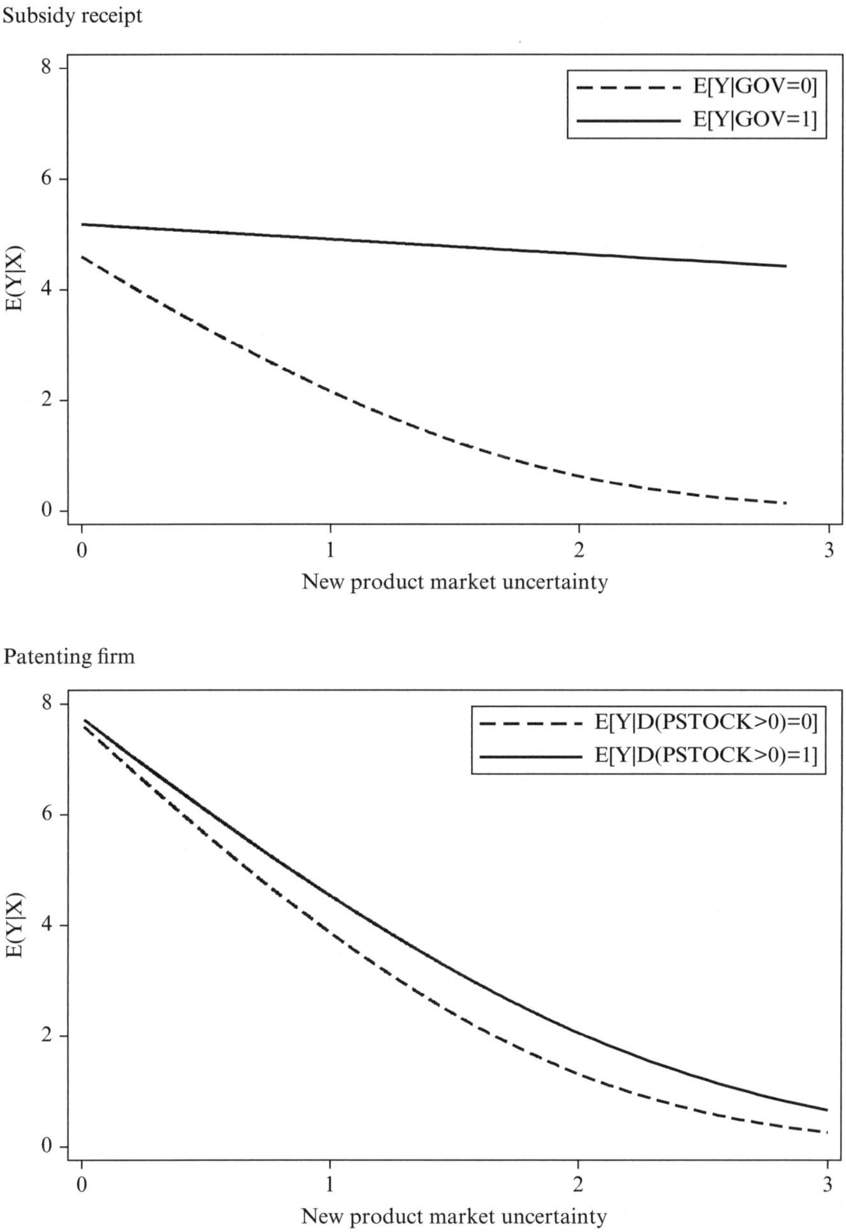

Figure 16.3 Estimated effects of uncertainty on expected R&D investment [ln(R&D)]

16.4 DISCUSSION

Drawing on the insights from the real options approach to investment under uncertainty, this chapter argues that government subsidy programs and patent policies are a means to purchase a portion of the firm's option value to wait. Although public innovation policies do not act directly to reduce innovative or product market uncertainties, they can offset the incentive effect of these uncertainties by increasing the expected return to the firm's R&D investment. Our empirical results suggest the real options mechanism is quantitatively important.

There are a number of implications of the analysis of uncertainty and its impact on R&D investment. First, public policies intended to increase private R&D investment can achieve this objective by reducing the degree of uncertainty in the innovative process or in the product market. While not tested empirically, Kremer and Glennerster (2000), Kremer (2001a, 2001b) and others have used this insight to argue that purchase precommitments and R&D prizes may be valuable mechanisms for stimulating R&D investment and innovation in areas ignored by private firms, such as malaria vaccines.

Second, the results concerning R&D subsidies suggest that firms may be using public programs to fund their most uncertain projects. It is widely known that program administrators have a difficult problem in picking proposals that have high social returns but insufficient private returns. While probably unintended, these administrators may still be stimulating private R&D by reducing the effect of uncertainty on private project returns. Furthermore, patents reduce product market uncertainty through granting the inventor a temporary monopoly to reap the economic returns of the investment.

While both policies reduce the sensitivity of firm-level investments to uncertainty, the mechanisms are inherently different: while patents protect successful project outcomes after the initial investment, subsidies facilitate the initial investments. These differences pose important questions for future policy. Unlike the arguments concerning market failures, we do not argue that sensitivity to uncertainty relates to any market failure. It is socially efficient and profit-maximizing for firms to delay investments in the face of uncertainties. Because real options investment behavior is efficient, the additional stimulus to R&D acting through this mechanism opens up the possibility that there may be overinvestment in R&D. Of course, this is very difficult to judge and most economists and policy-makers believe the underinvestment in R&D due to market failures is quite significant.

Regarding R&D subsidies, however, one potentially undesirable effect has to do with the selection process on the part of firms. Our results suggest that firms are likely to send their riskiest R&D projects to government agencies for subsidies. This puts an even greater burden on government administrators to select only those projects with high social returns. This is an adverse selection problem stemming from the low cost of applying for funds and the firm's desire to diversify its R&D portfolio at minimal cost. Since the government, in essence, underwrites the risk of these projects, it seems critical to have some kind of administrative mechanism(s) in place to limit adverse selection into the project application pool.

NOTES

1. Mazzoleni and Nelson (1998) discuss the various economic theories for patent protection and review some of the early empirical literature.
2. A detailed discussion of these studies is beyond the scope of this chapter. We refer the reader to a recent survey by Aerts et al. (2006).
3. There may also be significant financial resource issues related to patenting. For instance, there can be significant costs associated with enforcing patent rights. Marco (2005) examines some of these issues from a real options perspective.
4. Subsequent theoretical research has explored issues related to the firm's opportunity to delay investment. When investment has strategic value, Kulatilaka and Perotti (1998) show that the value of growth options increases with the level of uncertainty and offsets (at least partially) the affect of expandability options on the incentive for current investment. Weeds (2002) considers a real options model with R&D competition and finds an equilibrium outcome depends on the balance between the value of delay and the expected benefit of pre-emption. In a recent contribution, Novy-Marx (2007) finds that investment decisions are delayed in a perfectly competitive market when firm-level opportunity costs and heterogeneity are important.
5. Pindyck (1993) presents an alternative model with uncertainty about costs. He finds that higher technical uncertainty leads to earlier investment while higher input cost uncertainty leads firms to delay investment.
6. Minton and Schrand (1999) include R&D as one type of investment in their analysis of how cash flow volatility influences investment levels. There are a number of published empirical studies examining how uncertainty influences physical capital investment. Examples include Ghosal and Loungani (1996), Leahy and Whited (1996), Guiso and Parigi (1999), Von Kalckreuth (2000), Bulan (2005), Baum et al. (2008) and Bloom et al. (2007).
7. This empirical fact is actually consistent with the predictions of real options theory since some firms may choose not to perform R&D in the current year due to high levels of perceived uncertainty.
8. In the empirical literature studying the relationship between investment in physical capital and uncertainty, researchers have used a variety of measures, each with their own strengths and weaknesses. Carruth et al. (2000) and Lensink et al. (2001) review these. Following Leahy and Whited (1996), three recent studies use stock market volatility measures of uncertainty for publicly traded firms (Baum et al., 2008; Bloom et al., 2007; Bulan, 2005). Most of our firms are privately owned and not traded in the public market. Consequently, this type of uncertainty proxy is not possible in our context.
9. These are different measures of uncertainty than used in Czarnitzki and Toole (2007). In that paper, we use the standard deviation in the firm share of new product sales relative to the industry's share of new product sales. The measures we use in this chapter are

more intuitive, but not necessarily superior. Both uncertainty measures give the same qualitative results.

10. In this chapter, we do not present the details regarding these control variables (see Czarnitzki and Toole, 2006, 2007).
11. NACE is the European standard industry classification.
12. As a robustness check, Czarnitzki and Toole (2007) also estimated parametric treatment models which allow the subsidy dummy to be endogenous, as pointed out in the evaluation literature (for example David et al., 2000). The results regarding uncertainty also hold when estimating treatment models.
13. Tables 1 and 2 use different firm-level data sets, both of which are constructed from the MIP survey described above. The analysis in Czarnitzki and Toole (2006) relies on panel data controlling for firm-level unobserved heterogeneity. This alternative gives the same qualitative results.

REFERENCES

Abel, A.B., A.K. Dixit, J.C. Eberly and R.S. Pindyck (1996), 'Options, the value of capital, and investment', *Quarterly Journal of Economics*, **111** (3), 753–77.

Aerts, K., D. Czarnitzki and A. Fier (2006), 'Econometric evaluation of public R&D policies: current state of the art', unpublished manuscript, K.U. Leuven.

Almus, M. and D. Czarnitzki (2003), 'The effects of public R&D subsidies on firms' innovation activities: the case of Eastern Germany', *Journal of Business and Economic Statistics*, **21** (2), 226–36.

Arora, A., M. Ceccagnoli and W.M. Cohen (2008), 'R&D and the patent premium', *International Journal of Industrial Organization*, **26** (5), 1153–79.

Arrow, K.J. (1962), 'Economic welfare and the allocations of resources of invention', in NBER (ed.), *The Rate and Direction of Inventive Activity: Economic and Social Factors*, Princeton, NJ: Princeton University Press, pp. 609–25.

Baum, C.F., M. Mustafa and O. Talavera (2008), 'Uncertainty determinants of firm investment', *Economics Letters*, **98** (3), 282–7.

Bloom, N., S. Bond and J. Van Reenen (2007), 'Uncertainty and investment dynamics', *Review of Economic Studies*, **74** (2), 391–415.

Bulan, L.T. (2005), 'Real options, irreversible investment and firm uncertainty: new evidence from US firms', *Review of Financial Economics*, **14** (3–4), 255–79.

Butzen, R. and C. Fuss (2002), *Firms' Investment and Finance Decisions*, Cheltenham, UK and Northampton, MA: Edward Elgar Publishing.

Carruth, A., A. Dickerson and A. Henley (2000), 'What do we know about investment under uncertainty?', *Journal of Economic Surveys*, **14** (2), 119–53.

Cohen, W.M. (2005), 'Patents and appropriation: concerns and evidence', *Journal of Technology Transfer*, **30** (1–2), 57–71.

Cohen, W.M., R.P. Nelson and J.P. Walsh (2000), 'Protecting their intellectual assets: appropriability conditions and why US manufacturing firms patent (or not)', NBER Working Paper 7552, Cambridge.

Czarnitzki, D. (2006), 'Research and development in small and medium-sized German enterprises: the role of financial constraints and public funding', *Scottish Journal of Political Economy*, **53** (3), 335–57.

Czarnitzki, D., B. Ebersberger and A. Fier (2007), 'The relationship between R&D collaboration, subsidies and R&D performance: empirical evidence from Finland and Germany', *Journal of Applied Econometrics*, **22** (7), 1347–66.

Czarnitzki, D., B.H. Hall and R. Oriani (2006), 'The market valuation of knowledge assets in US and European firms', in D. Bosworth and E. Webster, *The Management of Intellectual Property*, Cheltenham, UK and Northampton, MA: Edward Elgar, pp. 111–31.

Czarnitzki, D. and G. Licht (2006), 'Additionality of public R&D grants in a transition economy: the case of Eastern Germany', *Economics of Transition*, **14** (1), 101–31.

Czarnitzki, D. and A.A. Toole (2006), 'Patent protection, market uncertainty, and R&D investment', ZEW Discussion Paper 06–056, Mannheim (revised version 2008).

Czarnitzki, D. and A.A. Toole (2007), 'Business R&D and the interplay of R&D subsidies and product market uncertainty', *Review of Industrial Organization*, **31** (3), 169–81.

David, P.A., B.H. Hall and A.A. Toole (2000), 'Is public R&D a complement or substitute for private R&D? A review of the econometric evidence', *Research Policy*, **29** (4–5), 497–529.

Dixit, A.K. (1992), 'Investment and hysteresis', *Journal of Economic Perspectives*, **6** (1), 107–32.

Dixit, A.K. and R.S. Pindyck (1994), *Investment Under Uncertainty*, Princeton, NJ: Princeton University Press.

Duguet, E. (2004), 'Are R&D subsidies a substitute or a complement to privately funded R&D? Evidence from France using propensity score methods for non experimental data', *Revue d'Economie Politique*, **114** (2), 263–92.

Ghosal, V. and P. Loungani (1996), 'Product market competition and the impact of price uncertainty on investment: some evidence from US manufacturing industries', *Journal of Industrial Economics*, **44** (2), 217–28.

Goel, R.K. and R. Ram (2001), 'Irreversibility of R&D investment and the adverse effect of uncertainty: evidence from the OECD countries', *Economic Letters*, **71** (2), 287–91.

González, X., J. Jaumandreu and C. Pazó (2005), 'Barriers to innovation and subsidy effectiveness', *RAND Journal of Economics*, **36**, 930–50.

Görg, H. and E. Strobl (2007), 'The effect of R&D subsidies on private R&D', *Economica*, **74** (2), 215–34.

Gusio, L. and G. Parigi (1999), 'Investment and demand uncertainty', *Quarterly Journal of Economics*, **114** (1), 188–227.

Hall, B.H. (2002), 'The financing of research and development', *Oxford Review of Economic Policy*, **18** (1), 35–51.

Hussinger, K. (2008), 'R&D and subsidies at the firm level: an application of parametric and semi-parametric two-step selection models', *Journal of Applied Econometrics*, **23**, 729–47.

Hyytinen, A. and O. Toivanen (2005), 'Do financial constraints hold back innovation and growth? Evidence on the role of public policy', *Research Policy*, **34**, 1385–403.

Klette, T.J., J. Møen and Z. Griliches (2000), 'Do subsidies to commercial R&D reduce market failures? Microeconometric evaluation studies', *Research Policy*, **29** (4–5), 471–95.

Kremer, M. (2001a), 'Creating markets for new vaccines: Part I: Rationale', in A.B. Jaffe, J. Lerner and S. Stern (eds), *Innovation Policy and the Economy*, Vol. 1, Cambridge, MA: MIT Press, pp. 35–72.

Kremer, M. (2001b), 'Creating markets for new vaccines: Part II: Design issues', in

A.B. Jaffe, J. Lerner and S. Stern (eds), *Innovation Policy and the Economy*, Vol. 1, Cambridge, MA: MIT Press, pp. 73–118.

Kremer, M. and R. Glennerster (2000), 'A better way to spur medical research and development', *Regulation*, **23** (2), 34–9.

Kulatilaka, N. and E.C. Perotti (1998), 'Strategic growth options', *Management Science*, **44** (8), 1021–31.

Lach, S. (2002), 'Do R&D subsidies stimulate or displace private R&D? Evidence from Israel', *Journal of Industrial Economics*, **50** (4), 369–90.

Lanjouw, J.O. (1998), 'Patent protection in the shadow of infringement: simulation estimations of patent value', *Review of Economic Studies*, **65** (4), 671–710.

Leahy, J.V. and T.M. Whited (1996), 'The effect of uncertainty on investment: some stylized facts', *Journal of Money, Credit and Banking*, **28** (1), 64–83.

Lensink, R., H. Bo and E. Sterken (2001), *Investment, Capital Market Imperfections, and Uncertainty*, Cheltenham, UK and Northampton, MA, USA: Edward Elgar Publishing.

Marco, A.C. (2005), 'The option value of patent litigation: theory and evidence', *Review of Financial Economics*, **14** (3–4), 323–51.

Mazzoleni, R. and R.R. Nelson (1998), 'Economic theories about the benefits and costs of patents', *Journal of Economic Issues*, **32** (4), 1031–52.

Minton, B.A. and S. Schrand (1999), 'The impact of cash flow volatility on discretionary investment and the costs of debt and equity financing', *Journal of Financial Economics*, **54** (3), 423–60.

Nelson, R.R. (1959), 'The simple economics of basic scientific research', *Journal of Political Economy*, **67** (3), 297–306.

Novy-Marx, R. (2007), 'An equilibrium model of investment under uncertainty', *Review of Financial Studies*, **20** (5), 1461–1502.

Pakes, A. (1986), 'Patents as options: some estimates of the value of holding European patent stocks', *Econometrica*, **54** (4), 755–84.

Pindyck, R.S. (1991), 'Irreversibility, uncertainty, and investment', *Journal of Economic Literature*, **29** (3), 1110–48.

Pindyck, R.S. (1993), 'Investment of uncertain cost', *Journal of Financial Economics*, **34** (1), 53–76.

Schankerman, M. (1998), 'How valuable is patent protection? Estimates by technology field', *RAND Journal of Economics*, **29** (1), 77–107.

Scotchmer, S. (2004), *Innovation and Incentives*, Cambridge, MA: MIT Press.

Toole, A.A (2007), 'Does public scientific research complement private research and development investment in the pharmaceutical industry', *Journal of Law and Economics*, **50** (1), 81–104.

Von Kalckreuth, U. (2000), 'Exploring the role of uncertainty for corporate investment decisions in Germany', Discussion Paper 5/00, Economic Research Group, Deutsche Bundesbank, Frankfurt.

Weeds, H. (2002), 'Strategic delay in a real options model of R&D competition', *Review of Economic Studies*, **69** (3), 729–47.

17. Innovation surveys and innovation policy

Jacques Mairesse and Pierre Mohnen

17.1 PRESENTING THE INNOVATION SURVEYS

In the late 1980s scholars of technological change were concerned about measuring more aspects of innovation than the mere information contained in the R&D surveys. They sat down under the auspices of the Organisation for Economic Co-operation and Development (OECD) and wrote the so-called *Oslo Manual*, which set out the guidelines for a new type of survey, the innovation survey (OECD, 1992).[1] In the EU countries under the coordination of Eurostat, the statistical office of the European Union, a common core questionnaire was agreed upon and surveys were launched under the acronym of CIS (Community Innovation Surveys). These surveys have been repeated every four years. So far there exist four waves of CIS (CIS 1 for 1990–92,[2] CIS 2 for 1994–96, CIS 3 for 1998–2000 and CIS 4 for 2002–04).[3] Similar surveys have been conducted in other countries, including emerging, transition and developing countries. In total, more than 50 countries have carried out at least one innovation survey.[4]

The innovation surveys provide us with three broad groups of measures: innovation inputs, innovation outputs and modalities of innovation. The innovation inputs encompass besides R&D, other expenditure related to innovation such as acquisitions of patents and licenses, product design, training of personnel, trial production and market analysis. Four types of innovation outputs are distinguished in the latest version of CIS, namely the introduction of new products (which can be new to the firm or new to the market), the introduction of new processes, organizational changes and marketing innovations. Whereas patents and bibliometrics measure the technical, scientific, inventive side of innovation, the innovation output measures contained in the innovation surveys measure the development, implementation and market introduction of new ideas; namely, they measure the introduction to the market of new products or services and the introduction of new ways of organizing production and distribution.

The modalities of innovation are the sources of information that lead to an innovation, the effects of innovation or the reasons for innovating, the perceived obstacles to innovation, the perceived strength of various appropriability mechanisms, and the cooperation in research and innovation.

The innovation surveys serve two purposes. First and foremost, they are used by policy-makers to monitor innovation and benchmark innovation performance. Their second utility is to provide statistical data to researchers in the economics of technological change in order to determine the reasons for innovating and the effects of innovation on economic performance. We shall discuss these two aspects with some illustrations of the usefulness of these data and a discussion of some of their limitations.

17.2 DIRECT USE OF INNOVATION SURVEYS FOR INNOVATION POLICY

The main use that has been made of the innovation surveys is for the purpose of monitoring and benchmarking the innovation performance in different countries. Some data from the CIS surveys have been included in the European Innovation Scoreboard (EIS) and in the construction of innovation indexes such as the Global Summary Innovation Index (see Sajeva et al., 2005; Arundel et al., 2007). The EIS 2006 included from the innovation surveys the percentage of enterprises receiving government support for innovation as an indicator of knowledge creation; the percentage of small and medium-sized enterprises (SMEs) with innovative activities, the percentage of SMEs cooperating with others, the ratio of innovation expenditure over total sales, the percentage of SMEs with organizational innovation as indicators of entrepreneurship; and the share in total turnover of new-to-firm or new-to-market products as indicators of innovation output. Innovation indexes are used by policy-makers to check whether there is an innovation gap between the European Union (EU) member states and some other parts of the world, a convergence in innovation between old and new member states of the EU, and the improvement in innovation performance on the way towards achieving the Lisbon Strategy.

Let us illustrate the utility of these indexes for policy-makers by giving some examples. The Global Summary Innovation Index 2005 showed that the EU, with an index value of 0.5, was lagging behind the average innovation performance of countries like Singapore, Israel, the Republic of Korea, Canada, Japan and the US. Comparing that same index over time reveals that there has been a process of convergence in innovation performance since the launching of the Lisbon Agenda, with old member states like France and Germany showing a decline in their index and many of the new member states improving their performance while being in the catching-up phase. The gap in innovation performance of the EU could be due to a lack of innovation activities, a deficiency in turning innovation inputs into innovation outputs, or a different sectoral composition, knowing that innovation intensities vary across sectors.

It is interesting for policy-makers to be able to compare their country's relative performance on a certain number of individual indicators like research and development (R&D), success in product innovations, importance of collaborations, and so on. A country may fare well in comparison to others in its R&D expenditure as a percentage of gross domestic product (GDP) but come up with a lower share of new products. This may suggest that the incentives for R&D are there but that a problem may exist in converting R&D into sales of innovative products. Or you can have a country where many enterprises declare receiving some kind of government support and yet few multinational enterprises (MNEs) innovate. Since government support for innovation often goes to MNEs, such a situation calls at least for a reconsideration of the effectiveness of those measures of support. A simple confrontation of some descriptive statistics drawn from the innovation surveys can help in refuting some hypotheses or identifying possible cases of government failure, although policy-makers should be aware that proximate causes may not reveal the ultimate explanations and that pairwise correlations may hide the mutual dependence on third factors. We shall get back to this point in the next section.

Aggregating these various indicators into a global innovation indicator, with specific weights and arbitrary choices of which indicators to include and which ones to exclude, is more debatable however. The choice of indicators entering the construction of an index is often based on the availability of data. The EIS 2002 was based on 17 indicators, the EIS 2006 on 26 indicators. At each new wave of CIS additional questions are asked to include new dimensions of innovation (like questions on knowledge management in CIS 3 or marketing innovations in CIS 4). Some components might be highly correlated, giving undue weight to certain dimensions. The interaction among indicators, precisely the idea behind the notion of complementarity or optimal policy mix, is largely ignored. It is even more difficult to aggregate qualitative data unless there is an underlying latent variable model or a constructed latent variable from a factor or principal component analysis (see Hollenstein, 1996). Moreover it is heroic to make international comparisons when the questionnaires differ in their content, the order of the questions and their formulations, and when the sampling of the respondents differs across countries. In countries with mandatory surveys, there may be an endogenous selection of respondents that have a tendency to respond in a certain way. The 2005 Canadian Survey of Innovation, in contrast to the CIS surveys, does not ask for quantitative information on output and labor from which labor productivity could be measured. Instead firms are asked to give an ordered categorical evaluation of the perceived effect of innovation on productivity growth.

The composite innovation indices can be useful insofar as they indicate how an economy performs compared to other economies and how this relative position varies over time. They do not, however, indicate which policies to put in place to overcome possible deficiencies (for a further discussion of some of these points, see Arundel and Hollanders, 2008). A careful analysis of causality needs to be done, followed by a reflection of the direct and indirect effects of possible policy measures including an evaluation of past policies to determine their effectiveness.

To improve the quality of the data and the ensuing policy analysis, we recommend the following points. First, as far as possible the survey questionnaires and the sampling procedure should be identical across countries. If this is not possible, information about the sampling should be provided in order to correct for possible biases when comparing performances across countries. Second, some of the questions asked should remain stable across waves so that a trend analysis can be performed. For example, between CIS 2 and CIS 3 the objectives of innovation were replaced by the impacts of innovation, making it impossible to continue examining the role of innovation objectives on innovation behavior. More specifically, we recommend the questionnaire to be split into three parts: (1) the core permanent part, as stable over time as possible and as identical as possible across countries; (2) a specific harmonized part, varying from one survey to another to analyse specific aspects, but strictly harmonized across countries; (3) an optional part in response to country-specific interests. Third, it would be useful to have more information about non-innovators, be it only to correct for possible selection biases when conducting an analysis on innovators.[5] Fourth, if at all possible, try to follow a core group of firms over time by making sure that they are part of successive samples. Fifth, it might be a good idea to make experiments about the sensitivity of the survey responses to the order in which questions are asked and the functional role of the respondents within an enterprise.

In summary, the innovation surveys have increased our information about the way innovation occurs, the reasons for innovating, the obstacles in the process of innovating, the sources of knowledge, the cooperation in innovation, the importance of intellectual property rights and the different ways of innovating. By coordinating as much as possible the contents of the questionnaire, not just within the European Union but also in other

OECD and non-OECD countries, it becomes possible to compare to some extent the innovation performances in different parts of the world. The survey questionnaires could be improved by constructing them in a more scientific way, learning from past experience in order to avoid repeating mistakes, and having in mind the kind of information and economic analysis that is intended to be performed with these data.

17.3 USE OF INNOVATION SURVEYS TO INCREASE OUR UNDERSTANDING OF INNOVATION

The innovation surveys have also been used by researchers to examine all sorts of aspects of innovation, ranging from the analysis of determinants (of innovation activities, innovation outputs, collaborations, obstacles, sources of information), to complementarities (between these same set of variables), to their mutual interrelations and effects on various measures of performance (exports, productivity, employment).

To illustrate the kind of econometric analysis that has been performed with the innovation survey data, we distinguish four kinds of studies: (1) a re-examination of the relationship between R&D and productivity; (2) testing the existence of complementarities; (3) evaluating the effectiveness of government interventions; and (4) exploring the dynamics of innovation. We present some selected examples of these studies and summarize some of the results obtained.[6]

17.3.1 R&D–Innovation Output–Productivity Relationship

The R&D–productivity relationship has been revisited using the additional information on the outputs and the modalities of innovation contained in the innovation surveys. With these data we can go a step further towards estimating a richer, more structural, and more informative model of the link between R&D and productivity. Crépon et al. (1998) (hereafter CDM) proposed and estimated such a model composed of three equations: first, an equation explaining the amount of R&D; second, an innovation output equation where R&D appears as an input (CDM had two alternative measures of innovation output: the number of patents and categorical data on the share of innovative sales); and, finally, a productivity equation, in which innovation output appears as an explanatory variable. The CDM model has been estimated for a number of countries individually – France, Germany, the Netherlands, Scandinavia, Estonia, Russia, Chile, the UK, China, Italy, Spain, Portugal . . . and the list keeps growing. It has also been run with the same specification to compare the performance in four countries: France, Germany, Spain and the UK (see Griffith et al., 2006). A larger project, which is presently being coordinated by the OECD (the NESTI/WPIA Innovation Microdata project), does the same cross-country comparison but on a much larger set of countries.

As Kremp et al. (2006) report, the results on the magnitude of the rates of return to R&D found in the early studies of the 1980s and 1990s are confirmed by the CDM model, as long as proper account is taken of selectivity and endogeneity in R&D and innovation output. The estimates are also robust to various measures of product innovation, in particular qualitative and quantitative measures, and new-to-firm versus new-to-market innovations. It is, however, true that innovation output statistics are noisier than R&D statistics (in part perhaps because they are subjective measures) and need to be instrumented to correct for errors in variables. On French data, process innovations yield higher returns than product innovations, but this is not always the case in other countries as reported in the international comparison study of Griffith et al. (2006). Indeed, we expect process innovation to affect directly the average cost of production, whereas product innovations can displace existing products and therefore have mixed effects on total sales and take more time to show up in the productivity statistics.

Among the determinants of innovation, these are some of the regular findings. In most studies size explains the propensity to innovate, but hardly affects, and if so negatively, the intensity of innovation, as measured for instance by the share in total sales due to the sales of new or improved products. Few countries (France is an exception) include in their questionnaire explicit questions regarding the demand pull and technology push hypotheses, respectively attributed to Schmookler and Schumpeter. Otherwise, proxies have been constructed for these two variables using information on the objectives and the sources of information for innovation. Both show up with a positive marginal effect, but demand pull is more often significant than technology push. The strongest explanation of innovation output, that indirectly feeds into productivity, is the R&D effort, especially the fact of performing R&D on a continuous basis. Blundell et al. (1999) find that the dominant firms innovate more not because they have cash on hand to finance the innovation, but because they have more to lose than newcomers by not innovating. Indeed, incumbents risk losing their monopoly position by not innovating.[7]

Although the innovation survey data reveal a lot of interesting information on the links between innovation inputs, output and productivity, our understanding of the innovation process is still far from perfect. Mairesse and Mohnen (2002) propose an accounting framework to compare innovation performance across regions, industries or countries, similar to the growth accounting for productivity decomposition. By linearly approximating the innovation performance function around a reference region, industry or country, it is possible to attribute cross-sectional differences in performance (innovation propensity or innovation intensity) to differences in its determinants. The unexplained residual, that is, the measure of our ignorance in matters of innovation, is very high, especially in low-tech sectors. The magnitude of the residual may not be unrelated to the voluntary or mandatory nature of the survey, calling for closer attention to the sampling issue, as mentioned earlier.

17.3.2 Complementarities

Many studies have tested the phenomenon of complementarity between different innovation strategies using the data from the innovation surveys. There is complementarity between innovation strategies when two strategies tends to be adopted together rather than in isolation because their joint adoption leads to better results. Some studies have tested the occurrence of joint adoption, others have tested whether indeed joint adoption leads to higher performance. This issue has been investigated for various aspects of innovation: (1) different types of innovation, for example product and process innovation (Cabagnols and Le Bas, 2002; Martínez-Ros and Labeaga, 2002; Miravete and Pernías, 2006); (2) internal and external technology sourcing (Cassiman and Veugelers, 2006; Belderbos et al., 2005; Catozzella and Vivarelli, 2007); (3) different types of cooperation strategies (Belderbos et al., 2006); and (4) internal skills and cooperations (Leiponen, 2005).

There are signs of complementarity in all these dimensions. Firms tend to innovate in both products and processes, to produce their own knowledge while acquiring knowledge from outside the enterprise; therefore they need to build up their own capacity to be able to absorb outside knowledge, and they tend to cooperate with different partners at the same time. There is not always full complementarity when more than two strategies are involved, that is, complementarity across all strategies. Firms may, for instance, collaborate with some partners and not with others. Another result that is often encountered in this literature is the importance of controlling for unobserved heterogeneity. Miravete and Pernías (2006) have clearly shown that not accounting for unobserved heterogeneity can lead to false conclusions as to a possible complementarity (supermodularity) in innovation strategies, because the unobserved heterogeneity can be falsely attributed to observed innovation strategies.

17.3.3 Innovation Policy

The innovation surveys contain qualitative information about whether firms receive government support for innovation. This information may be sufficient to check whether government support for innovation has a positive effect on performance (R&D, innovation output or productivity) and whether public and private funding for innovation are substitutes or complements to each other. In other words, does government support for innovation lead to a partial substitution of private funding for public funding or does it actually lead to more innovation than the amount of public funding involved? This can be done either by examining the effect of the presence of government support on innovation, by modeling at the same time the determinants of government support or, as is mostly done, by comparing the difference in innovation performance between matched pairs of supported and non-supported firms. For this evaluation of government support to lead to sensible results, enough observations must be available either to identify the determinants of government support for innovation, or to find good matches among the non-supported firms for all the firms that receive government support. Most studies conclude that government R&D support leads to additional private R&D, innovation expenditure or innovation outputs and not to crowding-out of private R&D by public R&D support.[8]

Just as complementarity has been examined between various innovation strategies, so it has also been examined between various innovation policies. The obstacles to innovation can be regarded as mirror images of failures in innovation policy. If an obstacle is perceived to be high by a respondent, it means that somewhere there is a deficiency in innovation policy. Although it may not be possible to pinpoint exactly which government policy should be acted upon to remove the perceived obstacle, especially as different policies may play out differently in different industries, an analysis of the complementarity of the obstacles nevertheless shows whether one or more policies should be adopted simultaneously to improve innovation. In other words, should there be a policy mix or not? If two obstacles are complements, they reinforce each other. Removing one will attenuate the other one. There might be less of a reason to remove both at the same time. If two obstacles are substitutes, however, the presence of one obstacle relieves the pressure from the other. In that case removing one obstacle will exacerbate the other. Both should be removed jointly. Mohnen and Röller (2005) conclude that when it comes to turning non-innovators into innovators, it is important to remove a group of obstacles at the same time: easing access to finance, making more skilled labor available or allowing for more collaboration. Governments should adopt a mix of policies, for instance easing access to finance and allowing firms to cooperate with other firms and technological institutions, or increasing the amount of skilled personnel and reducing the regulatory burden. When it comes to increasing the amount of innovation, one or the other policy will do.

17.3.4 Dynamics of Innovation

Another hypothesis that has been tested with the innovation survey data is the persistence of innovation. Does innovation breed more innovation? Such an analysis has not yet been done for many countries because it requires the existence of multiple observations per firm across successive waves of innovation surveys, with a sufficient amount of overlap of sampling across successive waves. The underlying models are dynamic precisely because the interest lies in testing whether firms tend to innovate conditional on past innovation. Clearly these studies will become more frequent in the future as the time-series dimension of the data increases.

A couple of studies based on patent data had concluded that there was no persistence in patenting (Geroski et al., 1997; Malerba and Orsenigo, 1999; Le Bas et al., 2003). With innovation data, Duguet and Monjon (2002) find a strong persistence in innovation, and Cefis (2003) finds that persistence in innovation is characteristic of major innovators. As mentioned by Duguet and Monjon (2002), persistence is more difficult to obtain with patent data because it requires innovation plus being the first to innovate. Peters (2009) finds persistence in innovation activities. Raymond et al. (2007) find persistence in innovation output, both in the appearance of new products and/or processes and the eventual share in total sales due to new products, in enterprises that belong to the high-tech category.

17.4 CONCLUSION

In the early 1990s countries started conducting innovation surveys. These surveys are structured and administered in a possibly comparable way in more and more countries. These surveys collect data on innovation inputs, innovation outputs and innovation modalities. International comparisons are still hampered by differences in coverage and wording of the questionnaires and intertemporal comparisons by additions and deletions of questions in successive waves of those surveys. Despite these hurdles, the information retrieved from these surveys allows governments better to monitor and benchmark the innovation performance of their economies.

The innovation surveys have also been widely used by researchers interested in estimating the determinants, interrelationships and effects of these various innovation indicators. Among the many topics investigated, we have selected four in relation to which some tentative conclusions seem to emerge. R&D is found to have an effect on the appearance of new products and processes. The rates of return on R&D estimated previously by linking directly R&D and productivity are confirmed even when innovation output is added to the models. There are signs of complementarity between different types of innovation and ways to obtain knowledge for innovating, but more work needs to be done especially with panel data to find out whether this complementarity is spurious or robust to the presence of unobserved heterogeneity. Evaluations of government support for innovation on the basis of data from the innovation surveys point to some additionality. Finally, as panel data become available it becomes possible to investigate the dynamics of innovation. Contrary to many previous studies using patent data as an innovation output measure, those based on the introduction of new products and processes as innovation output indicators reveal signs of innovation persistence.

In order to improve the availability and usefulness of the innovation surveys as both a guide to policy-makers and a tool of analysis for researchers and science and technology, we recommend a continued harmonization of the survey questionnaires across countries, the development of a core set of questions which do not change over time, the development of the possibility of merging these data with other firm data, and the improved availability of these data to individual researchers.

NOTES

1. The Oslo manual has since undergone two revisions (OECD, 1996 and 2005).
2. Some European countries had initiated their own surveys prior to CIS 1 (such as France, Germany, Italy, the Netherlands, Norway and Sweden). A few countries conduct their surveys more frequently than every four years (Germany, for instance, has a yearly survey, and the Netherlands conducts its surveys on a biannual basis). Some countries conduct innovation surveys that are specific to certain sectors (such as the 1996 Survey of Innovation in Service Industries and a survey on the construction industry in Canada) or to certain aspects of innovation (such as the French surveys on intellectual property rights, organizational changes and the financing of innovation).
3. In parallel, similar surveys were conducted, some even predating the innovation surveys. Probably the first one was conducted by the Science and Policy Research Unit (SPRU) at the University of Sussex. It collected information on specific innovations from firms and from a panel of experts (see, for example, Robson et al., 1988 and Geroski et al., 1997 for analyses based on the SPRU dataset). The Ifo Institute for Economic Research at the University of Munich has been conducting a yearly innovation survey in Germany since 1982 (see Lachenmaier and Rottmann, 2006 for a study on the Ifo data). The Ministry of Industry in Spain has conducted for about ten years the firm-level survey ESEE

(Encuesta Sobre Estrategias Empresariales) containing questions on innovation (see Huergo and Jaumandreu, 2004 and González et al., 2005). Besides innovation surveys, there exist literature-based innovation indicators such as the commercialized innovation data set collected from technology, engineering and trade journals at the US Small Business Administration (see Acs and Audretsch, 1988). In Italy, the investment firm Mediocredito Centrale has conducted a number of waves of the survey Indagine sulle Imprese Manifatturiere, in which firms are asked about their R&D and the incidence of product and process innovations.

4. While CIS-1 covered only 13 countries, CIS 4 has been implemented in all 25 EU member states, as well as in Iceland, Norway, Bulgaria and Romania. Innovation surveys exist also in Canada, Mexico (North America), Australia, New Zealand (Oceania), Norway, Switzerland, Russia, Turkey (other European countries), Argentina, Brazil, Chile, Colombia, Peru, Uruguay, Venezuela (South America), China, Japan, Malaysia, Singapore, South Korea, Taiwan, Thailand (Asia), Tunisia and South Africa (Africa). The United States is one of the major countries with no innovation survey, although the US National Science Foundation conducted a pilot innovation survey in 1985. Innovation surveys are being conducted in India and planned to be implemented in various African countries within the New Partnership for Africa's Development (NEPAD) initiative.
5. About non-innovators, all we know is their turnover, export and number of employees, in levels and growth rates, the main industry they belong to, and their potential affiliation to a group.
6. We have selected the studies that we know best, which are often those in which we were ourselves involved. A more exhaustive and complete survey is presently under way, which also goes more in depth into the econometric difficulties of handling the innovation survey data correctly.
7. For a synoptic table comparing the results on the determinants of innovation from different studies, see Raymond et al. (2009).
8. It is, however, only a partial picture of the justification for government intervention in private innovation. Spillovers are not taken into account. Spillovers can be positive if sequential innovation builds on past innovation or if innovation in one sector spurs innovation in another sector. But spillovers could also be negative if innovation puts pressure on the wages of researchers and thereby crowds out other research initiatives. We know nothing about the administration costs of government programs. Moreover, most of these studies do not evaluate the productivity of the additionally induced innovation efforts. It could be that only marginally productive or valuable research projects are stimulated by public incentives. See Arundel et al. (2008) for a summary of the findings regarding government support for innovation in various innovation surveys.

REFERENCES

Acs, Z. and D. Audretsch (1988), 'Innovation in large and small firms: an empirical analysis', *American Economic Review*, **78** (4), 678–9.

Arundel, A., C. Bordoy, P. Mohnen and K. Smith (2008), 'Innovation surveys and policy: lessons from the CIS', in C. Nauwelaers and R. Wintjes (eds), *Measurement and Strategy*, Cheltenham, UK and Northampton, MA, USA: Elward Elgar, pp. 3–28.

Arundel, A. and H. Hollanders (2008), 'Innovation scoreboards: indicators, policy use and future needs', in C. Nauwelaers and R. Wintjes (eds), *Innovation Policy in Europe: Measurement and Strategy*, Cheltenham, UK and Northampton, MA, USA: Elward Elgar, pp. 29–52.

Arundel, A., M. Kanerva, A. van Cruysen and H. Hollanders (2007), 'Innovation statistics for the European Service Sector', PRO INNO Europe paper No. 3, European Commission, Brussels.

Belderbos, R., M. Carree and B. Lokshin (2005), 'The productivity effects of internal and external R&D: evidence from a dynamic panel data model', *Oxford Bulletin of Economics and Statistics*, **70** (3), 399–413.

Belderbos, R., M. Carree and B. Lokshin (2006), 'Complementarities in R&D cooperation strategies', *Review of Industrial Organization*, **28** (4), 401–26.

Blundell, R., R. Griffith and J. van Reenen (1999), 'Market share, market value and innovation in a panel of Britisch manufacturing firms', *Review of Economic Studies*, **66** (3), 529–54.

Cabagnols, A. and C. Le Bas (2002), 'Differences in the determinants of product and process innovations: the French case', in A. Kleinknecht and P. Mohnen, (eds), *Innovation and Firm Performance. Econometric Explorations of Survey Data*, Basingstoke, UK and New York: Palgrave, pp. 112–49.

Cassiman, B. and R. Veugelers (2006), 'In search of complementarity in innovation strategy: internal R&D and external knowledge acquisition', *Management Science*, **52** (1), 68–82.

Catozzella, A. and M. Vivarelli (2007), 'The catalyzing role of in-house R&D in fostering complementarity among innovative inputs', IZA Discussion Paper No. 3126.

Cefis, E. (2003), 'Is there persistence in innovative activities?', *International Journal of Industrial Organization*, **21** (4), 489–515.

Crépon, B., E. Duguet and J. Mairesse (1998), 'Research, innovation and productivity: an econometric analysis at the firm level', *Economics of Innovation and New Technology*, **7**, 115–58.

Duguet, E. and S. Monjon (2002), 'Les fondements microéconomiques de la persistance de l'innovation: une analyse économétrique', *Revue Economique*, **53** (3), 625–36.

Geroski, P., J. van Reenen and C. Walters (1997), 'How persistently do firms innovate?', *Research Policy*, **26** (1), 33–48.

González, X., J. Jaumandreu and C. Pazó (2005), 'Barriers to innovation and subsidy effectiveness', *RAND Journal of Economics*, 36 (4), 930–50.

Griffith, R., E. Huergo, J. Mairesse and B. Peters (2006), 'Innovation and productivity across four European countries', *Oxford Review of Economic Policy*, **22** (4), 483–98.

Hollenstein, H. (1996), 'A composite indicator of a firm's innovativeness: an empirical analysis based on survey data for Swiss manufacturing', *Research Policy*, **25** (4), 633–45.

Huergo, E. and J. Jaumandreu (2004), 'Firms' age, process innovation and productivity growth', *International Journal of Industrial Organization*, **22** (4), 541–60.

Kremp, E., J. Mairesse and P. Mohnen (2006), 'Research, innovation and productivity: a new look', mimeo.

Lachenmaier, S. and H. Rottmann (2006), 'Employment effects of innovation at the firm level', Ifo working paper No. 27.

Le Bas, C., A. Cabagnols and C. Gay (2003), 'An evolutionary view on persistence in innovation: an empirical application of duration model', in P. Saviotti (ed.), *Applied Evolutionary Economics: New Empirical Methods and Simulation Techniques*, Cheltenham, UK and Northampton, MA: Edward Elgar, pp. 210–34.

Leiponen, A. (2005), 'Skills and innovation', *International Journal of Industrial Organization*, **23** (5–6), 303–23.

Mairesse, J. and P. Mohnen (2002), 'Accounting for innovation and measuring innovativeness: an illustrative framework and an application', *American Economic Review, Papers and Proceedings*, **92** (2), 226–30.

Malerba, F. and L. Orsenigo (1999), 'Technological entry, exit and survival: an empirical analysis of patent data', *Research Policy*, **28** (6), 643–60.

Martínez-Ros, E. and J.M. Labeaga (2002), 'Modelling innovation activities using discrete choice panel data models', in A. Kleinknecht and P. Mohnen (eds), *Innovation and Firm Performance: Econometric Explorations of Survey Data*, Basingstoke, UK and New York, Palgrave, pp. 150–71.

Miravete, E. and J. Pernías (2006), 'Innovation complementarity and scale of production', *Journal of Industrial Economics*, **54** (1), 1–29.

Mohnen, P. and L.-H. Röller (2005), 'Complementarities in innovation policy', *European Economic Review*, **49** (6), 1431–50.

Organisation for Economic Co-operation and Development (OECD) (1992, 1996, 2005), *Oslo Manual: Guidelines for Collecting and Interpreting Innovation Data*, Paris, 1st, 2nd, 3rd edition, Paris: OECD Publishing.

Peters, B. (2009), 'Persistence of innovation: stylized facts and panel data evidence', *Journal of Technology Transfer*, **34** (2), 226–43.

Raymond, W., P. Mohnen, F. Palm and S. Schim van der Loeff (2009), 'Persistence of innovation in Dutch manufacturing: is it spurious?', *Review of Economics and Statistics*, forthcoming.

Robson, M., J. Townsend and K. Pavitt (1988), 'Sectoral patterns of production and use of innovations in the UK: 1945–1983', *Research Policy*, **17**, 1–14

Sajeva, M., D. Gatelli, S. Tarantola and H. Hollanders (2005), 'Methodology report on European innovation scoreboard 2005', European Commission, Brussels, EIS 2005 Thematic Paper.

PART V

Technology Policy in Switzerland

18. How effective are the R&D-promoting activities of the Swiss innovation agency CTI? An evaluation based on matched-pairs analysis

Spyros Arvanitis and Nora Sydow

18.1 INTRODUCTION

In this chapter we investigate the impact of the innovation promotion policy of the Commission of Technology and Innovation (CTI), which is the most important government agency for the promotion of innovation in Switzerland. The CTI is supporting mainly research and development (R&D) cooperation projects from all scientific fields by funding the public partner of such a cooperation, a university or a public research institution, the private partner being an enterprise that agrees to contribute to this project on its own expenses by at least the amount of funds offered by the CTI (a private contribution of at least 50 per cent, a 'bottom-up' principle of support). The projects to be subsidized are selected by committees of experts that evaluate the applications by some 'excellency' criteria. Recently, programmes for the promotion of specific technologies (for example MedTech, TopNano21) have also been launched, but this kind of specific support has always been of minor importance. The principle of indirect R&D support of technologically high-quality projects, that are jointly undertaken by a private and a public partner, is fundamental for the Swiss technology policy. Its use as main instrument of promotion policy is, to our knowledge, unique in Europe.

Our main hypothesis was that enterprises that have been supported by the CTI would show on average a significantly higher innovation performance, measured by six innovation measures (for example sales share of innovative products), than structurally similar firms without such activities. To show this, we applied matched-pairs analysis for a set of CTI-supported firms and a control group of non-supported firms for the period 2000–2002.[1]

Recently, matching methods based on direct comparisons of participating and non-participating agents that were first used in evaluations of labour market policy measures, were also applied in the evaluation of technology programmes (for example Czarnitzki and Fier, 2002 and Almus and Czarnitzki, 2003 for Germany; Pointner and Rammer, 2005 for Austria, Görg and Strobl, 2007 for Ireland).[2] A major advantage of the matching methods versus the regression approach is that matching is non-parametric. As such, it avoids the functional form restrictions implicit in running a regression of some kind.

A brief description of the approach pursued in this chapter is as follows: (1) identification of the subsidized firms in the period 2000–2002 from the CTI database; (2) collection of innovation data for the promoted firms similar to those already existing for a sample of innovating firms of the Swiss Innovation Survey 2002; (3) estimation of propensity scores with respect to the likelihood of receiving a CTI subsidy; (4) application of four different matching methods in order to find the structurally similar, 'twin' firms for every subsidized firm; (5) test on the statistical significance of the difference of the means of six different innovation measures of the subsidized firms and the non-subsidized firms of the matched control group; (6) construction of a subsidy quotient measured by the amount of R&D promotion divided by the R&D budget of the firm in the same period; (7) distinction of firms with a high (higher than the median) and a low (lower than the median) subsidy quotient; and (8) test on the statistical significance of the difference of the differences of the means of the innovation variables of the subsidized firms and the matched non-subsidized firms.

For the period 2000–2002 we found (with one exception) for all six innovation measures and all four matching methods that the innovation performance of CTI-subsidized firms was on average significantly higher than that of the non-subsidized firms in the matched control group. Further, it was shown that the promotion effect was proportional to the magnitude of the subsidy quotient (that is, the promotion ratio measured by the ratio of R&D subsidies by CTI to a firm's own R&D expenditure).

New elements of our analysis are: (1) the use of innovation data for the subsidized firms collected by means of a survey; (2) the use of four different matching methods that allow testing of the robustness of our results; and (3) the investigation of the effect of promotion ratio as measured by the ratio of R&D subsidies by CTI to a firm's own R&D expenditure.

The chapter is structured as follows: section 18.2 deals with the data sources, section 18.3 presents some information on the patterns of CTI promotion in the reference period. In section 18.4 we describe the steps of our methodology for estimating the impact of CTI subsidies on firms' innovation performance. In section 18.5 we discuss the results. Section 18.6 contains a summary and some implications for technology policy.

18.2 DATABASE

Our information sources were: (1) a list of the firm projects that were subsidized by the CTI in the period 2000–2002; (2) additional information on the firms whose projects were subsidized by the CTI that was collected through a survey of the subsidized firms based on a shortened version of the questionnaire used in the Swiss Innovation Survey 2002; and (3) the data of firms that reported the introduction of innovations in the period 2000–2002 in the Swiss Innovation Survey 2002.

The CTI database contained information on 634 subsidized R&D projects that were finished between 1 January 2000 and 31 December 2002. Information was available on the scientific field of the project, the amount of the subsidy granted, and the name and address of the enterprise that conducted the subsidized project. These firms built our sample of subsidized firms. Start-ups, non-profit organizations and mergers were excluded from this sample because their specific characteristics could not be identified in our pool of control firms. Further, (a few) firms that ceased to exist by December 2003 were also taken out of the sample. The final sample of subsidized firms contained 307 firms. These firms received a shortened version of the questionnaire of the Swiss Innovation Survey 2002.[3] A total of 185 firms completed the questionnaire (see Table 18A.1 in the Appendix for information on the responding rates by scientific field). Fourteen more subsidized firms were identified among the participants of the Swiss Innovation Survey 2002. Hence, the sample we used for the study contained data for 199 firms (64.8 per cent of the firms subsidized by the CTI in the reference period). Additional information on the determinants of the propensity scores (see section 18.4) was collected through a telephone survey among the 122 subsidized firms that did not complete the postal survey. This additional information allowed us to estimate the propensity scores based on data for all 307 subsidized firms.

The 996 firms that participated in the Innovation Survey 2002 and reported the introduction of innovations in the period 2000–2002 built the pool of non-subsidized firms out of which a control group was constructed. Thus, we chose a wider basis for the control group and did not restrict it only to the firms conducting R&D.

The firms that finished their projects subsidized by the CTI during the first half of the period 2000–2002, that is, up to the middle of 2001, still would have had one and a half years until the end of the reference period to realize some impact of these projects on their innovation performance (for example, to introduce new products). One and a half years is an adequate time lag between doing R&D and realizing some R&D outcomes for most industries and for incremental innovations. However, for the firms that completed their subsidized R&D project(s) during the second half of the reference period, particularly in the year 2002, it is questionable whether they could have had enough time by the end of 2002 to realize any additional innovation gains. Table 18A.2 contains some information on the distribution of project finishing dates: 53 per cent of projects were finished by the middle of 2001, 78 per cent by the end of 2001. Hence, for the large majority of the projects there was enough time for a measurable impact of R&D on their innovation performance. For the remaining 28 per cent of the firms it is possible that only part of the impact could be realized by the end of 2002. In this sense our estimations of the impact of CTI promotion would be rather a lower bound of the possible effects.

18.3 PATTERNS OF CTI PROMOTION, 2000–2002

As already mentioned, 634 R&D projects were supported by the CTI in the period 2000–2002. Table 18.1 shows the scientific fields in which these projects were located and the amount of the granted subsidies by scientific field.

The projects in the fields of machinery and apparatus construction as well as information technology (software) amounted to about 33 per cent of all projects and received about 33 per cent of total subsidies. In general, the subsidies were rather broadly distributed among several scientific fields, which is in accordance with the general promotion policy of the CTI based mainly on the 'bottom-up' principle of support. So-called future-oriented technologies such as biotechnology (3.6 per cent of projects; 4.5 per cent of subsidies) and nanotechnology (5.7 per cent of projects; 3.8 per cent of subsidies) did not seem to have been particularly promoted. Totally about 120 million Swiss francs were invested in projects promoted by the CTI, that is, on average 60 million per annum. The mean subsidy amount per project was 190 000 Swiss francs, the mean amounts among scientific fields varying between 167 000 Swiss francs for information technology and 267 000 Swiss francs for microelectronics. This means that, including the firms' contribution of at least the same amount as the CTI subsidy, about 400 000 Swiss francs were invested per project.

Table 18.2 shows the distribution of subsidies among firms by scientific field. Enterprises with more than one project were classified by the scientific field of the project with the highest subsidy.

Table 18.1 Subsidized projects and volume of subsidy by scientific field, 2000–2002

Scientific field	Number of projects	%	CTI subsidy	%	CTI subsidy per project
Construction technology	27	4.3	3801686	3.1	140803
Biology	23	3.6	5462365	4.5	237494
Electrical machinery/ electronics	32	5.0	6477776	5.4	202431
Information technology	103	16.2	17235837	14.3	167338
Machinery, construction of apparatus	105	16.6	22735819	18.8	216532
Material sciences	56	8.8	13992873	11.6	249873
Microelectronics	48	7.6	12810767	10.6	266891
Nanotechnology	36	5.7	4537160	3.8	126032
Process engineering	41	6.5	8761137	7.2	213686
Production/management concepts	51	8.0	8406303	7.0	164829
Other	112	17.7	16631768	13.8	148498
Total	634	100.0	120853491	100.0	190621

Source: CTI database; authors' calculations.

The share of firms with projects in machinery, apparatus construction and information technology is about 22 per cent, significantly lower than the respective share of projects in these scientific fields. In contrast, material sciences are better represented among firms (about 24 per cent) than among projects (about 12 per cent).

In Table 18.3 the subsidized firms are further characterized by the industry affiliation and the number of employees in full-time equivalents (firm size).

Fifty-two per cent of the promoted firms belonged to mechanical and electrical machinery, electronics and instruments (column 4 in Table 18.3). This was the dominant group among the subsidized firms, quite in accordance with the high (relative) importance of these capital goods industries for Swiss manufacturing with respect to value added, employment and innovativeness; however, this group is rather over-represented in the sample. Chemical and pharmaceutical firms, which are on average the most innovative Swiss firms, are quite under-represented among the subsidized firms (4 per cent), reflecting the strong tendency of this branch of above-average investment in in-house R&D (compare also with the respective figures of the non-subsidized firms in column 2 in Table 18.3).

Table 18.2 Subsidized enterprises by scientific field, 2000–2002

Scientific field	Anzahl Firmen	%-Anteil
Construction technology	11	5.5
Biology	7	3.5
Electrical machinery/electronics	12	6.0
Information technology	21	10.6
Machinery, construction of apparatus	23	11.6
Material sciences	48	24.1
Microelectronics	21	10.6
Nanotechnology	6	3.0
Process engineering	16	8.0
Production/management concepts	14	7.0
Other	20	10.1
Total	199	100.0

Note: Enterprises with more than one project were classified by the scientific field of the project with the highest subsidy.

Source: CTI database; authors' calculations.

With the exception of wholesale trade the service sector is represented in the sample of the subsidized firms only by business services (computer services, engineering, business consulting, and so on; about 21 per cent). Small firms with up to 50 employees have a share of about 55 per cent, firms with more than 200 employees a share of only about 25 per cent, firms with more than 500 employees a share of about 10 per cent (column 4 in Table 18.3).

Both the distribution among industries and among firm size classes seem to be in accordance with the policy pursued by the CTI of promoting mainly small and medium-sized enterprises (SMEs) in all sections of the economy; there is even a tendency of promoting small firms rather than medium-sized firms.

18.4 METHOD

Our main hypothesis is that firms with CTI support, particularly through co-financed research projects in cooperation with universities, would show on average a significantly higher innovation performance, measured by output innovation measures (for example sales share of innovative products), than structurally similar firms without such support. To show this, we used several matching methods.

Table 18.3 Subsidized and non-subsidized enterprises, 2000–2002, by industry and firm size

Industry	Non-subsidized firms[1]	%	Subsidized firms	%
Food, beverage, tobacco	66	6.6	2	1.0
Textiles	24	2.4	2	1.0
Clothing, leather	9	0.9	0	0.0
Wood processing	20	2.0	4	2.0
Paper	18	1.8	1	0.5
Printing	27	2.7	3	1.5
Chemicals	63	6.3	8	4.0
Plastics, rubber	45	4.5	2	1.0
Glass, stone, clay	24	2.4	2	1.0
Metal	12	1.2	2	1.0
Metalworking	84	8.5	9	4.5
Machinery	153	15.5	36	18.1
Electrical machinery	38	3.8	12	6.0
Electronics, instruments	78	7.9	56	28.1
Watches	26	2.6	6	3.0
Vehicles	13	1.3	4	2.0
Other manufacturing	28	2.8	1	0.5
Energy	12	1.2	0	0.0
Construction	32	3.2	3	1.5
Wholesale trade	45	4.5	2	1.0
Retail trade	23	2.3	0	0.0
Hotels, catering	15	1.5	0	0.0
Transport, telecom	30	3.0	0	0.0
Banking, insurances	33	3.3	0	0.0
Real estate, leasing	3	0.3	0	0.0
Computer services	25	2.5	23	11.6
Other business services	45	4.5	19	9.5
Personal services	5	0.5	2	1.0
Size classes (number of employees)				
Up to 19	187	18.8	75	37.6
20–49	221	22.1	34	17.1
50–99	179	18.0	20	10.1
100–199	192	19.3	21	10.6
200–499	136	13.7	30	15.1
500–999	51	5.1	10	5.0
1000 and more	30	3.0	9	4.5
Total	996	100.0	199	100.0

Note: [1] The pool of firms out of which the firms of the control group were drawn for matching comes from the Swiss Innovation Survey 2002 (firms that introduced innovations in the period 2000–2002).

In order to measure appropriately the influence of CTI subsidies on a firm's innovation performance ('treatment effect')[4] we should be able to measure the performance difference of the two 'states' of a firm ('treated': subsidized by the CTI; 'non-treated': non-subsidized by the CTI), keeping all other things equal. In a cross-section framework mostly only one of these two possible states is observable: a firm is either subsidized or not subsidized. Thus, a proper comparison of these states is in most cases not possible. Heckman et al. 1998 developed a methodology to approximate this non-observable (counterfactual) state of a certain firm with the observable same state of another firm which is structurally similar to the first one with respect to a series of firm characteristics formally defined by a vector **X**. Thus, besides the group of firms that were subsidized by CTI in a certain time period, we need a pool of firms that were not subsidized in the same period, out of which structurally similar firms have to be selected according to a 'proximity' or 'distance' criterion (matched control group). The comparison of the two states for subsidized and non-subsidized firms is performed by comparing the means of the innovation performance variables for the treated firms and the 'twin' non-treated firms matched to the treated ones according to a proximity criterion. The multidimensionality of the matching problem (matching with respect to each single element of a vector **X** of firm characteristics) can be reduced under certain conditions (see Rosenbaum and Rubin, 1983) to a monodimensional (scalar) propensity score which comprehends the entire information of all relevant characteristics.[5]

If the Y_{1i} is a vector of innovation measures for the treated firm *i* and Y_{0j} the corresponding vector for a firm *j* belonging to the control group that is the 'twin' firm to firm *i*, then the performance difference between the two firms is defined as:

$$\Delta Y = Y_{1i} - Y_{0j}$$

In a first step, we estimated the propensity scores $P(X)$ by applying a probit model of the probability of a firm to have a research project subsidized by the CTI (see Table 18A.3 in the Appendix). As independent variables X we used: a variable characterizing a firm's R&D activities (permanent versus occasional), the degree of exposition to international competition (export activities, yes or no), firm size, firm age, industry affiliation and geographical location (region).

In a second step, all firms were distributed to adjustment cells according to the quintiles of the estimated propensity scores. The search for a 'twin' firm is then restricted only to the firms of the same adjustment cell, that is, the same quintile of propensity scores.

In a third step, based on a proximity or distance measure the structurally similar firm inside an adjustment cell was identified for each treated firm. In order to test the robustness of our results we used four different matching methods for identifying the structurally similar firms out of the pool of the non-treated firms (nearest neighbour, caliper, kernel, local linear regression; for details see Arvanitis et al., 2005).

In a fourth step, the means of the variables measuring innovation performance of the group of the treated firms and the group of the 'twin' non-treated firms were compared. We used six innovation variables covering the output side of the innovation process: (1) an ordinal measure of the technical importance of the introduced product and process innovations; (2) an ordinal measure of the economic importance of the introduced product and process innovations; (3) percentage reduction of average variable production costs due to process innovation; (4) sales of new products new to the firm or to the market as a percentage of total sales; (5) sales of significantly improved or modified (already existing) products as a percentage of total sales; (6) sales of products new to the market worldwide.

In a fifth and last step, we calculated a subsidy quotient for every subsidized firm by dividing the amount of the granted subsidy by the total R&D expenditure in the period 2000–2002. This subsidy quotient measured the relative magnitude of the subsidy.[6] We divided the subsidized firms into two groups, one group with firms with a subsidy quotient higher than the median ('high-subsidy' firms) and a second one with firms with a subsidy quotient lower than the median ('low-subsidy' firms). Then, we calculated the difference of the means between subsidized and non-subsidized firms separately for the high-subsidy and the low-subsidy firms. We tested whether the difference in the former case was significantly larger than the difference in the latter case. If this was the case, we interpreted this result as empirical evidence that the impact of the CTI subsidies was positively correlated to the magnitude of the subsidy quotient. Hence, high-subsidy firms would show a larger impact than the low-subsidy ones.

18.5 RESULTS OF THE MATCHED-PAIRS ANALYSIS

18.5.1 Comparison of the Innovation Performance of Subsidized Firms and Non-Subsidized Firms

Table 18.4 shows a qualitative summary of the results of the comparison of the innovation performance, as measured by six different indicators, of the subsidized and the non-subsidized firms for four different matching methods.

Table 18.4 Summary of results for various matching methods

Variable	Significantly higher means of subsidized than of non-subsidized firms (after matching)			
	'Nearest neighbour'	'Caliper'	'Kernel'	'Local linear regression'
Importance of introduced innovations from a technical point of view	yes	yes	yes	yes
Importance of introduced innovations from a economic point of view	no	yes	yes	yes
Percentage reduction of average variable production costs due to process innovation	yes	yes	yes	yes
Sales of significantly improved or modified (already existing) products as a percentage of total sales	yes	yes	yes	yes
Sales of products new to the firm or to the market as a percentage of total sales	yes	yes	yes	yes
Sales of products new to the market worldwide as a percentage of total sales	yes	yes	yes	yes

Note: Statistical significance: 5%-test level.

We calculated the difference in the means of the two categories of firms (subsidized, non-subsidized) for six innovation variables and four matching methods, that is, for 24 different cases. With one exception (importance of introduced innovations from an economic point of view; nearest neighbour method) we found that the subsidized firms showed a significantly higher innovation performance than non-subsidized firms (at the 5 per cent test level). Hence, these results seem to be quite robust across various methods and innovation indicators. Having controlled for firm size and firm age, sector affiliation, region, export propensity and the existence of continuous R&D activities in the propensity equation, these performance differences have to be traced back to the main difference between the two groups of firms, namely having or not having received CTI subsidies in the reference period.[7] Of particular interest for the effectiveness of CTI promotion policy is the result for the sales of products new to the market worldwide, because it shows that supported firms can significantly outperform structurally similar non-supported firms not only with respect to incremental innovations but also in terms of market novelties.[8]

18.5.2 Comparison of the Innovation Performance of 'High Subsidy' and 'Low Subsidy' Firms

Table 18.5 contains a qualitative summary of the results of the comparison of the differences of the innovation performance of high-subsidy and low-subsidy firms from that of the respective groups of non-subsidized firms.

Table 18.5 Summary of results with respect to the magnitude of the subsidy quotient for various matching methods

Variable	Significantly higher differences of differences of means of subsidized and non-subsidized firms (after matching) for subsidized firms with a subsidy quote > median than for subsidized firms with subsidy quotient < median			
	'Nearest neighbour'	'Caliper'	'Kernel'	'Local linear regression'
Importance of introduced innovations from a technical point of view	yes	yes	yes	yes
Importance of introduced innovations from a economic point of view	no	no	no	no
Percentage reduction of average variable production costs due to process innovation	yes	yes	yes	yes
Sales of significantly improved or modified (already existing) products as a percentage of total sales	yes	yes	yes	yes
Sales of products new to the firm or to the market as a percentage of total sales	yes	yes	yes	yes
Sales of products new to the market worldwide as a percentage of total sales	yes	yes	yes	yes

Note: Statistical significance: 5%-test level.

For five innovation indicators we found that the difference of the means of the high-subsidy and the non-subsidized firms for all four matching methods is significantly higher (at the 10 per cent level) than the respective differences for the low-subsidy firms (that is, significantly positive difference of the differences). Hence, for these cases we have empirical evidence that the impact on innovation performance is proportional to the relative magnitude of the granted subsidy. The larger the amount of the subsidy relative to a firm's own R&D investment, the stronger is the impulse for the innovation performance of a firm. For one innovation variable (importance of introduced innovations from an economic point of view) we could not find any significant effect.

18.6 SUMMARY AND IMPLICATIONS FOR THE SWISS TECHNOLOGY POLICY

Based on a matched-pairs analysis of 199 firms supported by the CTI in the period 2000–2002 and a control group of 996 firms that were not supported by the CTI, we found that the CTI promotion significantly improved the innovation performance of supported firms with respect to six different measures of innovation performance. This could be shown by four different matching methods. A further finding was that the magnitude of the impact correlated positively with the relative size of financial support as measured by the quotient of the volume of financial support to the volume of a supported firm's own R&D expenditure.

The present analysis yields some information on three policy-related issues: (1) kind of enterprises that received subsidies from the CTI; (2) effectiveness of CTI promotion policy; (3) relationship between subsidy quotient and policy effectiveness. The results of the study show a positive picture of the CTI promotion policy. Subsidized firms are mainly SMEs (perhaps too many micro firms among them) whose promotion is an explicit goal of CTI policy. The technological orientation of subsidized projects is quite broad, covering also currently 'fashionable' fields such as biotechnology and nanotechnology. Further, subsidized firms represent a wide spectrum of manufacturing firms, the concentration in firms of machinery, electronics and instruments reflecting the structure of Swiss manufacturing. The 'bottom-up' principle applied by the CTI for allocating funds seems to be quite effective in avoiding the weaknesses of policy measures focusing on specific technologies, that bear the additional risk of promoting what experts (instead of the markets) think to be the technological future. An additional positive element is that policy effectiveness is proportional to the amount of financial support. All this is quite in accordance with the general principles of the Swiss technology policy tending to be 'non-activist', providing primarily for the improvement of the framework conditions for private innovation activities.

Even if a policy measure is successful from a microeconomic point of view, it still remains an open question whether this policy measure is also relevant in macroeconomic terms. In the case of the CTI policy investigated in this chapter it is questionable whether an amount of 60 million Swiss francs of additional R&D support per annum could have a discernible impact on an economy that invested about 19 billion Swiss francs in R&D in 2004. A further open question is of course whether some kind of 'functional equivalent' of this policy at a broader base, for example R&D tax incentives, would do better, but such a discussion would be beyond the scope of this empirical chapter.

APPENDIX

Table 18A.1 Survey of the subsidized enterprises: structure of answering enterprises by scientific field

Scientific field	Number of addressed enterprises	Number of answering enterprises	% share of answering enterprises
Construction technology	16	11	68.8
Biology	13	7	53.8
Electrical machinery/ electronics	18	12	66.7
Information technology	38	20	52.6
Machinery	70	46	65.7
Material sciences	33	20	60.6
Microelectronics	27	16	59.3
Nanotechnology	6	5	83.3
Process engineering	29	15	51.7
Production/management concepts	23	14	60.9
Other	34	19	55.9
Total	307	185	60.3

Table 18A.2 Termination date of CTI projects of the subsidized enterprises; for firms with more than one project, the project that was terminated at the latest date was considered

Termination date	Number of enterprises	%
1. half-year 2000	29	14.6
2. half-year 2000	45	22.7
1. half-year 2001	31	15.7
2. half-year 2001	51	25.4
1. half-year 2002	29	14.6
2. half-year 2002	14	7.0
	199	100.0

Source: CTI database; authors' calculations.

Table 18A.3 Propensity of having a research project subsidized from the CTI as a function of various firm characteristics (probit estimation; dependent variable: research project subsidized by the CTI, 2000–2002, yes/no)

Firm characteristics	Test level 5%	Test level 10%
Firm size		
20–49 employees	–0.31	–0.30
	(0.11)	(0.11)
50–99 employees	–0.52	–0.51
	(0.13)	(0.13)
100–199 employees	–0.45	–0.45
	(0.12)	(0.12)
200–499 employees		
500–999 employees		
1000 employees and more		
Other characteristics		
Continuous R&D activities	0.40	0.40
	(0.10)	(0.10)
Export activities	0.43	0.45
	(0.11)	(0.11)
Firm founded before 1996	–0.86	–0.86
	(0.14)	(0.14)
Sector		
Traditional manufacturing	–0.54	–0.51
	(0.10)	(0.10)

Table 18A.3 (continued)

Firm characteristics	Test level 5%	Test level 10%
Traditional service industries	–1.23	–1.26
	(0.23)	(0.23)
Modern service industries		
Region		
Region of Geneva lake		0.32
		(0.17)
Espace midlands		
North-western Switzerland	–0.30	–0.35
	(0.14)	(0.14)
Eastern Switzerland		–0.21
		(0.12)
Central Switzerland		
Ticino		
Language of questionnaire		
French	0.56	0.32
	(0.10)	(0.14)
German		
N	1317	1317
Adj. McFadden-R^2	0.14	0.14
% concordance	76.50	77.30

Notes: In the table only the coefficients of variables reported that were significant at the 5%- and 10%-level respectively after a backward elimination procedure was applied. All variables in the table are dummy variables. Reference group for firm size: up to 19 employees; reference sector: high-tech manufacturing; definition: High-tech manufacturing: chemistry, plastics, machinery, electrical machinery, electronics/instruments; modern service industries: banking/insurance, computer services; other business services; traditional manufacturing: food/beverage/tobacco, textiles, clothing/leather; wood processing, paper, printing, glass/stone/clay, metal, metalworking, watches, other manufacturing, energy; traditional service industries: wholesale trade, retail trade, transport/telecommunication, hotels/catering, personal services; reference region: Zurich; Reference language: Italian.

NOTES

1. In Arvanitis et al. (2005) we report on a similar analysis for the period 1994–96.
2. See for example Bozeman (2000) and Georghiou and Roessner (2000) for recent reviews of the central issues related to the evaluation of the effectiveness of technology programmes; for reviews of the related econometric issues see for example Klette et al. (2000) and Hall and Van Reenen (2000); see also OECD (2006) for an analysis rather from the point of view of policy-makers. For Switzerland, Donzé (2002) conducted a matched-pairs analysis for the evaluation of the impact of computer-integrated manufacturing (CIM) support programmes on the diffusion rate of such technologies in the 1990s; Arvanitis et al. (2002) used a traditional econometric analysis for estimating the impact of CIM programmes on the diffusion rate of such technologies.

3. The questionnaire is available upon request in German, French and Italian.
4. The expression 'treatment effect' comes from the labour market research, where individuals are 'treated' via a concrete policy measure. It is used here analogously for firms subsidized by the CTI.
5. See Heckman et al. (1999) for a survey on various matching procedures, and Smith (2000) for a critical non-technical survey of these methods. Caliendo and Huber (2005) and Caliendo and Kopeinig (2005) give overviews of recent developments with respect to matching methods.
6. There is a measurement error in this calculation due to the time incongruence between subsidies granted before the beginning of 2000 and R&D expenditure strictly referring to the period 2000–2002 that unfortunately cannot be quantified and corrected.
7. Of course we cannot exclude that other factors that are not specified in the propensity equation could be responsible for the better performance of the subsidized firms. The variables included in our equation can explain about 14 per cent of variance, which is not a bad fitting for cross-section analysis.
8. The detailed results are found in Arvanitis et al. (2005). These show that there are substantial differences with respect to innovation performance. The differences vary from a 9–11 per cent larger magnitude for the qualitative self-assessment of the technical importance of the introduced innovations, up to a threefold to fivefold larger magnitude in the case of sales of products new to the market.

REFERENCES

Almus, M. and D. Czarnitzki (2003), 'The effects of public R&D subsidies on firms' innovation activities: the case of Eastern Germany', *Journal of Business and Economic Statistics*, **21** (2), 226–36.

Arvanitis, S., L. Donzé and N. Sydow (2005), 'Wirksamkeit der Projektförderung der Kommission für Technologie und Innovation (KTI). Analyse auf der Basis verschiedener "Matched-Pairs"-Methoden', KOF Working Papers Nr. 103, April, Zurich.

Arvanitis, S., H. Hollenstein and S. Lenz (2002), 'The effectiveness of government promotion of advanced manufacturing technologies (AMT): an economic analysis based on Swiss micro data', *Small Business Economics*, **19** (4), 321–40.

Bozeman, B. (2000), 'Technology transfer and public policy: a review of research and theory', *Research Policy*, **29** (4), 627–55.

Caliendo, M. and R. Huber (2005), 'The microeconomertric estimation of treatment effects: an overview', IZA Discussion Paper No. 1653, Bonn.

Caliendo, M. and S. Kopeinig (2005), 'Some practical guidance for the implementation of propensity score matching', DIW Discussion Paper No. 485, Berlin.

Czarnitzki, D. and A. Fier (2002), 'Substitutive or complementary? Innovation subsidies in the German service sector', ZEW Discussion Paper No. 02-04, Mannheim: ZEW.

Donzé, L. (2002), 'Matched-pair analysis based on business survey data to evaluate the policy of supporting the adoption of advanced manufacturing technologies by Swiss firms', KOF Working Papers No. 65, July, Zurich.

Georghiou, L. and D. Roessner (2000), 'Evaluating technology programmes: tools and methods', *Research Policy*, **29** (4), 657–78.

Görg, H. and E. Strobl (2007), 'The effect of R&D subsidies on private R&D', *Economica*, **74** (294), 215–34.

Hall, B. and J. Van Reenen (2000), 'How effective are fiscal incentives for R&D? A review of the evidence', *Research Policy*, **29** (4), 449–69.

Heckman, J., H. Ichimura, J. Smith and P. Todd (1998), 'Characterizing selection bias using experimental data', *Econometrica*, **66** (5), 1017–98.

Heckman, J.J., R.J. Lalonde and J.A. Smith (1999), 'The economics and econometrics of active labour market programmes', in A. Ashenfelter and P.E. Todd (eds), *Handbook of Labour Economics*, Amsterdam: Elsevier Publishers, pp. 1865–2097.

Klette, T.J., J. Moen and Z. Griliches (2000), 'Do subsidies to commercial R&D reduce market failures? Microeconometric evaluation studies', *Research Policy*, **29** (4), 471–95.

OECD (2006), *Government R&D Funding and Company Behaviour: Measuring Behavioural Additionality*, Paris: OECD Publishing.

Pointner, W. and C. Rammer (2005), 'Wirkungsanalyse', in W. Pointner and W. Polt (eds), *Diffusionsorientierte Technologiepolitik ⊠ Eine vergleichende Wirkungsanalyse für Österreich, die Schweiz, Deutschland und die USA*, Vienna: Leykam, pp. 67–108.

Rosenbaum, B.R. and D.B. Rubin (1983), 'The central role of the propensity score in observational studies for causal effects', *Biometrika*, **70** (1), 41–55.

Smith, J. (2000), 'A critical survey of empirical methods for evaluating active labour market policies', *Schweizerische Zeitschrift für Volkswirtschaft und Statistik*, **136**, 247–68.

19. Characteristics of foreign R&D strategies of Swiss firms: implications for policy

Heinz Hollenstein

19.1 INTRODUCTION

Since the early 1980s the internationalization of Swiss firms' research and development (R&D) activities has strongly increased. Similar trends are observed in other countries (Narula and Zanfei, 2005; Veugelers et al., 2005). As a result there is increasing concern in Switzerland (and in other countries as well: see Håkanson and Nobel, 1993; OECD, 1998; Veugelers et al., 2005) that foreign R&D activities may substitute for domestic ones. On the other hand, it is argued that foreign R&D is a means to support production and sales activities in foreign markets and to tap into the worldwide pool of knowledge. In this view, foreign R&D complements and augments the domestic knowledge base, given that the transfer of knowledge to the headquarters works sufficiently well. Whether one or the other hypothesis holds true depends to a large extent on the strategies firms pursue by investing abroad in R&D.

According to the classical model of international trade and investment, differences among countries with respect to (relative) costs are the driver of foreign investments (Mundell, 1957). Reducing costs (increasing efficiency) is the prime motive for performing foreign R&D. In this theoretical setting, foreign and domestic R&D are substitutes.

In contrast, the experience with foreign direct investment (FDI) in the 1960s showed that some R&D in foreign locations was often required for successfully penetrating and developing local markets. Foreign R&D primarily served to modify products that basically were the result of domestic R&D according to local needs. This strategy driven by market-oriented (demand-side) motives is emphasized by the product cycle model of international trade and investment (Vernon, 1966). In this case, foreign and domestic R&D are complements.

In the 1990s observers increasingly became aware of the relevance of supply-side motives of foreign R&D as a growing number of companies started to perform R&D abroad in order to profit from (specialized) knowledge (only) available at foreign locations.[1] Knowledge-seeking as a means to augment a headquarters' knowledge base fits well into the dynamic capability view of the firm proposed by evolutionary economics (see Teece and Pisano, 1998). In this theoretical perspective, foreign and domestic R&D again are complements, at least to the extent that knowledge transfer to the domestic headquarters works sufficiently well.

Granstrand et al. (1993) reviewed the empirical evidence with respect to the internationalization of R&D, primarily reflecting work done during the 1980s and the early 1990s. Since then quite a few empirical studies have been published that specifically deal with knowledge-seeking activities, the relatively new element of the internationalization of R&D (see, among others, Cantwell, 1995; Florida, 1997; Kuemmerle, 1999; Patel and Vega, 1999; Frost, 2001; Le Bas and Sierra, 2002). A main objective of this work was to show the growing relevance of this type of foreign R&D ('asset-augmenting') and/or to compare its prevalence with the more traditional market-seeking strategy ('asset-exploiting'). Moreover, this research showed that geographic proximity to universities and highly innovative firms, in accordance with the asset-augmenting strategy, offers great opportunities for profiting from knowledge spillovers in various forms (access to specific human capital, exploiting local high-tech networks, and so on; see for example Cantwell and Piscitello, 2005). Besides, it was shown empirically that some foreign affiliates upgraded their market-oriented R&D activities by using locally available firm-internal and firm-external knowledge for creating new products not only for the local market but for the world market as well. This extended market-oriented role of foreign affiliates has been documented in various studies (see, among others, Pearce, 1992, 1999; Pearce and Papanastassiou, 1999).[2]

The different motives of foreign R&D, as stressed by distinct theoretical models, were incorporated by Dunning in his well-known OLI paradigm. Its most recent version (Dunning, 2000; Cantwell and Narula, 2001; see also Dunning, 1994) is well suited to accommodate for FDI in R&D activities. 'Ownership-specific advantages' (O) capture market-seeking as well as knowledge-seeking foreign R&D. 'Location-specific advantages' (L) represent the classical cost-reducing, efficiency-seeking motive. 'Internalizing advantages' (I) are not directly linked to a certain motive for performing R&D abroad. Internalizing transactions in imperfect markets for knowledge may explain FDI in R&D, but can be realized only if a firm disposes of specific O-advantages (for example particular expertise in international knowledge management and firm-internal knowledge transfer).

In this chapter I aim, firstly, at identifying a number of specific strategies that firms pursue by investing in R&D in foreign locations, expecting that firms are mostly driven by a combination of several motives ('mixed strategies'). Secondly, I ask whether foreign and domestic R&D are substitutes or complements. Thirdly, I discuss some policy implications.

In order to identify foreign R&D strategies of Swiss firms, I perform, in a first step, a cluster analysis based on firm-level information of the relevance of a set of motives for foreign R&D investments as assessed by the firms themselves. The four clusters resulting from this exercise represent specific combinations of the underlying motives and are thus interpreted as different types of foreign R&D strategies ('mixed' strategies). In a second step, I characterize the clusters based on a large number of variables that, in the first place, represent the most important aspects of the OLI paradigm. In this way it is possible to check whether the statistical classification procedure of the first step effectively yields types of foreign R&D strategies that clearly differ from each other and are consistent with the OLI framework. The analysis is based on firm-level data stemming from the Swiss Innovation Survey conducted in 2002.

The relative importance of the different R&D strategies enables an assessment of whether foreign R&D, on balance, substitutes domestic R&D, or whether these two components of R&D are complements. By discussing the direct home-country effects of the various strategies and also considering indirect effects (knowledge spillovers to domestic firms) additional evidence is obtained on the relative merits of the two hypotheses. Based on these results I derive some policy implications and discuss what type of policies are required to maximize the benefit of foreign R&D for the Swiss economy.

The chapter complements (and adds to) previous work in several respects. Firstly, I apply a methodological approach for identifying specific foreign R&D strategies, which, to my knowledge, has been employed so far only in one study (Håkanson and Nobel, 1993). This approach is particularly suited to accommodate for 'mixed' strategies that are based on a combination of motives for foreign R&D. By combining a statistical classification procedure (cluster analysis) with a theory-based characterization of the clusters (variables representing the OLI paradigm) I am quite confident that the clusters effectively represent specific types of foreign R&D strategies. Secondly, as the database contains a large number of variables suitable to characterize different R&D strategies it allows a more differentiated analysis of foreign R&D strategies at the firm level than is usually the case. Moreover, the database includes small and medium-sized enterprises (SMEs) and service sector firms, which are not considered in most studies dealing with foreign R&D. Thirdly, the study contributes to the analysis of the home-country effects of foreign R&D, which did not gain much attention till the early 1990s (Granstrand et al., 1993) and still remains a question not clearly answered to date (Veugelers et al., 2005). Fourthly, taking into account the characteristics of the different R&D strategies allows a differentiated policy analysis. Finally, the Swiss case may be of special interest as the process of the internationalization of R&D has progressed very far in this country.

The structure of the chapter is as follows. In the next two sections I briefly describe the database and the method I apply in order to identify specific foreign R&D strategies. In section 19.4 I present the empirical results. Finally, I discuss the implications of the empirical results for economic policy in Switzerland.

19.2 DATA

The data used in this study were collected as part of the Swiss Innovation Survey 2002. The firms were asked to fill in a large questionnaire (downloadable from www.kof.ethz.ch) on their innovative activities. Among many other topics, the survey provided information on a firm's foreign R&D expenditure. Moreover, the companies were asked to assess on a five-point Likert scale, ranging from 'practically irrelevant' (value 1) up to 'very important' (value 5), the importance of specific motives for performing R&D abroad. This information is used to identify alternative foreign R&D strategies. The survey also provided data on a large number of variables that I used to characterize these strategies in terms of the well-known OLI paradigm.

The survey was based on a stratified sample of firms with at least five employees (28 manufacturing and services industries; three industry-specific firm size classes, with full coverage of large companies). The questionnaire that was sent to 6524 companies yielded valid data for 2583 firms (response rate 40 per cent). A total of 1078 firms performed R&D (42 per cent of the respondents), among which 156 (15 per cent) also did so at foreign locations. Foreign R&D activity is more concentrated than total R&D on high-tech manufacturing and, to a lesser extent, on knowledge-intensive services. Large companies more often perform foreign R&D than smaller ones. Nevertheless, more than 20 per cent of the firms investing abroad in R&D have less than 50 employees.

The industry composition of the data set of responding firms is quite similar to that of the underlying sample; some over-representation of manufacturing is noticed at the expense of the 'traditional' part of the service sector. As the structure of the sample and that of respondents is sufficiently similar, unit non-response is no serious problem, as is confirmed by a survey among a sample of non-respondents (Arvanitis et al., 2004). In contrast, I had to correct for item non-response by replacing missing by imputed values ('multiple imputation'; see Rubin, 1987).

19.3 METHOD

In order to identify the strategy a firm pursues by investing abroad in R&D I apply a two-step procedure. Firstly, I perform a non-hierarchical cluster analysis of seven motives of foreign R&D, which capture the most important 'pull' and 'push' factors that may induce foreign R&D, as proposed by the different theoretical approaches mentioned above. By applying (non-hierarchical) cluster analysis (see Manly, 1986), I classify firms into a number of categories, which, in terms of the combination of motives of foreign R&D, are as homogenous as possible (small within-cluster variance) and at the same time as different as possible (large between-cluster variance). Therefore, we may conclude that firms of a specific category pursue very similar foreign R&D strategies. However, since cluster analysis is a (purely) statistical classification procedure, such an interpretation is preliminary.

Secondly, in order to check whether the clusters identified in the first step really may be interpreted as specific foreign R&D strategies, I compare the cluster-specific means of a large number of variables not used in clustering ('external plausibility check'). These variables represent core elements of the OLI paradigm, the firms' market environment and some structural firm characteristics.

More specifically, I characterize the clusters, in addition to the motives of foreign R&D, based on four groups of variables:

1. 'Ownership-specific advantages' (O): (a) several types of innovation indicators based on firm-internal and firm-external factors; (b) supply-side determinants of innovation performance (complemented by some demand-side determinants which are only partly related to O-advantages); (c) firm size and productivity (capturing not explicitly specified O-advantages).
2. 'Location-specific disadvantages' of Switzerland (L): obstacles to innovation.
3. 'Internalizing advantages' (I): R&D cooperation and firm size (which, as mentioned, also reflects some not explicitly specified O-advantages).
4. Structural firm characteristics such as, for example, firm size, industry affiliation, and so on (with firm size, as mentioned, also capturing some O- and I-advantages).

19.4 EMPIRICAL RESULTS

19.4.1 Identifying Foreign R&D Strategies

The identification of foreign R&D strategies is based on the seven motives for performing R&D at foreign locations shown in Table 19.1. These reflect the various theories of international trade and investment as integrated in the OLI paradigm. The first item (supporting local production and sales) reflects market-seeking motives of foreign R&D. The next three items (proximity to leading-edge universities; proximity to highly innovative firms; knowledge transfer to the headquarters) represent several dimensions of knowledge-seeking. Exploiting low R&D costs, and high government support for R&D investments, both as compared to Switzerland, reflect the motive of cost-reduction. Finally, making use of an ample supply of R&D personnel at foreign locations may represent cost-reducing but also knowledge-seeking motives (access to specific human capital). The importance of the seven motives, as assessed by the firms themselves, is measured on a five-point Likert scale.

The cluster analysis based on these 'motive variables' yielded four clusters. The statistical properties of the classification (relationship between within-cluster and between-cluster variance) is satisfactory in statistical terms. The value of the approximate expected overall R^2 of 0.47 suggests an acceptable fit of the data to the underlying cluster model.

Table 19.1 shows for the whole sample and the four clusters the share of firms for which a specific motive is highly relevant. It turns out that the first cluster (column 1) contains a particularly high percentage of companies for which profiting from geographic proximity to universities, from an ample supply of R&D personnel and – to a lesser extent – from high government support for R&D investments are at the core of their strategy; hence, this cluster is labelled UNIV_HC (universities, human capital). Firms of the second cluster emphasize geographic proximity to innovative firm networks and the knowledge transfer to the headquarters (NETWORK). The third cluster highlights R&D as a means to support local production and sales (MARKET), and the fourth one stresses low R&D costs and access to an ample supply of R&D-related human capital (COST_HC). I conclude that the four clusters systematically differ in terms of the seven 'motive variables'.

By taking the sum of the motive-specific frequencies (see the last row of the table) we get some idea of the breadth of the strategy the firms of a specific cluster pursue. It turns out that firms of type UNIV_HC are by far most diversified in their strategic orientation as they pursue several objectives in parallel (strongly 'mixed strategy'). At the other end, we find

Table 19.1 Motives for performing R&D at foreign locations by type of R&D strategy (% share of firms assessing a specific motive as highly important – score 4 or 5 on a five-point Likert scale)

Motives	R&D strategies (cluster means)				All Firms N = 156
	UNIV_HC N = 39	NETWORK N = 37	MARKET N = 56	COST_HC N = 24	
Supporting local production/sales	26	30	61	29	40
Geographic proximity to leading universities	67	5	21	0	26
Geographic proximity to highly innovative firms (networks)	44	59	16	29	35
Transfer of knowledge and technology to the domestic headquarters	28	59	13	0	26
Low R&D costs	38	14	4	79	26
High government support for R&D	26	0	9	13	12
Ample supply of R&D personnel	64	30	11	71	38
Sum of percentage shares (columns)	293	197	135	221	203

Note: The labels of the four clusters are more or less self-evident as they reflect the relative importance of the seven motives.

Source: Swiss Innovation Survey 2002.

the firms of the cluster MARKET whose strategy is very focused on one motive (market-seeking R&D).

19.4.2 Characteristics of the Foreign R&D Strategies

In order to check the appropriateness of the classification resulting from cluster analysis (step 1 of the procedure), the four clusters are characterized and compared in terms of the variables not used in clustering. To this end I refer to a large number of variables representing the OLI paradigm and the firms' market environment, as well as to some structural firm characteristics. In so doing, it is possible to assess whether the clusters effectively represent specific R&D strategies.

O-advantages are represented by three sets of variables. Firstly (see Table 19.2a), based on the view that innovation performance is an important element of a firm's competitive advantage, I use information on 14 innovation indicators. These capture different aspects of the innovation process: (1) innovation input (R&D and innovation expenditure); (2) innovation output (patent-related indicators); and (3) market-oriented innovation measures (sales of innovative products).

A second category of O-advantages pertains to firm-external knowledge inputs that have become more important in the process of increased specialization in knowledge production (Haagedoorn, 1996). External knowledge inputs have a direct (positive) impact on firm productivity and also increases indirectly the effectiveness of a firm's internal innovation input (Arvanitis and Hollenstein, 1998). I dispose of information capturing the intensity of use of 14 external sources of knowledge (see Table 19.2b): customers; suppliers of components, of software, of equipment; competitors; firms of the same enterprise group; universities; other research institutions; consultancy firms; institutions promoting technology transfer; patent disclosures; fairs, exhibitions, professional conferences, (scientific) journals; computer-based networks. I synthesized the information contained in the 14 sources of knowledge by use of factor analysis, with five factors turning out as the optimal solution. The resulting factor pattern is convincing in statistical terms (the five factors account for 63 per cent of total variance) as well as with respect to the interpretation of the factors: science-related knowledge sources, supplier-related sources, generally accessible sources, market-related sources and, finally, group-internal knowledge flows.

As a third group of O-advantages (Table 19.2c), I include some supply- and demand-side determinants of innovation as considered in the literature (see for example Cohen, 1995). On the supply side, technological opportunity is proxied by the firms' assessment of the potential of novelties to be generated in and around its field of activity. Besides, I consider a measure of the appropriability of knowledge (again as assessed by the firms themselves). Human capital intensity (share of highly qualified personnel) is used to capture a firm's capacity to absorb knowledge from outside the firm. These supply-side variables are complemented by four demand-side determinants of a firm's innovation performance, which are only partly related to O-advantages: medium-run market prospects (growth of a firm's relevant markets in the period 2000–2005), the intensity of price

Table 19.2a Innovative activities, 2000–2002

Innovation indicators	R&D strategies (cluster means)				All firms N = 156
	UNIV_HC N = 39	NETWORK N = 37	MARKET N = 56	COST_HC N = 24	
a) Input-oriented measures					
Qualitative measures[1]					
Research expenditure	36	41	21	29	31
Development expenditure	82	70	68	67	72
Quantitative measures					
Sales share of innovation expenditure (%)	7.6	5.2	5.3	8.9	6.4
Sales share of R&D expenditure (%)	5.5	5.0	3.4	2.9	4.2
Employment share of R&D personnel (%)	13.8	11.8	9.7	9.0	11.1
b) Output-oriented measures					
Share of firms with patent applications (%)	59	43	57	54	54
Number of patent applications per employee	0.058	0.033	0.023	0.024	0.034
c) Market-oriented measures					
Sales share of innovative products (%)					
Worldwide novelties	9.0	4.3	6.7	6.8	6.7
New or fundamentally improved products	20	17	18	21	19
New and all kind of improved products	43	35	36	41	38

Note: [1] Percentage share of firms assessing expenditure for research and development respectively as high (score 4 or 5 on a five-point Likert scale).

Source: Swiss Innovation Survey 2002.

and non-price competition on a firm's product markets and, finally, the number of principal competitors (market concentration). The intensity of non-price competition is measured by a composite indicator (based on factor analysis) of the relevance of eight elements of non-price competition (firm assessments) such as product quality, product differentiation, after-sales services, and so on.

Finally, in order to take account of O-advantages I could not explicitly specify, I use labour productivity and firm size. The latter (among other

Table 19.2b Sources of external knowledge and R&D cooperation

External knowledge sources / R&D co-operation	R&D strategies (cluster means)				All firms N = 156
	UNIV_ HC N = 39	NETWORK N = 37	MARKET N = 56	COST_ HC N = 24	
a) Use of external knowledge sources[1]					
Users	51	54	59	83	60
Suppliers of materials/ components	38	54	45	58	47
Suppliers of software	18	24	13	29	19
Suppliers of machinery/ equipment	28	19	18	17	21
Competitors	38	43	30	54	39
Firms of the same group	36	35	41	50	40
Universities	59	43	41	21	43
Other research institutions	36	27	18	13	24
Consulting firms	15	8	7	0	8
Technology transfer organizations	10	8	4	8	7
Patent documents	23	32	25	25	26
Fairs and exhibitions	51	43	29	75	45
Scientific and trade journals; conferences	54	57	32	46	46
Computer networks	38	46	21	29	33
b) Aggregate measure of the use of external knowledge sources (mean of factor scores)[2]					
SCIENCE (science-related knowledge)	0.34	–0.13	–0.03	–0.18	0
SUPPLIER (supplier-related knowledge)	0.01	0.05	–0.10	0.13	0
GENERAL (general accessible knowledge)	0.17	0.18	–0.28	0.10	0
MARKET (market-related knowledge)	0.02	–0.14	–0.13	0.49	0
GROUP (group-internal knowledge flows)	0.03	–0.15	0.06	0.04	0
Sum of the five mean scores	0.57	–0.19	–0.48	0.48	0

Table 19.2b (continued)

External knowledge sources / R&D co-operation	R&D strategies (cluster means)				All firms N = 156
	UNIV_HC N = 39	NETWORK N = 37	MARKET N = 56	COST_HC N = 24	
c) R&D co-operation					
Share of firms cooperating in R&D with other firms or research institutions (%)	41	49	48	33	44

Notes:
[1] Percentage share of firms assessing the input of external knowledge as high (score 4 or 5 on a five-point Likert scale).
[2] Factor scores based on a principal component analysis of the use of the fourteen external knowledge sources listed in the upper part of the table (five-factor solution). The table shows the mean scores by cluster and for the full sample (which is zero as a result of standardization). In addition we show the sum of the mean scores of the five categories of knowledge sources as a measure of the total input of external knowledge. For detailed results see Table A.2 in Hollenstein (2006).

Source: Swiss Innovation Survey 2002.

Table 19.2c Other innovation-related characteristics, factor input and productivity

Indicators	R&D strategies (cluster means)				All firms N = 156
	UNIV_HC N = 39	NETWORK N = 37	MARKET N = 56	COST_HC N = 24	
a) Supply-side determinants of innovation					
Technological opportunities[1]	56	51	48	33	49
Appropriability[1]	46	41	30	42	38
b) Demand-side determinants of innovation					
Market growth 2000–2005[1]	36	46	45	33	41
Intensity of price competition[1]	74	65	82	79	76

Table 19.2c (continued)

Indicators	R&D strategies (cluster means)				All firms N = 156
	UNIV_ HC	NETWORK	MARKET	COST_ HC	
	N = 39	N = 37	N = 56	N = 24	
Intensity of non-price competition[2]	0.19	0.00	–0.16	0.07	0
c) Market concentration (number of principal competitors)					
0–4	26	32	39	21	32
5–10	33	32	29	21	29
11–15	15	6	16	21	14
16 and more	26	30	16	37	25
d) Factor input and productivity 2001					
Human capital intensity (employment share of highly qualified personnel, %)	25.9	31.1	25.5	29.0	27.5
Physical capital intensity (gross capital income per employee)[3]	117	87	106	72	99
Labour productivity (value added per employee)[3]	203	189	200	157	192

Notes:
[1] Percentage share of firms assessing technological opportunities, appropriability, market growth and intensity of price competition, respectively, as high (score 4 or 5 on a five-point Likert scale).
[2] Factor scores based on a principal component analysis (one-factor solution) of the importance of eight dimensions of non price competition as assessed by the firms themselves (5-point Likert-scale). The table shows the mean scores by cluster and for the full sample (which is zero as a result of standardization). For detailed results see Table A.3 in Hollenstein (2006).
[3] Mio. SFR.

Source: Swiss Innovation Survey 2002.

things) may capture size-dependent O-advantages (for example advantages of large firms in international marketing), whereas the former should represent not explicitly specified O-advantages in general (high learning capacity, and so on).

Table 19.2d Obstacles to innovation

Obstacles	R&D strategies (cluster means)				All firms N = 156
	UNIV_HC N = 39	NETWORK N = 37	MARKET N = 56	COST_HC N = 24	
a) Obstacles[1]					
High taxation	31	13	13	11	17
Insufficient availability of R&D personnel	69	50	63	41	54
Insufficient availability of highly qualified employees in general	64	39	58	35	47
Restricted access to the EU market	33	14	38	27	26
Excessive regulation of the domestic product market	23	13	13	19	17
Restrictive access of foreigners to the domestic labour market	31	18	46	22	26
Lack of public research programmes	28	18	25	19	22
Lack of R&D subsidies	28	14	17	11	17
Severe protection of environment	33	13	17	27	22
Restrictive regulation of land use and construction	31	13	25	22	21
b) Aggregate measure of the importance of ten obstacles to innovation (mean of factor scores)[2]					
REGULATION (restrictive regulatory environment)	0.26	*–0.29*	0.08	0.12	0
SUPPORT (tax- and subsidy-related obstacles)	0.32	–0.11	–0.08	–0.12	0
LABOUR (lack of highly qualified personnel)	0.19	–0.12	0.45	*–0.31*	0
Sum of the three mean scores	0.77	–0.52	0.45	–0.31	0

Table 19.2d (continued)

Notes:

[1] Percentage share of firms assessing the obstacles as highly important (score 4 or 5 on a five-point Likert scale).

[2] Factor scores based on a principal component analysis of the ten obstacles to innovation listed in the upper part of the table (three-factor solution). The table shows the mean scores by cluster and for the full sample (which is zero as a result of standardization). In addition, we show the sum of the mean scores of the three categories of obstacles to innovation as a measure of the total level of hindrances. For detailed results see Table A.4 in Hollenstein (2006).

Source: Swiss Innovation Survey 2002.

L-disadvantages of Swiss locations are captured by a set of variables representing obstacles to innovation that may drive firms to perform R&D at foreign rather than at domestic locations. I take account of the relevance of ten obstacles as assessed by the firms themselves (see Table 19.2d): high taxation; insufficient supply of R&D personnel and of other highly qualified workers; restricted access to the EU market; excessive regulation of domestic markets; entry barriers for foreigners on the Swiss labour market; lack of public research programmes and of R&D subsidies; environment protection; restrictive regulation of land use. Again I synthesized the information by use of a factor analysis, with three factors turning out as the optimal solution. The factor pattern is convincing in statistical terms (the three factors account for 68 per cent of total variance) as well as with regard to the interpretation of the three factors: restrictive regulatory conditions, tax- and subsidy-related obstacles and shortage of highly qualified labour.

I-advantages reflect gains a firm may realize by internalizing market relationships in order to reduce transaction costs (Buckley and Casson, 1985). In the present context such costs may primarily stem from high risks involved in imperfect markets for knowledge and technology (for example limited access to tacit knowledge). I-advantages, however, are difficult to measure. Since cooperation in R&D is an increasingly used means for internalizing knowledge-related market transactions, I use as a proxy the dummy variable 'R&D cooperation yes or no' (see Table 19.2b). As another indicator of I-advantages, I include firm size (which is also used to capture some unspecified O-variables). Large firms are likely to be superior to small ones, for example, with regard to international innovation management, which is an important instrument for internalizing knowledge-related market transactions.

Finally, I include a set of structural firm characteristics: firm size and age, industry affiliation, degree of export orientation and company status (Table 19.2e).

Table 19.2e Selected structural characteristics of firms, 2001

Characteristics	R&D strategies (cluster means)				All Firms N = 156
	UNIV_ HC	NETWORK	MARKET	COST_ HC	
	N = 39	N = 37	N = 56	N = 24	
a) Firm size (share of firms (%) by size class; number of employees)					
5–49	23	43	13	13	22
50–149	31	24	27	50	31
150–499	33	11	32	29	27
500 or more	13	22	28	8	20
b) Industry/sector (share of firms, %)					
Low-tech industries	26	22	27	21	24
Pharmaceuticals, chemicals/plastics	13	26	11	13	15
Mechanical engineering, vehicles	30	14	29	28	27
Electrical engineering, electronics, instruments	10	16	20	25	17
Services	21	22	13	13	17
c) Export orientation (share of firms (%), based on the export to sales ratio)					
0–29	18	38	27	29	28
30–74	31	30	18	25	25
75–100	51	32	55	46	47
d) Company status					
Independent	36	43	32	38	37
Mother	28	22	29	29	27
Affiliate	36	35	39	33	36
e) Firm age (number of years)					
Less than 20 years	23	24	7	13	16
20 or more	77	76	93	87	84

Source: Swiss Innovation Survey 2002.

In the following I do not comment upon each table. It is more sensible to describe each cluster briefly in terms of the groups of variables shown in Tables 19.2a to 19.2e. In this way I can synthesize the very detailed information, so that we get a clear picture of the main characteristics of the four strategies. For more details, I ask the reader to study the individual tables.

19.4.3 A Portrait of the Four R&D Strategies

Strategy 1

Firms pursuing a broad-based foreign R&D strategy in terms of motives, with tapping into knowledge available at foreign universities and embodied in specialists as the core elements (UNIV_HC).

This cluster consists of 39 companies (25.0 per cent of firms, 11 per cent of employment). These firms dispose of strong O-advantages. They are very innovative with special emphasis on the generation of world novelties based on high internal R&D and other innovation-related expenditure, extended patenting activities as well as a very intensive use of external knowledge (in particular science-related sources). Innovative activities are supported by very favourable supply-side conditions (large technological opportunities, high appropriability of knowledge), while demand-side factors are somewhat less advantageous as the relevant markets are only moderately expanding. I-advantages (R&D cooperation, firm size) are about average. The firms of this cluster suffer from all kind of locational disadvantages (L) of Switzerland, which might increase the propensity to invest in R&D abroad at the expense of domestic locations. Such disadvantages pertain to excessive regulation, insufficient financial incentives (taxes, public support for R&D) and shortage of highly qualified personnel. This cluster contains an above-average share of highly export-oriented, medium-sized firms (with only very few large firms), which are slightly over-represented in mechanical engineering and services. The share of rather young firms is also above average. Labour productivity is the highest among all clusters, and the same holds, accentuated even more, for physical capital intensity.

Strategy 2

Firms strongly embedded in networks of highly innovative companies and transferring a substantial part of the knowledge obtained abroad to the domestic headquarters (NETWORK).

This cluster consists of 37 firms (23.7 per cent of firms as well as of employment) characterized by strong O- and I-advantages. Innovative activities of these firms, which are endowed with excellent staff, are strongly research-oriented. Output- and market-oriented measures of innovations (patents, sales share of innovative products) are below average. The same holds true for the use of external knowledge, with the exception of some elements of (generally accessible) science-related sources (patent documents, scientific journals). This pattern and the widespread practice of formal R&D cooperation are in line with the strongly research-based firm-internal innovative activities. Supply-side conditions for generating novelties (technological opportunities, appropriability), somewhat surprisingly, are not better than average. On the other hand, firms of this cluster benefit from excellent demand conditions (high market growth, low intensity of price competition). L-disadvantages of Switzerland are very low; in other words, these firms are not pushed to perform R&D abroad but choose foreign locations in order to complement their capabilities by knowledge available in foreign networks of highly innovative firms. This cluster contains a large share of very small, often young companies; however, we also find in this cluster four large multinational enterprises (MNEs) of the chemical, pharmaceutical and food industry. Export orientation is low, reflecting the high share of small companies. Among the sectors, the chemical and pharmaceutical industry and, to a lesser extent, services are over-represented. Labour productivity is about average, while physical capital intensity is low.

Strategy 3

Firms pursuing a strongly focused strategy, with foreign R&D almost exclusively used as a means to extend local markets (MARKET).

This cluster is the largest one and consists of 56 companies (35.9 per cent of firms, 57.8 per cent of employment). In terms of O-advantages, these firms are weaker than the average firm, and, in particular, the average company of the first two clusters. Innovation capacity is based primarily on development expenditure; patent activity is low and market-oriented innovation measures point to only average innovation content of sales. The moderate intensity of internal innovation activities is not matched by an intensive use of external knowledge. Therefore, it is not very surprising that the supply-side conditions for innovation are not more than average (technological opportunities) or even below average (appropriability). In contrast, the firms benefit from operating in strongly growing markets, where non-price competition is low; price competition, however, is fierce, perhaps reflecting the rather low number of competitors (oligopolistic competition). As far as I-advantages are concerned, the firms of this cluster are in a good position. L-disadvantages are concentrated on shortages of highly skilled personnel. This cluster contains a very high proportion of large, well-established rather old firms, which are export-oriented to an extremely high extent. The sectoral pattern is characterized by some over-representation of manufacturing (with the exception of pharmaceuticals and chemicals). Labour productivity and, even more so, physical capital intensity are above average.

Strategy 4
Firms pursuing, in terms of motives, a rather narrow-based foreign R&D strategy that aims at reducing R&D costs and gaining access to highly skilled personnel (COST_HC).

This cluster consists of only 24 companies (15.4 per cent of firms, 7.5 per cent of employment). O-advantages of the firms of this cluster are slightly below average. Innovation activities show a specific pattern. The firms are characterized by quite substantial innovation expenditure that reflects high outlays for engineering and innovation-related follow-up activities rather than R&D investments. As a result, these firms primarily generate incremental innovations. The supply-side as well as the demand-side environment for generating innovations is unfavourable (low technological opportunities and appropriability; slow growth of highly price-sensitive markets). In contrast to the only moderate internal innovation activities, these firms draw substantially on external knowledge available from other companies operating along the same value chain (suppliers, competitors, customers, firms of the same group). With regard to I-advantages the firms of this cluster are in a rather weak position. L-disadvantages seem to be no problem, which is somewhat surprising as the firms' foreign R&D activities are motivated by cost-reduction and getting access to human skills. This cluster contains a very high share of small, mostly old firms (with only one really big company). There is some over-representation of electrical engineering and electronics. Export orientation is about average, whereas labour productivity and physical capital intensity are much lower than in the other clusters.

Assessment
We conclude from this sketch of the four portraits that the four clusters reflect distinct patterns of motives for investing in foreign R&D and are clearly different in terms of the theory-based categories of variables I have used to characterize them (OLI-related variables, structural firm characteristics). Therefore, the four clusters may safely be interpreted as specific foreign R&D strategies. Some of the clusters represent mixed, broad-based strategies as they are driven by several motives (particularly strategy UNIV_HC), whereas others are more focused, in particular strategy MARKET.

In view of these results it is sensible to analyse foreign R&D strategies in terms of a combination of motives ('mixed strategies') rather than investigating the individual motives separately. The two-step procedure based on cluster analysis (step 1), complemented by a theory-based characterization of the clusters (step 2), proves to be a suitable procedure to identify and assess such strategies.

19.5 IMPLICATIONS FOR ECONOMIC POLICY IN SWITZERLAND

An assessment of the impact of foreign R&D of Swiss firms on the domestic economy is a precondition to drawing policy conclusions and to recommending policy measures. The literature distinguishes two types of effects on the home country. Firstly, knowledge and technology transfer from foreign affiliates to the headquarters company may strengthen the knowledge base of the domestic economy (positive direct home-country effects). Secondly, the domestic economy may profit from knowledge spillovers from the headquarters company to other domestic firms such as suppliers or users and (public) institutions such as universities (positive indirect home-country effects). Empirical evidence related to the two types of home-country effects is scarce, particularly with respect to spillover effects (Veugelers et al., 2005).[3]

Direct effects, in the first instance, reflect the prevalence of the four foreign R&D strategies (number of firms, employment) as these have a different impact on the knowledge base of the headquarters:

- Strategy 3 (MARKET): market-oriented strategies are the dominant feature of Swiss firms' foreign R&D. This strategy gives rise to firm-specific economies of scale at the headquarters. The concomitant higher return to domestic R&D is an incentive to spend more on R&D (positive direct effect). However, according to the scarce empirical evidence, the direct home-country effects of market-oriented R&D strategies seem to be rather weak.
- Strategies 2 (NETWORK) and 1 (UNIV_HC): knowledge sourcing is an essential element of these two strategies. The direct effects are positive only if the knowledge acquired abroad is transferred to a significant extent to the domestic headquarters. In the case of strategy 2, where affiliates source knowledge by operating in foreign networks of highly innovative firms, technology transfer works well according to the surveyed firms. The direct effects of strategy 1, which emphasizes knowledge sourcing based on geographical proximity to universities and access to human capital, is not so obvious.

In the case of this strategy, knowledge transfer to the headquarters takes place but it is not the prime feature. This result, however, does not imply that knowledge transfer is not relevant. It rather indicates that in the frame of this broad-based strategy other motives are more important. Moreover, as shown in Table 19.1, knowledge transfer of firms pursuing this strategy is more important by far than in the case of strategies 3 and 4. Therefore, I presume that at least part of the knowledge gained abroad will flow back to the headquarter company. To sum up, I conclude that both strategies for which knowledge sourcing is a constituent element strengthen the domestic knowledge base (positive direct home-country effect). The results from other empirical studies tend to support this assessment.

- Strategy 4 (COST_HC): firms pursuing this strategy primarily seek to lower their R&D costs. As the cluster analysis yields no evidence for a significant reverse knowledge transfer, the direct home-country effects are probably negative (relocation of R&D activities).

Based on the prevalence of the four strategies and the assessment of their direct home-country effects I conclude that foreign and domestic R&D, on balance, are complements. The unambiguously complementary strategies 2 and 3 are pursued by 60 per cent of firms employing 81 per cent of workers, whereas only 15 per cent of firms (8 per cent of employment) adhere to strategy 4 which may have a negative effect on domestic R&D. This interpretation is a cautious one as it does not consider strategy 1, where the impact on the headquarters' knowledge base is not so straightforward but is probably positive as well. My overall assessment is in line with the findings of my earlier work (Arvanitis and Hollenstein, 2001, 2007; Hollenstein, 2005), which was based on an econometric analysis of a firm's decision to invest in foreign R&D.

If indirect home-country effects (knowledge spillovers) are positive as well, the balance would tilt even further towards the complementarity of foreign and domestic R&D. The extent of knowledge spillovers is determined by several factors such as the firms' ability to prevent know-how from leaking to competitors, or their willingness to share knowledge with local suppliers and users in order to improve their own market position. Most importantly, however, spillovers are the larger, the higher the capacity of domestic firms to absorb external knowledge.

As already mentioned, there is not much evidence with respect to the size of knowledge spillovers. Nevertheless, I argue that in the Swiss economy, as compared to other countries, domestic firms are likely to benefit a lot from such spillovers. Firstly, the absorptive capacity of Swiss firms is particularly high, since SMEs are more innovative than firms of the same size class in all EU member states.[4] The highly distributed knowledge base of the economy substantially fosters technology diffusion. The large share of highly qualified personnel in science and technology employed by Swiss firms also facilitates the absorption of external knowledge (OECD, 2007). Secondly, firms performing R&D in foreign locations are well embedded in the domestic innovation system, as (domestic) R&D cooperation is more widespread than in most EU countries (with Scandinavian countries as the main exception), and technology transfer between science (which is of a very high standard in Switzerland) and industry works well (Arvanitis et al., 2008). Moreover there are some important clusters of knowledge-intensive industries such as pharmaceuticals–biotechnology–chemicals, banking–insurance and scientific instruments. I conclude that, in the Swiss case, indirect home-country effects of foreign R&D (knowledge spillovers) are likely to add substantially to the positive direct home-country effects.

Notwithstanding this positive assessment, policy may support the Swiss economy to capitalize even more on foreign R&D activities. The aim of such a policy basically should be to secure the attractiveness of Switzerland as a location for R&D-intensive headquarters of firms pursuing an active foreign R&D strategy, and to facilitate knowledge spillovers from headquarters companies to other domestic firms.

There is a wide range of policies which may contribute to reaching these objectives. Without making a claim to be complete, I propose five lines of action:

- Measures to increase the insufficient domestic supply of highly qualified labour, which is no higher than the Organisation for Economic Co-operation and Development (OECD) average. The intensive use of human capital in the Swiss economy is highly dependent on immigration and the inflow of cross-border workers, which in a long-run perspective is not feasible. Therefore, tertiary education must have top priority in public spending. Moreover, it is necessary to promote the labour market participation of women (investment in the social infrastructure) and to mobilize the untapped intellectual potential of the large number of foreign children living in Switzerland (integration policy).
- It is necessary to maintain the high standard of university research, in particular in science and engineering, and to foster new frontier research (science policy).
- Policy should promote the usage of the results of science in the business sector; favourable intellectual property rights (IPR) regulations; avoiding a too restrictive regulatory framework for the application of fundamentally new technologies such as biotechnology and

nanotechnology; promoting science–industry cooperation; providing an environment conducive to start-ups in high-tech industries; and so on.

- Strengthening the linkages between the domestic MNEs and other local companies by means of cluster-oriented policies ('embeddedness').
- Finally, general policy measures to make Switzerland an even more attractive location for doing business (for example low, incentive-oriented taxation, deregulation of markets, and so on).

These measures are part of a framework-oriented policy design rather than of a more interventionist concept.

NOTES

1. For some early evidence see Ronstadt (1978).
2. Some indication of the evolution of R&D activities of foreign affiliates from product adaptation for the local market to product development for other markets is already documented in Håkanson (1981).
3. In the following, when commenting on the available evidence, I refer to the survey of these authors; I thus refrain, with some exceptions, from citing other references.
4. The comparisons with the EU countries are based on the results of the most recent Community Innovation Survey (CIS 4) and the Swiss Innovation Survey 2005 (see Arvanitis et al., 2007).

REFERENCES

Arvanitis, S., J. von Arx, H. Hollenstein and N. Sydow (2004), *Innovationsaktivitäten in der Schweizer Wirtschaft. Eine Analyse der Innovationserhebung 2002*, Bern: Staatssekretariat für Wirtschaft.

Arvanitis, S. and H. Hollenstein (1998), 'Firm performance, innovation, and technological spillovers: a cross-section analysis with Swiss firm data', in G. Eliasson, C. Green and C.R. McCann (eds), *Microfoundations of Economic Growth: A Schumpeterian Perspective*, Ann Arbor, Michigan: University of Michigan Press, pp. 271–84.

Arvanitis, S. and H. Hollenstein (2001), 'Technologiestandort Schweiz im Zuge der Globalisierung. Eine explorative Analyse der F&E-Aktivitäten schweizerischer Industrieunternehmen im Ausland', *Schweizerische Zeitschrift für Volkswirtschaft und Statistik*, **137**, 129–48.

Arvanitis, S. and H. Hollenstein (2007), 'Determinants of Swiss firms' R&D activities at foreign locations: an empirical analysis based on firm-level data', in G.R.G. Benito and H.R. Greve (eds), *Progress in International Business Research*, Vol. 1, Amsterdam: Elsevier, pp. 61–90.

Arvanitis, S., H. Hollenstein, U. Kubli, N. Sydow and M. Wörter (2007),

Innovationsaktivitäten in der Schweizer Wirtschaft. Eine Analyse der Innovationserhebung 2005, Bern: Staatssekretariat für Wirtschaft.

Arvanitis, S., N. Sydow and M. Woerter (2008), 'Is there any impact of university–industry knowledge transfer on innovation and productivity? An empirical analysis based on Swiss firm data', *Review of Industrial Organization*, **32**, 77–94.

Buckley, P.J. and M.C. Casson (1985), *The Economic Theory of the Multinational Enterprise*, London: Macmillan.

Cantwell, J. (1995), 'The globalisation of technology: what remains of the product cycle model?', *Cambridge Journal of Economics*, **19** (1), 155–74.

Cantwell, J. and R. Narula (2001), 'The eclectic paradigm in the global economy', *International Journal of the Economics of Business*, **8** (2), 155–72.

Cantwell, J. and L. Piscitello (2005), 'Recent location of foreign-owned research and development activities by large multinational corporations in the European regions: the role of spillovers and externalities', *Regional Studies*, **39** (1), 1–16.

Cohen, W.M. (1995), 'Empirical studies of innovative activity', in P. Stoneman (ed.), *Handbook of the Economics of Innovation and Technological Change*, Oxford and Cambridge, MA: Basil Blackwell, pp. 182–264.

Dunning, J.H. (1994), 'Multinational enterprises and the globalization of innovatory capacity', *Research Policy*, **23** (1), 67–88.

Dunning, J.H. (2000), 'The eclectic paradigm as an envelope for economic and business theories of MNE activity', *International Business Review*, **9** (2), 163–90.

Florida, R. (1997), 'The globalization of R&D: results of a survey of foreign-affiliated R&D laboratories in the USA', *Research Policy*, **26** (1), 85–103.

Frost, T.S. (2001), 'The geographic sources of foreign subsidiaries' innovations', *Strategic Management Journal*, **22** (2), 101–23.

Granstrand, O., L. Håkanson and S. Sjölander (1993), 'Internationalization of R&D: a survey of some recent research', *Research Policy*, **22** (5/6), 413–30.

Haagedoorn, J. (1996), 'Trends and patterns in strategic technology partnering since the early seventies', *Review of Industrial Organization*, **11** (5), 601–16.

Håkanson, L. (1981), 'Organization and evolution of foreign R&D in Swedish multinationals', *Geografiska Annaler. Series B, Human Geography*, **63** (1), 47–56.

Håkanson, L. and R. Nobel (1993), 'Foreign research and development in Swedish multinationals', *Research Policy*, **22** (5–6), 373–96.

Hollenstein, H. (2005), 'Determinants of international activities: are SMEs different? An empirical analysis based on Swiss survey data', *Small Business Economics*, **24** (5), 431–50.

Hollenstein, H. (2006), 'Strategies pursued by Swiss firms in investing in R&D at foreign locations: an empirical analysis based on firm-level data', KOF Working Paper No. 154, KOF Swiss Economic Institute, Zurich.

Kuemmerle, W. (1999), 'The drivers of foreign direct investment into research and development: an empirical investigation', *Journal of International Business Studies*, **30** (1), 1–24.

Le Bas, C. and C. Sierra (2002), 'Location versus home country advantages in R&D activities: some further results on multinationals' locational strategies', *Research Policy*, **31** (4), 589–609.

Manly, B.F.J. (1986), *Multivariate Statistical Methods: A Primer*, London: Chapman & Hall.

Mundell, R.A. (1957), 'International trade and factor mobility', *American Economic Review*, **47** (3), 321–47.

Narula, R. and A. Zanfei (2005), 'Globalization and innovation: the role of multinational enterprises', in J. Fagerberg, D.C. Mowery and R.E. Nelson (eds), *The Oxford Handbook of Innovation*, Oxford: Oxford University Press, pp. 318–47.

OECD (1998), *Internationalisation of Industrial R&D: Patterns and Trends*, Paris: OECD Publishing.

OECD (2007), *OECD Science, Technology and Industry Scoreboard 2007. Innovation and Performance in the Global Economy*, Paris: OECD Publishing.

Patel, P. and M. Vega (1999), 'Patterns of internationalization of corporate technology: location vs. home country advantages', *Research Policy*, **28** (2–3), 145–55.

Pearce, R.D. (1992), 'World product mandates and MNE specialization', *Scandinavian International Business Review*, **1** (2), 38–58.

Pearce, R.D. (1999), 'Decentralised R&D and strategic competitiveness: globalised approaches to generation and use of technology in multinational enterprises (MNEs)', *Research Policy*, **28** (2), 157–78.

Pearce, R.D. and M. Papanastassiou (1999), 'Overseas R&D and the strategic evolution of MNEs: evidence from laboratories in the UK', *Research Policy*, **28** (1), 23–41.

Ronstadt, R.C. (1978), 'International R&D: the establishment and evolution of research and development abroad by seven US multinationals', *Journal of International Business Studies*, **9** (1), 7–28.

Rubin, D.B. (1987), *Multiple Imputation for Nonresponse in Surveys*, New York: John Wiley & Sons.

Teece, D.J. and I. Pisano (1998), 'The dynamic capabilities of firms', in G. Dosi, D.J. Teece and J. Chytry (eds), *Technology, Organisation, and Competitiveness. Perspectives on Industrial and Corporate Change*, Oxford: Oxford University Press, pp. 193–212.

Vernon, R. (1966), 'International investment and international trade in the product cycle', *Quarterly Journal of Economics*, **80** (2), 190–207.

Veugelers, R., B. Dachs, S. Mahroum, B. Nones, A. Schibany and R. Falk (2005), 'Internationalisation of R&D: trends, issues and implications for S&T policies: a review of the literature', Background Report Presented at the Forum on the Internationalisation of R&D, 29–30 March, Brussels.

20. Small and medium-sized enterprises: the promotion of R&D and innovation behaviour in Switzerland

Beat Hotz-Hart

Switzerland consistently holds a leading position in international comparisons of innovation performance of the economy. According to several international surveys, including the innovation scoreboard of the European Union (EU) or the global competitiveness report of the World Economic Forum, Switzerland is amongst the innovation leaders together with Sweden and Finland.

Some particular characteristics which distinguish Switzerland from other countries might help to explain this success:

- The share of expenditure on research and development (R&D) of gross domestic product (GDP) is high: 2.9 per cent. This is first and foremost because of the high engagement of private companies in R&D such as Novartis and Hoffmann-LaRoche; their coverage of more than 70 per cent of total R&D funding is unique in international comparison. And there is hardly any military spending on R&D at all.
- R&D activities of the Swiss economy are highly internationalized with more than half located abroad in the world's most highly regarded research centres.
- Private companies get no public subsidies or funding for their R&D from public authorities whatsoever. This is in contrast to the practice of most other countries and the EU promotion of R&D.
- The relatively small amount of public support for R&D is given exclusively to public institutions such as universities, including universities of applied science, and is granted according to the bottom-up principle. There are (almost) no politically chosen and targeted promotion areas of R&D activities by public funds. If there are any focal points, they develop within the bottom-up mechanism.

- Public innovation policy strongly relies on the excellence of Swiss universities including the federal institutes of technology and universities of applied science in order to provide the labour market with well-trained talent and be attractive partners for companies, enabling knowledge and technology transfer.

All these characteristics mean that the allocation of R&D resources is directed according to market forces and competition amongst companies to a larger extent than in any other economy and not according to political priorities. Risks are taken by the units responsible for R&D resources. The innovative behaviour in companies is mainly a consequence of market incentives. The positive impact of these characteristics is strengthened by the small size of the country and a good mix of small and large companies.

Differences within R&D and innovation activities can be identified according to firm size (Arvanitis et al., 2007, p. 33):

- The larger the size of a company, the larger the share of those companies that are innovative. Looking at companies in different size classes, the share of innovative companies within a class is higher the larger the size class. Larger companies are more likely to be innovative. On average, companies in the service sector are less innovative than those in the industrial sector.
- The propensity of a company to invest in R&D activities depends to a much larger extant on company size than its propensity to innovate.
- The larger the company, the more likely it is that it might cooperate with a university (Arvanitis et al., 2005, p. 21).

Nonetheless, Swiss small and medium-sized enterprises (SMEs) are more innovative than the international average:

- Most SMEs pursue their own innovation strategy. Assessed according to the share of turnover a SME has with its main contractors, Swiss companies are independent to a larger extent than the SMEs for example in Japan. They pursue their own business and innovation strategy.
- They pursue incremental innovations more often than radical ones. And these focus mainly on rationalization.
- Radical innovations are realized mainly by start-up companies. In cases of success they are often taken over by larger companies.

Aspects of financing of innovation are of particular interest. Evidence can be found in the surveys of the Swiss Institute for Business Cycle

Research, Swiss Federal Institute of Technology, Zurich (KOF ETHZ) (Arvanitis et al., 2007, p. 69). The major restrictions on all companies participating in the survey are costs, risks and amortization. These restrictions are more relevant for small than for larger firms. Small firms are restricted in a more substantial way by financial bottlenecks – including tax loads – than larger firms.

- In 2005 small firms with fewer than 50 employees saw their major restriction on R&D activities resulting from a lack of internal (30.6 per cent of all answers) and external (24.9 per cent) financial resources and from a high tax load. This category covers 98 per cent of Swiss companies.
- Medium-sized companies (from 50 to 499 employees) saw the lack of R&D personnel and qualified collaborators to be as restrictive as the scarcity of financial resources.
- For large companies, financial resources for R&D activities were nearly irrelevant (respectively 6.8 per cent and 5.8 per cent for lack of internal for lack of external financial resources). Major restrictions for them were costs, risks and the acceptance of new technologies.

In the 1990s restrictions on innovation activities became less and less influential. This was particularly the case with respect to aspects such as costs and risks, scarcity of qualified labour and state regulations. The framework conditions for innovation generally improved. Only financial bottlenecks restricted innovation activities increasingly up to the mid-1990s. Since then they have come to be seen as the second most important disadvantage for innovations after the cost factor.

With respect to the financing of innovation activities, self-financing is a problem for 30 per cent of all companies which replied to the survey. It is more relevant than debt financing which is stated by 25 per cent. Self-financing is a major problem particularly for SMEs, and amongst them specially for SMEs in the machine and apparel sectors.

Swiss companies intend to finance R&D whenever possible with free cash flow (cash flow sensitivity >0). It is within the tradition of Swiss companies that they want to avoid financial dependency if possible. However, that makes their innovation activities more dependent on the business cycle and therefore more cyclical. This can be documented with the time series from innovation tests.

A survey of 1998 indicates some particular problems of financing the creation of new companies (Arvanitis and Marmet, 2001, p. 124): 27.7 per cent of all new companies reviewed had difficulties with self-financing. But only 10.5 per cent saw a major problem for the creation of the new company in a lack of venture capital, while 23 per cent saw a problem in the conditions of debt-financing a major restriction on the foundation. New firms in fast-growing sectors have fewer difficulties in obtaining debt financing than do new companies in traditional sectors, which illustrates the behaviour of investors.

Next we will take a closer look at the role of institutional investors with respect to the R&D activities and innovative behaviour of Swiss companies. In Switzerland, institutional investors such as pension funds are a major economic factor because of their enormous amount of assets; in 2006 Swiss pension funds managed a portfolio of CHF 581 billion, that is, 1.2 times the GDP. Common stocks play a minor role in these portfolios: 12 per cent Swiss shares, 16.9 per cent foreign shares. These investments are made with the primary purpose of an adequate return, without any focus on innovation and its promotion. Bonds and investments in real estate dominate. Their investment in new ventures, start-up companies or particularly innovation active firms is marginal. With some few exceptions, they do not take on any managerial decision rights based on their investments. The reasons for this are associated with institutional characteristics of the governance structure of pension funds: employees are obliged to pay into a particular fund allocated by their employer and have no right to choose another fund, for example, according to its return on investment. Therefore, there is no competition between funds for members. Federal law determines the room for manoeuvre for the major categories of assets and therefore restricts the investment policy of the funds. Their policy is generally conservative.

20.1 COMMENTS ON POLICY

- In the case of promotion of R&D, now and in the future, Swiss authorities do not pay any subsidies directly to private companies. The rules concerning intellectual property rights with respect to results from R&D efforts where public money is involved are to a large extent designed in the interest of private companies. Rules similar to the Bayh–Dole Act of the USA have been rejected.
- The framework conditions for start-ups could be improved further. Reforms in order to support innovation and start-up companies may be more possible and are discussed in fiscal policy: for example leaner rules and a reduction of the tax load on options for managers and employees. This could help to ease problems of financial liquidity for young companies. Another improvement could be a simplification of the rules of value added tax.

- There are no particular policy measures in order to activate the assets of pension funds for start-up projects. The few existing measures to give tax incentives for private funds to invest in start-up projects have had no substantial impact. What is needed is better rules for the corporate governance of pension funds which support and make their asset management more professional and modern and increase competition. Although there are ideas and proposals in this respect, reforms develop only slowly and gradually.
- In order to promote innovative activities, in Switzerland public procurement plays almost no role at all. Public procurement is controlled by policy agents. And politicians do not take risks, they are highly risk-averse.
- The Innovation Promotion Agency CTI runs a federal programme to give coaching support for start-up projects: CTI Start-up and CTI Invest. Start-up projects can benefit from services paid by the federal programme, for example advice for any kind of legal affairs such as the protection of intellectual property or licensing, further development of the technology used, market research and/or improving the business plan of the project. Projects which achieve a certain quality standard according to a jury get the chance to be presented to a community of venture capitalists: CTI Invest. Members of CTI Invest have agreed to invest a minimum amount (CHF 0.5 million) over the years in projects which are presented in that context. This initiative reduces the information and transaction costs of potential investors, and therefore increases the chance of a project obtaining financing. There is a kind of public–private partnership: the public authorities help to build up the project and to improve its quality; the private side are the investors who allocate seed and venture capital.

This chapter has outlined some particularities of the Swiss innovation system. They go together with a high innovation performance of the Swiss economy. This shows that there is not only one way, but different ways for success in the international innovation race.

REFERENCES

Arvanitis, S. and D. Marmet (2001), *Unternehmensgründungen in der schweizerischen Wirtschaft: Studie im Auf trag des Staatssekreteriats für Wirtschaft*, Bern: Seco–Staatssekreteriat für Wirtschaft.

Arvanitis, S., U. Kubli, N. Sydow and M. Wörter (2005), 'Knowledge and technology transfer (KTT) activities between universities and firms in Switzerland: the main facts. An empirical analysis based on firm-level data', Working Papers No. 115.

Arvanitis, S., H. Hollenstein, U. Kubli, N. Sydow and M. Wörter (2007), 'Innovationsaktivitäten in der Schweizer Wirtschaft. Eine Analyse der Ergebnisse der Innovationserhebung 2005', Strukturberichterstattung Nr. 34, Bern.

PART VI

Technology Policy in the European Union

21. Nature of the European technology gap: creative destruction or industrial policy?[1]

David Encaoua

21.1 INTRODUCTION

In the technology race, can Europe catch up with its competitors, in particular the US? This is a central question on the European agenda, and the response depends on the diagnosis of the sources and the nature of the technology gap. First, let us recall why the technology gap poses an important question. Economic welfare, measured at first glance by per capita gross national product (GNP) is the product of two constituents: average productivity of labor and the employment rate among the working age population.[2] In the last ten years (1995–2005), Europe has faced a two-sided problem: on the one hand, Europe is behind the US in its labor productivity and employment rate; and on the other, it has witnessed growth in only one of these constituents of economic well-being. Labor productivity growth has been obtained at the expense of employment rate, or the inverse. The consequent slowdown in European hourly productivity growth has awakened fears that the European social model is unsustainable. Of course there is heterogeneity in growth trajectories across member countries, but particularly in eurozone countries and taken as a whole, they incite serious worry despite the grandiose objectives and expectations declared at the Lisbon Summit in 2000.

Among the most significant stylized facts is the now widely recognized downward shift in productivity growth in Europe in the middle of the 1990s. A period of technological divergence in which the productivity gap between Europe and the US widened began in 1995, following a long period of technological catch-up since World War II. This shift may be seen in basic statistics (Gordon, 2004). With respect to a base level of GNP per hour worked of 100 in the US, the mean among European countries increased from 44 in 1950 to 70 in 1973, 94 in 1995, then declined to 85 in 2003. Catch-up and divergence phases are also evident in annual productivity of labor per hour: higher in Europe from 1950 to 1973 (4.77 percent in Europe compared with 2.77 percent in the US), and from 1973 to 1995 (2.25 percent versus 1.48 percent), before inverting between 1995 and 2003 to arrive at a growth rate of 1.15 percent in the European Union (EU) versus 2.33 percent in the US.

Which structural policies would be most appropriate in Europe to reverse these trends? This is a difficult question but of critical interest. To simplify, we might say that two conceptions in the literature seem to give contradictory diagnoses.

The first (Dosi et al., 2006) highlights insufficiency of public funds dedicated to research and private investment in research and development (R&D) in Europe coupled with a weak position of European firms in global, oligopolistic markets. According to this view, the implications for economic policy are that Europe should increase public investment in human capital formation and research and embark on a voluntary industrial policy to reinforce leadership in large firms and to define priority areas for state intervention in innovation.

The other conception (Aghion, 2006; Encaoua and Guesnerie, 2006) emphasizes structural rigidities that prevent the process of 'creative destruction' from stimulating growth of the knowledge-based economy as the source of European weakness. These often disputed rigidities involve many issues including the labor market, the insufficient integration of the product markets, the under-realization of potential growth in services, the maintenance of underperforming university systems, a poor pairing of fundamental research and technological innovation and the insufficiently developed public–private partnership. The economic policy implications thus consist of a set of complementary structural remedies to alleviate these rigidities (Sapir et al., 2004; Kok, 2004).

A large part of the literature that has developed around the observed shift in productivity growth in the mid-1990s underlines the difference between structural conditions necessary for 'catch-up' versus for 'leapfrogging'. One important conclusion drawn from this literature affirms that even if the structural conditions necessary for catch-up were present collectively in the first phase, in the second, those needed for creation, innovation, and leadership in a knowledge economy were absent in Europe while they worked to significant effect in the US.

To move from these observations to economic policy recommendations is difficult for at least three reasons. First, because there is a great deal of heterogeneity not only across countries within the European Union, but also across sectors within a given country, as well as across firms within a given sector. Accounting for the nature of this heterogeneity would seem to be a preliminary requirement to understand the nature of the technological gap. Second, structural economic policies in the research and innovation arena are complex, numerous and complementary. Their complementarity, a necessary condition to their success, is difficult to establish (Aghion et al., 2006). The final difficulty lies in the choice of how to implement these structural policies. Should policies and their implementation be decentralized and left to the initiative of individual member countries, or should they be centralized at the level of the EU or at least coordinated between the European countries of the eurozone? After all, the heterogeneity among these countries could prevent successful coordination of an integrated program.

In short, moving from a European single market to a European knowledge economy is an enormous challenge. To treat these questions, I start with two methodological detours that allow some refinement of the technology gap diagnosis.

In the first detour, I turn attention toward studies based on disaggregated sectoral data. The sectoral decomposition obtained from two different taxonomies sheds light on some aspects of the productivity gap diagnosis. The first sectoral decomposition is based on the production or the use of information and communication technologies (ICT). It allows a first assessment of the strengths and weaknesses of the European industries according to the intensity of their production or their usage of ICT. The second taxonomy is based on the nature of the technological regimes, built according to Pavitt's classification (1984). This taxonomy yields insight into whether the strengths of Europe are concentrated in traditional manufacturing sectors in which innovation results from the adoption of innovative equipment, while its weaknesses are concentrated in sectors in which internal R&D underlies the production of new goods and services. These questions are discussed in section 21.2.

In the second detour, I examine how the characteristics of industrial dynamics differ on the two sides of the Atlantic. In the Schumpeterian analysis of economic growth, industrial dynamics are at the heart of the 'creative destruction' process and thus the source of growth. The outcome of this process in the industrial dynamics is obtained by using comparisons performed on longitudinal firm-level data. These comparisons try to evaluate to what extent variations in labor productivity derive from demographic movements that affect the population of firms. Some of these variations are internal to incumbent firms, while others consist in inter-firm movements that result in reallocation of market shares as well as new entry and exit of firms. This approach is quite demanding in terms of the firm-level time series needed. As a result, there are few comparative studies, but the few that are available do yield results that are of enough interest to merit making this methodological detour. I present these results in section 21.3.

In terms of the diagnosis of the nature of the technology gap revealed in the two previous detours, I return to the question of structural policy, particularly as informed by the two conceptions mentioned above. Besides the nature of the appropriate structural policies, I focus on two questions: the complementarity between these policies, and the appropriate implementation mechanisms. The identification of the complementarity is essential for two reasons: first, because no single isolated policy can be sufficient in a knowledge economy; and second, because the objective of these policy reforms is itself multidimensional, in particular with respect to productivity and the employment rate. The question of how to implement policies is just as crucial. Here there is conflict between proponents of centralized coordination and those who favor loose coordination, devolved to the member countries. In the revised version of the Lisbon Agenda introduced in 2005, the European Council expressed support for the second option, leaving aside the recommendations of Kok's report (2004). Will this option succeed in correcting the failure of the initial version of the Lisbon Agenda? I discuss these different questions in section 21.4.

21.2 THE SECTORAL LOCUS OF THE TECHNOLOGY GAP: A TAXONOMY APPROACH

I begin my inquiry by looking for the sectoral locus of the technology gap and its dynamics. The contrast in labor productivity growth between the EU and the US hides important differences across sectors and time. In some sectors, the US holds a long-established leading edge, while in others, US leadership is only the result of recent acceleration there and/or recent deceleration in the EU.

Analyzing the sectoral specificities of the labor productivity growth accelerations and decelerations requires some disaggregated evidence. Among different studies, a recent analysis, commissioned by the Enterprise Directorate General of the European Commission and directed by O'Mahony and van Ark (2003) compares labor productivity growth in the US and the EU-15 at a disaggregated sectoral level. The overall data cover 56 sectors over the period 1979–2001, including details on output, number of hours worked, and labour productivity levels and growth rates in each sector for all 15 EU countries and the US.[3] Some interesting industrial regroupments, according to different taxonomies, are examined.

The first taxonomy is based on information and communication technologies (ICT). Sectors are divided into ICT-producing, ICT-using and non-ICT sectors, with a distinction in each group between manufacturing and services. This taxonomy is important because it is often claimed that the difference between the EU and the US is largely explained by their different patterns in their production and use of ICT.

The second taxonomy (innovation) is based on Pavitt's classification (1984). This classification distinguishes four groups of industries, according to the channels through which innovation takes place. The first group contains sectors in which innovations are mainly embodied in equipment goods ('supplier-dominated industries'). The second group includes sectors where innovation is based on internal R&D that is strongly oriented towards process innovations ('scale-intensive industries'). The third group consists of sectors in which innovation is mainly oriented toward quality improvement rather than cost reduction ('specialized suppliers'). The last group includes sectors in which the main sources of technology derive from internal R&D based on basic knowledge ('science-based industries'). For each group, a distinction is made according to whether the industry is a supplier of goods or services.[4]

21.2.1 Labor Productivity Growth According to the ICT Taxonomy

The results reported in Table 21.1 lead to three observations. First, there has been no productivity revival in the sectors that are neither ICT-producing nor ICT-using products (row 3, decomposed in rows 3a and 3b). The EU had a starting advantage in terms of productivity in non-ICT manufacturing sectors (row 3a) but there has been a dramatic deceleration

Table 21.1 Annual labor productivity growth in industries according to the ICT taxonomy

Annual labor productivity growth	1979–90		1990–95		1995–2001	
	EU	US	EU	US	EU	US
Total economy	2.2	1.3	2.3	1.1	1.7	2.2
1. ICT-producing sectors	7.2	8.7	5.9	8.1	7.5	10.0
1.a Manufacturing	12.5	16.6	8.4	16.1	11.9	23.7
1.b Services	4.4	2.4	4.8	2.4	5.9	1.8
2. ICT-using sectors	2.2	1.2	2.0	1.2	1.9	4.7
2.a Manufacturing	2.4	0.5	2.4	–0.6	1.8	0.4
2.b Services	2.1	1.4	1.8	1.6	1.8	5.3
3. Non-ICT sectors	1.8	0.5	2.1	0.3	1.0	–0.2
3.a Manufacturing	3.0	2.1	3.6	2.7	1.6	0.3
3.b Services	0.6	–0.2	1.2	–0.5	0.5	–0.3

Source: O'Mahony and van Ark (2003).

in the European labor productivity growth from a rate of 3.6 percent per year during the period (1990–95) to a rate of 1.6 percent per year in the period 1995–2001. These sectors represent the core of the Eureopan economy (their value added represents more than 63 percent of the EU-15 total economy). They include a large variety of traditional industries such as motor vehicles, chemicals, oil refining, food, drink and tobacco.

Similar cross-country and dynamic patterns are observed in the category of non-ICT services (row 3.b). The labor productivity growth rate is still higher in the EU-15, but it also exhibits a significant deceleration over time. This group includes a heterogeneous list of sectors such as sale and maintenance of motor vehicles, hotels and catering, air transport, and travel agencies.

The second observation is that labor productivity growth in ICT-producing manufacturing industries (row 1.a) is the highest compared to the other groups, both in the US and the EU. This observation confirms the important role of ICT in productivity growth. The dynamics are similar in the US and the EU-15, but in the US the initial level was higher and the growth path accelerated in the last period. This category includes different high-tech sectors such as office machinery, electronic valves and tubes, telecommunication equipment, radio and television receivers, and scientific instruments.

In contrast, the group of ICT-producing services (row 1.b) that includes software, computer and related services, exhibits higher growth rates in the EU during the three periods. It is interesting to note that despite the absence of software protection by a patent in Europe, the software industry is the only ICT service for which the EU outperforms the US. The value added of this ICT producing services group represents no more than 5 percent of the total value added in the EU-15.

Third, the group of ICT-using service sectors (row 2.b) is the locus of a very sharp labor productivity acceleration in the US from 1995 (5.3 percent per year), that is not matched by the EU-15 (1.8 percent per year). This finding confirms that the gap in ICT-using services explains a large part of the overall technological gap between the EU-15 and the US. A large part of the recent acceleration in US labor productivity since 1995 is accounted for by a small number of industries, including wholesale and retail trade (Doms et al., 2004) and financial securities, in which a large productivity premium appears in the US. The changes in the retail trade sector in the US have been analyzed extensively by Foster et al. (2005), to which we will return later.

21.2.2 Labor Productivity Growth According to Patterns of Innovation: Pavitt's Taxonomy

Pavitt's taxonomy, based on the innovation patterns previously described, leads to some interesting evidence, presented in Table 21.2. I begin by

Table 21.2 Annual labor productivity growth according to Pavitt's innovation taxonomy

Annual labor productivity growth Pavitt decomposition (Patterns of Innovation)	1979–90		1990–95		1995–2001	
	EU	US	EU	US	EU	US
A. Manufacturing Sectors						
A1 Supplier-dominated	3.1	1.8	2.7	0.3	1.9	1.8
A2 Scale-intensive	2.8	2.2	3.7	2.8	1.5	–0.3
A3 Specialized suppliers	5.8	8.7	5.4	9.7	5.5	14.5
A4 Science-based	4.0	3.1	4.3	2.4	2.9	1.1
B. Services Sectors						
B1 Supplier-dominated	2.8	2.2	3.0	2.0	3.9	6.7
B2 Specialized suppliers	1.0	0.3	0.6	0.1	0.9	–0.7
B3 Organizational innovation	2.3	0.4	2.5	1.1	1.7	1.5
B4 Client-led	0.5	1.3	1.3	1.2	0.3	4.0

Source: O'Mahony and van Ark (2003).

presenting the results obtained from the classification made in manufacturing sectors. In the group of 'supplier-dominated sectors' (row A1) which contains traditional industries that use embedded innovative equipment and are defined by cost-cutting technological trajectories, productivity growth rates have been higher in the EU than in the US during the three periods. But as these rates decline in the EU, productivity converges to the same value in the two continents. This group of industries, including construction, clothing, furniture, printing and publishing, and agriculture, represents around 10 percent of the total value added in each continent.

The group of 'scale-intensive sectors' (row A2) represents products that are price sensitive, belong to large-scale technological trajectories and assembly production, and in which in-house process innovations seek mainly to reduce cost. These include mining and quarrying, food, drink and tobacco, oil refining, motor vehicles, ship and boat building, and basic metals. In these sectors, the EU experienced higher levels of labor productivity growth than the US in all periods. Here, the recent trend is still largely in favor of Europe. The value added produced by these industries represents the same order of magnitude in both continents (around 10 percent).

The group of 'specialized suppliers' (row A3) consists of high-tech industries (mechanical engineering, office machinery, electronic valves and tubes, telecommunications equipment, scientific instruments, and so on) where in-house innovation is strong and due mainly to small and specialized firms developing technologies that are more oriented towards quality improvement than to cost reduction. Three observations arise from this group. First, the levels of productivity growth are highest in this group, in both the EU and the US. Second, the EU lags behind the US in each period and the gap is even greater after 1995. Third, the value added of this group of industries is particularly low in the EU (3 percent). Thus, evidence from this group points towards an insufficient number of innovative small and medium-sized enterprises (SMEs) in Europe. The diagnosis made here is consistent with the diagnosis made in the ICT-producing industries category because the specialized supply goods category is dominated by the same ICT-producing manufacturing firms. These two categories of industries, in which the superiority of the US is manifest, suggest that a structural policy in favor of innovative SMEs must be an important objective in the EU.

Finally, in the 'science-based innovation' category (row A4) which contains industries where the main technological improvements come from basic research in public laboratories and universities (for example chemicals, biotechnology, electronics, radio and television receivers), we note surprisingly that the EU has experienced higher labor productivity growth than the US during the three periods. However, there has been a slowdown in recent productivity growth in the EU, leading to some convergence across the two continents. We note also that the value added of this category represents a small share of the total economy in Europe (around 3 percent).

Hence, in manufacturing, the EU appears to have some productive advantage in the production of traditional manufacturing goods, except in the 'specialized supply' category, where the role of very innovative SMEs is crucial. Moreover, in the three other categories where the EU had some initial advantage over the US, there has been a recent slowdown in European productivity growth, except in the non-ICT industries where the EU maintains some advance. This raises the general question of whether traditional manufacturing industries may continue to retain their role of 'powerhouse' of the European economy (O'Mahony and van Ark, 2003).

I turn now to innovation patterns in services from which I retain two observations. The first concerns the category of 'supplier-dominated services' (row B1). This category regroups all services in which there is little scope for suppliers to influence directly the technological innovative pattern that comes mainly from upstream manufacturers (hardware and software). Suppliers of these services must adopt organizational changes in order to offer a higher-quality service (for example retail trade, repair of personal and household goods, and communications). The recent acceleration of the labor productivity growth in the US in these services is rather impressive (6.7 percent per year) compared to that in the EU-15 (3.9 percent). It confirms the previous finding that globally, the productivity gap between the US and the EU comes largely from the retail trade sector which dominates this category of services. We note also that this category of services represents more than 9 percent of the US total value added and only 7.5 percent of the EU-15 value added. These findings give some credibility to the emphasis of the European Commission on the services liberalization process.

The second result concerns the so-called 'client-led innovation services' group (row B4) in which suppliers innovate on the basis of a specific need expressed by their clients. A supplier of a service in this category innovates according to the needs of specific segments of the mass market. This category includes a heterogeneous list of sectors, such as wholesale trade, hotels and catering, travel agencies, financial intermediaries, and household services. In this category, the US has recently experienced an impressive labor productivity growth rate (4 percent per year since 1995) while globally the performance in the EU has been decelerating.[5] The value added of this category is rather high (around 17 percent in both continents).

Finally, in the two remaining categories, 'specialized suppliers services' (row B2) and 'organizational innovative services' (row B3), the EU and the US are more or less even, but the labor productivity growth rate is slightly declining in the EU, while performance has strongly improved in the US, particularly in banking.

The evidence on productivity growth in services, that shows a strong acceleration of US productivity growth in 'supplier-based services' (row B1), dominated by retail trade, and in 'client-led services' (row B4) dominated by wholesale trade, suggests that a better exploitation of potential productivity gains depends both on the success of the services liberalization process and on country member characteristics.

21.3 THE TECHNOLOGY GAP IN TERMS OF THE CREATIVE DESTRUCTION PROCESS

I turn now to the evidence concerning the microeconomic process of creative destruction. Many empirical studies, using longitudinal firm-level data, provide interesting results on industry changes that occur through different channels including variation within firms' activity, resource reallocation between firms, entry of new firms and exit of old ones. These studies lead to the general conclusion that the dynamic efficiency of an economy in dealing with the churning process is important not only for the turnover rate and productivity growth but also for the dynamics of product and labor markets (Caves, 1998; Ahn, 2000; Bartelsman and Doms, 2000; Foster et al., 2005; Bartelsman et al., 2004). Some stylized facts emerge concerning the evolution of an industrial structure over time, its effects on the labor productivity growth and on the employment variation.

First, all industries are characterized by a skewed distribution of firms according to their size as measured by their employment. This distribution is the result of the churning process induced by market reallocation, entry, exit and turnover. Second, the churning process has substantial effects on labor productivity because a large proportion of productivity growth is accounted for by output and input reallocations from less productive firms to more productive firms. Entry and exit also have important roles in labor productivity variations. Third, although precise cross-country comparisons remain difficult, preliminary results suggest that the industries and/or the countries where the churning process is inhibited exhibit lower productivity levels and employment rates. Fourth, distortions in industry dynamics have diverse origins: regulation and public policy, business environment and labor market institutions. Whatever their origin, these distortions have important implications in the long run that are impossible to capture at the aggregate level.

Some studies suggest also that the intensity of the churning process differs across industries and countries. Most of studies proceed on a country-by-country basis, using mostly firm-level data for the US. However, there are now some studies that achieve international comparisons. One such study by Bartelsman et al. (2004), combines firm-level longitudinal data for 24 countries (ten industrial economies, five central and Eastern European economies and nine emerging economies in Latin America and East Asia) over the period 1990–2000. Some sources of firm heterogeneity in terms of churning and its consequences for productivity levels and growth rates persist in the manufacturing sector, which is the most exposed sector to international competition. The results can be presented under four headings:

- Firm demography.
- Structural variations: assessment of entry, exit and turnover.
- Labor productivity variations across countries: the creative destruction process.
- Labor productivity variations across sectors.

21.3.1 Firm Demography

Firm demography is captured through both the firm size distribution and movements that affect the variation of this distribution over time.

One of the most robust results obtained in many empirical studies is that, in each industry, firms' size distribution is very skewed, but skewness varies across countries. While the number of small firms is generally very large in each country, the aggregate share of employment accounted for by small firms differs significantly across countries. The international comparisons in Bartelsman et al. (2004) confirm this result. Firms with fewer than 20 employees represent a substantial proportion of the overall population of the firms in the manufacturing industry (between 72 percent and 89 percent across countries). However, the weight of these small firms in terms of employment differs largely across countries, ranging from 5 percent (in some of the transition economies still dominated by large public firms) to 31 percent (in Nordic countries like Denmark). Across countries, micro units with less than 20 employees in manufacturing account for about 80 percent of the firm population on average, but their share in total employment has a very large spread across countries. For instance, firms in the French manufacturing industry with less than 20 employees represent more than 78 percent of the overall number of firms and their employment share is around 20 percent, whereas in the US manufacturing sector, firms with less than 20 employees represent less than 73 percent of the overall number of manufacturing firms and their employment share is less than 7 percent. The same orders of magnitude appear when one compares the US with other European countries such as Italy, Germany and UK.

These findings are summarized in the following statement. Very small firms are more numerous in the European manufacturing sector than in American industry and their share in terms of employment is much more important in Europe. The EU tends to have a marginally greater concentration than the US of employment inside very small firms.

Sectoral specialization or invariance across industries?

The previous finding may have two origins. It may be either the consequence of some sectoral specialization in the European economy or it may occur within each sector. The first alternative would mean that European countries are more oriented towards industries with a smaller efficient scale, while the second alternative would mean that there is no sectoral bias in the sense that the average size is smaller in each European manufacturing sector with respect to the corresponding American sector.

To resolve this issue, Bartelsman et al. decompose the difference between the average size $\bar{s}_j$ of the manufacturing firms in country j and the overall mean $\bar{s}$ across all the countries as the sum of three terms:

$$\bar{s}_j - \bar{s} = \sum_i (w_{ij} - \bar{w}_i)\bar{s}_i + \sum_i (s_{ij} - \bar{s}_i)w_{ij} + \sum_i (s_{ij} - \bar{s}_i)\,(w_{ij} - \bar{w}_i)$$

$$= \Delta_w + \Delta_s + \Delta_{ws} \qquad (21.1)$$

The weighted average firm size in manufacturing in country j is defined by $\bar{s}_j = \Sigma_i w_{ij} s_{ij}$ where w_{ij} is the employment share of the subsector i in country j and s_{ij} is the average firm size in subsector i with respect to the total number of manufacturing firms in country j. The overall weighted mean size in manufacturing across countries is equal to $\bar{s} = \Sigma_i \overline{w}_i \bar{s}_i$ where $\overline{w}_i$ is the employment share of sub-sector i in the manufacturing industry over all countries and $\bar{s}_i$ is the average size of the firms in subsector i.

In this decomposition, the first term, $\Delta_w = \Sigma_i (w_{ij} - \overline{w}_i)\, \bar{s}_i$ accounts for differences in the sectoral composition of firms, the second term, $\Delta_s = \Sigma_i (s_{ij} - \bar{s}_i) w_{ij}$ accounts for cross-country differences in firm size within each sector, and the third term $\Delta_w = \Sigma_i (s_{ij} - \bar{s}_i)\ (w_{ij} - \overline{w}_i)$ is a covariance term which indicates whether size and sectoral composition deviate from the benchmark in the same direction or in opposite directions.

The results of this decomposition are summarized in Table 21.3, giving the contributions coming from differences in the sectoral composition, from differences in average firm size inside each sector, or from the interactive term, for some selected countries. The last column (Total) is the sum of the three terms and represents the percentage deviation of average size from the cross-country average.

Observations from Table 21.3 can be summarized as follows. Within-sector size differences make the largest contribution to explaining differences in overall firm size across countries: US firms have a larger size in each sector. This confirms the idea that the large American market serves to promote larger firms. In contrast, the firms in European countries do not seem to benefit to the same extent from the European internal market, despite the fact that the European market has roughly the same size as the US market. In other words, the internal market effect is weaker in Europe than in the US.

Table 21.3 Components of firm size distribution in manufacturing across countries

Country	Sectoral contribution	Within contribution	Interactive contribution	Total
	Δw	Δs	Δws	
France	0.08	–0.05	–0.05	–0.02
UK	–0.01	–0.02	–0.03	–0.06
Canada	0.01	0.03	–0.02	0.01
US	0.00	0.42	–0.07	0.34

Source: Bartelsman et al. (2004).

We note however that the sectoral composition effect plays a non-negligible role in some countries, as in France where the manufacturing industry is more oriented towards sectors in which average size is larger. Finally, we note that the sectoral composition effect and the within-sector effects are not highly correlated.

Dispersion of firm size and cross-country differences

It is interesting to analyze the dispersion of firm size within each sector of the economy in order to understand cross-country differences. The coefficient of variation of firm size, normalized by the overall cross-country coefficient of variation delivers an interesting information. If technological factors were the main explanation of the firm size heterogeneity across countries, the value of the normalized coefficient of variation should be concentrated around one. If, on the contrary, the size differences were explained by national factors inducing a specific bias within sectors, the value of the normalized coefficient of variation should be different from one. Table 21.4 delivers interesting insights.

These results may be summarized. Within each sector of the manufacturing industry, industrialized countries have greater dispersion in firm size than other countries. Among the industrialized countries, the United States shows a wider dispersion in firm size, even after controlling for the greater average size of firms in the US. Thus, not only do US manufacturing firms have a larger size than their European counterparts, but they also exhibit wider dispersion. Differences in the normalized coefficient of dispersion are particularly large in some high-tech sectors and in the wholesale and retail trade sector. The differences are particularly acute across the US

Table 21.4 Within-industry normalized coefficient of variation of firm size across countries

Sectors	Cross-country average	Industrialized countries	Other countries	France	USA
Manufacturing	7.5	1.28	0.74	1.04	2.83
Motor vehicles	6.6	1.46	0.58	0.76	3.48
Machinery & equipment	4.7	1.19	0.77	1.02	2.86
Services	15.9	0.94	1.05	0.72	1.83
Wholesale & retail trade	10.0	1.35	0.68	0.93	4.20

Source: Bartelsman et al. (2004).

and other industrialized countries, as in France where the within-industry dispersion is not very large. These results point to the potential influence of business environment conditions in shaping the degree of heterogeneity of the firms. Conditions of entry are less stringent in the US than in some European countries, as in France where institutional and technological factors limit the heterogeneity of firm size distribution.

21.3.2 Structural Variations: Assessment of Entry, Exit and Turnover

The quantitative and qualitative features of the process of firm entry and exit are important determinants of the creative destruction process.[6]

Entry, exit and net entry

The entry rate at a given date is defined as the number of new firms divided by the total number of incumbents and entrant firms producing at that date. The exit rate is the number of firms exiting the market in a given period divided by the incumbents in the preceding period. These rates, averaged over the last decade (1990–2000), have been compared across countries and some interesting findings emerge from Bartelsman et al. (2004).

Focusing on manufacturing firms with at least 20 employees, firm turnover (the unweighted sum of entry and exit rates) appears to vary between 3 and 8 percent in most Western industrialized countries and exceeds 10 percent in transition and Latin America economies.

Net entry (entry minus exit rate) is far less important, implying that the entry of new firms in the market is not equivalent to an increase of the number of competitors in the market, as a naive view could suggest. Net entry is negative in all industrialized Western countries, whereas it is positive in most transition economies where the role of market forces in shaping industrial dynamics is crucial in the transition phase.

The comparison between the US and France leads to the following observation. Exit rates outweigh entry rates by around 2 percent in France, while the difference is less than 0.5 percent in the United States. The exit rate is more or less compensated by the entry rate in the US, a sign of a more active creative destruction process, while in France the destructive process component is less than compensated by the creative counterpart.

Entry size

It is interesting to compare the average size of entrants relative to the average size of incumbents in terms of employment. The question is whether entry conditions differ across countries. It appears that the average size of entrants is much smaller in the United States and Canada than in other countries. In the United States, the ratio of the average size of new firms to the average size of incumbents in manufacturing is less than 20 percent, while in France this ratio is around 50 percent. This difference reflects economic and institutional factors linked to the entry cost: a lower entry cost in the US allows the start-up of relatively small businesses while a higher entry cost in European countries, like France, permits entry only at a larger scale.

Summing up the patterns of entry by firm size, it appears that the US environment is more favorable than the European environment to entry by small firms.

Gross turnover rates

Cross-country comparisons of the sectoral gross turnover rates (entry plus exit rates weighted by employment), normalized by the average over all countries, deliver interesting indications. First, variability of turnover rates across countries in a sector is comparable in magnitude to that across sectors in the same country. Turnover rates are significantly higher in some specific sectors: retail and wholesale trade, accounting and computing machinery, construction, and radio, TV and communication equipment. The turnover is above 10 percent in these sectors while its average is around 7 percent in overall manufacturing industry. Second, turnover rates differ across countries in these sectors. The value of the normalized gross turnover rate in the retail and trade sector is largely higher in the US than in any other country. To illustrate, the value is 0.64 in France and 0.95 in the US. The gross turnover rate is higher in the US, particularly in the services sectors.

Entry and exit: two hypotheses

In order to analyze the links between entry and exit, two competing hypotheses are confronted. The first hypothesis is that entry and exit rates are mainly driven by specific 'sectoral shocks': a positive shock induces entry while a negative shock induces exit. According to this hypothesis, the cross-industry correlation between entry and exit rates should be negative. The alternative hypothesis is that both entry and exit are driven by the 'creative destruction process' in each sector. Consequently, the correlation between entry and exit should be positive.

The most striking observation from Table 6 in Bartelsman et al. (2004) is that the cross-industry correlation is positive in almost all countries, except in some European economies such as France where the correlation is significantly negative. This result confirms previous similar findings in Geroski (1991) and Baldwin and Gorecki (1987).

The entry and exit process observed in European countries, especially in France, seems to be driven by sectoral shocks or cyclical conditions, whereas the creative destruction process plays a higher role in the US.

Post-entry performances

Does post-entry performance differ across the two sides of the Atlantic? Survival rates evaluated two, four or seven years after the date of entry reveal interesting differences across countries and sectors.

Variations in survival rates are larger across countries than across sectors. In the US, two years after the entry date, survival rates are very low, but after this market experimentation period, the conditional survival rate of successful firms becomes very high. This suggests that the delay after which the market selects the most successful small size entrants is shorter in the US.

In addition, the size of a firm that survives after two years of experimentation in the market increases at a significantly higher rate in the US than in other industrialized countries. The comparison with France is illustrative: the size of a French start-up that survives seven years after its entry in the market is the same as its initial size, whereas the size of the small American start-up that survives is multiplied by seven during the same period.

The smaller entry size, greater opportunities to experience the market and higher growth rate of the successful US start-ups indicate that the process of entry and market selection works better in the US than in European countries. Besides barriers to entry, there are significant barriers to growth in European economies: there is greater scope for expansion amongst young firms in American markets than in Europe.

21.3.3 Labor Productivity Variations across Countries: The Creative Destruction Process

To what extent does the churning process among firms contribute to the labor productivity growth?

Starting from firm-level labor productivity, Bartelsman et al. (2004) propose the following decomposition for aggregate labor productivity variation in manufacturing industry during a period of three or five years, measured for each country:

$$\Delta LP_t = \sum_{e \in C} s_{et-1} \Delta LP_{et} + \sum_{e \in C} (LP_{et-1} - LP_{t-1}) \Delta s_{et} + \sum_{e \in C} \Delta LP_{et} \Delta s_{et} + \sum_{e \in N} s_{et}(LP_{et} - LP_{t-1}) - \sum_{e \in X} s_{et-1}(LP_{et-1} - LP_{t-1}) \quad (21.2)$$

Labor productivity LP_{et} of firm e at period t is measured by sales divided by employment. Weighted average labor productivity in manufacturing is denoted $LP_t = \sum_e s_{et} LP_{et}$, while its variation between two periods is given by $\Delta LP_t = \sum_e s_{et} \Delta LP_{et}$, where individual employment shares (s_{et}) are used as weights. The index C designates the set of continuing firms during the period, and the indexes N and X correspond respectively to the sets of new firms and exiting firms in the period.

The first term in (21.2) is the 'within-firm effect'. It captures the contribution made by continuing firms to the aggregate labor productivity growth, each firm being weighted by its initial employment share.

The second term is the 'between-firm effect'. It captures the contribution of market reallocation between continuing firms to aggregate labor productivity. The expected result from the creative destruction mechanism is that market reallocation operates through transfers from less efficient firms towards more efficient ones. Thus reallocation should be beneficial to average productivity in manufacturing for continuing firms.

The third term is the 'cross effect'. It captures the component of aggregate labor productivity that comes from an employment expansion of a high productivity growth firm or from an employment reduction of a low productivity growth firm. The productivity growth of a firm is evaluated relative to the previous period's average productivity level.

The fourth term is the 'entry effect'. It captures the contribution of each entry to aggregate productivity. It is measured by the difference between each entering firm's productivity and the initial productivity level in the manufacturing sector, each entering firm being weighted by its employment share. A negative sign would mean that entrants enter with a lower productivity level than the average productivity level before entry.

The last term is the 'exit effect'. It captures the contribution of each exit to aggregate labor productivity. It is measured by the difference between each exiting firm's productivity and the initial productivity in the manufacturing industry, each exiting firm being weighted by its previous employment share.

This decomposition of the overall labor productivity growth in the manufacturing sector is computed for 24 countries. It leads to the following observations (Bartelsman et al., 2004).

1. The 'within-firm' effect is the most important effect: aggregate labor productivity growth in manufacturing is largely driven by 'within-firm' performance in almost all the industrialized countries, particularly when one focuses on a short horizon (period of three years). In a longer horizon (period of five or seven years) the reallocation and entry effects play a stronger role in promoting productivity growth.

2. The 'between effect', which measures the impact on aggregate labor productivity due to the reallocation of employment across existing firms, varies significantly across countries. It is largely higher in the US than in European countries.
3. The 'cross effect', term which combines changes in productivity with changes in employment shares, is generally negative, implying that firms that experienced an increase in productivity obtained this result by downsizing their employment rather than by expanding it. However, in Nordic countries the covariance term is positive, suggesting a positive job market turnover effect induced by specific labor markets rules ('flexi-security' regime) in these countries.
4. The 'net entry effect', which measures the impact of the difference between entry and exit rates on overall labor productivity growth, is generally positive in most countries, accounting for between 20 percent and 50 percent of total productivity growth. Moreover, for most countries, while the contribution of net entry is positive, it is less than proportionate to the share of employment accounted for by firm turnover.

The decomposition of the net entry effect leads to more insights. The exit effect is always positive which means that exiting firms are the least productive firms, helping to increase the labour productivity level of the manufacturing sector. The entry effect tends to be negative in most Organisation for Economic Co-operation and Development (OECD) countries, and is positive in transition economies where the entry of new firms makes a positive and often strong contribution to productivity. Some differences across OECD countries are noteworthy. In European countries, new firms generally make a positive contribution to overall productivity growth, although the effect is generally of small magnitude. In contrast, entry makes a negative contribution in the US where a stronger than average contribution tends to come from the exit of low productivity firms.

Focusing on total factor productivity (TFP) growth in US manufacturing establishments during the ten-year period 1977–87, other studies (Bartelsman and Dhrymes, 1998; Bartelsman and Doms, 2000) illustrate the strength of the creative destruction process in the US. They show that the net entry effect represents more than 25 percent of aggregate productivity growth over a ten-year period, while the within-establishment component is almost 50 percent. They also show that, while at the aggregate manufacturing level, rising labor productivity is often accompanied by reductions in employment, the negative correlation does not hold at the plant level. Among plants with increasing labor productivity in the ten-year period, the same proportions of firms increased employment as decreased employment. This means that overall, about a third of the aggregate labor productivity growth of 3 percent per year in the US is attributable to upsizing firms, about a third to downsizers and the remaining third to the net effect of entry and exit.

In other words, productivity growth has not been detrimental to the employment rate in the US, as it has been in various European countries.

21.3.4 Labor Productivity Variations across Sectors

Some other results from the decomposition of labor productivity growth in subsectors of the manufacturing industry according to the technological intensity are interesting.

In low-tech industries, the within effect is dominant in all countries while the between effect is insignificant except in the US where it is high. The cross effect is negative in these industries in all countries: firms that experienced strong productivity growth downsized their employment. Some differences across countries are significant. The contribution of entry to productivity growth is very modest in France, UK and Germany while it is small and negative in the US. The contribution of exit to productivity growth is rather modest in France and UK and very high in the US.

All of these features go in the same direction: in low-tech industries, the creative destruction process leads to stronger selection effects in the US than in European countries.

In medium- and high-tech industries, the within effect is also dominant in all countries and very high in Germany. The between effect is insignificant except in Germany, which means that the transfer of productive resources from less efficient to more efficient firms has been relatively absent in this country. The cross effect is insignificant or negative. Once again, firms that experienced an increase in productivity in this group of industries obtained this result by downsizing their employment rather than by expanding it. The entry effect is positive and this suggests an important role for new firms in more technologically intensive industries.

The most striking result is that in medium and high-tech industries, the entry effect is largely stronger in the US than in European countries.

Regulatory barriers and ICT diffusion: the retail trade sector in the US

The importance of the net entry effect in the US is particularly significant in the retail trade sector in which almost all labor productivity growth in the 1990s is accounted for by more productive entering establishments displacing less productive exiting establishments. 'The productivity gap between low productivity exiting single unit establishments and entering high productivity establishments from large national chains plays a disproportionate role in these dynamics' (Foster et al., 2005). It is important to stress that this productivity revival in US retailing goes beyond a simple more intensive use of computers, software and ICT technology. According to Gordon (2004), Europe has fallen behind because European firms are less free to develop 'big box' retail formats (like Wall Mart, Home Depot, Best Buy, Circuit City, and so on):

> Impediments include land use regulations that prevent the carving out of new 'greenfield' sites for 'big box' stores in suburban and exurban locations, shop closing regulations that restrict the revenue potential of new investments, congestion in central-city locations that are near the nodes of Europe's extensive urban public transit systems, and restrictive labor rules that limit flexibility in organizing the workplace and make it expensive to hire and fire workers with the near total freedom to which US firms are accustomed. (Gordon, 2004)

In total accordance with this diagnosis, other empirical studies indicate that more restrictive product market regulation lowers the productivity growth (Nicoletti and Scarpetta 2003; Conway et al., 2006). In industries and services that use ICT intensively, the gap in productivity improvement that follows a shift of the technological frontier allowed by this general purpose technology reaches a level as high as 40 percent between the countries with the more restrictive regulatory framework and the countries with the less restrictive regulation. This suggests that regulatory barriers are also barriers to technology diffusion and, as a result, to productivity growth.

A summing-up

The overall findings of the previous sections can be summarized around two series of observations. First, the aggregate superiority of the US in terms of labor productivity growth is not uniform across industries: the sectoral regroupments obtained by the ICT taxonomy and the innovation taxonomy reveal slight differences. It is in the ICT-producing and-using sectors on the one hand and in the client led innovation services on the other hand that the US–EU productivity gap is the most accentuated. While labor productivity growth in ICT-producing manufacturing industries has been particularly high both in the US and the EU, the US benefited from a leading initial position and an accelerated growth path in the last period. ICT-using services have been the locus of the most profound technological gap, particularly in the retail and wholesale sectors and in the banking and finance sectors where more restrictive regulatory barriers in European countries have been detrimental to the diffusion of ICT worldwide. In contrast, in traditional non-ICT-producing nor ICT-using manufacturing industries (motor vehicles, chemicals, oil refining, food, drink and tobacco), which still form the core of the European manufacturing industry, the EU keeps some leadership despite a declining average labor productivity growth rate. These results raise concerns about the relative competitive positions of the European economies. The innovation taxonomy leads to a distinction between two groups of sectors according to their innovation patterns. In high-tech industries where in-house innovation is strong and comes mainly from small and specialized firms developing higher-quality products rather than cost-reducing technologies, the EU lags behind the US in each period and the gap is still higher after 1995. In contrast, in industries where the main sources of technology improvement come from basic research, the EU has experienced higher labor productivity growth than the US during the three periods, despite a recent slowdown. These are indications of the weakness of the private R&D effort rather than of the public–private transfer of knowledge.

Second, the more important differences between the US and European countries are attributable to the less effective microeconomic creative destruction process in Europe that appears through the firms' demography and the sources of labor productivity growth. The firms' demography is slightly different between the two continents. In all the European industries, the number of small firms and their employment share are higher than in the US. But European SMEs seem to benefit much less from the size of the internal market in Europe than US firms do from their own market. While entry and exit rates are roughly of the same order of magnitude across Europe and the US, the average size of entrants is much more smaller in the US. Entry by very small firms is easier in the US than in Europe, mainly because lower entry costs in the US increase the incentives to start up small businesses, allowing them to benefit from the experimentation process supplied by the market. Post-entry performances also differ markedly between Europe and the US. While the short-term survival rate for US entrants is very low, those firms that survive four or seven years after their date of entry grow at a substantially higher rate in the US than in the European countries. Besides higher barriers to entry in the European markets, these results are a clear indication that there are also higher barriers to growth for SMEs in Europe. Finally, the impact of the creative destruction process on manufacturing labor productivity growth is much more significant in the US than in continental Europe. While the overall labor productivity growth comes mainly from the within-firms growth component, both in the US and the European manufacturing sector, the between-firms reallocation effect and the net entry component are largely higher in the US. This seems to be a clear indication that the creative destruction processes arising through the reallocation of resources towards more productive uses and through market contestability are less effective in European countries than in the US. Less significant creative destruction mechanisms in Europe are observed in both the low-tech and high-tech industries.

21.4 STRUCTURAL POLICIES IMPLICATIONS

Drawing policy implications from all these observations is not an easy task. Different contributions built upon more or less similar diagnoses have been presented.[7] The economic policy debates turn around two questions: what structural policies, and what governance method to implement them? Based on the above observations, some views around these two headings are presented.

21.4.1 Complementary Structural Policies to Improve the Creative Destruction Process

Two contrasting views on the nature of the appropriate structural policies have been mentioned in the introduction.

Arguing against the conjecture expressed in the so-called 'European paradox', according to which Europe succeeds in research but fails in innovation, Dosi et al. (2006) present convincing evidence that Europe's weakness occurs in both its system of scientific research and its corporate innovative capacity. Europe combines lower performance both in basic research leading to scientific discoveries and in applied research leading to marketable innovations. This statement is by no way contestable but the authors draw from it a policy implications that is less evident. Dosi et al. rightly argue that it would be a mistake to believe that an exclusive effort to improve the public–private partnership could be sufficient to bridge the technological gap, without reforming both the higher education system and the organization of the public research system. This implies that much more effort towards public and private research must be realized, accompanied by reforms of the higher education system in Europe.[8] However, the policy implication is much more controversial. It states that the weak innovative performance of the European economy is explained by the lack of an appropriate industrial policy at the EU level to strengthen European corporate actors.

The evidence on the weakness of Eureopan industry, collected so far in the two previous sections, does not support this implication, despite the fact that the evidence from which Dosi et al. draw their policy implication is not so different from the evidence reviewed in the previous sections.

They consider first the evolution (1990–2001) of the world market shares held respectively by European, US and Japanese firms (Figure 3 in Dosi et al.) in eight different ICT sectors. The EU lags behind the US in all the sectors, even in the telecommunications industry where Europe had a big advantage in the 1990s. In order to draw more precise policy implications, Dosi et al. observe that the US lead has decreased in industries in which European countries had a voluntary industrial policy approach. From an observation concerning the evolution of the radio communications and radar equipment, Dosi et al. draw the following conclusion: 'This has probably been the outcome of the formation of a few European companies, especially in the military sector, with sizes and capabilities that begin to be comparable with those of their American counterparts.'

A second observation compares export market shares in some high-tech industries excluding intra-EU trade. The authors find that while European firms had lower trade performances in instruments and pharmaceuticals, they gained in airline and aerospace industries, probably due to the public funding of Airbus and Ariane.

As a third observation, Dosi et al. note that among the top 250 ICT firms, only 13 percent are based in the EU while 56 percent are based in the US.

According to Dosi et al. all these observations 'support the conjecture that . . . potential corporate recipients in Europe are generally smaller, weaker and slower in seizing novel technological opportunities than their transatlantic counterparts'. However, if the technological advance of US firms is confirmed, the authors do not really explain the origin of this advance.

While Dosi et al. argue in favor of public interventions to strengthen European champions through a voluntarist industrial policy, by recalling its successes but forgetting its failures, the present chapter argues in favor of structural policies that improve the creative destruction process by removing the barriers to growth that inhibit the development of new innovative firms in Europe, the barriers to technology diffusion due to institutional obstacles, and the labor market rigidities. In other words, the structural conditions of the growth process in a market economy are emphasized, whereas Dosi et al. focus on what they consider as being the tools of the corporate success. They think that the potential success of European corporate actors depends on some voluntarist industrial policy in favor of national or European champions, while this chapter argues that this success should come from the introduction of more favorable environments to allow the creative destruction process to play its role.

The main implication that can be drawn from the diagnosis of the technology gap made in previous sections is that an agenda for growth in a knowledge-based economy must take into account the conditions that favor the microeconomic creative destruction process that affects the industry dynamics at the firm and sectoral levels. Phelps (2003) provides a unifying framework for analyzing these conditions. According to Phelps, economic dynamism is fostered by policies that promote competition and flexible equity finance, while it is retarded by corporatist institutions designed to protect incumbents and inhibit new entry or impede growth by successful entrants. Phelps also emphasizes numerous cultural and institutional attributes that inhibit the development of innovation in Europe. These attributes include the lack of a common language, an inefficient and inequitable education system, a fragmented scientific community, an insufficient inclination towards entrepreneurship particularly among teenagers and young adults, a less favorable climate towards business, especially SMEs, and last but not least, the institutional obstacles that restrict labor market adaptability in a globalized economy.

According to Phelps (2003): 'some of these impediments to economic growth are inbred and likely to persist'. Even if all the conditions that fostered the development of a knowledge-based society in the US cannot be gathered in Europe, because European structural policies cannot and must not simply try to mimic the American way of life, some structural reforms or supply-side policies to improve the creative destruction process seem absolutely inevitable. They include labor market reform, a reorganization of the public research system and the higher education system, an increase in the European R&D budget and a more efficient funding process, the construction of a genuine intellectual property system at the European level, an acceleration of the services liberalization process including banking and finance activities, the definition of a common energy policy, and a common regulatory framework for European public utilities. The chapter does not review all of these policy reforms, but one has to start from a political presumption: European citizens are not against the statement of common objectives intended to stimulate a knowledge-based society, so long as these objectives are clearly explained and not simply presented as the result of an official European Council meeting. The construction of an internal market was at the time a strong common objective implemented through a common competition policy instrument. But it is clear that this instrument is no longer sufficient for a knowledge-based economy. To be more precise, a strong emphasis on a coordinated competition policy is still necessary, but in no way a sufficient condition to improve the creative destruction process (Encaoua and Hollander, 2002; Encaoua and Guesnerie, 2006; Aghion and Griffith, 2005). European structural policies must build on economic incentives, be assessed at a microeconomic level and not only at a macroeconomic one, and present an overall consistency requirement expressed through some complementary conditions. Two of them, that I examine below, are particularly relevant: the complementarity between productivity growth and employment, and the complementarity between public and private R&D funding.

Productivity and employment

The first complementary requirement relates to the relationship between labor productivity and the rate of employment. Until now, these two performance indices have been achieved only as substitutes in most European countries, while they have been realized as complements in the US. European firms that experienced an increase in their labor productivity too often succeeded by downsizing employment. This unfortunate result is socially supportable only if the job turnover mechanism operates in such a way that job creation compensates job destruction. The failure in realizing this condition is the main European problem. The need to increase simultaneously the productivity and the employment requires interdependent product market and labor market reforms.

The usual drivers of productivity growth, essential for this purpose, involve many factors, including physical investment and investment in knowledge, transformation of knowledge into innovative products and technologies, improvement of skills by education and training, more favorable management practices and labor relationships, dynamic competition in the product and service markets, and removal of barriers to entry and barriers to growth. There is evidence that higher administrative costs of entry are associated with: lower aggregate labor productivity; more capital-intensive production; and lower firm turnover. Moreover, the effect of entry on productivity depends on how far the firms are from the knowledge technological frontier (Aghion et al., 2003; Aghion and Griffith, 2005). The positive effect of entry on productivity growth is all the more significant when an industry is closer to the technological frontier. In addition, the effect of entry on productivity and employment depends mostly on the removal of barriers to growth to which are currently confronting innovative small entrants in European markets. A policy reform involving some of these productivity drivers could consist in combining the creation of a genuine environment favorable to European SMEs and the achievement of the internal market, both in the product and services markets. Such reform could enhance the rate of growth of new entrants, the intensity of competition and the rate of employment. The opportunity to create in Europe some equivalent of the US Small Business Act and the Small Business Innovation Research (SBIR) Program is now largely debated (see Wallstein, 2000; Connell, 2006). The corresponding European programs should involve such institutional innovations as the creation of a judicial statute for a genuine

European enterprise, the creation of a trans-European equity market, the creation of a special European agency devoted to defense public procurement in European countries, a simplified public funding organization for R&D investment by young innovative firms, a genuine European patent at low cost, and the development of economic incentives to form partnerships with public laboratories and universities, as in the European CRAFT program (Cooperative Research Action for Technology).

But the drivers of productivity growth are not sufficient. The effects of all these reforms would be ineffective without some deep structural reforms of labor market regulation. Until now, ambitious labor market policy reforms in many European countries have been largely inhibited by institutional obstacles. New labor market policy packages should combine the two components of the so-called 'flexi-security regime': an institutionalization of the personal rights for a permanent training during work life with a combination of some insurance schemes for transitory unemployment on one hand, and more flexible labor laws allowing labor mobility between firms and between countries on the other hand. Despite the fact that such policies could increase European integration and deliver higher benefits to European workers, only gradual transformations and uncoordinated policies between member countries have so far been delivered, resulting in fragmented labor markets, and institutions that vary a great deal across countries with respect to the structure of wage negotiations and the features of unemployment insurance.[9]

The difficulties of achieving a coordinated labor market framework are illustrated by the controversial European Services Directive (Delgado, 2006). Since the presentation of the first draft of this Directive in 2004, there has been a vigorous debate throughout Europe: workers of the wealthier member states consider the Directive as an open door to service providers from new member states where wages are lower and social protection less developed. Moreover, as many services are supplied by state-owned enterprises, many citizens perceive the Services Directive as an attempt to privatize these public services, despite the fact that the Directive is simply a generalization of the free trade principle to include European services. It is clear that services liberalization in Europe cannot succeed without deep reforms in the labor markets. This illustrates once more the complementarity that must exist between labor markets and product and services markets. The recent European Parliament vote in 2006, which opted to remove any reference to labor market reform from the Services Directive, avoided direct confrontation but did not solve the problem. The liberalization of services remains an unavoidable objective in Europe for at least two reasons discussed in the previous sections. First, the service sector now represents more than two-thirds of economic activity and employment in the

European Union and is the main driving force for growth within European economies. Second, we have seen that services are the main locus of the technological gap between the US and the EU, particularly in wholesale and retail trade and the financial services sectors.

Public–private partnerships

The second complementarity is related to the decomposition of the R&D effort between public and private actors. The Lisbon objective of making the EU the most competitive knowledge-based economy in the world by 2010 has been popularized in terms of R&D intensity through the famous 3 percent level. But clearly, this objective is not under the exclusive control of public authorities, insofar as a substantial portion of it depends on private R&D decisions. The private R&D effort is largely below the target.

Three questions arise. First, insofar as national budgets are under tight constraints in different member countries, is the research effort at the European Community level sufficient? Second, to what extent can indirect European public funding through incentive schemes complement the direct public funding? Third, does private R&D investment compensate the weakness of public R&D investment?

The direct R&D funding instruments available from the European Union budget include four sources: the research Framework Program (FP) and three smaller programs: the Competitiveness and Innovation Framework Programme, Structural Funds for regional development, and European agencies funds dedicated to specific programs as Galileo. Despite a substantial increase in Europe's Seventh Research Framework Program (FP7) for the 2007–13 period, the European Community public funds devoted to R&D remain largely insufficient. The recent 5 percent increase per year during the FP7 period will not be sufficient to catch up the US leadership. One figure is sufficient to illustrate the gap: the global budget devoted to R&D by the FP7 is around €50 billion over the seven years of the 2007–13 period, whereas the budget of the US National Institutes of Health (NIH) devoted exclusively to medical research for one year was around $28.4 billion in 2007. Thus the NIH budget represents by itself more than one-half the global FP7 budget for seven years. It is clear that the European Union R&D still falls behind that of the US by a significant margin.

Of course, efforts by individual member countries must be added to the centralized effort at the European level. Some simple figures illustrate, however, that member countries do not sufficiently compensate the weakness of the R&D Community effort. In 2007, the aggregate UE-27 R&D is around €200 billion while the Community-level R&D is around €18 billion (representing 0.17 percent of the overall GNP). Thus, even if member countries' R&D expenses represent more that ten times the Community level R&D effort, the global R&D investment in Europe still lags behind that of the US: its value in the EU-27 is only two-thirds of its value in the US.

It has been claimed that an indirect public funding by the European Bank of Investment (EBI), initiated in 2000 at the Lisbon meeting, could significantly supplement the R&D European Union budget. This claim is supported by some evidence showing that loans and collateral financing by the EBI increased in the period 2000–2006 at a higher rate than the direct public funding. The catalytic role of the EBI, in collaboration with FP7, in funding public–private partnerships and providing risk-sharing mechanisms, should be increased in the future.

Finally, the allocation across private and public R&D efforts raises another question. Private R&D investment is still too low in Europe. It represents only 55 percent of total R&D investment in the EU-27 while the corresponding figure for the US is around 65 percent. In addition, in most European countries, private R&D expenses are mainly realized by the largest firms, which together benefit mostly from the public R&D subsidies. Once again, this raises the question of the choice of an appropriate structural policy in favor of innovating SMEs.

21.4.2 Implementation Level

At what level should the structural policy reforms, discussed so far, be implemented? The Lisbon Summit (2000) introduced the so-called open method of coordination (OMC) as a way to implement a large number of structural policy reforms in areas where the European Union has no constitutional competence and which are the preserve of member states. Under the OMC process, the EU countries agreed to voluntarily cooperate in the implementation of structural policy reforms customed to their national circumstances. The European Commission's role was simply to coordinate this process in an advisory role by ensuring a benchmarking framework.

Five years after its launch, the failure of the Lisbon Agenda led to the Kok High-Level Group report (Kok, 2004), recommending a new system of governance based on three key changes: an emphasis on more limited policy goals, the provision of appropriate EU funding, and a 'carrot and stick' implementation mechanism in which poor performing member states would be be 'named and shamed', while the best-performing countries would be 'rewarded'. However, the 2005 European Council retained only the first of these recommendations in the renewed Lisbon Agenda. The revised[10] Lisbon 2 still involves National Reform Programmes (NRPs) in which country members retain the political responsibility for implementing 'less but the same' objectives as in Lisbon 1.[11]

The revised OMC mechanism to implement structural policy reforms in Europe raises two questions. First, what are the economic justifications for maintaining 'national political ownership' of these reforms, particularly in countries that have the same currency unit and share the same monetary policy? Second, is it possible and desirable to coordinate some common structural policies, given the heterogeneity between country members?

Concerning the first question, the theoretical justification underlying the frontier between what should be implemented under common responsibility and what should be left under the country's control is built on the grounds of budget federalism theory. Tabellini and Wyplosz (2004) introduce the notion of pecuniary externalities distinguishing between two categories of supply-side policies: those that do not need centralized coordination and those for which strong coordination is needed.

Any policy in a single country belonging to a free trade community involves externalities insofar as it has cross-border effects, but these effects may be more or less circumscribed. An externality of a pecuniary type arises from a country's specific policy when its effects are mainly restricted to price and wage variations. A country that unilaterally adopts a structural policy of the pecuniary type is thus rewarded by better market performance, while a country that is reluctant loses without necessarily harming other countries. This suggests that a structural policy involving an externality of a pecuniary type should be left to the control of individual countries. For instance, Tabellini and Wyplosz argue that a unilateral labour market reform that lowers the structural rate of unemployment is presumed to be of the pecuniary type because it does not significantly impact its neighbors while its success benefits its own citizens. In addition, the OMC governance allows mutual learning of individual reforms to reduce unemployment insofar as it allows other countries to benefit from the most successful policy reform. Similarly, a country which improves its labor productivity essentially boosts its own growth while signalling the successful method to other countries.

In contrast, individual policies exhibiting externalities of the non-pecuniary type must be internalized through a common implementation mechanism for two reasons: their cross-border effects are strong and their outcomes are interdependent. For instance, competition policy involves externalities of the non-pecuniary type because, in a free trade area, a more stringent competition policy in country B than in country A would have significant cross-border effects. Not only does it harm country B's producers while benefiting country B's consumers and harming A's consumers, but more significantly, it distorts trade exchange between the two countries.

This approach, founded on the nature of externalities, does not lead to a precise frontier between what policies must be centralized and those that must be left decentralized. First, it is not clear why, in a free trade area, economic and social differences in labor market conditions do not affect cross-border performance through the transfer of some businesses into countries where wages are lower and social protection is weaker. We observe such relocations every day in the enlarged European Union. We observe also that despite its intrinsic interest, services liberalization in Europe is inhibited insofar as the global labor market reforms are not achieved. Second, it is no more evident whether a policy for reforming the system of higher education is of the pecuniary type or not. Mobility among students and academics calls for more compatibility between the higher education systems. Third, the OMC mechanism to coordinate National Reform Programmes rests on the conviction that each country may learn from other country experiences with the presumption that this learning could be sufficient to stimulate adoption by other countries. However, this argument ignores the fact that comparing structural reform policies in member countries is more complicated than the learning provided by yardstick competition mechanisms in regulated industries, from which the OMC mechanism borrows its inspiration. Strong national preferences, misunderstanding of foreign experiences, and many other contextual factors that affect the success of structural policies may lengthen the period of time necessary for the OMC learning procedure to succeed. Despite the fact that the 2006 Spring European Council decided to focus on stronger action to drive forward the higher education Lisbon Agenda, few member countries made them their own national priority.

For all these reasons, as Pisani-Ferry (2005) argues:

> The decision by the European council of March 2005 to base the monitoring on 'National Reform Programmes' geared to the member states 'own needs and specific situations' risks watering down the whole exercise and may weaken even further the incentive to conform to the commonly agreed agenda.

This view calls for a better coordination process of the structural policy reforms. For instance, the common target of reaching a level of R&D spending of 3 percent of gross domestic product (GDP) cannot be achieved without a high cooperation level between member countries, through a common agreement to reallocate public funds towards R&D activities and a political commitment to convince some categories of workers (farmers for example) that less subsidies for their activities are a short-term sacrifice that will be compensated by medium- and long-term benefits. For all these reasons, Pisani-Ferry and Sapir (2006) argue for a more intensive cooperation between the eurozone member countries. Moreover, economic and social interdependence across countries with the same currency create more spillover effects because an increase of their rate of employment and their productivity growth may have short- and medium-term positive impacts on their neighbors through demand and revenue effects.

Despite all these arguments in favor of more cooperation in the implementation of structural reforms, the structural heterogeneity of the member states, especially after the enlargement of the European Union, remains a strong argument against common implementation. Take for instance the overall target for R&D spending. Some European countries are already above target while others remain far behind. The different starting positions are such that defining the same target for every country would be completely inappropriate. In addition, letting each European country implement its own structural policy may be more appropriate because we know from the recent endogenous growth literature (Acemoglu et al., 2006) and from empirical evidence (surveyed in Aghion and Griffith, 2005, Chapter 4) that the nature of innovation policies depends crucially on the country's distance to the technological frontier. While investment in research and higher education is an essential determinant of growth in countries that are close to the technological frontier, capital accumulation and technology adoption are more beneficial policies in countries that are still far from this frontier. More generally, the catch-up process and the leapfrogging process that lead to improvements in the global technology frontier depend on different structural policies (Griffith et al., 2004). Therefore, the structural heterogeneity between the EU country members requires some flexibility, allowing different policy reforms with a specific agenda according to the peculiarities of each country. The revised Lisbon Agenda policy is designed in such a way that every country could choose its own structural reforms, by keeping political ownership of its reforms, by turning away from the 'one size fits all' principle and by abandoning incentives to monitor individual performance. At the same time, the agenda addresses the same long-term objectives for the EU.

Finally, even if it is too early to know whether the revised Lisbon Agenda will deliver the expected results, some doubts on its effectiveness cannot be discarded. While some transformations aimed at reducing the technological gap may be implemented at the national level, a clear orientation towards common policies designed to improve the creative destruction process at the microeconomic level is still lacking. Moreover the complementary aspects of the correponding policies must be emphasized, particularly with regards to labor market regulation, higher education reform and services liberalization. A reinforcement of the implementing instruments by common procedures among the member states, as suggested in Kok's report, seems unavoidable.

NOTES

1. I am most grateful to Faye Steiner for several helpful comments and suggestions. I also thank Luc Soete who presented a very rich discussion of this chapter at the Monte Verità Conference. The comments by Luc Soete, in this book, appear thus as a genuine complementary piece to this chapter. Many thanks also to Dominique Foray who invited me to the conference and organized a special session for the presentation and the discussion of this chapter.
2. Average productivity of labor can be itself decomposed as labor productivity per hour times average working hours duration.
3. The data are built from the OECD Structural Analysis (STAN database) and the estimates produced by the Groningen Growth and Development Center/The Conference board (available from http://www.eco.rug.nl/ggdc/homeggdc.html). The methodology is described in O'Mahony and van Ark (2003), Chapter 7. See also McGuckin and van Ark (2003).
4. The detailed list of sectors in each group is presented in O'Mahony and van Ark, (2003).
5. Except in some Nordic countries as Belgium, Denmark and Sweden.
6. See Boone (2000) for a theoretical approach and Chen (2006) for a large survey of empirical results.
7. Among the huge amount of policy papers devoted to the appropriate structural reforms in the EU, one can quote the Phelps lecture at the Royal Institute of International Affairs (Phelps, 2003), the analysis made in the Sapir (Sapir et al., 2004) and Kok (2004) reports, the comments by Pisani-Ferry and Sapir (2006) on the new Lisbon agenda, the lecture by Aghion and Howitt (2005) at the Schumpeterian Society, the contribution by Aghion et al. (2006), the report by Encaoua and Guesnerie (2006) on competition policy in Europe and the alternative views by Dosi et al. (2006) on the technological gap.
8. The higher education reform has been largely documented in the literature (see for instance van der Ploeg and Veugelers, 2007; Jacobs and van der Ploeg, 2006).
9. For a more elaborated analysis of the relative merits of gradual transformations of the labor markets versus global policy packages, see Eichorst and Konle-Seidl (2007), Eichorst (2007), Cahuc and Postel-Vinay (2002) and Abowd et al., (2000).
10. The revised version of Lisbon objectives is presented in the European Commission's Communication to the Council (2005) and in the integrated guidelines 'National Reform Programs for Growth and Jobs' (2005).
11. The simplified objectives are regrouped around three goals, namely growth, innovation, and employment and social cohesion. The program recommends the pursuit of economic integration, a better coordination of domestic labor markets and pension reforms and a restructuring of public spending in the direction of R&D and higher education.

REFERENCES

Abowd, J., F. Kramarz, D. Margolis and T. Philippon (2000), 'The tail of two countries: minimum wages and employment in France and the United States', IZA Discussion Paper 203, Bonn, IZA.

Acemoglu, D., P. Aghion and F. Zilibotti (2006), 'Distance to frontier, selection and economic growth', *Journal of the European Economic Association*, **4**, 37–74.

Aghion, P. (2006), 'A primer on innovation and growth', *Bruegel Policy Brief*, Issue 2006/66, October, Bruegel, Brussels, available at: http://www.bruegel.org.

Aghion, P., R. Blundell, R. Griffith, P. Howitt and S. Prantl (2003), 'Entry and productivity growth: evidence from micro-level data', *Journal of the European Economic Association*, **2**, 265–76.

Aghion, P., P. David and D. Foray (2006), 'Linking policy research and practice in "STIG Systems": many obstacles, but some ways forward', Stanford Institute for Economic Policy Research Discussion Paper No. 06-009.

Aghion, P. and R. Griffith (2005), *Competition and Growth, Reconciling Theory and Evidence*, Cambridge, MA: MIT Press.

Aghion, P. and P. Howitt (2005), 'Appropriate growth theory: a unifying framework', Lecture delivered at the 20th Annual Congress of the European Economic Association, Amsterdam.

Ahn, S. (2000), 'Firm dynamics and productivity growth: a review of micro evidence from OECD countries', OECD Economics Department Working Paper 297, Paris.

Baldwin, J. and P. Gorecki (1987), 'Plant creation versus plant acquisition: the entry process in Canadian manufacturing', *International Journal of Industrial Organization*, **5** (1), 27–41.

Bartelsman, E. and M. Doms (2000), 'Understanding productivity: lessons from longitudinal microdata', *Journal of Economic Literature*, **33**, 569–94.

Bartelsman, E. and P. Dhrymes (1998), 'Productivity dynamics: US manufacturing plants, 1972–1986', available at: http://ssrn.com/abstract=5901.

Bartelsman, E., J. Haltiwanger and S. Scarpetta (2004), 'Microeconomic evidence of creative destruction in industrial and developing countries', NBER Working Paper.

Boone, J. (2000), 'Competitive pressure: the effects on investments in product and process innovations', *RAND Journal of Economics*, **31** (3), 549–69.

Cahuc, P. and F. Postel-Vinay (2002), 'Temporary jobs, employment protection and labor market performance', *Journal of Labor Economics*, **9** (1), 63–91.

Caves, R. (1998), 'Industrial organization and new findings on the turnover and mobility of firms', *Journal of Economic Literature*, **36**, 1947–82.

Chen, Z. (2006), 'Rivalry, market structure, and industrial competitiveness: issues and evidence', Report for Micro-Economic Policy Analysis Branch, Industry Canada.

Connell, D. (2006), '"Secrets" of the world's largest seed capital funds', Centre for Business Research, University of Cambridge.

Conway, P., D. De Rosa, G. Nicoletti and F. Steiner (2006), 'Regulation, competition and productivity convergence', *OECD Economic Review*, **43**, 45–87.

Delgado, J. (2006), 'The European Services Directive', US–Europe Analysis Series No. 34, Washington, DC: The Brookings Institution, available at: http://www.brookings.edu/papers/2006/04europe_delgado.aspx.

Doms, M., R. Jarmin and S. Klimek (2004), 'Information technology investment and firm performance in US retail trade', *Economics of Innovation and New Technology*, **13** (7), 595–614.

Dosi, G., P. Llerena and M. Sylos-Labini (2006), 'The relationship between science, technologies and their exploitation: an illustration through the myths and realities of the so-called "European Paradox"', *Research Policy*, **35**, 1450–64.

Eichorst, W. (2007), 'The gradual transformation of continental European labor markets: France and Germany compared', IZA Discussion Paper 2675, Bonn, IZA.

Eichorst, W. and R. Konle-Seidl (2007), 'The interaction of labor market regulation and labor market policies in welfare state reform', *Comparative Labor Law and Policy Journal*, **28** (1), 1–41.

Encaoua, D. and R. Guesnerie (2006), *Politique de la Concurrence*, Conseil d'Analyse Economique (CAE), 060, Paris, La Documentation Française.
Encaoua, D. and A. Hollander (2002), 'Competition policy and innovation, *Oxford Review of Economic Policy*, **18** (1), 63–79.
Foster, L., J. Haltiwanger and C. Krizan (2005), 'Market selection, reallocation and restructuring in the US retail trade sector in the 1990s', NBER Working Paper.
Geroski, P. (1991), *Market Dynamics and Entry*, Oxford: Basil Blackwell.
Gordon, R. (2004), 'Why was Europe left at the station when America's productivity locomotive departed?', Nothwestern University and CEPR, CEPR version.
Griffith, R., S. Redding and J. van Reenan (2004), 'Mapping the two faces of R&D: productivity growth in a panel of OECD countries', *Review of Economics and Statistics*, **86** (4), 883–95.
Jacobs, B. and F. van der Ploeg (2006), 'Guide to reform of higher education: a European perspective', *Economic Policy*, **47**, 535–92.
Kok, W. (2004), 'Facing the challenge: the Lisbon strategy for growth and employment', Report from the High-Level Group, http://ec.europa.eu/growthandjobs/pdf/kok_report_en.pdf.
McGuckin, R. and B. van Ark (2003), 'Performance 2002: productivity, employment, and income in the world's economies', New York: Conference Board.
Nicoletti, G. and S. Scarpetta (2003), 'Regulation, productivity and growth', *Economic Policy*, **36**, 11–72.
O'Mahony M. and B. van Ark (eds) (2003), 'EU productivity and competitiveness: an industry perspective. Can Europe resume the catching-up process?', http://www.ggdc.net/pub/EU_productivity_and_competitiveness.pdf.
Pavitt, K. (1984), 'Sectoral patterns of technical change: towards a taxonomy and a theory', *Research Policy*, **13** (6), 343–74.
Phelps, E. (2003), 'Economic underperformance in continental Europe: a prospering economy runs on the dynamism from its economic institutions', Lecture at the International Institute of Royal Affairs, 18 March.
Pisani-Ferry, J. (2005), 'What's wrong with Lisbon?', mimeo.
Pisani-Ferry, J. and A. Sapir (2006), 'Last exit to Lisbon', *Bruegel Policy Brief*, Issue 2006/02, March, Bruegel, Brussels, available at: http://www.bruegel.org.
van der Ploeg, F. and R. Veugelers (2007), 'Higher education reform and the renewed Lisbon Strategy: role of member states and the European Commission', CESifo Working Paper 1901, Category 1: Public Finance.
Sapir, A., P. Aghion, G. Bertola, M. Hellwig, J. Pisani-Ferry, D. Rosatti, J. Viñals and H. Wallace (2004), *An Agenda for a Growing Europe, The Sapir Report*, Oxford: Oxford University Press.
Tabellini, G. and C. Wyplosz (2004), *Réformes Structurelles et Coordination en Europe*, Conseil d'Analyse Economique (CAE), 051, Paris: La Documentation Française.
Wallstein, S. (2000), 'The effects of government–industry R&D programs on private R&D: the case of the Small Business Innovation Research program', *RAND Journal of Economics*, **31** (1), 82–100.

22. Innovation, growth and structural reforms: what role for EU policy?[1]

Reinhilde Veugelers

22.1 EU GROWTH AND ITS COMPONENTS

GDP growth in the EU rebounded markedly in 2006 and 2007 (see Table 22.1). Although the financial market turbulence has seriously revised the economic prospects for 2008 downward, an important feature of the recent recovery in the EU is that both employment has increased and the decline in productivity growth has come to an end. This has raised the question of the extent to which this rebound was a purely cyclical phenomenon or is related to and reflects structural improvements, and especially improvements associated with the reforms of the Lisbon Strategy, the centrepiece of reform policy in the EU.

22.2 A STRUCTURAL REBOUND?

Employment growth has been accompanied by widespread declines in unemployment and increasing participation rates, particularly of women and older workers. This suggests that the gains in employment were structural, consistent with labour market reforms aimed at bringing into and keeping more people in the labour market (ECFIN, 2007). But on the structural character of the labour productivity rebound, the empirical evidence is less clear. Since 2003, the rate of decline, which commenced in the mid-1990s, and is discussed at length by Encaoua (Chapter 21 in this

Table 22.1 Real GDP growth rates

	2004	2005	2006	2007
EU-27	2.5	1.9	3.0	2.9
US	3.6	3.1	2.9	2.2
Japan	2.7	1.9	2.4	2.1

Source: Eurostat website: http://www.pro-inno-europa.eu, accessed March 2008.

volume), has been halted and labour productivity growth has stabilized at around 1 per cent per year (ECFIN, 2007). Whether this development was cyclical or structural is virtually impossible to tell at this juncture – the evidence is too recent to permit drawing confident conclusions.

22.3 SOURCES OF PRODUCTIVITY GROWTH (DIFFERENTIALS): LESSONS FROM THE RECENT PAST

The uncertainties on how to interpret the recent productivity data do not preclude feeding policy with insights from research. By now a large set of studies is available which uses sectoral and firm-level data from the 1990s, examining which factors critically determined productivity growth during this period. The role of information and communication technology (ICT), innovation and firm dynamics are prominent among the sources for productivity growth and for explaining cross-country differentials. This evidence from the 1990s, nicely reviewed by Encaoua (Chapter 21 in this volume), suggests that the global positive technology shock induced by ICT in the US during the 1990s has not been matched to its full extent in key countries in the EU. ICT-using services have been the locus of the most profound productivity growth gap with the US, particularly in the retail and wholesale sectors and in banking and finance.

The more recent evidence suggests that the European Union (EU) is catching up with the US on ICT expenditure and broadband penetration. Nevertheless, recent firm-level analysis (Van Reenen et al., 2007) shows that US firms manage to obtain a higher return from their ICT investments as compared to their EU competitors. And since this holds also for subsidiaries of US firms operating outside the US, this suggests that other firm-specific advantages are important, such as the quality of management practices (Bloom and Van Reenen, 2007).

An important question in the present context is the extent to which the example of ICT (the failure, that is, of EU enterprises to reap the full benefits associated with ICT) is an isolated case or is the symptom of a more general problem of the EU and its innovation infrastructure (in terms of the resources devoted, rates of return and industry focus).

22.4 INNOVATION DEFICIT

The European Innovation Scoreboard (EC-ENTR 2007) (Figure 22.1a) – which traces countries on a number of innovation input and input

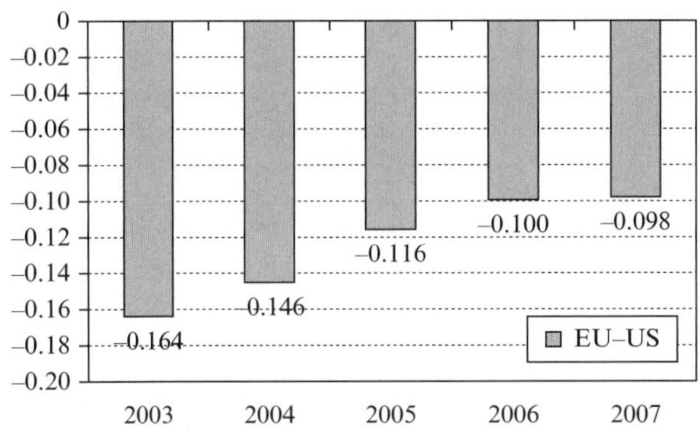

Figure 22.1a European Innovation Scoreboard: trend in EU–US gap

indicators – provides both good (Figure 22.1b) and bad news (Figure 22.1c) on the innovative capacity of the EU.

On the positive side, the EU is slowly catching up with the US. It outperforms its global competitors in the number of science and engineering graduates. Also new applications to the European Patent Office, new Community trademarks and designs have increased significantly.

But in a number of important aspects, Europe is lagging behind the US, and with relatively little signs of progress. The EU's innovation environment remains weak in a number of key 'input' indicators, such as the stock of science and technology (S&T) researchers. The proportion of the population in tertiary education in the EU is smaller compared to the US and Japan, with funding allocated to education lower, particularly private funding. General weaknesses of the higher education system are often mentioned to explain weaknesses on the capabilities side, with poor governance of universities and research centres, rigid structures and lack of rewards, autonomy and accountability in a non-integrated education and research market. Also, on research and development (R&D) investment, the EU continues to trail the US, despite the Barcelona 3 per cent target.

The EU's R&D deficit problem is mostly due to the business sector. The EU's private R&D deficit compared to the US primarily manifests itself in ICT goods and services. This is both because of a lower specialization of the EU economy in these R&D-intensive, high-growth sectors, but also because of a lower R&D intensity of firms within these sectors. In terms of firm behaviour, based on the limited evidence available, the deficit in ICT reflects constraints on the rapid growth of new, technology-based entrants in the EU as compared with the US (O'Sullivan, 2007).

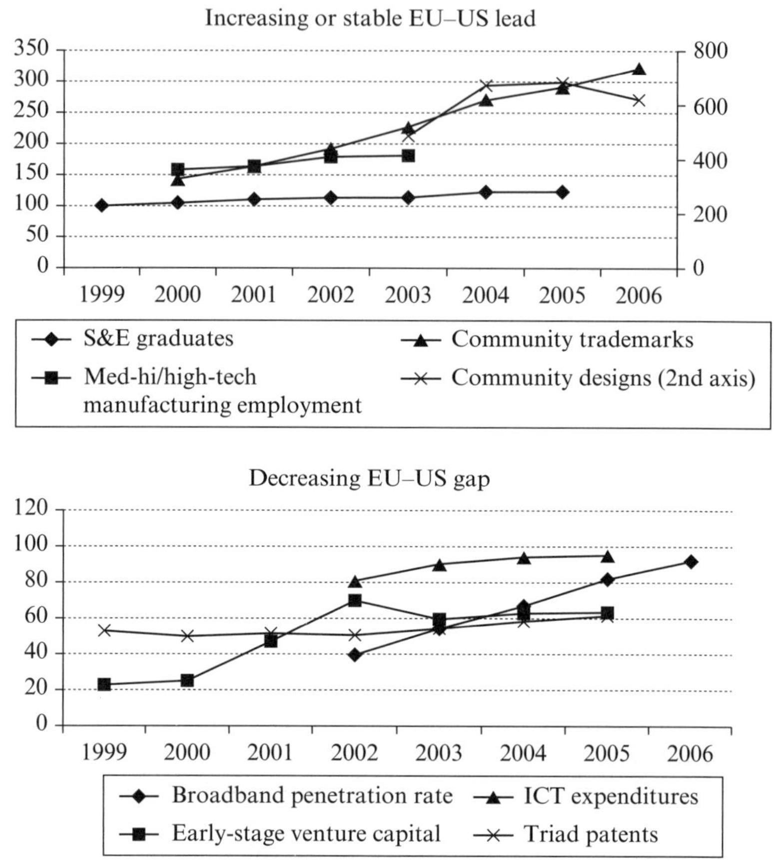

Figure 22.1b Decomposing the EU–US Innovation Score: the dimensions with the good news (increasing/stable EU–US lead and decreasing EU–US gap)

From this perspective, the business R&D deficit is a symptom rather than a cause of a weakness in the EU's capacity to innovate; the cause is rooted in the structure and dynamics of industry and enterprise. Europe's innovation gap relative to the US results partly from a lack of specialization in high-tech sectors, a larger share of small and primogeniture family-owned firms and especially a lack of fast-growing, efficient innovative entrants that can challenge incumbents. The churning that characterizes the creative destruction process in a knowledge-based economy is hindered by a variety of barriers. Product markets insufficiently open to competition, including competition from abroad, as well as excessive

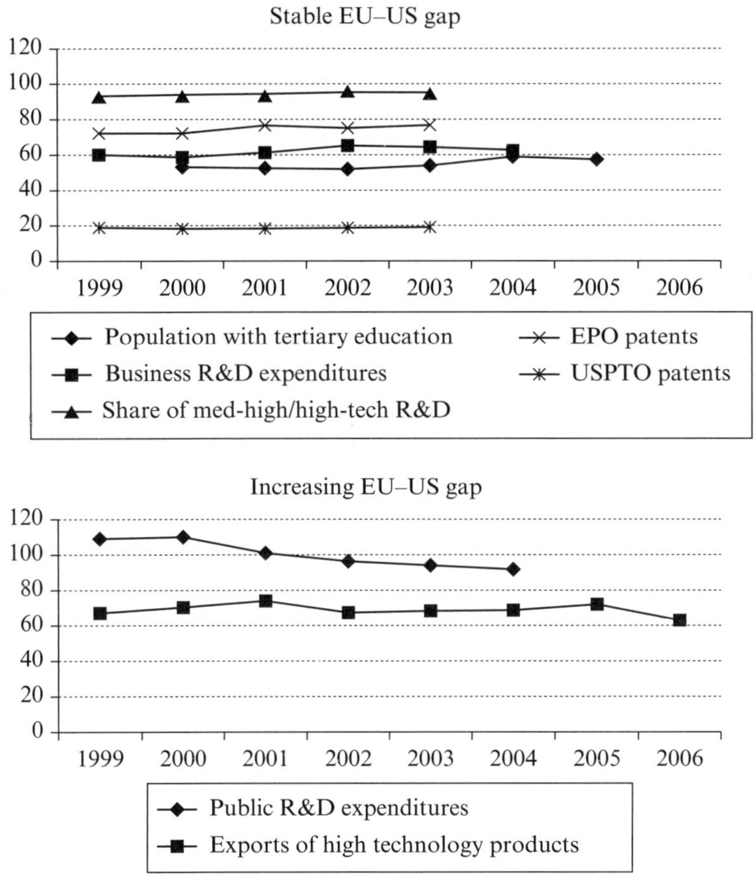

Note: Values for the EU relative to the US = 100.

Source: EC-ENTR (2007).

Figure 22.1c Decomposing the EU–US Innovation Score: the dimensions with the bad news (stable and increasing EU–US gap)

regulation and the lack of a clear intellectual property rights (IPR) regime are important barriers for firms in the EU to enter, grow, innovate, adopt new technologies and implement good management practices. These factors also inhibit the exit of inefficient firms, thereby preventing the reallocation of resources to more productive uses. Also the EU's linking capacity is deficient, with hampered industry–science links, less well-functioning (venture) capital markets and more rigid labour markets.

22.5 THE IMPACT OF REGULATION AND PRODUCT MARKET REFORMS ON INNOVATION AND PRODUCTIVITY

A number of studies show the substantial negative effects of bad regulation, too-slow reforms and insufficient product market competition, especially in countries far from the technology frontier, and in ICT-intensive sectors (Nicoletti and Scarpetta, 2003; Conway et al., 2006). It is particularly interesting to see how the average effects of high regulation materialize through keeping 'alive' badly performing firms and sectors (see Figure 22.2).

Furthermore, these studies show that a large part of the impact on productivity runs through indirect effects, affecting dynamic efficiency. For instance, the gains from further product market reforms are estimated to be largest in innovation-intensive ICT sectors. In industries and services that use ICT intensively, the gap in productivity improvement that follows a shift of the technological frontier allowed by this general purpose technology reaches a level as high as 40 per cent in the more restrictive countries. This indicates that regulatory barriers may not only have a direct restrictive effect on growth, but are also barriers for innovation and technology diffusion and as a result inhibit dynamic efficiency.

22.6 WHAT POLICY AGENDA DO WE NEED?

The previous sections have tried to demonstrate that addressing the deficient EU innovative capacity requires going beyond stimulating the research inputs from the public and the private sector. It is important that structural reforms aimed at improving the functioning of labour, product and financial markets are part of the policy agenda to improve the EU's innovative capacity. To address the problem of poor innovative performance and industry dynamics, a full set of structural policies is required that strengthen the creative destruction mechanism, remove barriers to entry, exit and growth and provide smooth access for dynamic firms to markets, capital and skills.

Competition policy and market liberalization and integration, particularly in service sectors, are crucial components of this policy agenda. But these will not yield the expected improvements without structural reforms in the market for higher education and research, and in Europe's capital and labour markets.

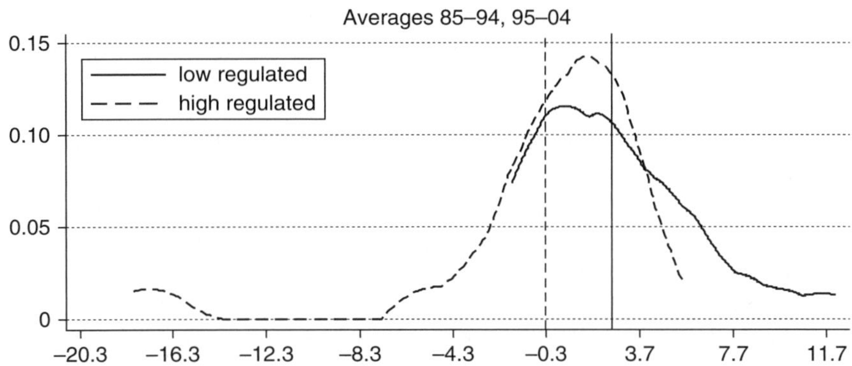

Source: OECD (2007).

Figure 22.2 Comparing productivity growth in ICT using sectors: low versus highly regulated subsectors

22.7 THE EU LISBON AGENDA

At the March 2000 Lisbon European Council, the EU launched a comprehensive set of integrated structural reforms. The scope of the Lisbon Strategy has been wide from the outset in terms of the policy tools to be used, combining investments in the knowledge-based economy (education, training, R&D, innovation, ICT) with product and capital market reforms (improving the functioning of the internal market, promoting EU financial integration, improving the business environment) and labour market reforms (increasing labour market flexibility and incentives to participate in the labour market).

The Lisbon Strategy was renewed in 2005, with a greater focus on growth and jobs, recognizing R&D and innovation as a key priority and with an improved policy governance structure. Member states were asked to draw their own National Reform Programmes (NRPs) on the basis of common integrated guidelines. The Community Lisbon Programme (CLP) includes the set of actions taken at the level of EU in support of the Strategy, relabelled as the Growth and Jobs Strategy. The CLP includes the Community Patent Regulation, Directive on Services, the DOHA multilateral trade agreements, a proposal on the Common Consolidated Tax Base, revised guidelines on State Aid for R&D and risk capital, changes in the Company Law Directive, legislation on portability of pension rights, recognition of professional qualifications and a set of funds to support the Lisbon Agenda. This renewed Lisbon Strategy and its priority actions on

R&D, innovation and a dynamic business environment have been continuously endorsed by the heads of states in subsequent Spring Councils.

22.8 PROGRESS ON STRUCTURAL REFORMS

With the (renewed) Lisbon Strategy in place, Europe continues to make progress in structural reforms, both in product markets and in labour markets, according to the Organisation for Economic Co-operation and Development (OECD) (2007). Nevertheless, the reform process has yet to be advanced decisively. While most progress has been recorded in product market reforms with the Internal Market Program, a more detailed analysis reveals that these reforms are nevertheless slow-paced, not broadly based across sectors (most notably the services sectors) and across member states, and not always targeted to the most binding bottlenecks. Labour market reforms have started later, are still relatively restricted, but seem to have started to pay off more visibly, particularly in those countries where product market reforms have preceded them.

The own evaluations made by the EU of the first round of NRPs reveal that, on the reforms that matter most for improving Europe's creative destruction processes, the NRPs (and also the CLP for that matter) could and should go further. On the Community Patent no marked progress has been made. Also the functioning of the internal market and the need to enhance competition and market access in general deserve greater attention, for example the effective opening of energy markets, access to public procurement contracts or effective competition in services. Better regulation is crucial to creating a more competitive business environment and removing obstacles to innovation and change. Much of the rule-making affecting business, for example in taxation, social security or regional planning, is done at national (or local) level. Nearly all member states address parts of this agenda but in many cases a more integrated approach is necessary.

22.9 IMPLICATIONS FOR EUROPEAN POLICY-MAKING

At this stage, it is too early to know whether the revised Lisbon Agenda is delivering and will continue to deliver expected results. Nevertheless, some transformations that could increase the likelihood of success include: a more focused implementation; a clearer orientation towards policies designed to improve the creative destruction process, particularly by removing barriers to growth for innovative, young enterprises; a higher emphasis on the complementary aspects of these policies, particularly with regard to research mobility, higher education reforms, services liberalization and a reinforcement of the implementing instruments and common procedures among the member states.

All this is well known and does not require any major change in objectives and instruments, only a focused commitment and a systemic approach. Mastering the full set of policy instrument, breaking down the barriers across policy departments and between member states and Community policy levels, has been and remains a constant challenge in the Lisbon Strategy. It also requires a regular evaluation of progress made, both of the National Reform Programmes and Community Lisbon Programme. This calls for more evidence and analysis to motivate and improve the effectiveness of policy actions, investing in a monitoring capacity that can build on up-to-date facts and analysis to evaluate and, where needed, redirect policy actions and priorities. At this juncture, with a less benign economic climate, mounting fears of globalization driving protectionism, stalling trade liberalization and a backlash against competition, Europe needs innovative, well-informed policy-makers.

NOTE

1. Financial support from FWO (ESF-STRIKE and G.0523.08), Belgian Federal Government PAI (P6/09), KUL-OF (OT/07/11) and the EC(SSHT-CT-2008-217436 Scifi-glow) is gratefully acknowledged. The article was largely written when the author was an adviser at EC-BEPA, on leave from the university, where various BEPA colleagues and BEPA/GEPA meetings provided useful inputs. This article does not necessarily reflect the view of the EC. All views, omissions and errors are on the account of the author only.

REFERENCES

Bloom, N. and J. Van Reenen (2007), 'Explaining management practices across firms and nations', *Quarterly Journal of Economics*, **122** (4), 1351–1408.

Conway P., D. de Rosa, G. Nicoletti and F. Steiner (2006), 'Regulation, competition and productivity convergente', OECD Economics Department Working Paper 509.

EC-ENTR (2007), European Innovation Scoreboard, Luxembourg: European Commission.

ECFIN (2007), 'EU economy 2007 review: moving Europe's productivity frontier', Luxembourg, European Commission.

Nicoletti, G. and S. Scarpetta (2003), 'Regulation, productivity and growth', *Economic Policy*, **36**, 11–72.

O'Sullivan, M. (2007), 'The EU's R&D deficit and innovation policy', Report of the Expert Group on Knowledge for Growth, EC-RTD.

OECD (2007), *Going for Growth: Economic Policy Reforms*, Paris: OECD Publishing.

Van Reenen, J., N. Bloom and R. Sadun (2007), 'Americans do IT better: US multinationals and the Productivity Miracle', CEP Discussion Paper 788, Centre for Economic Policy, London School of Economics.

PART VII

Technology Policy and New Models of Innovation

23. Adapting policy to user-centered innovation

Eric von Hippel

23.1 OVERVIEW

At least since Schumpeter (1934 [1974]), economists and policy-makers have assumed that the dominant mode of innovation is a 'producers' model'.[1] That is, it has been assumed that economically important innovations originate from producers who need to be able to protect these innovations through intellectual property rights in order to secure monopolies over their innovations for some period of time (Arrow, 1962). Differences found in the social versus private rates of return for innovations also suggested that drawing forth more innovations would increase public welfare (for example, Mansfield et al., 1977).

Accordingly, around the world, policies have been developed and progressively elaborated to support producers in their innovation-related efforts. Prominent among these are various kinds of government subsidy for the 'properly documented' research and development expenditure of private firms, and intellectual property law protections to increase the profits of those who introduce innovations into the marketplace.

If, as we now are discovering, users are an important – and perhaps the most important – developers of innovations, two things must be done: (1) present, producer-centric innovation policies must be re-examined to determine their possible impacts on user innovation; and (2) new policies should be considered that might provide valuable additional support to user innovation.

In what follows, I first very briefly summarize what we know about the importance of user innovation (section 23.2). Then I suggest that user innovation must be better measured by governments, and offer an example of how this can be done (section 23.3). Next I describe an important form of user innovation – collaborative innovation by user communities (section 23.4). Finally I suggest some relevant arenas for policy-making that could help support user innovation (sections 23.5 and 23.6).

23.2 CASE STUDIES CLEARLY SHOW THE UBIQUITY OF USER INNOVATION

Users, as we use the term in this chapter, are firms or individual consumers that expect to benefit from using a product or a service. In contrast, manufacturers expect to benefit from selling a product or a service. A firm or an individual can have different relationships to different products or innovations. For example, Boeing is a manufacturer of airplanes, but it is also a user of machine tools. If we were examining innovations developed by Boeing for the airplanes it sells, we would consider Boeing a manufacturer-innovator in those cases. But if we were considering innovations in metal-forming machinery developed by Boeing for in-house use in building airplanes, we would categorize those as user-developed innovations and would categorize Boeing as a user-innovator in those cases.

23.2.1 Many Users Modify or Develop New Products

It is now well documented that many product users innovate to modify or develop *de novo* products that they use in many fields. Consider the sampling of studies shown in Table 23.1.

23.2.2 Innovations Developed by 'Lead Users' are often a Source of Commercially Attractive Products for Manufacturers

Users that innovate have been found to typically be 'lead users' – defined as having two characteristics: (1) expecting major benefits from solutions to the novel needs they encounter; and (2) being at the leading edge of important marketplace trends. It has been shown that, because 'necessity is the mother of invention' (characteristic 1), many lead users will innovate to solve the problems they have encountered. It has also been shown that innovations that lead users develop to solve problems they encounter at the leading edge of the market (characteristic 2) will later also be wanted by others – and therefore will be potentially profitable products for manufacturers. Studies of innovations commercialized by manufacturers in a range of fields bear out this expectation (Franke et al., 2006; Luethje et al., 2005; von Hippel, 2005).

23.2.3 User-Developed Products are often Important on Several Dimensions

Studies also show that innovations developed by users are by no means trivial relative to manufacturer-developed innovations. Indeed, many of

Table 23.1 Studies of user innovation frequency

Innovation area	Number and type of users sampled	% developing and building product for own use
Industrial products		
1. Printed Circuit CAD Software (a)	136 user firm attendees at a PC-CAD conference	24.3
2. Pipe Hanger Hardware (b)	Employees in 74 pipe hanger installation firms	36
3. Library Information Systems (c)	Employees in 102 Australian libraries using computerized OPAC library information systems	26
4. Medical Surgery Equipment (d)	261 surgeons working in university clinics in Germany	22
5. Apache OS server software security features (e)	131 technically sophisticated Apache users (webmasters)	19.1
6. Twenty six 'Advanced Manufacturing Technologies' introduced into Canadian plants (f)	4200 Canadian manufacturing plants Nine Manufacturing Sectors (less food processing) in Canada, 1998	28
Consumer products		
7. Outdoor consumer products (g)	153 recipients of mail order catalogs for outdoor activity products for consumers	9.8
8. 'Extreme' sporting equipment (h)	197 members of 4 specialized sporting clubs in 4 'extreme' sports	37.8
9. Mountain biking equipment (i)	291 mountain bikers in a geographic region known to be an 'innovation hot spot'	19.2

Sources: (a) Urban and von Hippel (1988); (b) Herstatt and von Hippel (1992); (c) Morrison et al. (2000); (d) Lüthje (2003); (e) Franke and von Hippel (2003); (f) Arundel and Sonntag (1999); (g) Lüthje (2004); (h) Franke and Shah (2003); (i) Lüthje et al. (2005).

the innovations judged to be most important in a field with respect to both improved functionality over previous best practice and commercial value are in fact developed by users rather than manufacturers. Thus Enos (1962) reported that nearly all the most important innovations in oil refining were developed by user firms. Freeman (1968) found that the most widely licensed chemical production processes were developed by user firms. Von Hippel (1988) found that users were the developers of about 80 percent of the most important scientific instrument innovations, and also the developers of 67 percent of the major innovations in semiconductor processing. Pavitt (1984) found that a considerable fraction of invention by British firms was for in-house use. Shah (2000) found that the most commercially important equipment innovations in four sporting fields were developed by innovating users.

Innovations developed by users are also often of high technical quality. In a 2007 study of 26 000 medical device patents, Chatterji and Fabrizio (2007) found that 20 percent were filed by physician inventors – users. They compared patents filed by user-inventors to those of inventors who were not users, and concluded that the user patents were of higher technical quality on several separate dimensions. First, the user-inventors cited the scientific literature to a greater degree than did patents developed by non-physician inventors. Second, user patents were ahead with respect to important 'technical trajectories'. Third, they had more claims than non-user inventors, suggesting broader scope. Fourth, patents filed by user inventors were more frequently cited by succeeding patents than were patents filed by non-user inventors, and also were more frequently cited by patents outside of the patent's own technology class.

A study by Lettl et al. (2007) examined 2795 patent families in 'surgical instruments, devices or methods'. They found that citations of user inventor patents were lower than for manufacturer patents in terms of immediate impact on subsequent technological developments in a focal technological domain. Later in the patent's life, however, this gap was closed. Their study also shows that user patents cited more classes than did manufacturer patents – that is, were broader. The subset of user patents that were narrowly focused on a particular technical field were as technically important (cited as frequently) as patents filed by manufacturer inventors who were on the leading edge of that discipline.

23.3 BETTER MEASUREMENT OF USER-CENTERED INNOVATION NEEDED

To paraphrase Robert Solow's famous quip about computers: 'One can see user innovation everywhere – except in the statistics!' (Solow, 1987). One important thing governments can do, therefore, is to improve the measurement of innovation by users. Until the actual levels of user innovation and expenditure are made clear, it will be difficult to get academics and policy-makers to take the policy-making needs of user innovators seriously.

For example, Community Innovation Survey (CIS)-type innovation surveys currently ask manufacturers about 'sources' of important information to their innovation projects. Manufacturers invariably report that customers were a source of important information – but the 'sources' questions do not go into any detail on the content of that important information. As a consequence, the true locus of innovation cannot be inferred from the responses given. For example, the actual content of an 'important information input' from a customer can range from: 'I have an important need that is not yet fulfilled – can you develop a solution?' to 'I have developed a new machine and used it successfully in my factory. Here is a roll of blueprints. Build me 50 more.' But, in the absence of this type of content information, one can only conclude that customers are an important source of information to manufacturer innovation projects.

It is possible for government statistical agencies to address the current bias against the reporting of innovations by users by changing the questions asked, and changing whom one asks them of. We are aware of one survey in which users, rather than manufacturers, were asked by a government statistical agency to report on an innovation 'adoption' process from their point of view. In 1998 Fred Gault of Statistics Canada directed a survey to Canadian plants using advanced manufacturing technologies (AMTs) rather than to, as was customary practice, AMT equipment suppliers. This survey covered nine manufacturing sectors in Canada (food processing was excluded) and inquired about the methods plants had used to introduce any of 26 AMTs they were using.

In the Statistics Canada survey, two questions were asked about possible user innovation: (1) had the plants introduced an AMT 'by customizing or significantly modifying existing technology?' and (2) had the plants introduced an AMT 'by developing brand new advanced technologies?' Data were obtained from 4200 manufacturing plants, and the data were analyzed by Arundel and Sonntag (1999) and by Sabourin and Beckstead (1999) (see Table 23.2).

As can be seen in Table 23.2, this survey showed extensive innovation by users. Fully 29 percent of plants – AMT users – reported introducing advanced technologies into the plant 'by developing brand new advanced technologies'. Fully 50 percent reported that they did this 'by customizing or significantly modifying existing technology'. This finding fits the case data in Table 23.1 which shows a similar proportion of users innovating in a range of product categories. Note especially that study 1 in Table 23.1 deals with an 'advanced manufacturing technology' – a type of computer-aided design (CAD) system – that is on the Canadian list of advanced technologies. That study reported that 24.3 percent of users developed their own CAD systems. Further experiments are now under way within

Table 23.2 Results of a Statistics Canada survey of users of advanced manufacturing technologies

Method of introducing advanced technologies into a plant (Establishment Weighted)		
METHOD	YES	NO
	(percentage of establishments)	
a) by purchasing off-the-shelf equipment	84	16
b) by licensing new technology	18	82
c) by customizing or significantly modifying existing technology	50	50
d) by developing brand new advanced technologies	29	72

Source: Sabourin and Beckstead (1999), Table 5.1.

Statistics Canada and elsewhere to learn how to improve the measurement of innovation expenditure by corporate users.

23.4 HOW COLLABORATIVE USER-CENTERED INNOVATION WORKS

In order to understand how government policies might better support innovation by users – and/or hinder it less – we need to understand a bit more about how user innovation works. All the data shown in Table 23.1 link innovations to a single user individual or firm. However, recent research shows that users often tend to develop their innovations via informal collaboration with others (Franke and Shah, 2003; Baldwin et al., 2006). In this 'users' collaborative innovation model', users divide up the tasks (and thus the costs) of innovation and then share their results without demands for payment enforceable by intellectual property rights (Harhoff et al., 2003).

User-innovators that do informally collaborate and freely reveal innovations to each other in this manner gain advantages over 'Robinson Crusoe' users that innovate independently. (Baldwin and Clark, 2006 showed this in the case of open source software development projects.) In essence, since innovation-related information is a non-rival good, when user-innovators are not in direct competition with each other, each participant gains a private benefit by using its own innovation. Innovators also often gain additional private benefit from freely revealing their innovations as a public good, via network effects, reputational advantages and so on. All interested users then additionally gain benefit from innovations freely revealed by other contributors (Allen, 1983; von Hippel, 2005). Benkler (2006) makes very similar points in his explorations of the functioning of information networks.

23.5 CONDITIONS FAVORABLE TO COLLABORATIVE USER-CENTERED INNOVATION

As was noted above, a very effective and widely practiced form of user innovation is a collaborative and distributed process involving the free revealing of individually created contributions, with contributors both drawing from and contributing to an information and innovation commons. With the advent of the Internet and collaborative design tools, the fixed and variable costs of enabling individual contributors to make timely and useful contributions to many types of innovation projects have decreased greatly (Benkler, 2006):

> The great success of the Internet generally, and peer-production processes in particular, has been the adoption of technical and organizational architectures that have allowed them [individual contributors] to pool such diverse efforts effectively. The core characteristics underlying the success of these enterprises are their modularity and their capacity to integrate many fine-grained contributions . . . 'Granularity' refers to the size of the modules, in terms of the time and effort that an individual must invest in producing them . . . The granularity of the modules therefore sets the smallest possible individual investment necessary to participate in a project. If this investment is sufficiently low, then 'incentives' for producing that component of a modular project can be of trivial magnitude. . . . If the finest-grained contributions are relatively large and would require a large investment of time and effort, the universe of potential contributors decreases. (Benkler, 2006, pp. 100–101).

23.6 POLICIES NEEDED TO SUPPORT COLLABORATIVE INNOVATION BY USERS

Given the above brief description of collaborative, user-centered innovation, what is it that these innovation processes need to function efficiently? Since each user-contributor to a collaborative innovation has to make his or its contribution yield justifiable private benefit without aggregation of demand across multiple users – it is key to the success of user distributed user innovation to make the fixed and variable cost of making micro-contributions as low as possible. An example of a fixed or 'set-up' transaction cost would be acquiring a computer or learning a new computer language. An example of a variable or 'frictional' transaction cost would be the costs associated with submitting code in that language to solve a specific problem.

There are several aspects to making innovation contribution transaction costs as cheap as possible. In what follows I offer some suggestions. I hope policy-makers will refine or change or add to these, and comment on the potential they see for government policy-making:

1. Issue. Widely distributed potential innovation contributors need cheap access to each other and to problems and to exchange problem-solving content. They also need tools to enable and ease collaborative work.

   Discussion questions for policy-makers. Should Internet access be supported by government – for the same reasons that roads are supported by government as a public good? Should channel neutrality (perhaps by mandated separation of ownership of channel and content) be supported by government? Should the development of Internet-related tools for collaborative innovation work be supported?
2. Issue. Contributors need open standards and open interfaces to enable them to innovate with the fullest information and the fewest interface constraints possible. There is marketplace pressure towards open standards in many fields, but firms with sufficient market power may prefer proprietary standards (for example, Apple iTunes.)

   Discussion questions for policy-makers. Does government policy-making and/or funding support for open standards and open interfaces make sense? (For example, I am told that currently standards-writing is not an allowable expense in the US in National Science Foundation (NSF) grants – although it may be in Europe. This may leave the funding of standards-writing up to entities with large economic interests in the outcome.)
3. Issue. In order to build the efficiency of collaborative user innovation over time, contributors to collaborative innovation processes need to be able freely to reveal, deposit and withdraw solution information to and from information commons at low cost. Today the intent and design of present-day copyright and patent law and other legislation and policy such as the Digital Millennium Copyright Act (DMCA) is to create strong property rights. These enable owners of intellectual property to put all sorts of barriers and toll booths in the path of those who would freely access and use information. (An unpleasant example: owners of patented property can deposit it in a commons

without revealing its ownership status, wait for its value to increase as people build upon it – and then sue.)

Discussion question for policy-makers. How can intellectual property policy be changed to allow commons-based and 'owned' property to exist in parallel and without mutual interference? Should the range of property for which ownership is allowed be reduced (software patents, business method patents)?

NOTE

1. Schumpeter even regarded producers as the primary generators of new needs among consumers, saying: 'Yet innovations in the economic system do not as a rule take place in such a way that first new wants arise spontaneously in consumers and then the productive apparatus swings round through their pressure. We do not deny the presence of this nexus. It is, however, the producer who as a rule initiates economic change, and consumers are educated by him if necessary; they are, as it were, taught to want new things, or things which differ in some respect or other from those which they have been in the habit of using' (Schumpeter, 1934, p. 65).

REFERENCES

Allen, R.C. (1983), 'Collective invention', *Journal of Economic Behavior and Organization*, **4** (1), 1–24.

Arrow, K. (1962), 'Economic welfare and the allocation of resources for inventions', in NBER (ed.), *The Rate and Direction of Inventive Activity: Economic and Social Factors*, Princeton, NJ: Princeton University Press, pp. 609–25.

Arundel, Anthony and Viki Sonntag (1999), 'Patterns of advanced manufacturing technology (AMT) use in Canadian manufacturing: 1998 AMT survey results', Catalogue No. 88F0017MIE, No. 12, Ottawa: Statistics Canada.

Baldwin, Carliss Y. and Kim B. Clark (2006), 'The architecture of participation: does code architecture mitigate free riding in the open source development model?', *Management Science*, **52** (7), 1116–27.

Baldwin, Carliss Y., Christoph Hienerth and Eric von Hippel (2006), 'How user innovations become commercial products: a theoretical investigation and case study', *Research Policy*, **35** (9), 1291–1313.

Benkler, Yochai (2006), *The Wealth of Networks*, New Haven, CT: Yale University Press.

Chatterji, Aaron K. and Kira Fabrizio (2007), 'User innovation in the medical device industry', Working Paper, Fuqua School of Business, Duke University.

Enos, J. L. (1962), *Petroleum Progress and Profits: A History of Process Innovation*, Cambridge, MA: MIT Press.

Franke, N. and S. Shah (2003), 'How communities support innovative activities: an explanation of assistance and sharing among end-users', *Research Policy*, **32** (1), 157–78.

Franke, Nikolaus and Eric von Hippel (2003), 'Satisfying heterogeneous user needs via innovation toolkits: the case of Apache Security software', *Research Policy*, **32** (7), 1199–1215.

Franke, Nikolaus, Eric von Hippel and Martin Schreier (2006), 'Finding commercially attractive user innovations: a test of lead-user theory', *Journal of Product Innovation Management*, **23**, 301–15.

Freeman, C. (1968), 'Chemical process plant: innovation and the world market', *National Institute Economic Review*, **45** (August), 29–57.

Harhoff, Dietmar, Joachim Henkel and Eric von Hippel (2003), 'Profiting from voluntary information spillovers: how users benefit from freely revealing their innovations', *Research Policy*, **32** (10), 1753–69.

Herstatt, Cornelius and Eric von Hippel (1992), 'From experience: developing new product concepts via the lead user method: a case study in a "Low Tech" field', *Journal of Product Innovation Management*, **9**, 213–21.

Lettl, Christopher, Katja Rost and Iwan von Wartburg (2007), 'Technological merit of user inventions: achieving impact by exploitation', Working Paper, IOU, University of Zurich.

Lüthje, C. (2003), 'Customers as co-inventors: an empirical analysis of the antecedents of customer-driven innovations in the field of medical equipment', Proceedings from the 32th EMAC Conference 2003, Glasgow.

Lüthje, C. (2004), 'Characteristics of innovating users in a consumer goods field: an empirical study of sport-related product consumers', *Technovation*, **24** (9), 683–95.

Lüthje, Christian, Cornelius Herstatt and Eric von Hippel (2005), 'User-innovators and "local" information: the case of mountain biking', *Research Policy*, **34** (6), 951–65.

Mansfield, E., J. Rapoport, A. Romeo, S. Wagner and G. Beerdsley (1977), 'Social and private rates of return from industrial innovations', *Quarterly Journal of Economics*, **91** (2), 221–40.

Morrison, P.D, J.H. Roberts and E. von Hippel (2000), 'Determinants of user innovation and innovation sharing in a local market', *Management Science*, **46** (12), 1513–27.

Pavitt, K. (1984), 'Sectoral patterns of technical change: towards a taxonomy and a theory', *Research Policy*, **13** (6), 343–73.

Sabourin, D. and D. Beckstead (1999), 'Technology adoption in Canadian manufacturing', Catalogue No. 88F0006XPB, No. 05, Ottawa: Statistics Canada.

Schumpeter, Joseph A. (1934), *The Theory of Economic Development*, New York: Oxford University Press, Reprinted 1974.

Shah, Sonali (2000), 'Sources and patterns of innovation in a consumer products field: innovations in sporting equipment', MIT Sloan School of Management Working Paper 4105 (March).

Solow, Robert (1987), 'We'd better watch out', *New York Times*, Book Review Section, 12 July, p. 36.

Urban, G.L. and E. von Hippel (1988), 'Lead user analyses for the development of new industrial products', *Management Science*, **34** (5), 569–82.

von Hippel, Eric (1988), *The Sources of Innovation*, New York: Oxford University Press.

von Hippel, Eric (2005), *Democratizing Innovation*, Cambridge, MA: MIT Press.

24. Technology policy, cooperation and human systems design

Yochai Benkler

The decade since the late 1990s has seen an increase in the salience of commons-based production of information, knowledge and culture in general, and peer production in particular. Most prominent and extensively studied by economists has been free and open source software.[1] Since the early 2000s, the applicability of commons-based peer production more generally has been recognized, through the increasing salience of Wikipedia, Slashdot and, more recently, the Web 2.0 phenomenon generally (Benkler, 2002a). These phenomena raise two types of policy considerations. First, there are policy implications even if these practices were purely limited to creative and innovative practices in the networked environment. Second, they raise further policy considerations given that they represent salient examples of broader trends or characteristics of innovation, such as the congruence of the new forms of peer production with Eric von Hippel's long-standing work on user innovation. In particular, I will suggest a need for more systematic work on mechanism design for cooperation, based primarily on experimental economics of cooperation and reciprocity, and some strands in organizational sociology.

24.1 COMMONS-BASED PRODUCTION, PEER PRODUCTION AND POLICY

Commons-based production refers to production without exclusion from the outputs of innovation efforts. A 'commons' is an institutional arrangement whereby a resource is managed so that access to, or use of, it as a resource is available under rules that give a set of people symmetric rights or powers, rather than based on asymmetric power to determine their disposition, as in the case of property. Trucking, by comparison to railroads, is partly a commons-based model of shipping, because it relies for a core input on a system of roads that are open to all on symmetric rules. Commons-based production can be commercial or non-commercial, individually pursued or cooperative. Information production is only commons-based when a producer utilizes mechanisms other than exclusion through asserting patents or copyrights, or retaining secrecy, to appropriate the value of the information produced. The policy significance of commons-based production is that, where it is sustainable for a given information production activity, the standard tension underlying the policy of copyrights and patents, between the need of producers to see a positive return and the inefficiency of positive pricing of information, is resolved.

Peer production is a subset of commons-based production. It refers to large-scale collaboration among contributors, which is not coordinated through a price system or a managerial model. A site built on professional contributors paid to blog, for example, so as to draw readers, which distributes its contents free of constraints on reuse, accompanied by advertising, is engaged in a commons-based commercial model, but not in peer production. A site like Slashdot that sells advertising but neither pays contributors nor appropriates the value of the contents or comments on the site by exclusion, is engaged as a commercial platform for harnessing peer production. Wikipedia is a non-commercial commons-based peer production enterprise. The touchstone for commons-based production is not the absence of money, but the absence of exclusion. The touchstone for peer production is not the absence of some form of appropriation, including monetary, but the fact that communications and social cooperation, not prices or commands, coordinate action.

Much work on open source software has focused on two basic questions: 'What are the incentives motivating people to contribute to open source software?' And 'What are the comparative advantages, in terms of efficiency or innovation, of this model of development?' The basic insight on motivation is that open source software development projects draw on a variety of people, operating from a diverse set of motivations, engaged in diverse levels of effort.[2] Because the software services industry is so large, there are relatively many opportunities for non-proprietary commercial appropriation of the investments in open source software by comparison to other types of innovation and creativity. In survey evidence from Europe, for example, about half of the contributors surveyed claimed not to make any money from contribution to free software, and the other half split roughly evenly between those paid directly to develop, administer or support free software, and those paid indirectly, because of experience or other, more remote connections to their contributions (Ghosh et al., 2002). The half that is not paid, as well as a greater portion of participants in many non-software peer production efforts, require other explanations. At the macro level, the answer to the question, 'Are there sufficient motivations to achieve a sustained flow of information production in this model?' is likely some combination of the answers with regard to user-driven innovation (von Hippel, 2005), and the claim that with sufficient diversity of motivation and excess capacity (time, insight) in the population, modularizing tasks (Baldwin and Clark, 2006) in sufficiently fine-grained modules, and allowing integration of efforts of diverse granularity, will tap a sufficient number of contributions to achieve a steady flow of contributions (Benkler, 2002a; Benkler, 2004a). It was this macro-level question that strained credulity, and invited the answers for why peer production as a broad phenomenon was stable. At the micro level, answering the question, 'What will make this project more or less likely to draw contributions?' more work is required. I will suggest one avenue to approaching it in the second part of this chapter. The second question concerns the advantages of open source software development, or peer production more generally. Economists, following more informal claims by Eric Raymond, focused on the ability of users to invest in improving their software and customizing it to their own heterogeneous needs (Franke and von Hippel, 2003). My own argument, applicable more broadly to peer production than specifically to software, was based on transaction costs and the incontractibility of knowledge work. Decentralized capacity to act, created by the decentralization of physical capital (computers and network connections), together with decentralization of authority to act (the commons), allows people with diverse insights and availability as to what projects can be pursued, with which resources, in which collaborations, to sense the environment for potential projects, and pursue those projects with those resources in those potential collaborations, without encountering the burdens of transaction costs or knowledge management shortfalls that similar efforts to bring together people, resources and projects encounter within explicit markets or firms (Benkler, 2002a; Benkler, 2004a).

From a policy perspective, the rise of commons-based production in general, and peer production in particular, as a significant solution space to innovation and creativity, exacerbates a pre-existing policy concern with patents and copyrights as technology policy. At root, peer production should be understood against the background that we have always had diverse models for appropriating the benefits of innovation and creativity, both by commercial entities and through the very large role of government and non-profit sectors. The different roles and advantages of, most famously, patent-based commercial firms and academic science, have long been and continue to be a subject of study and emphasis (Nelson, 1959; Aghion et al., 2006). For patents, a long line of survey studies show persistent differences among industries in terms of dependence on patents

(Mansfield et al., 1981; Levin et al., 1987; Cohen et al., 2000 [2004]). For basic science, government funding, cross-subsidies from teaching, and the university prestige system were, and continue to be, primary drivers. With regard to creativity covered by copyright, different industries and different forms require very different models. Jazz is different from pop, is different from classical music, but live performances play a large role in funding artists in all these categories. Television is different from movies; documentaries, from action movies. Academic research books are different from textbooks and trade books. In almost all the cases of the former in these binary comparisons, royalties play a smaller role than 'service'-like models: live performance, teaching, consulting; as well as advertising for most of the mass media.

The critical point from a policy perspective is that patents and copyrights affect different appropriation models differently, and can therefore cause shifts in appropriation strategy before they affect overall innovative or creative activity (Benkler, 2002b). The anchor to this point is the 'on the shoulders of giants' effect (Scotchmer, 1991). Because patents and copyrights raise the input costs of all information producers, but increase appropriability only for producers who rely on exclusion as their appropriation model, these regulatory mechanisms change the pay-offs to different appropriation techniques independently of their effect on overall levels of innovation.

The rise of user-driven innovation and peer production exacerbates the problem presented by a regulatory preference for patent- and copyright-based strategies over appropriation strategies that are not based on exclusion. Because these mechanisms of innovation and creativity depend in significant part on voluntary contributions and free revealing, without any form of monetary appropriation, or on forms of indirect appropriation, such as human capital accrual and non-definite improvement in future employment, they are particularly sensitive to higher information input costs. The basic dynamic inefficiency associated with positive pricing of non-rival goods as inputs is not counterbalanced in these projects by increased incentives. Cumulatively, the transaction costs associated with licensing of participation in highly distributed projects composed of many small-grained contributions, mean that the cost burden per contribution, relative to the value of the contribution to the overall project, are high. The resistance to software patents in Europe, for example, centers precisely around the ecological effect of patents on open source development. While large Free and Open Source Software (FOSS) developers, like IBM or Red Hat, could afford to negotiate for and pay for a non-exclusive license, the thousands of contributors who might want to patch any given bug could not, depriving the open innovation system as a whole of its lifeblood. The primary policy emphasis around commons-based production generally and peer production in particular has therefore been deregulatory. That is, the rise of commons-based and peer production has been one of the reasons given for the need to retreat from the emphasis on stronger copyright and patent protection, such as with software patents in Europe, technology mandates, such as the Digital Millennium Copyright Act or the *Grokster* decision in the United States, the creation of rights in data, such as the Database Directive in the EU or the introduction of rights to prohibit automated data collection, like 'trespass to chattels', in some states in the US, and the international harmonization of these exclusive rights regimes.

Work has also been done on affirmative interventions that could support user-driven innovation or peer production. Most extensive has been work on licensing. The basic question here is whether and when cooperation efforts need some form of 'copyleft' protection. 'Copyleft', a term coined by Richard Stallman, is a licensing provision originally implemented in the most widely used free software license, the General Public License, or GPL, which requires those who distribute modified versions of the code to distribute the modified code under the same terms that the original version was distributed. Given that one of the most famous examples of open source software, the GNU/Linux system, is distributed under GPL, while another, Apache, is distributed under a license that does not have such a requirement, there has been some discussion about the advantages and disadvantages of this approach (Lerner and Tirole, 2005). Within the community of programmers, the debate is as much, if not more, political than economic. One aspect of this question that has not been studied by economists or other social scientists is the choice of license as a 'political' or community-minded signal or statement of commitment. A similar debate has arisen over 'creative commons' licenses: standardized license terms for more-or-less free distribution of other forms of copyrighted materials. The emphasis in creative commons is on author choice, providing a menu of options as to limitations on downstream users: ranging from 'attribution', through 'non-commercial' (which limits permission to non-commercial use) and 'sharealike' (which is a copyleft provision), to 'sampling', which is a very narrowly defined privilege to sample digitally a work for purposes of remixing it. There is debate over whether the creative commons model of control plus choice, rather than a constrained set of sharing requirements on the background of a broad culture of implied permission, is most conducive to a culture of freely shared creative work and peer production (Elkin-Koren, 2005).

Some work has also been done on applying peer production, or 'open source'-like models to other areas of innovation. In particular, this has been true of open science (Rai and Boyle, 2007; Maurer et al., 2004; Benkler, 2004b), open scientific publication, open archiving and libraries, and open source educational materials. Science, certainly in its ideal, Mertonian rendition, has always been 'open source'. The effort is to see the extent to which scientific inquiry can be reorganized from its present, relatively silo-based and increasingly patent-focused model, to one where scientists can collaborate across institutions more effectively and in ways that reduce the costs of research and perceived dependence on patents. Unsurprisingly, early work in this vein suggests that different kinds of scientific inquiry, requiring different capital investments or biological materials, and implemented with greater or lesser necessity for a point of industrial output, are amenable in different ways and to different degrees to peer production. At one end of the spectrum is bioinformatics, which increasingly does seem to be organized along the lines of open source software development. Still, it needs to find ways to penetrate conservative university attitudes toward promotion and tenure, which dampen participation in projects, such as annotating gene sequences as part of the International Haplotype Mapping project, which are enormously important to science but do not fit the traditional publication model for recognition and funding. A similar problem occurs for open scientific publication, as was seen in the US when the original Public Library of Science commitment not to publish in closed journals collapsed under the needs of young scientists to place their papers. At the other end of the spectrum seems to lie biomedical innovation, in particular research of biologics, where the present seemingly insurmountable barrier is the distribution, consistency, availability and know-how-intensive use of biological materials. Although in biomedical innovation, too, it is not obvious that all efforts are equally dependent on insufficiently available materials or machines. Agricultural research, on the other hand, because of the role of public efforts and farmers, may present a more tractable problem.[3] In all, this new trend should be juxtaposed to the zeitgeist (if not consistently the practice) (Mowery et al., 2004; Owen-Smith and Powell, 2001) that followed Bayh–Dole, according to which the university would move closer to the patent-based industry model. As with the case of the extent of necessity of copyrights and patents, one of the core insights is that detailed studies of sectors, their costs and available appropriation models, will yield better insights than more abstract models.

There have also been efforts to look at the adoption of open innovation and creativity approaches to questions of innovation, creativity and human development in low- and middle-income countries. Most prominent here have been calls for developing-nation governments to require open source software in their procurement policy. This is advocated as a mechanism for allowing local talent to develop and be able to compete in a global software services market. Beyond this specific claim, there has been a broader push, led most prominently by Brazil, for using peer production as a way of enhancing local knowledge, innovation and creativity. In Brazil, this focuses on projects to support indigenous music development. The extent to which open innovation and creativity strategies are available as a development strategy remains an important subject of study.

In all, commons-based and peer production, online and offline, has achieved a new salience in the information production and innovation system of networked economies. It is likely stable. Because of networked computers, it appears to have a larger potential role in current information, culture and innovation systems than it was able to play in the past. For any given traditional question of technology and innovation policy, one therefore now needs to ask two new questions: (1) Is there a commons-based (whether cooperative or not) or peer production substitute or complement? And (2) If so, how does whatever solution or policy condition exists or is proposed affect its actual or possible existence, and the interaction effects between it and proprietary models?

24.2 A BROADER RESEARCH AGENDA ON SYSTEMS DESIGN FOR COOPERATION

The observable emergence of online cooperation coincides with several academic trends in thinking about human cooperation. These go beyond a selfish rational actor model, emphasizing a diverse set of motivational profiles, not all selfish, on the one hand, and the centrality of communication and human interaction to forming preferences for cooperation and the commitment to ongoing cooperative processes, on the other hand. Where implemented, cooperation-based systems seem primarily aimed to construct human systems capable of observing a complex and rapidly changing environment, to learn about new conditions and practices within it, and to pursue them in flexible, adaptive ways.

One anchor of this trend is the large literature in several disciplines on the prevalence of observations of human cooperation inconsistent with the predictions of the selfish rational actor model. In experimental economics we see a line of work on human proclivity to cooperate in patterns inconsistent with uniformly selfish preferences, rather than on the more mainstream concern of experimental economics: behavioral deviations from rationality.[4] From this literature we get that somewhat over half the population predictably behaves as cooperators or reciprocators in social dilemma and altruism-adducing games, and about one-third act as selfish actors. (The remainder are too noisy to characterize.) Various manipulations are associated with decay of cooperation, while others are associated with increasing cooperation. These findings suggest that, under appropriate designs, cooperators cooperate, reciprocators cooperate and invest in punishing defections by selfish agents or rewarding cooperation, and selfish agents increase cooperation over time to avoid that punishment or gain the rewards. While the literature itself is not oriented toward characterizing design levers for systems of cooperation, it is possible to synthesize these out of it. Parallel work in experiments and field studies has been done in political science, in particular around governance of the commons (Ostrom, 1998; Cardenas et al., 2000; Frolich and Oppenheimer, 2003). Aiming to fix proximate causes for the experimental observations, there is crossover work in neuroeconomics to support some of the observations of the experimental work (Camerer, 2005; Fehr et al., 2005). As to ultimate causes of cooperation, evolutionary biology has seen the introduction of multilevel selection, including group selection, as a more complex model of evolution, that explains forms of altruism that need not rely on selfishness at all (Sober and Wilson, 1999), as well as developments in the theory of reciprocity, building on early work on 'kin selection' and 'reciprocal altruism' to extend to 'indirect reciprocity' and 'network reciprocity', which operate at such remove from direct payoffs to the individual that they are entirely consistent with thoroughly other-regarding phenotypic expressions of what can still be modeled as 'selfish' underlying evolutionary dynamics (Nowak, 2006). This work has been applied to human evolutionary biology, suggesting why a proclivity to cooperate would develop and establish in a human population under conditions thought to apply in the Pleistocene, given the development of reciprocity-enforcing cultural practices like ostracism (Bowles, 2006; Bowles and Gintis, 2004), and was further coupled with culture in theories of gene-cultural co-evolution, which allow for more rapid development of cooperation practices and for the variation in practice observed in historical societies by anthropologists (Boyd and Richerson, 1988; Richerson and Boyd, 2004).

A second, distinct line is seen within organizational sociology. Growing from the work on post-Fordism, trust and increasing knowledge-intensity in firms, sociologists had observed an increasing adoption of networked organization models emerging within firms, and in some cases across firms in supply relationships (Heckscher and Adler, 2006). Globalization and rapid technological change put organizations under increasing pressure to innovate in their processes, adapt to changes, learn about a rapidly changing environment and increasingly complex processes, and implement learning continuously. Under a variety of names, such as total quality management (TQM), team production, quality circles, and so on, a variety of business processes have emerged that depend heavily on communication, on relatively higher responsibility in the hands of employees, or on the emergence of what Sabel has called new routines for trust-based collaboration, replacing the traditional models of market and hierarchies to govern internal relations within firms and between firms.[5] The two critical points, from the perspective of innovation policy, are that the turn to cooperative models and decentralization of action is seen as driven by a need to improve the learning and adaptation capabilities of organizations and interorganizational networks, and that many of the characteristics of successful collaborations fit those that one sees coming out of the experimental work.

A third trend is the emergence, within software systems design, of an effort to characterize 'social software': that is, software intended to be run for and by a group of people, and that takes fostering their interaction, including its social dynamics, as its design objective (Shirky, 2003). This literature at the moment is in an early stage, but nonetheless offers a good basis for observing cooperation in practice, running on a designed system with, therefore, relatively easily characterizable design features.

These lines of work do not generally speak to each other, yet they all point to the increasing importance of human cooperation across multiple domains, arrived at from a wide-ranging and diverse set of approaches and methods. They allow us to begin to characterize what design elements would be necessary to foster cooperation, and therefore allow us to design systems for cooperation more systematically. To the extent that innovation is a public goods problem, a classic social dilemma game, to the extent that cooperation fosters engaged learning within and across organizations to allow them to innovate their processes and practices, and to the extent that online cooperation platforms can foster greater cooperation in the production of information and innovation, a systematic approach at the micro level toward understanding why people cooperate, and how to build systems that would foster a cooperative stance and sustain cooperation as practice, would be valuable.

First, what is 'cooperation'? The working definition proposed here is based on distinguishing 'cooperation' from the predictions of the selfish rational actor model that has dominated economics for so long. The definition needs to characterize behaviors that are poorly accounted for within that framework, and yet are commonly observed in practice and experiments. For this purpose, cooperation here shall mean one of the following three attitudinal and behavioral states: (1) committed mutualism: a commitment to success of the other consistent with success of self (this can be behaviorally similar to straight trade, but with the added commitment to care about the pay-off to the other; its distinguishing characteristic emerges when the particular actions required of that commitment go beyond what straight trade and monitoring account for, and covers the role that some economists assign to trust in the context of trades where information and transaction costs make perfect pricing impossible); (2) collective efficacy: action intentionally oriented toward the success of a common goal that transcends the agent's specifiable individual success; or (3) altruism: action aimed to achieve the flourishing of the other as self, irrespective of success of self.

To dispel misinterpretations: 'cooperation' does not mean 'behaving nicely'. It means acting in ways that are beyond what a selfish and self-centered person would be predicted to do. Gang members are often highly cooperative. Suicide bombers exhibit high degrees of self-sacrifice for collective efficacy. Learning the dynamics of cooperation is important in order to disrupt successful cooperation that we judge normatively harmful, as much as it is important in order to learn how to construct successful cooperation with outcomes and processes that we normatively affirm. The question becomes general: how do we develop an approach as general and flexible in its applicability as mechanism design, but that relies on a more behaviorally realistic view of the dynamics of human cooperation, and can be optimized not purely to motivate and regulate selfish actors, the least cooperative 30 percent of the population, but can actually provide diverse motivational constraints and affordances that allow cooperators to cooperate, reciprocators to reciprocate (both at and above the minimum predicted and elicited by mechanism design), and keeps selfish actors no less in line with the cooperators than they would have been under traditional mechanism design?

Synthesis of the experimental and observational work suggests several design levers whose implementation can increase the probability of cooperative outcomes (Table 24.1). These levers characterize targets of institutional and platform design, and include: communication, empathy, humanization and solidarity; norms and fairness; trust; efficacy; discipline and punishment; transparency and reputation; exit and entry; cost; and leadership. At this stage, these levers are still in some cases at too high a level of abstraction to implement, but they are intended as a mid-level abstraction framework, general enough to capture most of the underlying experimental and observational literature, and concrete enough to inform design decisions aimed to achieve and apply one or another of the design levers. Future work will require case studies to test the applicability of the design levers and to characterize a toolbox of micro-mechanisms that can trigger these levers, as well as experimental studies and computational modeling intended to test and refine both the levers and approaches to their implementation and utilization. For now, however, the first task is to

Table 24.1 Design levers for cooperation

Design Lever	Description
Communication	Allowing participants to communicate, without any additional enforceable commitment, increases cooperation
Empathy/ humanization	Participants who identify with the counter-party to a game increase cooperation in social dilemma games, and even altruistic giving in Dictator Games
Solidarity	Participants who see themselves as part of a common identity group increase cooperation
Fairness	Participants consistently appear to care about the fairness of the outcomes, of the intentions of other participants, and of the processes
Norms	The presence of even minimal coordination focal points, or Schelling norms, can improve cooperation by clarifying what is expected from whom, and what counts as defection or cooperation. Beyond that, self-chosen norms appear to improve cooperation, as will, likely, background norms already encoded by participants as 'values'
Trust	Trust as a design lever refers to an attitudinal stance participants can have toward each other. As a design lever it is narrower than the term is usually applied, and characterizes a belief agents have about the likely actions of others when unconstrained by other system elements. When it functions, it acts as a form of anticipatory cooperation, which agents can 'reciprocate' by themselves cooperating in their first move
Efficacy	Individuals are internally driven to act with competence and efficacy. Providing a sense of efficacy in the cooperation likely improves intrinsic commitment to the cooperative project
Punishment/ reward	There is consistent evidence that introduction of a possibility of punishment into social dilemma games increases cooperation. This is consistent with the presence of some portion of the population who are selfish, and others who are reciprocators and overcome second order public goods problem of 'Who will punish?' and keep the former group in check by threatening or imposing punishment for defection
Crowding-out	Systems can crowd each other out, and elements within a given system can crowd each other out. There is significant evidence that the introduction of money into an interaction can limit participation motivated by intrinsic motivations. There is also evidence that introducing punishment can crowd out trust. Crowding out renders design more complex, because not all potential interventions interact positively

Table 24.1 (continued)

Design Lever	Description
Transparency (reputation)	Transparency of cooperation platforms enables agents to observe what others are doing, characterize actions, intentions, and outcomes, and identify cooperation for positive reciprocity and defection for negative reciprocity. Reputation is a core instance of transparency
Cost	Cooperation in this approach continues to be modeled for rational actors. The level of cooperation is sensitive to the cost of cooperation, although it is not dominated by it
Exit/entry	Whether a system is easy or hard to enter will affect the mix of types that participate and the level of trust participants will have. The direction of the effect will depend on whether exit itself is a form of defection and on whether there are significant opportunities for appropriation within the interaction
Leadership/ asymmetric contribution	Case studies and work in organizational sociology and management science suggest that leadership is important in creating and sustaining cooperation

provide a plausible provisional mid-level framework to form the basis of this future work.

24.2.1 Communication

The first thing we see is the critical role of communication in fostering cooperation. Communication is an input into causing people to cooperate more often (Sally, 1995), and can itself be a form of cooperation: the sharing of knowledge and insight. The particularly salient role of communication is important, because it locates the work on cooperation in the tradition of dialogic theories of the self: that the self comes to know its interests, desires and meaning through communication with others, rather than through solipsistic or egocentric views. Communication is therefore both a dynamic in its own right, through which people come to see their own goals, preferences and policies in conversation with others with whom they interact, and a mechanism for achieving the cooperation dynamic through facilitating most of the design levers I describe below. The effect of communication is a very robust finding in these literatures, and an obvious target for design interventions. It has a large effect in experimental work, and its routinization is one of the core design principles of the organizational shift to collaborative models.

24.2.2 Empathy, Humanization and Solidarity

The first step in cooperation is recognition (social psychologists often call this situational construal): mapping the particular interaction, seeing the individual other or group as a potential cooperator or partner in cooperation. Since I treat cooperation as attitudinal, in part, the moment at which an individual can actually recognize the other or the group as worthy of cooperation in this sense is germinal. This largely relates to two mechanisms – individual empathy, or humanization, and group solidarity. One clear experimental finding is that humanization – mechanisms to assure that participants know and recognize the humanity of their counterpart – improves the number of cooperators and the degree of 'generosity' they are willing to show others (Bohnet and Frey, 1999). Neuroscientific studies support the proposition that agents' brains respond differently to cooperation with humans than to 'cooperation' (that is, playing strategies that in game theory count as cooperative) with computers (Rilling et al., 2002; Rilling et al., 2004). But not all cooperation is at an individual level of committed mutualism or altruism. Much that is interesting occurs through commitment to collective efficacy of a symbolically marked group. This feature appears in the work on human evolutionary biology and anthropology that I have already mentioned. It is also consistent with the concept in organizational sociology of 'affiliation-based trust' (Zucker, 1986) and with claims in social network theory that social similar flock together (the phenomenon called homophily) (McPherson et al., 2001), and it plays a central role in organizational psychology (Haslam, 2001). The basic intuition is that the more someone has a sense of being part of the team (the clan), the more one is willing to sacrifice one's own good for the group. Solidarity and its instigation is, then, another important mechanism for design, and is directly part of the dynamic of recognition.

24.2.3 Fairness, Norms, Trust and Efficacy

Another consistent finding of the experimental literature is that fairness is endogenous to the cooperative dynamic. Mechanism design based on a selfish rational actor puts fairness of outcomes aside, focusing on whether an individual, looked at individually, is made better or worse off by an interaction as a way of predicting an agent's behavior. Consistent with this, fairness is usually separated in policy analysis from efficiency, and left to be dealt with after the desired level of activity has been induced through egocentrically defined incentives. A consistent finding of the experimental literature is that this approach fails to take account that people care about the fair distribution of outcomes, the perceived fairness of the intentions of others in the interactions, and probably the fairness of the process of the interaction (Fehr and Schmidt, 2003). A distinct and substantial literature is the literature on social norms (Ellickson, 1991). That literature deals with long-standing, usually tightly knit communities, which combine many of the design levers I try to separate into discrete building blocks into ongoing, stable, social relations. When thinking of designs for systems that may be as new as a collaborative wiki launched yesterday, social norms must play a different role. At a minimum, they refer not to long-standing internalized norms, but to instances of more-or-less clearly specified behavioral expectations about what counts as 'cooperative' in a given system. Once participants know what counts as cooperation, and what is defection, they can adjust their own actions, as well as judge the actions of others. At the simplest levels, these could be Schelling coordination norms. Beyond that, they can be explicitly stated expectations about behavior, like those that anchored Wikipedia and made it unique among cooperation models in its early days on being purely norms-based. There is evidence that norms that are self-consciously chosen by a group enjoy high adherence with minimal enforcement requirements (Ostrom et al., 1994). Where these norms evoke background, already ingrained social norms, they may enjoy the status of those already internalized norms, or the norms can themselves be the object of enforcement through another design lever, punishment. A third type of finding, central to the organizational sociology but strongly present also in the experimental work, is the importance of trust. Trust is the subject of its own immense literature, and has been used in many different ways (Gambetta, 1988). Often, it is used to characterize the success of a system that removes the possibility of human defection or error. Here, 'trust' is not a design lever at all. It is a description of the outcome that signifies confidence in its performance. Trust as design lever should be seen as an attitude that agents possess; it is a belief agents in a relationship have about how others in the system will behave when those others do in fact have a choice to act in ways harmful or helpful to the trusting agent, not when they do not. Constructing a system to allow trust in this sense to be built will usually be improved by breaking down cooperative actions into observable chunks, where participants can lower their exposure to each other while observing the proclivities of others to cooperate or defect, for example. Finally, there is a significant psychological literature suggesting that people need a personal sense of competence or efficacy in their action, and pursue activities that satisfy that need (Deci and Ryan, 2000); and in a parallel observation of social software also suggests that people will join a clearly effective project and abandon one that seems to be going nowhere. Working to assure and visibly perform efficacy appears to be important to stabilizing levels of contribution.

24.2.4 Discipline, Punishment, Transparency and Crowding-Out

The first set of design levers all operate at the level of intrinsic motivations. That is, they all work to cause participants to want to cooperate for reasons that are internal to their own psychological and social needs and desires, rather than in response to external rewards or constraints. Because, however, both the observational and the experimental work suggest a significant diversity in motivational profiles, and a substantial presence of selfish actors, stable cooperation systems require elements that can use extrinsic motivations to keep in line those who are not driven to cooperate by intrinsic motivations, and to prevent the unraveling of cooperation in those situations (which are not all situations) where the presence of selfish actors can undermine the efficacy, fairness, solidarity, or any of the other mechanisms that might sustain cooperation among cooperators even in the presence of defectors.

The presence and design of mechanisms for disciplining defectors and punishing are therefore important to the design of cooperation platforms. The experimental literature finds that: (1) with the right design, reciprocators can solve the second-order public goods problem of punishment without intervention from an external body, such as the state or management; but (2) punishment can backfire if it is not properly designed, leading to deterioration (Bowles and Gintis, 2004; Fehr and Gächter, 2002; Fehr and Rockenbach, 2002; Falk et al., 2005). It is important to understand that punishment does not collapse the analysis back to selfish rationality. It is neither necessary (we see cooperation without it, most importantly in the second-order public good problem created by the need to impose costly punishment on defectors) nor sufficient (we see instances where it reduces cooperation, probably through crowding-out) to explain cooperation. But it is one design lever available to systems designers to work with to improve compliance by selfish actors with the cooperative behavior of the other agents in the system.

The ambiguous effects of punishment bring to the fore one more design focus, or constraint, and that is the phenomenon of crowding-out. Crowding-out can occur inter-system or intra-sytem. Intra-system crowding out refers to situations when the use of one design lever would reduce the efficacy of another. For example, the introduction of punishment can, under certain circumstances, crowd out trust, and thereby undermine, rather than improve, cooperation (Yamagishi, 1986). Inter-system crowding-out can occur when one tries to mix and match elements from cooperative systems with elements from other systems, such as market mechanisms. There is a large literature on crowding-out caused by the introduction of money into otherwise cooperation-based interactions

(Frey and Jege, 2001). Given that we observe many mixed systems, such as open source software innovation and the introduction of cooperative models into firms, mixing is not impossible. But it requires attention to the interactions between the motivational and organizational forms, rather than a simple assumption of additive effect. One last design lever that obviously contributes to structuring an appropriate framework for extrinsic motivation is transparency (Fehr and Gächter, 2000).[6] It is necessary for trust to form, for fairness to be observed and judged, and for discipline to be imposed. The most common particular instantiation of transparency is the introduction of reputation systems into cooperative platforms.

24.2.5 Self-Selection, Cost and Leadership, or Asymmetric Contribution

Three additional design levers appear to be important. First, people seem to cooperate more when they have easy exit and entry from and into a social context.[7] The voluntariness of participation may increase the willingness to contribute. More systematically, a well-functioning cooperation platform with easy exit would tend, all things considered, to draw cooperators and repel selfish actors. Cooperators and reciprocators will tend to select into a cooperative framework in which behavior is rewarding for them, whereas selfish actors will select out of it unless there are opportunities for gainful abuse. Note, however, that in the context of organizational sociology, easy exit tends to leave firms with easier recourse to market-based mechanisms to structure their relationship, which undermines trust (MacDuffie and Helper, 2006). More broadly, this suggests that ease of entry and exit is a design focus with no single 'right' setting, but rather, as social software designers are finding out, focusing on how easy or hard it is to enter and become a full participant is an important design intervention, and the right level depends on the type of activity and how easy it is to undermine a group by appropriating its efforts to the purposes of an individual.

Second, one of the things that distinguishes the experimental literature on cooperation from behavioral economics more generally is that it does not challenge rationality itself. People will cooperate more when the cost of doing so is lower, such as when the opportunity cost of cooperating in a prisoner's dilemma is lower because of pay-off structure (Camerer and Fehr, 2004), or because the task has been modularized or chunked into sufficiently fine-grained modules to make the cost of contribution smaller (Benkler, 2002a).

Finally, leadership is important. This does not come out of the experimental work, which does not examine leadership, but it is a consistent feature of the organizational sociology (Maccoby and Heckscher, 2006), is emphasized in the study of open source software (Weber, 2005), and repeatedly crops up in field studies of online cooperation. It is important to recognize, however, that 'leadership' does not mean 'hierarchy'. Rather, what we see in this observational work is that people contribute at widely diverse levels, and systems need to be designed so as to accommodate these divergent patterns and to find fulfilling ways for participants to be recognized for their asymmetric contribution, often through a greater say in the collective governance of the enterprise, or through symbolic means of expressing honor and respect. What is required of leadership, and how asymmetric contribution leads to leadership and motivates it, are important areas of research into cooperation platforms.

24.3 CONCLUSION

Cooperation begins with a different model of human beings than the selfish rational agent model. It emphasizes the diversity of human motivational profiles, and the importance of the interaction to determining actual behavior. To the extent that these literatures better predict human behavior under differently designed systems, they hold the promise of improvement in the design of systems for human action. Just as the selfish rational actor model was applied in very different contexts, so too can cooperation be applied to very different systems. Technical systems, such as online collaboration forums, business processes and organizational strategies, legal regimes and constructed social contexts are all systems of affordance and constraint for human action. They can all benefit from cooperation-based design approaches. One may wish to analyze whether a GPL free software license, which implements a copyleft requirement to share back one's improvements of software that one modifies, is better than a Berkeley Software Design (BSD) license, which allows users more or less free rein to use the software and share or decline to share modifications as they please, or whether trade-secret law should, or should not, include the inevitable disclosure doctrine. The questions one would ask would be different under the cooperative or the selfish model. Similarly, if one is trying to decide whether it is important to include a profile page on a collaborative wiki site, or whether to allow anonymity, introduce tiered privileges based on length of time that a user has been part of a cooperative effort, or introduce explicit pricing into one's technical platform, these are all amenable to cooperation-based analysis. So too, of course, with business processes. This has not been done as much in the interpretation of universities and science policy, although some of the efforts to suggest that Bayh–Dole undermines the Mertonian norms of science is a way of getting at the question of crowding-out and systemic effects of discrete design elements. My point is merely to emphasize that refining our approach to system design based on the large and diverse empirical and theoretical literature on cooperation holds the promise of significant improvement in our ability to design human systems for cooperation. Better knowledge of how to build such systems, in turn, will improve our ability to build systems of learning, innovation and knowledge creation.

NOTES

1. A good basic edited volume that provides a good overview of the work is Feller et al. (2005).
2. On motivations, early works included Lerner and Tirole (2002), Lakhani and von Hippel (2003) and Ghosh (1998).
3. For a study comparing the applicability of open source-like models to agriculture and biomedical, see Hope (2007). For an analysis of applicability of open innovation to these, as well as to publication, educational materials, and so on, as development policy, see Benkler (2006), Chapter 9.
4. An entry point into these materials is Henrich et al. (2004), in particular Chapter 3, Camerer and Fehr (2004) and Gintis et al. (2005).
5. Note the parallel between these empirical, case study-based claims and the formal analysis in Acemoglu et al. (2006).
6. Partner treatment yields higher levels of cooperation.
7. For a collection of these see Ostrom (1998).

REFERENCES

Acemoglu, D., P. Aghion, C. Lelarge, J. Van Reenen and F. Zilibotti (2006), 'Technology, information and the decentralization of the firm', unpublished.

Aghion, P., M. Dwatripont and J.C. Stein (2006), 'Academic freedom, private sector focus, and the process of innovation', unpublished.

Baldwin, C. and K. Clark (2006), 'The architecture of participation: does code architecture mitigate free riding in the open source development model?', *Management Science*, **52** (7), 1116–29.

Benkler, Y. (2002a), 'Coase's Penguin, or Linux and the nature of the firm', *Yale Law Journal*, **112** (3), 369–446.

Benkler, Y. (2002b), 'Intellectual property and the organization of information production', *International Review of Law and Economics*, **22** (1), 81–107.

Benkler, Y. (2004a), 'Sharing nicely: on shareable goods and the emergence of sharing as a modality of economic production', *Yale Law Journal*, **114** (2), 273–358.

Benkler, Y. (2004b), 'Commons-based strategies and the problems of patents', *Science*, **305**, 1110–11 (August 20).

Benkler, Y. (2006), *The Wealth of Networks: How Social Production Transforms Markets and Freedom*, New Haven, CT: Yale University Press.

Bohnet, I. and B. Frey (1999), 'The sound of silence in prisoner's dilemma and dictator games', *Journal of Econonomic Behavior and Organization*, **38**, 43–57.
Bowles, S. (2006), 'Group competition, reproductive leveling, and the evolution of human altruism', *Science*, **314** (5805), 1569–72.
Bowles, S. and H. Gintis (2004), 'The evolution of strong reciprocity: cooperation in heterogeneous populations', *Theoretical Population Biology*, **65** (1), 17–28.
Boyd, R. and P.J. Richerson (1988), *Culture and the Evolutionary Process*, Chicago: University of Chicago Press.
Camerer, C.F. (2005), 'Neuroeconomics: how neuroscience can inform economics', *Journal of Economic Literature*, **43** (1), 9–64.
Camerer, C.F. and E. Fehr (2004), 'Measuring social norms and preferences using experimental games: a guide for social scientists', in J. Henrich, R. Boyd, S. Bowles, C. Camerer, E. Fehr and H. Gintis (eds), *Foundations of Human Sociality: Economic Experiments and Ethnographic Evidence from Fifteen Small-Scale Societies*, Oxford: Oxford University Press, pp. 55–95.
Cardenas, J.C., J.K. Stranlund and C.E. Willis (2000), 'Local environmental control and institutional crowding out', *World Development*, **28** (10), 1719–33.
Cohen, W.M, R.R. Nelson and J.P. Walsh (2000), 'Protecting their intellectual assets: appropriability conditions and why US manufacturing firms patent (or not)', Working Paper 7552, February, National Bureau of Economic Research, Cambridge, MA, revised 2004.
Deci, E.L. and R.M. Ryan (2000), 'The "what" and "why" of goal pursuits: human needs and the self-deterimination of behavior', *Psychological Inquiry*, **11** (4), 227–68.
Elkin-Koren, N. (2005), 'What contracts cannot do: the limits of private ordering in facilitiating a creative commons', *Fordham Law Review*, **74** (2), 375–422.
Ellickson, R.C. (1991), *Order Without Law: How Neighbors Settle Disputes*, Cambridge, MA: Harvard University Press.
Falk, A., E. Fehr and U. Fischbacher (2005), 'Driving forces behind informal sanctions', *Econometrica*, **73** (6), 2017–30.
Fehr, E. and S. Gächter (2000), 'Cooperation and punishment in public goods experiments', *American Economic Review*, **90**, 980–94.
Fehr, E. and S. Gächter (2002), 'Altruistic punishment in humans', *Nature*, **415**, 137–40.
Fehr, E. and B. Rockenbach (2002), 'Detrimental effects of sanctions on human altruism', *Nature*, **422**, 137–40.
Fehr, E. and K. Schmidt (2003), 'Theories of fairness and reciprocity, evidence and economic applications', in M. Dewatripont, L.P. Hansen and S.J. Turnovsky (eds), *Advances in Economics and Econometrics: Theory and Applications: Eighth World Congress of the Econometric Society*, Vol. 1, Cambridge: Cambridge University Press, pp. 208–57.
Fehr, E., U. Fischbacher and M. Kosfeld (2005), 'Neuroeconomic foundations of trust and social preferences: initial evidence', *American Economic Review: Papers and Proceedings*, **95** (2), 346–51.
Feller, J., B. Fitzgerald, S.A. Hissam and K.R. Lakhani (eds) (2005), *Perspectives on Free and Open Source Software*, Cambridge, MA: MIT Press.
Franke, N. and E. von Hippel (2003), 'Satisfying heterogenous user needs via innovation tool kits: the case of Apache Security software', *Research Policy*, **32** (7), 1199–1215.

Frey, B.S. and R. Jege (2001), 'Motivation crowding theory: a survey of empirical evidence', *Journal of Economic Surveys*, **15** (5), 589–611.
Frolich, N. and J.A. Oppenheimer (2003), 'Optimal policies and socially oriented behavior: some problematic effects of an incentive compatible device', *Public Choice*, **117** (3–4), 273–93.
Gambetta, D. (ed.) (1988), *Trust: Making and Breaking Cooperative Relations*, Oxford: Basil Blackwell.
Ghosh, R.A. (1998), 'Cooking pot markets: an economic model for the trade in free goods and services on the Internet', *First Monday*, **3** (3), 2 March, available at: http://firstmonday.org/htbin/cgiwrap/bin/ojs/index.php/fm/article/view/580/501.
Ghosh, R.A. et al. (2002), *Free/Libre and Open Source Software: Survey and Study, FLOSS Final Report*, International Institute of Infonomics, University of Maastricht, the Netherlands, June.
Gintis, H., S. Bowles, R. Boyd and E. Fehr (eds) (2005), *Moral Sentiments and Material Interests: The Foundations of Cooperation in Economic Life*, Cambridge, MA: MIT Press.
Haslam, S.A. (2001), *Psychology in Organizations: The Social Identity Approach*, Thousand Oaks, CA: Sage Publications.
Heckscher, C. and P. Adler (2006), *The Firm as A Collaborative Community: Reconstructing Trust in the Knowledge Economy*, Oxford: Oxford University Press.
Henrich, J., R. Boyd, S. Bowles, C. Camerer, E. Fehr and H. Gintis (eds) (2004), *Foundations of Human Sociality: Economic Experiments and Ethnographic Evidence from Fifteen Small-Scale Societies*, Oxford: Oxford University Press.
Hope, J.E. (2007), *Biobazaar: The Open Source Revolution and Biotechnology*, Cambridge, MA: Harvard University Press.
Lakhani, K. and E. von Hippel (2003), 'How open source works: "free" user-to-user Assistance', *Research Policy*, **32** (6), 923–43.
Lerner, J. and J. Tirole (2002), 'Some simple economics of open source', *Journal of Industrial Economics*, **50** (2), 197–234.
Lerner, J. and J. Tirole (2005), 'The scope of open source licensing', *Journal of Law, Economics, and Organization*, **21** (1), 20–56.
Levin, R.C., A.K. Klevorick, R.R. Nelson and S.G. Winter (1987), 'Appropriating the returns from industrial research and development', *Brookings Papers on Economic Activity*, **3**, 783–831.
Maccoby, M. and C. Heckscher (2006), 'A note on leadership in collaborative community', in C. Heckscher and P. Alder (eds), *The Corporation as a Collaborative Community*, Oxford: Oxford University Press, pp. 469–78.
MacDuffie, J.P. and S. Helper (2006), 'Collaboration in supply chains with and without trust', in C. Heckscher and P. Alder (eds), *The Corporation as a Collaborative Community*, Oxford University Press, pp. 417–66.
Mansfield, E., M. Schwartz and S. Wagner (1981), 'Imitation costs and patents: an empirical study', *Economic Journal*, **91** (364), 907–18.
Maurer, S.M., A. Rai and A. Sali (2004), 'Finding cures for tropical diseases: is open source the answer?', *PLoS Medicine*, **1** (3), e56.
McPherson, M., L. Smith-Lovin and J.M. Cook (2001), 'Birds of a feather: homophily in social networks', *Annual Review of Sociology*, **27**, 415–44.
Mowery, D.C., R.R. Nelson, B.N. Sampat and A. Ziedonis (2004), *Ivory Tower*

and Industrial Innovation: University–Industry Technology Transfer Before and After the Bayh–Dole Act, Stanford, CA: Stanford University Press.
Nelson, R.R. (1959), 'The simple economics of basic scientific research', *Journal of Political Economy*, **67** (3), 297–306.
Nowak, M.A. (2006), 'Five rules for the evolution of cooperation', *Science*, **314** (5805), 1560–63.
Ostrom, E. (1998), 'A behavioral approach to the rational choice theory of collective action', *American Political Science Review*, **92** (1), 1–22.
Ostrom, E., R. Gardner and J. Walker (1994), *Rules, Games, and Common Pool Resources*, Ann Arbor, MI: University of Michigan Press.
Owen-Smith, J. and W.W. Powell (2001), 'Career and contradictions: faculty ıesponses to the transformation of knowledge and its uses in the life sciences', in S. Vallas (ed.), *The Transformation of Work: Research into the Sociology of Work*, Vol. 10, Oxford: JAI/Elsevier Press, pp. 109–40.
Rai, A. and J. Boyle (2007), 'Synthetic biology: caught between property rights, the public domain, and the commons', *PloS Biology*, **5** (3), e58.
Richerson, P.J. and R. Boyd (2004), *Not by Genes Alone: How Culture Transformed Human Evolution*, Chicago: University of Chicago Press.
Rilling, J.K., D.A. Gutman, T.R. Zeh, G. Pagnoni, G.S. Berns and C.D. Kilts (2002), 'A neural basis for social cooperation', *Neuron*, **35** (2), 395–405.
Rilling, J.K., A.G. Sanfey, J.A. Aronson, L.E. Nystrom and J.D. Cohen (2004), 'Opposing bold responses to reciprocated and unreciprocated altrusim in putative reward Pathways', *Neuroreport*, **15** (6), 2539–43.
Sally, D. (1995), 'Conversation and cooperation in social dilemmas', VII *Rationality and Society*, **7** (1), 58–92.
Scotchmer, S. (1991), 'Standing on the shoulders of giants, cumulative research and patent law', *Journal of Economic Perspectives*, **5** (1), 29–41.
Shirky, C. (2003), 'Social software and the politics of groups', March, unpublished.
Sober, E. and D.S. Wilson (1999), *Unto Others: The Evolution and Psychology of Unselfish Behavior*, Cambridge, MA: Harvard University Press.
von Hippel, E. (2005), *Democratizing Innovation*, Cambridge, MA: MIT Press.
Weber, S. (2005), *The Success of Open Source*, Cambridge, MA: Harvard University Press.
Yamagishi, T. (1986), 'The provision of a sanctioning system as a public good', *Journal of Personality Social Psychology*, **51**, 110–16.
Zucker, L. (1986), 'Production of trust: institutional sources of economic structure, 1840–1920', *Research in Organization Behavior*, **8**, 53–111.

25. Comments

David Encaoua

Even if the preceding two chapters do not deal exactly with the same notions, their topics overlap to some extent. This allows a joint discussion with specific comments, when necessary, to either one or the other chapter.

Both chapters contribute to open the discussion on two very interesting and general issues:

1. What is the role of collaborative user-centered innovators (Eric von Hippel terminology) or peer production (Yochai Benkler terminology) in the dynamics of innovation?
2. Do we need specific public policies to support or to favor this form of collaborative research based on the principle of non-exclusion and free disclosure? And if the answer is yes, what should these policies be?

I will structure my discussion around the following questions:

1. Is it possible to draw some boundary between projects for which research activity could be organized around collaborative user-centered or peer production principles and those that could not? In other words, what are the main drivers of the development of the open cooperative research regime?
2. Can the agents' behavior in the peer production system be characterized as a form of 'involuntary altruism' or is it better to describe their behavior as reflecting specific preferences towards equity and fairness?
3. Finally, what can we say on government policies to support or favour the open regime?

25.1 THE BOUNDARY BETWEEN DIFFERENT RESEARCH REGIMES

Let me begin by recalling the main notions. According to Eric von Hippel terminology, user innovators are either firms or individuals that develop innovations for their own usage rather than selling them to the market to obtain a revenue. Different works by Eric von Hippel present evidence on the user innovation frequency for both industrial and consumer products (von Hippel, 2005; Chapter 23 in this volume). There is no doubt that the user innovation phenomenon is ubiquitous across industries at least in the US, where I suspect that the phenomenon has a larger spread than in Europe. It would be interesting to learn more about cross-country and cross-industry variations. Deepening our understanding of the sources of innovation which are currently poorly informed in the Community Innovation Survey would be a very valuable task.

The main point is that innovative users develop their innovations not only in isolation, but most often through informal collaboration with others, with tasks, costs and results allocated according to open access principles, without enforceable payments from intellectual property rights (IPR). Some innovations led by users become later commercial products. Baldwin et al. (2006) present a model to explain this evolution and to test it against the history of the rodeo kayak industry.

The notion of users as collaborative innovators is thus not very far from the notion of peer production used by Yochai Benkler. A peer production regime is defined by two properties: non-exclusion of others (which does not imply the absence of rewards) and collaboration based on voluntary information exchanges, not coordinated by market mechanisms nor hierarchies.

Thus peer production is totally different from a Research Joint Venture (RJV) in which collaboration is obtained through contractual rules that exclude those outside the RJV members and in which revenue is obtained by selling the result of the joint research.

By crossing the two criteria of exclusion and cooperation, one obtains thus four regimes, as illustrated in Table 25.1.

The main question is to know under what conditions peer production is both feasible and efficient, when compared to other regimes. In other words, what are the boundaries of peer production?

This is a difficult question, but some advances have been made in order to understand the development of the open source software, considered as a prototype of peer production.

According to Carliss Baldwin and Kim Clark (2006), the open source software may be characterized by some simple features:

1. The architecture design of an open source system has a modular structure, in which various independent software programs are linked to some platform via an open interface.
2. Each software code has value to its own producer (as a user) as well as to other users or producers; it is a non-rival good which is costly to produce.

Table 25.1 Innovation regimes by crossing the two criteria of exclusion and cooperation

	Exclusion	Non-exclusion
Cooperative	Common property: patent pool, RJV	Peer production: Wikipedia, Slashdot, Open-Source, etc.
Non-cooperative	Individual property: patent, copyright	Commons-based production: private provision public good

3. The construction of the modular system is a sequential process that involves uncertainties, resolved only after achievement. Any software code thus involves option values: before its construction, it is not certain that it will improve on its predecessors. Modular architectures add value to systems designs by creating options to improve the system by substituting or experimenting in individual modules.
4. Free disposal is facilitated through both the existence of individual incentives to reveal information, and low transaction costs due to the development of worldwide exchange instruments.

One must note at this stage that this overall set of conditions is not satisfied by all technological processes. For instance, the so called 'O-ring technology' introduced by Michael Kremer totally contrasts with these conditions (Kremer, 1993). A shuttle will not work if only one of its components fails.

According to different contributions, these conditions allowed the successful development of the open source system in the software industry.

A first question arises. Are these conditions sufficient to justify a peer production process or a user collaborative innovation process in other industries? Answering this question could be an important step to foster the development of these processes in the economy. In other words, given a specific project, it would be very interesting to know whether its characteristics would make it more or less likely to draw contributions from a community of producers or users working under peer production principles.

25.2 INVOLUNTARY ALTRUISM OR PREFERENCES FOR FAIRNESS?

The works by Johnson (2002) and Baldwin and Clark (2000) give a first answer to this question. They stress the architecture or the design of a project as the most crucial aspect for the prospective features of its development. Baldwin and Clark represent the development of a peer system as a game of private provision of a public good in which each member of a community chooses either to free-ride or to contribute to the provision of one component of the public good, given that the supply of the public good is organized around a modular architecture and presents some option values.

Two results emerge from this game. One is that with modular architecture, joining and staying in the collective development effort by a community of developers is a strategy that strictly dominates acting in isolation, for both active players and free-rider players. The second result is that modularity and option value act as economic complements: more of one makes the other more valuable in mitigating the free-riding effect. More uncertainty reduces the number of free-riders as the number of components increases.

In other words, under the assumption that players voluntarily reveal their information, a cooperative development effort is both sustainable and efficient if the system is modular and has enough option value relative to the cost of individual action.

The individual incentive to reveal freely comes from the benefit of using the information produced by others. Another feature that enables individual contributors to reveal their information is the very low communication cost induced by the advent of the Internet. Overall, the incentives to reveal correspond to what Baldwin and Clark call 'involuntary altruism'.

Lerner and Tirole (2002) describe this form of altruism in terms of a reputation effect in the labour market. Writing a program and disclosing the code signals the ability or the capacity of its author. This also corresponds to the main incentive that pushes a researcher to publish, as a publication is the main signal to improve the reputation and consequently the career of the researcher in the open science system.

In his contribution in Chapter 24, Yochai Benkler emphasizes other aspects of human cooperation, derived from experimental economics, that depart from selfish rational actors. At this stage, there is some ambiguity. First, rationality does not imply selfishness: it is well known that strategic behavior of rational agents in an interactive situation yields to outcomes that are totally different from those that would result in the absence of interaction (see Gintis, 2000). Second, the big lesson from experimental economics is not that agents are irrational, but that the perception they have from the experimental situation may be different from the perception that the instructor has in mind. So, I wonder if more work on experimental economics would deliver 'the promise of improvement in mechanism design of systems for human action', as Yochai Benkler argues.

I would prefer to say that the mechanism design is the choice made by the society to implement in a decentralized way some social preference.

If rational agents behave interactively under the appropriate mechanism design, their individual actions will be compatible with the desired social preference. In other words, if the society (the principal) wants a research project to be realized under peer production principles, because these principles are welfare-improving, the best that it can do is to design the architecture of the project according to a modular structure allowing individual micro-contributions, modularizing tasks in sufficiently fine-grained modules to reduce the cost of each contribution, and allowing users or producers to integrate their efforts.

The architecture of the project is what matters the most. Some research projects could be designed around these principles, but certainly not all of them.

What happens if in the same industry the two forms of organization coexist, namely peer production and proprietary production? The question is important. It particularly concerns the software industry in which open source software and proprietary software are two competing products. Analyzing the technology dynamics in this industry is a promising topic of research (see Malerba et al., 2001 for the computer industry).

25.3 POLICY QUESTIONS

One of the main policy issues, raised by Eric von Hippel in Chapter 23, relates to the question, 'How to reduce the micro-contribution transaction costs?' This is a necessary requirement for the development of a users' collaborative innovation model.

In my view, this question is very often related to the well-known indirect network effects that arise in various networked activities, because of the feedback between applications development and demand. Typically, in a network industry, there exist different platforms (such as a game console or a computer operating system) permitting or not the use of different applications, according to whether access to the interface is allowed or not. Access to interface software code is therefore crucial to allow interoperability. Since the interface is the component that allows applications to run on the platform, one may distinguish two categories of objects: the first includes the platform and applications that may be matters for intellectual property (IP) protection since they correspond to real inventions; the second category includes applications programming interfaces (API) that are pure technical standard devices, and as such they should be discarded from intellectual protection.

Proprietary standards, or in other words closed standards, too often tip a market towards a single platform monopoly. This is illustrated by the Microsoft cases, both in the US and in the EU. Once Microsoft held a dominant position with the Windows platform, it increased its capabilities by creating its own closed version of Java and its own Internet browser, and it also increased the number of applications exclusive to Windows. These actions led to reducing the role of the open platforms Java and Netscape, as potential competitors to Windows.

The European case against Microsoft also involves a restrictive access to the interface between Windows and non-Microsoft work group servers. Whether the specifications for accessing to the interface are covered or not by IPR is a complex and technical issue. Even if the European Commission did not rule out the possibility that these specifications may be covered by copyright, it maintained the argument that their access by others does not constitute a breach of copyright since they lead to clearly distinct works. In 2003, the European Commission issued a preliminary injunction requiring that Microsoft provide clear access to non-microsoft work group servers, and this injunction has been upheld by the recent Court of First Instance (CFI) decision (2008).

The Microsoft cases, both in the US and in the EU, illustrate the benefits that can be obtained by enlarging the technology policy perspective towards a competition policy perspective. For instance, defining the conditions under which access would be mandatory, whether access is covered by IPR or not, could be an important step. These conditions to mandatory access could also be considered as necessary exemptions to the usual intellectual protection provisions under some conditions. First, when access is indispensable for providing a product on a secondary market or for using the knowledge in a process of follow-up innovation; second, when there is an objective demand for the would-be product; and third, when there are no objective justifications for the access refusal. However, even if these conditions are met, other questions remain unresolved. For instance, what would be the reasonable price for licensing of the disclosed information if access and interoperability were made compulsory? My own view is that interfaces in network systems should be considered as commons-based property rather than proprietary systems.

Finally, let me say just one word concerning a general problem that arises in the digital economy. The introduction of the Digital Millenium Copyright Act (DMCA) in the US in 1998 has been an indication of a worrying change: the protection system has evolved from a system that protects content to a system that protects technical access to the content. Indeed, the DMCA creates legal protections for technical protections, insofar as it prohibits circumventions of technical protection systems themselves. It thus expresses a significant extension of the protection. Similar patterns are observed in other areas such as biotechnology, and raise many concerns. I think that this volume offers a big opportunity to rethink the appropriate balancing of access and appropriation in the future of IP policy.

REFERENCES

Baldwin, C. and K. Clark (2000), *Design Rules, Vol. 1: The Power of Modularity*, Cambridge, MA: MIT Press.

Baldwin, C. and K. Clark (2006), 'The architecture of participation: does code architecture mitigate free-riding in the open source and development model?', *Management Science*, **52** (7), 116–27.

Baldwin, C., C. Hienerth and E. von Hippel (2006), 'How user innovations become commercial products: a theoretical investigation and case study', *Research Policy*, **35** (9), 1291–1313.

Gintis, H. (2000), *Game Theory Evolving*, Princeton, NJ: Princeton University Press.

Johnson, J. (2002), 'Open source software: private provision of a public good', *Journal of Economics and Management Strategy*, **2** (4), 637–62.

Kremer, M. (1993), 'The O-Ring theory of economic development', *Quarterly Journal of Economics*, **108** (3), 551–75.

Lerner, J. and J. Tirole (2002), 'Some simple economics of open source', *Journal of Industrial Economics*, **52**, 197–234.

Malerba, F., R. Nelson, L. Orsenigo and S. Winter (2001), 'Competition and industrial policies in a "history friendly" model of the evolution of the computer industry', *International Journal of Industrial Organization*, **19** (5), 635–4.

von Hippel, E. (2005), *Democratizing Innovation*, Cambridge, MA: MIT Press.

PART VIII

Technology Policy for Development

26. Innovation policy for development: an overview[1]

Manuel Trajtenberg

26.1 INTRODUCTION[2]

This chapter is meant to provide a framework for thinking systematically about innovation policies for development, without venturing into specific, recipe-like policy recommendations. It does so by highlighting and dissecting the key issues that arise in this context, and by examining in some detail the case of innovation policy in Israel, which sheds light on both the promise and the limitations of such policies. There are a few guiding principles that inform the discussion. First, innovation for economic development has to be construed as a much broader notion than just the creation of new, technologically fancy gadgets; indeed, economic growth stemmed historically from widely distributed innovations of all kinds, both in products and in processes, generated by rank-and-file workers as much as by research and development (R&D) labs. The issue then is not just how to elicit say patentable innovations resulting from formal R&D, but how to provide both incentives and basic means for would-be entrepreneurs and small enterprises to engage in productivity-enhancing investments.

Second, the economic rationale for government support of R&D, while universal and hence applicable to developing economies as much as to developed ones, needs to be expanded and adapted to the economic environment and idiosyncratic problems of developing countries. In particular, the notion of spillovers should be re-examined in view of globalization, which makes the actual benefits from spillovers depend upon the relative intensity of inwards versus outwards flows. The working of 'general purpose technologies' (GPTs) is also contingent upon the level of development, and therefore the extent to which GPTs play their role as 'engines of growth' depends upon economic policies promoting the adoption of GPTs and the unfolding of innovational complementarities. It is not true that in the realm of innovation there is only the issue, in the sense of innovating for global markets as part, say, of the network of multinationals; there is such a thing as local needs and local markets, which are not necessarily well served, and may require enhanced incentives from the government.

The Israeli economy offers a fascinating illustration of extraordinary success in innovation, particularly in information and communication technology (ICT), which came largely as a result of a concerted, long-term strategy of government support for commercial R&D, which levered the potential of a highly skilled labor force. Yet, the benefits from the rapid growth of the high-tech sector eluded the rest of the economy, thus giving rise to a 'dual economy' and a mediocre growth rate for the economy as a whole. Understanding this seemingly contradictory outcome may provide valuable insights for the design of growth-promoting innovation policies, which should focus on the trajectory and end destination of the knowledge generated by innovations, as much as in promoting innovation per se.

Section 26.7 of this chapter discusses the broad policy corollaries that emerge from the analysis, and in particular the main levers which innovation policies for development should act upon: skills formation, provision of incentives, access to information and the availability of finance. The chapter stops short of sketching actual policies, both because that would be too presumptuous at this still preliminary stage, and because it is a basic tenet of the analysis that heterogeneity is key, and no sensible policy can be designed without paying due attention to the idiosyncratic characteristics of each country.

26.2 THE SCOPE OF INNOVATION IN THE CONTEXT OF DEVELOPMENT

We commonly associate 'innovations' with the development of new products that represent discrete improvements over existing ones in performing known functions (for example a CD versus a magnetic tape), or that open up entirely new functional categories (for example global positioning system (GPS), cardiac stents). These are labeled 'product innovations' and are typically more visible to consumers than 'process innovations', which lower the costs of producing given products (for example hybrid corn, computerized machine tools). This typology is sufficiently broad to accommodate virtually any type of innovation, yet we are naturally inclined to focus attention on innovations that are both technologically salient, and that have had (or have the potential for) a significant economic impact. In particular, nowadays we tend to associate innovations with improvements in information and communication technologies (ICT), no doubt the leading 'general purpose technology' of our era. Yet the notion of innovation relevant for policy-making in developing countries ought to be much broader, and the same goes for the related notion of spillovers. Indeed, understanding what innovation entails in countries that are technologically laggards, and exploring how a surge of innovation in them may generate wider ripple effects, may well be the key for the design of sound innovation policies in these countries.

Widely construed, innovation means conceiving, designing and implementing changes in the available set of products and production processes, which have a positive expected value for the innovator and/or for society. Innovation may thus consist of redesigning the goods produced so as to make them more appealing to buyers or cheaper to manufacture. It may entail altering the production process by rearranging the sequence or timing of tasks, the composition of material inputs, the kind and mixture of skills deployed, the nature of upstream and downstream linkages, and so on. Innovation may bring in new, more efficient machinery that triggers a reorganization of work, or new ways of transporting inputs and outputs that in turn require complementary changes in them. All these as well as a myriad of other small, scattered improvements throughout the whole spectrum of economic activity are part and parcel of what innovation consists of, and as Mokyr (1990) has convincingly argued, when taken together these may be the true unsung heroes of economic growth.

There are two important empirical regularities to highlight in this context. The first is that the cumulative effect of widely distributed small improvements has been as significant for secular growth as the impact of discrete, 'higher-order' innovations (in the sense of entirely new products and production processes). The second is that innovations entail a great deal of interdependencies, necessitating and triggering further complementary innovations in order to reap their full benefits (see Rosenberg, 1982, Chapter 3). This is certainly the case for 'general purpose technologies' (GPTs),[3] but similar interdependencies happen also locally, on a small scale, and not just for the dominant technology of an era.

These two features have far-reaching implications for thinking about and designing innovation policies. Indeed, it is clear that in developing countries such policies should encompass more than just promoting and supporting formal R&D projects, and certainly more than doing so in technologically advanced ('high-tech') sectors. Again, the cumulative impact of 'small' and/or 'informal' innovations (in the sense of innovations that are not the result of preconceived R&D projects) has been historically as large as that of innovations driven by formal R&D. Furthermore, most of economy activity takes place either in 'traditional' sectors or in services, which do not qualify as 'high-tech'. Technological change surely brings about structural transformations which in turn alter the composition and relative weights of the different sectors of the economy, yet in order for sustained growth to take place, most existing sectors have to experience innovation. A recurrent theme in this chapter is thus that narrowly localized innovations are unlikely to result in economy-wide growth, even if the few sectors that do innovate are 'high-tech' and highly successful in themselves. I turn now to the economic rationale for government support of innovation on purely analytical grounds, that is, regardless of whether the economic setting is that of a developed or of a developing country – in later sections I shall focus on the specific issues that arise in developing economies.

26.3 THE ECONOMIC RATIONALE FOR GOVERNMENT SUPPORT OF INNOVATION

Ever since the path-breaking research of Robert Solow (1957), economists have known that secular growth is due mostly to technological change rather than to factor accumulation, as previously thought. Indeed, a vast array of subsequent empirical research over half a century has conclusively shown that at least half of the growth in per capita income in virtually every country studied is associated with the growth of total factor productivity (TFP) rather than with other, more traditional factors. However, attaching to the famous 'residual' (that is, TFP growth) the label of technological change begs the question of what exactly it contains, and more importantly, what are the economic forces that determine its course and pace.

Indeed, one of the frustrating aspects of the early phase of economic thinking about these matters was that the growth of TFP appeared to economists as an impenetrable 'black box', and seemed to occur outside the realm of economic forces. A long and very fruitful research agenda pioneered by prominent economists such as Griliches, Jorgenson, Denison, Rosenberg and their associates sought to pierce open this black box in order to provide it with empirical content. With the advent of endogenous growth theory in the late 1980s (Romer, 1986, 1990; Grossman and Helpman, 1991, and so on) the economic profession as a whole came to accept the view that innovation, spillovers and R&D were indeed the key factors driving self-sustained, long-term economic growth and, moreover, that these factors were generated from within the economic system, responding to economic incentives. This is then the conceptual framework that molds our analysis: namely, on the one hand the view of the centrality of innovation and knowledge creation in the growth process, and on the other hand the understanding that these are economic factors that may thus be shaped and influenced by properly designed economic policies.

One of the corollaries of the developments just sketched was the emergence of a soundly based and carefully articulated economic rationale for public support of R&D and innovation, which is by now widely accepted among both academic economists and practitioners. The basic argument for government support to R&D is that, while innovation is clearly a critical factor for growth (and hence *inter alia* for poverty alleviation), a well-functioning market economy cannot generate by itself the optimal levels of investment in innovation.[4] That is so primarily because of two sources of market failures (see Arrow, 1962): (1) partial appropriability due to spillovers; and (2) information asymmetries which lead to a serious 'funding gap.' These failures inhibit private firms from investing enough in innovation and R&D, thus depriving the economy from one of the key levers of sustained growth.[5] I proceed now to discuss these failures in detail.

26.3.1 Partial Appropriability and Spillovers

A basic feature of knowledge creation is that the returns from investments in it are not fully appropriable. Knowledge has significant public good attributes: once created it costs little to reproduce and distribute, and it can be used repeatedly by multiple actors without impairing the amount available to others. This implies that firms making investments in knowledge creation capture only a portion of the benefits so generated, since they do not receive compensation for the spillovers that their innovative efforts generate: that is, for the positive externalities of their actions on other firms and agents. Further, new technologies confer benefits to the purchasers of new products (consumers and producers alike) that often exceed any increase in the selling price that can be sustained; these non-appropriable benefits are also commonly referred to as spillovers to consumers. Both type of spillovers, namely the purely technological externalities and the excess benefits to buyers, imply that the social returns from innovations may be far larger than the private returns.

As a result of this gap, innovators operating in a market economy will invest in innovative activities less than the socially optimal amount; the extent of underinvestment depends of course on the extent to which social returns exceed private returns, and that may vary widely across fields, technologies, stages in the innovation cycle, and so on. Empirical studies have shown that the social rate of return on R&D expenditure is typically very large, and often exceed private returns by as much as a factor of three (see for example Jones and Williams, 1998). Moreover, these studies show that the returns to R&D exceed by a wide margin the returns from other types of investment, in particular from investment in physical capital. This implies that there are wide margins to increase the amount of resources devoted to R&D at the economy-wide level, and that the government should play a role in doing so.

Spillovers may occur in many different ways, one of them being the mobility of R&D personnel. The process of innovation and its commercialization in an enterprise significantly enhances the human capital of its employees. Indeed, employees acquire R&D skills and understanding of technologies and markets which are partly general, that is, which go beyond the knowledge embodied in any specific innovation that they have developed, and that cannot be fully protected by intellectual property rights (IPR). Employees that move from one firm to another carry with them this human (or innovation) capital, which may benefit their new employers beyond the increment in wages that the mobile employees may receive. If mobility takes the form of migration, then the origin countries may be unwittingly subsidizing the destination countries through these spillovers; thus the mobility of inventors is an important transmission mechanism for spillovers, and hence a channel that should be closely monitored as it may have both positive and negative effects on any given country. Spillovers may also occur through economic transactions, such as trade: countries can increase their productivity by importing goods, particularly capital equipment embedding more advanced technologies (see Coe et al., 1997), as well as through foreign direct investment (FDI) (for example see Blomstrom and Kokko, 1999).

26.3.2 Information Asymmetries and the 'Funding Gap'

A second source of market failure in the creation of knowledge has to do with asymmetric information between inventors and external agents (for example funding bodies such as banks). Innovative activities entail by necessity a fundamental information asymmetry, certainly at the early stages when the inventor formulates the idea and seeks funds to develop it. Presumably the inventor has intimate knowledge of the technology and of the details of the planned innovation, of his or her true abilities to carry it out, and of the efforts he or she is willing to put into developing the innovation. However, there will always be a significant gap between what the inventor knows and what an external agent can gauge, even if the information on those crucial matters is well documented. In particular, there will be significant information asymmetries in this respect between the inventor and mainstream financial intermediaries like banks and institutional investors, who lack the capacity to verify the information and claims of the entrepreneur. Potential investors will therefore be skeptical of the likely returns on investments in developing new technologies, and therefore entrepreneurs who could offer attractive returns may have no credible way of conveying such potential to risk-averse investors.

The information asymmetry makes it very hard for a creditor or equity investor to predict the returns from a potential investment in new innovative ventures, which implies that such funding is not likely to be forthcoming. Thus in the absence of cash flows or other collateral, a typical start-up company or individual innovative entrepreneur will not have access to traditional sources of finance – this is the so-called 'funding gap'. At the most basic level then the funding gap implies that entrepreneurs face stiff constrains in the funding of innovations, and therefore will not invest (or will invest too little) in innovative projects that may have high social returns.

The information asymmetries are particularly stringent at the very early stages of the innovative process (the so-called 'early-stage technological development' – ESTD), that is, going from the raw idea to the formulation of a business plan. Not surprisingly, it is at these stages that the funding gap is most acute, and where the market may be particularly prone to failure. Indeed, a study by Branscomb and Auerswald (2002) shows that the three most important sources of funding for ESTD in the US were: internal corporate funds (32–47 percent), the federal and state government (23–30 percent), and 'angel' investors (24–28 percent). Venture capital accounted only for 2–8 percent, and universities the remaining 3–4 percent.[6] Equally telling, mainstream intermediaries like banks, private equity and other institutional investors are entirely absent from these early stages.

It is not surprising that internal funds account for the biggest share of ESTD financing, since this is the most straightforward way of overcoming information asymmetries. Established enterprises know the track record of their own inventors and employees, and typically have a better understanding of the market and the commercial potential of internally proposed innovations than outside agents. Thus enterprises use cash flows generated by established operations to finance innovation, or source external funds on the basis of their balance sheet strength.

The typical profile of 'angel' investors is that of successful entrepreneurs who look for new opportunities to invest private funds (earned from their own previous innovations), and are willing to invest in early-stage projects in technological fields that they understand well (having 'been there and done that'). They tend to get deeply involved in the funded ventures, providing managerial guidance and contacts, and acquiring significant overall control.

Early-stage financing of innovation thus requires specialized investors with the skills to evaluate and directly manage the risks, or governments with broader public objectives, such as generating and internalizing spillovers that may benefit the economy as a whole. In the absence of internal cash flows and 'angel' investors, even if appropriability is adequate to yield a reasonable profit expectation, it may be impossible to secure the capital necessary to develop a new technology. Quite clearly, the information asymmetries and funding cap problem are typically much more acute in developing countries than in developed economies.

26.4 ZOOMING IN: INNOVATION IN DEVELOPING ECONOMIES

26.4.1 Local versus Global Spillovers

The spillover-based argument clearly holds for large economies having a moderate ratio of exports and imports to gross domestic product (GDP), the prototypical case being of course the US: being large increases the probability that other local economic agents will benefit, and trading internationally a relatively small proportion of its GDP lowers the risk of spillovers slipping out. For small open economies this is more complex: on the one hand spillovers may easily spill out of the country, and benefit external firms and consumers rather than the local economy.[7] Thus, increasing local innovation and R&D may not necessarily result in faster growth for the economy as a whole, even if it does propel the R&D-intensive sectors, and benefit the global economy. On the other hand, being small and wide open increases the probability of being the recipient of spillovers that originate elsewhere: indeed, as Coe and Helpman (1995) have shown, these types of economies tend to benefit the most from international spillover flows (in relative terms of course), mediated by trade. It is much harder to know what happens in terms of 'net effects': to be able to capture these international spillovers the country needs to develop 'absorptive capacity' (see Cohen and Levinthal, 1989), which entails *inter alia* investing in local R&D. At the same time, the locally generated spillovers from this same R&D may end up diffusing away from the local economy.

Any policy designed to promote R&D should pay close attention to this issue; namely, it should aim not just at increasing total R&D, but to do so in a way that incentivizes local spillovers rather than external leakages, develops absorptive capacity and ultimately impacts the productivity of a wide range of sectors in the local economy. None of this can be taken for granted in small open economies, certainly not in developing countries.

26.4.2 General Purpose Technologies

Technological change contributes to growth wherever it happens, but there are certain technological advances that have played a critical role in fostering growth in the economy as a whole over the long haul. Indeed, in any era there are a handful of (or even a single) 'general purpose technologies' that drive growth, by spreading over the different sectors of the economy and prompting them to innovate as well.[8] Progress in the adopting sectors feeds back into the GPT sector, providing incentives for further advances in the GPT itself, and thus setting up a positive, self-sustained loop.

From the 1990s onward, innovation has commonly been associated with the tremendous technological advances that have taken place in what is loosely referred to as 'high-tech', and in particular in information and communication technology (ICT). Indeed, the advent of the personal computer and the Internet, mobile phones, the digitization of words, voice and image in a wide array of existing and newly created media, and above all the inexorable march of Moore's Law, have revolutionized the way by which we produce and consume virtually everything. The pre-eminent general purpose technology of our era is undoubtedly ICT, and as such it is enabling and fostering economic growth in developed countries, as well as in many transition and developing countries.

Yet, the way a GPT fosters economy-wide growth is not simply and not mainly by innovation taking place just in the GPT itself; rather, economy-wide growth occurs when a wide and ever-expanding range of other sectors adopt the advancing GPT, and as a consequence improve their own technology. A telling example is the revolution in retailing brought about by Wal-Mart, primarily via the massive adoption of ICT-based methods; in fact, the gains in productivity of the retailing sector by itself made a sizable contribution to the total productivity growth of the US economy during the second half of the 1990s. The GPT sector itself is bound to be small relative to the economy as a whole, and however fast it innovates and grows in itself, it can never on its own pull the whole economy (for example think of the steam engine-producing sector in the nineteenth century, or the electricity sector in the first decades of the twentieth century). In that sense, the often-used analogy of the GPT as a 'locomotive' pulling the other sectors is wrong and misleading: if the rest of the economy fails to adopt widely the GPT, or fails to make complementary innovations in the adopting sectors, economy-wide growth just will not materialize.

A key issue then in 'secondary countries,' that is, in countries that are not at the frontier of the GPT, is how to allocate R&D and other innovative inputs so as to lever the growth potential of the prevalent GPT. What is clear is that just trying to jump onto the bandwagon of ICT innovation per se is far from enough, and may not necessarily be the most effective strategy. Again, what needs to happen is that ever-expanding segments of the economy adopt ICT in ways that increase their own productivity.

These types of complementary actions (that is, adoption of ICT, local innovations in traditional sectors, and so on) may well be less 'flashy', less overtly 'innovative', and therefore may not be deemed as worthy of support or encouragement, and yet these ultimately constitute the key to economy-wide growth.

Still, developing a local ICT industry, joining forces with ICT multinationals, and otherwise encouraging the ICT-producing sectors may play an important role in the process of development. This is so both because of the concomitant development of local technological skills, managerial expertise and world-class standards in ICT, and because such strategies require the wide opening of the economy, which in itself brings inflows of capital, expands trade, and so on. In both dimensions, then, the spillovers of a thriving local ICT sector may play a crucial role in prompting the rest of the economy to follow suit. The point is that this latter stage may not happen by itself (or may take too long), and may therefore require government intervention.

Thus, growth-oriented innovation policies have to proceed from a far wider perspective than just promoting the ICT sector per se, and GPTs may well provide the guiding conceptual framework for that purpose. To repeat, the key point is not that ICT in and of itself 'causes' growth, but rather that 'innovational complementarities' in the adopting sectors ought to materialize for economy-wide growth to take place. The development of the ICT sector itself may in some cases be an effective stepping stone, but by no means the final destination. In fact, the recalcitrant problem may lie in eliciting adoption and innovation, not in ICT producers but in those that could benefit from its use (see for example Jorgenson and Vu, 2005).

26.4.3 Export-Oriented versus Local Market-Oriented Innovation

The discussion above of 'high-tech' versus the rest of the economy has already touched upon the issue of export-oriented innovations versus innovations aimed primarily at local markets; the two issues are connected and yet the latter is conceptually distinct and deserves further scrutiny. Widely held perceptions have it that in the era of globalization there is no such thing as 'local needs' or 'local markets', particularly not in innovative technologies, but rather that virtually all relevant markets are global, and hence local innovators should aim at serving global demand rather than local niches. There is no denying of course that the ICT sector is preeminently global in both inputs and outputs, and that the extent of global specialization and cost arbitrage is increasing over time, leading to further productivity gains and faster innovation. To repeat, linking up with this

earlier stages of development, in terms of both income and human capital. Thus, it may be justified in those countries to support early adopters of new technologies (particularly those that can potentially enhance productivity in a wide range of sectors), since in so doing widespread adoption is accelerated, and with it the benefits of the innovation are brought forward.

26.6.3 Emulation and Positive-Sum Norms in Historical Perspective

There is yet another, more general aspect of demonstration effects, and that is early innovators providing a new role model for entrepreneurial individuals to emulate, and thus paving the way for a shift from a zero-sum to positive-sum type of norms and institutions. As Joel Mokyr (2003) has forcefully argued, up to the seventeenth century Europe was characterized by and large by rent-seeking behavior, supported by the fragmentation of society into rent-extracting institutions such as guilds, and semi-autonomous regions (hence internal tariffs), and so on. In such an environment entrepreneurial individuals found it most profitable to devote their inventiveness and creativity to perfecting rent-seeking activities, which were of course detrimental for growth. Thus they sought to strengthen barriers to entry (into guilds, local markets, and so on), impede mobility, increase taxation, and the like. The intellectual revolution brought about by the Enlightenment sought to free society from these shackles, and instead promote openness, of ideas as much as of trade. The important point is that once the prevailing norms, substantiated by vivid examples, shifted towards positive-sum type of accepted behaviors, and once institutions changed accordingly, productivity-enhancing innovations became powerful attractors, displacing innovativeness in rent extraction. This was, according to Mokyr, a fundamental precondition for the Industrial Revolution to unfold.

In this sense the Enlightenment has yet to take hold in many developing countries, where rent-seeking is still the predominant norm. Why invest in developing uncertain and costly new technologies or in improving production processes, if ingenuity can bring higher returns by further exploiting the system? The traits that typically define an entrepreneur can become very handy for engaging in rent extraction as well (often bordering on corruption), and surely will be deployed there rather than in innovation, if simple cost–benefit considerations so indicate. Changing such basic, deeply rooted patterns is extremely difficult, but not impossible. Demonstration effects can help a great deal: what is needed is the emergence of a local Thomas Edison, a local Steven Jobs, that is, highly successful innovators who may serve as models to emulate. Skilled, young, aspiring would-be innovators need to convince themselves that coming up with better products and production processes may be as promising a route to upward mobility and to economic success as tricking the system.

There are of course innumerable obstacles to overcome on the way to legitimate innovation, since those that have a stake in the prevailing regime of tight control over markets would do their outmost to keep it that way. On the other hand, the more zealously players cling to the zero-sum, rent extraction mold, the wider the disparity between it and more efficient technologies, products and market configurations, and hence the more attractive the legitimate innovation alternative becomes. Indeed, one of the benefits of openness (in the flow of ideas and knowledge) is that the tensions between obviously inefficient and efficient economic patterns cannot be hidden. Thus, policies that help inventors, market pioneers and early adopters succeed, in spite of the efforts to the contrary of stakeholders, may have wide ripple effects and benefits, far beyond those stemming from the original innovation itself. In particular, the government should aim at dismantling the web of regulations that often afflict markets in developing countries, and that constitute 'barriers to innovation', very much as the traditional 'barriers to entry' impede competition in the static sense.

26.7 POLICY INSTRUMENTS

The discussion so far offers as corollaries a few principles that should guide the design of innovation policies in developing countries:[20]

1. Innovation should be widely distributed over the whole spectrum of economic activity, that is, across sectors (not just 'high-tech'), and type of innovations (not just formal R&D projects).
2. Policies should be bottom-up and not top-down: the point is to provide the enabling conditions and to strengthen the incentives, but growth-enhancing innovation should spring from ever-widening cohorts of aspiring, would-be entrepreneurs and inventors.
3. Policies should alter the balance between innovation's aim at rent creation versus ingenuity in rent extraction; it is often more feasible to do so by enhancing the former than by penalizing the latter.

There are many ways by which those principles may be implemented; here I wish to focus on the following four areas, which may provide key levers for policy: skills, incentives, access to information and availability of finance.

26.7.1 Skills

The wide availability of skills is of course a basic precondition for any innovation-based growth strategy to succeed: basic skills are necessary for innovative ideas to arise in the first place, advanced skills are required for would-be innovators to be able to search for and absorb the necessary information, and yet more sophisticated skills are typically called for in order for inventors to be able to tackle the technological and business-related problems that stand along the way. Skills in this context thus refer to a wide spectrum of capabilities, to be acquired both through formal education, and through learning by doing. They range from basic literacy to advanced science and technology (S&T), and include also managerial abilities, business acumen and computer skills. Many of these should arise endogenously, that is, once innovation gets going the demand for skills increases, presumably prompting more individuals to acquire them, and there is more room for learning by doing. What is important for policy in this respect is a two-pronged strategy, consisting of the supply of the traditional public good type of education and skills formation on the one hand, and ensuring the responsiveness of vocational and advanced skills supply on the other hand.

The first and foremost policy goal in this respect is of course the provision of universal access to literacy and basic numeracy, and also the rudiments of English and of computer literacy. The later two are essential as a gateway to ICT and to global markets, which sooner or later need to be accessed for innovation to succeed. Furthermore, this baseline education should be periodically revised and upgraded in response to a changing environment, particularly if innovation becomes widespread. That is, success in triggering innovation requires continuous, concomitant changes in the institutions supplying human capital, otherwise these will soon turn into bottlenecks holding back further innovation. The initial conditions of many developing countries are far removed from the baseline alluded to here, and therefore they should seek creative ways of short-circuiting the process of providing for it. One generic approach is to rely increasingly on ICT to impart basic skills, through for example distance learning, Internet-mediated short courses, and so on. There is plenty of room for innovation also in this sense, and indeed in some countries such as India (which suffers from high rates of illiteracy), this may be a highly promising route.

The second aspect of the strategy is to make sure that endogeneity kicks in, that is, that the institutions and markets responsible for the supply of skills indeed respond to changes in demand. In particular, vocational schools, training programs, colleges and universities should be made highly responsive to shifts in the demand for skills. This is by no means to be taken for granted, and in fact in many cases the educational system is isolated from the (changing) demands of the economy, and prides itself on being so. While some of it should indeed operate according to its own norms (such as basic scientific research), most of the system should not only adapt and respond to demand shifts (for example, train more computer programmers, less mechanics), but even anticipate and stay ahead of the changes. Rosenberg and Nelson (1994) have extensively documented the very important role that universities have played in fostering innovation in the US since the early twentieth century, as opposed to their European counterparts – a disparity that continues, if slightly diminished, to this day. The key is the high responsiveness of US universities to the technological and scientific needs of industry, a classic example being the fact that shortly after the invention of the transistor in 1948, Massachusetts Institute of Technology (MIT) and Stanford were offering courses in solid state physics, taught not by resident professors but by outside adjunct faculty coming from industry, whereas in Europe it took years for such courses to be introduced.

26.7.2 Incentives

Behind any innovation, be it the most trivial or the most sophisticated, there is of course an innovator that discerns the problem to be solved, envisions the innovative solution and carries it through its initial stages. These activities are costly, often very much so, and hence entrepreneurial individuals would engage in them only insofar as they foresee that the expected rewards from the innovation would be significantly larger than those upfront costs.[21] Thus, incentives in this context refer to the extent to which potential inventors can anticipate sufficiently high rewards. A traditional aspect of this issue is the availability of suitable mechanisms of appropriability, such as effective patents and other means of protecting intellectual property. This is surely a highly relevant issue for developing countries, not for the reasons typically alluded to by developed countries (that is, that their IP is not properly protected) but rather because weak local IP regimes may discourage local inventors. I am not going to dwell on IP since that would take us far afield, but rather focus on other aspects of incentives.

In particular, the question is whether potential inventors can expect to be properly rewarded, given the nature of the institutions in which they operate. As mentioned before, innovation in developed countries has been historically very widely distributed, which means that innovators came from all sorts of occupations, ranks and sectors. For that to happen, would-be innovators within enterprises, whatever their rank, should either have a stake in the success of the company and/or foresee internal upward mobility. Furthermore, labor markets should be very fluid, in the sense of offering opportunities of mobility across firms, sectors, and geographical area. Likewise, as previously argued, 'barriers to innovation' within markets should be low, in the sense of both officially sanctioned regulations and tacit collusion. Lastly, the alternative course of tinkering with rent-extraction mechanisms should be made less attractive.

Incentives for innovation in less developed countries thus mean first and foremost promoting policies of inclusion and openness. If workers on the production line of traditional manufacturing as much as in software design do not have a stake in the results of their efforts, or if avenues of internal or external mobility are foreclosed for them, they can hardly be expected to unleash their creativity to enhance productivity. Policies to improve incentives in this sense are difficult to articulate, let alone implement: first, such policies are likely to run into stiff opposition from those that benefit from the inertia and stagnation of the system; and second, by definition these policies should provide incentives not for what is currently done (which is observable), but for what could be done, which is typically ill-defined and unobservable (such as potential mobility), and hence much more difficult to mold and codify.

R&D labs in large, well-established enterprises are well aware of these issues, and typically handle them well, as reflected in the incentives provided for in the contracts with their scientists and technicians. However, that is only part of the story, and in developing countries a rather small part of it: R&D labs can be expected to spring up only within a small number of enterprises within yet fewer sectors, whereas innovation as envisioned here should be much more generalized and pervasive, touching virtually every corner of economic activity. It is possible that labor markets, organizational structures, promotion practices and related institutional molds will eventually react endogenously to an upsurge of innovations, making adaptive changes. However, initial conditions matter, endogeneity in this sense cannot be taken for granted, and hence it is the role of government to give the initial push to such changes.

26.7.3 Access to Information

Access to knowledge stocks and to up-to-date information flows is a necessary condition for there to be innovation, primarily access to information about technology, and about markets for inputs and outputs. Consider for example a potential innovation that entails enhancing the functionality of a product, such as increasing the ruggedness of a bicycle for countries devoid of paved streets. Would-be innovators need to understand the wider technological context (for example the physical properties of various materials, including their durability), the relationship between design and manufacturing requirements and materials used (for example very heavy metals cannot be used, even if they are more durable, and likewise for materials that are not sufficiently malleable), and other such issues. They need also know what is 'best practice' in those dimensions, both in bicycle design and manufacturing and in other, unrelated products whereby similar issues may arise (for example golf clubs or car seats). In fact, innovation often comes from the 'recombination of ideas' as Weitzman (1998) has convincingly argued, and hence knowledge of a wide variety of both immediately related as well as of 'distant' issues is extremely important.

Intimate knowledge of the market for the (improved) product is required, as well for the innovation to have reasonable chances of commercial (and not just technological) success. This entails gathering information on the market for existing close substitutes, and for forming estimates of market size for the new or improved product. The innovator also needs to gather information on prices and availability of inputs, typically covering a wide range of alternatives that may affect profitability, and to assess future competition, both local and international, that may arise as a consequence of the innovation.

Access to such wide range of information is thus key for inventors to be able to formulate and work out their innovations, and yet it may elude big segments of the population of potential inventors. There is a great deal that can be done policywise to increase access, including encouraging knowledge intermediaries, promoting competition and openness in various kinds of media, developing channels for continuing education at various levels, making sure that data on markets are widely publicized, and so on. Providing for Internet access to the population at large is perhaps one of the most effective means of securing widespread access to relevant information. However, that goes beyond deploying a fiber optics network, having access to personal computers (PCs) and to Internet service providers (ISPs): users need to be taught rudimentary computer skills, as well as search techniques. Moreover, and as mentioned earlier, a basic working knowledge of English may be a *sine qua non*.

26.7.4 Availability of Finance

As already discussed, one of the economic features of knowledge creation is that it entails information asymmetries that lead to a funding gap. In developing countries this problem is gravely compounded by the fact that capital markets are typically not well developed, and in particular by the dearth of funding for small enterprises and individual entrepreneurs. The inherent risks associated with innovative projects, the absence of collateral for such projects (as opposed, say, to investment in physical capital, equipment or structures), and the lack of expertise to screen them make it extremely hard for inventors to secure the necessary financial resources. Providing such funding is then a pre-eminent role for the government to play in the context of virtually any plausible innovation policy. The question is how to structure financial support so as provide strong incentives to inventors, while at the same time avoiding the ills of corruption on the one hand, and of moral hazard (of inventors) on the other hand. These difficulties notwithstanding, this is an area where there exists a great deal of accumulated cross-country experience, which can be tapped in order to design sensible policies and support programs.[22]

NOTES

1. My thanks to Nadine Baudot-Trajtenberg for providing insightful comments, and to Yitzhak Goldberg of the World Bank for having prodded me into applying myself to research in this area, and having conducted highly stimulating brainstorming sessions at the World Bank. A previous version of this chapter was presented at the Latin America/Caribbean and Asia/Pacific Economics and Business Association (LAEBA) 2005 second annual meeting, Buenos Aires, Argentina.
2. An upfront disclaimer is in place: I am not a development economist, neither by training nor by practice; rather, my research so far has focused on technological change, innovation, patents and industrial organization themes, either in the abstract or in the context of developed countries. This is my first venture into development, an area that is increasingly capturing my intellectual interests. Yet, I have so far had little exposure to the relevant literature and acquired but a scanty expertise in it; thus, I am sure that I am overlooking in this chapter a great deal of pertinent previous work, as much as established common wisdom in this area. Nevertheless, I hope that this 'crossing of research lines' will eventually render fruitful outcomes.
3. As discussed below, the defining feature of GPT-driven processes is 'innovational complementarities', which entails strong interdependencies between the GPT and the application sectors; see Bresnahan and Trajtenberg (1995).
4. Investments in innovation are often used interchangeably with 'research and development' (R&D), yet the former is a more general concept: R&D typically refers to formal investments in dedicated research labs, whereas there are many ways by which innovative activities may take place outside the lab. One has to bear this distinction in mind particularly in the context of developing countries, where formal R&D is much less common.
5. Clearly, though, it is not enough to spell out such economic rationale: in order for it to lead to policy, it must be weighed against the costs of government intervention, namely the well-known problems associated with 'industrial policies', capture, corruption and the like.
6. The study was based on a 1998 survey and other data, and the wide range of estimates stems from the alternative use of restrictive or inclusive definitional criteria for the various components. There was a wide variance in these percentages across sectors and geographical areas.
7. 'Small' here refers not to the size of GDP per se, but to the relative size of the relevant sectors in the economy, that is, those sectors that could potentially benefit from technological spillovers from innovation. Thus, countries such as Brazil or Indonesia would likely be considered 'small' in this respect, whereas Finland or Taiwan would be 'large'.
8. See Bresnahan and Trajtenberg (1995) and Helpman and Trajtenberg (1998).
9. For background on innovation in Israel see Trajtenberg (2001, 2002).

10. Spillovers became an explicit criterion only recently, following a rewriting of the R&D Law.
11. Yozma means 'initiative' in Hebrew.
12. There was no explicit exclusion of these sectors, but as suggested the equilibrium that emerged was such that it de facto favored electronics, communications, computerized equipment, and the like, and not processes-based sectors.
13. In fact the R&D Law of 1984 explicitly favored export-oriented R&D projects.
14. Much more empirical research is needed, though, to shed light on this set of issues.
15. The R&D done by these labs account for about 15 percent of business sector R&D, and hence for ~ 0.5 percent of GDP.
16. In some cases, though, the multinational has a large operation in Israel, with 'lateral' connections between the different parts of the operation (for example R&D and manufacturing) so that local spillovers are much more likely to occur.
17. The extent of this effect depends of course upon the labor supply elasticity; in the late 1990s for example it proved to be quite inelastic, with overall increases in R&D spending by the business sector causing more of a spiraling rise in salaries rather than an increase in the amount of real R&D performed.
18. Notice that I am not referring here to the well-known question of the relationship between the extent of competition in the market and the *ex ante* incentives to innovate – the so-called 'Schumpeterian hypothesis' – but to the *ex post*, competitive response to innovation.
19. Such as complementary developments that are triggered by the initial adopters (for example the emergence of repair services for new computers or mobile phones; a wide variety of software for new hardware, and so on), or direct externalities in the sense that the number of adopters (that is, the size of the network) directly affects the utility of a new adopter, for example the number of fax machine users.
20. This is of course not an all-inclusive list, but rather it includes those principles that I regard as particularly important for policy-making.
21. The reason to expect what Schumpeter called 'extraordinary' rewards is simply to compensate for the high risk that usually accompanies innovations.
22. I shall not expand on this extensive topic here – see Goldberg et al. (2006).

REFERENCES

Arrow, Kenneth J. (1962), 'Economic welfare and the allocation of resources for inventions', in NBER (ed.), *The Rate and Direction of Inventive Activity: Economic and Social Factors*, Princeton, NJ: Princeton University Press, pp. 609–25.

Avnimelech, Gil and Morris Teubal (2005), 'Evolutionary innovation and high tech policy: what can we learn from Israel's targeting of venture capital?', Samuel Neaman Institute STE Working Paper Series, 25.

Blomstrom, M. and A. Kokko (1999), 'How foreign investment affects host countries', Policy Research Working Paper No. 1745, World Bank.

Branscomb, Lewis M. and Philip E. Auerswald (2002), 'Between invention and innovation, an analysis of funding for early-stage technology development', Advanced Technology Program, National Institute of Standards and Technology, November.

Bresnahan, T. and M. Trajtenberg (1995), 'General purpose technologies: engines of growth?', *Journal of Econometrics*, **65** (1), 83–108.

Coe, David T. and Elhanan Helpman (1995), 'International R&D spillovers', *European Economic Review*, **39** (5), 859–87.

Coe, David T., E. Helpman and A.W. Hoffmaister (1997), 'North–South R&D spillovers', *Economic Journal*, **107** (440), 134–49.

Cohen, Wesley M. and Daniel A. Levinthal (1989), 'Innovation and learning: the two faces of R&D', *Economic Journal*, **99**, 569–96.

Comin, Diego and Bart Hobijn (2004), 'Cross-country technological adoption: making the theories face the facts', *Journal of Monetary Economics*, **51** (1), 39–83.

Goldberg, Itzhak, Manuel Trajtenberg, Adam B. Jaffe, Thomas Muller, Julie Sunderland and Enrique Blanco Armas (2006), 'Public Financial support for commercial innovation: Europe and Central Asia Knowledge Economy Study Part I', World Bank.

Griliches, Zvi (1957), 'Hybrid corn: an exploration in the economics of technological change', *Econometrica*, **25** (4), 501–22.

Grossman, Gene M. and Elhanan Helpman (1991), *Innovation and Growth in the Global Economy*, Cambridge, MA: MIT Press.

Helpman, Elhanan and Manuel Trajtenberg (1998), 'A time to sow and a time to reap: growth based on general purpose technologies', in E. Helpman (ed.), *General Purpose Technologies and Economic Growth*, Cambridge, MA: MIT Press, pp. 55–84.

Jones, C.I, and J.C. Williams (1998), 'Measuring the social returns to R&D', *Quarterly Journal of Economics*, November, 1119–35.

Jorgenson, Dale W. and K. Vu (2005), 'Information technology and the world economy', *Scandinavian Journal of Economics*, **107** (4), 631–50.

Mansfield, Edwin (1968), *Industrial Research and Technological Innovation*, New York: Norton.

Mokyr, Joel (1990), *The Lever of Riches: Technological Creativity and Economic Progress*, New York: Oxford University Press.

Mokyr, Joel (2003), 'The great synergy: the European enlightenments as a factor in modern economic growth', Keynote address, European Association for Political and Evolutionary Economics, Maastricht, November.

Romer, Paul (1986), 'Increasing returns and long-run growth', *Journal of Political Economy*, **94**, 1002–37.

Romer, Paul M. (1990), 'Endogenous technological change', *Journal of Political Economy*, **98** (5), Part 2, S71–102.

Rosenberg, Nathan (1982), *Inside the Black Box: Technology and Economics*, Cambridge: Cambridge University Press.

Rosenberg, Nathan and Richard R. Nelson (1994), 'American universities and technical advance in industry', *Research Policy*, **23**, 323–48.

Solow, Robert (1957), 'Technical change and the aggregate production function', *Review of Economic and Statistics*, **39**, 312–20.

Trajtenberg, Manuel (2001), 'Innovation in Israel 1968–97: a comparative analysis using patent data', *Research Policy*, **30** (3), 363–90.

Trajtenberg, Manuel (2002), 'Government support for commercial R&D: lessons from the Israeli experience', in A. Jaffe, J. Lerner and S. Stern (eds), *Innovation Policy and the Economy*, Vol. 2, National Bureau of Economic Research, Cambridge, MA: MIT Press, pp. 35–72.

Weitzman, Martin (1998), 'Recombinant Growth', *Quarterly Journal of Economics*, **113**, 331–60.

27. Discussion of Manuel Trajtenberg's 'Innovation policy for development: an overview'

Richard R. Nelson

This informed and thoughtful chapter by Trajtenberg deals with a range of topics. In these comments I will focus on two of them. One is the relative isolation of Israel's 'high-tech' sector from the rest of the economy, with the former doing very well, while economic growth more generally is sluggish. The other is Trajtenberg's observation that innovation in developing countries needs to be understood as involving a lot more than high-tech. And I will draw some connections between these two themes.

The conventional wisdom these days is that economic growth is driven by technological advance in the leading industries of the era, an argument that was put forth a long time ago by Joseph Schumpeter, but which only recently has caught on widely. Trajtenberg makes the interesting observation that in recent years Israel has been doing very well in R&D-intensive industries, particularly those associated with the complex of information technologies. However, counter to the conventional wisdom, the overall growth rate of Israel has not been rapid, and there has been a tendency in recent years for the income distribution to be breaking apart, with the highly trained Israelis working in industrial R&D and related activities achieving very high incomes, but with much of the rest of the population experiencing little gains in income.

Trajtenberg's account suggests that there are two different aspects to the isolation. One is that much of the production and marketing of the new products made possible by R&D and innovation done in Israel is not being undertaken in Israel. Researchers at Israeli universities are important sources of ideas for new products. Foreign companies are attracted by the high level of scientific and technical skills available in Israel to set up R&D laboratories there. A strong venture capital industry enables Israeli firms to spring up to develop new products. But after the R&D is done, the follow-on economic activity, which accounts for most of the employment generated by new technologies, is set up abroad.

While he is less explicit here, I suspect that a second reason is that, where production and marketing do go on in Israeli firms, there is little in the way of upstream and downstream linkages to other Israeli firms. And the level of economic activity of the those progressive Israeli firms is not large enough so that they generate a broad multiplier effect.

Trajtenberg's story of a developing dualism in Israel's economy, despite considerable prowess in innovating in high-tech industries, has a familiar ring to a US citizen. While I do not think the causes highlighted by Trajtenberg explain adequately what has been happening in the United States, some of them certainly are there, and active. I believe the same very unequal sharing of the fruits of progress in high-tech is going on in several other high-average income countries. On the other hand I do not think the same syndrome obtains in the countries of Northern Europe, at least not to the same extent. To my knowledge, there has been too little recognition of this phenomenum, and why it seems to be occurring in some high-income countries but not others. There is a real challenge here for scholars studying economic growth.

Which brings me to Trajtenberg's observations on the kinds of innovation that are necessary to drive the economic development of countries that are significantly behind the world's economic and technological frontier. His basic argument is that it is a mistake for policy-makers to think that the key to economic development is the building of innovative capabilities in high-tech industries. At the very least such a position overlooks the wide range of innovations in many economic sectors that can contribute effectively to economic development.

Indeed, if one defines innovation in the way Schumpeter did – as the introduction of ways of doing things that are new to the order in which they enter – then the heart of the process of economic development of countries behind the frontier involves innovation. That is what the modernization process is all about. And from this point of view the lion's share of the innovating that necessarily goes on in successful development is not going to be in high-tech, but rather in the economic activities that account for the lion's share of employment: farming, construction, transportation, manufacture of standard consumer products, and so on. I think there is a lot to this conception.

I also think the current focus of policy-makers on high-tech is misguided in that the high-tech sectors generally are the ones that countries significantly behind the frontiers have the greatest difficulty in building. And the lesson of Israel is especially relevant here. By focusing policy attention on somehow attracting foreign branches of high-tech firms, or pushing venture capital, developing countries are courting the kind of isolated enclaves of economic prosperity that Trajtenberg points to in Israel.

Of course there are developing countries where investments in high-tech have been the driver of widespread economic development; South Korea and Taiwan quickly come to mind. On the other hand there are several developing countries that have clear signs of the syndrome highlighted by Trajtenberg in the case of Israel: a strong, small high-tech sector whose development has had little effect on most of the economy. India and Brazil are cases in point. Again, an important question for economists is how to explain the differences; there has been little research on this question.

I like Trajtenberg's chapter very much. It saddens me, however, that Trajtenberg obviously has read very little of the now considerable literature on technological change and economic development that is written from the perspective of evolutionary economic theory. I urge him to do more reading there. I believe that if he does he will find that literature highly relevant to the questions that interest him.

PART IX

Conclusions

28. Research without frontiers

Luc Soete

28.1 INTRODUCTION

Contrary to national policy belief, typified for example by the emphasis in the European Union (EU) on the so-called Barcelona 3 per cent research and development (R&D) investment norm, that research and science policy is essentially a local affair – that is, consisting primarily of funding and fiscally supporting research at domestic university, public and private research laboratories – in the modern world of the Internet and digital libraries, science is increasingly a global affair. For most countries in the world, the contribution of domestic sources to the global stock of academic knowledge is relatively small; its contribution to domestic productivity growth equally small. By contrast, there is little doubt that the largest part of worldwide productivity growth over the last decade has been associated with an acceleration in the diffusion of technological change and global access to codified knowledge. The role of information and communication technologies has been instrumental here, as has been that of more capital and organizational embedded forms of technology transfer such as foreign direct investment.

There remains of course a huge worldwide concentration of research investments in a relatively small number of rich countries and regions, but it is important, certainly from a national science and technology policy perspective, to realize that such activities, whether privately or publicly funded are increasingly becoming global in focus. Furthermore, today it is no longer the direct impact of the transfer of industrial technologies on economic development which is at the centre of the debate but rather the broader organizational, economic and social embedding of such technologies and the way they unleash or block particular specific growth and development opportunities. The latter is closely associated with levels of development as has become recognized in the endogenous growth literature. In the high-income, developed-country context the innovation policy challenge seems increasingly directed towards questions about the sustainability of processes of 'creative destruction' within environments that give premiums to insiders, to security and risk-aversiveness, and to the maintenance of income and wealth. In emerging country contexts, by contrast, the challenge appears directed towards the more traditional, 'backing winners', industrial science and technology policies, bringing also to the forefront the importance of engineering and design skills and accumulating 'experience' in particular. Finally, in developing countries characterized by 'disarticulated' knowledge systems, the endogenous innovation policy challenge is most complex of all.

In this chapter an overview will be given of the gradual shift in thinking about research and innovation policy and the current need for a further renewal in the direction of more global concerns. More than any other field of economic policy, research and innovation policy is running behind the facts.

28.2 FROM INDUSTRIAL TO 'KNOWLEDGE' POLICY

From the 1950s onwards there have been major shifts in the recognition amongst policy-makers about the effectiveness of various forms of industrial, technology and, today, innovation policy. Back in the early post-war period, industrial policy rapidly became one of the cornerstones of economic policy with the need felt in many national policy circles, and most notably in those economies which had been most devastated by the war, to support a more rapid structural transformation of their economies towards internationally stronger, large industrial sectors and complexes.

In Europe, this included alongside the traditional heavy, capital- and scale-intensive industrial sectors such as coal mining and steel – the European Coal and Steel Community, created in Paris in 1952 and dismantled (formally integrated in the European Community) in 2001 – the agricultural sector, with the development of national, and in the case of Europe, a Common Agricultural Policy. Over time with the subsequent General Agreement on Tariffs and Trade (GATT) rounds of international trade liberalization, industrial policy became gradually more dominated by the need to assist the international 'adjustment', as it was called euphemistically, of an increasing number of sectors towards stronger technological performance: from the old coal mining and steel sectors to more traditional labour-intensive sectors suffering increasingly from increased international competition. The political awareness of having to shift industrial policy from its negative, job-reducing image towards a more dynamic, sunrise image was of course very much inspired by the success of Japan in rapidly catching up in many industrial sectors from motor vehicles to semiconductors in the 1970s and 1980s. At the political level, the

US–Japanese semiconductor trade agreement, providing breathing space to the US industry, became one of the most clear-cut examples of what appeared to become the example of a new form of strategic industrial and trade policy with major long-term implications for the competitiveness of the US semiconductor industry. Hence not surprisingly, in Europe too, the strategic nature of industrial and technology policy became its central new justification.

With the Lisbon Strategy, as set out by the European Council in March 2000, and the broad policy acknowledgement of the crucial role of knowledge for Europe's economic development contained therein, a much wider set of horizontal policies emerged, shifting the analysis away from the strong sectoral focus of European industrial and technological policies. It is important to realize that this shift in focus cannot be seen independently from the major shifts in the world economy, and in particular the much greater readiness to rely on 'abroad' to bring about domestic structural change, whether in the form of international trade competition, foreign direct investment, foreign mergers or acquisitions. At the same time the large European, so-called 'national champion' firms had themselves gradually been transformed into sometimes truly multinational companies with increasingly multinational, as opposed to national interests. This actually holds both for the Organisation for Economic Co-operation and Development (OECD) world as well as for many emerging countries. It explains the eagerness with which the latter have become members of the World Trade Organization (WTO). In short, the predominance of the absolute faith, as expounded since the beginning of the 1990s, in the benefits of international markets, capital and technology flows as the means of allocating sectoral resources cannot be seen outside of the broader context of the fundamental changes in the global political, institutional and technological environment which took place over the same period.

It is within this context that one should see the emergence over the last decade of innovation policy as a much broader policy framework bringing to the forefront the local systemic features anchoring, so to say, industrial production nationally and regionally. Since the formulation of the Lisbon Strategy, there is, I would argue, broad recognition that a sectoral focus on international competitiveness needs to be complemented by a much broader look at the systemic 'congruence' between various other policy domains. The relevant policy term coined here is the 'national system of innovation', made popular in the 1990s by scholars such as Freeman, Lundvall and Nelson. Over the past two decades the institutional matching between the various components of countries' national systems of innovation has become gradually weaker, not least because of globalization pressures, which have acted differently on each of the components of the national system of innovation. Elsewhere, I have dubbed for example the growing mismatch between the key public and private knowledge components of the national system of innovation, the 'Dutch knowledge disease'. From this latter perspective the innovation policy focus should be on the 'crowding-in' in Europe of such knowledge-based activities, in both the private and the public sector.

28.3 INNOVATION IN INNOVATION

At the same time, the 1990s brought also another significant shift in understanding of the relationships between technology, innovation and socio-economic development. With the growing importance of service sectors in the economy, and the emergence of information and communication technologies as a general purpose technology, the actual perception of the nature of innovation processes changed significantly. Innovation capability became seen less in terms of the ability to discover new technological principles, than in terms of the ability to exploit the effects produced by Schumpeter's old notion of 'neue Kombinationen' and the use of pieces in the existing stock of knowledge. This new model, neatly described by David and Foray (2002), became closely associated with the emergence of numerous knowledge 'service' activities. It implied often routine use of a technological base allowing for innovation without the need for particular leaps in science and technology, sometimes also referred to as 'innovation without research'. It required systematic access to state-of-the-art technologies from anywhere in the world, something made possible by new information and communication technologies.

In short, whereas traditional R&D-based technological progress, still very much dominant in many industrial sectors, had been characterized by the science and technology system's ability to organize technological improvements along clear agreed-upon criteria, a continuous ability to evaluate progress and an 'ability to hold in place', to replicate at a larger industrial scale and to imitate experiments carried out in the research laboratory environment; the new, more recent mode of technological progress would be more based on flexibility and confronted with intrinsic difficulties in replication. Learning from previous experiences or from other sectors is difficult and sometimes even misleading. Evaluation is difficult because of changing external environments: over time, among sectors, across locations. It will often be impossible to separate out specific context variables from real causes and effects. Progress will in other words be much more on a trial-and-error basis yet without, as in the life sciences, providing 'hard' data which can be scientifically analysed and interpreted.

Following this shift in understanding of innovation, removing as David and Foray put it the dichotomy between R&D and production, a further shift has been occurring more recently, removing (partially) the distinction between production – as a locus for innovation – and consumption. The notion of user-driven innovation has existed of course for a long time (see for example Nuvolari, 2004 on the development of the Cornish pumping engine in the late eighteenth century), but it has only recently been used within a much broader international context to explain the emergence of such new industries as open source software (von Hippel, 2005). More broadly, blurring the distinction between production and consumption allows one to understand the increasing importance of collaboration among multiple producer-consumers, with incremental, sometimes called 'open' innovation contributed by several producers resulting in a single end-product. The more complex the interaction is among contributors, the more sophisticated can be the innovation, as resources and skills can be matched to needs with lower search and transaction costs. This may require adjustments in attitudes to ownership and the control of rights. This form of collaborative ownership and production (von Hippel, 2005) can be found in several domains beyond software.

In short, there is a significant degree of innovation within the process of innovation itself. Innovation policy appears consequently confronted with continuously moving policy targets. As has become well recognized by endogenous growth theorists (see in particular Aghion and Howitt's Schumpeter lecture, 2005), the innovation policy challenge with its characteristic Schumpeter mark 1 versus mark 2 features appears closely associated with levels of development. In a high-income, developed country context such as the old EU-15, the innovation policy challenge will have increasingly to address questions about the sustainability of processes of 'creative destruction' within ageing environments that increasingly give premiums to insiders, to security and risk-aversiveness, and to the maintenance of income and wealth.

28.4 INNOVATION FOR DEVELOPMENT

In an emerging, developing-country context, by contrast, the challenge might well appear at first sight more similar to the old, more traditional, industrial science and technology policy concerns, bringing also to the forefront the development of engineering and design skills and accumulating 'experience' in particular. However, in the old industrial science and technology (S&T) model, the focus within a context of development was naturally on technology transfer and imitation. Imitation to some extent is the opposite of innovation: allowing for a rapid catching-up process being accompanied by a systematic copying or where necessary the adoption of 'appropriate' technologies from developed countries. In the new model, every innovation is to some extent unique with respect to its application, also within a developing-country context. As argued at greater length elsewhere (Ghosh and Soete, 2006), there are quite specific innovation needs in most developing countries across many sectors. These so-called 'bottom of the pyramid' innovations have increasingly become a strategically interesting and challenging new area of research for many companies, including many international, globally operating firms from developed countries.

Going back though to the common feature of collaborative innovation, the most important enabling feature is access. Access is not required to knowledge alone, but to the tools and (legal) ability to replicate and improve upon knowledge. In the old model, developing countries were often treated as consumers who do not have the ability to innovate, perhaps due to the lack of technical skills, and must therefore passively consume products of developed countries (with subsidies, if required) or if they are more industrially advanced, imitate production methods developed elsewhere. Apart from being patronising, this view does not fit with the new mode of technological progress for development, for two reasons.

First, empirical research has shown (Ghosh and Soete, 2006) that in the case of software, open collaboration provided by access to modifiable technology may not be problematic due to a lack of skills; rather, it leads to the development of technical, business and legal skills. Such skills are often better than those learnt on formal courses and proven participation in open source development may compensate for the lack of formal degrees. Second, the premise of the new mode of technology development is that lowering entry barriers for the modification of technology reduces search costs, allowing participants in the market of producer-consumers more efficiently to allocate skills and other resources to needs for improvement. This leads to more efficient and perhaps faster technical innovation, with the entrepreneurial risks of innovation spread widely. Thus, providing access to technology need not be seen as charity or aid for developing countries, but as enlarging the resource base of potential innovators.

While access to knowledge as a passive process is politically framed within the language of development aid, access to technology as a way of providing the right and ability to participate is analogous to the arguments favouring free trade: developing countries can then be seen as providing a resource of potential innovators, rather than merely using existing innovations from the developed world.

28.5 CONCLUSIONS

The national and, in the case of Europe, European focus on the need for investments in knowledge accumulation, as exemplified by the Barcelona targets, is not just at odds with the global decision-making about knowledge investments of multinational firms, it appears also to ignore the increasingly global nature of long-term sustainable problems likely to affect directly the future welfare of the EU and its Member States.

Most of the national and European framework programmes were designed at a time when strengthening the international competitiveness of particular European high-tech firms and sectors was considered essential for Europe's long-term welfare. It led to the strengthening of a number of industrial firms and sectors, some of which became successful at the world level, while others failed dramatically. Today most EU research programmes benefit equally firms of European or foreign origin, as long as they are located in Europe. The same holds for universities and other public research institutes. No one though has ever calculated the inherent knowledge 'diversion' and European 'cocooning' implications of this territorially based research networking strategy, but it could be argued that they are likely to have been significant. Achieving technological international competitiveness might well, to paraphrase Paul Krugman (1994), have become today a dangerous European obsession, certainly when viewed against the global challenges and threats to national welfare.

In many research areas, European welfare will in the long term be directly influenced not by the development of national or local knowledge, its international commercial exploitation and intellectual appropriation, but rather by global access to such knowledge, the development of joint global standards and the rapid worldwide diffusion of new technologies to other, non-EU countries. One may think of energy-saving technologies, research on sustainable development and climate change, health and the spreading of diseases, food safety, security, social sciences and humanities, and so on. In all these areas, the territorial limitation of the funding of research and innovation to academic, public and private research agents appears contrary to the need for global solutions to safeguard European welfare in the long term.

In short, is it not time for research and innovation policy to recognize much more explicitly that research is intrinsically without borders, whether national or European?

REFERENCES

Aghion, P. and P. Howitt (2005), 'Appropriate growth policy: a unifying framework', the 2005 Schumpeter Lecture, 20th Annual Congress of the European Economic Association, Amsterdam.

David, P. and D. Foray (2002), 'An introduction to the economy of the knowledge society', *International Social Science Journal*, **54** (171), 9–23.

Ghosh, R. and L. Soete (2006), 'Information and intellectual property: the global challenge', UNU-MERIT Working Paper 029.

Krugman, P. (1994), 'Competitiveness: a dangerous obsession', *Foreign Affairs*, **73** (2), 28–44.

Nuvolari, A. (2004), 'The making of steam power technology', Dissertation, ECIS, Eindhoven University.

von Hippel, E. (2005), *Democratizing Innovation*, Cambridge, MA: MIT Press.

29. The rumblings of a paradigm shift: concluding comments

Manuel Trajtenberg

I would like first of all to thank Dominique Foray for having done a great job in organizing the very exciting conference that gave rise to this book. Indeed, Dominique managed to put together a highly stimulating volume, by assembling contributions from a superb group of scholars that come from varied backgrounds and hold eclectic views, yet share common concerns about research and development (R&D) and innovation.

I will try to frame my remarks in this closing chapter so as to reflect common threads that emerged in many of the contributions to this volume, particularly in Luc Soete's chapter. In fact, I can think of three key issues that underlie a great deal of current concerns in this area:

1. What should be the unit of analysis for policy formation in the global economy, given that science, technology and R&D are also swept by the winds of globalization? Should the individual state or country be (still) the prime unit, or rather a wider or narrower regional entity? What about meta-state institutions such as the European Union (EU)? How do the geographical, the political and the economic dimensions fare in this respect?
2. Which fundamental premises should inform science and technology (S&T) policy, and what should be corresponding goals of such policy? Does the 1960 Nelson–Arrow paradigm still constitute the basic economic rationale for S&T policy?
3. What are the policy instruments that could best serve those goals, in light of their underlying economic rationale? In particular, is the support of formal R&D an effective way of fostering innovation? What about the drive and motivations of would-be innovators?

Until not long ago, we focused our attention primarily on the third issue, relying on accepted wisdom for the first two. That is, for the most part we regarded the individual state as the relevant unit for policy formation and implementation, which meant that implicitly we had in mind a model by which technology and innovation are primarily country-bound phenomena. Thus, we implicitly assumed that individual countries could control the input side (for example R&D, the supply of scientists and engineering) and, moreover, be on the receiving side of the benefits from innovation, be it in terms of spillovers, productivity, consumer welfare or profits.

Likewise, we had a very clear set of premises regarding the economic rationale that underlies policy in this area, going back to the famed NBER 1962 volume, *The Rate and Direction of Inventive Activity* (NBER, 1962). Thus, the disparity between social and private rates of return that characterizes R&D and more so academic research, and the consequent underinvestment in these activities, constituted for decades the predominant rationale that informed and shaped policy. Having thus framed the issue in terms of country-bounded policies in a Nelson–Arrow conceptual context, we could focus on policy instruments, be it intellectual property (IP), patent systems or R&D grants, and their supporting empirics, such as the scope of knowledge spillovers or the additionality of innovation subsidies.

The contributions to this volume have made it clear that we can no longer proceed in this manner, that in this brave new world swept by ever stronger gales of globalization, we cannot keep assuming that the ebb and flow of innovation inputs and outputs respect political borders, or that the innovation bandwagon that has caught up with so many countries is still congruent with the view that there is underinvestment in R&D. Something fundamental has changed in this area, and luckily enough this community of scholars has been wide open and attuned to the winds of change. Thus what we have in this volume may turn out to be the first signs of a paradigm shift, or rather the trembling of the ground that typically precedes such shifts. Whether or not we will see a nascent paradigm is still an open question, but at least the incisive questioning that is an essential prerequisite is amply displayed here.

Let me dwell a bit more on the first question, namely, what constitutes the relevant unit of analysis for policy formation. Luc Soete in Chapter 28 expanded on the implications of globalization, and I agree with virtually everything he said in that respect. Clearly there is a basic incongruence between the fact that policies are formulated for the most part at the national level, and the fact that the objects of these policies (for example science, R&D, innovation) take place in a global dimension, and are governed by forces that to a large extent escape national control. Suppose for example that a particular country wants to attract multinational corporations, and in particular offers incentives to set up R&D labs in it. If that happens, who will actually benefit from the R&D done there? Will it be mostly the local economy? Who will ultimately own the IP generated in such a lab? The answers to these and similar questions are far from clear, and yet in the absence of hard evidence or reasonable presumptions in that respect we cannot assess or design policies. One can easily replicate this dilemma in virtually all other areas of science and technology policy: the fact is that both the inputs and the outputs of research and innovation do not respect borders, are increasingly mobile and fluid, and devoid of clear institutional or geographic anchors. To reiterate, this creates a fundamental incongruence between country- or national-level policies and the objects of such policy.

One telling aspect of this incongruence is the fact that virtually all players, big and small, developed or emerging, are deeply concerned about the implications of globalization in science, technology and R&D. Thus the USA is concerned about the fact that significant portions of innovative activities have moved away from the US to other countries, driven by the wide availability of talent elsewhere. On the other hand, emerging economies are disturbed by the fact that innovations generated in their midst by guest multinationals end up benefiting somebody else. As we have seen in this volume, 'host' and 'guest' (for R&D) countries can easily be discussing the same sort of concerns from diametrically opposed standpoints. Likewise, brain gain for one is obviously brain drain for others, but then in a further twist returning diaspora scientists and engineers may undo the flow and generate opposite anxieties. The proliferation of government support to R&D in ever more countries is certainly good for world innovation, but for individual players it assumes at times the nature of a race that only a few can win.

We know very little about this brave new global world, we do not possess enough data, our models are not yet tailored to fit the bare contours of these evolving phenomena, and hence can offer little help for framing policies. This is not surprising, since we have been proceeding for decades under the assumption that the first two of the three issues that we posed were long ago solved, and we could thus afford to ignore them. No longer.

One interesting aspect of R&D policy that has been repeatedly mentioned in this volume (and that is particularly relevant for Europe), is that of cooperation versus competition at the national level. There are plenty of good arguments either way. On the one hand, the need for critical mass in many areas of research, the fact that costs keep escalating, and that the benefits are hardly confined to the host country, favor cooperation. On the other hand, the need for strong incentives typically calls for stiff competition, and makes cooperation a doubtful proposition. We are of course in no position to shed too much light on this issue, let alone resolve it. However, let me venture some raw thoughts in this respect, evoked in part by the chapters in this volume.

Cooperation is perceived at times as a way to bring about uniformity among the players, and that can be devastating, since it might destroy the creative force of diversity. Let us not forget that important ideas and innovations tend to spread by themselves, without need for explicit coordination or cooperation, and without imposing uniformity. Consider for example key innovations in the realm of socio-economic policy and institutions over the twentieth century, such as universal education, the welfare state, social security, health insurance, countercyclical fiscal policies, and even all-encompassing market mechanisms. These and many other ideas and policies have spread relentlessly over most of the world, without explicit cooperation, let alone attempts to harmonize or ensure compliance. As a consequence, we see enormous diversity in the midst of equally strong commonalities: each country has developed its own version of the policies that reflects its idiosyncrasies, and that is essential for success: it enriches the set of possibilities, it encourages continuous experimentation. The command 'Let a thousand flowers bloom' is as essential for economic policy in general and for R&D policy in particular, as it is for the arts and the sciences. We should resist the (legitimate and often justified) lure of harmonization whenever it may endanger the powerful forces of diversity.

I turn now to the second issue, namely, what should be the goals of science and technology policies. As already mentioned, the received wisdom stemming from the Nelson–Arrow paradigm is now being called into question, not because there is anything wrong with its logic, but because it has become increasingly at odds with current trends. Thus, it could be that there is too much protection of IP, too many patents, and even too much R&D. Imperfect appropriability is still imperfect, but it is not clear that it should be the key consideration in designing policy. Moreover, it is not clear that focusing policy on those inputs that we have grown used to observe, quantify and use in empirical research (primarily formal R&D) is really what makes a difference in terms of innovation. We should never forget that it is the latter that we are interested in: innovation in every realm of economic activity and in the widest sense of the term, and not just the narrow notion of quantifiable innovation such as patent counts. It could well be that we are witnessing a world whereby too many resources are devoted to (duplicative, bureaucratized) R&D, to the formalization and enforcement of highly fragmented IP, to the creation and maintenance of intermediaries (such as offices of technology transfer at universities), and at the same time there is too little innovation, too little creativity, too much implicit collusion in research.

Policies designed to encourage R&D often overlook the fact that further R&D brings about increased demand for the key underlying input, namely scientific and technological talent, and not just for a higher headcount of R&D personnel. We know little about talent as an economic good, but we do know that its distribution is highly skewed, and it is becoming increasingly scarce. Thus, a policy-induced increase in R&D that results in higher demand for S&T personnel is not necessarily going to result in more innovation, and may even have pernicious side-effects. Thus, we should examine what happens to the distribution of scientific talent and productivity as demand increases – does it become more skewed, widening the disparity between the mean and the median, and if so, what are the implications for policy, direct and indirect?

The notion of a 'Republic of Science', admirably advocated by Dasgupta and David (1994), is highly appealing, and I am for the most part a proud citizen of such a republic. However, we can not ignore the fact that at times this republic is self-serving, self-contained and self-referential. Thus, we may be pleased by the fact that there is an expanding community of scholars who publish ever more papers in a growing number of journals, that we continue to bring up good students who follow in the steps of our work and cite it profusely, and take all this as a sign of scientific progress, important and relevant for economic progress, for humanity at large. Well, I am not so sure – what do we truly think would happen if we were, for example, to halve the number of academic economists? Would the true output of economic science diminish in any real sense? Perhaps, but we should not avoid asking hard questions in this regard – it may well be that the Republic of Science is in need of institutional reform itself.

As suggested above, ultimately what matters for S&T policy is the extent to which an economy can produce, adopt and sustain innovation in every conceivable realm. Innovation in turn requires some observable inputs (such as formal R&D), but equally important, it goes hand in hand with entrepreneurship. In fact, in a deeper sense the commercialization and deployment of innovation are undistinguishable from entrepreneurship. Indeed, the creation of new technologies, the introduction of products or processes that embed them into new markets, and their adoption into exciting enterprises, entail entrepreneurial acts that require a set of talents very different from purely scientific or technical skills. The twin phenomena of innovation and entrepreneurship have to do first and foremost with two distinct sets of human qualities: drive and ambition on the one hand, talent and skills on the other. As said before, we know little about talent and its determinants, but we can impact skills to some extent via education, and hence we possess some leverage in that respect. The more serious issue is how we can affect drive, how we can generate or induce entrepreneurship.

Every society at every point in time needs a set of goals, of challenges, to motivate its young generation, to ignite its imagination, to set off its drive. That is the key for any society, for any economy, to flourish. We can try to fine-tune the institutions of R&D policies forever, but if we do not have talented youth that want to take on the challenges, if there is nothing compelling enough to call upon their latent creative energies, nothing will happen. In my view this is not mainly about the cost side: one can easily subsidize higher education or R&D, but it is much more difficult to fire off the demand side.

Ten years after having set the 'Lisbon Agenda', Europe is still searching for effective instruments to do precisely that. Of course, I do not presume to know any better how to make it happen in an affluent, peaceful, relatively content and secure society. I am doubtful that the 'conventional' driving forces of economic gain or scientific curiosity or the attainment of status or upward mobility are powerful or appealing enough in the twenty-first century. Many students consult with me about what to study, and I often find myself at a loss; I fail to find the right button to push. Typically they are financially well off, they are not too eager to take risks, they seem to be rather hedonistic, they do not hold strong beliefs or convictions, and hence everything looks pretty much the same, nothing is exciting enough.

Unfortunately, societies in which this is the situation will not see great innovations and entrepreneurship, it just will not happen. Years ago a title of a book (or an article, I am not sure about it) caught my attention: 'God is dead, Marx is dead, and I am not feeling too well either'. Well, if that is still an allegoric but accurate portrayal of our society then we are in trouble in a very real sense – it is not the 3 percent of R&D gross domestic product (GDP) that is critical, but the motivating forces of those who should dream up and implement innovation.

Pressing, incredibly interesting and challenging issues are not lacking: ageing, immigration, inequality, sustainable development, renewable energy, a multipolar world, terrorism, ethical aspects of genetic research, and so on. The question is how to turn them into appealing challenges to light up the creative forces of the young generation. Each of these issues has also tremendous implications for science, technology and innovation, and we as economists interested in this field could and should have our hands full with tackling them.

In 1960 the groundbreaking conference that led to the volume *The Rate and Direction of Inventive Activity* was held. Almost 50 years later the paradigm that was established then with enormous success has worked itself out, and cries for renewal. I would like to suggest that a conference should be planned for 2010, exactly 50 years later, in order to set the stage for new directions of innovative activity. By then we should be able not just to pose the questions, but to venture some innovative answers. I sense that we are on the verge of a paradigm shift, and I think we should grab the occasion, be daring and let the intellectual forces of creative destruction work out their way also among the followers of Schumpeter.

REFERENCES

Dasgupta, P. and P.A. David (1994), 'Toward a new economics of science', *Research Policy*, **23** (5), 487–521.

NBER (ed.) (1962), *The Rate and Direction of Inventive Activity: Economic and Social Factors*, A conference of the Universities, Special Conference Series vol. 13, Princeton, NJ: Princeton University Press.

David Mowery, Dietmar Harhoff, Alfonso Gambardella, Luc Soete and Nathan Rosenberg

Edward Steinmueller

Richard Nelson and Dominique Foray

Philippe Aghion

David Mowery and Iain Cockburn

Giovanni Dosi and Dietmar Harhoff

Index